AF334721

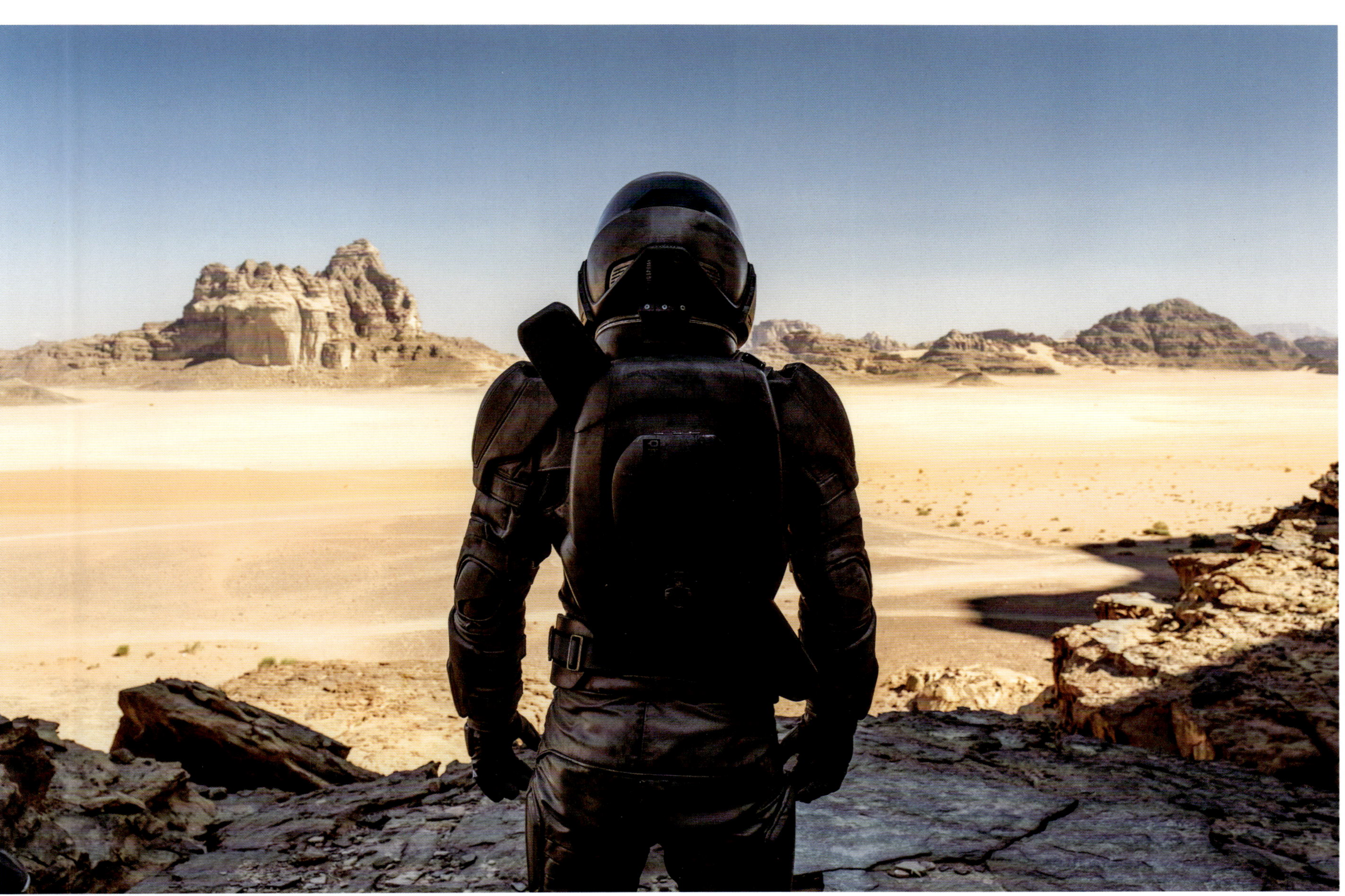

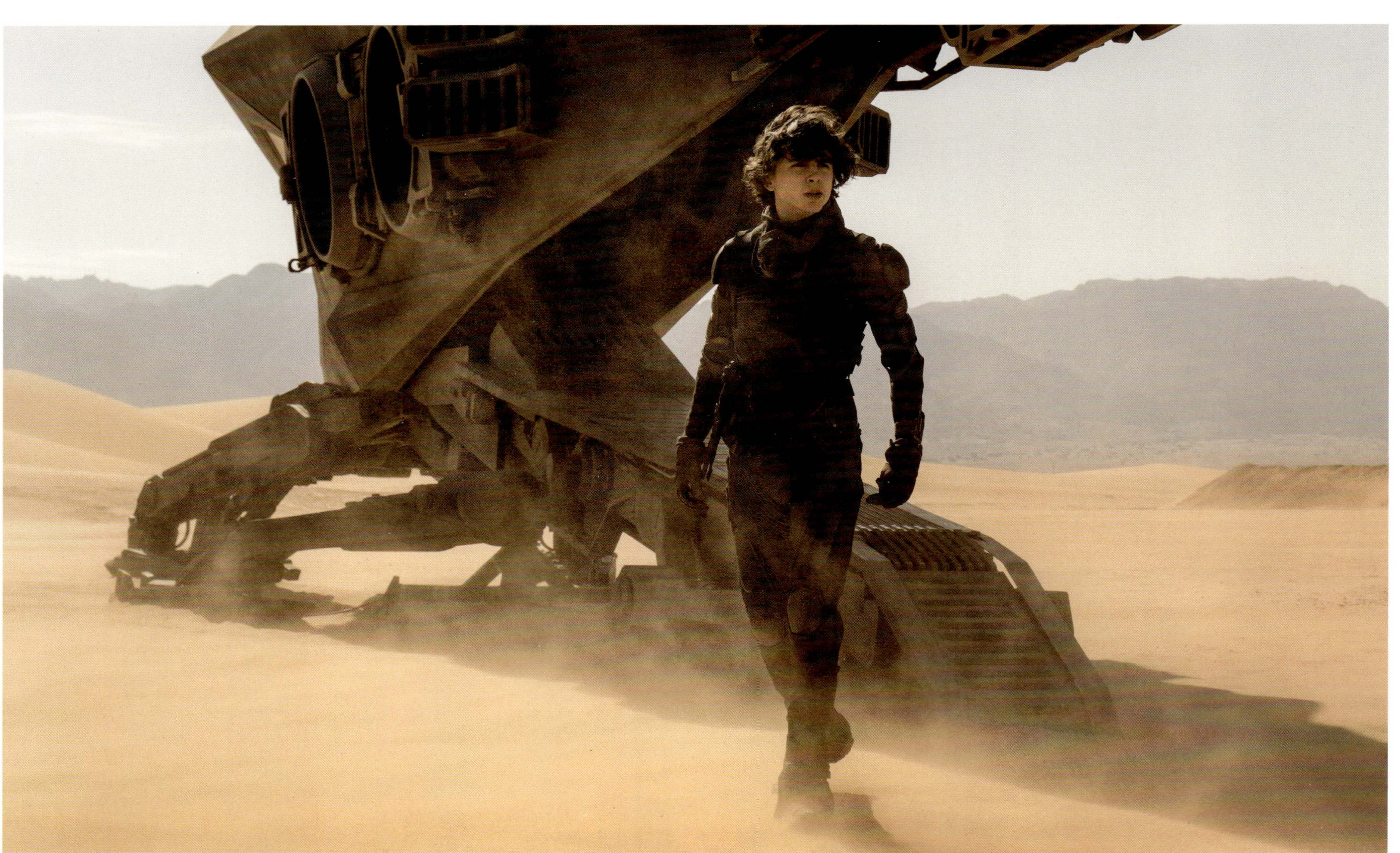

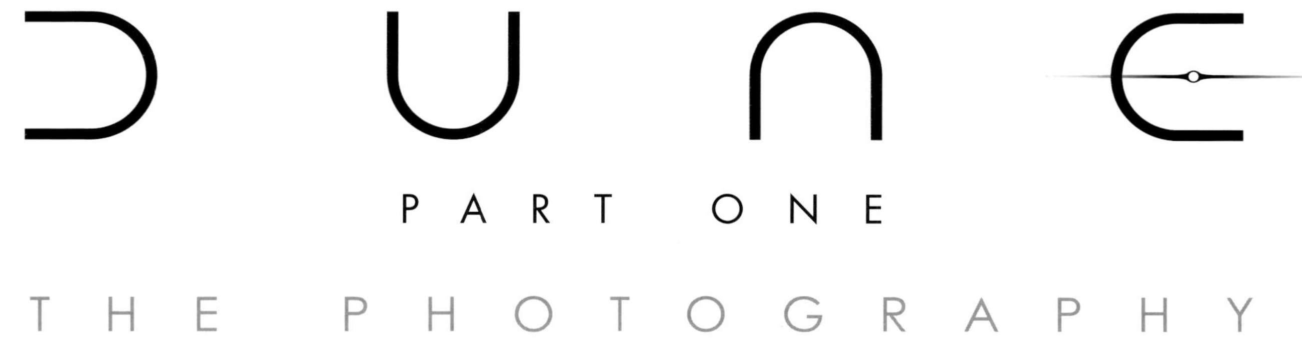

DUNE
PART ONE

THE PHOTOGRAPHY

PHOTOGRAPHY AND TEXT BY
CHIABELLA JAMES

FOREWORD BY TANYA LAPOINTE

PREFACE BY REBECCA FERGUSON

AFTERWORD BY BRIAN HERBERT

DUNE: PART ONE IS BASED ON THE NOVEL BY FRANK HERBERT

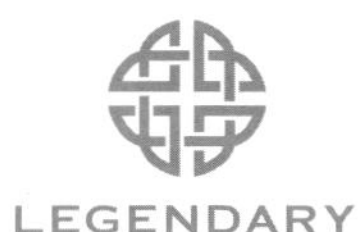

LEGENDARY

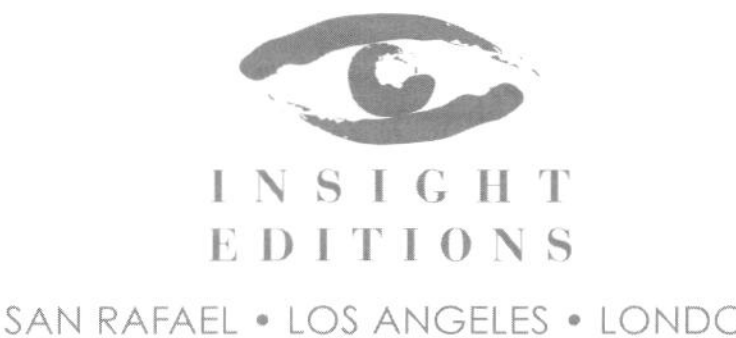

INSIGHT
EDITIONS

SAN RAFAEL • LOS ANGELES • LONDON

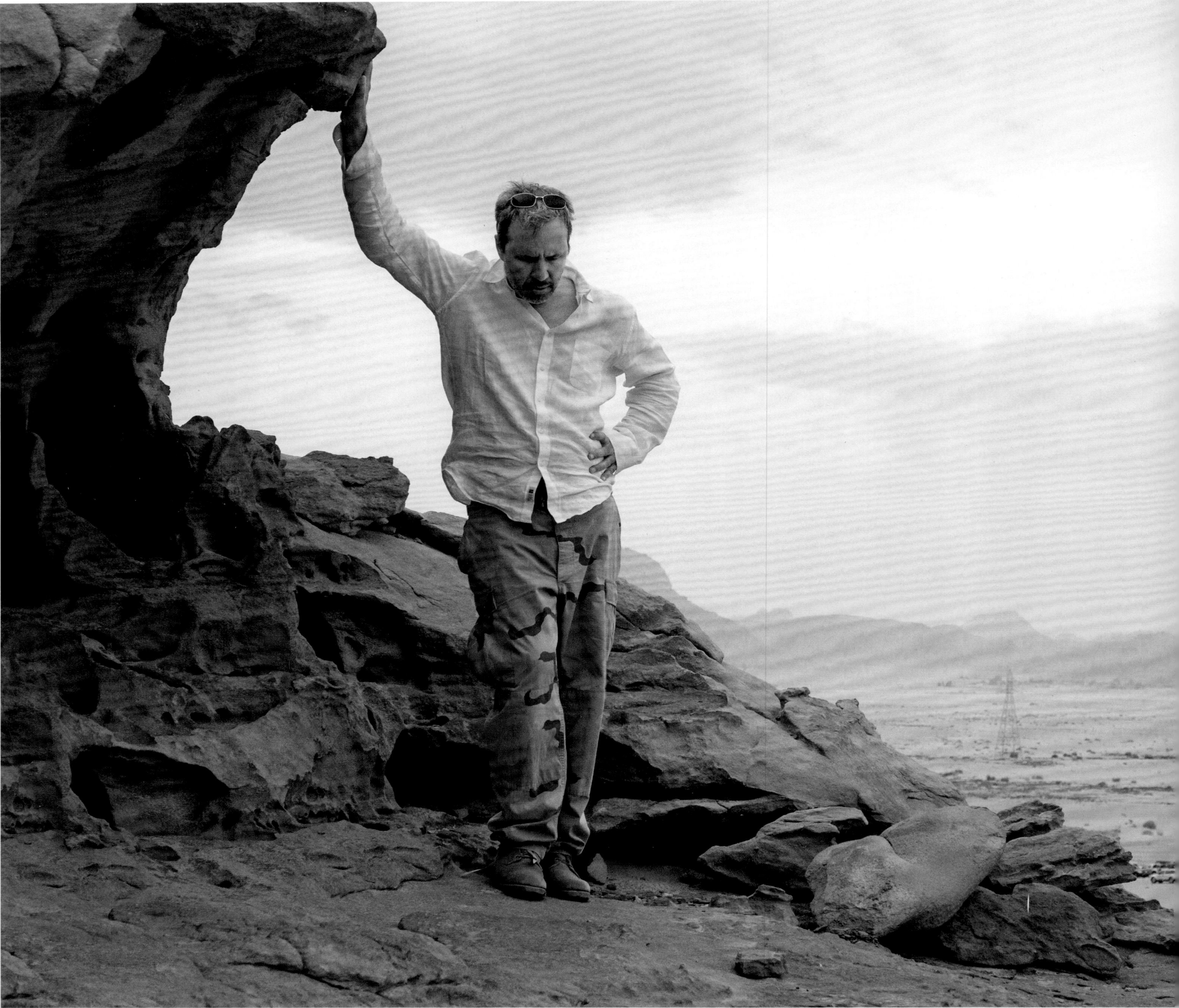

CONTENTS

FOREWORD.........................7

INTRODUCTION....................8

PREFACE........................13

WADI RUM.......................14

BUDAPEST.......................86

ABU DHABI.....................240

NORWAY........................264

AFTERWORD.....................271

CAPTIONS......................277

ACKNOWLEDGMENTS...............282

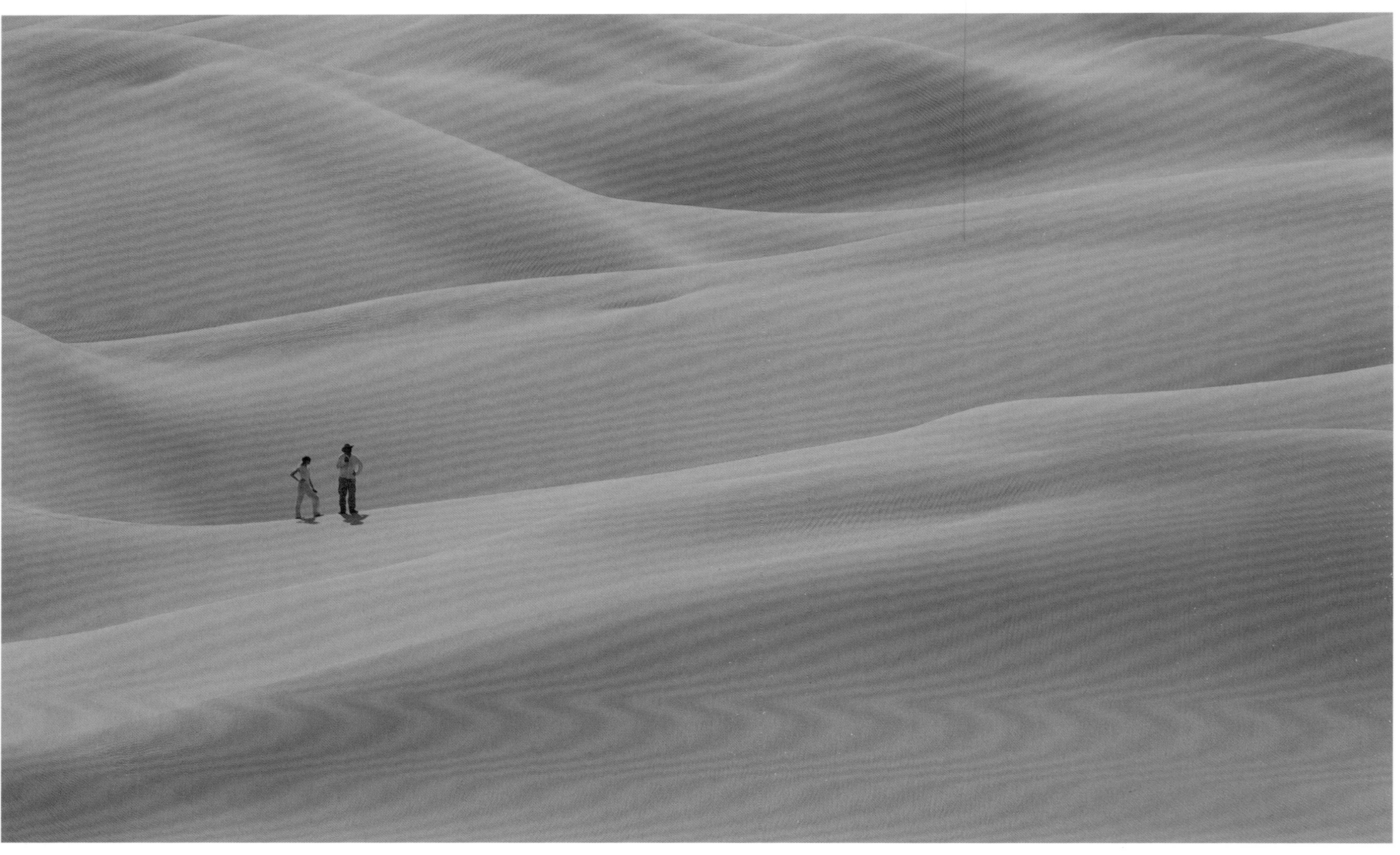

FOREWORD

DUNE: THE PHOTOGRAPHY features the work of Chiabella James who joined the *Dune* crew in early 2019 as the production's still photographer. It's a position I've long been fascinated by. First of all, let's be clear, this is a difficult and delicate job. Filmmaking is not designed to make a photographer's life easy. Even though *Dune*'s cinematographer Greig Fraser was a great ally in this regard, Chiabella still had to navigate the reality of capturing beautiful imagery in the midst of the whirlwind that occurs while shooting a movie.

I vividly remember our first day on set—it was a pre-shoot day. We were filming a scene with Lady Jessica meditating in the Atreides castle, and as Rebecca Ferguson transformed into her character in front of the movie camera, Chiabella captured every moment behind her lens. She was an impressive sight to see with her multiple cameras strapped onto a leather shoulder harness. She was clearly ready for anything coming her way, discreetly moving in the shadows and diligently immortalizing the creative process.

When I finally saw her pictures, I was blown away. They were not only stunning, but they also expressed mystery and emotion. Chiabella captured the subtleties of the actors' performances, the breathtaking desert locations, and the overall uniqueness of this world coming together. Some of my favorite shots are perhaps those which offer an intimate access into a life in cinema. These are much more than "behind the scenes" images, they are imbued with poetry. They are art.

You may not realize it, but you are probably already familiar with Chiabella James's work. Her *Dune* images have been published and shared millions of times in magazines, newspapers, and social media. The picture of Timothée Chalamet and Rebecca Ferguson in stillsuits gazing into the sunset, which you'll find later in this book, was first published by *Vanity Fair* in April 2020. It was one of the "first look" images ever shared with the world, offering an exclusive glimpse into the *Dune* visual universe we had created, based on Frank Herbert's epic novel. Chiabella was, in a way, the portal for audiences to peak into the creative space we fiercely protected.

While many of Chiabella's pictures were used to promote the film, they don't even begin to reveal the breadth of her work on *Dune*. She captured thousands of photographs which have never before been seen. That is why this book came to be. As you delve into it, I urge you to keep in mind the eye behind the lens. Capturing these images required patience, a heightened sense of observation, and strong instincts. It takes a millisecond to snap actors bursting into laughter but you have to be ready for it when it occurs.

For five months, Chiabella James brought her cameras to set observing every movement, every breath. She captured precious fleeting moments encapsulating them into single images that will draw you in. You can spend hours poring over these pages, yet you will discover something new every time you revisit them. Enjoy the journey into her photography.

TANYA LAPOINTE

INTRODUCTION

THE BEAUTY OF ART and literature is their ability to touch and move us in ways unique to us as individuals. In his 1965 novel, *Dune*, Frank Herbert wrote, "The person who experiences greatness must have a feeling for the myth he is in." For me, that line sums up my experience as a photographer for films. I am part of a traveling circus, mysterious to the outside world and, at times, even to those of us within it. A team of creative and technical experts come together as a crew of storytellers to produce a theatrical experience of images, characters, sounds, and emotions that take audiences on a journey to worlds beyond their own. These artisans come from all walks of life, full of stories and experiences of their own, with a love for storytelling and a respect for the magic of the silver screen.

To photograph a film like Denis Villeneuve's *Dune* is a once-in-a-career opportunity. This is not your average blockbuster movie. It is a collision of genres within an epic story, dear and familiar to so many but foreign to a new generation, told by one of the greatest visual storytellers of our era. I received a call from producer Joe Caracciolo, asking me to photograph Denis's film less than two weeks before filming began. I barely had a chance to get my life in order before I was on a plane, beginning a six-month journey into another world that took me from the dusty valleys of Jordan to the beating heart of Budapest, the endless dunes of Abu Dhabi, and the crisp coast of Norway.

Before we started filming, I met with Denis and his producing partner, Tanya Lapointe, and asked him to share his vision for the film with me so I could learn his perspective and start to channel my own vision for the photography accordingly. I wanted to capture the spirit of the story, the production, and the people creating it as authentically and accurately as possible. From day one, Denis opened his world to me. He enthusiastically shared his plans to tell Herbert's story in a way that was true to the novel that he respected so much but relevant to today's audiences and carry it forward into a new generation. I left that meeting with anticipation for the challenge ahead of me, genuinely inspired by Denis's authentic passion for storytelling and his unique vision for this big studio film. This wasn't going to be just a movie; it was going to be art.

As a movie photographer, my priority is to produce images for the film's publicity campaign, giving audiences a glimpse into the world we've created for them and enticing them to want to see more. It is also my job to document and share a front-row view of the process and people that bring it all together. Photographs are not fleeting like the moments they capture. Time stands still in the frame, immortalizing both the story and the journey.

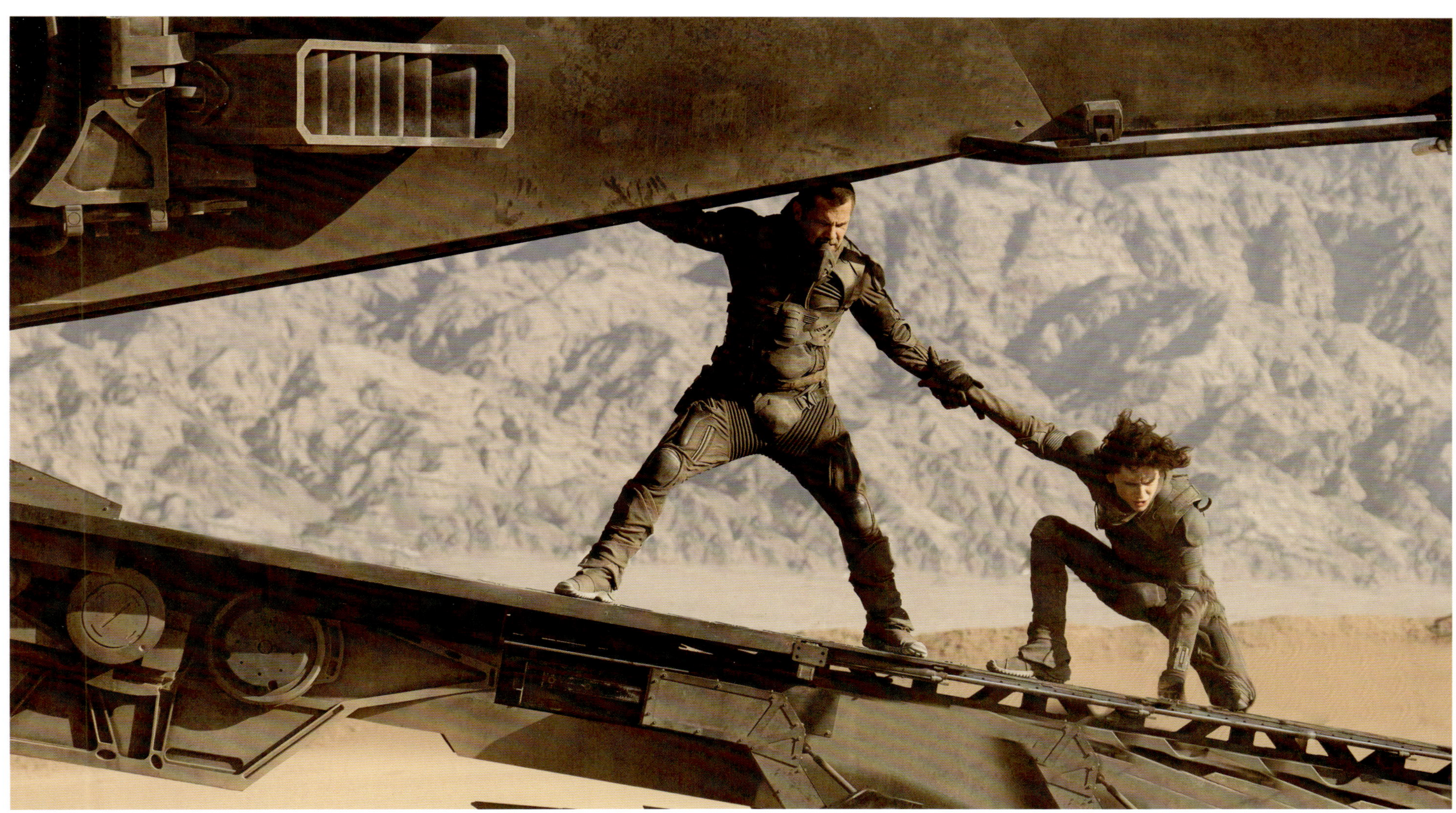

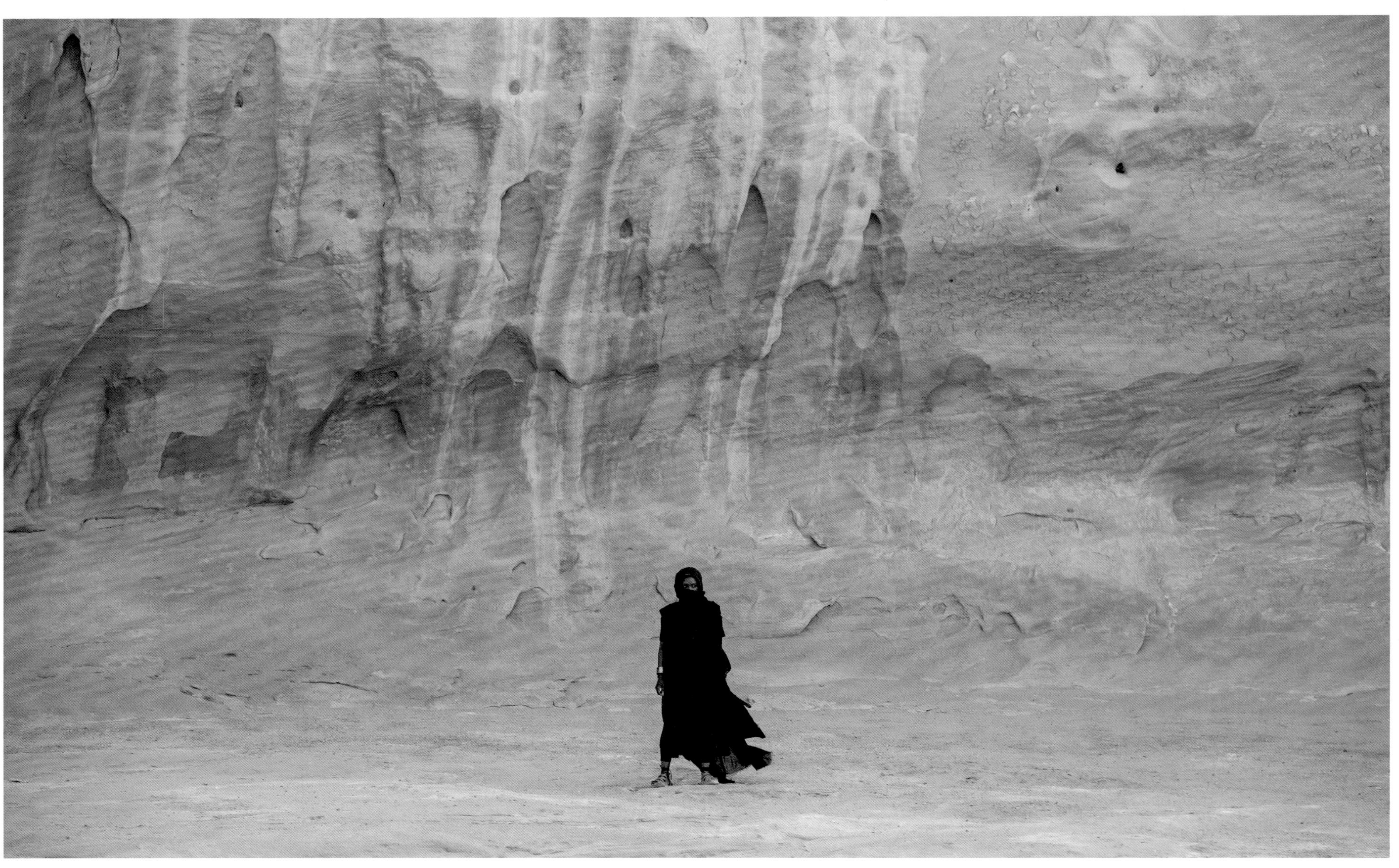

Photographs give us the opportunity to pore over the details, keeping a record for posterity but also giving us a window to explore these worlds and dive into new cultures. With each photograph, my goal is to tell a story in a single frame. I seek out the moments that surpass words or explanation and translate to a visual language of gesture and emotion. Although the focus may be on the plot of the film, there is just as much narrative to tell behind the scenes. The personal stories of artists, technicians, and laborers intersect on a film set in the process of telling a larger story, one that will bring audiences around the world together.

As a photographer, you don't get time to prep: You don't get to set the blueprint of the frame or the direction of the scene. You have split seconds to see a moment, decide if you're going to shoot it, and then frame, light, adjust, and capture, because once the moment is gone, it's lost and becomes a memory.

The *Dune* film set had 360 degrees of visual potential. To narrow that down in my viewfinder was my first round of editing. I had to let go of the desire to shoot in every direction and focus on my responsibility to the film by finding the frames that expressed Denis's intentions, did justice to the beauty of the locations, and displayed the artistry and depth of the production design. I had to find ways to cut into and isolate pieces of a scene that would show audiences the magnitude and scale of the story without the magic of the visual effects (which I wouldn't even see until I was an audience member myself, two years later).

The next round of editing was narrowing down thousands of photographs and choosing what to share with the world. After the first week of shooting, I pulled together a selection of images. I chose one or two from each scene and sent them to Denis for his review of the direction I had taken. A couple of days passed before Denis approached me on set, and I could see in his face that this was the moment I had been anticipating. He reached out his arms, put his hands on my shoulders, and said, in his elegant Québécois accent, "My friend, we are making the same movie. Thank you. Thank you very much." While I exhaled with relief, I felt the jolt of adrenaline and excitement for the adventure ahead of us.

Dune is an action-filled science fiction adventure made for the big screen, but unlike other films of its size, it is a work of cinematic art, worthy of art house cinemas and IMAX theaters alike. Movie photography is mostly generated for use in the marketing of a film and is almost never presented as art, but *Dune* gave me the rare chance to capture movie imagery that crossed into the world of art photography.

The stunning visuals and performances under the brilliant direction it took to tell this renowned story are unmissable for anyone watching the film, but I hope this collection of photographs will convey the visual journey that a group of incredible artisans took together to bring this production to life. Not every face is featured, but their art and efforts are in every frame. The details in the images on these pages are not only a celebration of their contribution but also a record of the ability of a big blockbuster movie to retain its truth as an art form.

CHIABELLA JAMES

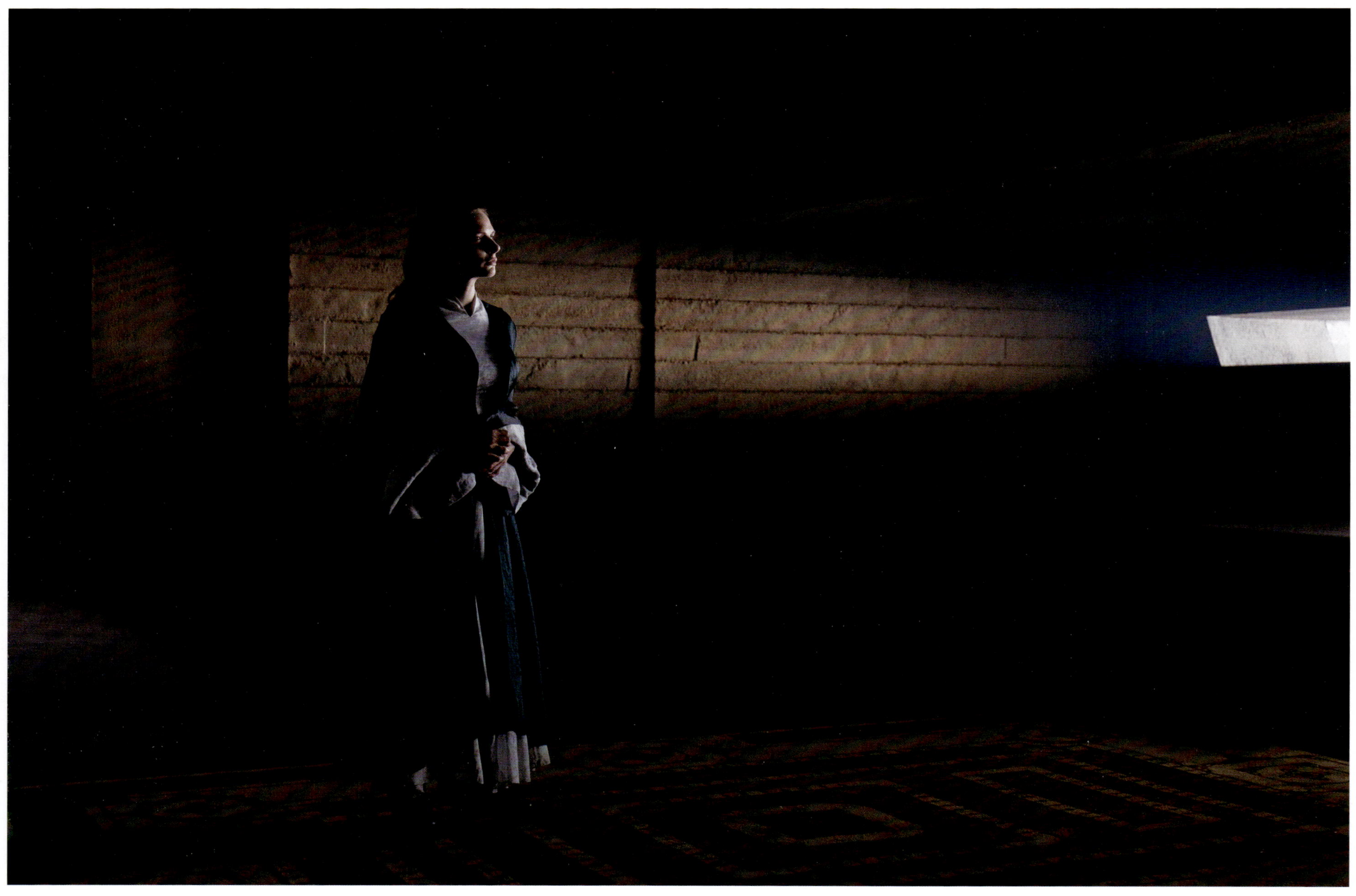

PREFACE

SHE HAD AN ENERGY about her that made me want to get to know her, be in her presence, listen to her stories, and share mine. It's not often we come across people who make us feel the way Chiabella does. There she was, this happy, vibrant person who somehow seemed to know everyone. I would see her outside, engaged in great conversations with cast or crew, but it turned out she was also the one hidden in the shadows on set, grabbing not only the beauty but also the "rawness," the reason, and the emotion behind each moment.

It really amazes me that someone so charismatic can become completely invisible while being in the center of where it all happens.

Rocking a ridiculously cool leather harness with multiple cameras attached to it, this pretzel-like woman with a semi-split stance knows instinctively which camera to use to capture the action as well as the most intimate moments—both whilst shooting the scenes, but most importantly, in between takes without anyone knowing or feeling her presence. An artist catching the best of what we all are trying to do and letting us forever enjoy the memories in the work she leaves behind before moving on to her next target.

For me, personally, it is the most wonderful experience to see your friend in action, whether completely immersed in her work or in between takes—such as when I decided to start tap dancing on the dunes in Abu Dhabi carrying an umbrella, only to see her once again seizing the moment and, this time, making it ours.

I once watched as she silently fashioned together her own miniature canopy hoods. I asked why, assuming it was for the glare of the sun, but no, no, no. Cool as anything and seemingly unfazed, she replied, "My cameras are melting in the heat."

Chiabella's mind never stops, even when her lenses are resting. You can see the magic dancing inside her head, ready to activate next time she puts that finger on the trigger.

I hope everyone gets the chance to play with this extraordinary creature of an artist!

REBECCA FERGUSON

WADI RUM

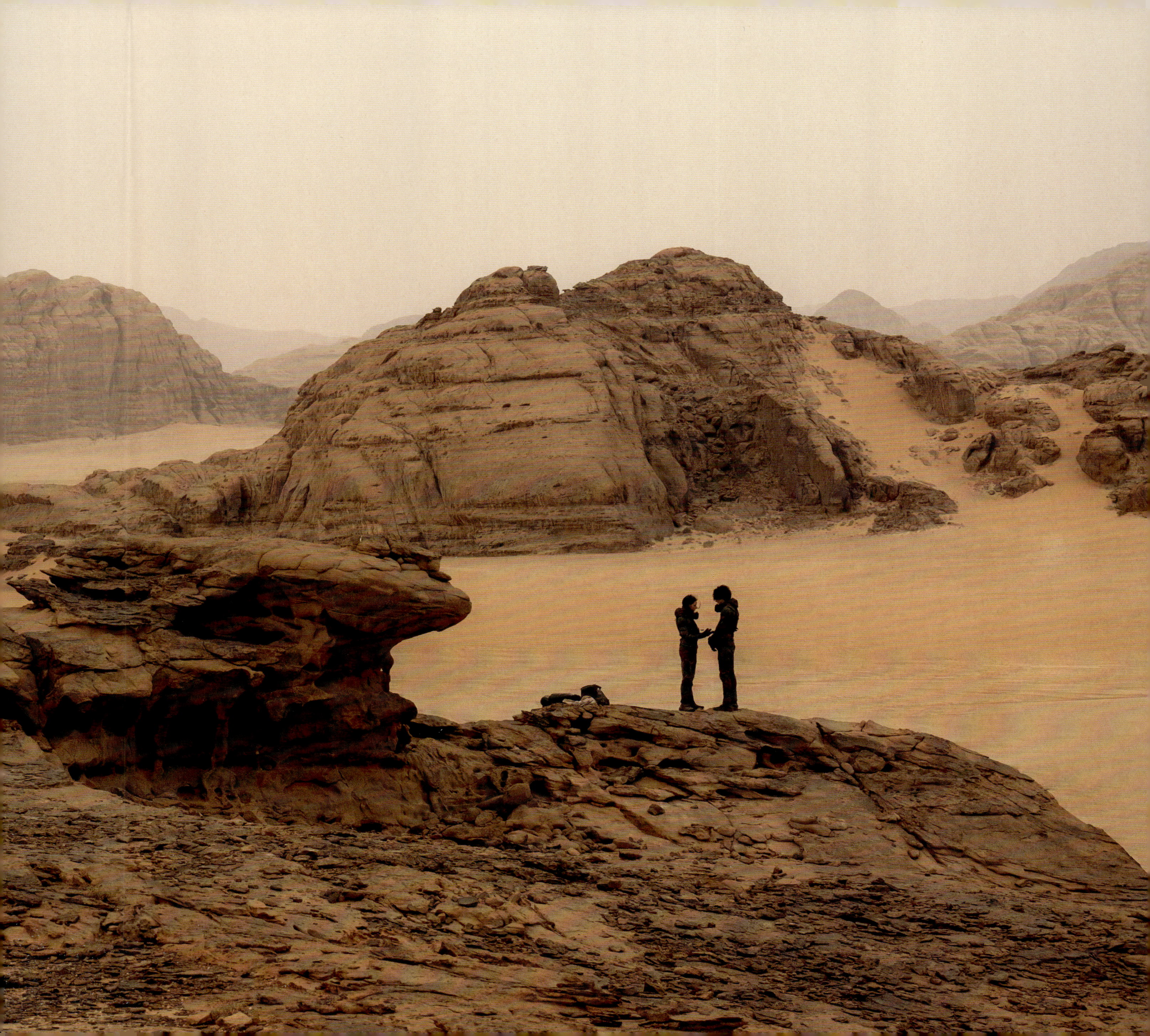

THE WARMTH OF THE people in Jordan is matched only by
the colors of the vast expanse of dusty red and golden rock
formations that glow in Wadi Rum's sunsets. Gorges etched
through the rock allowed us to venture inside, where every
fracture felt foreboding and the layers in the rock told stories of
the generations here long before us. As we approached, we
became smaller and smaller at the foot of ancient skyscrapers.
These fragile, ominous rocks became our home for weeks. We
froze at night and in the shadows but then shed layers in the
heat of the sun, taking refuge beneath umbrellas as the shadows
moved past us.

The Jordanian landscape became Arrakis, the desert world
first created by Frank Herbert. We watched ornithopters take off
and land at the hands of the special effects teams. The extras,
melting in their costumes under the desert sun, had the faces of
real spice workers who had been there for decades. In order to
film the scenes from different angles over multiple takes, we had
to protect the untouched desert floor from being blemished by
footprints. A chorus line of departments filed in and out of the
set via roped pathways, compelling the crew to find new forms
of collaboration; even the cast took up brooms to sweep away
their footprints between takes.

The sandworms seen in the final film may have been a
creation of visual effects, but we frequently endured the reality
of sandstorms. With sand whipping every inch of exposed skin,
leaving us unable to see more than a foot ahead, we threw
ourselves into the experience, giving everything to the shot. We
carried that sand with us in our clothes, our equipment, even our
ears, for months after we left Jordan.

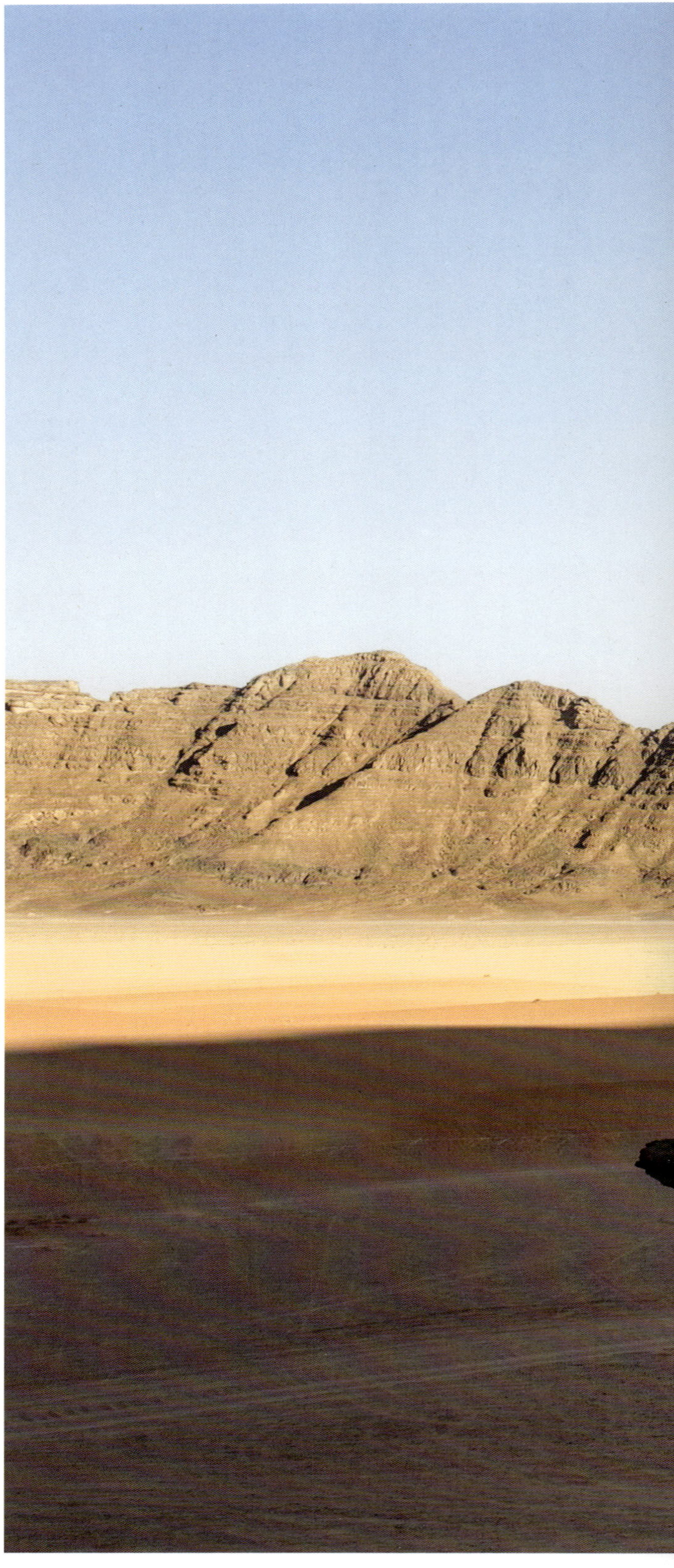

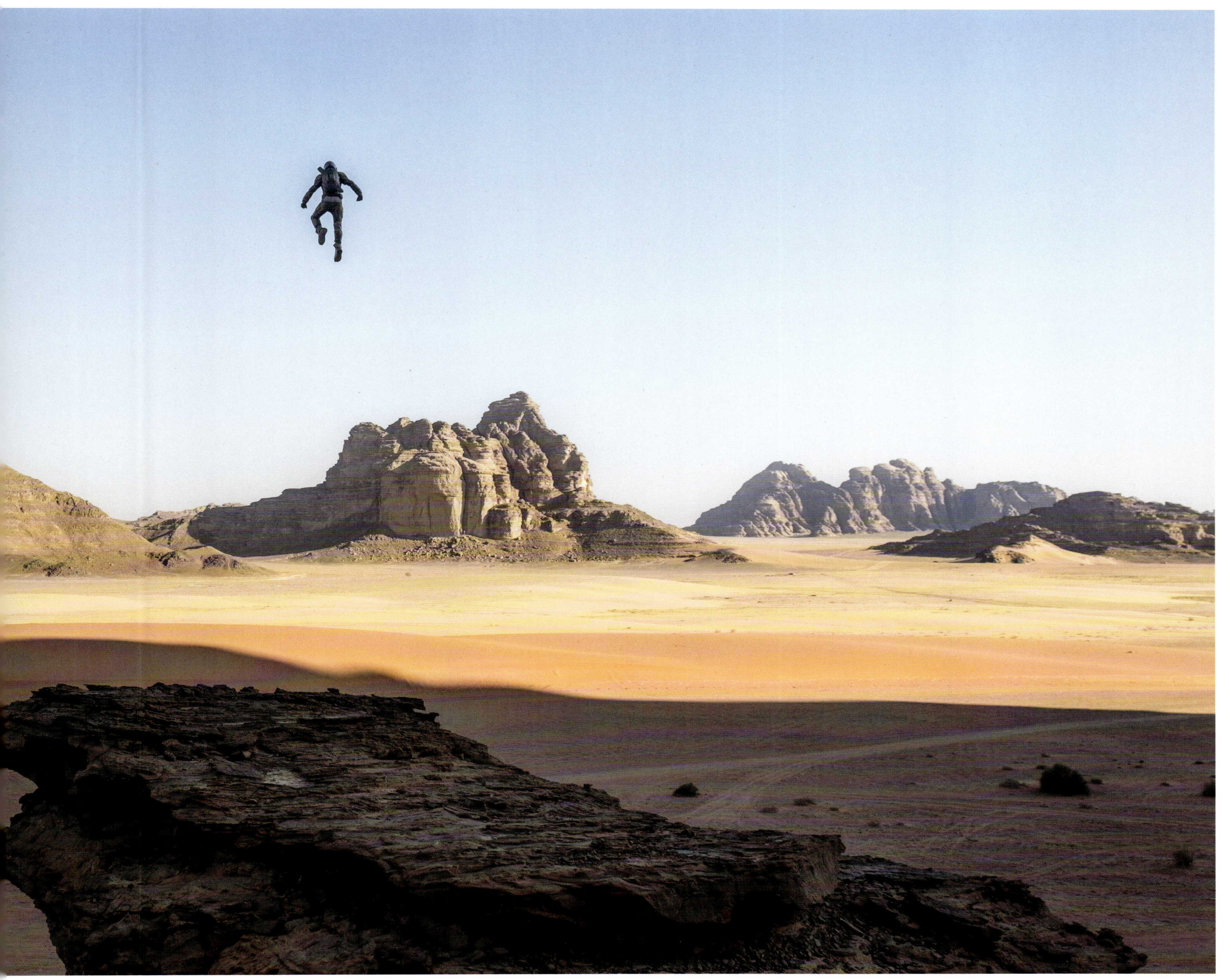

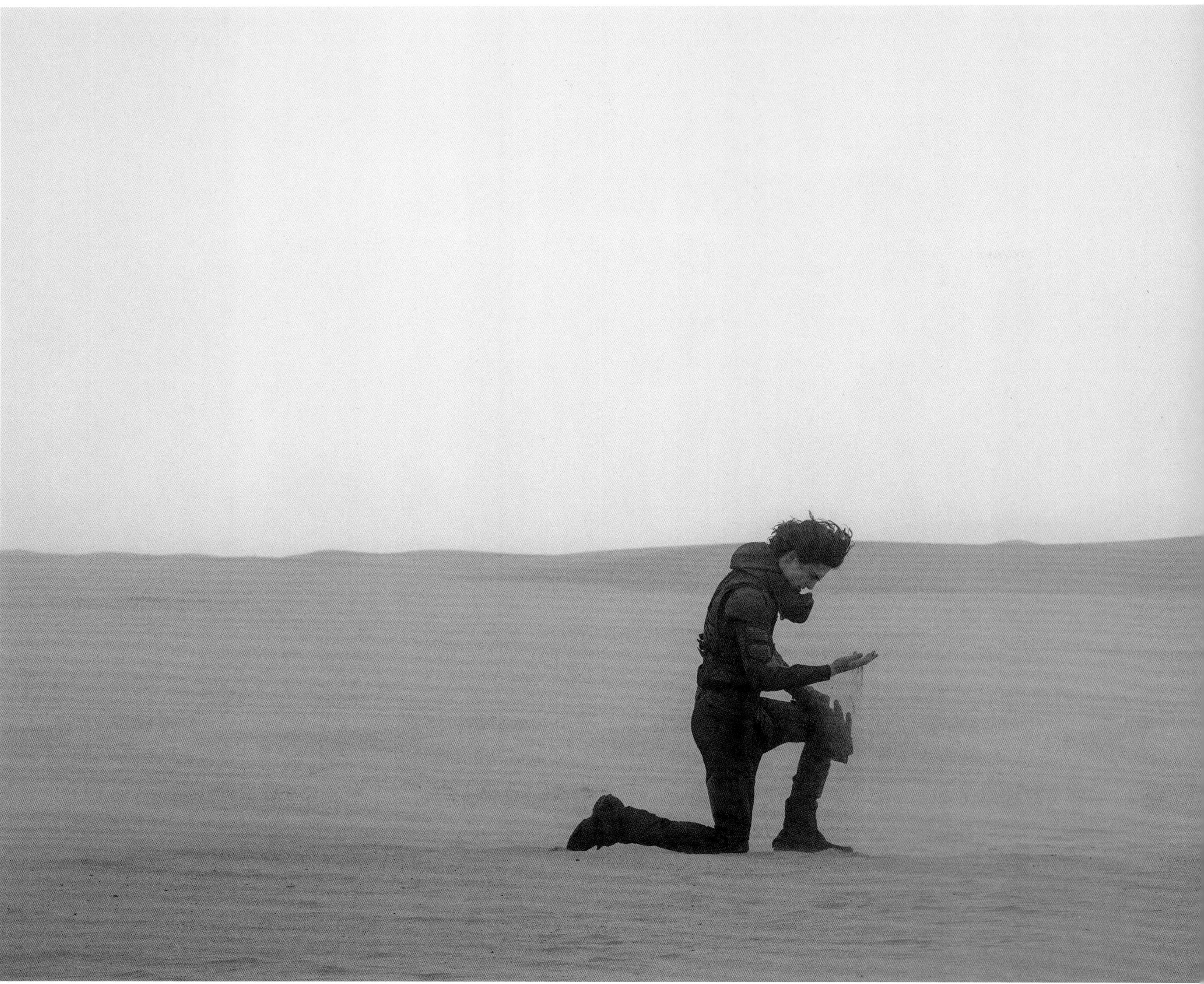

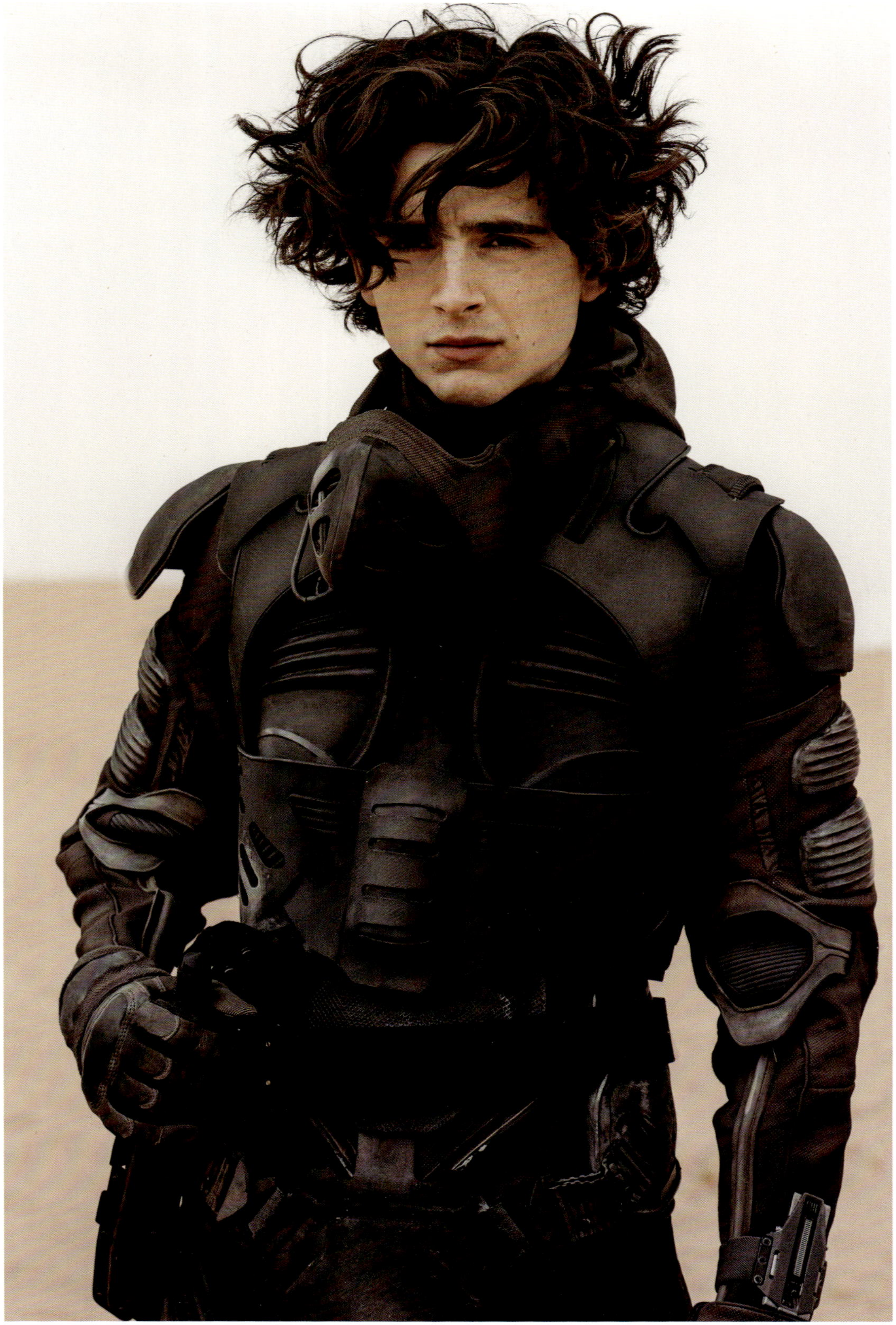

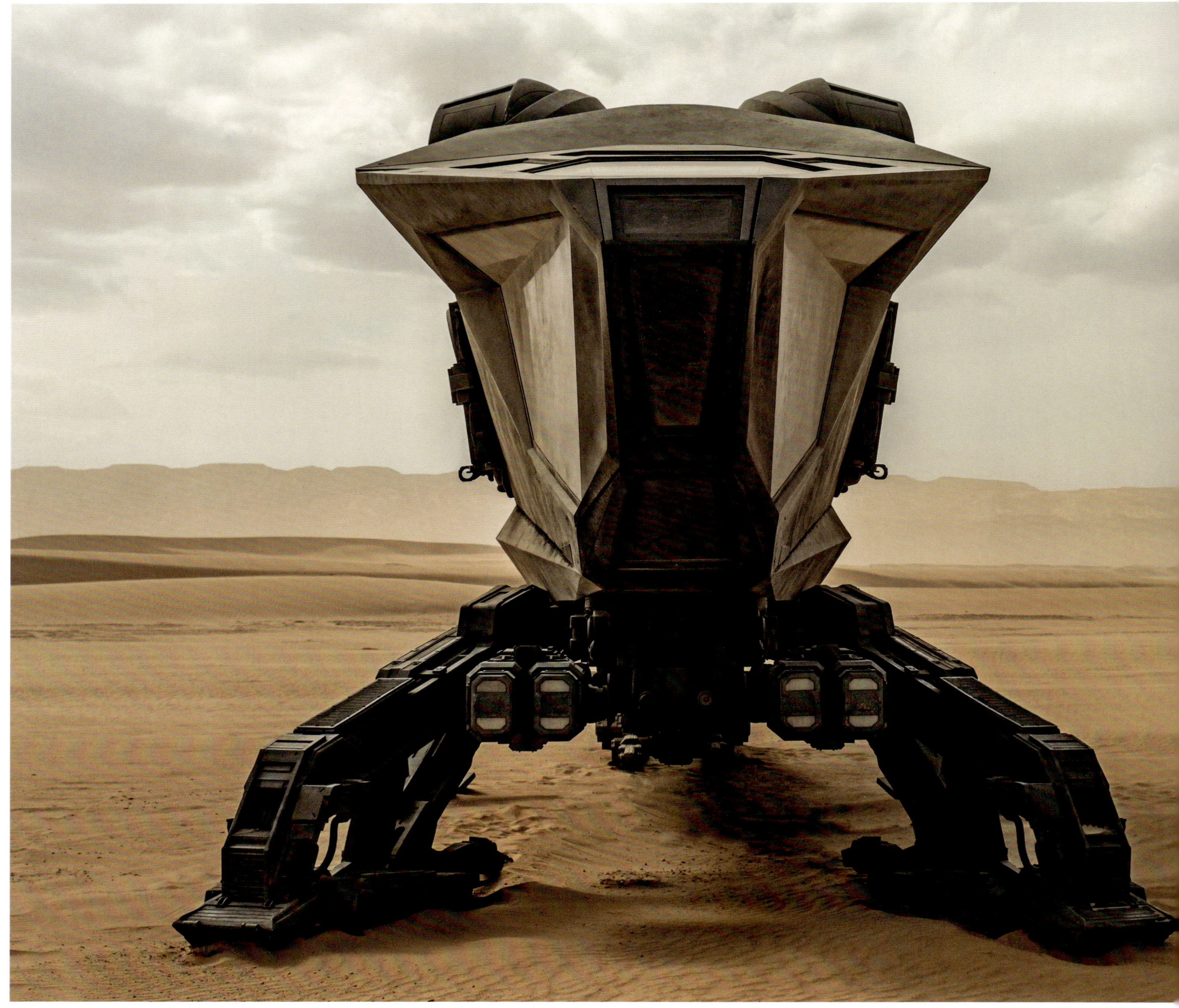

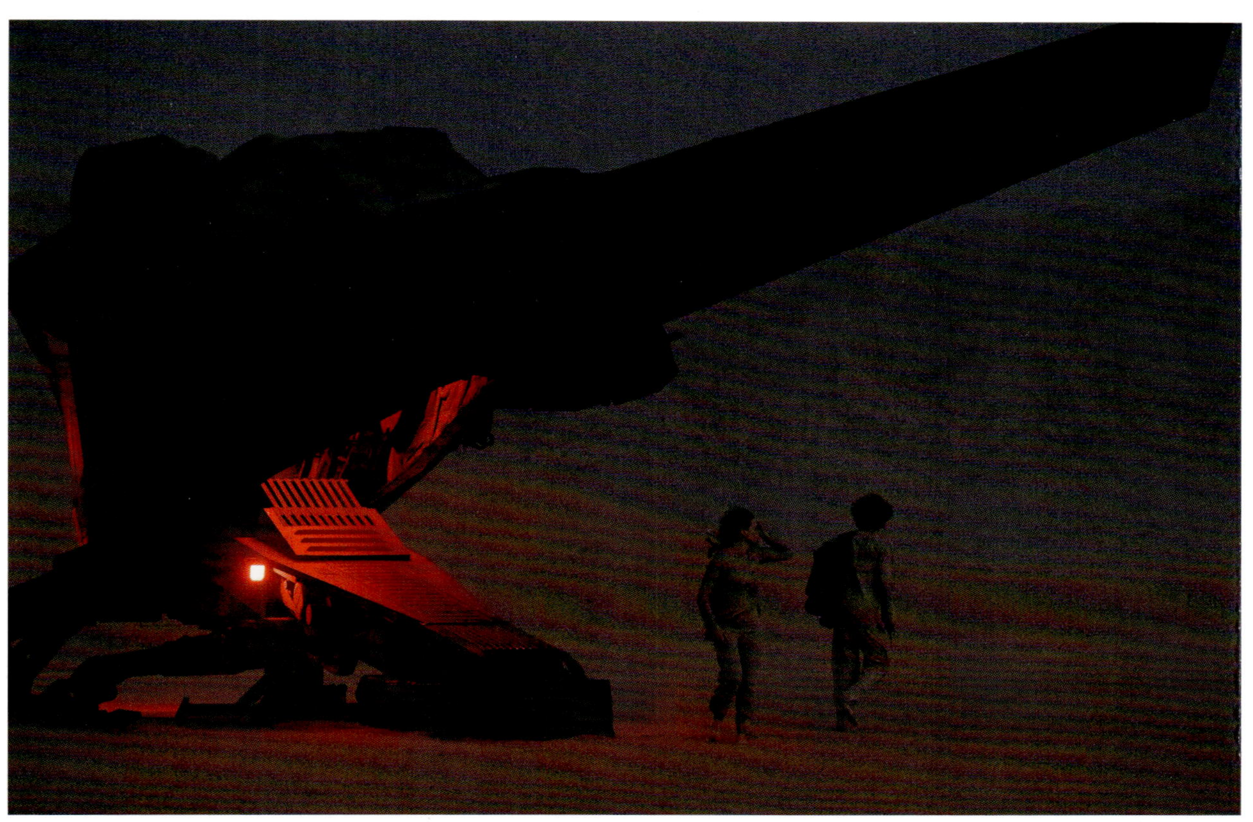

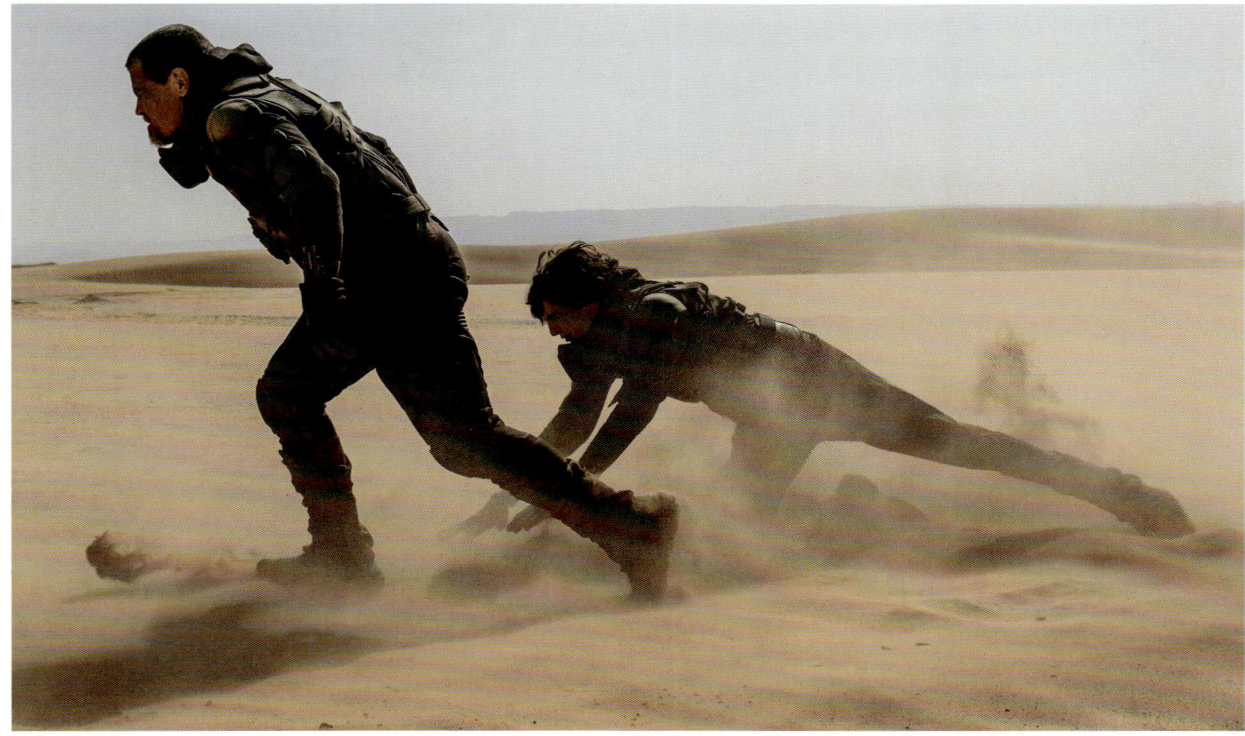

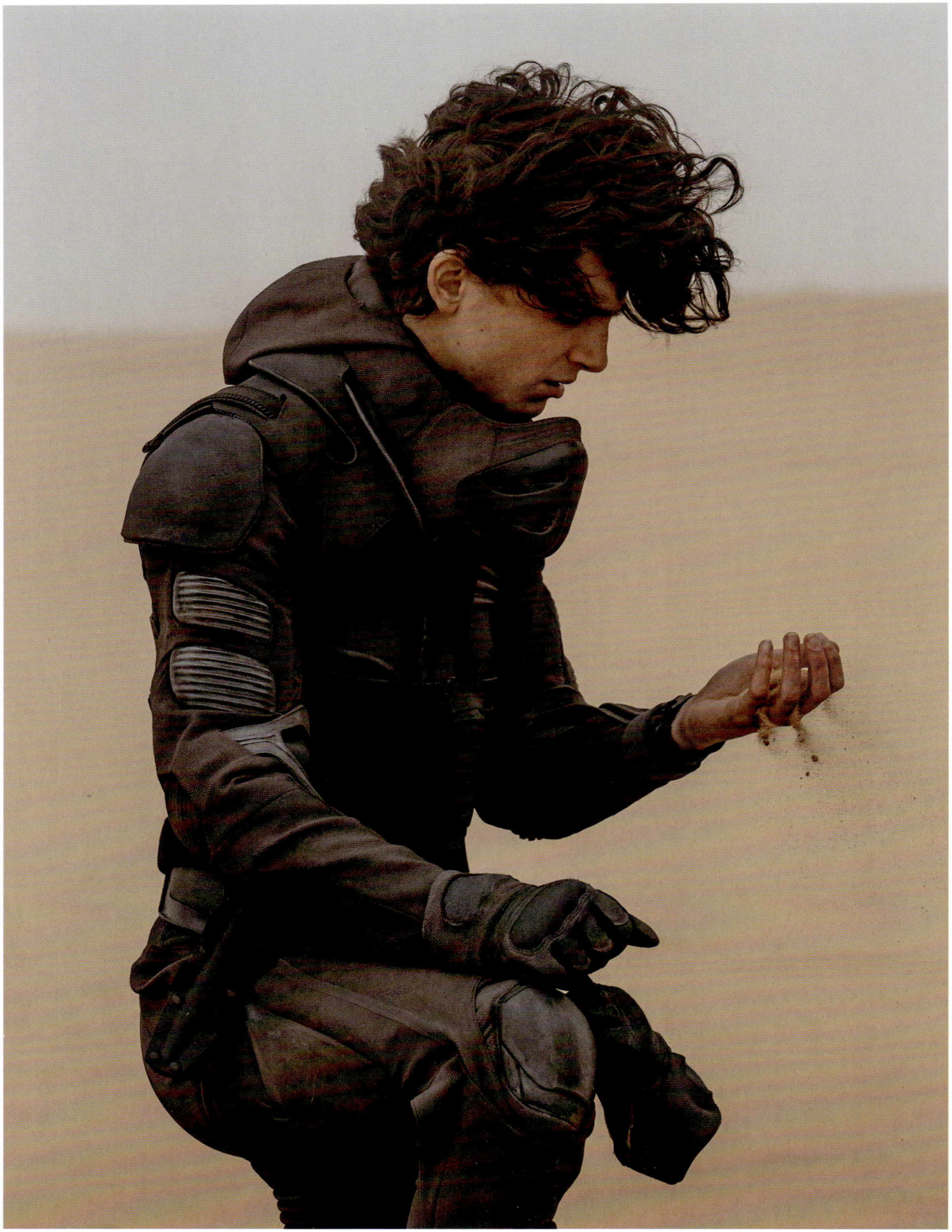

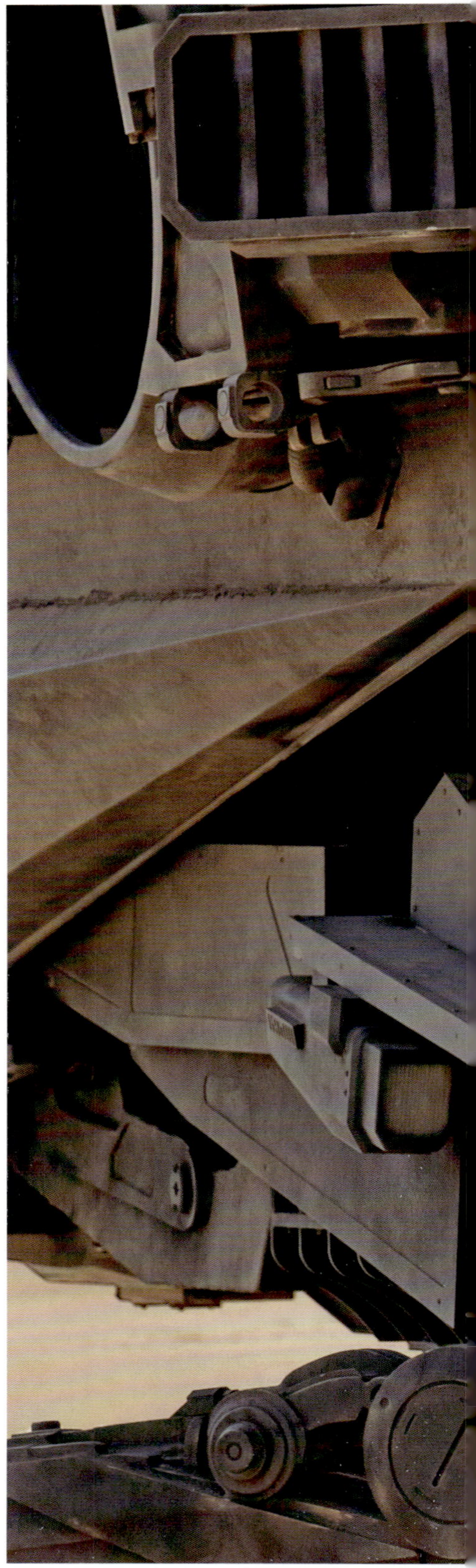

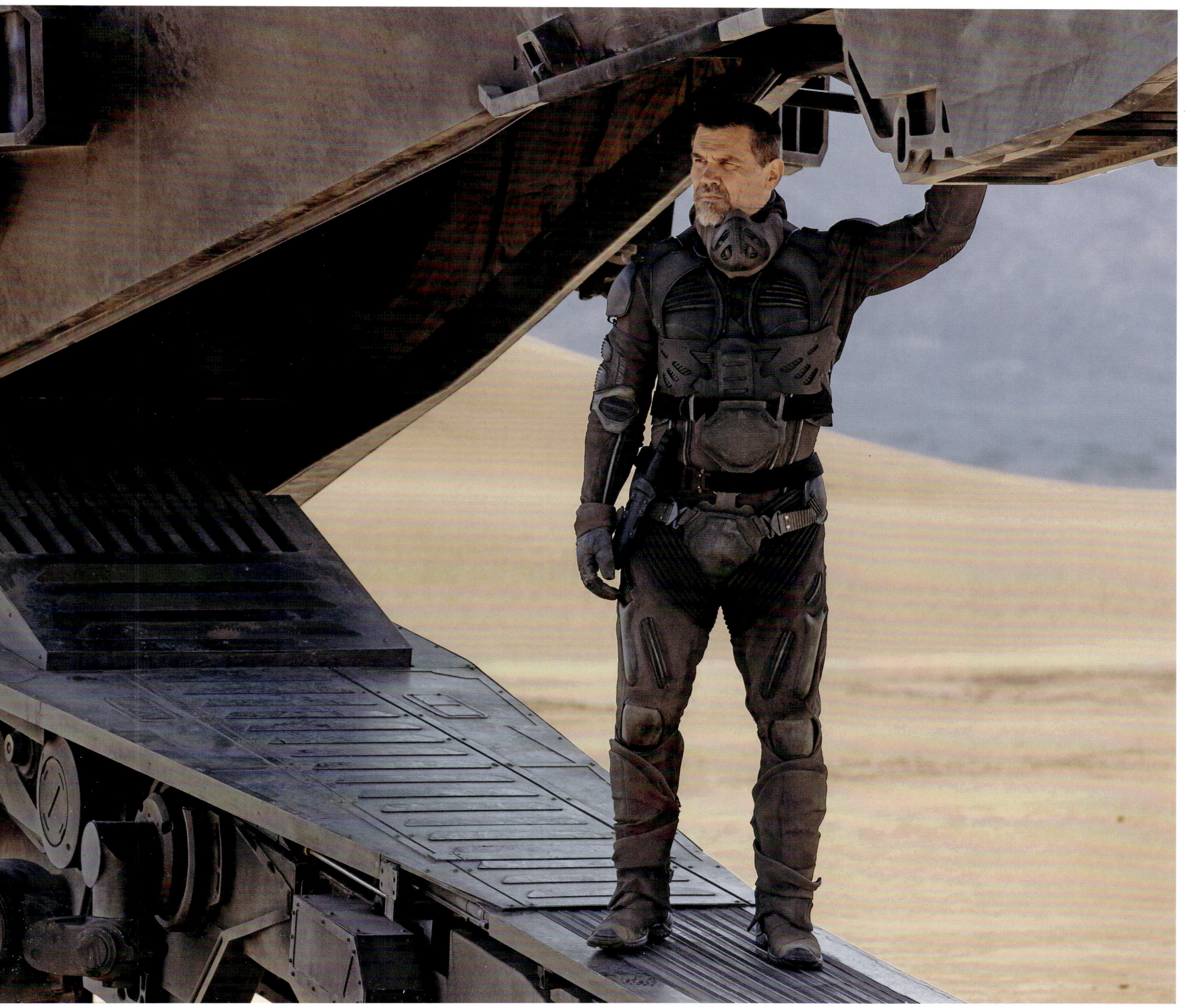

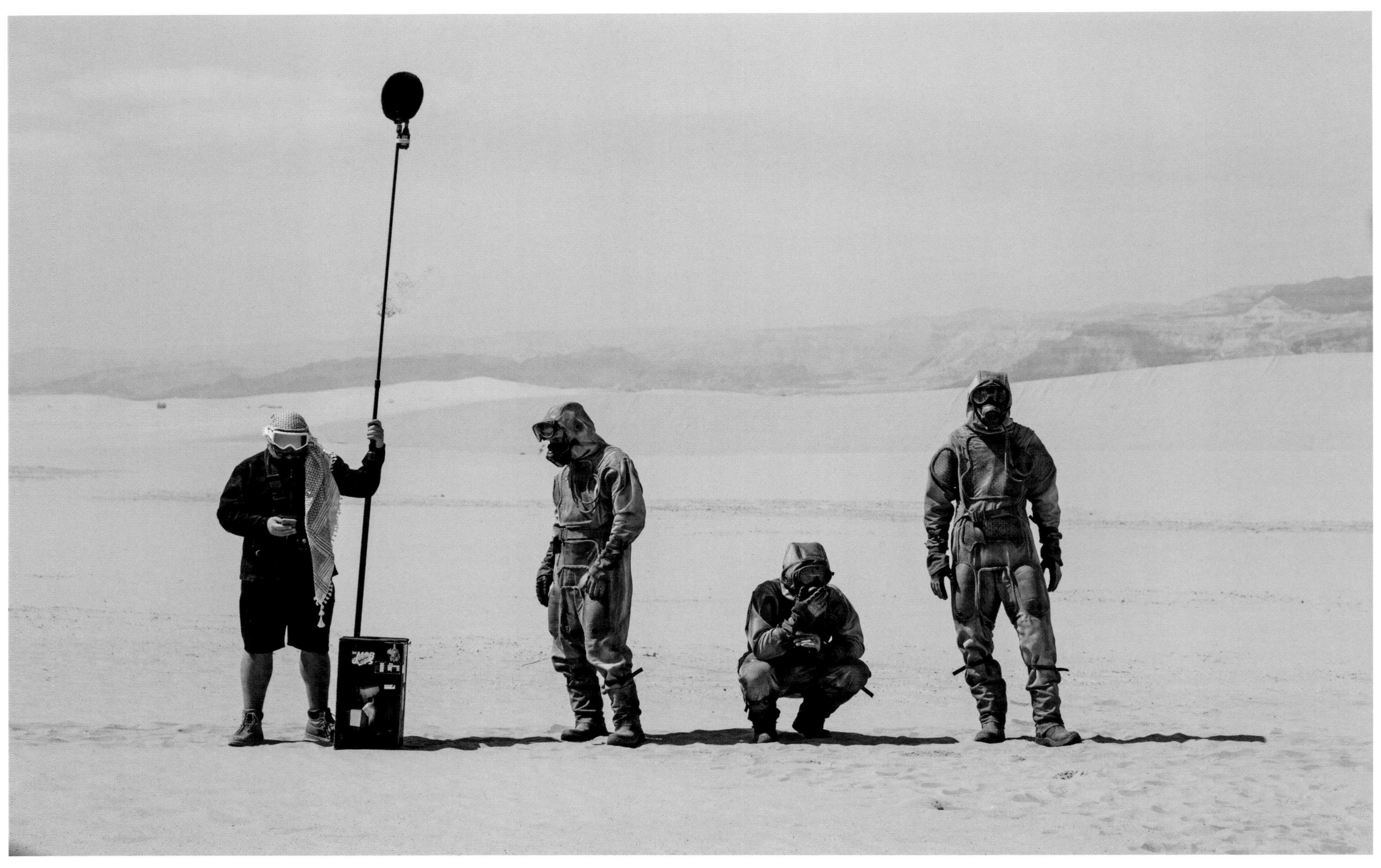

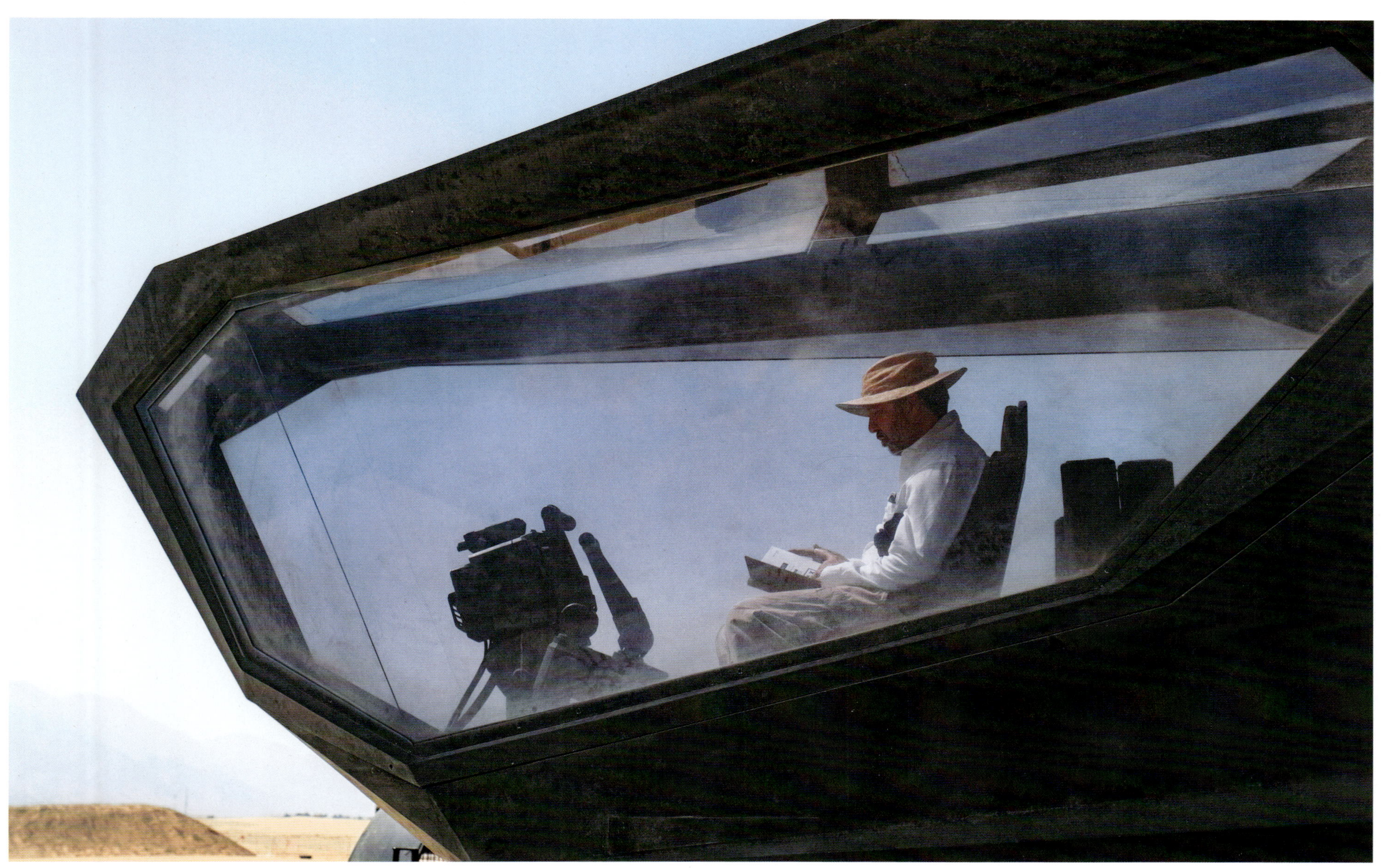

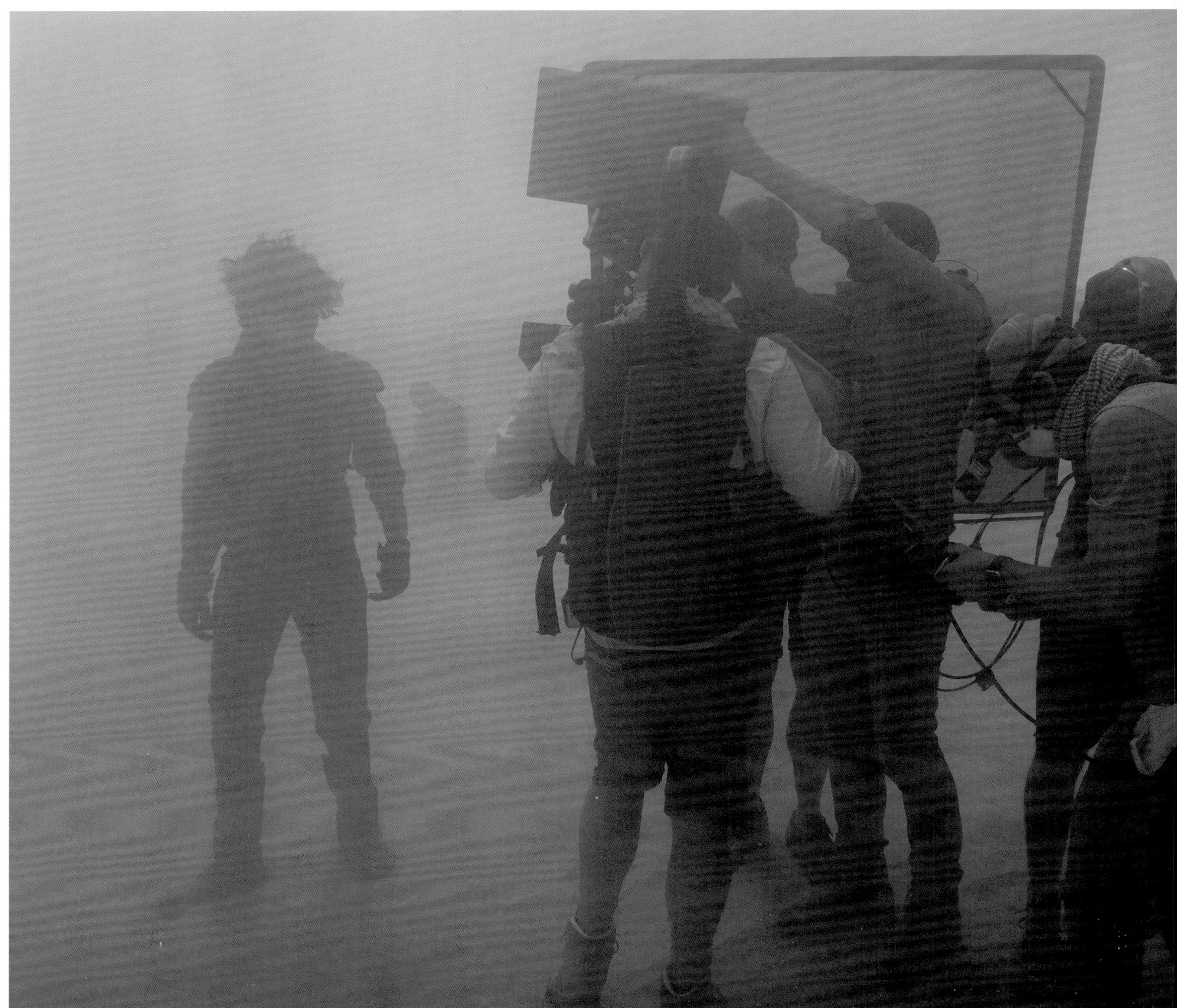

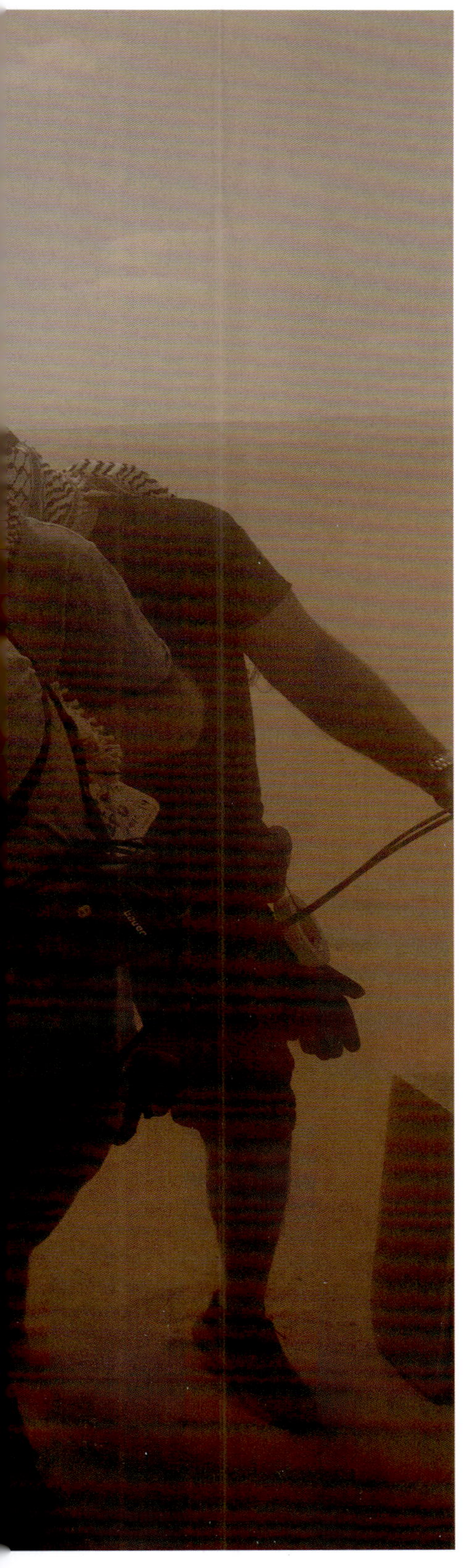

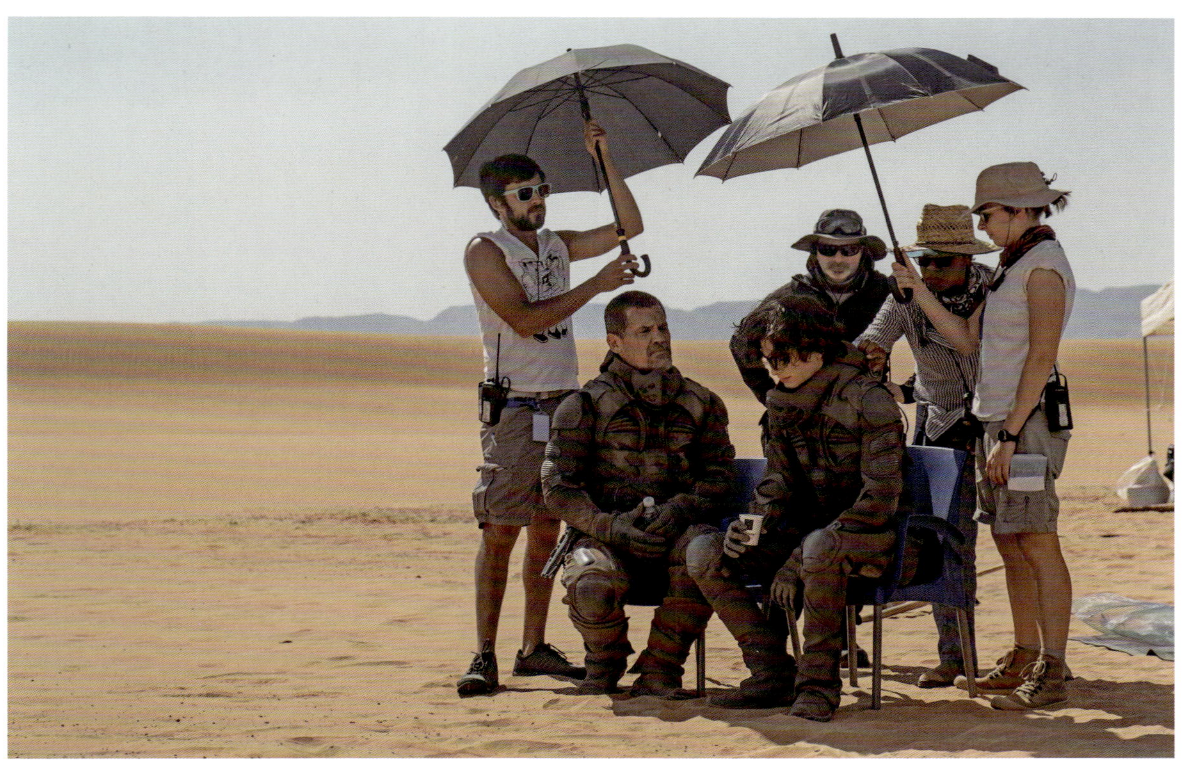

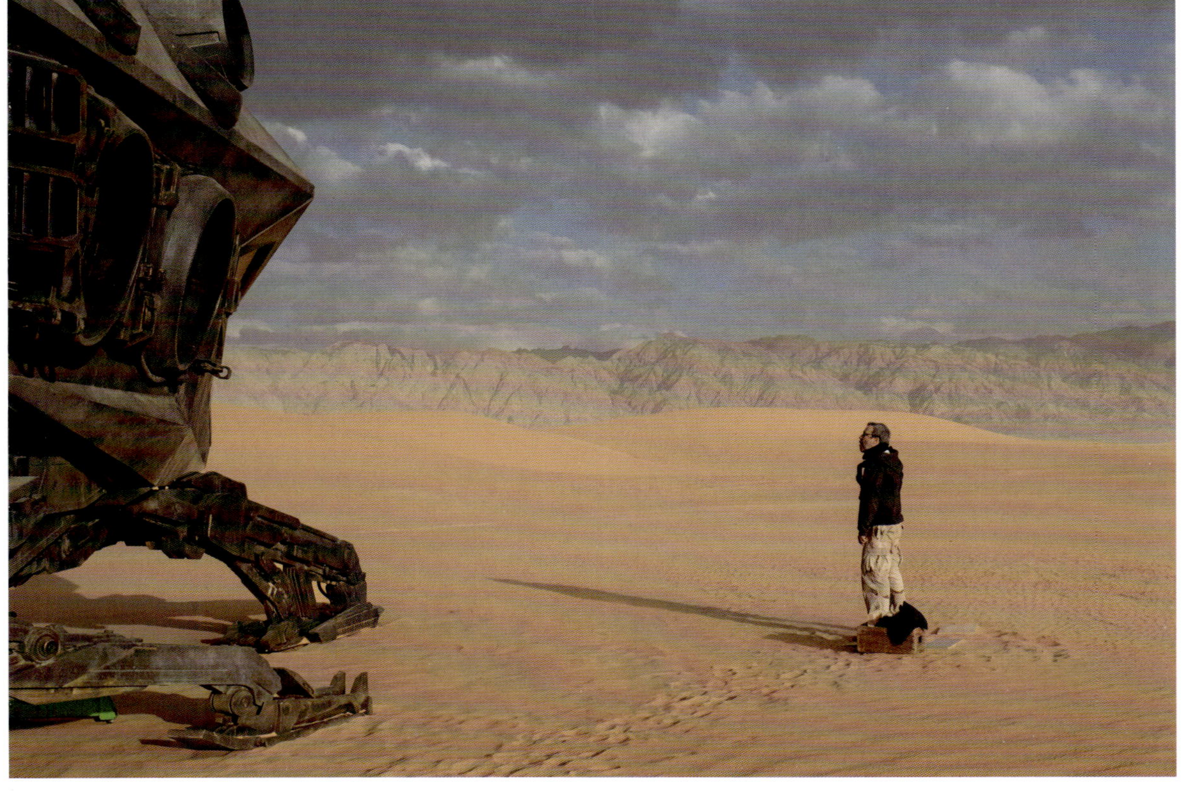

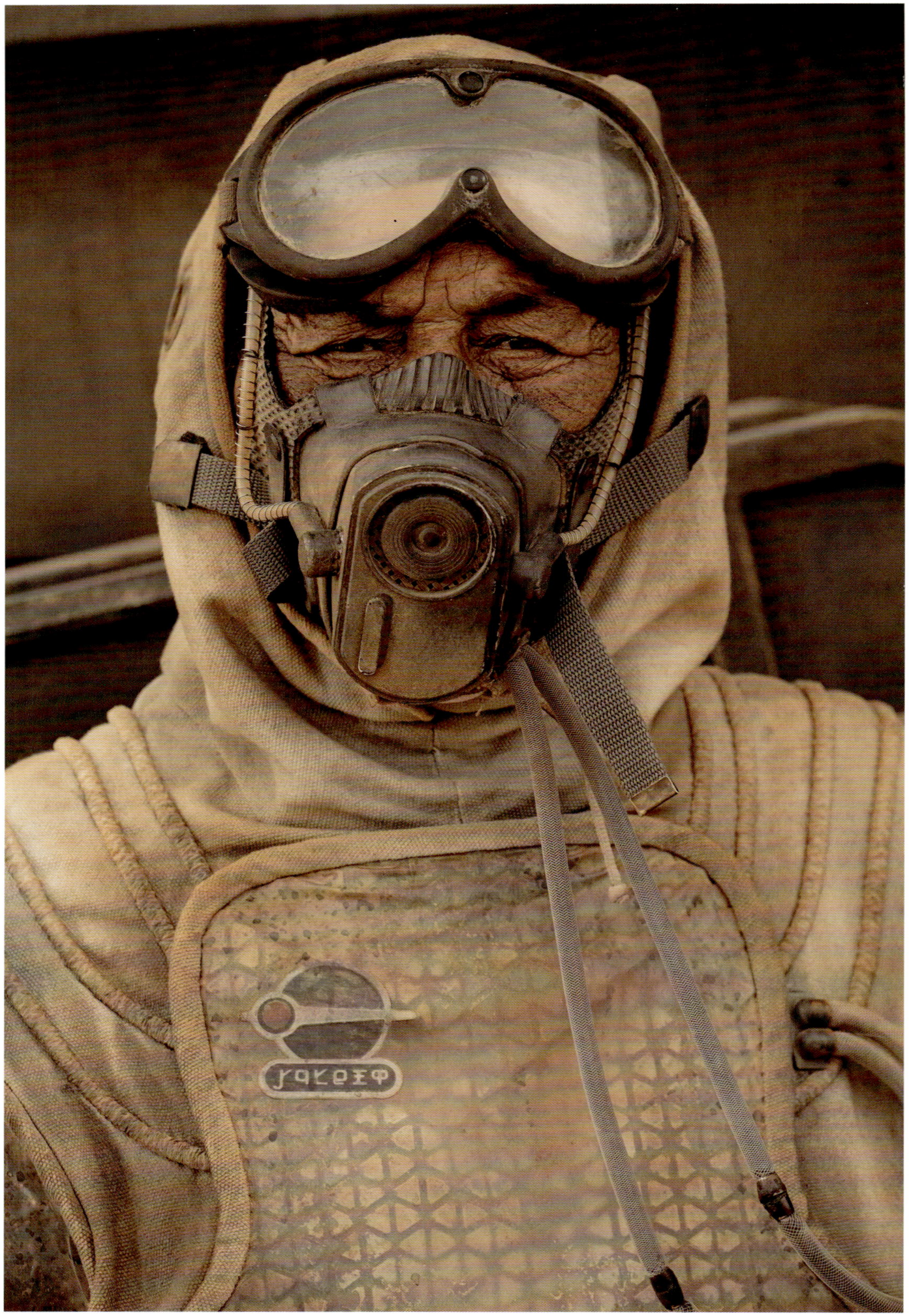

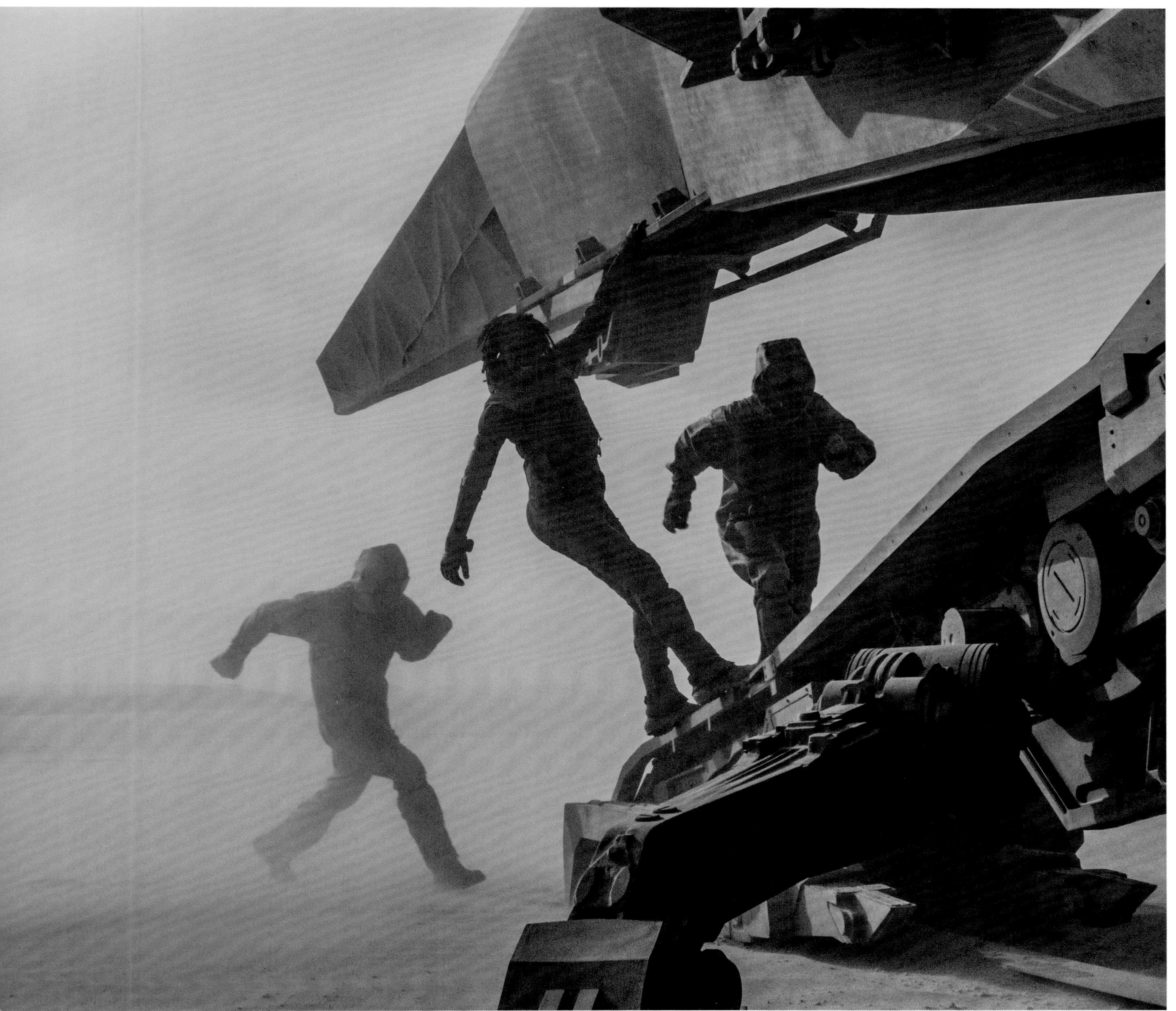

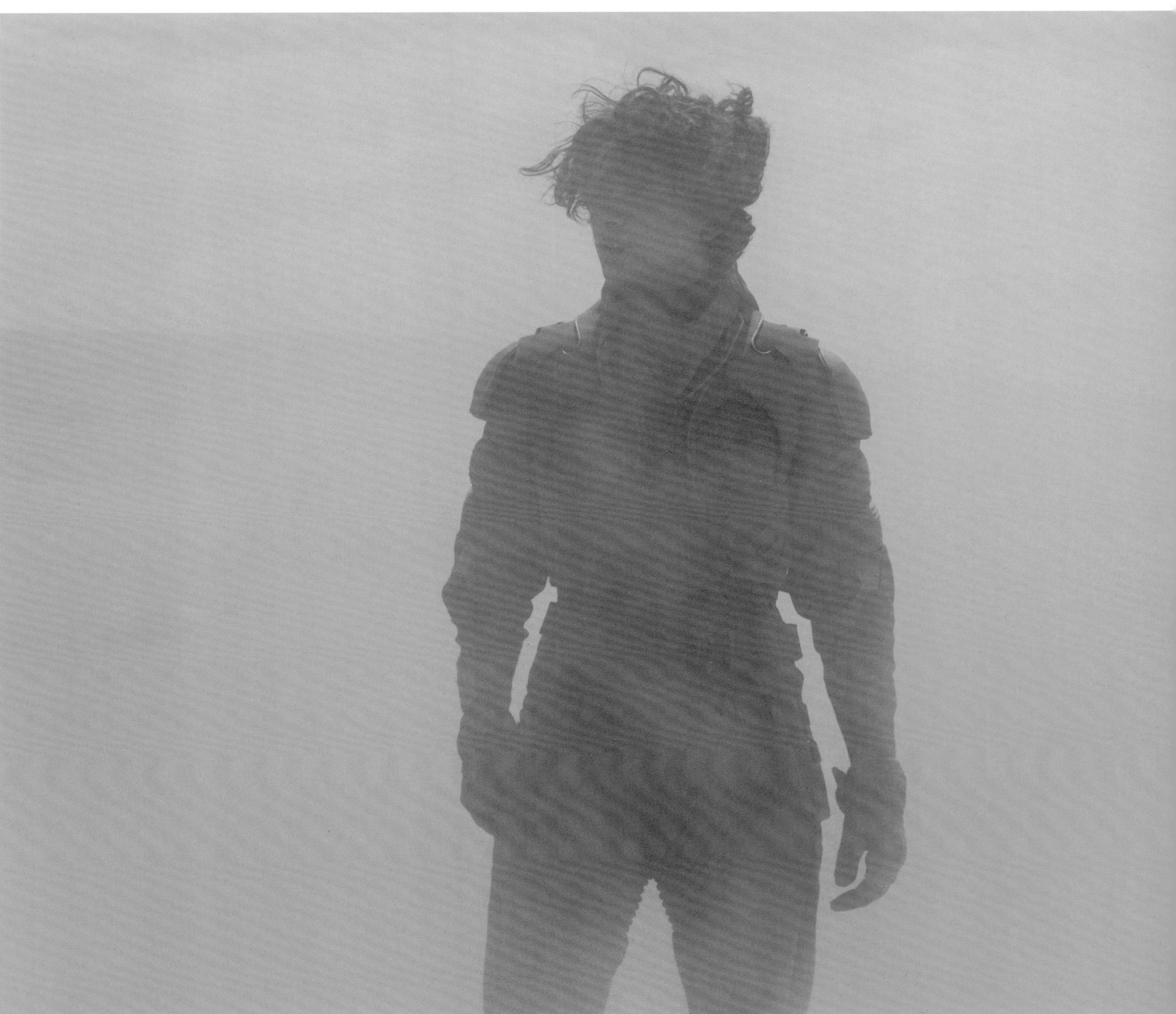

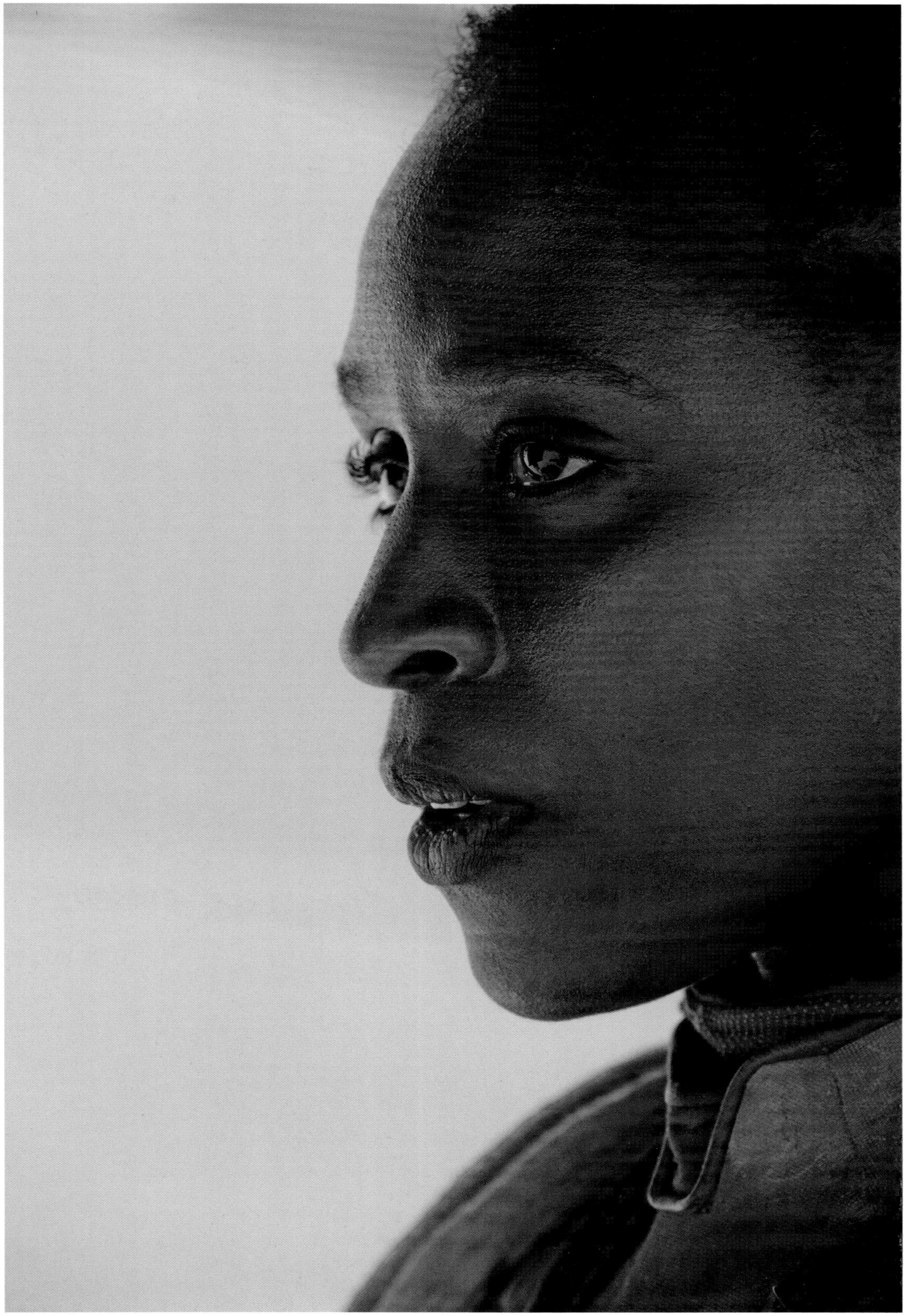

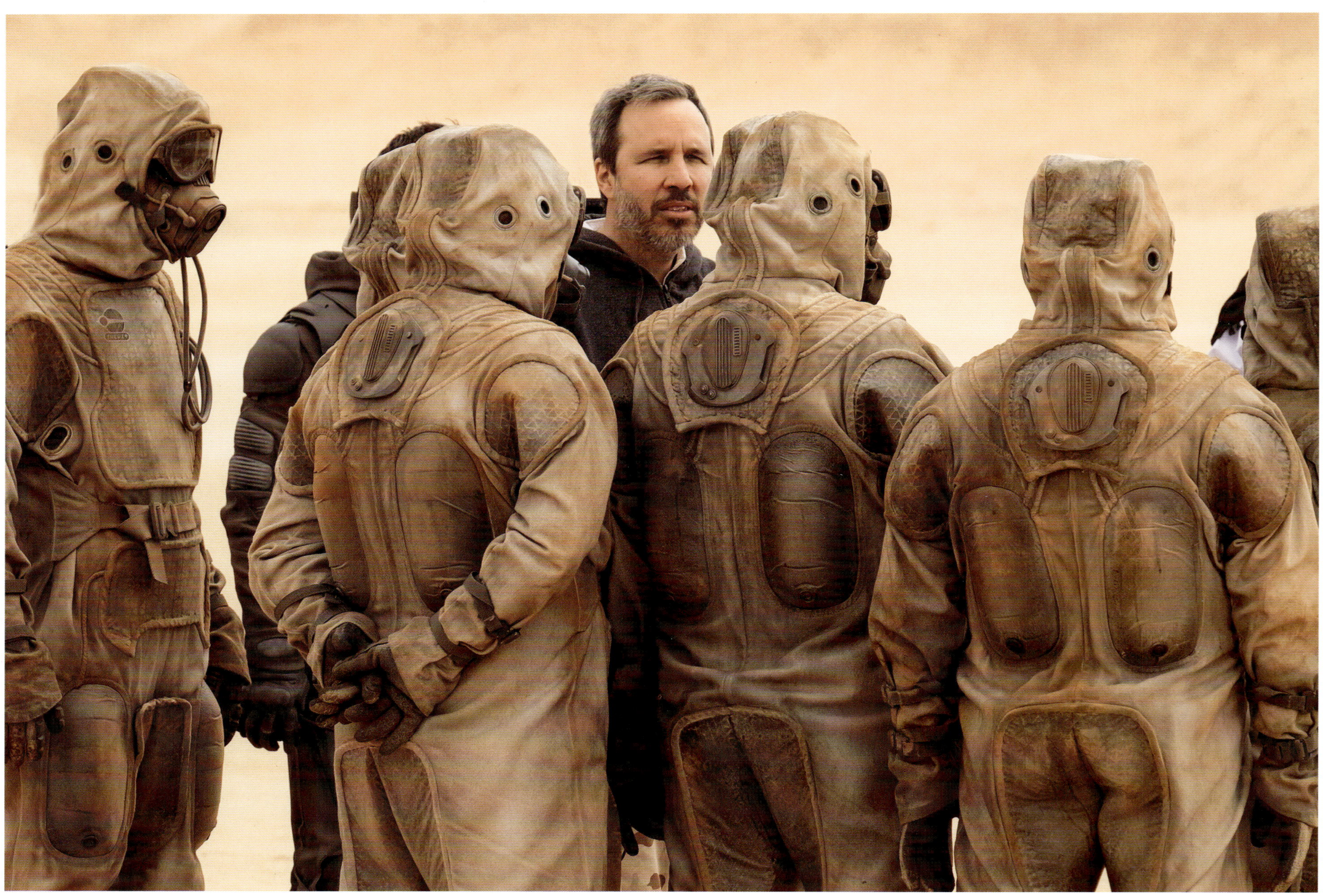

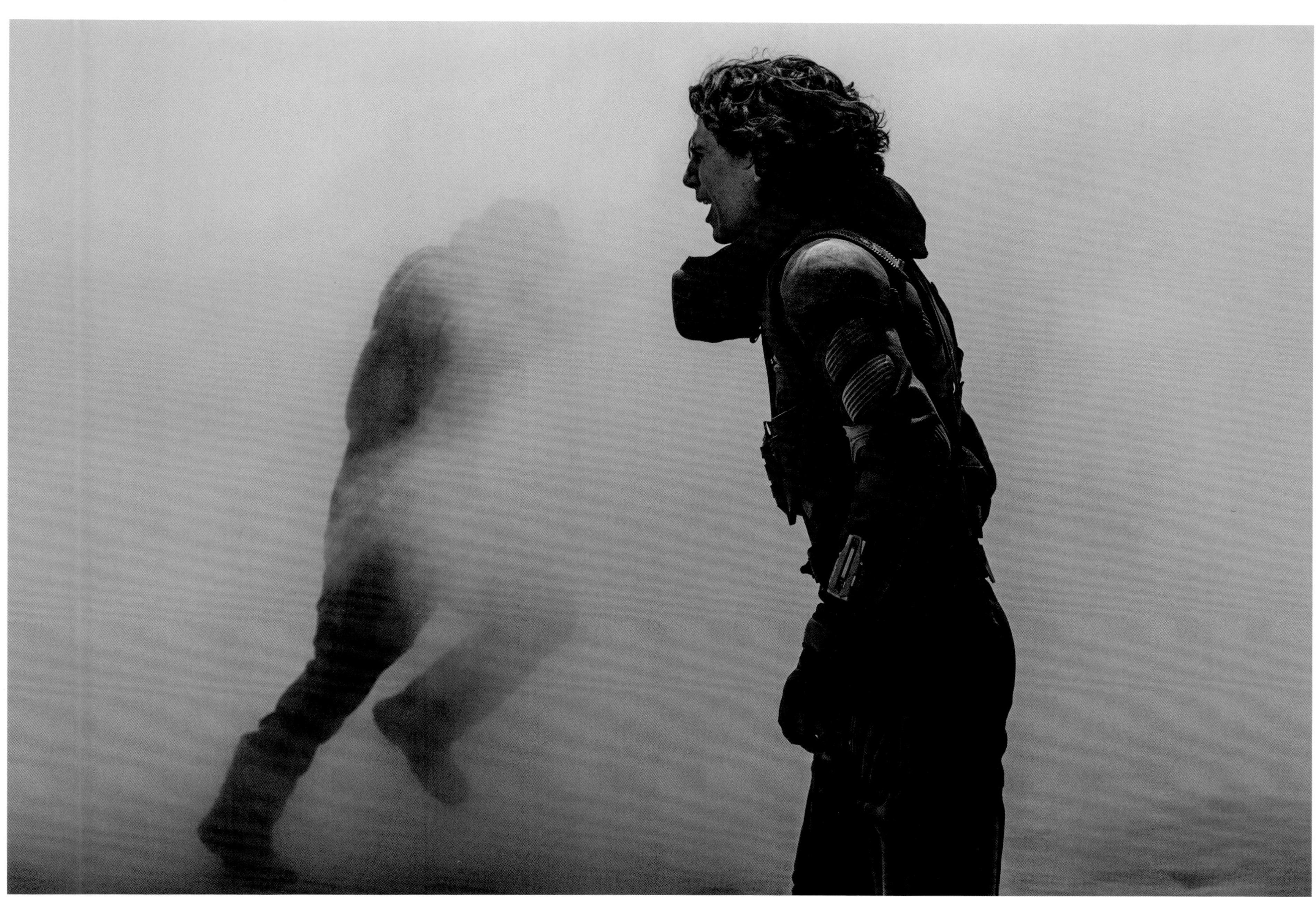

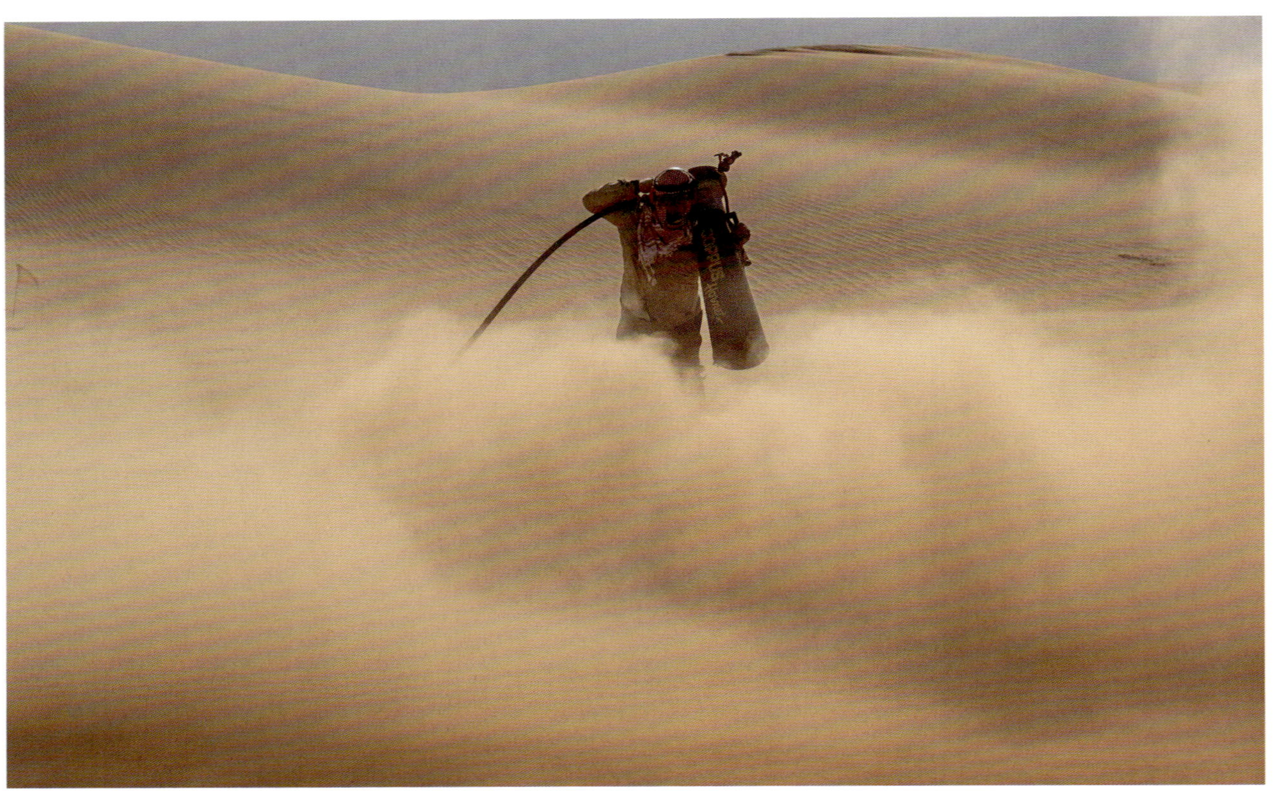

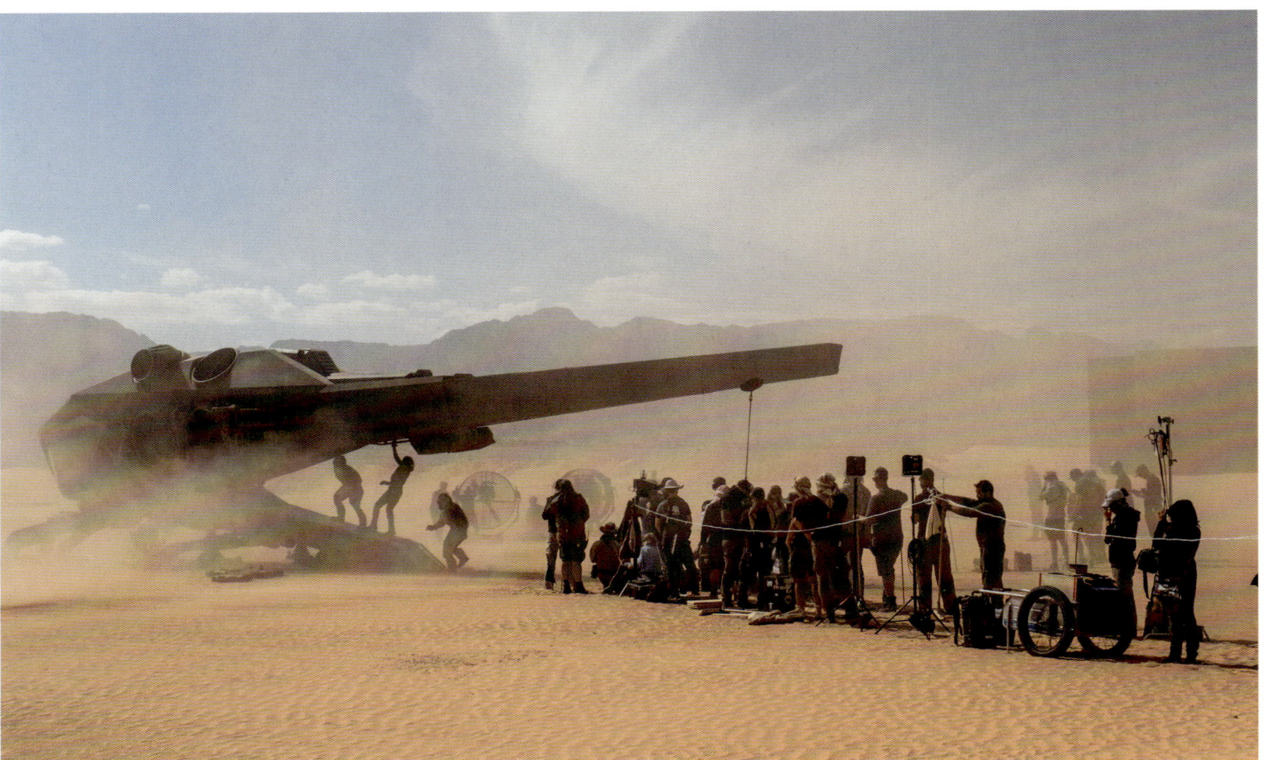

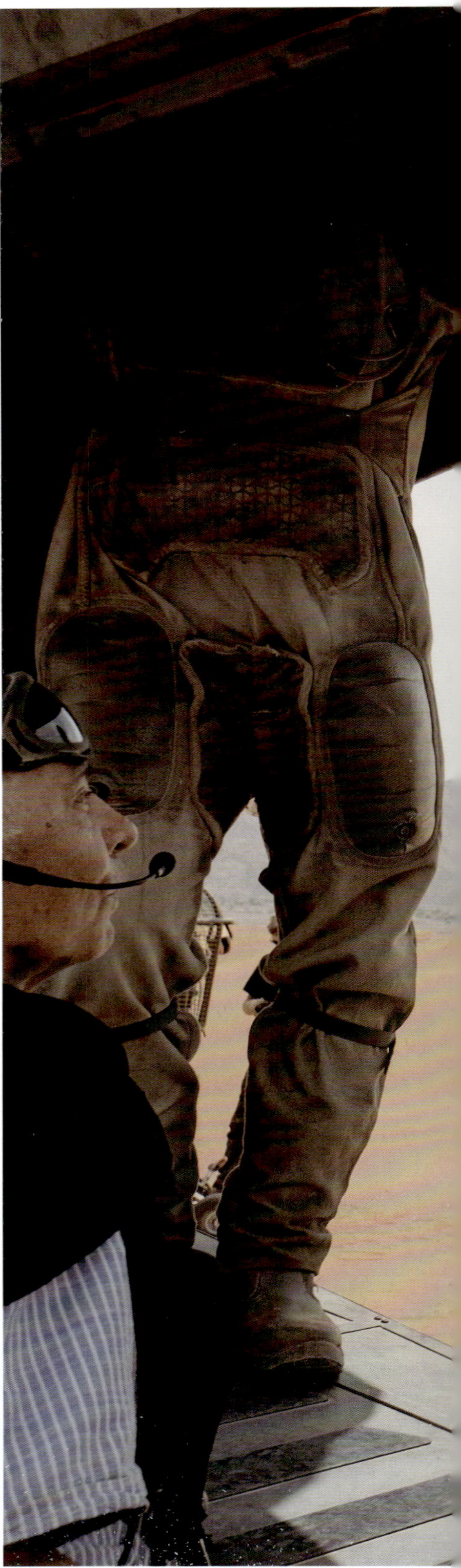

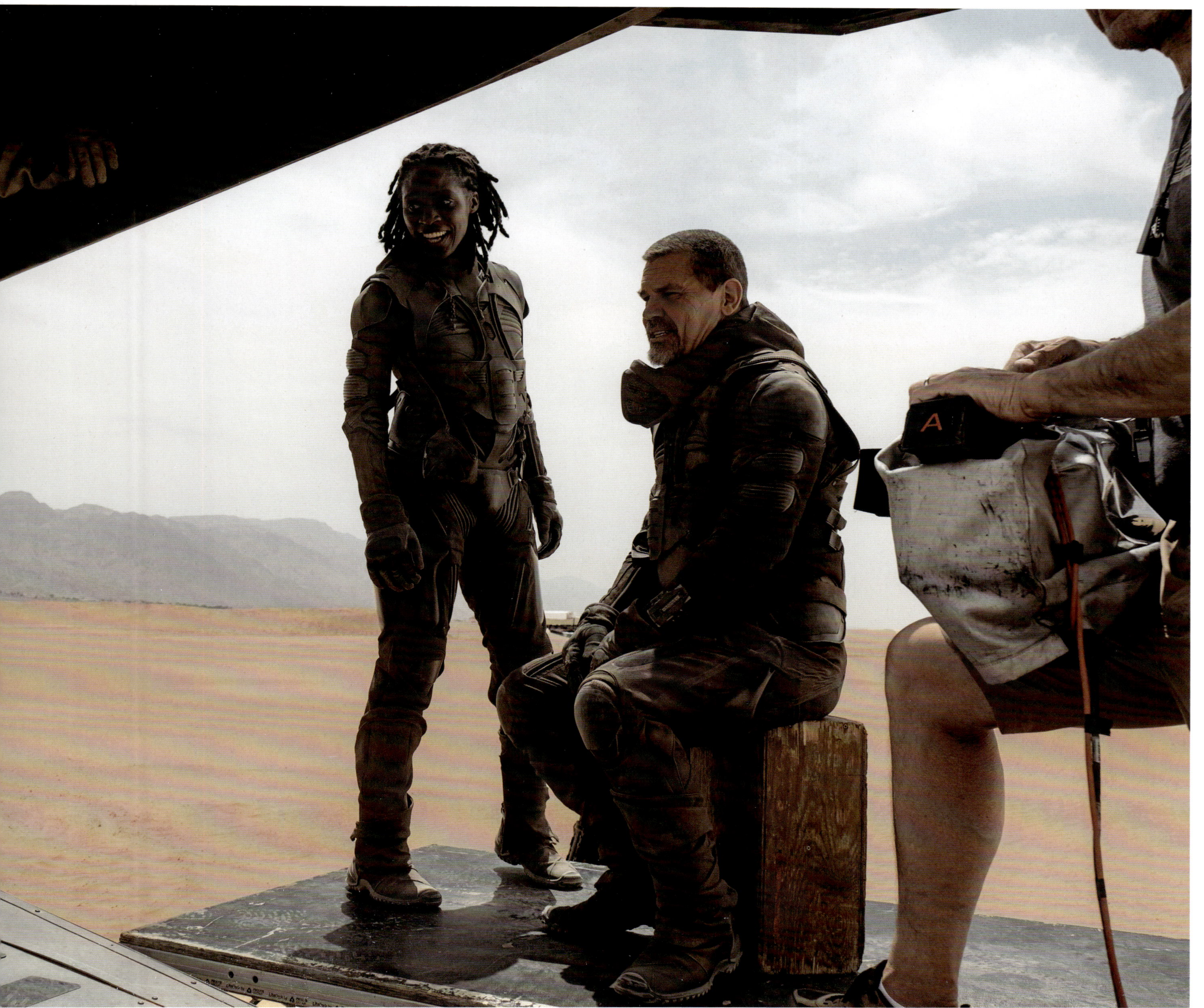

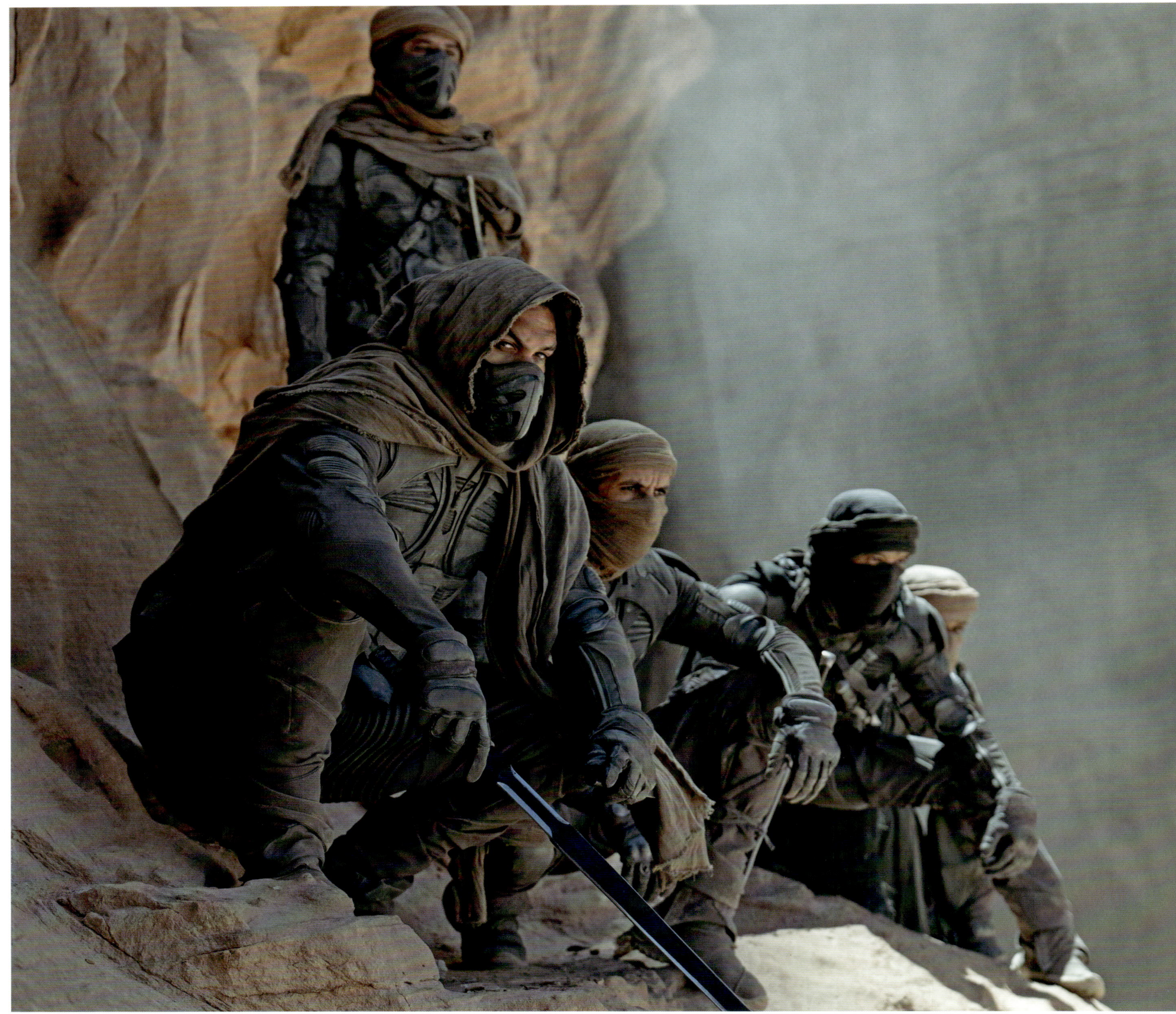

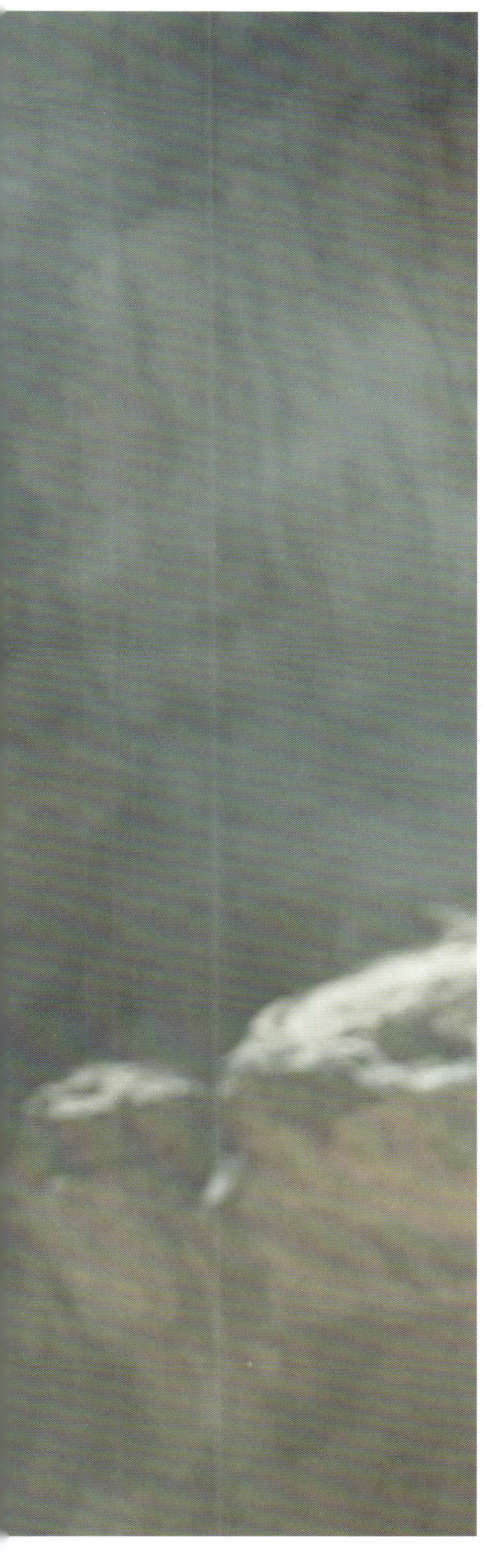
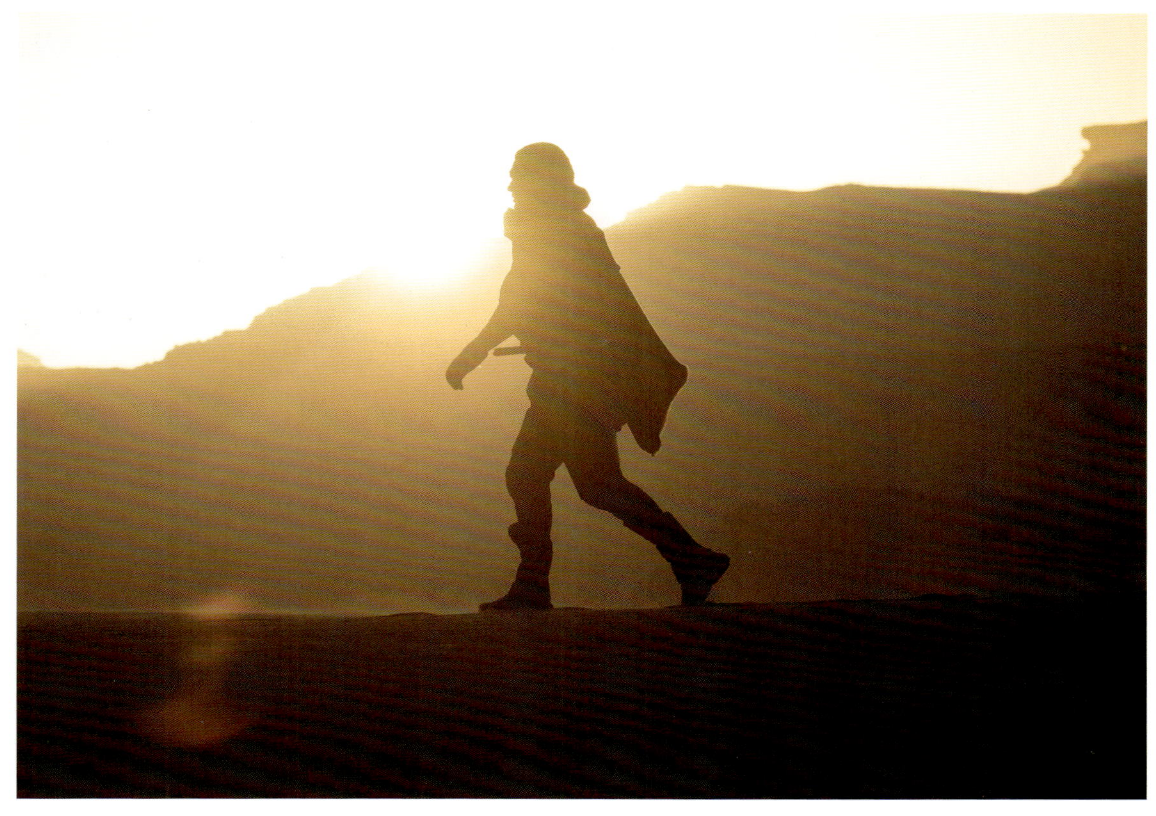
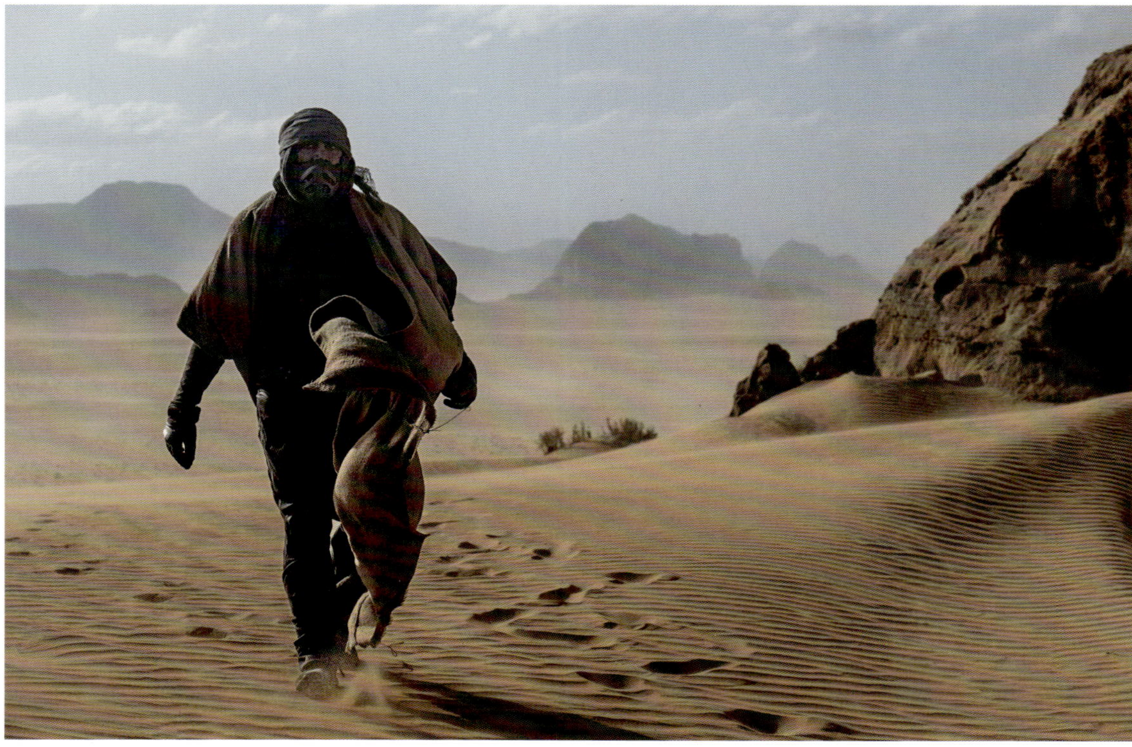

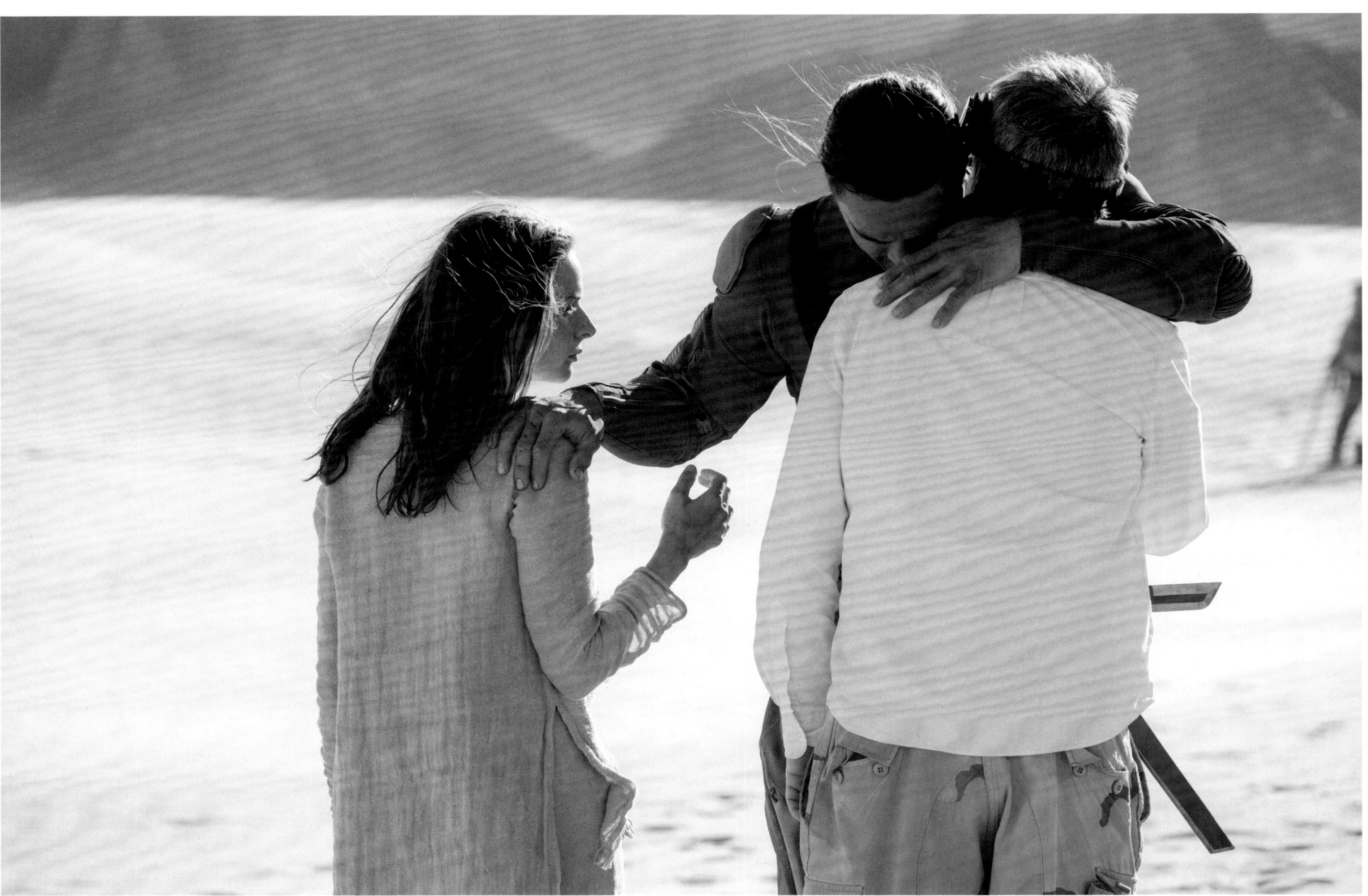

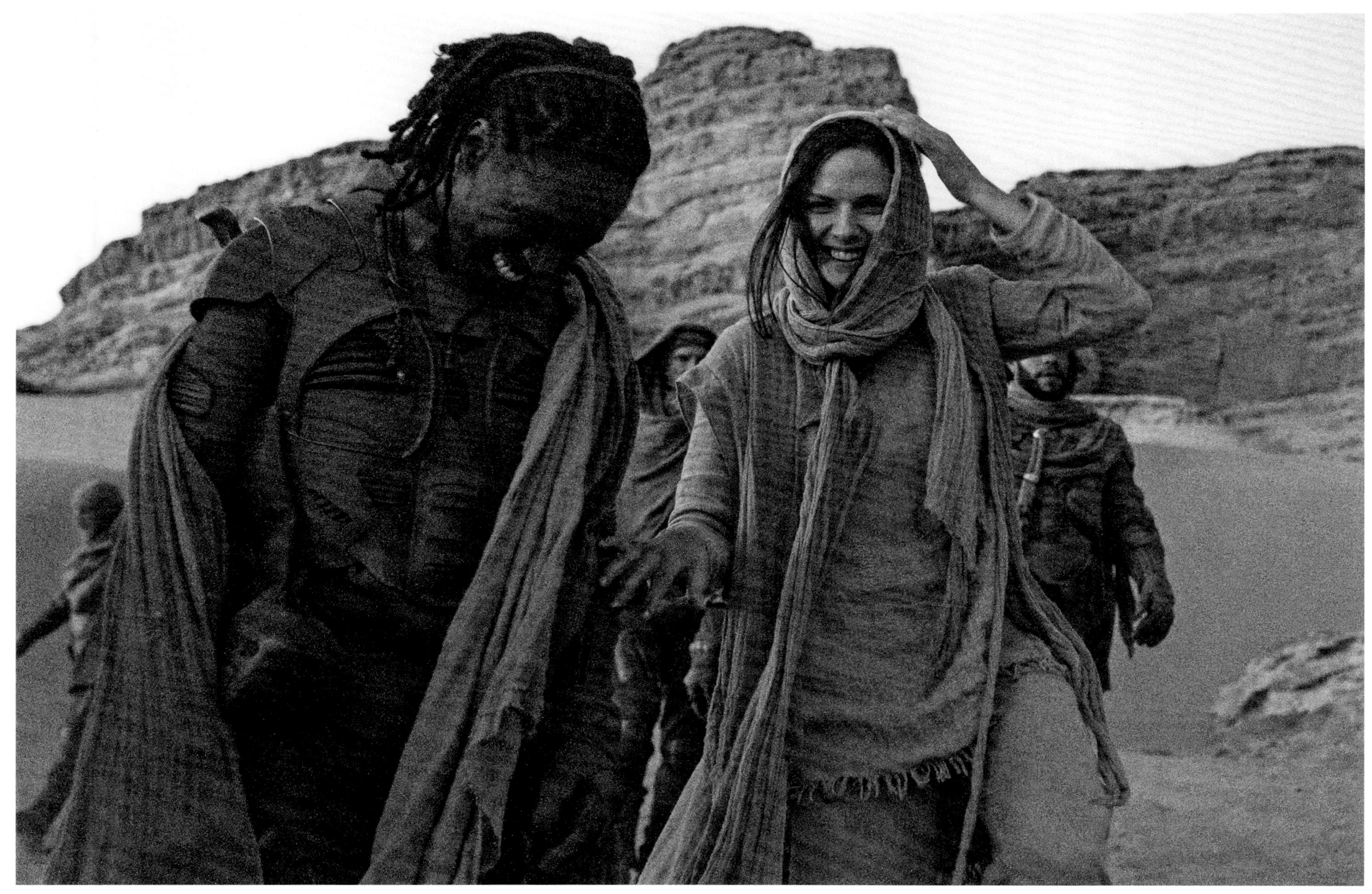

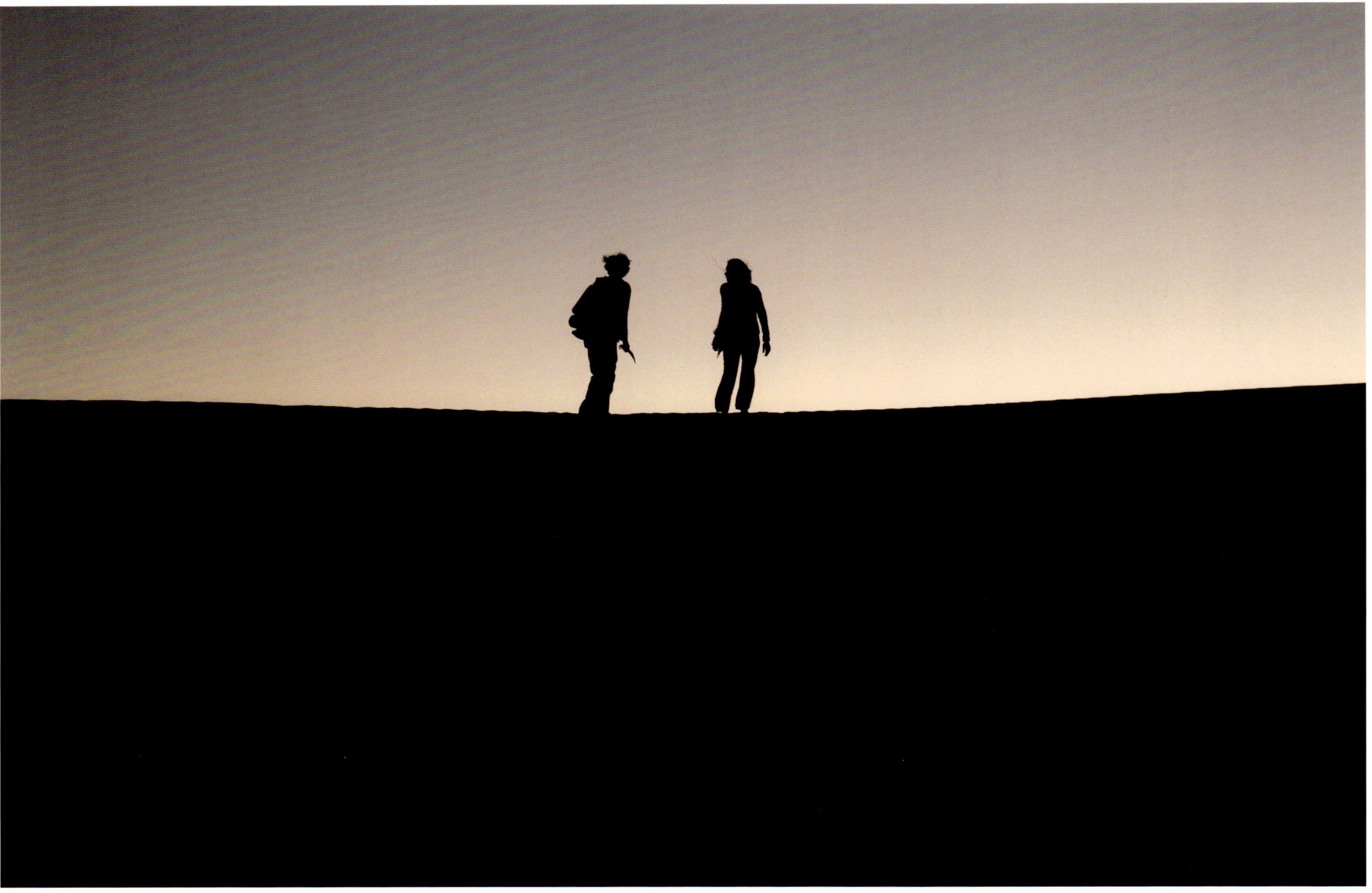

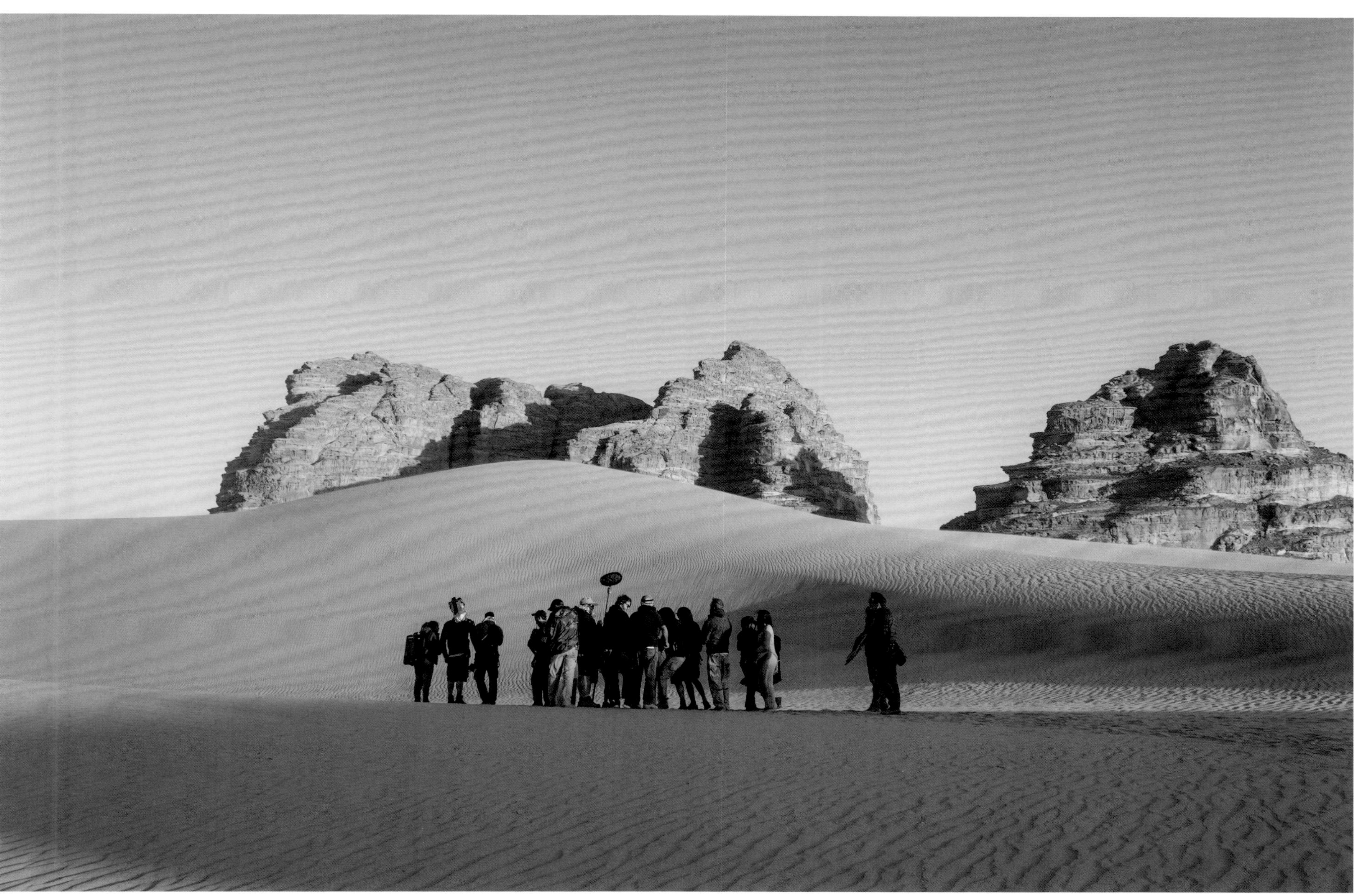

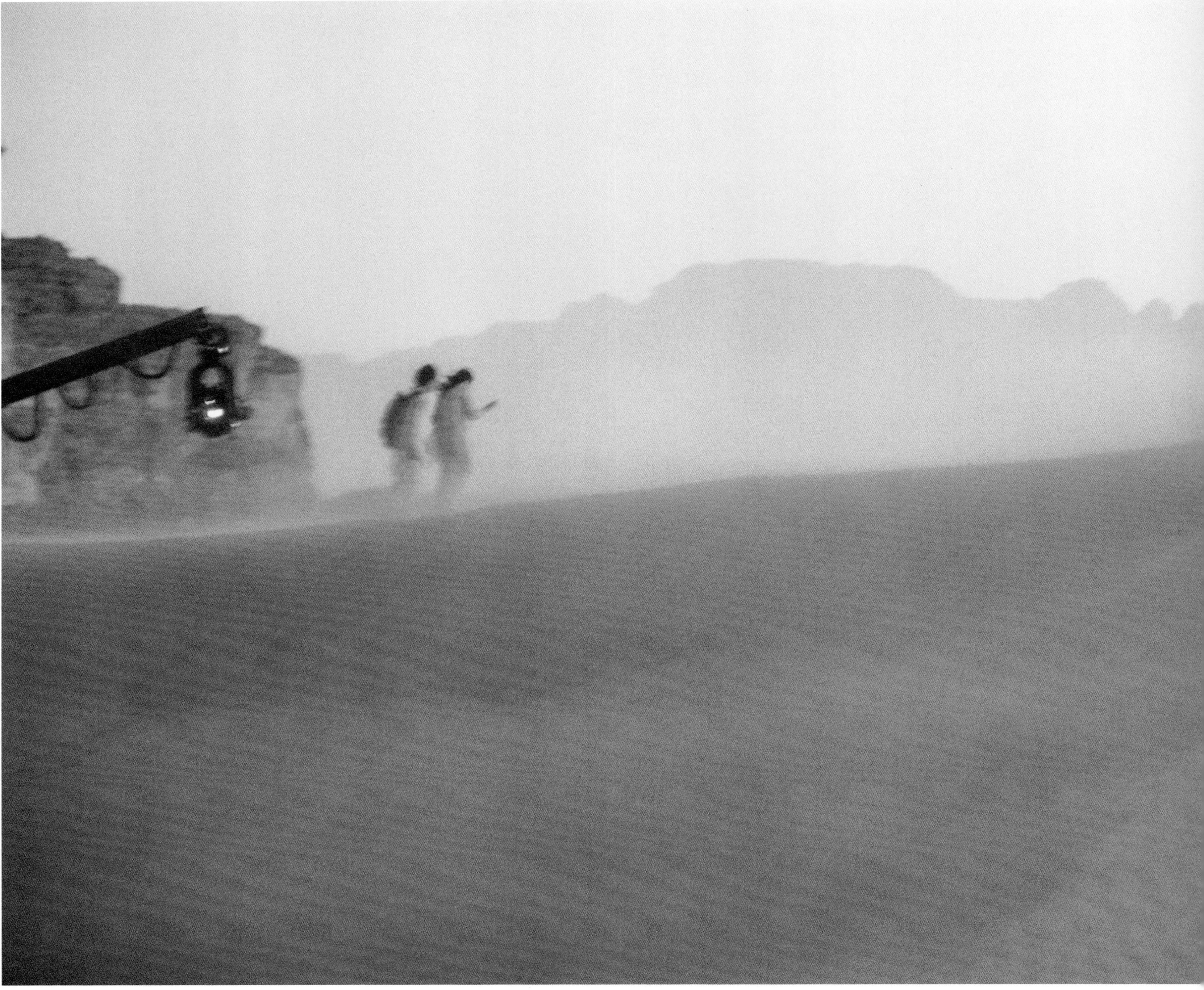

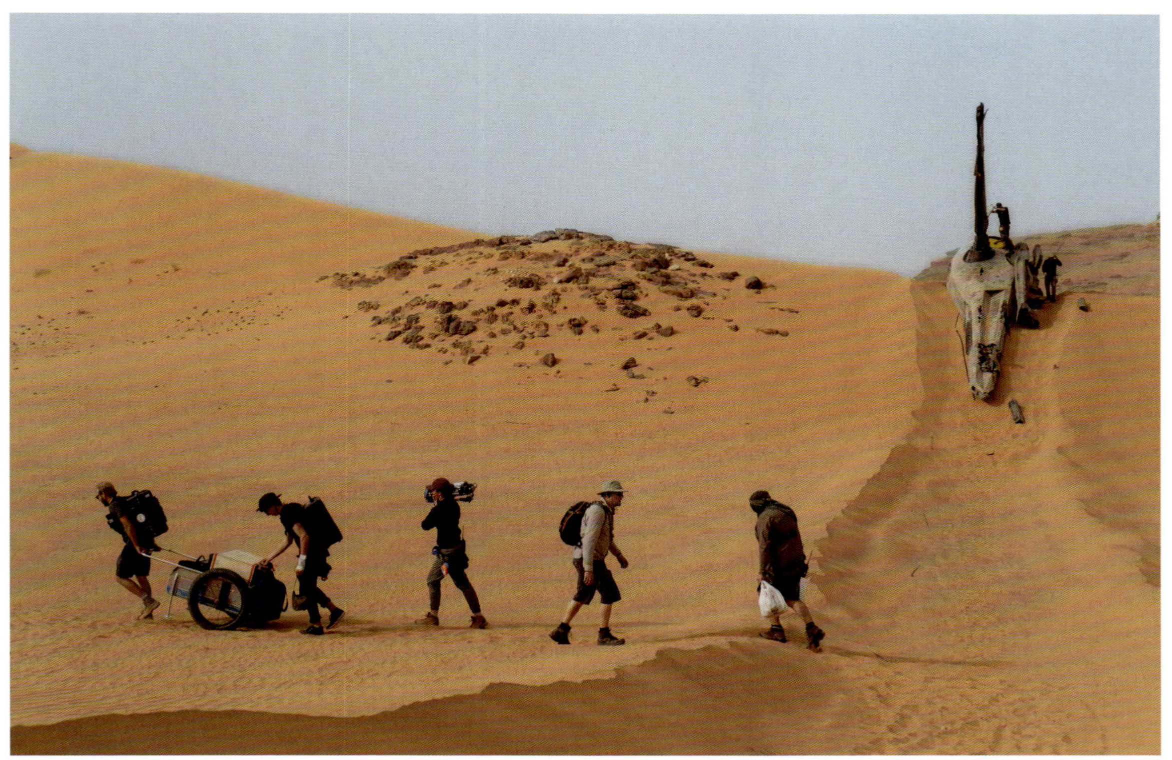

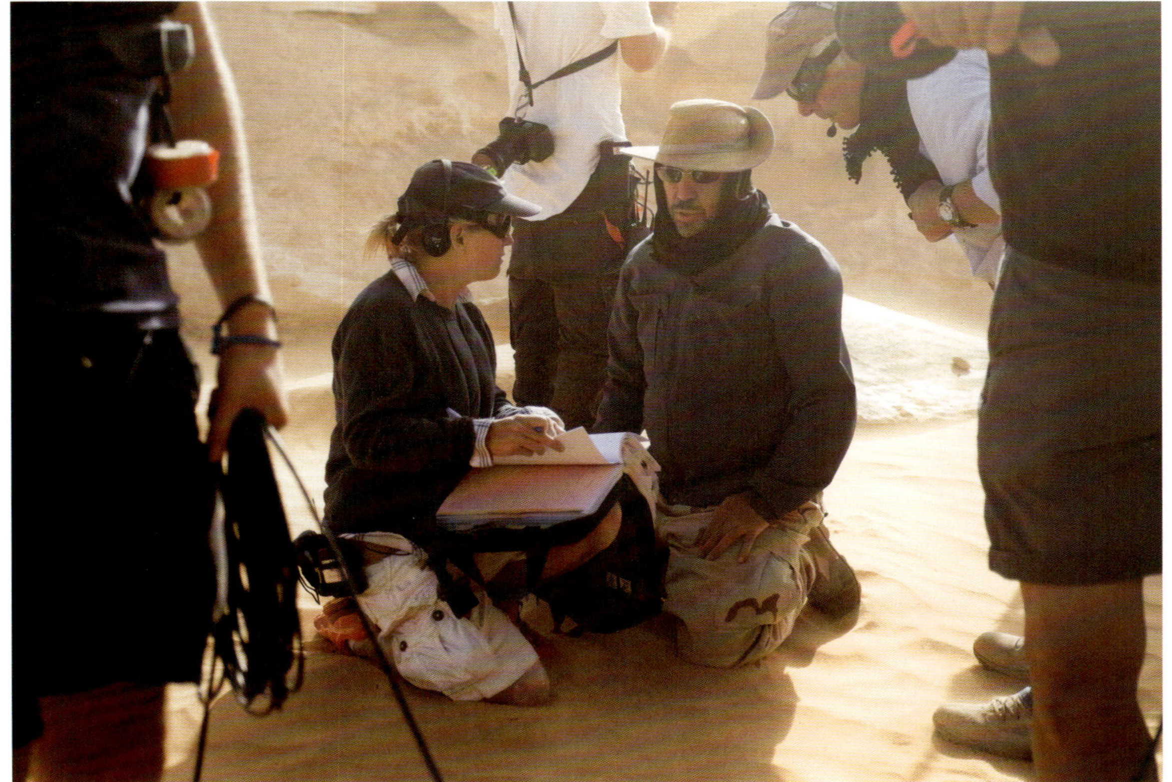

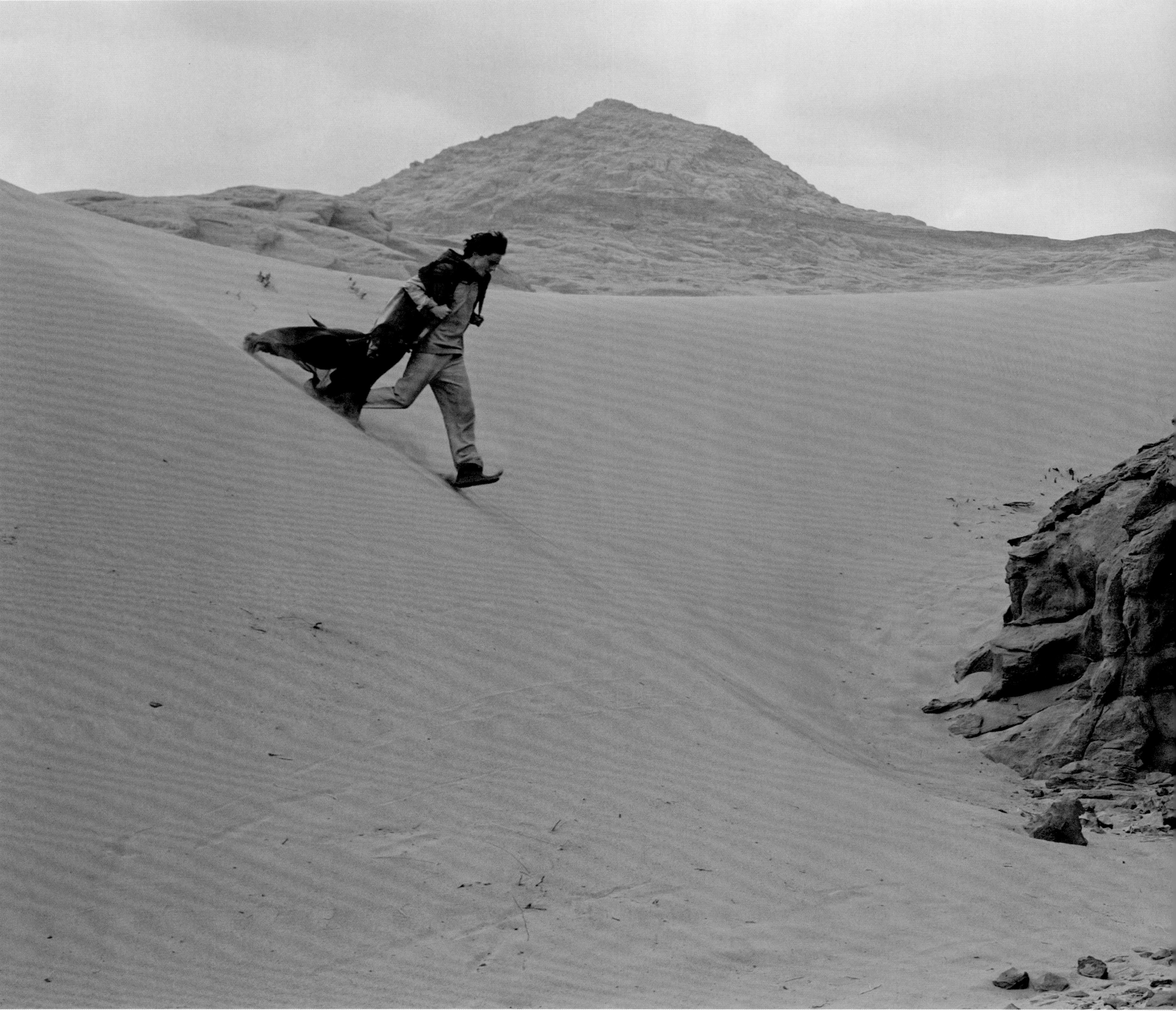

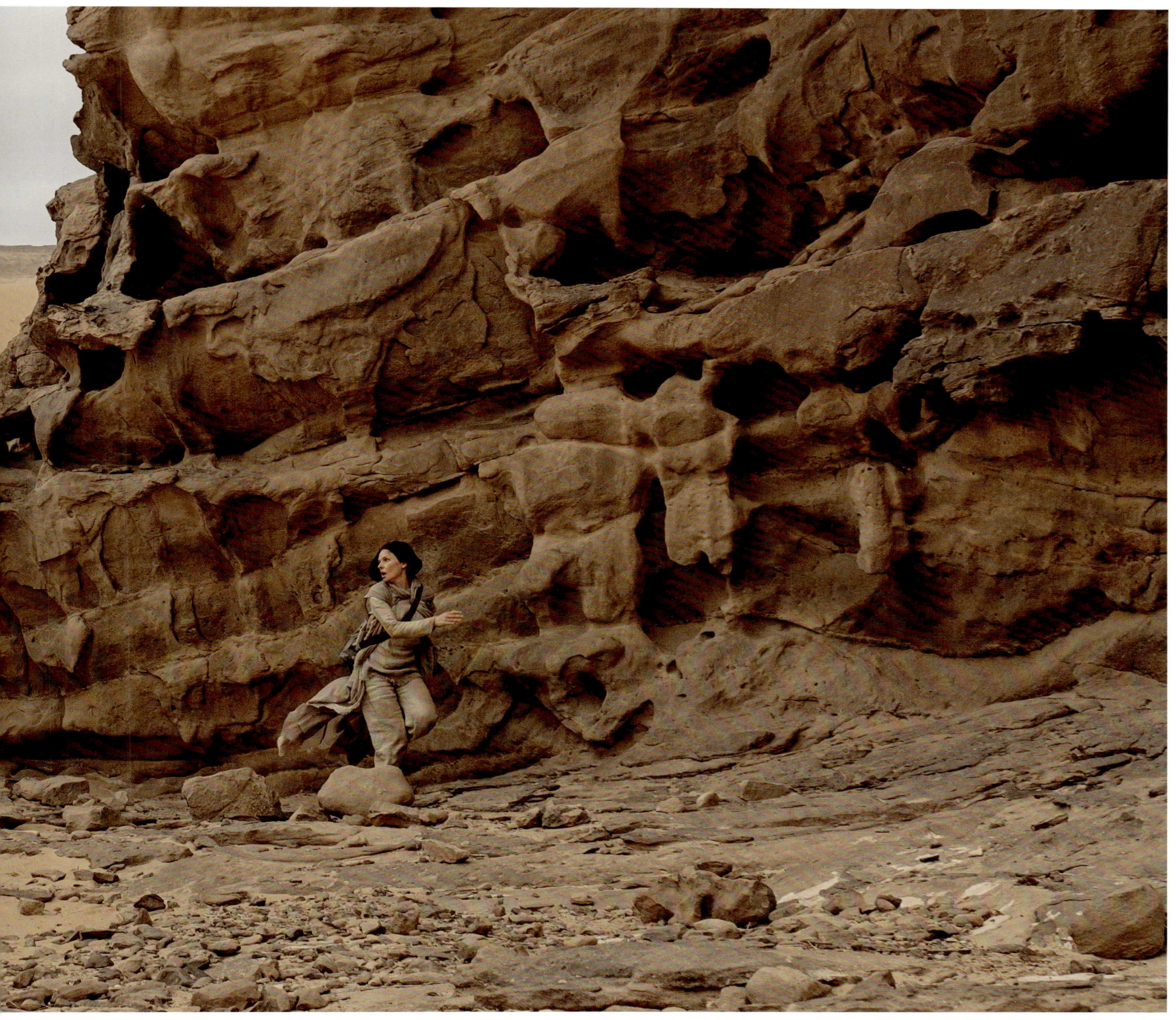

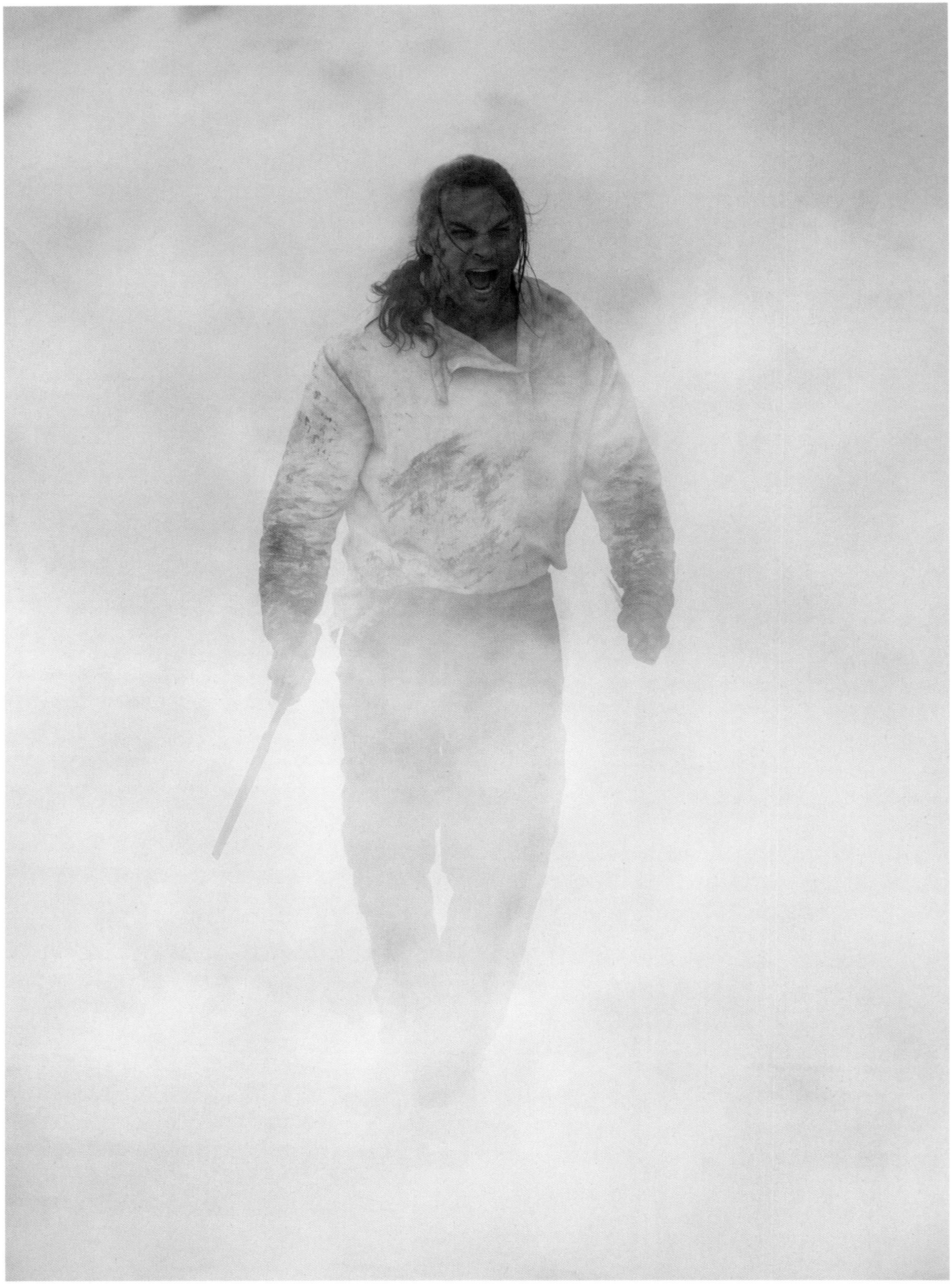

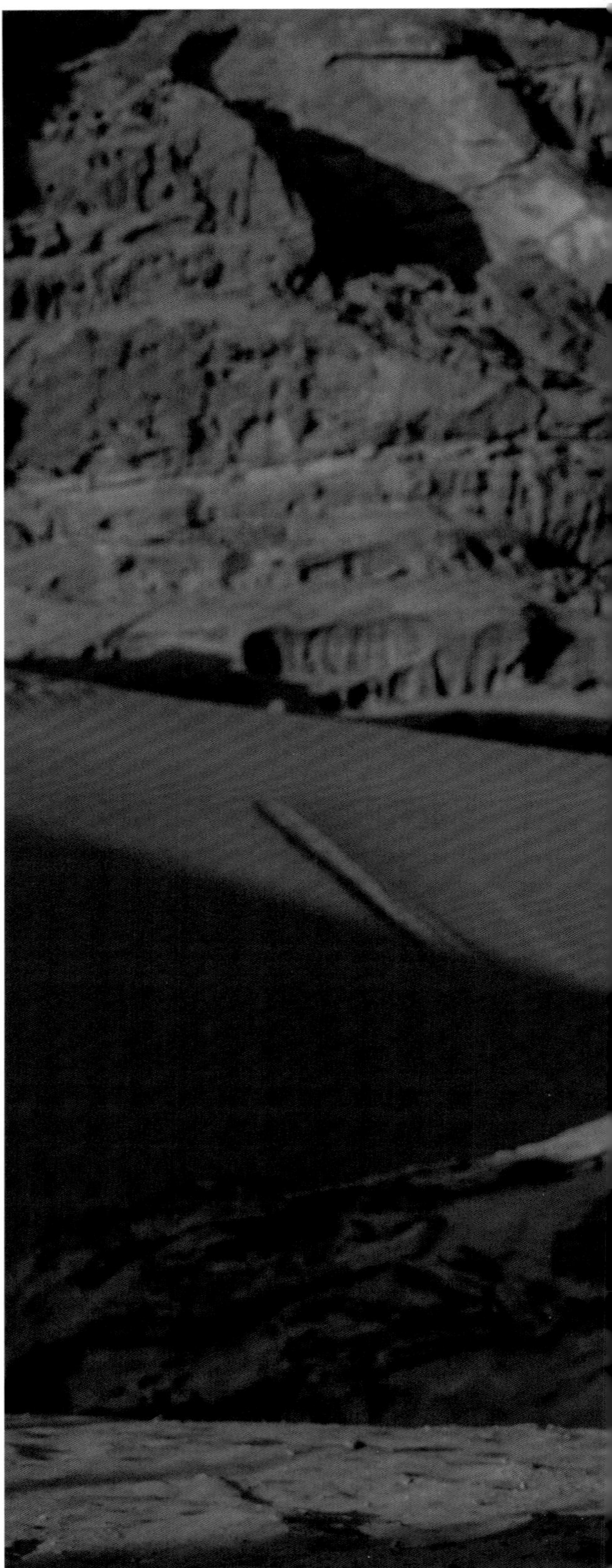

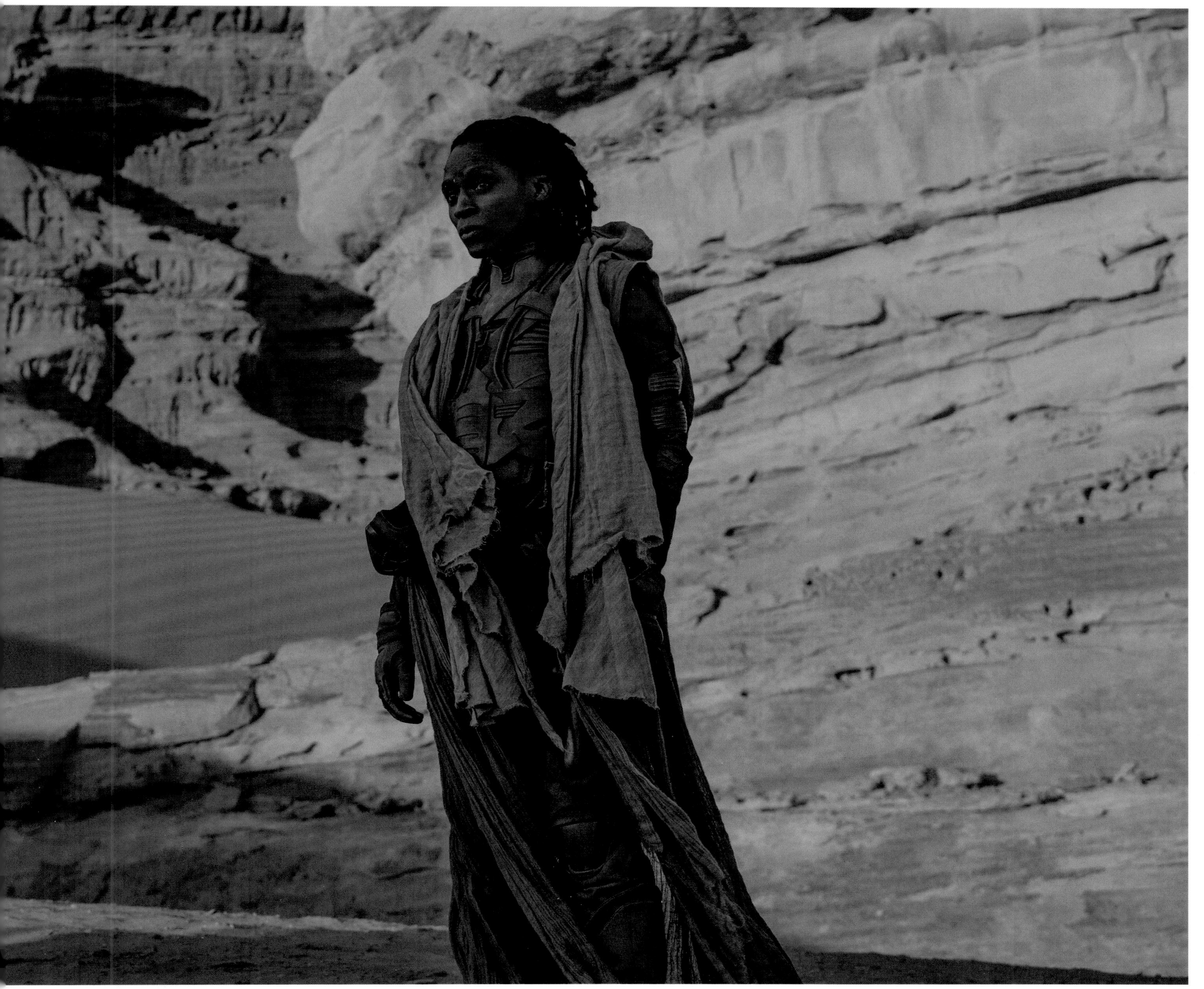

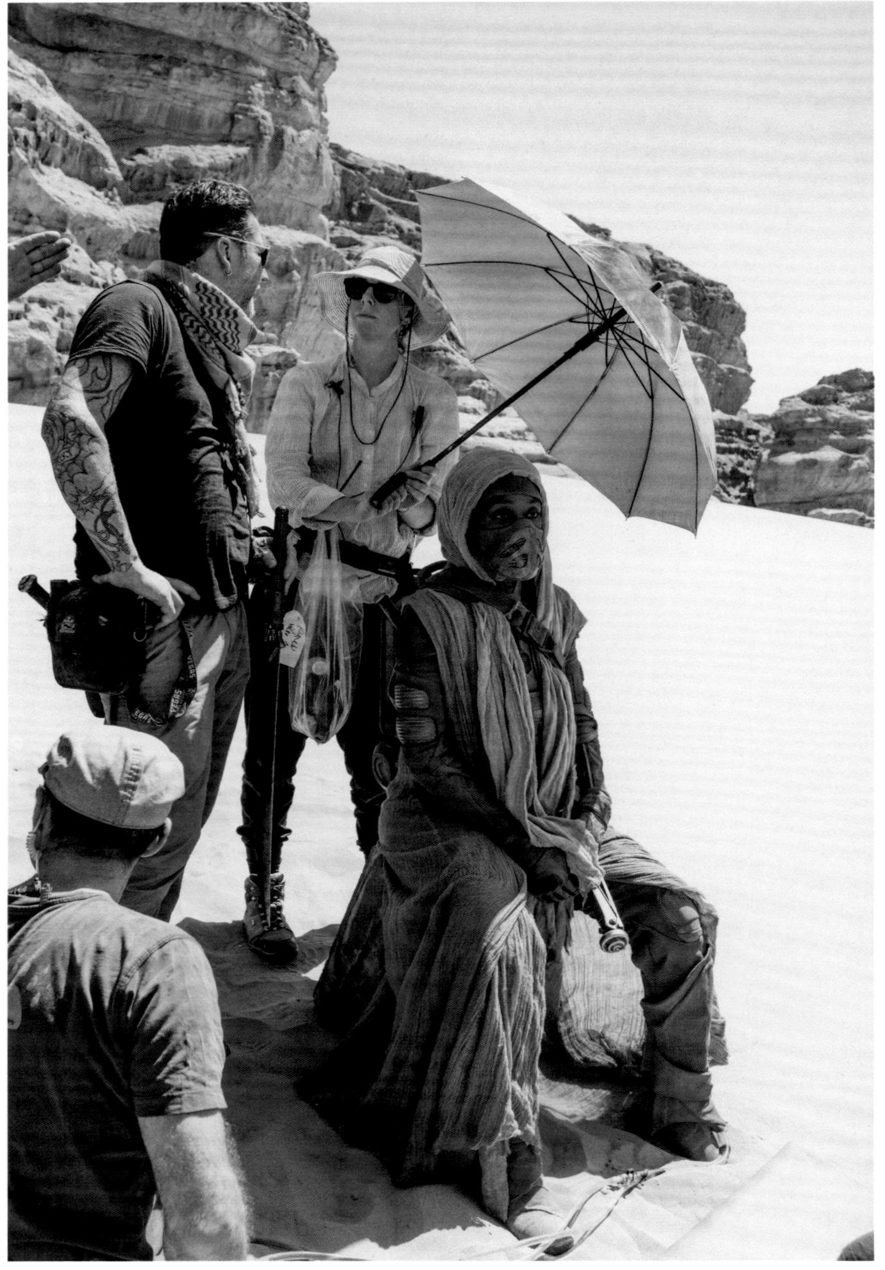

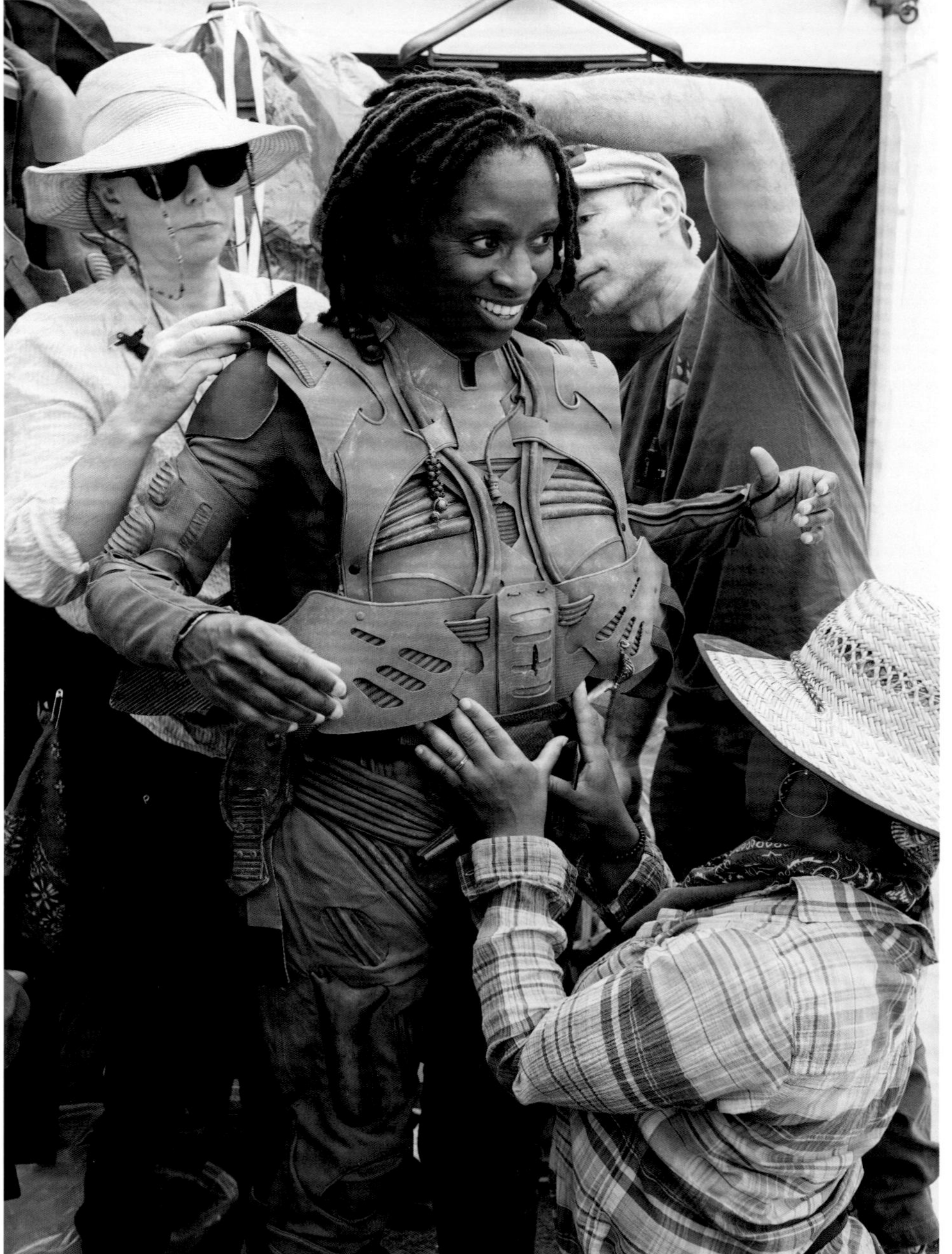

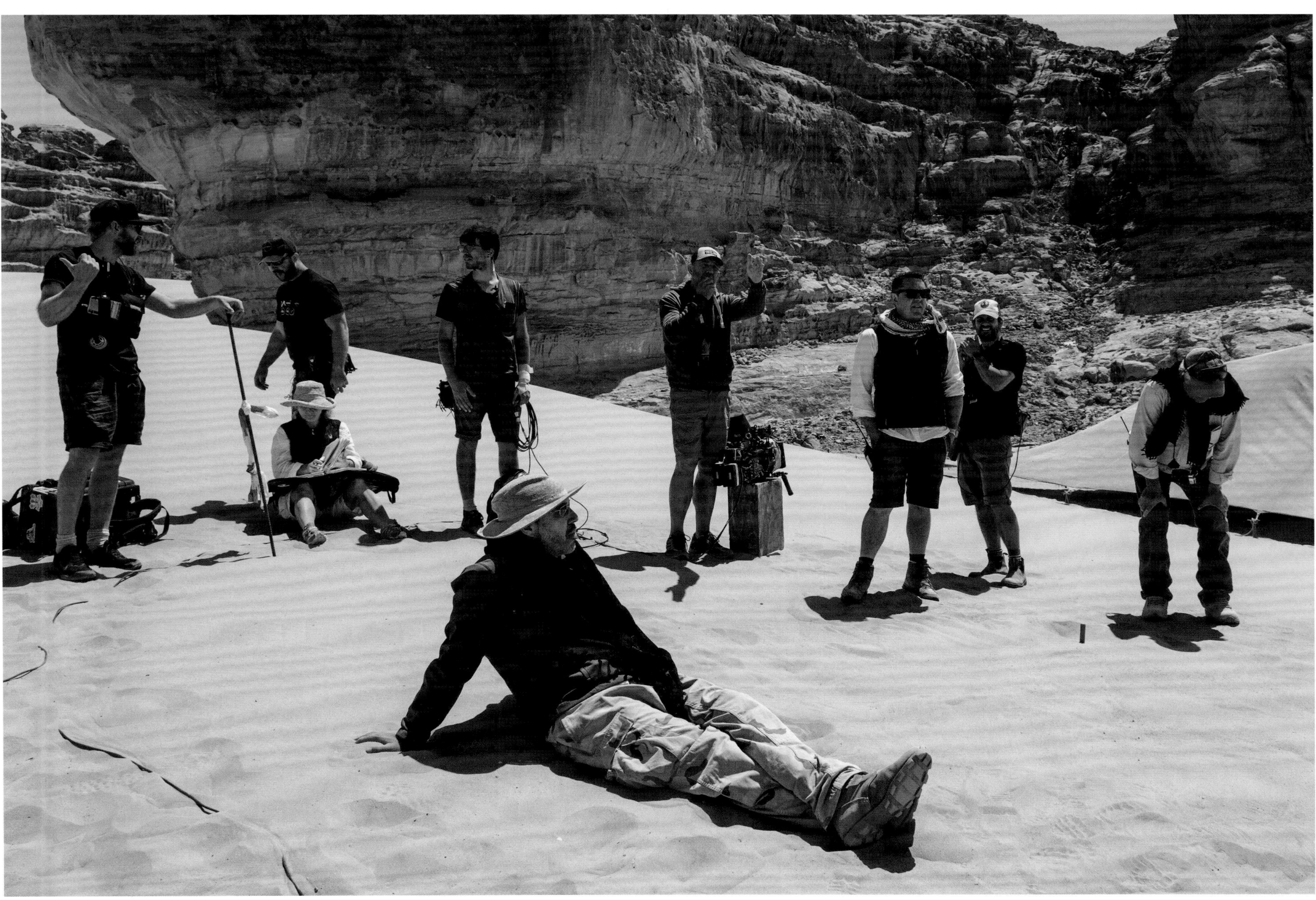

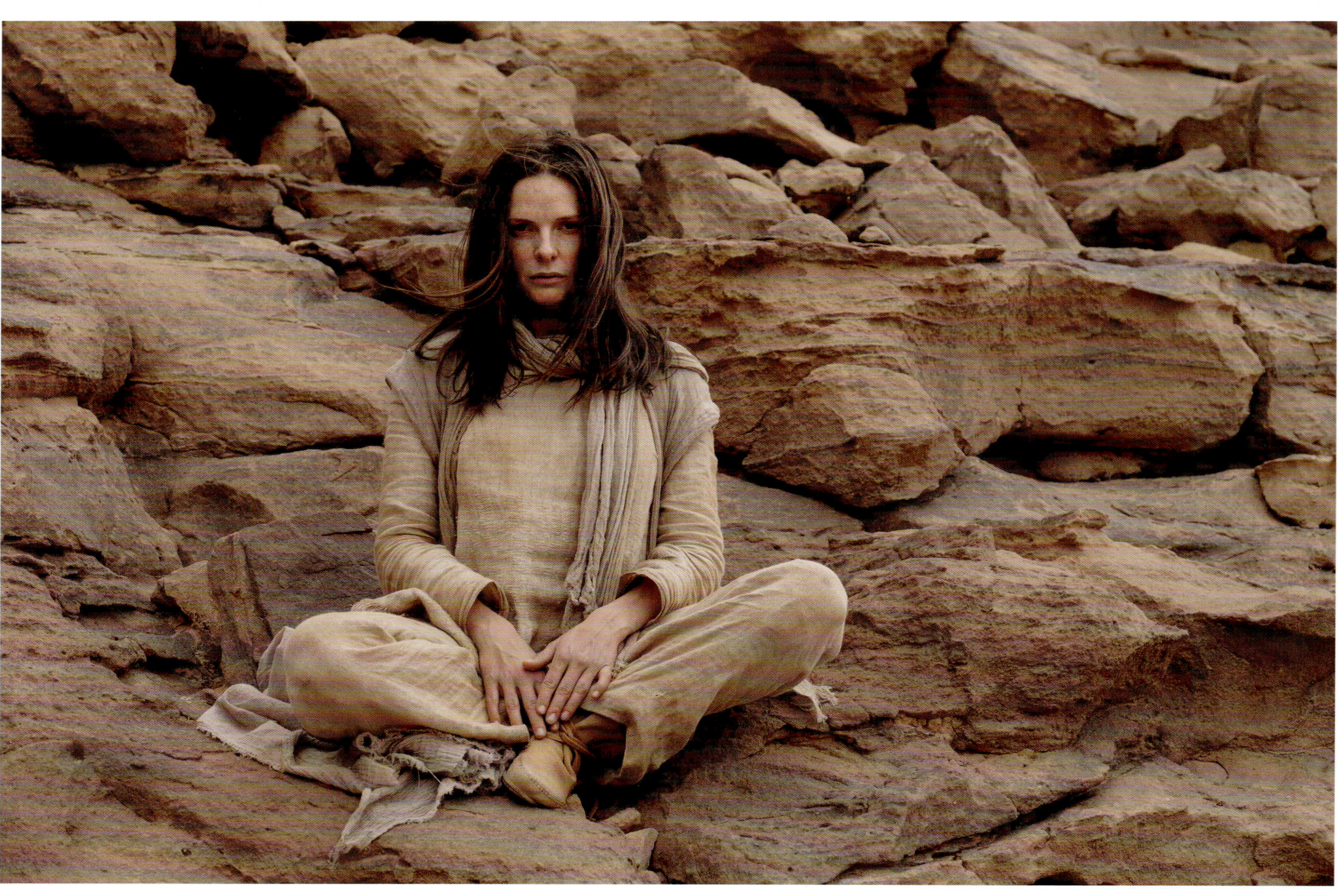

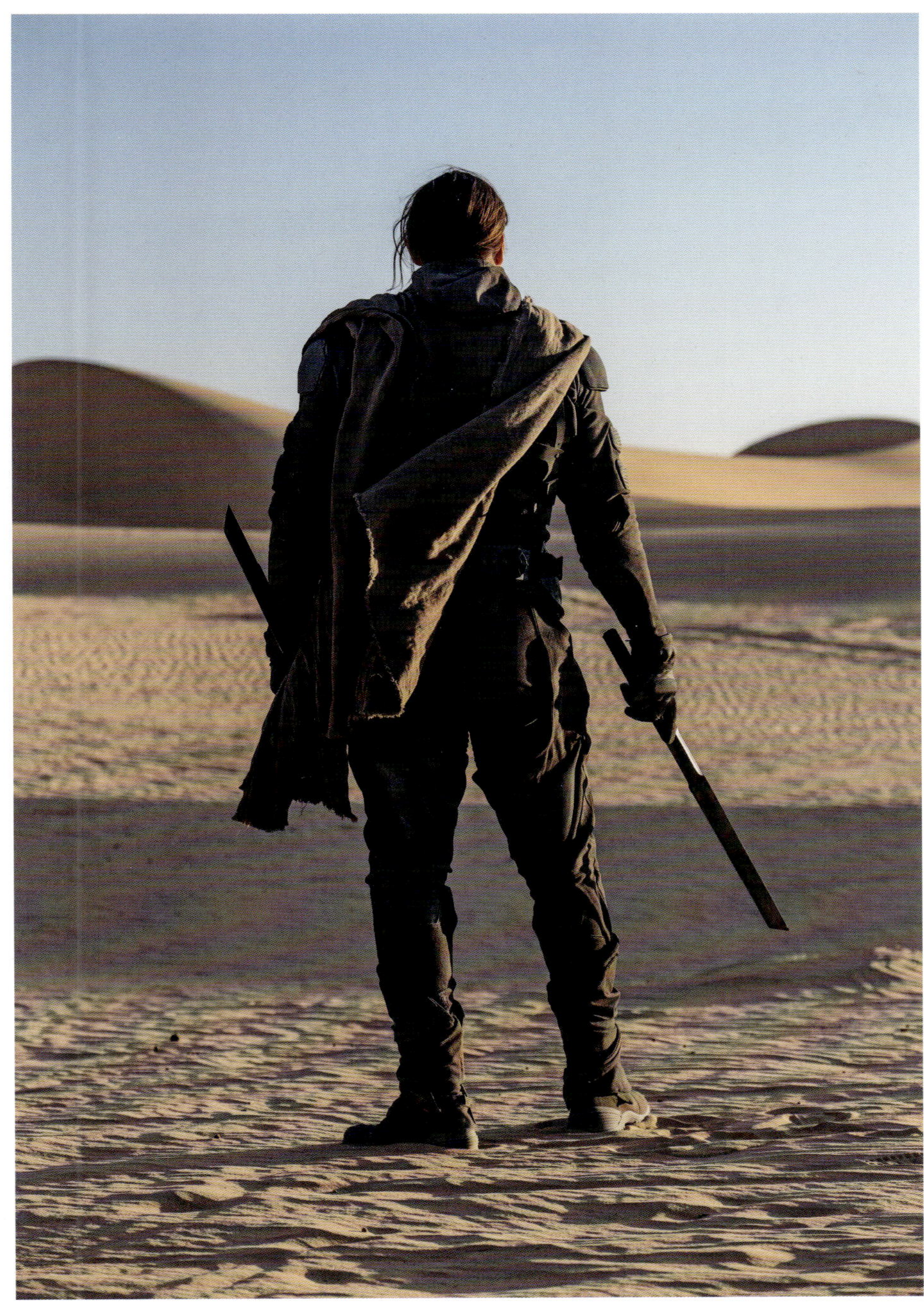
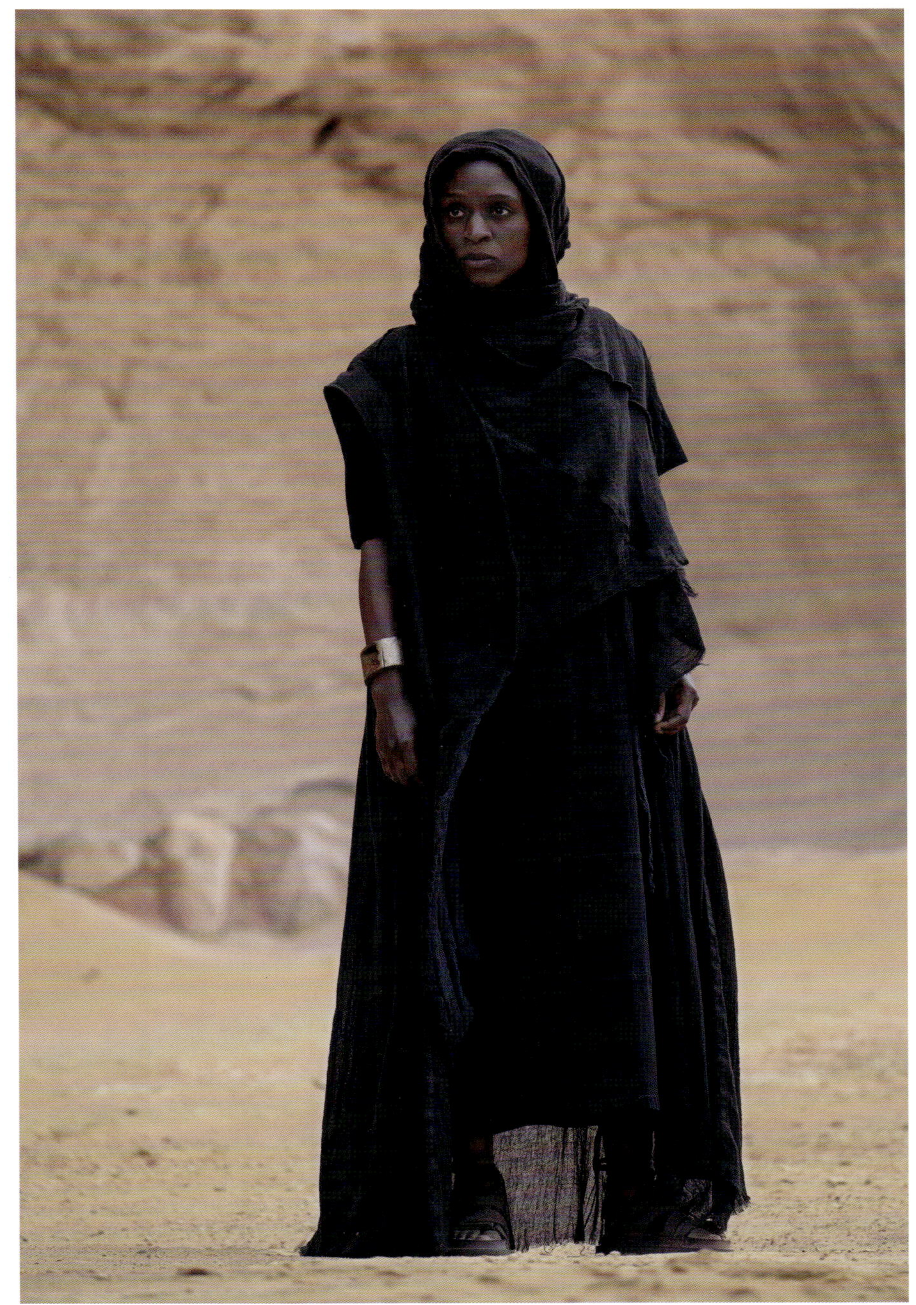

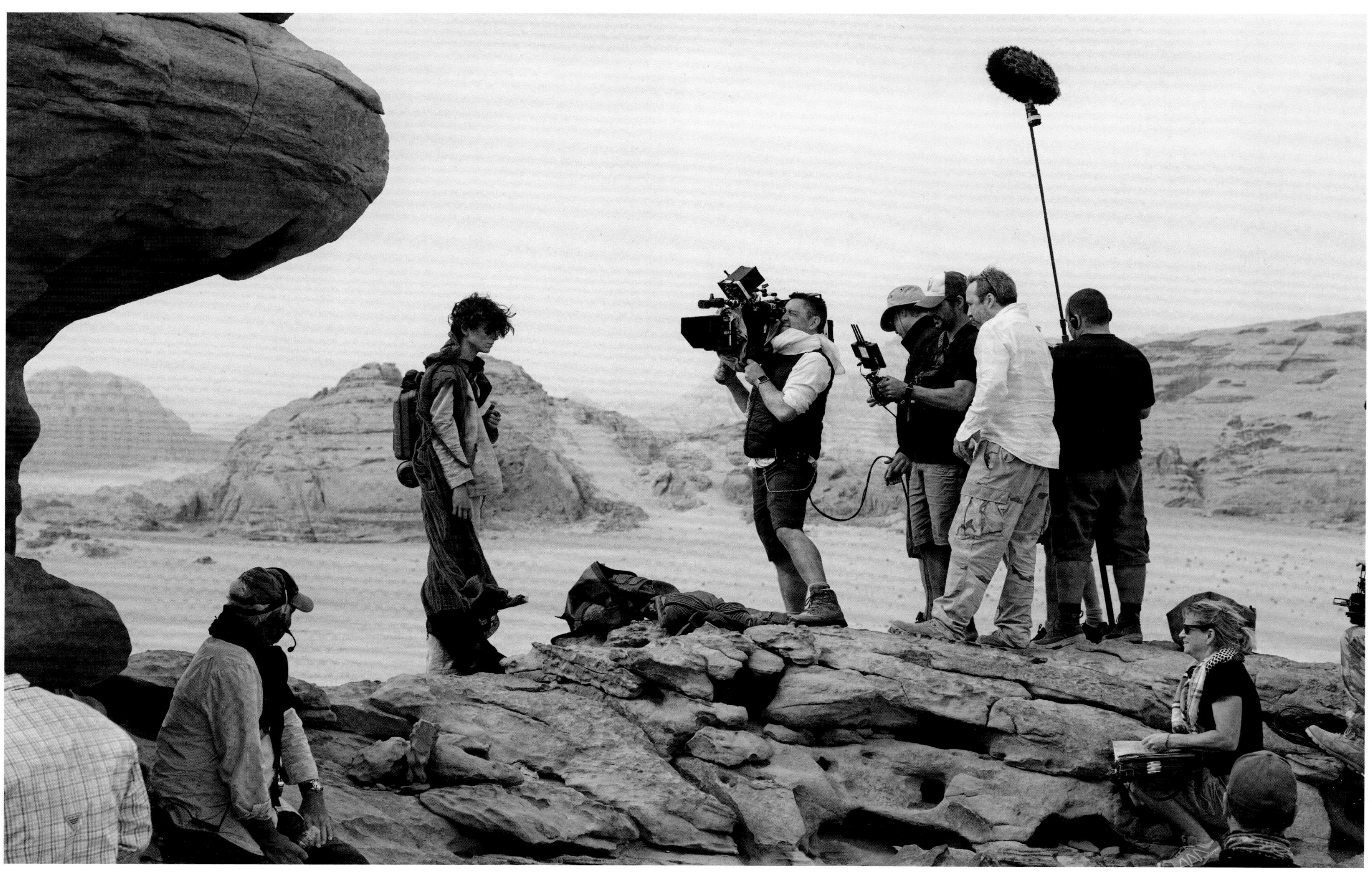

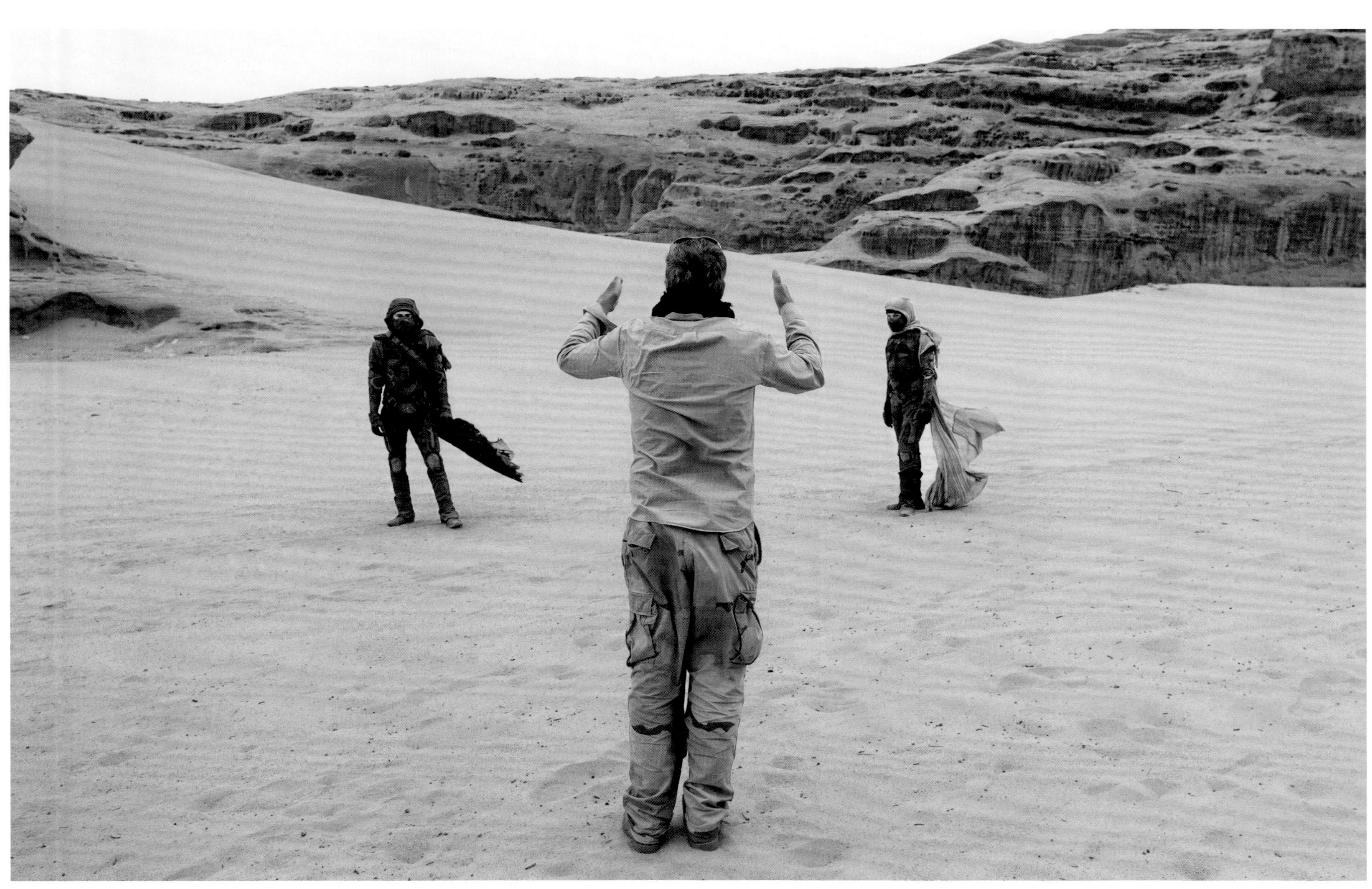

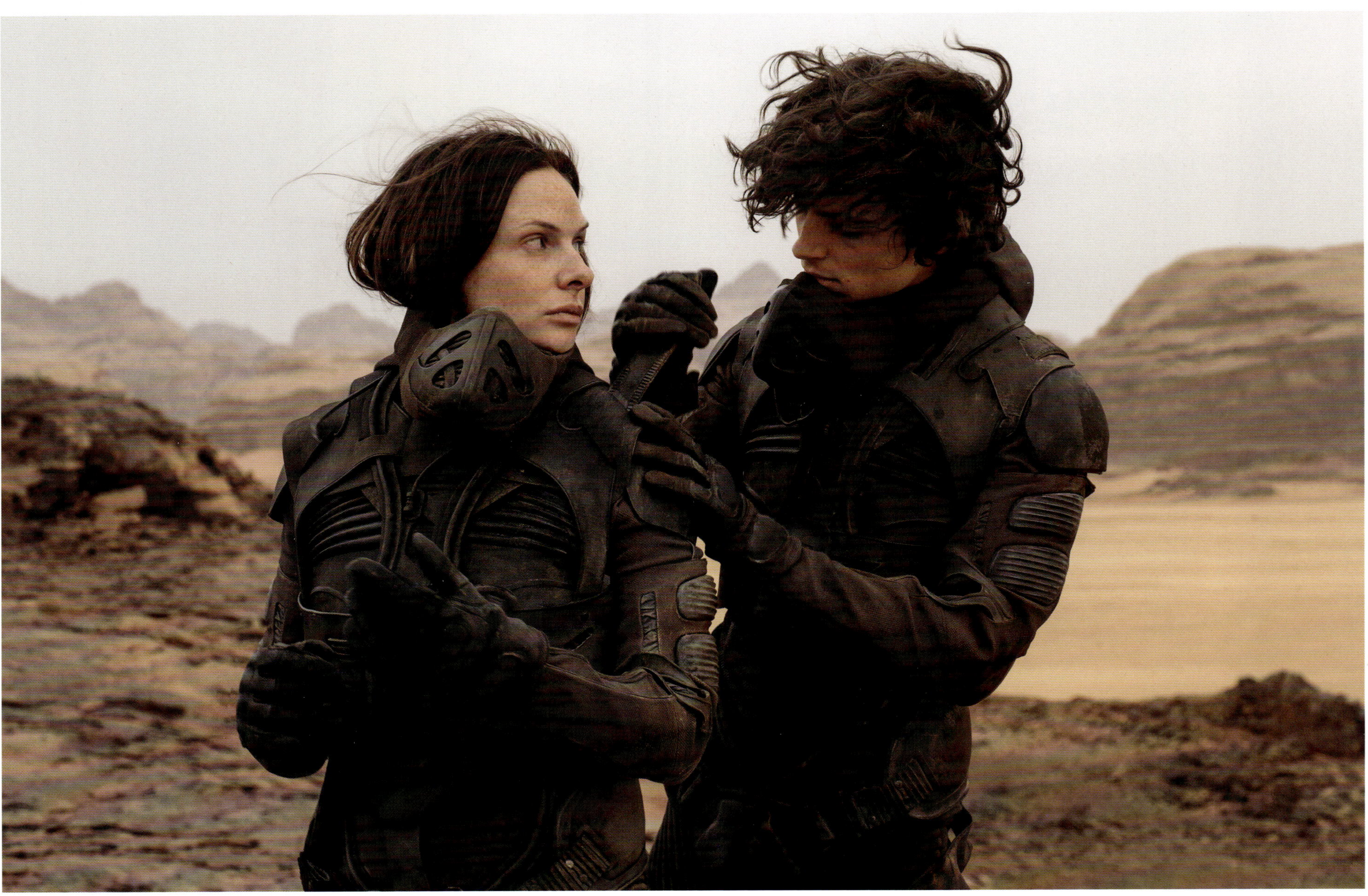

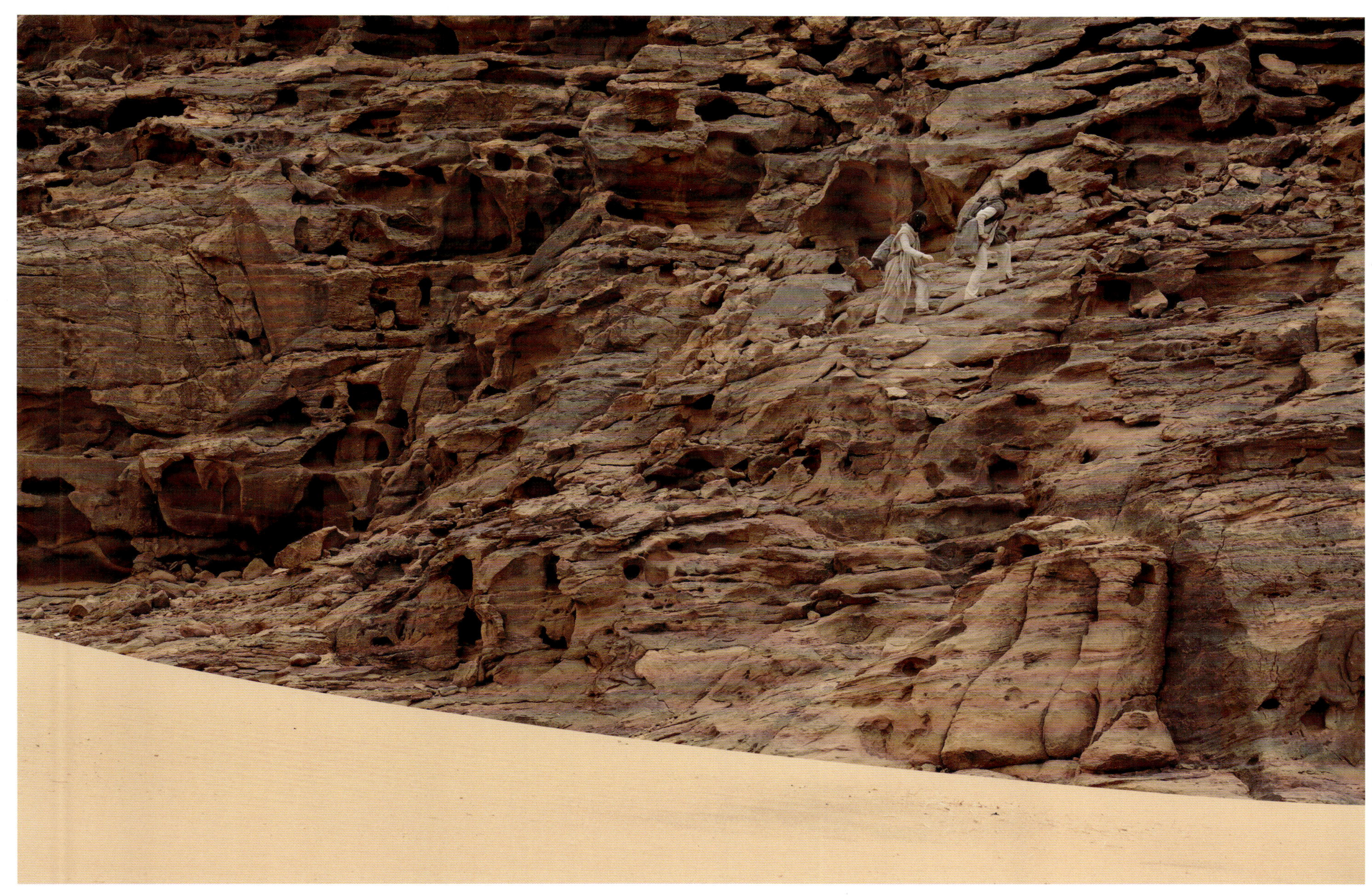

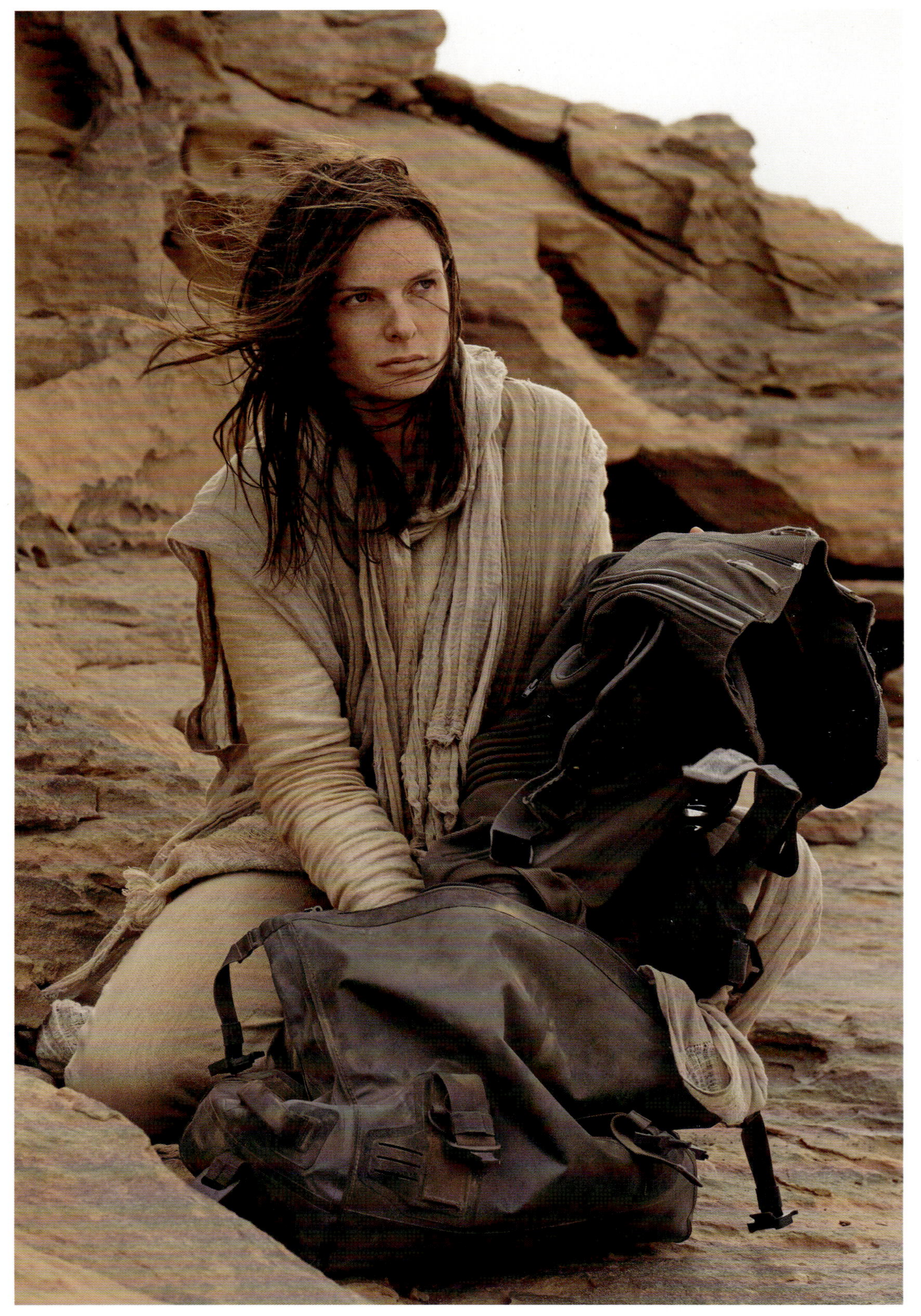

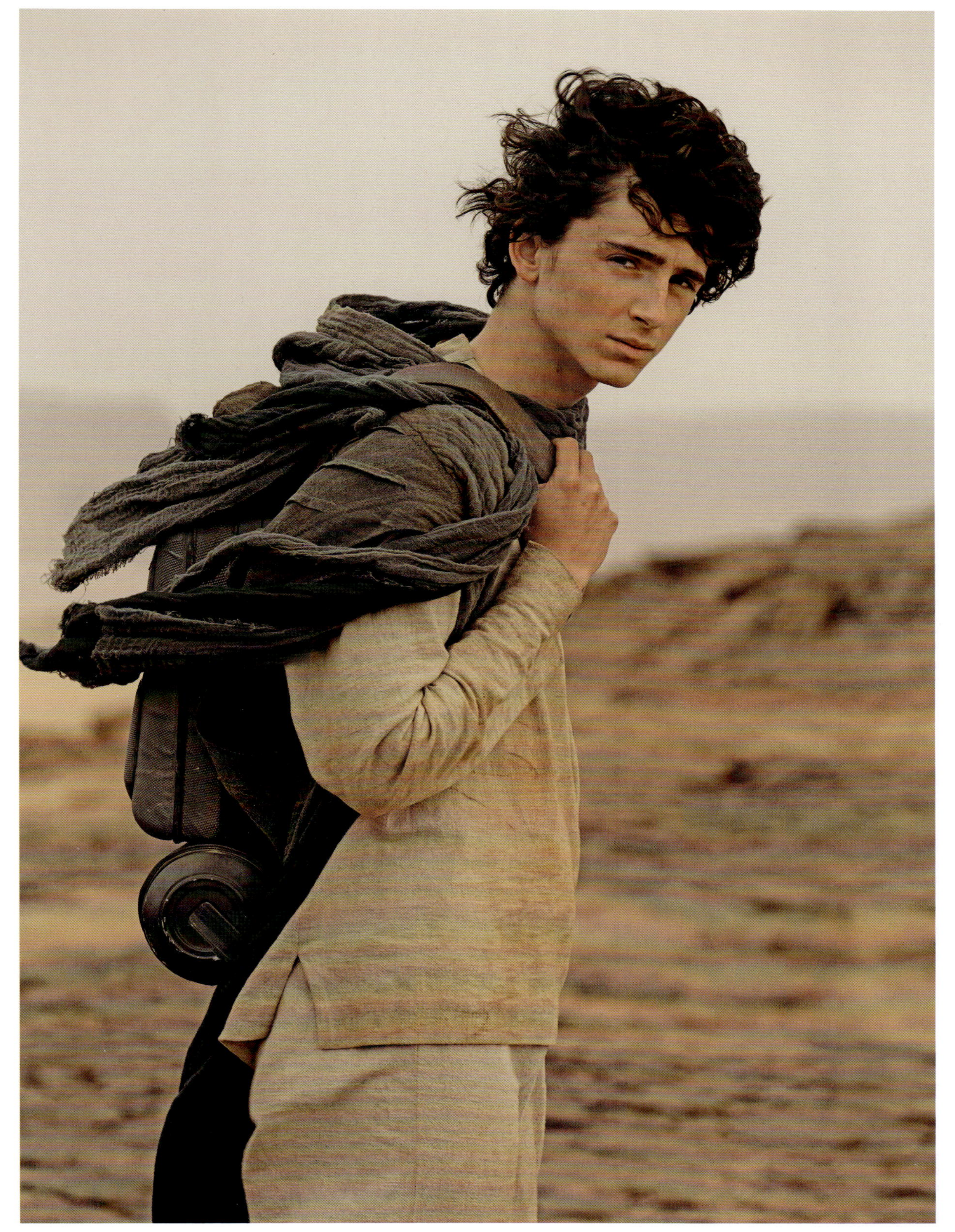

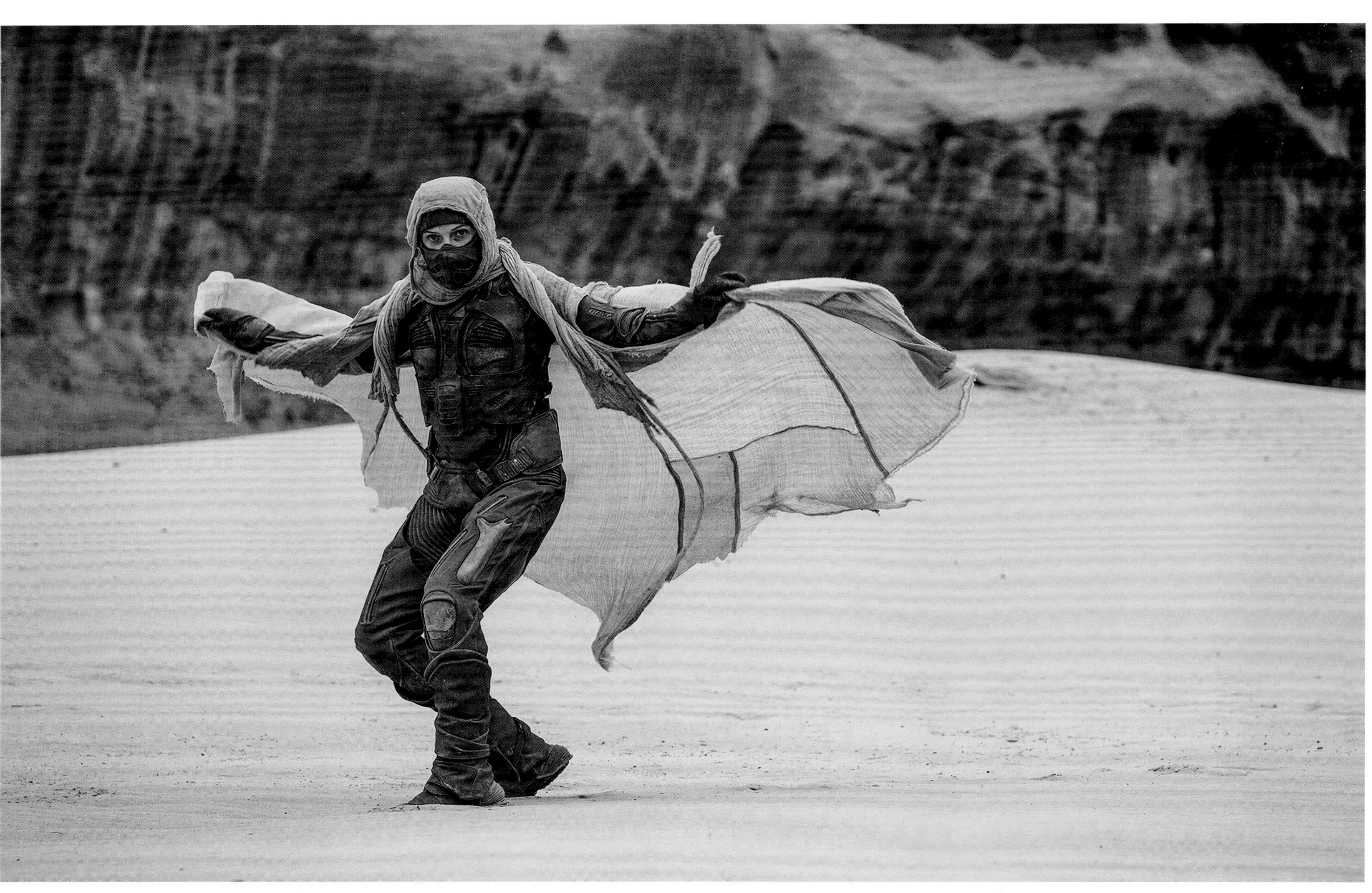

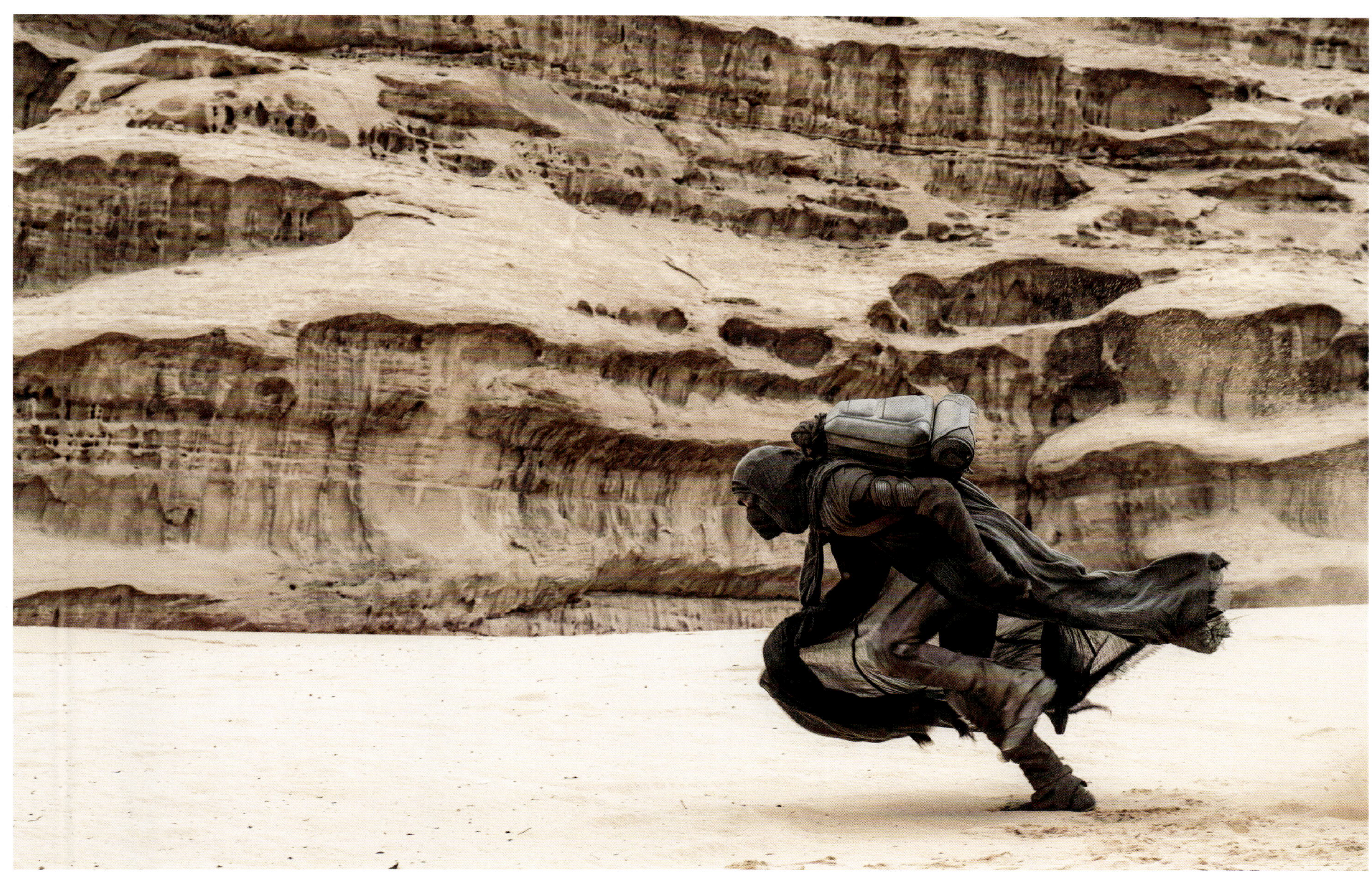

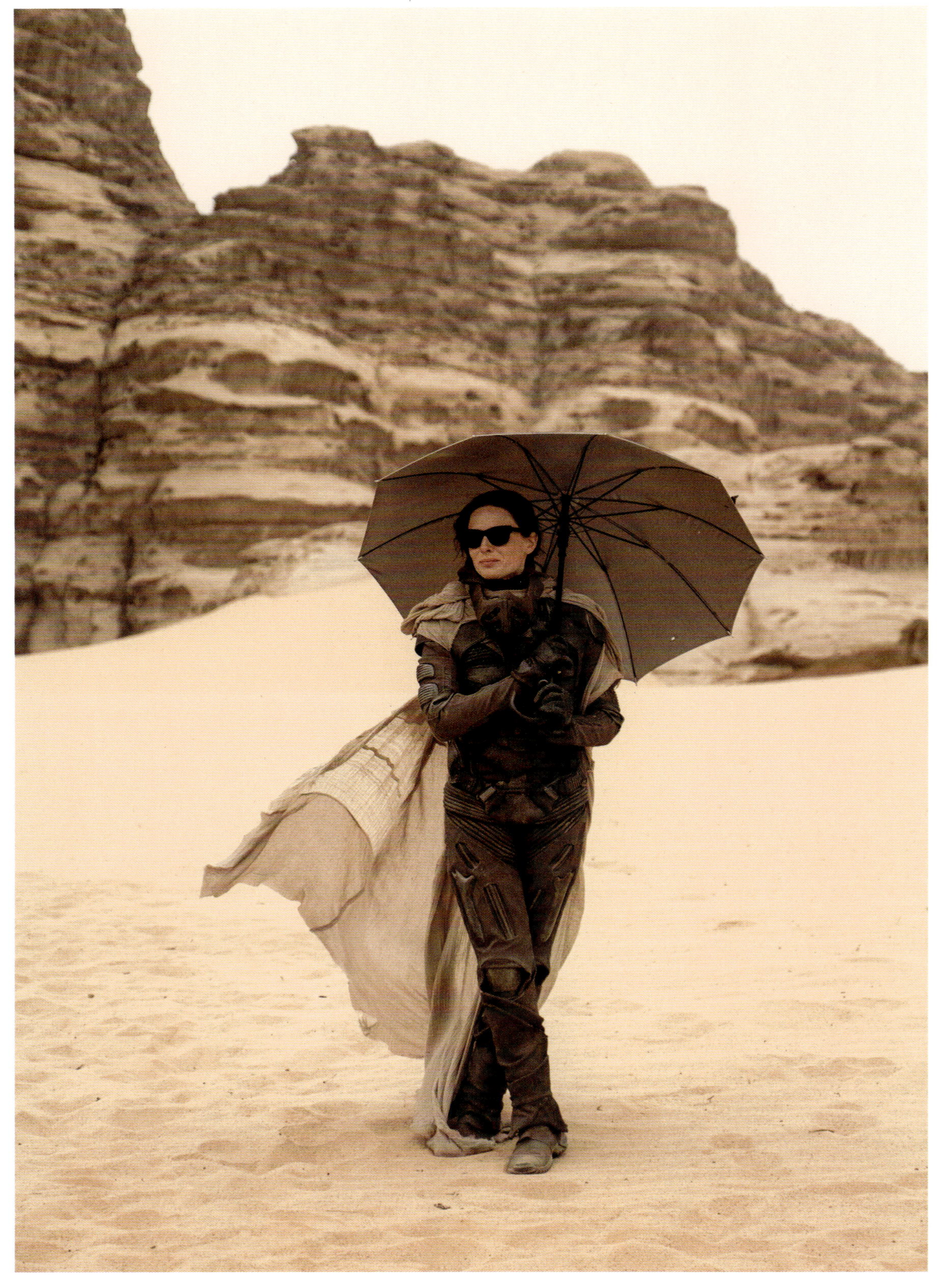

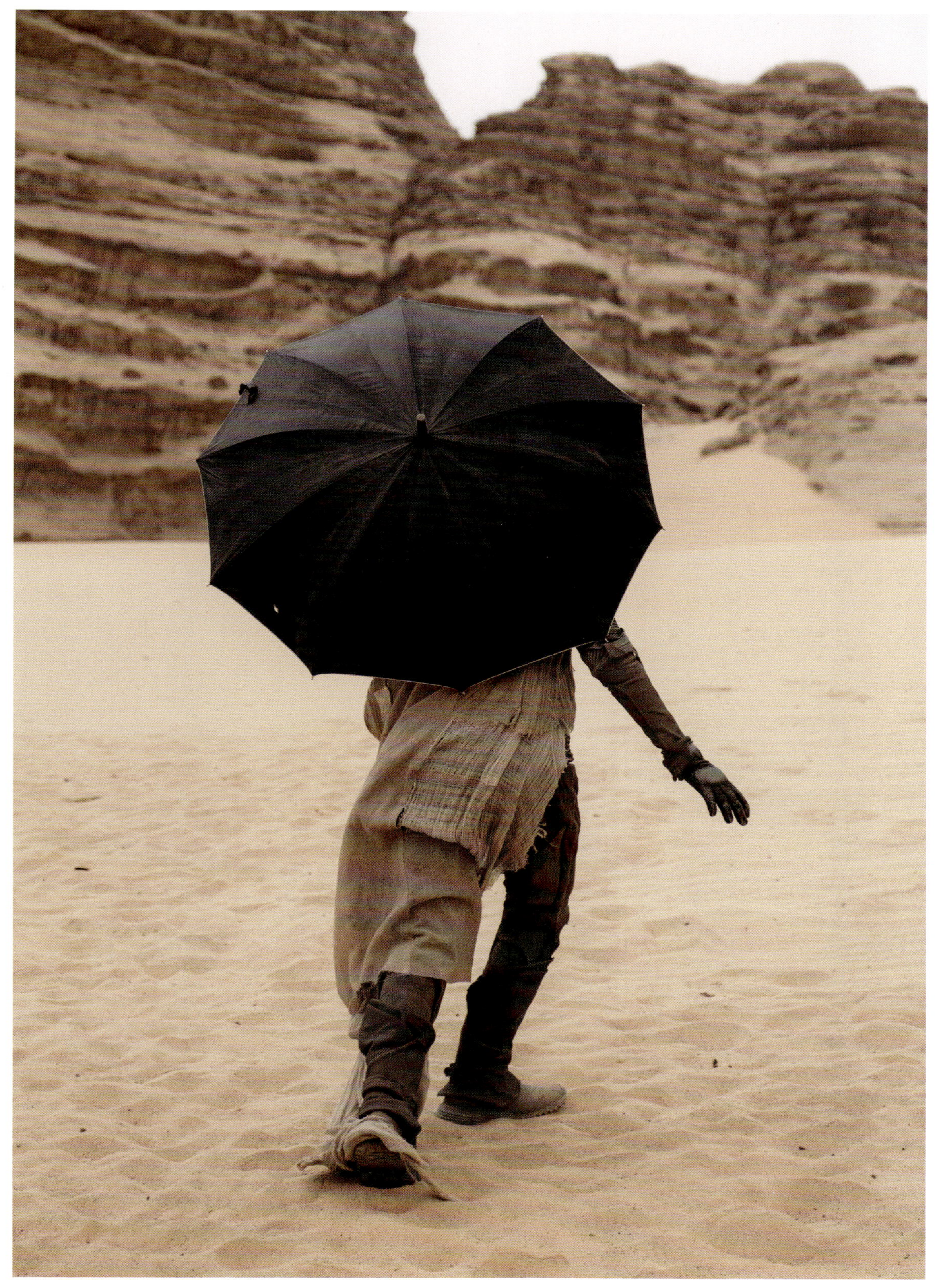

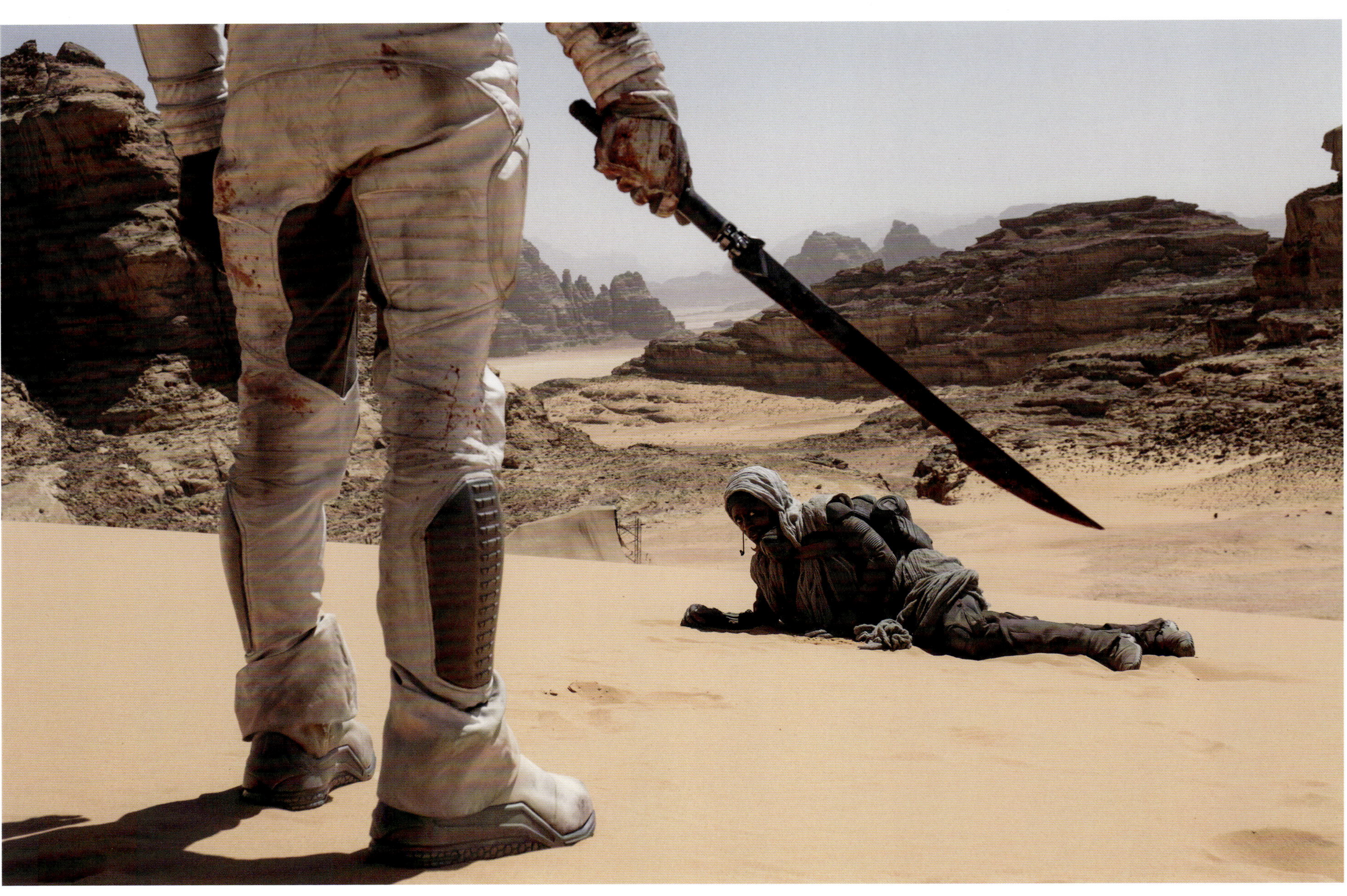

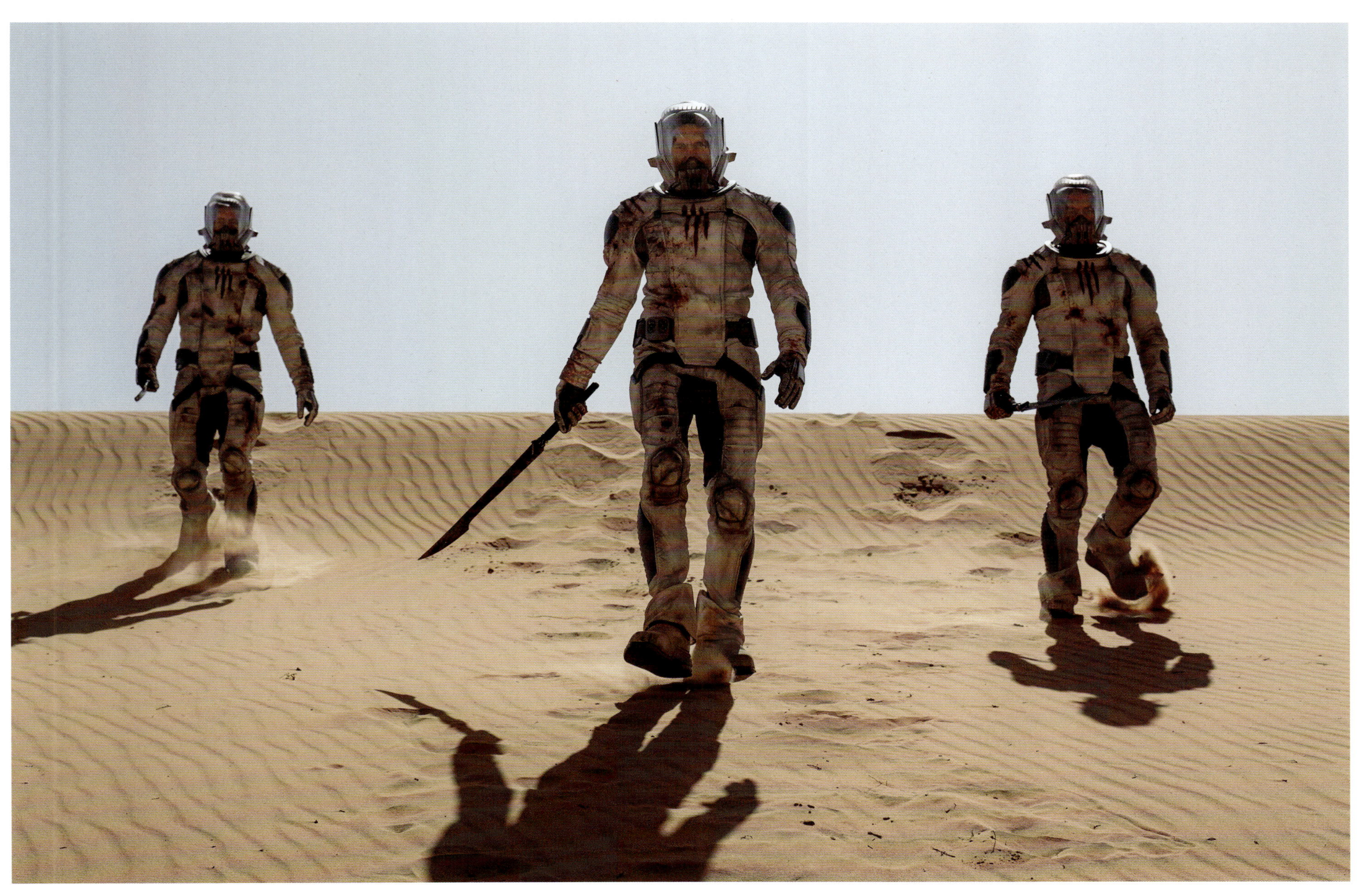

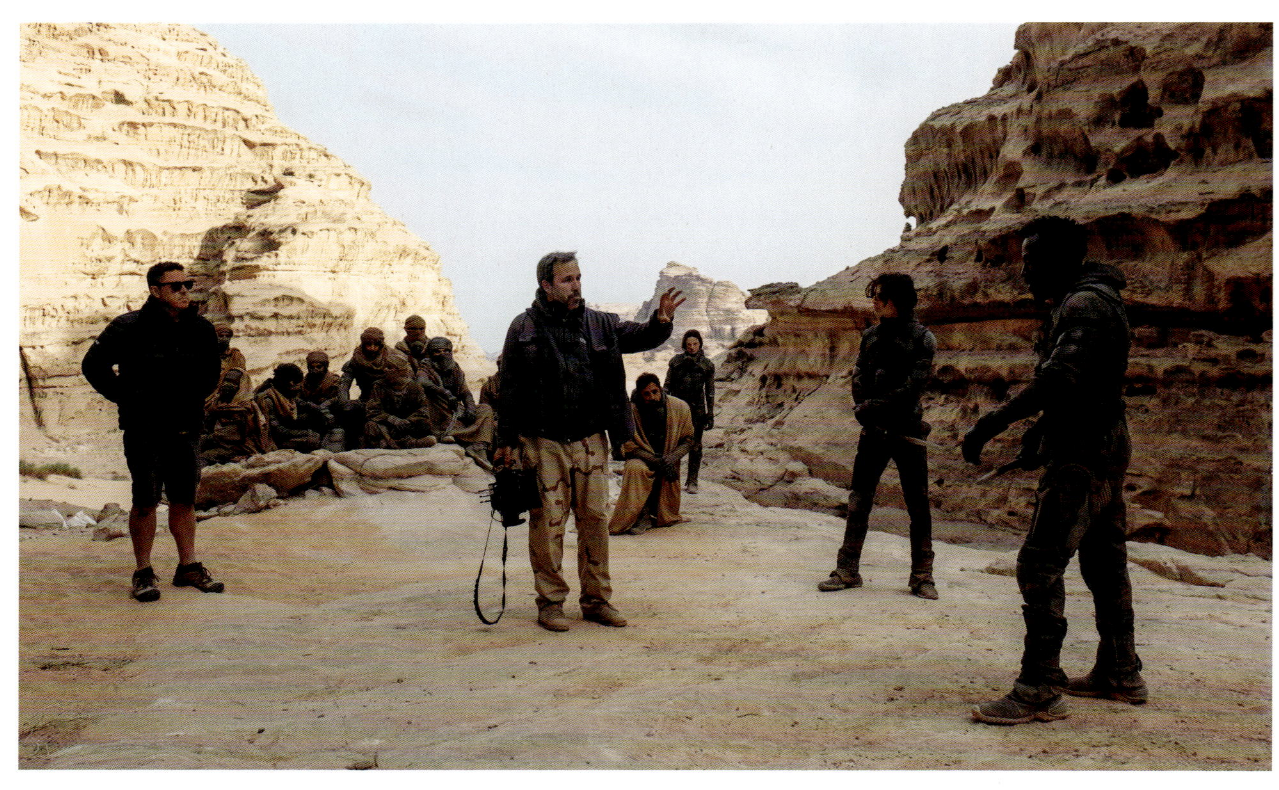

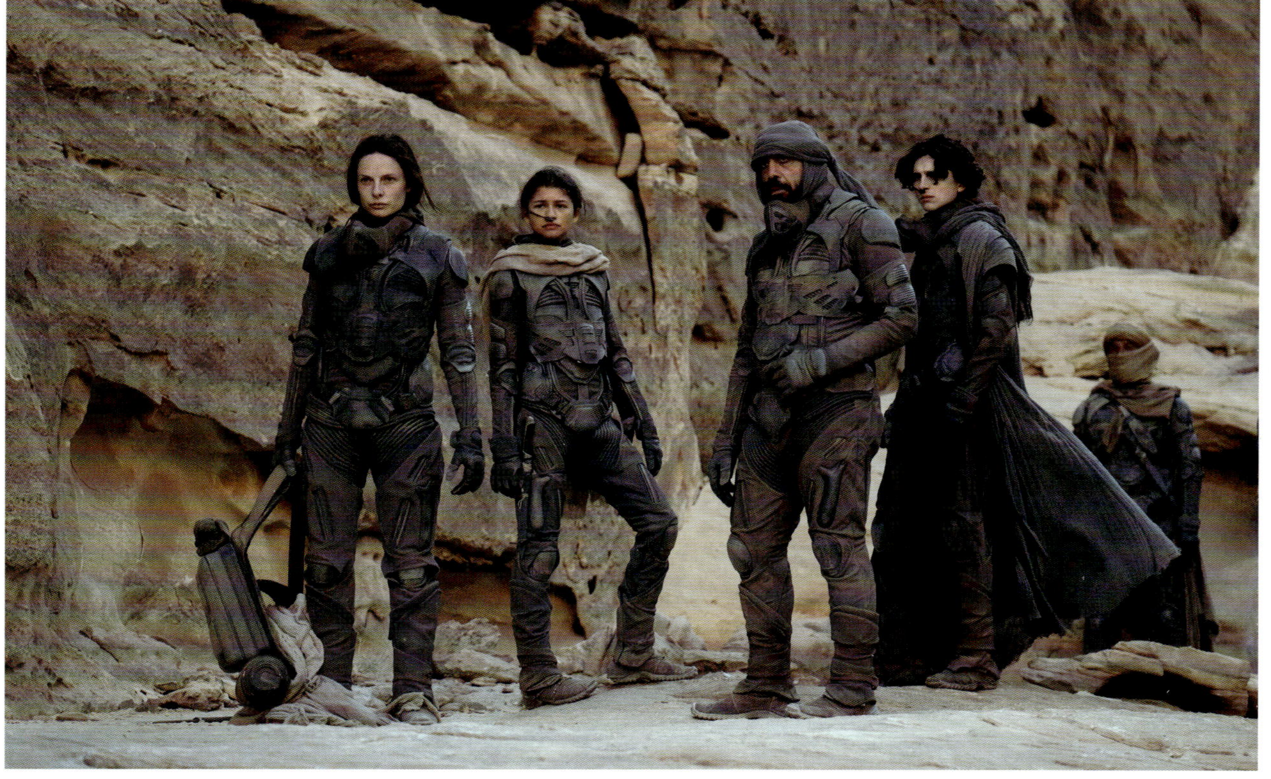

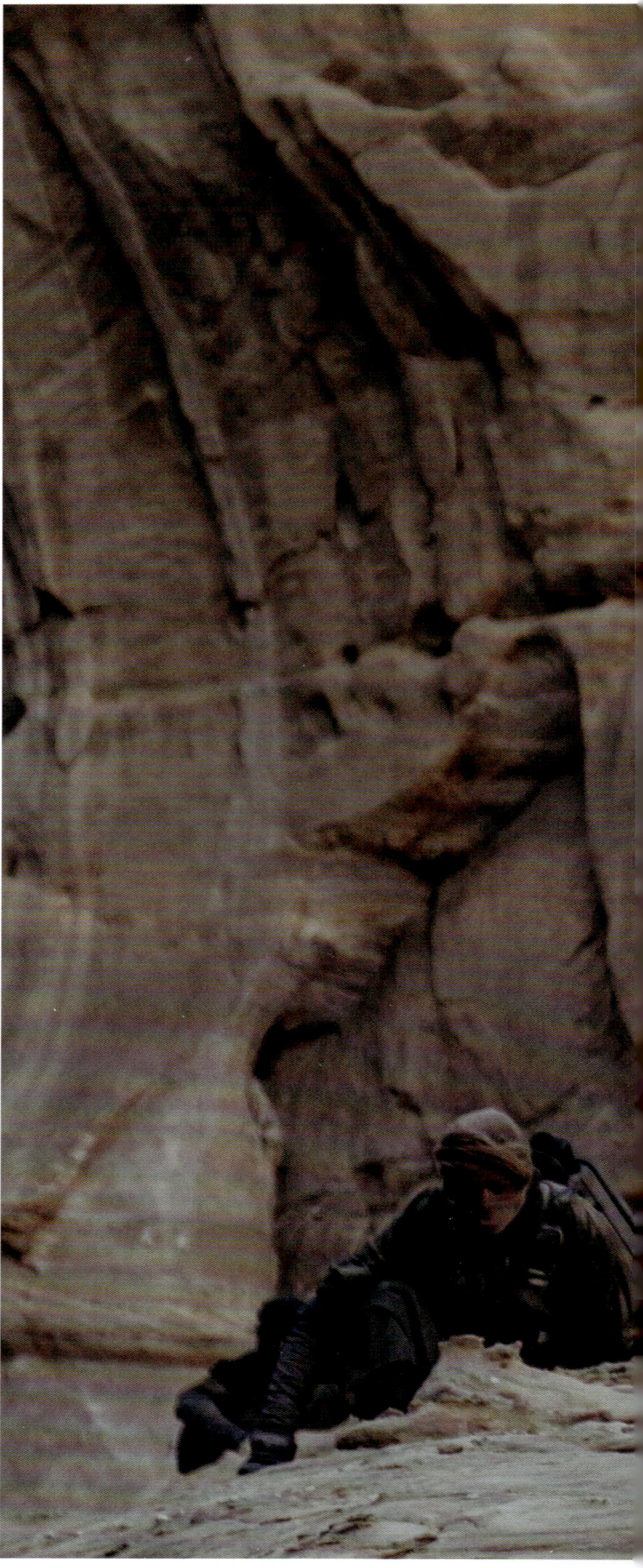

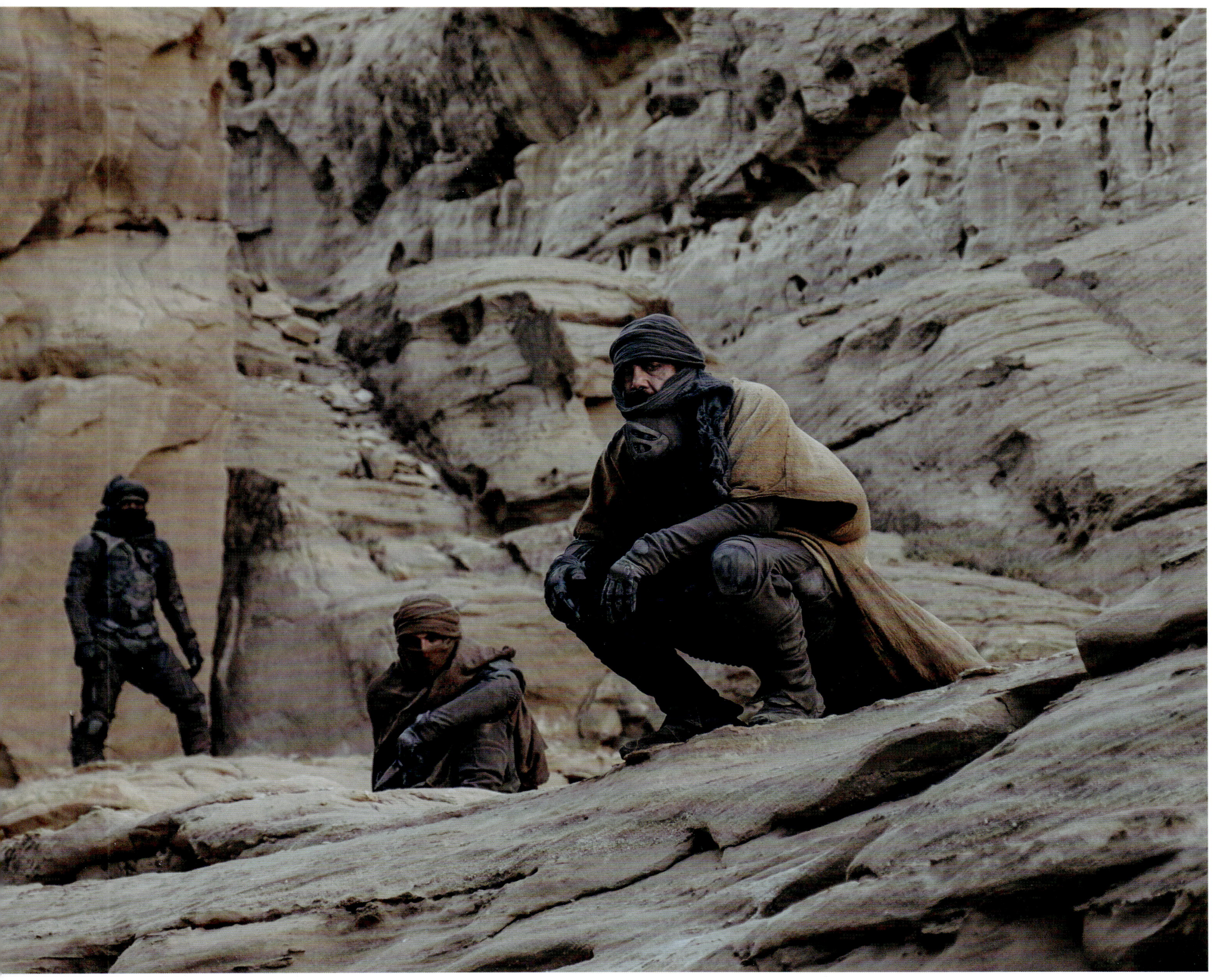

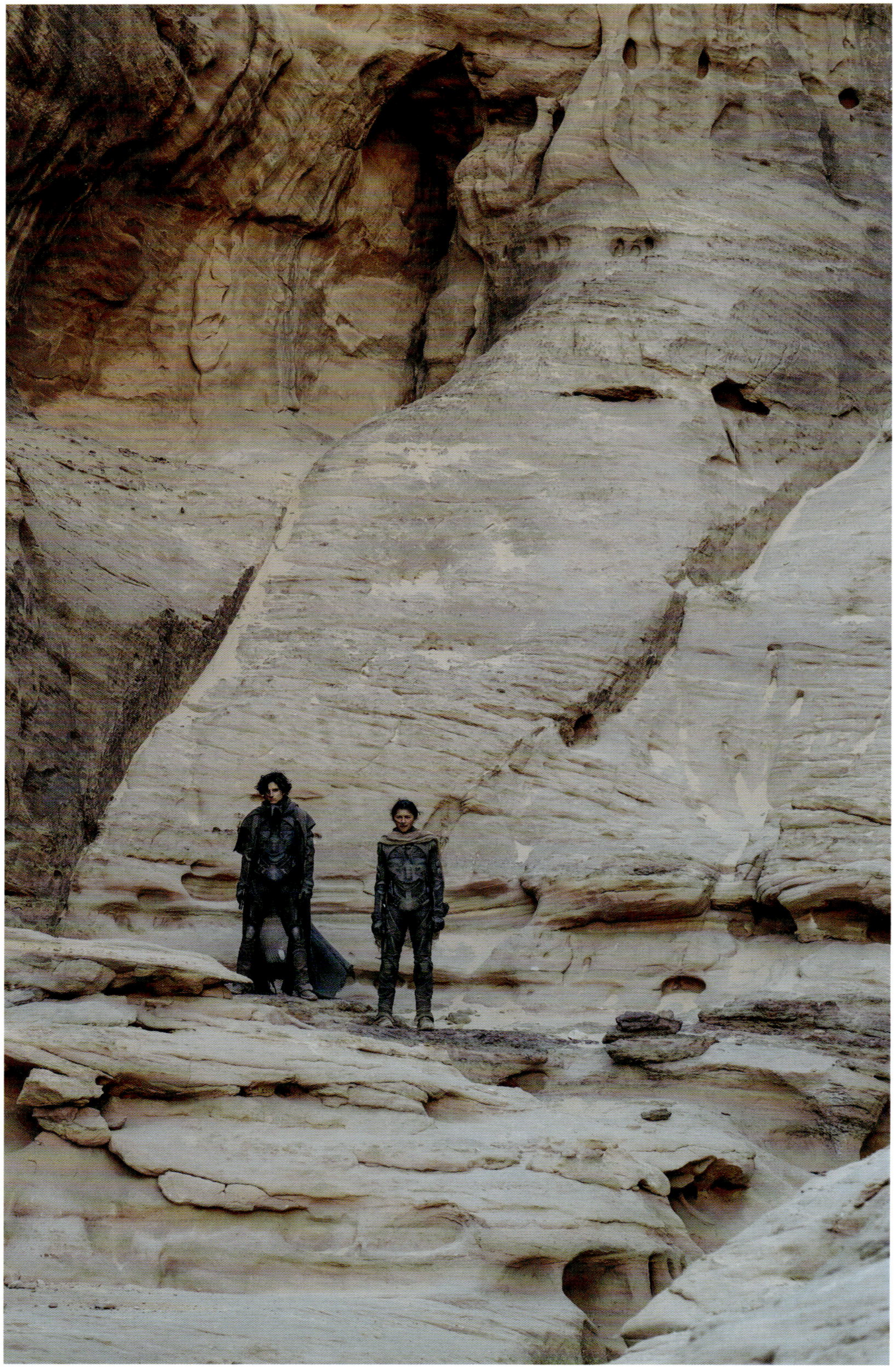

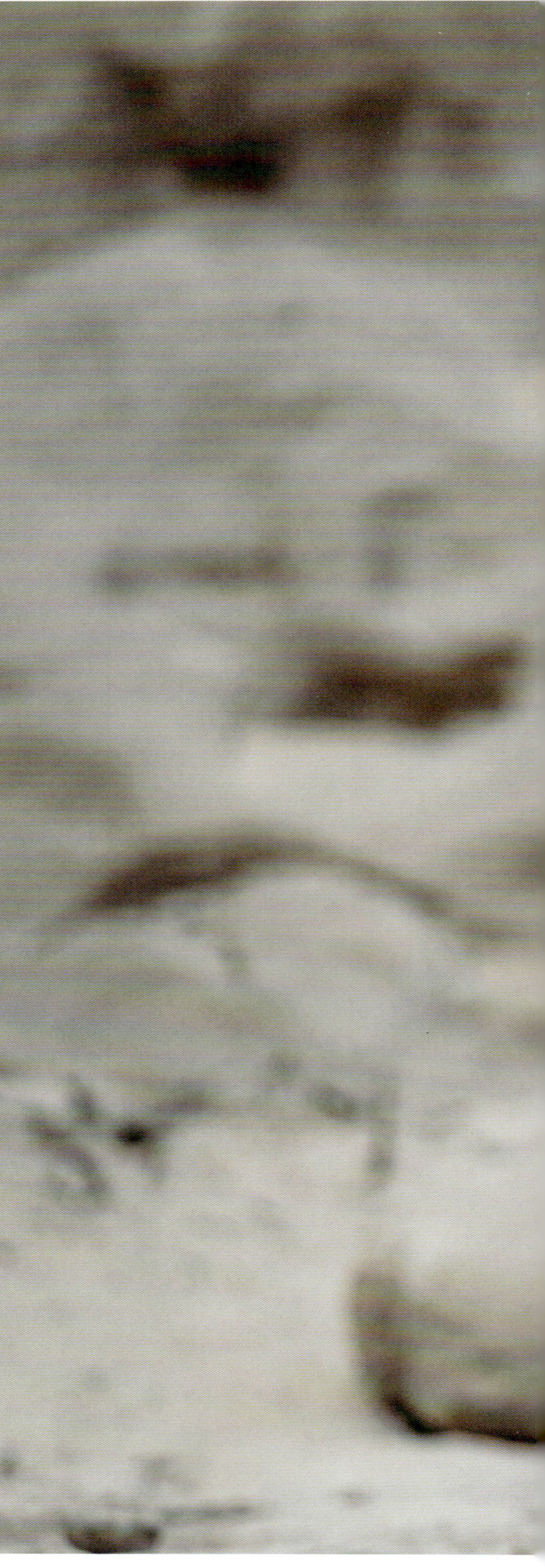

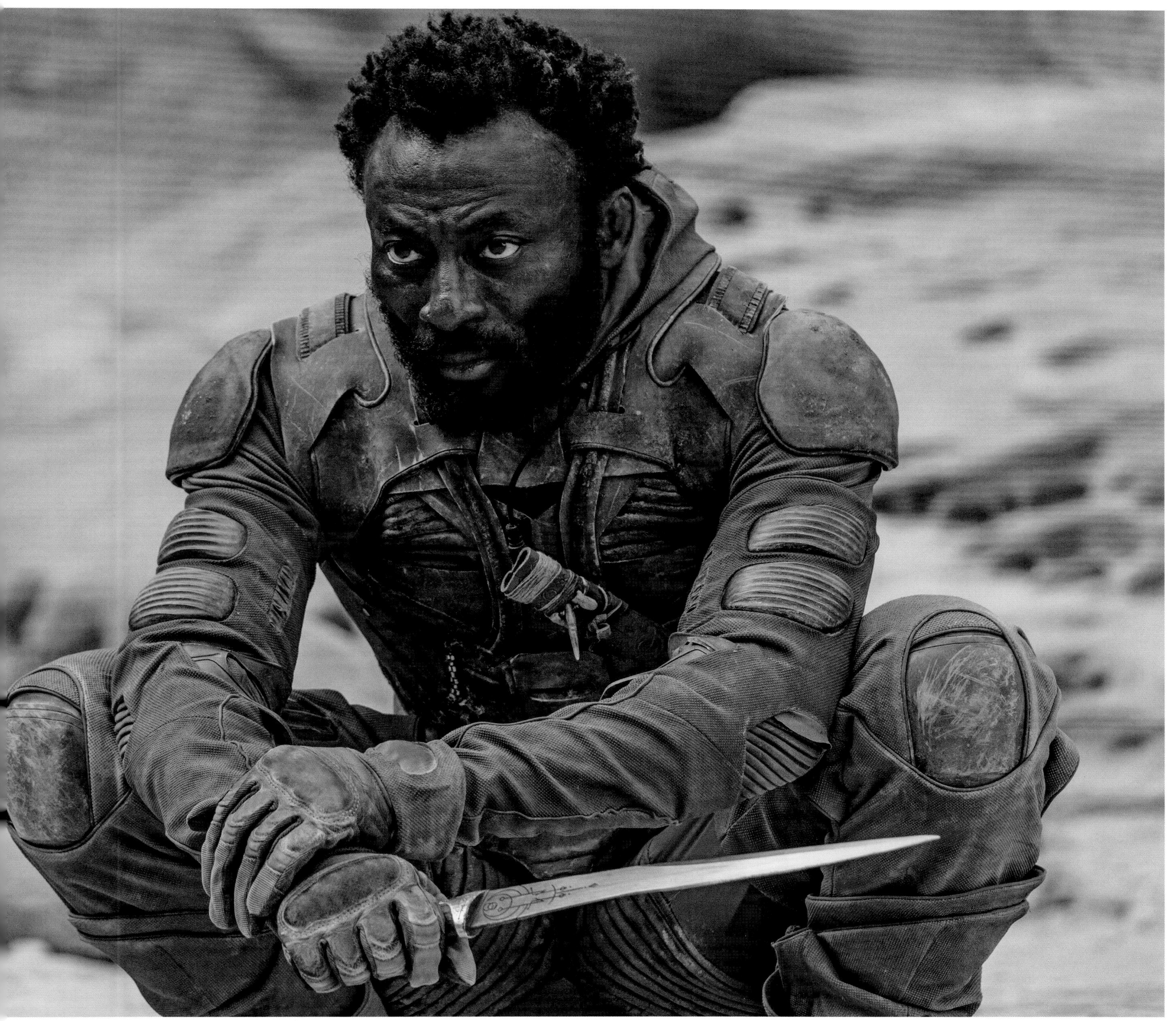

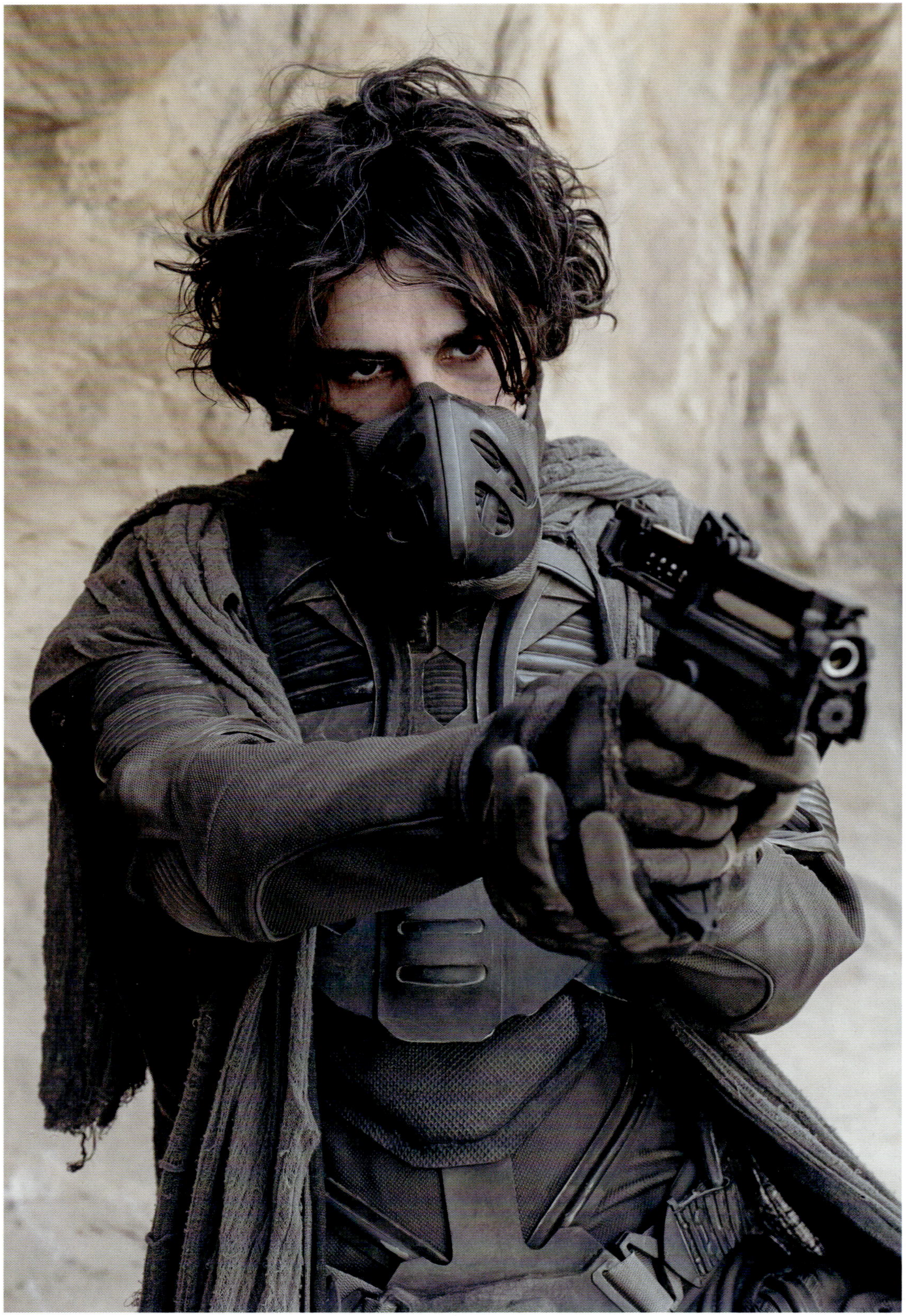

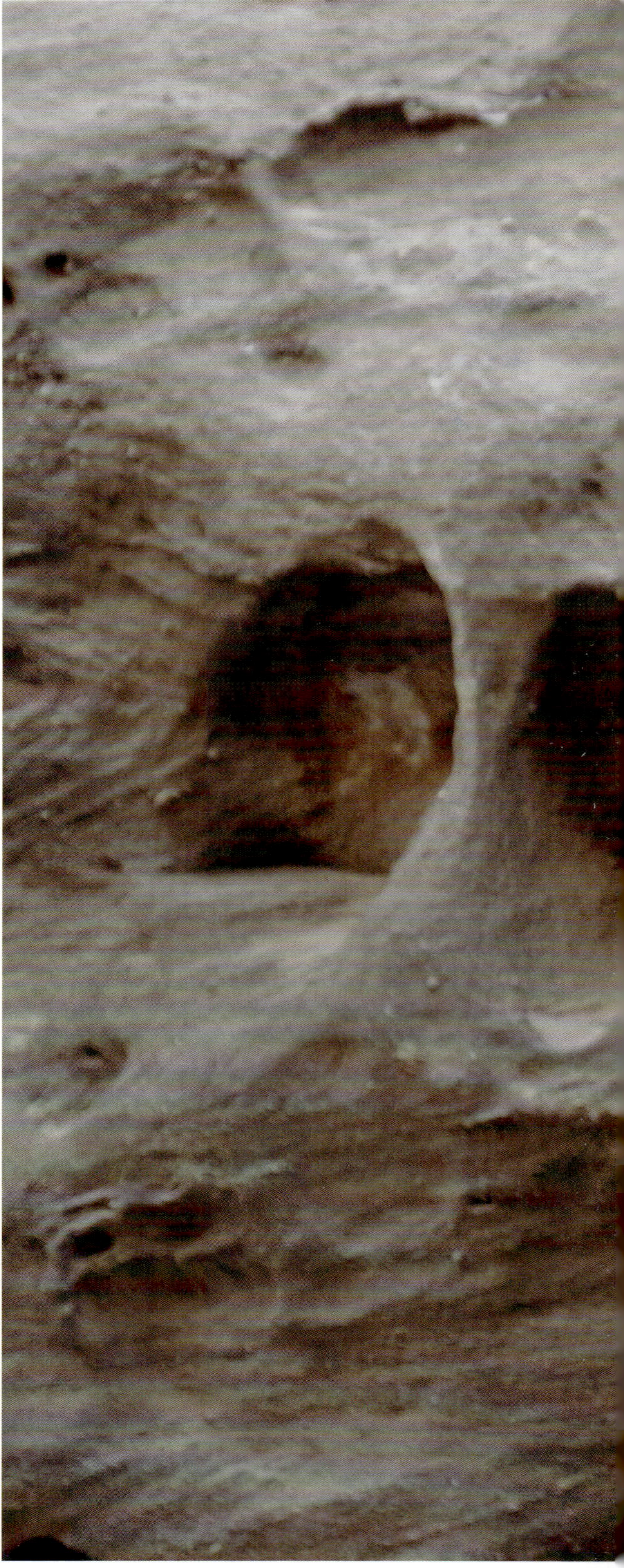

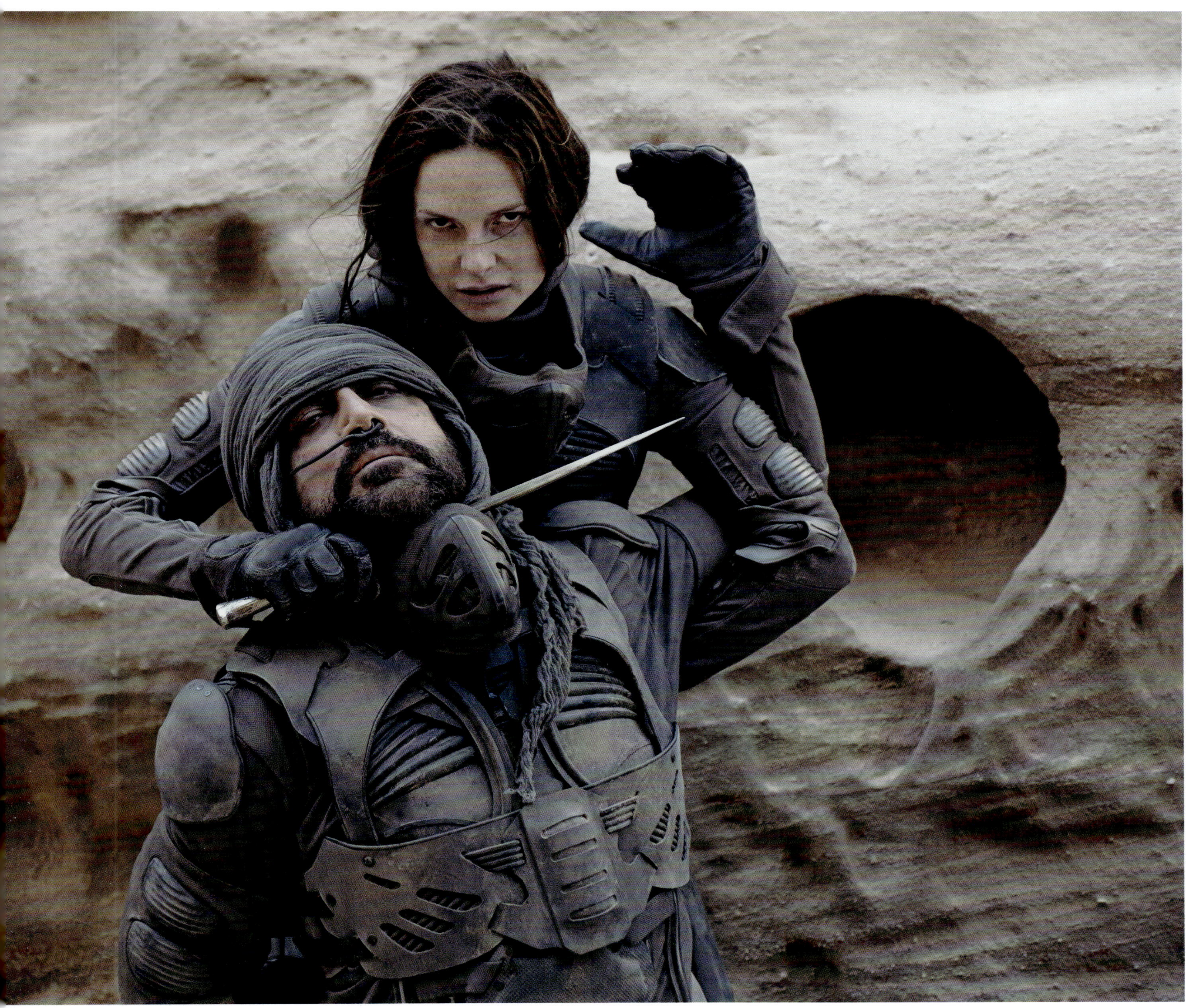

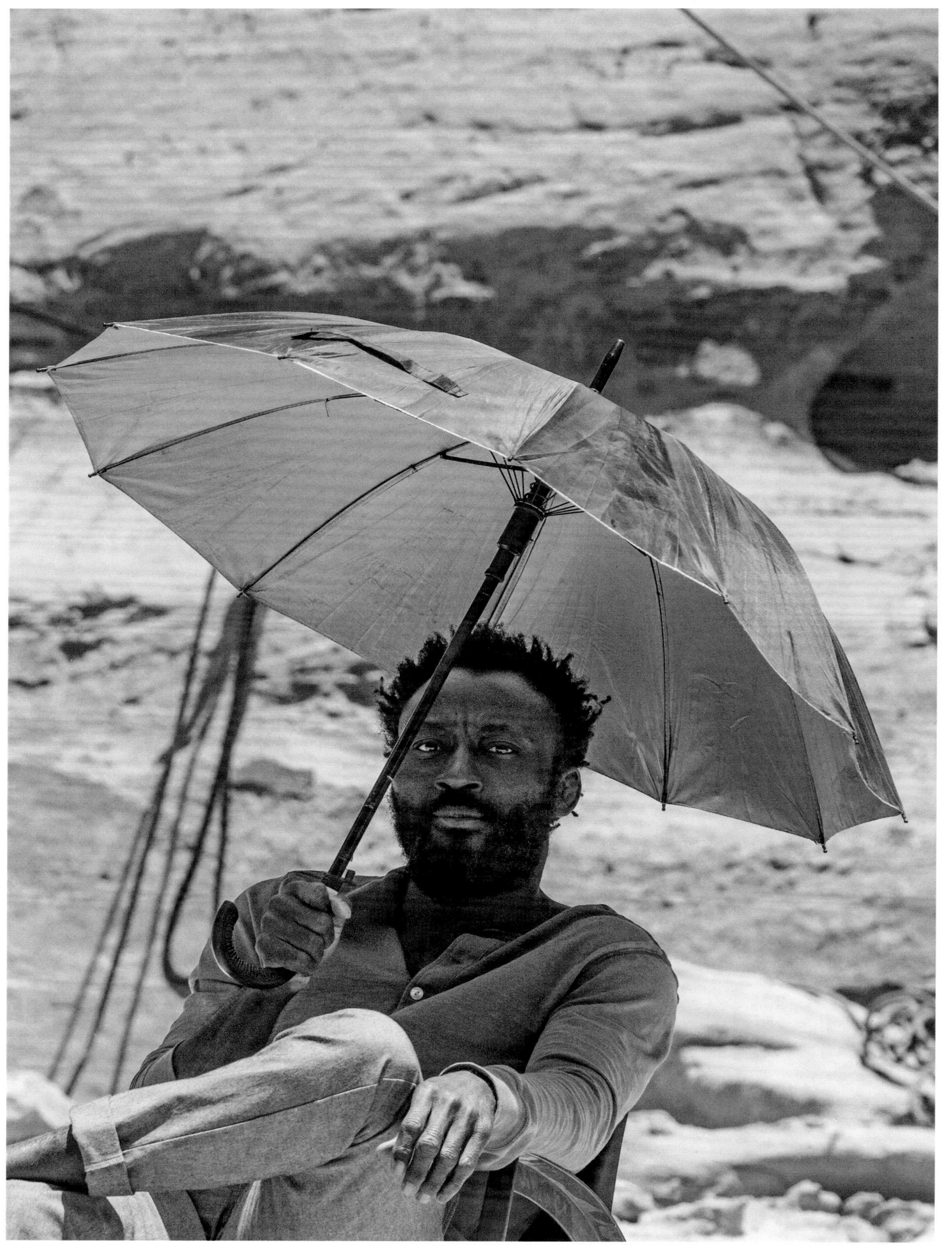

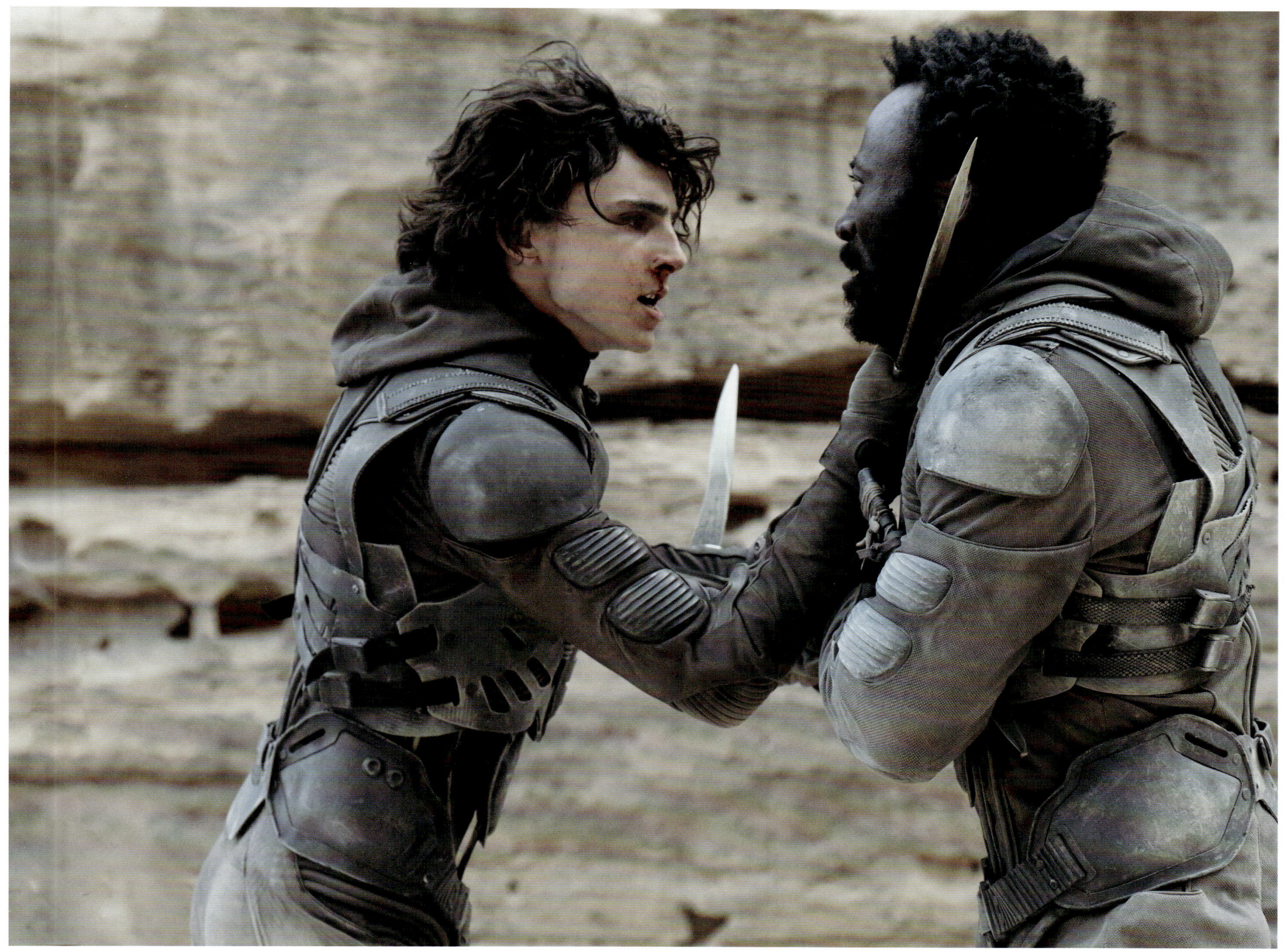

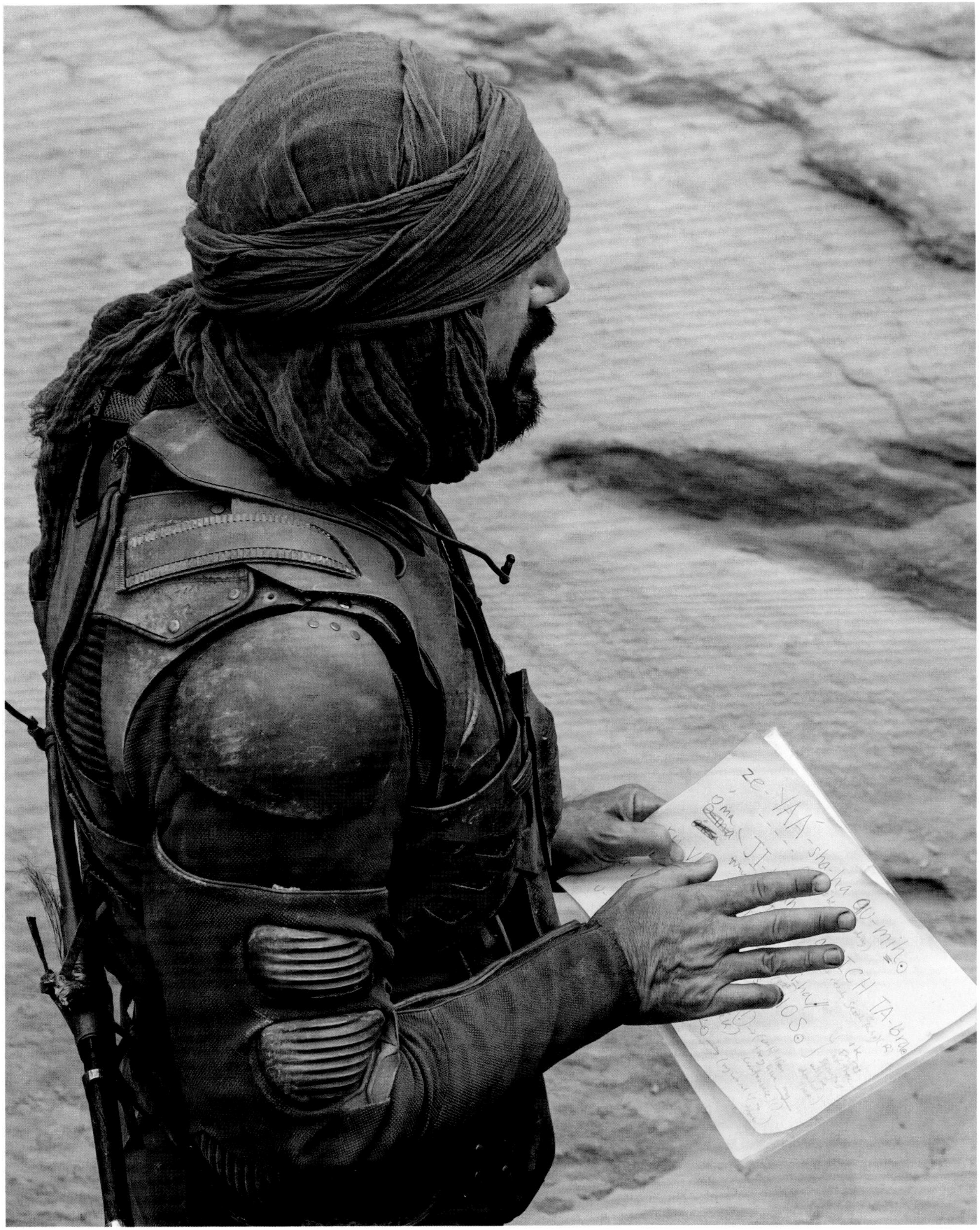

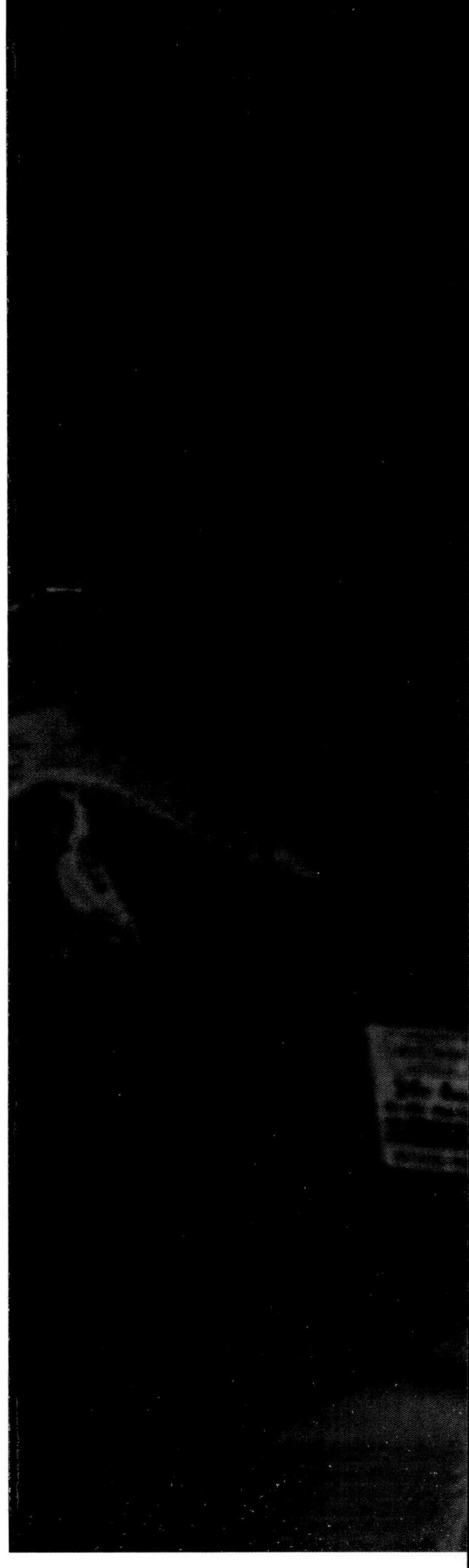

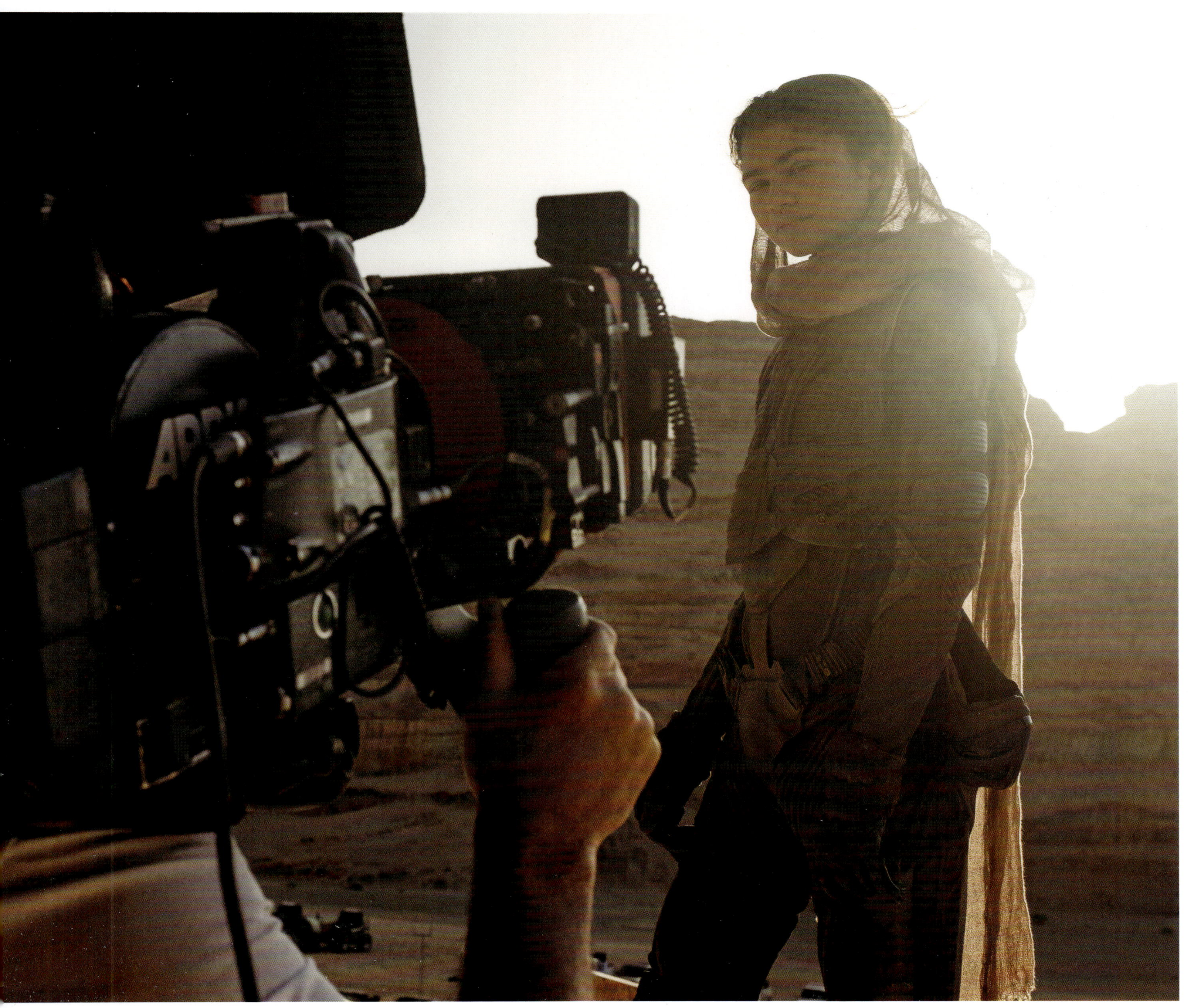

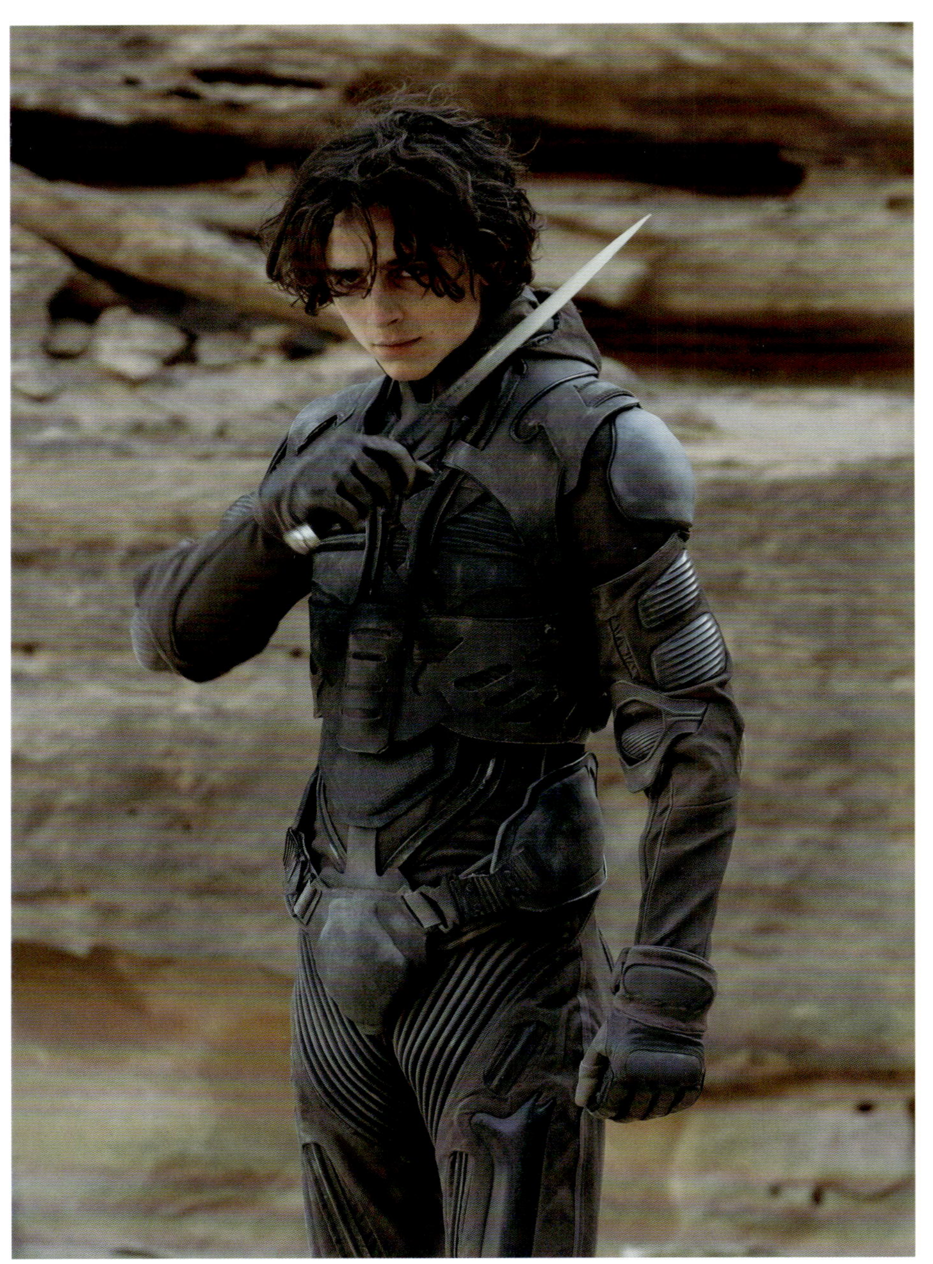

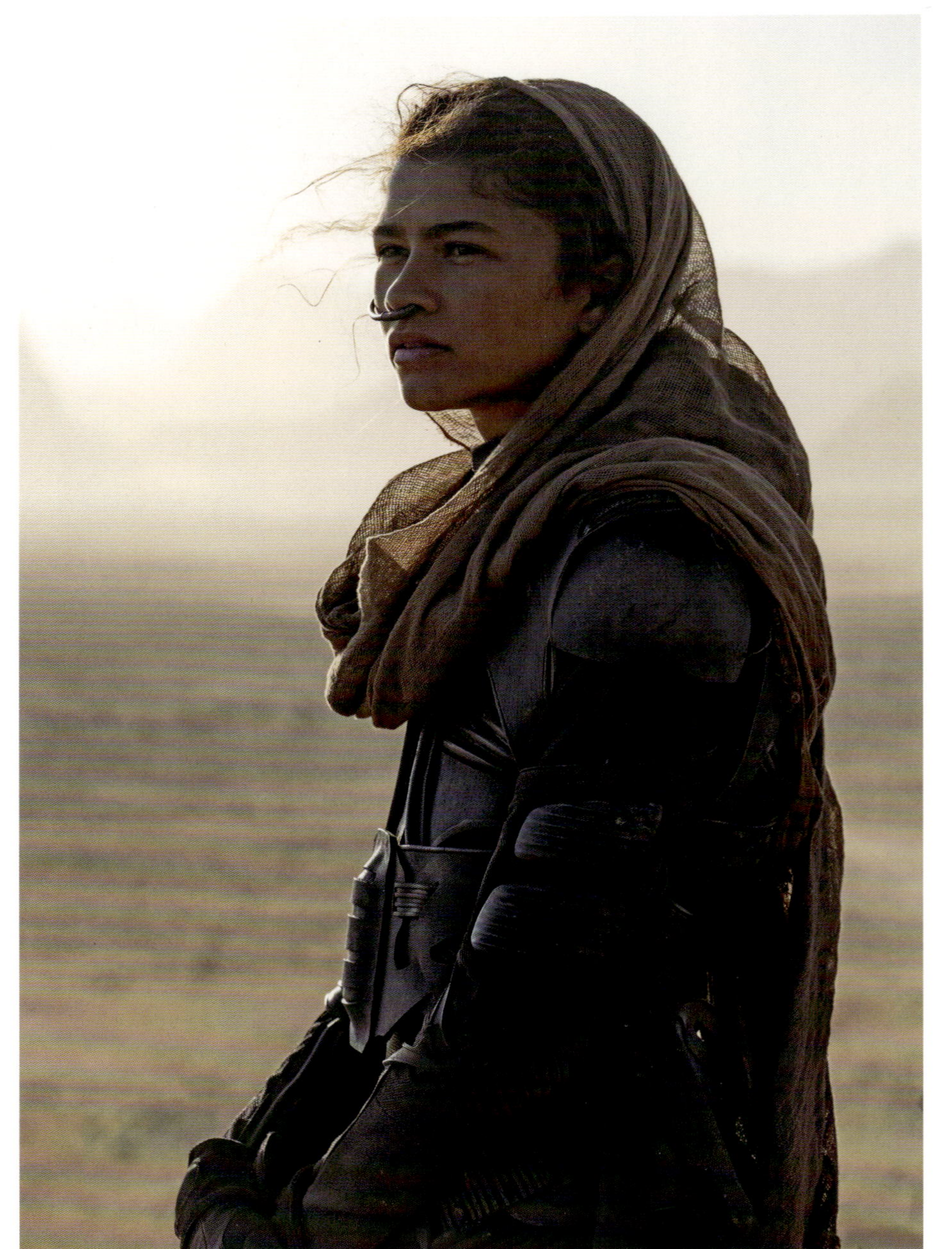

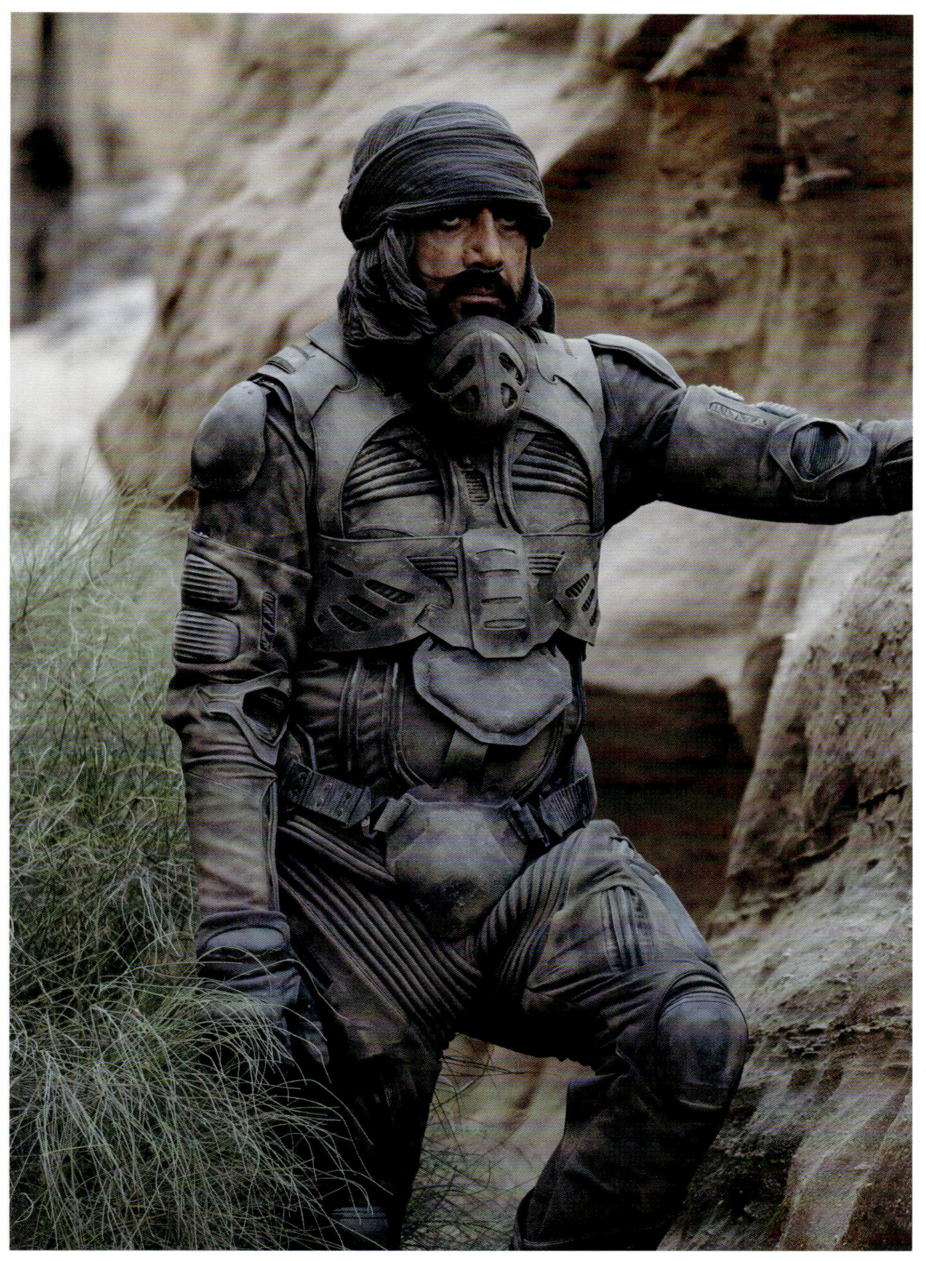

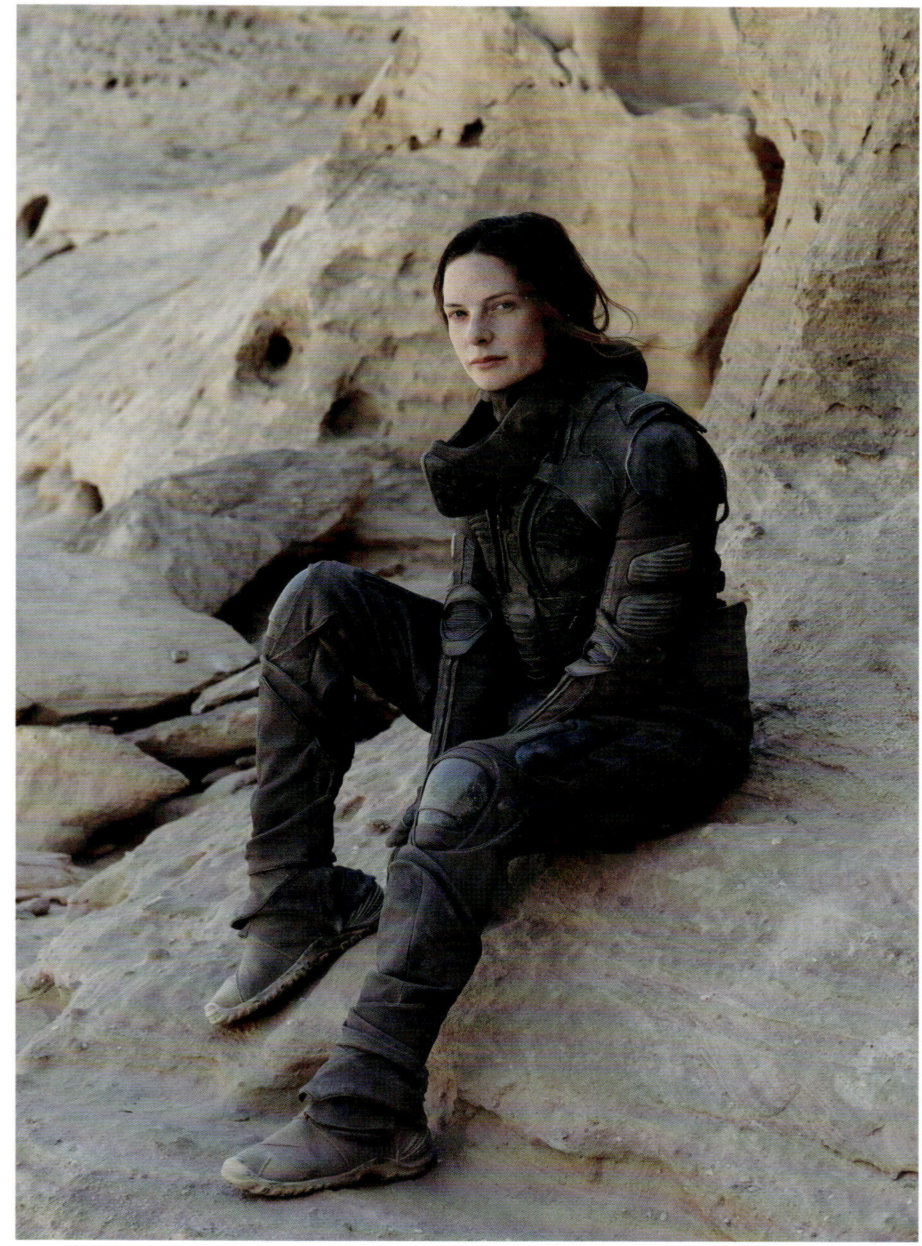

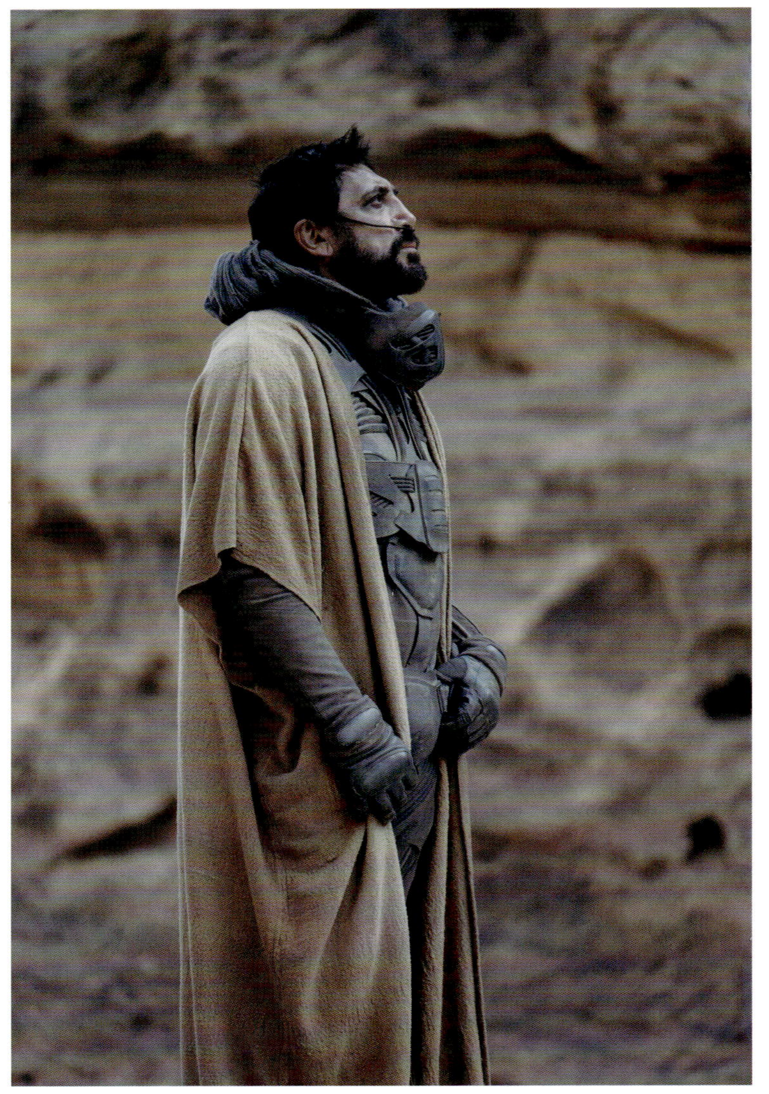

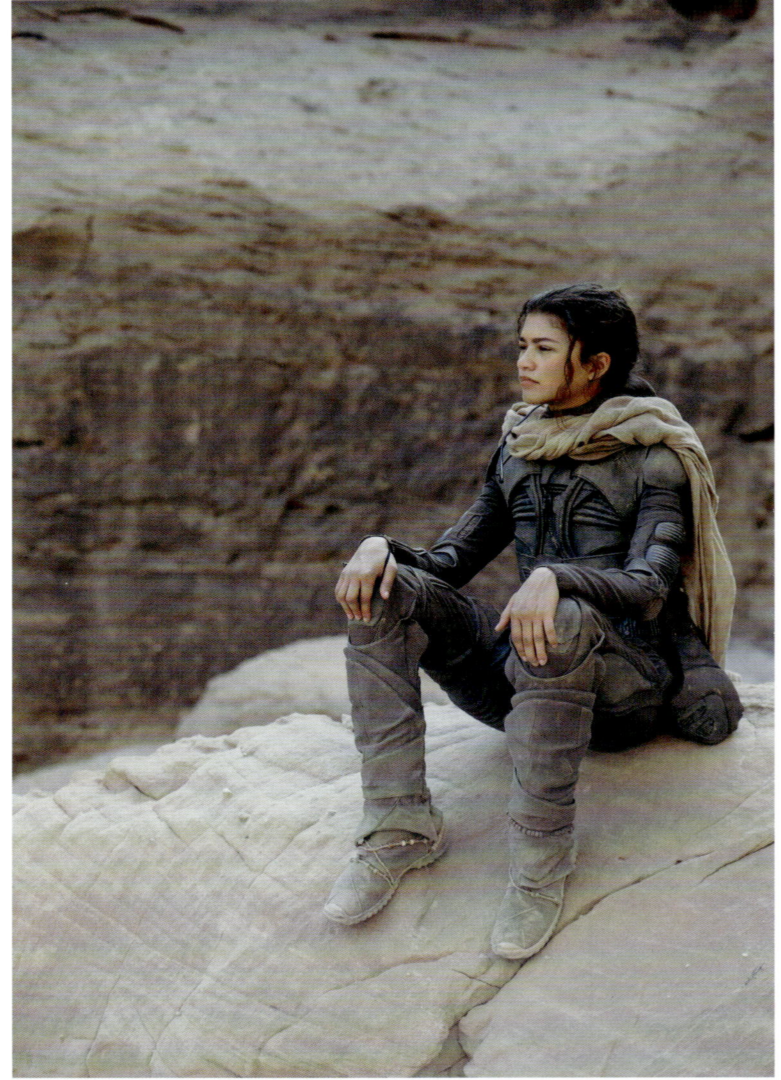

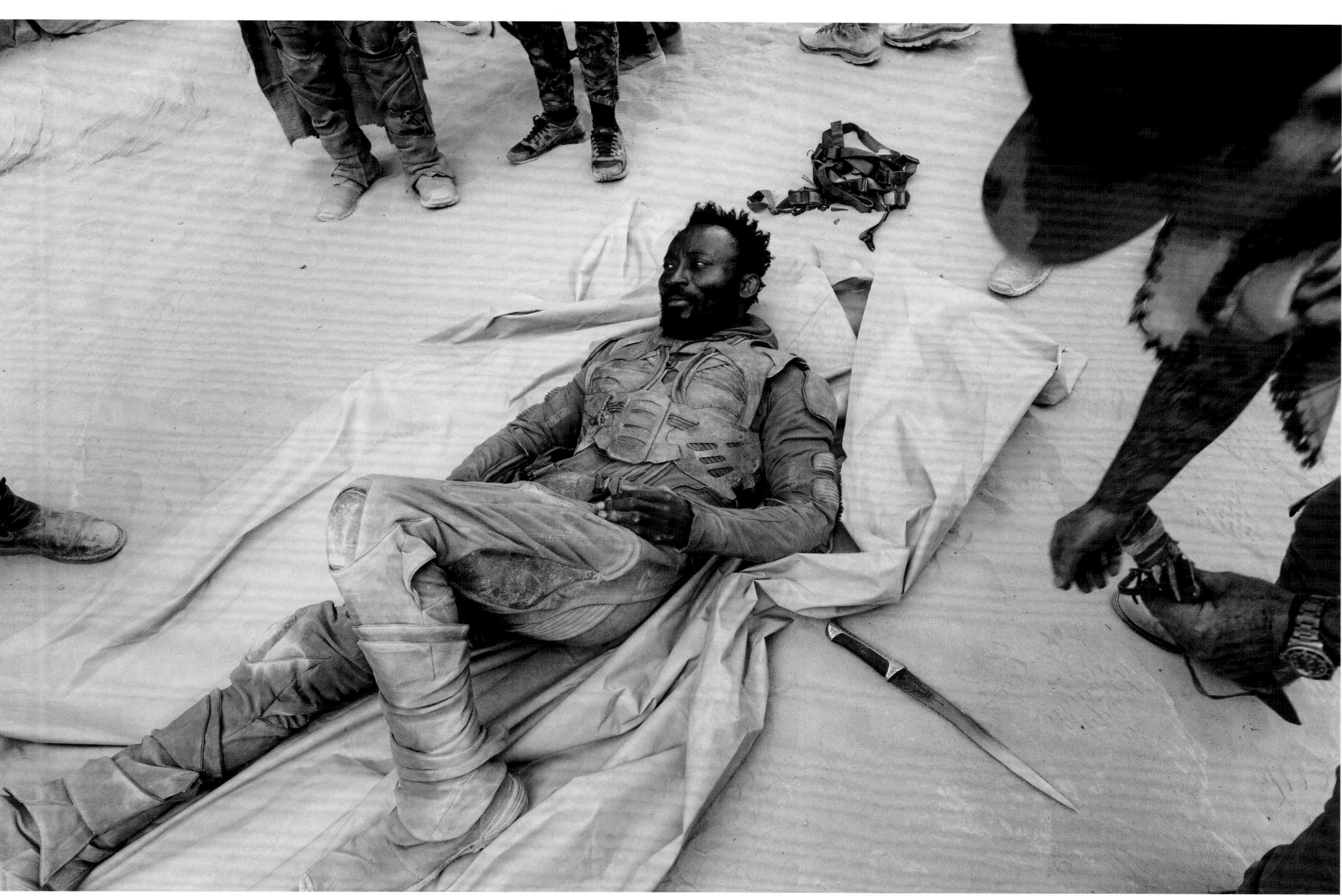

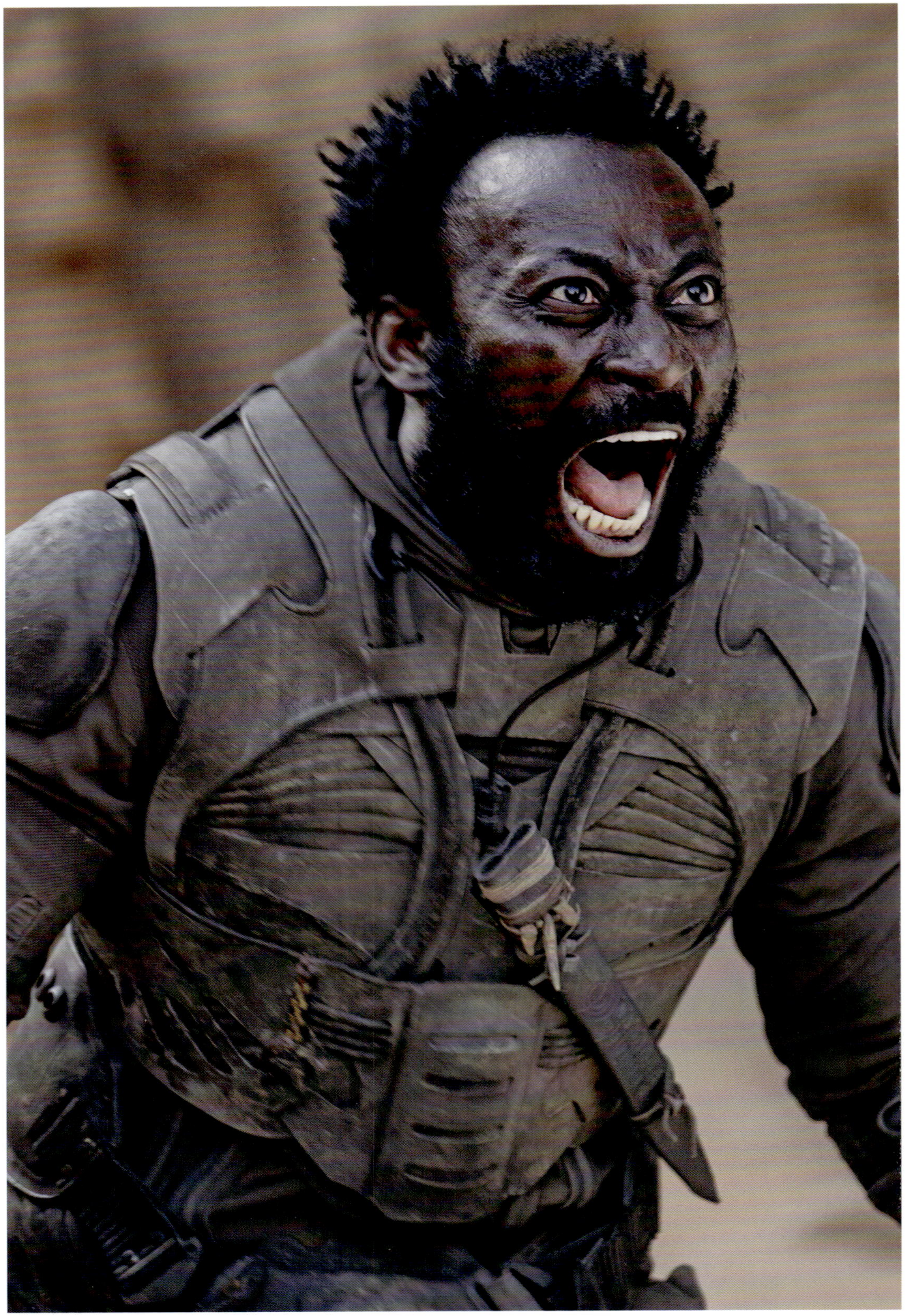

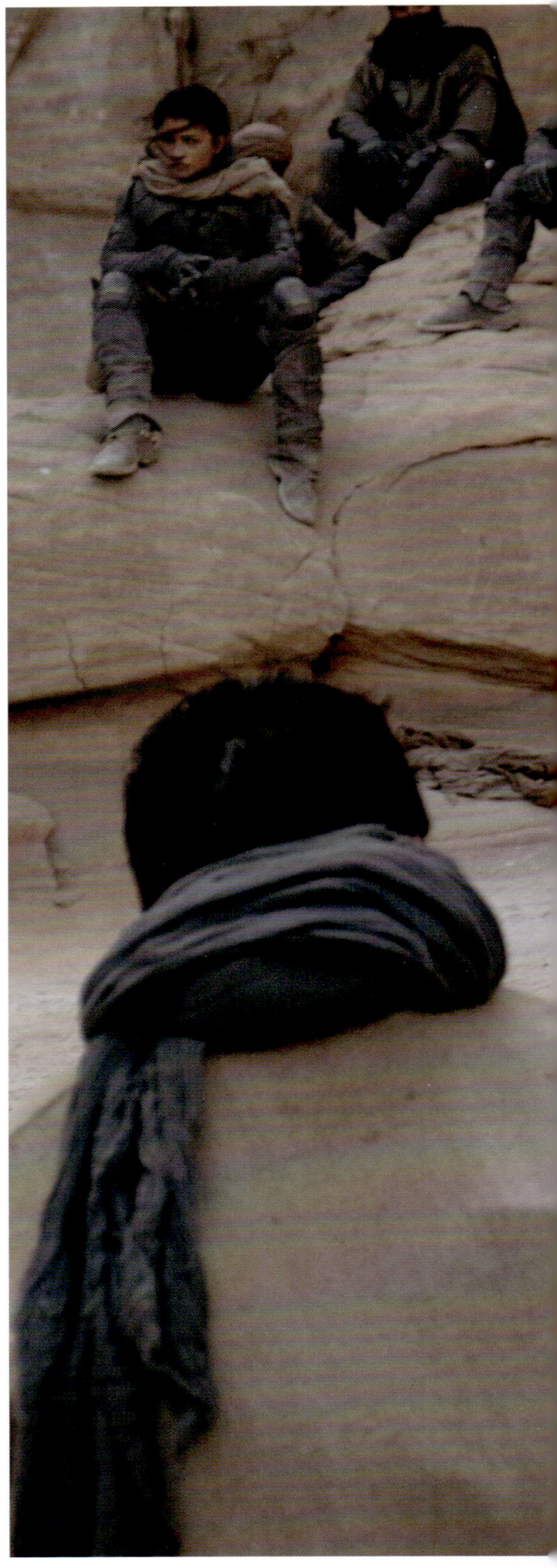

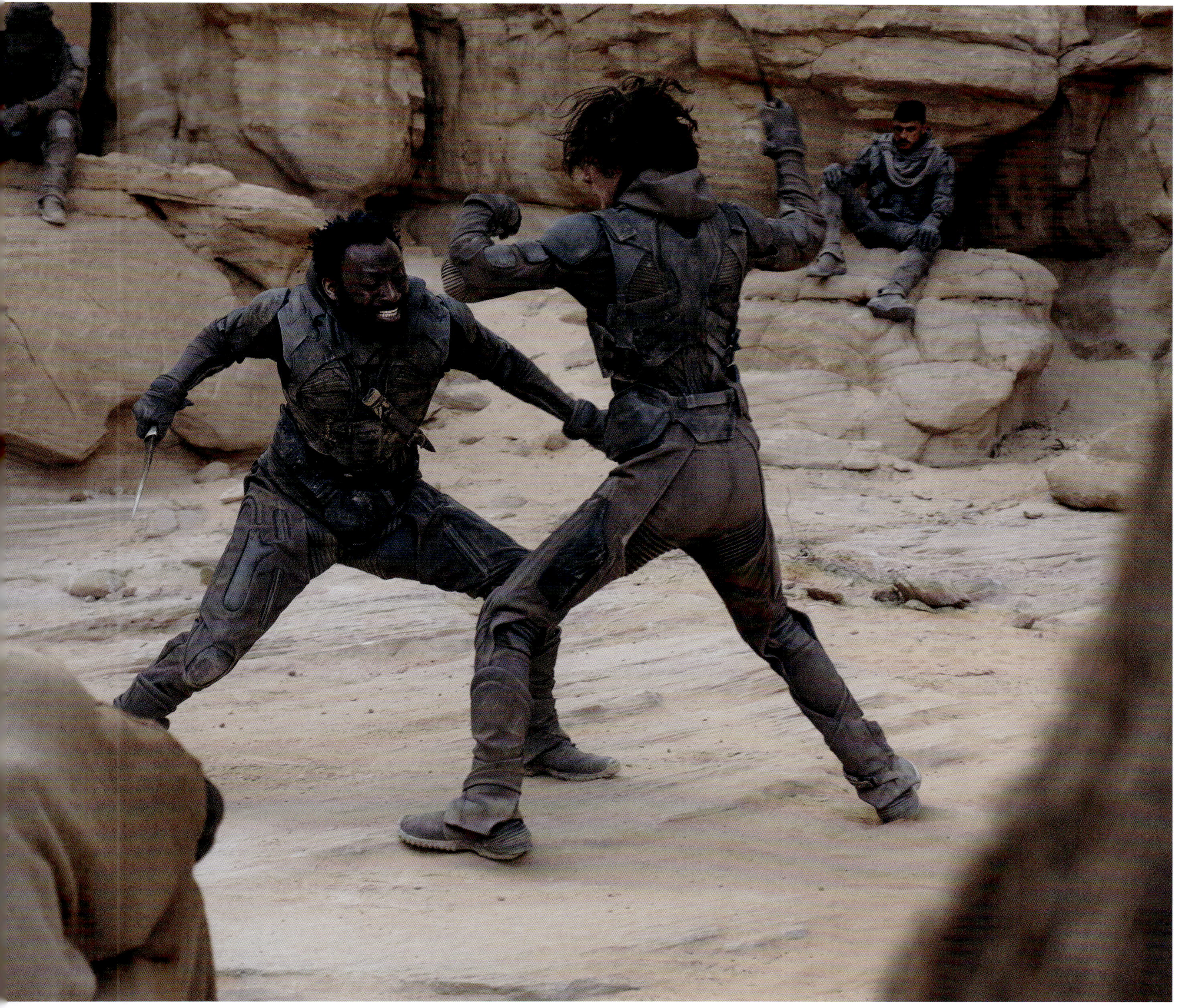

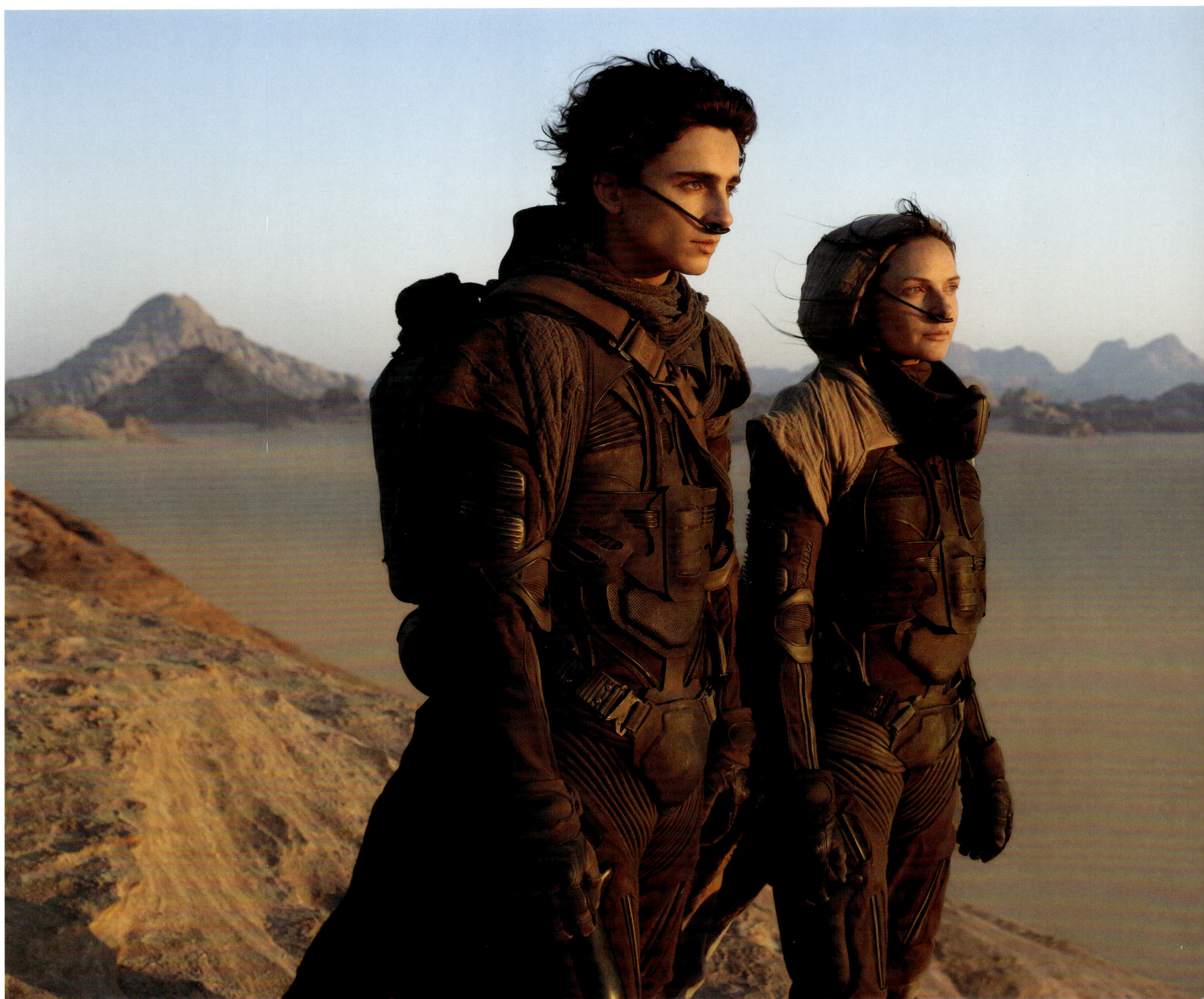

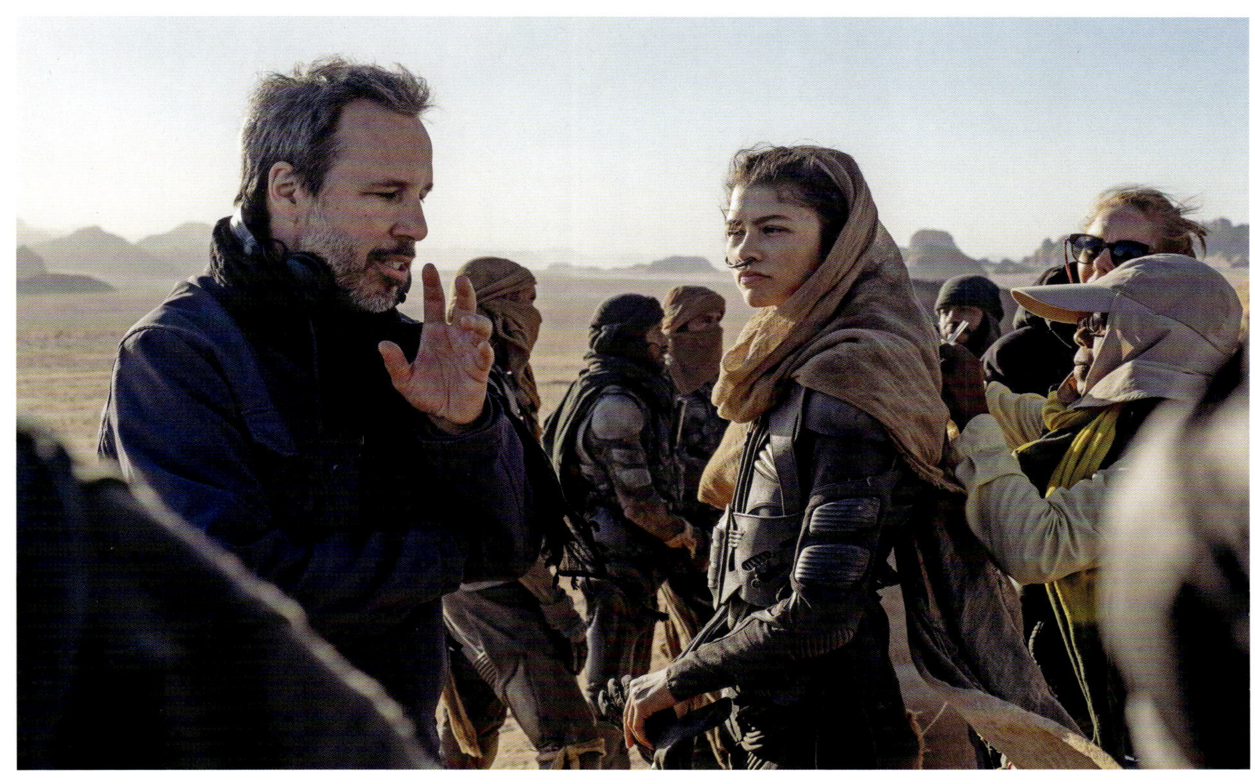

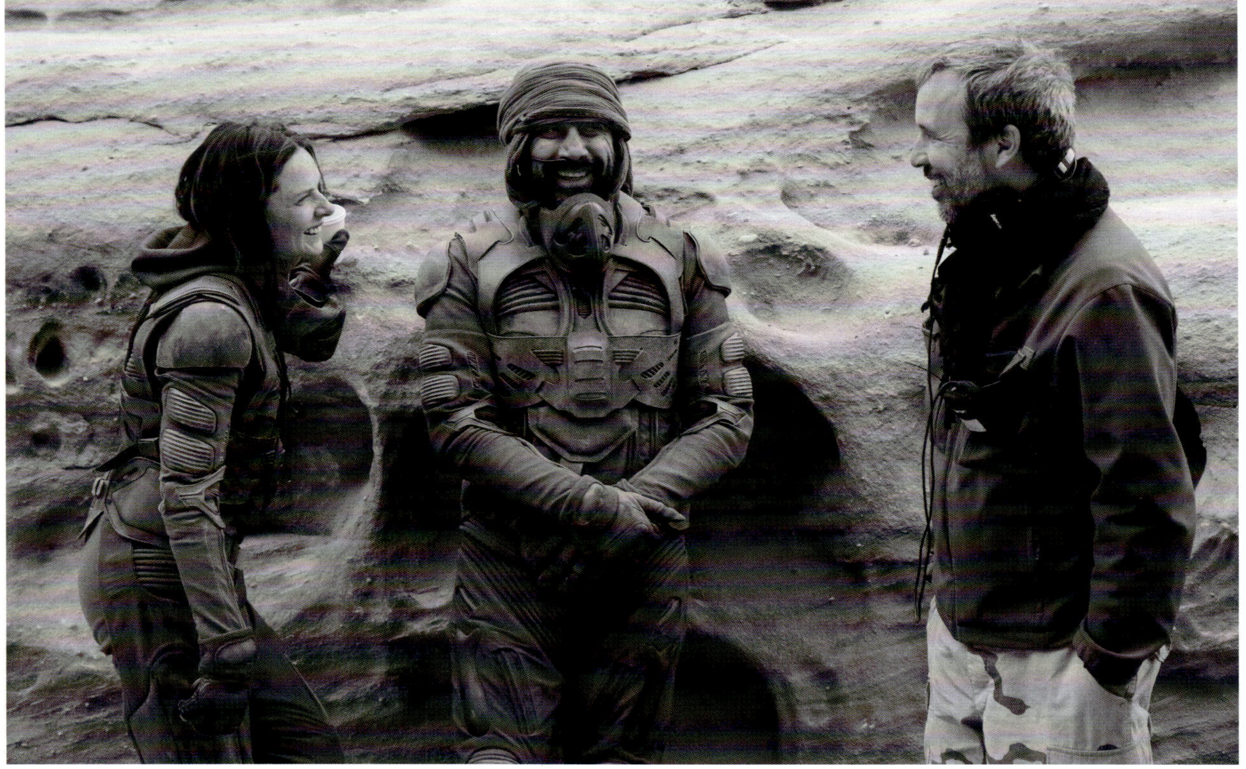

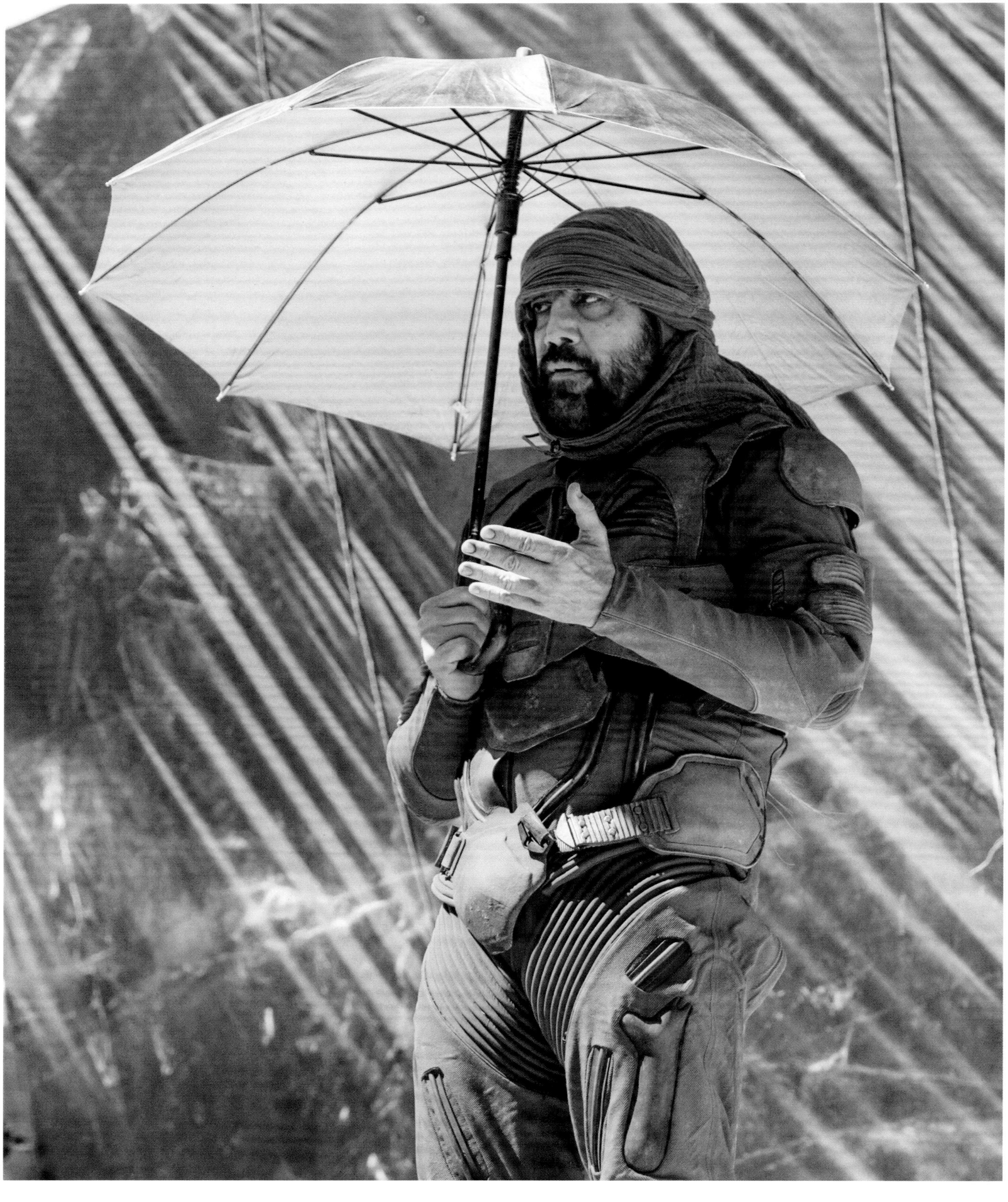

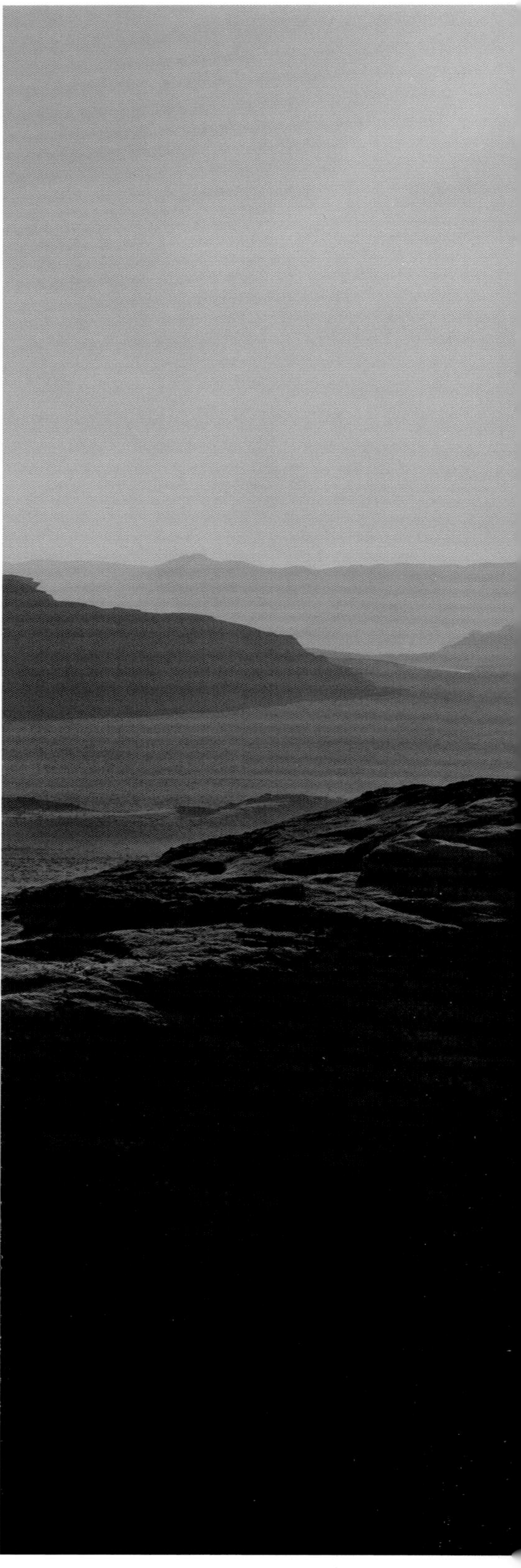

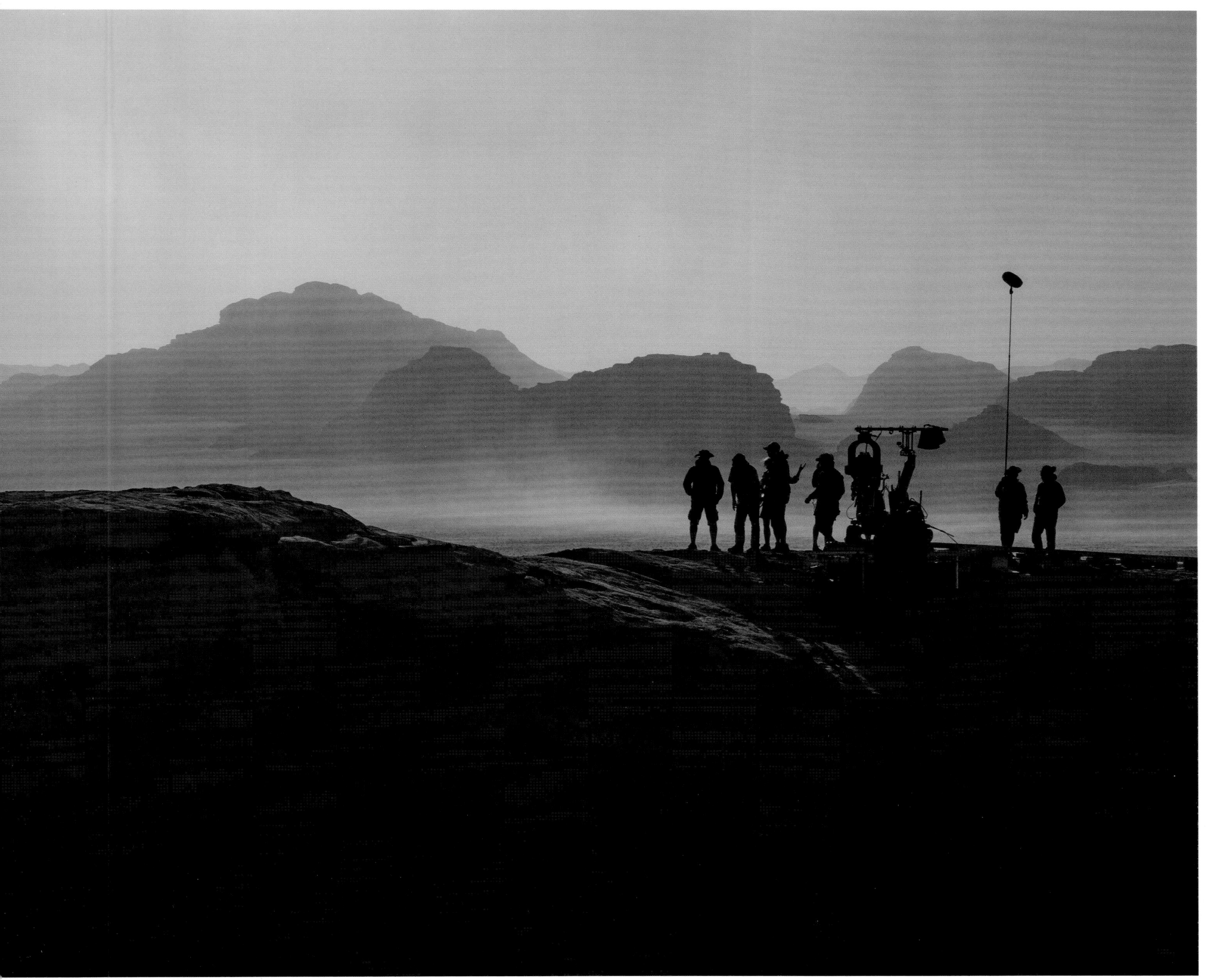

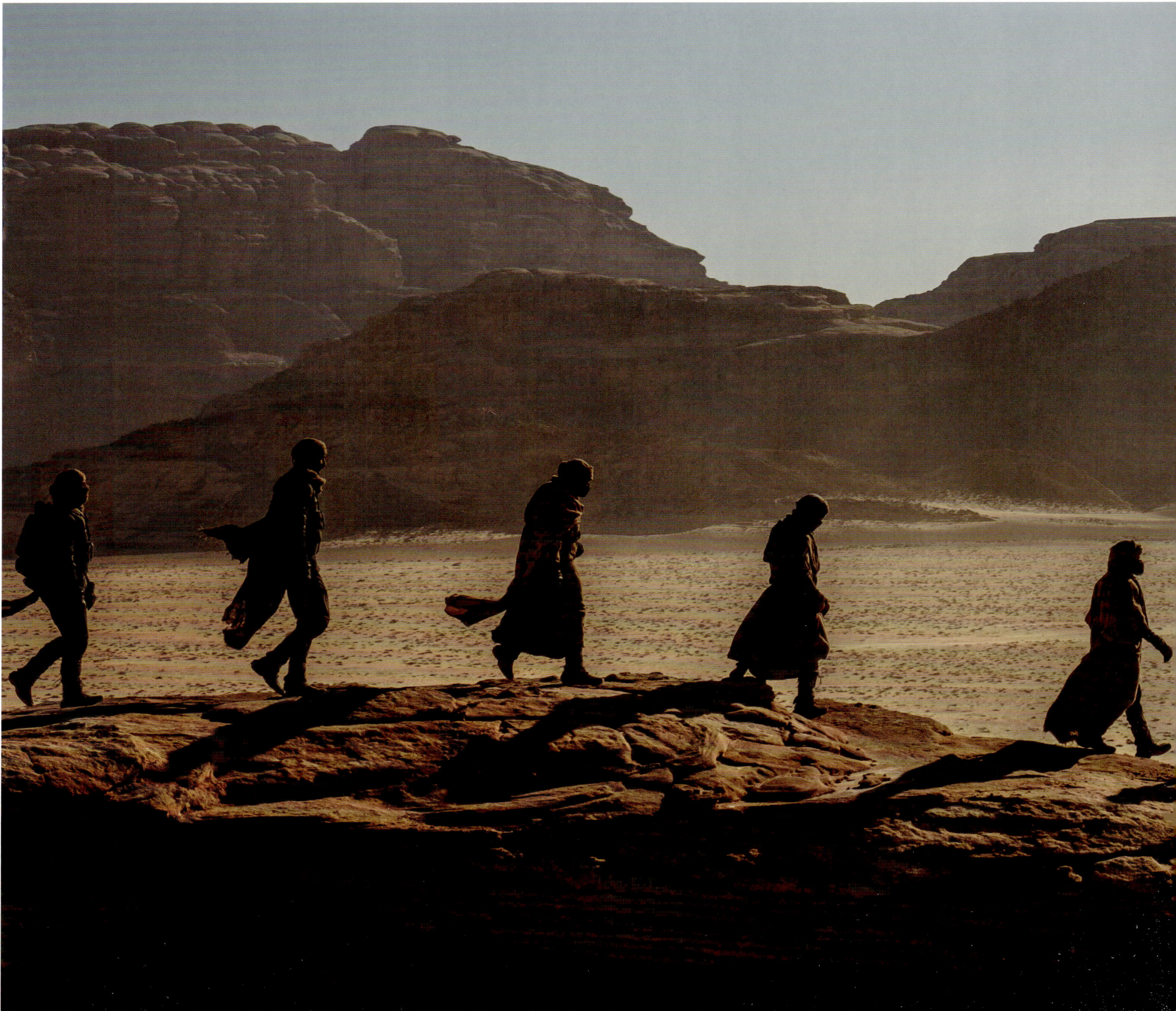

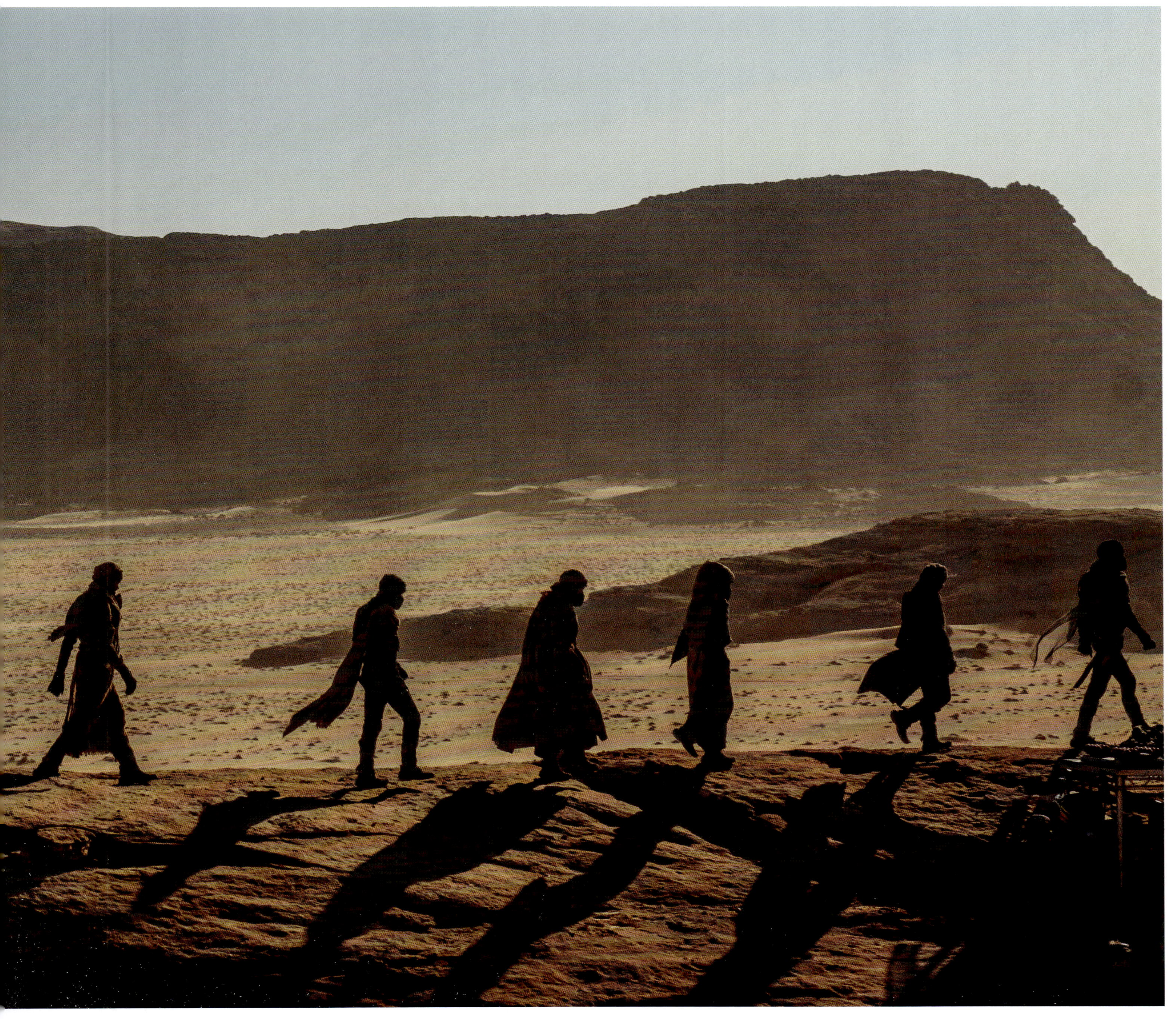

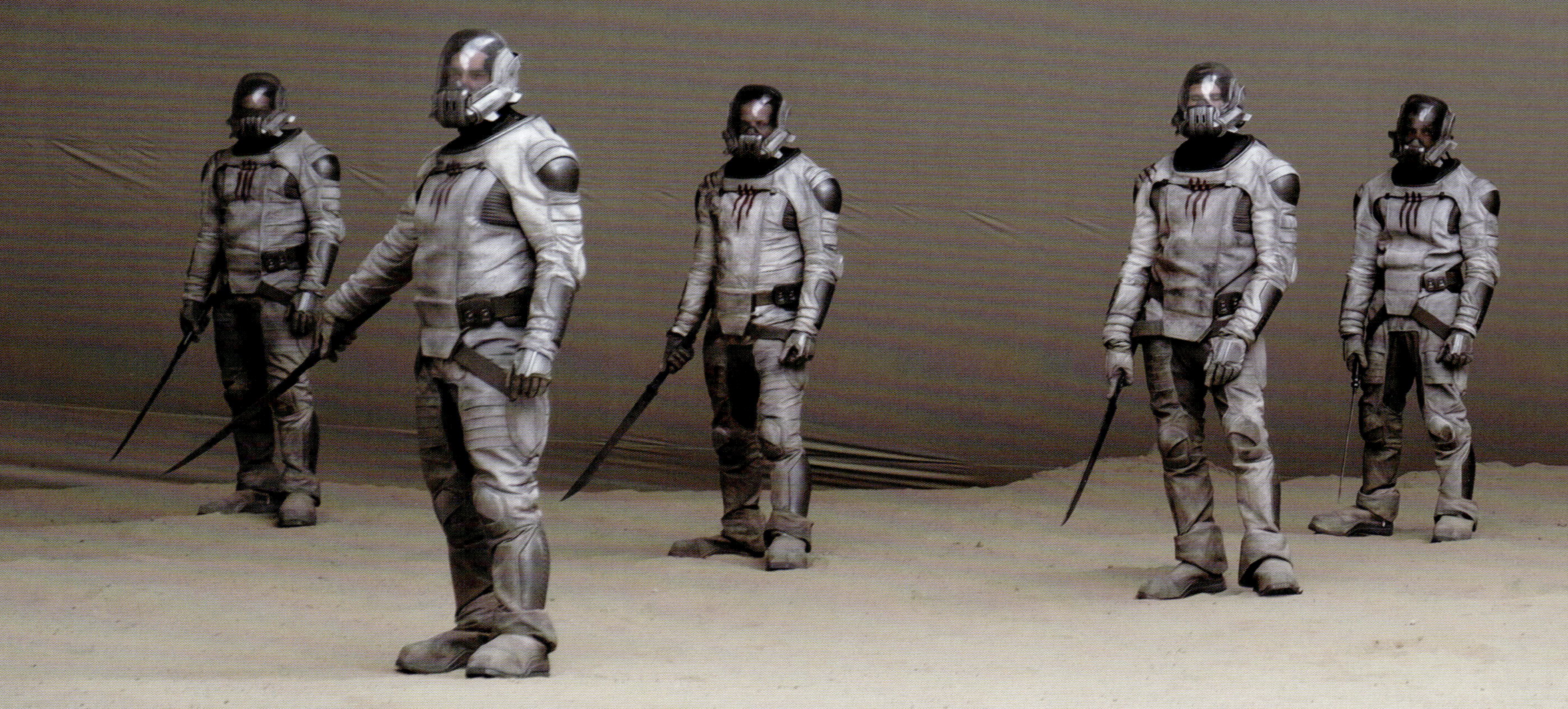
BUDAPEST

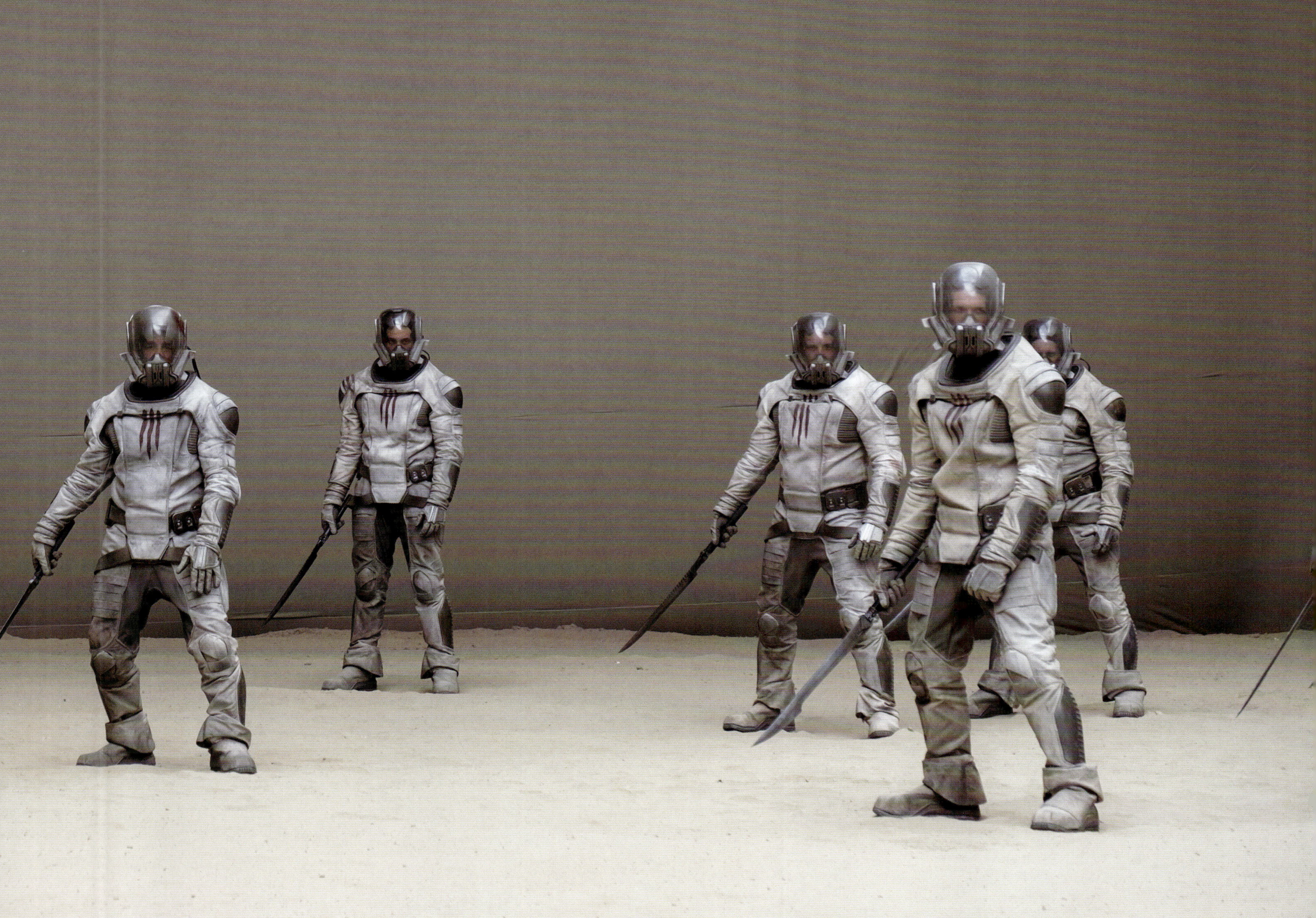

BUDAPEST WAS OUR HOME for several months, and many of our crew were Hungarian locals who welcomed our international film family with open arms. Within the stages of Origo Studios, we traveled through locations first dreamed up by Frank Herbert and brought to life by Denis Villeneuve, from the misty medieval hues of Castle Caladan to the creepy chill of the Baron's bathroom on Giedi Prime. We moved between the sun-baked backlot and the dark halls of Arrakeen, the city that housed the transition of power between the Harkonnens and the Atreides. On occasion, we ventured out of the soundstages into the local areas around Budapest. We followed Liet Kynes into the ecological testing station, built in an old steel mill, climbed aboard the flight rig built to fly the ornithopters on a secluded hilltop, and worked in the rain on a grassy highland dressed with gravestones as the Caladan cemetery.

Photographing both main and second unit simultaneously often required me to be in two places at once. One minute, I would be outside on the muddy backlot, pummeled by the special effects' torrential rain, photographing an ominous scene of the Sardaukar soldiers on Giedi Prime; the next, I would step across into an eerily quiet, almost pitch-black stage to photograph the Baron floating through the halls of the Arrakeen Residency. It often took a moment for my eyes to adjust, but I was always in awe of the passport that movies give us, both as crew members and as audiences, to travel between these disparate worlds.

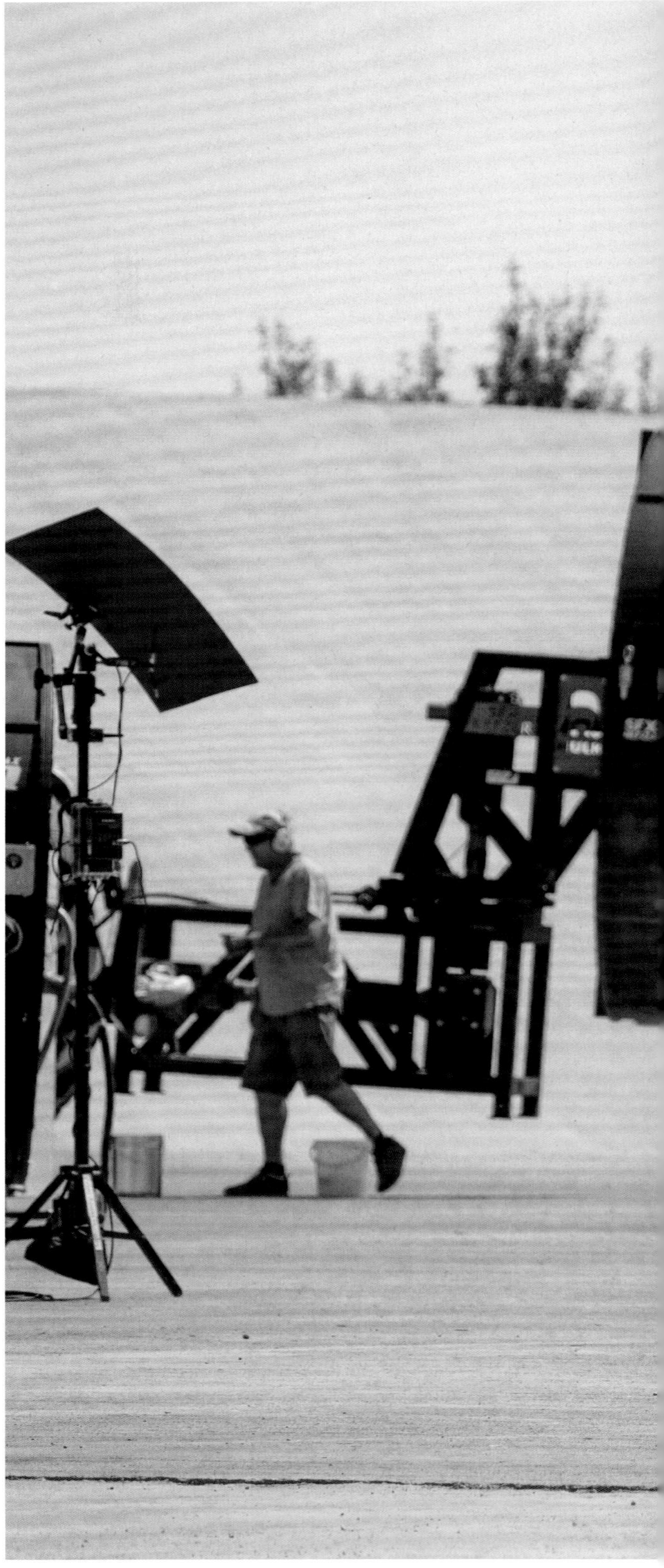

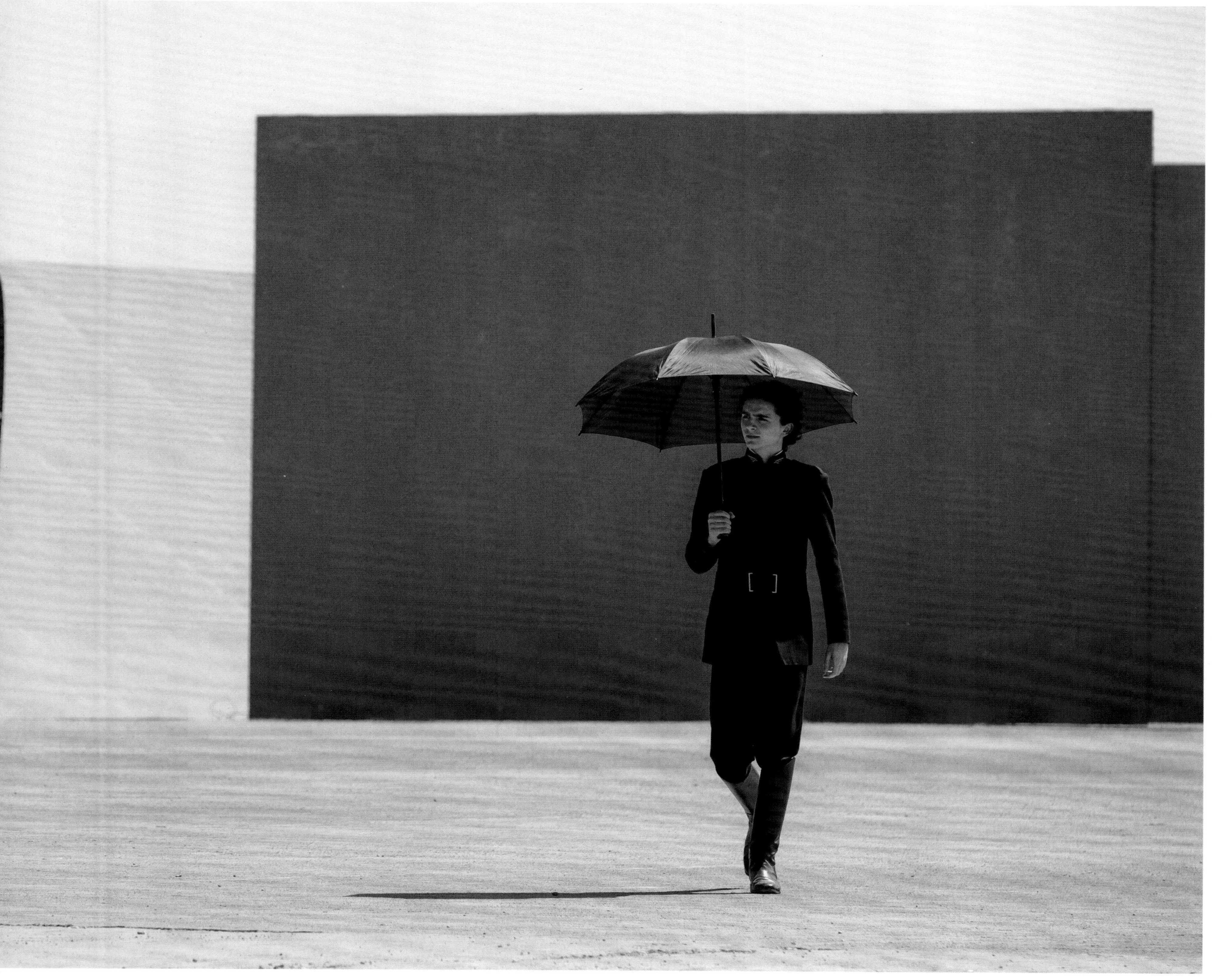

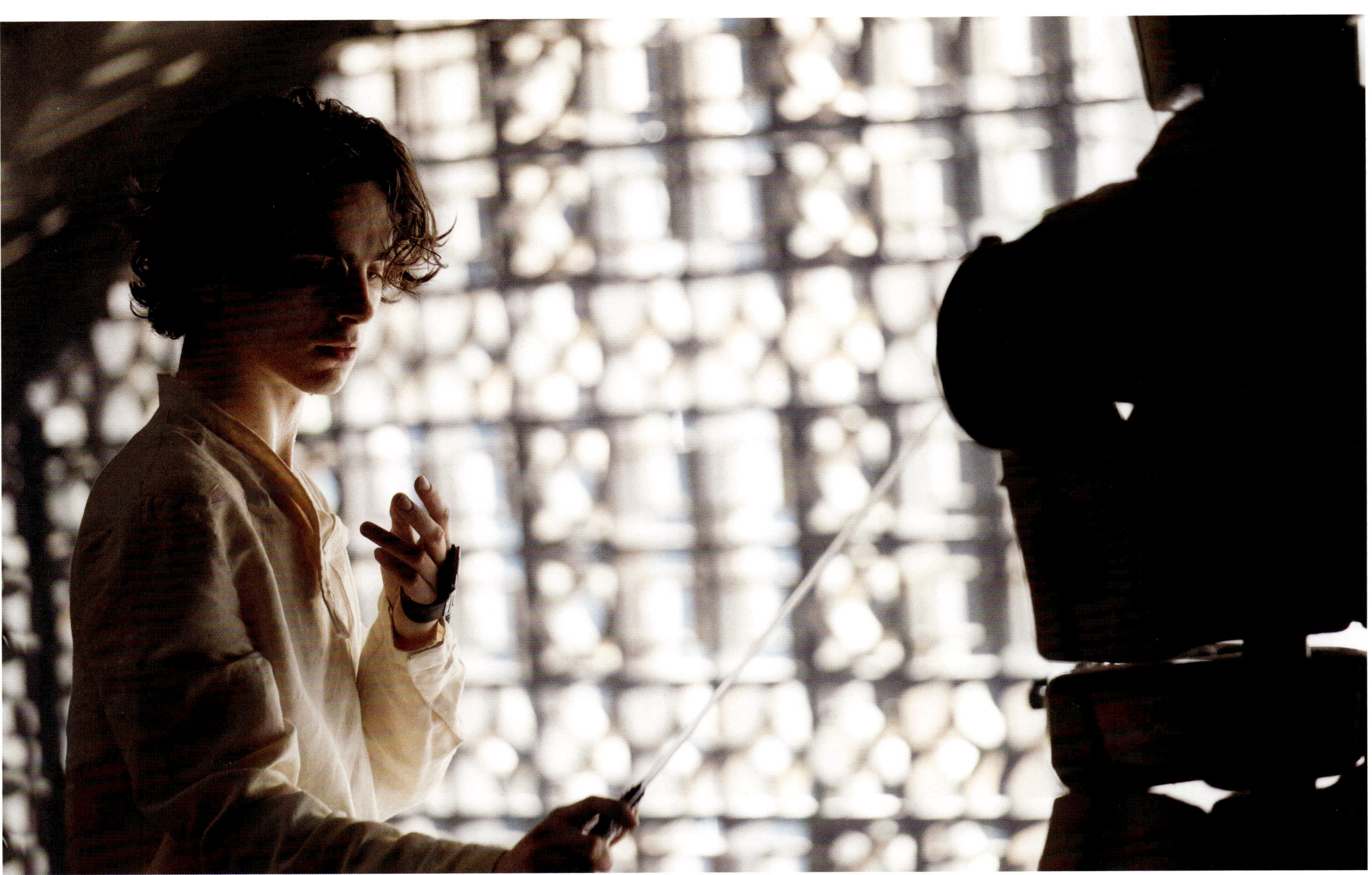

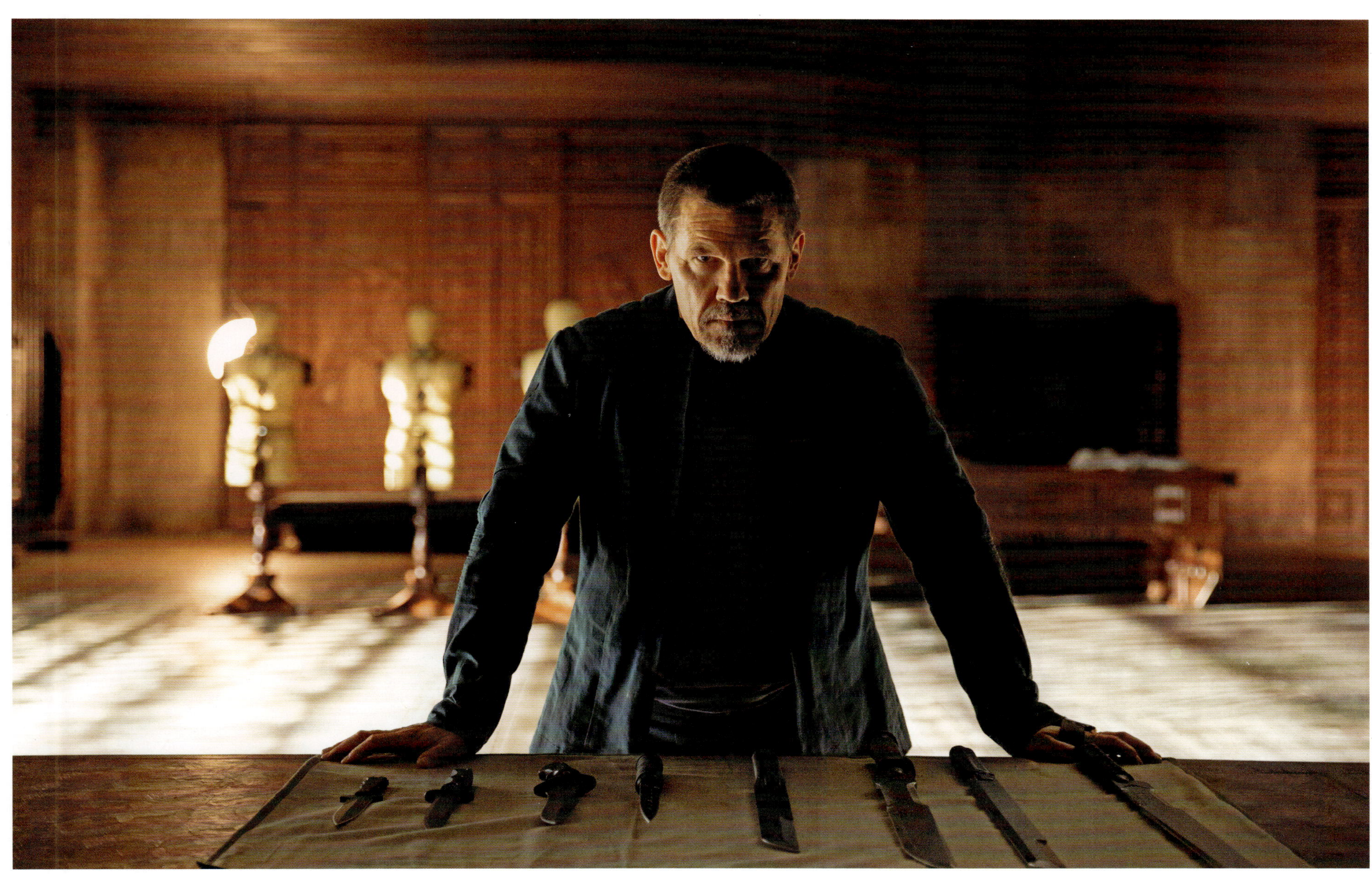

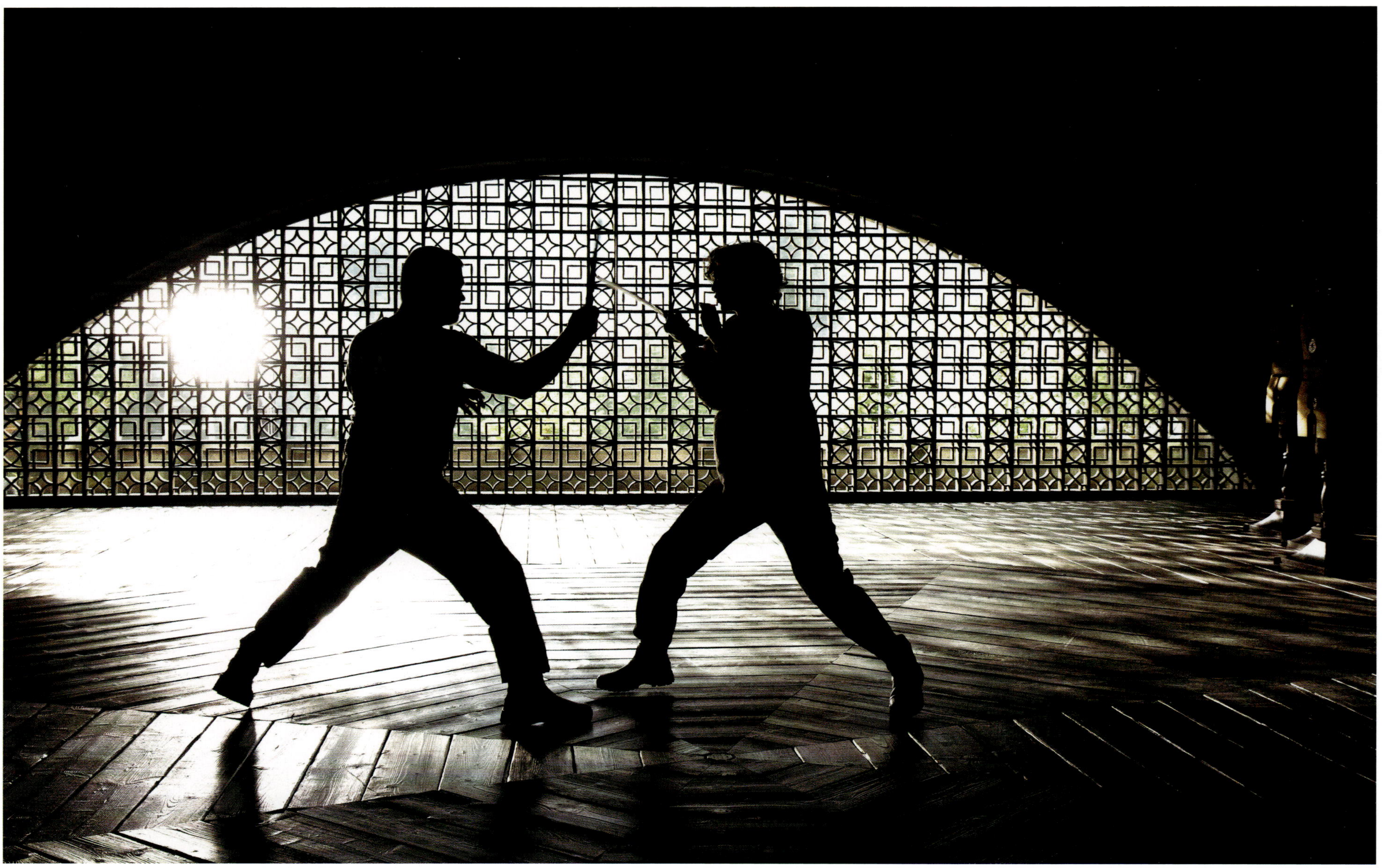

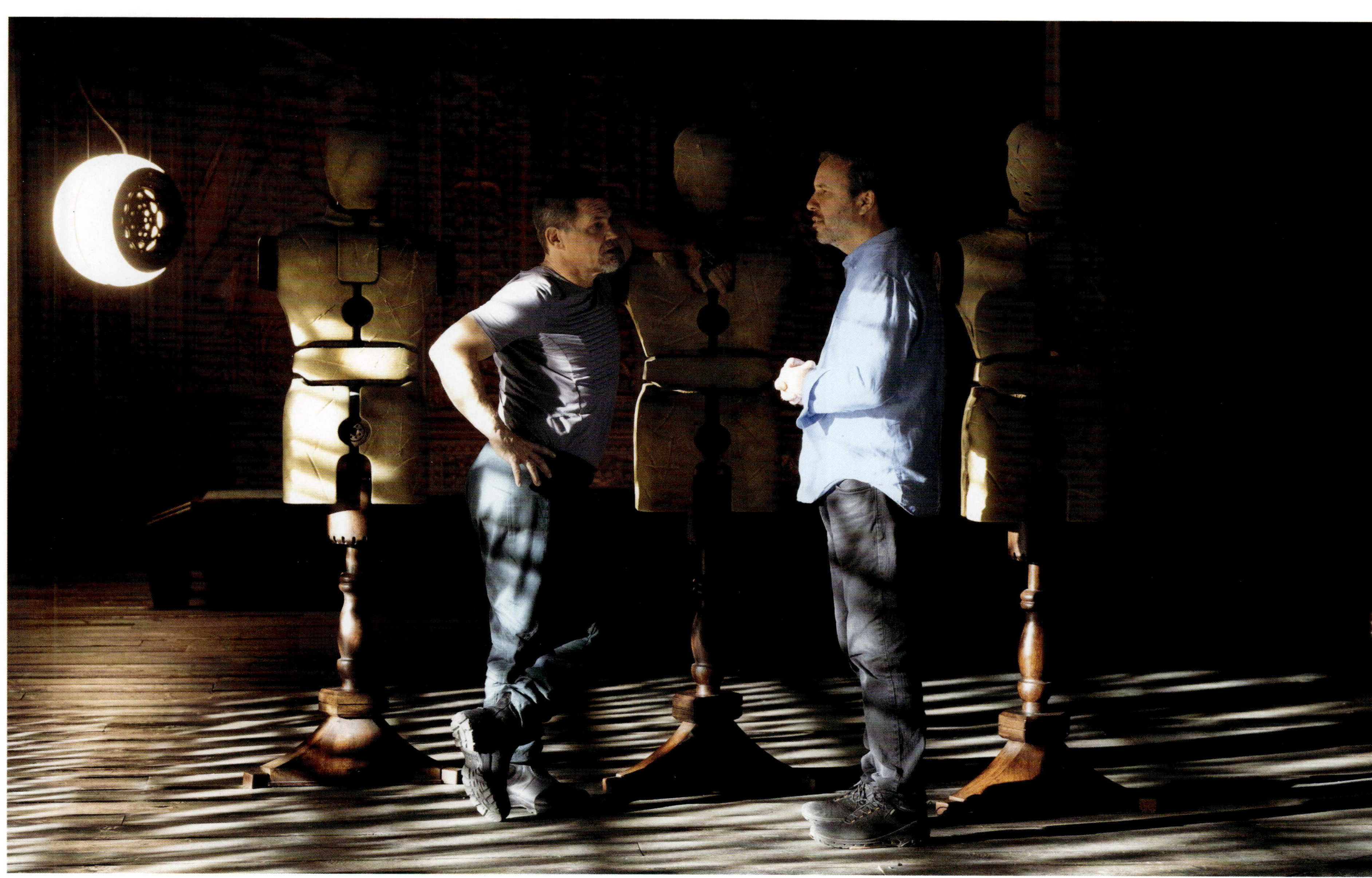

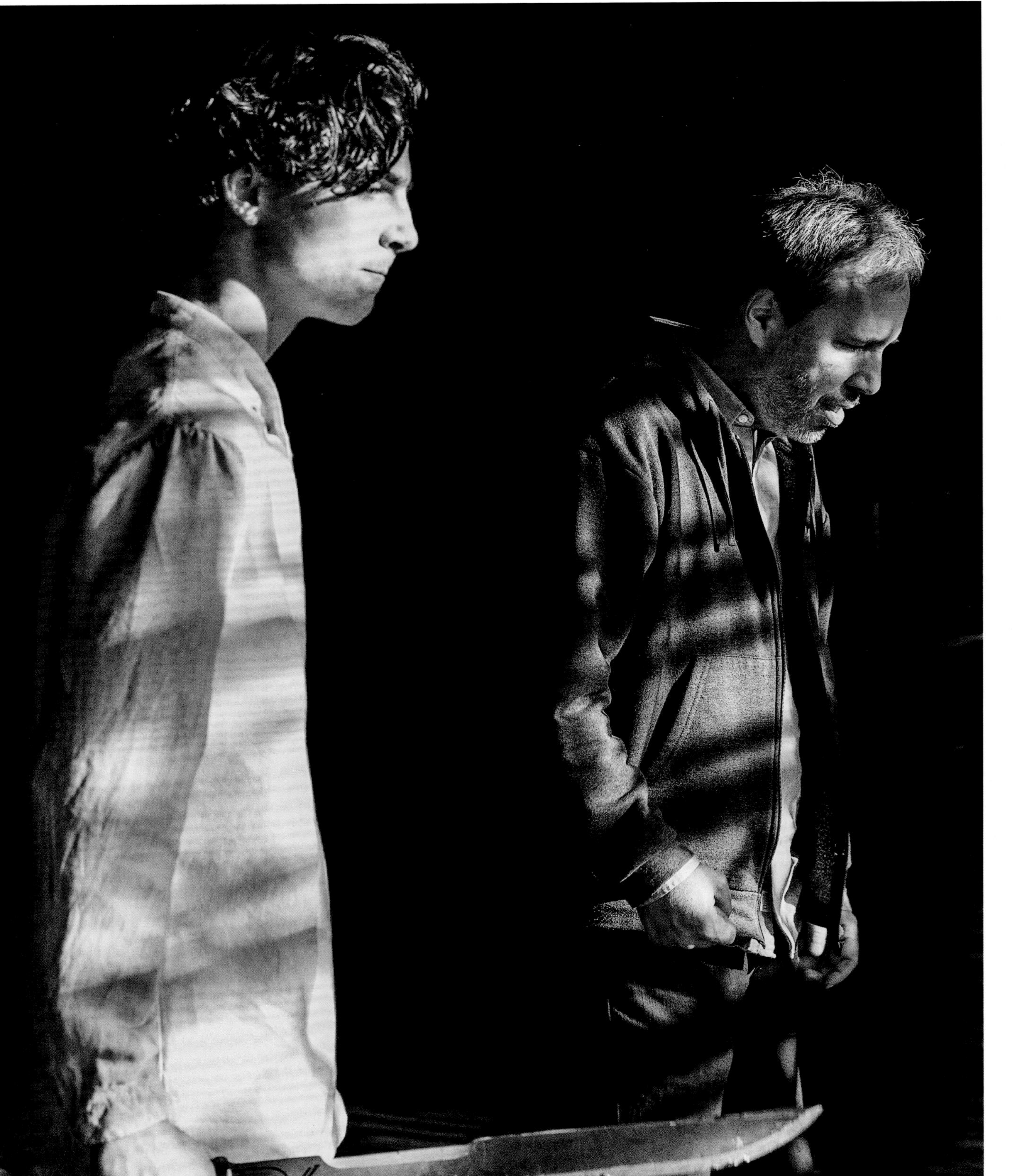

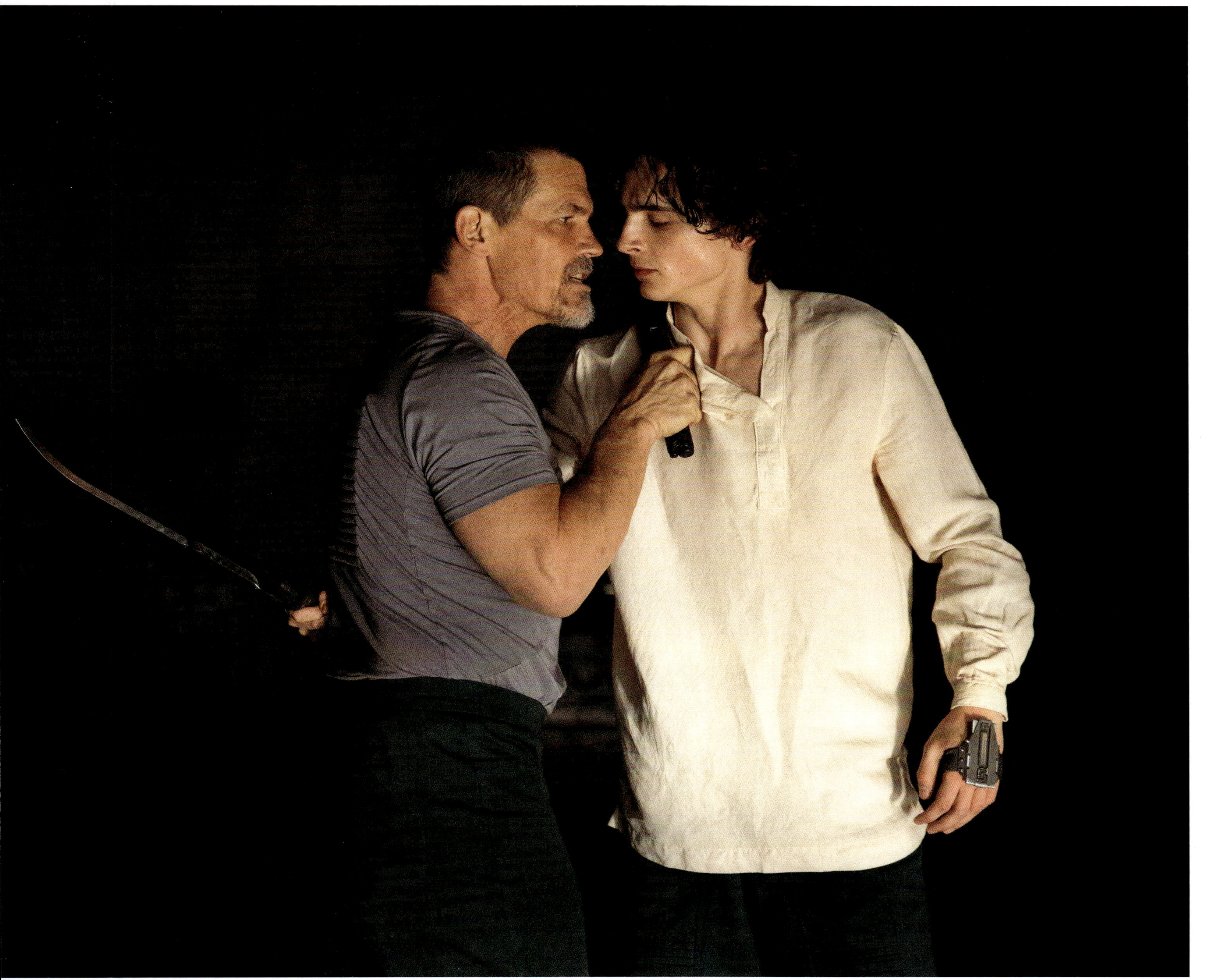

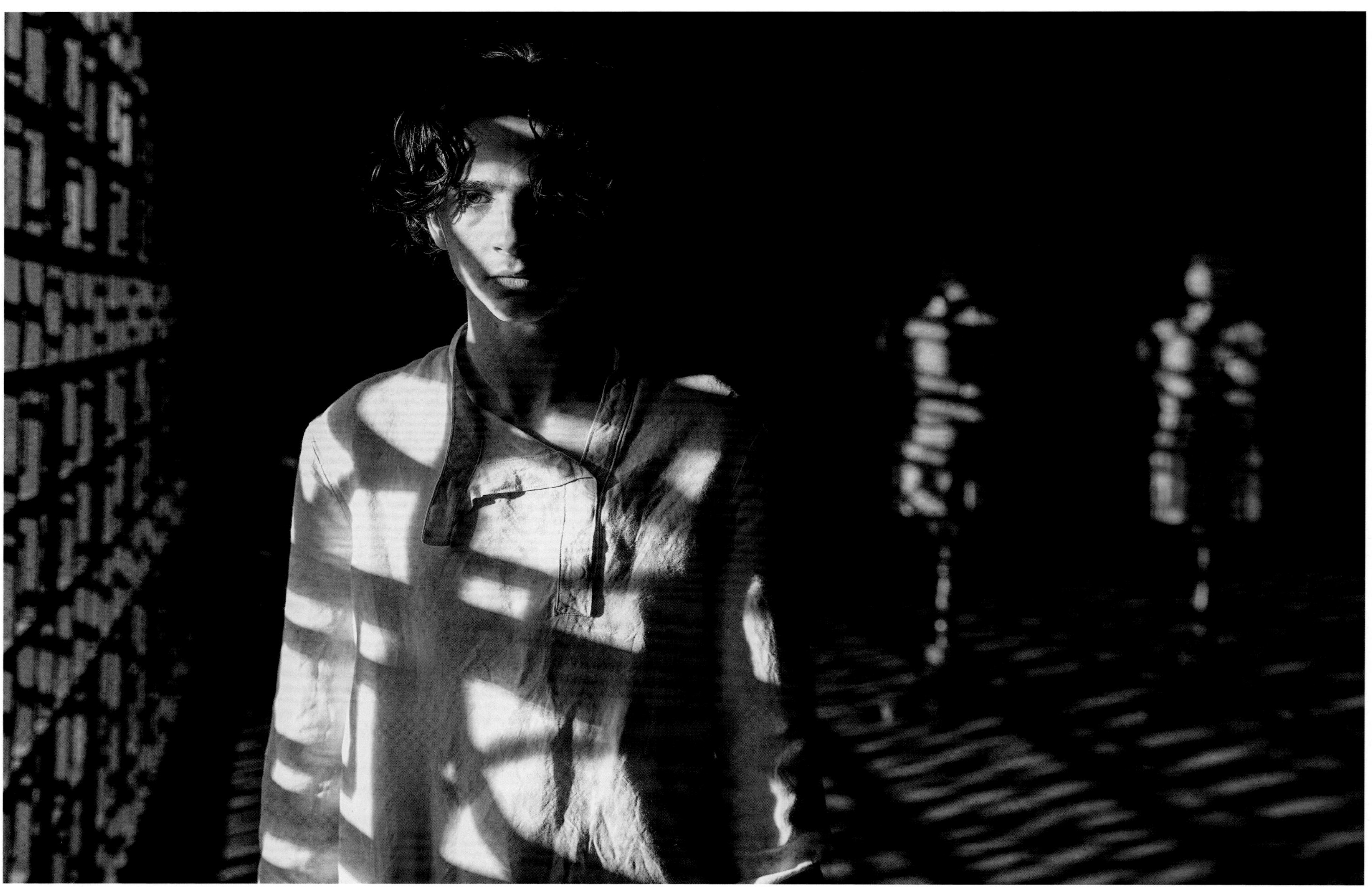

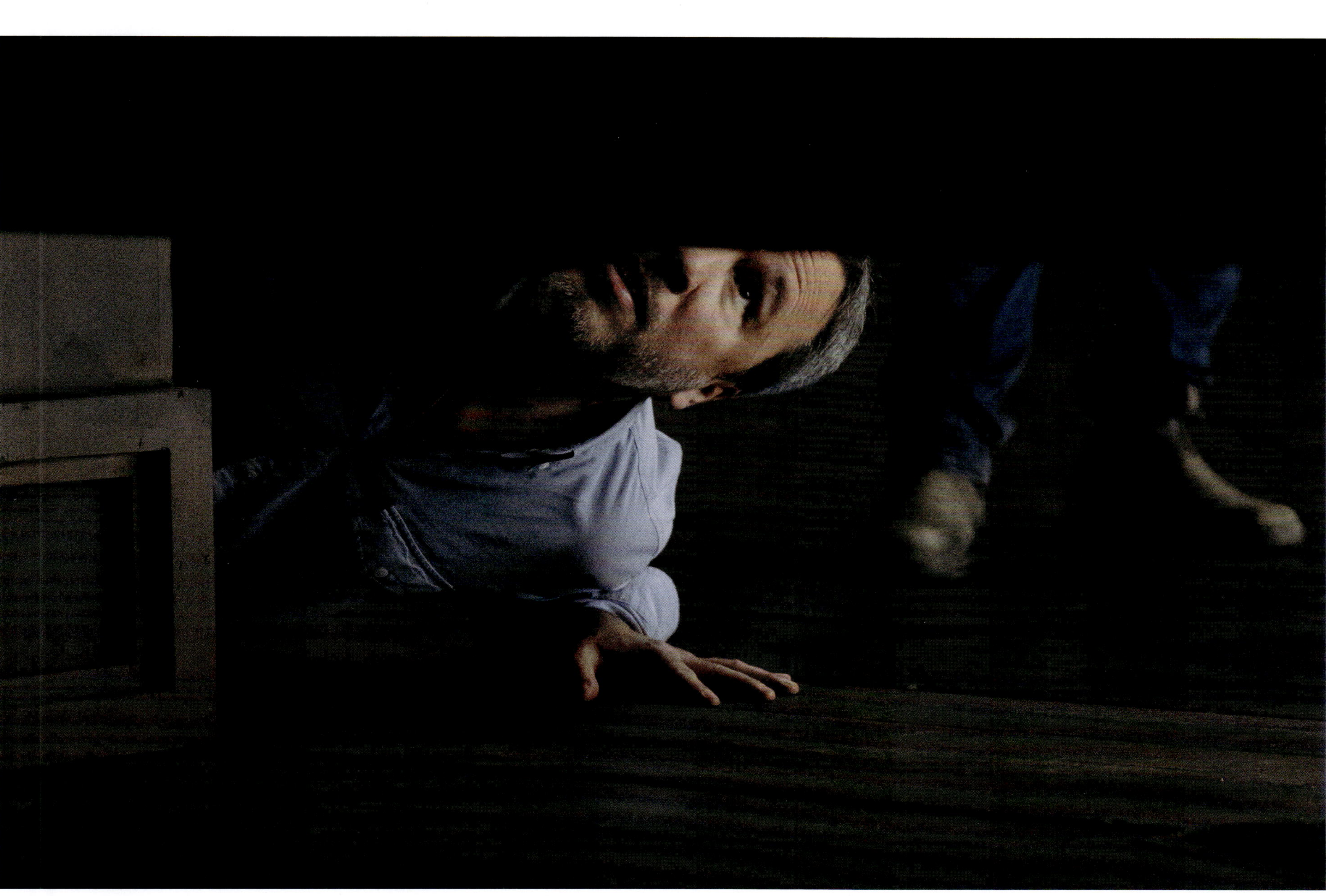

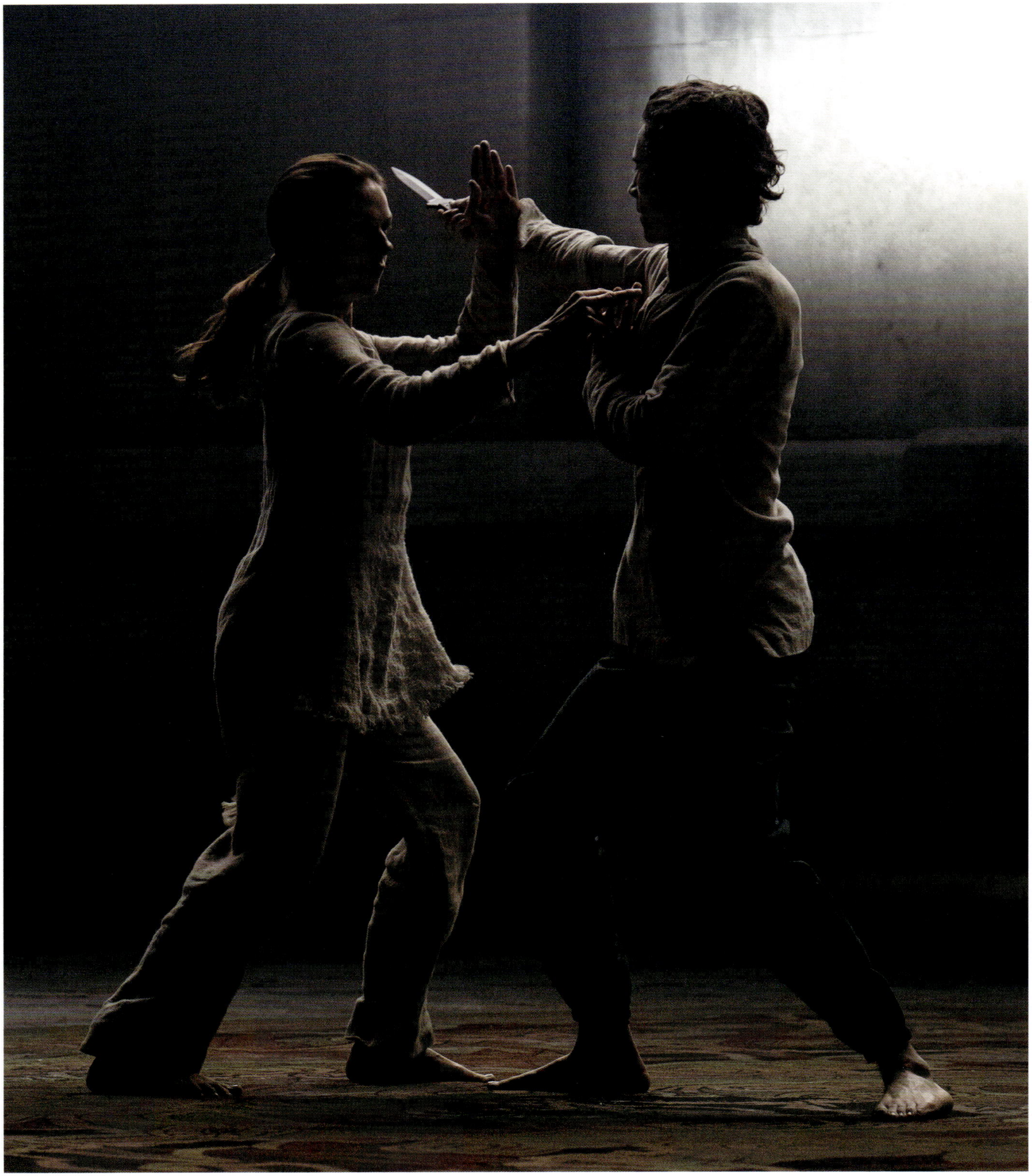

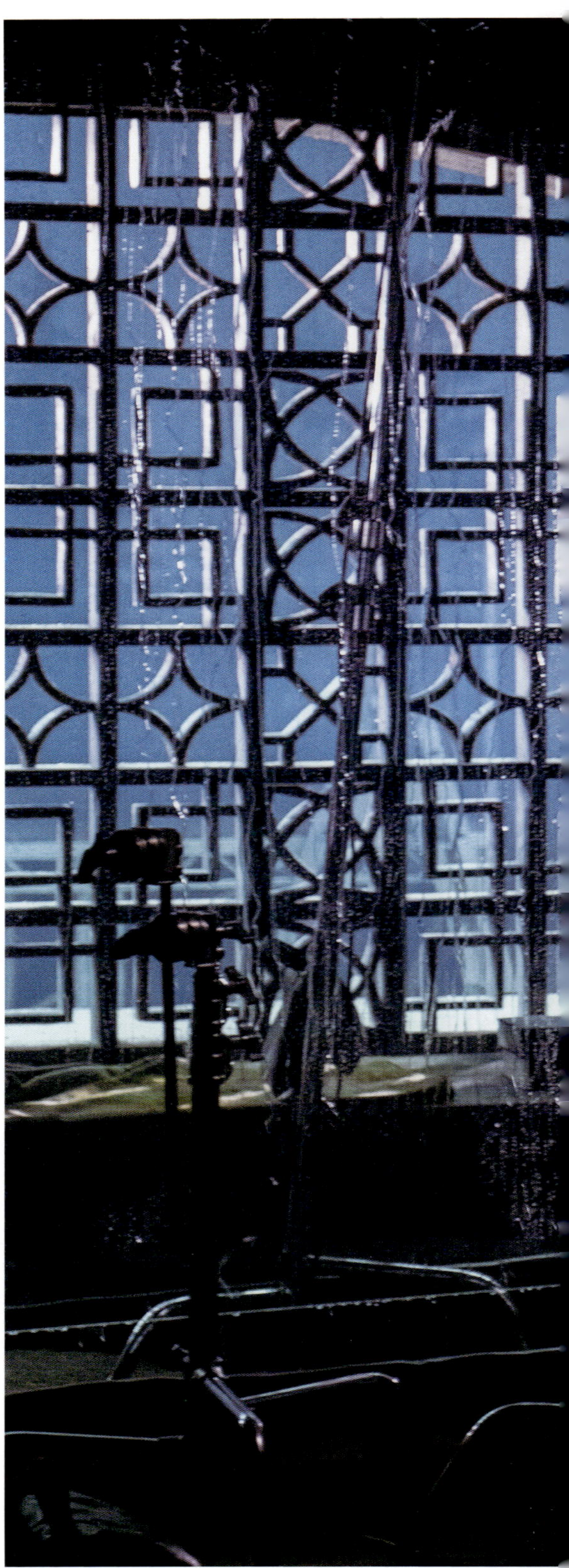

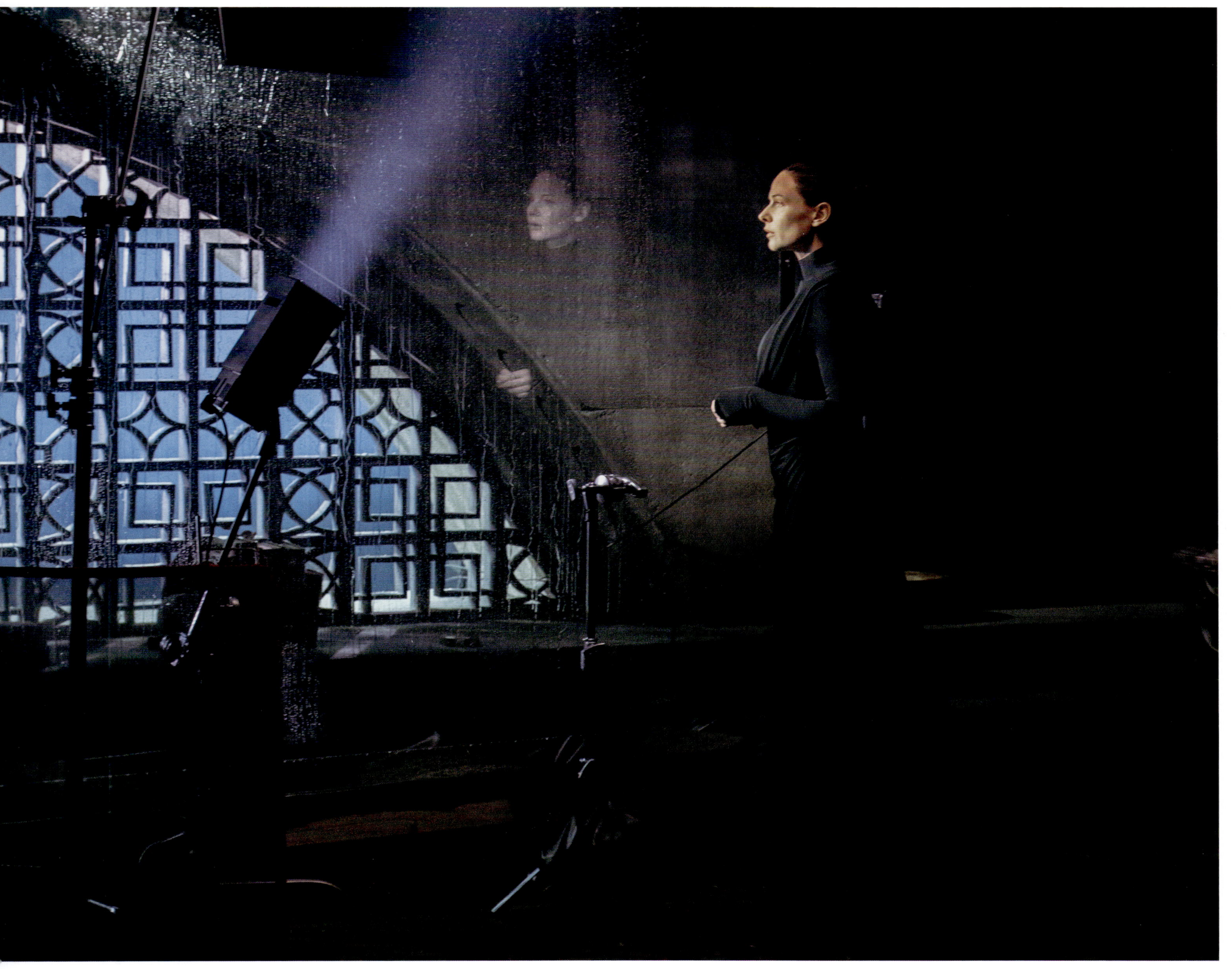

I HAVE SPENT MOST of my life in the movie circus, on sets, among famous names and award-winning talents, but I have rarely experienced the connection or sense of family our crew had on *Dune*. We spent months away from home, working long, physical days, but found ourselves among friends and family, holding each other up and pushing each other forward.

My personal journey on this film was one that I could sum up by the collaboration and support of the crew around me. Camera, lighting, and grip departments made space for me, offering their support with a reflector or a grovel pad, or a shoulder to lean on. The art, props, special effects, sound, costume, hair, and makeup departments all gave me access to their domains so I could document and share their talents with the world in a way that would do them justice. The cast gave their time, performances, and personal insight to the photography because they understood its importance.

There was also an incredibly strong female presence among our cast and crew and, in our very own parallel to the Bene Gesserit, a sisterhood developed between us, creating a bond made even stronger by the gentlemen who stood beside us, contributing to and encouraging our success.

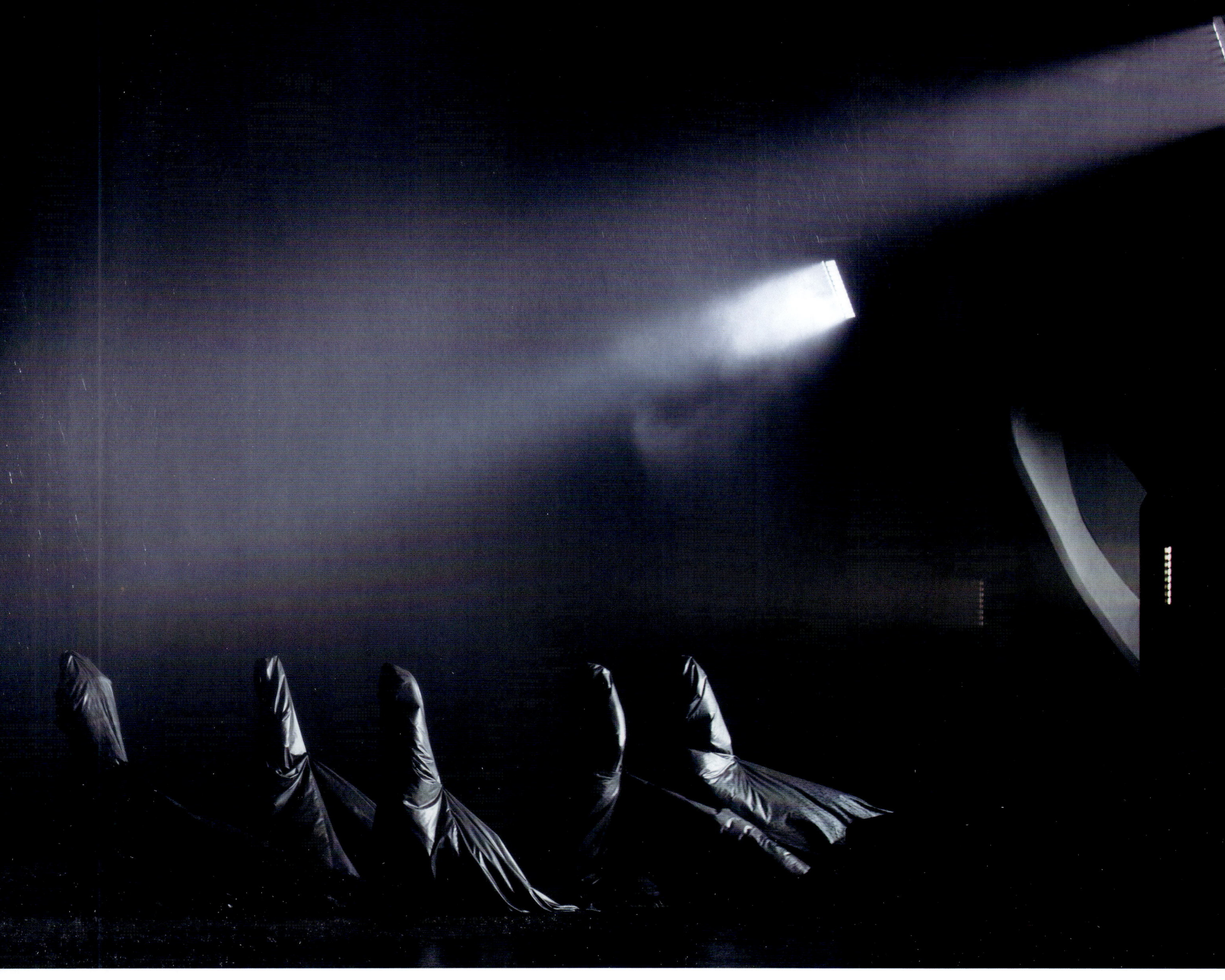

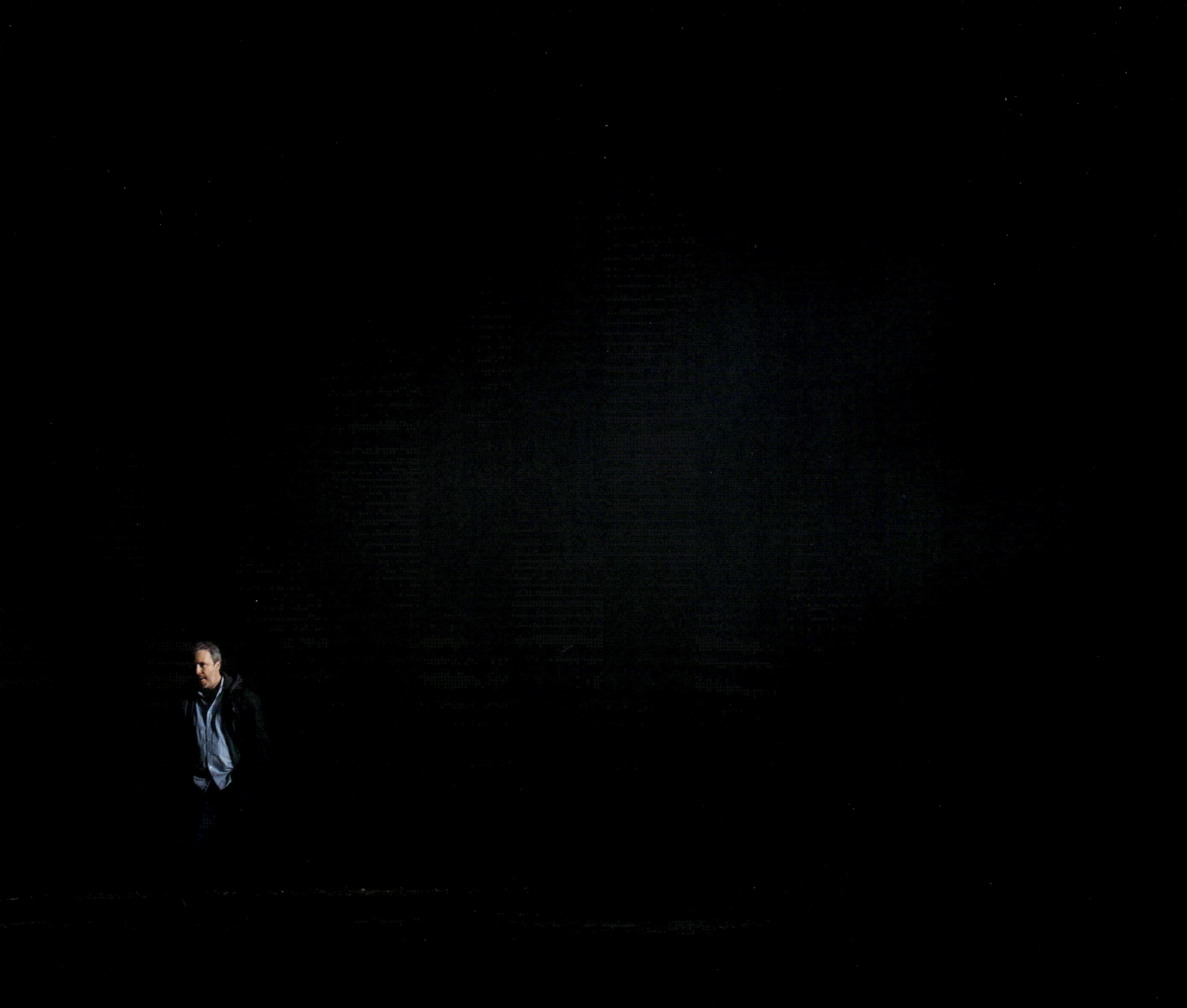

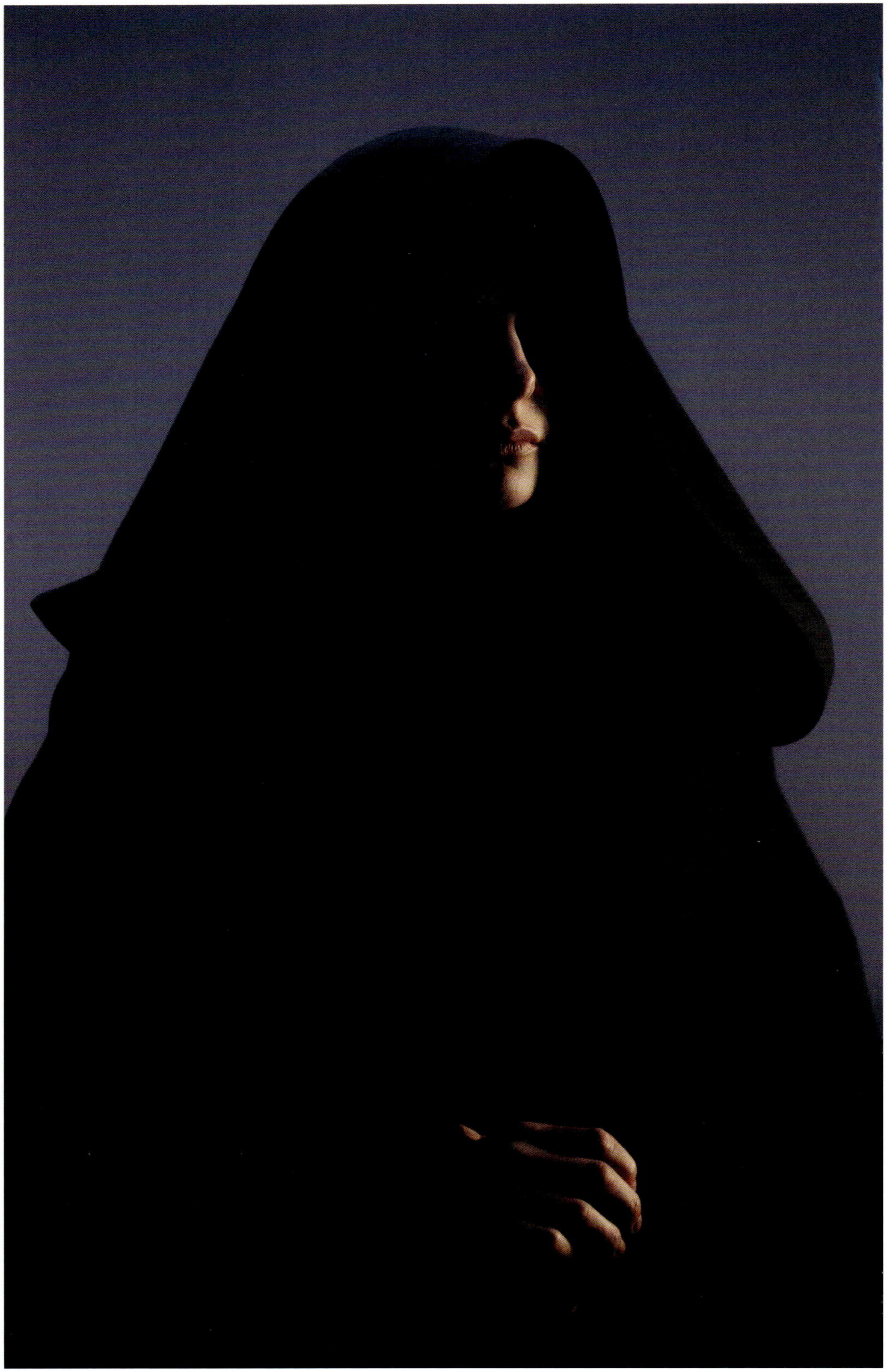

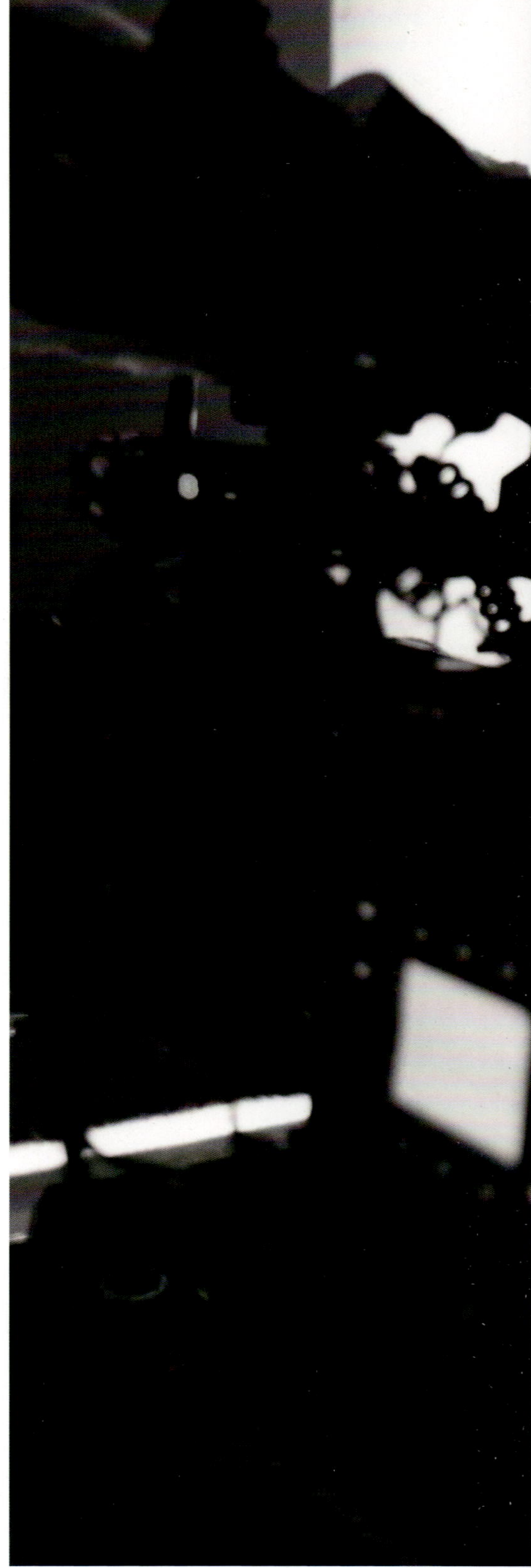

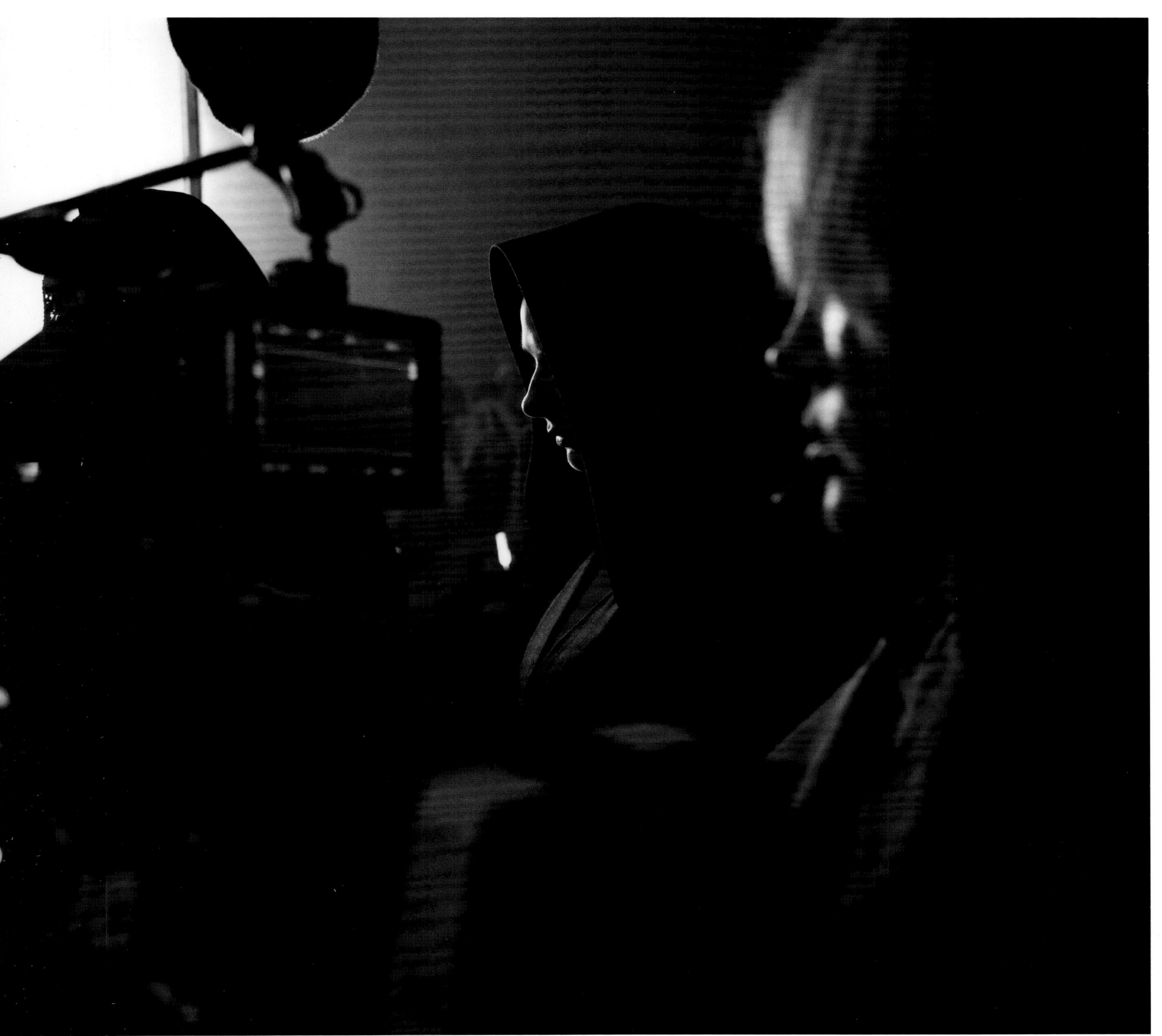

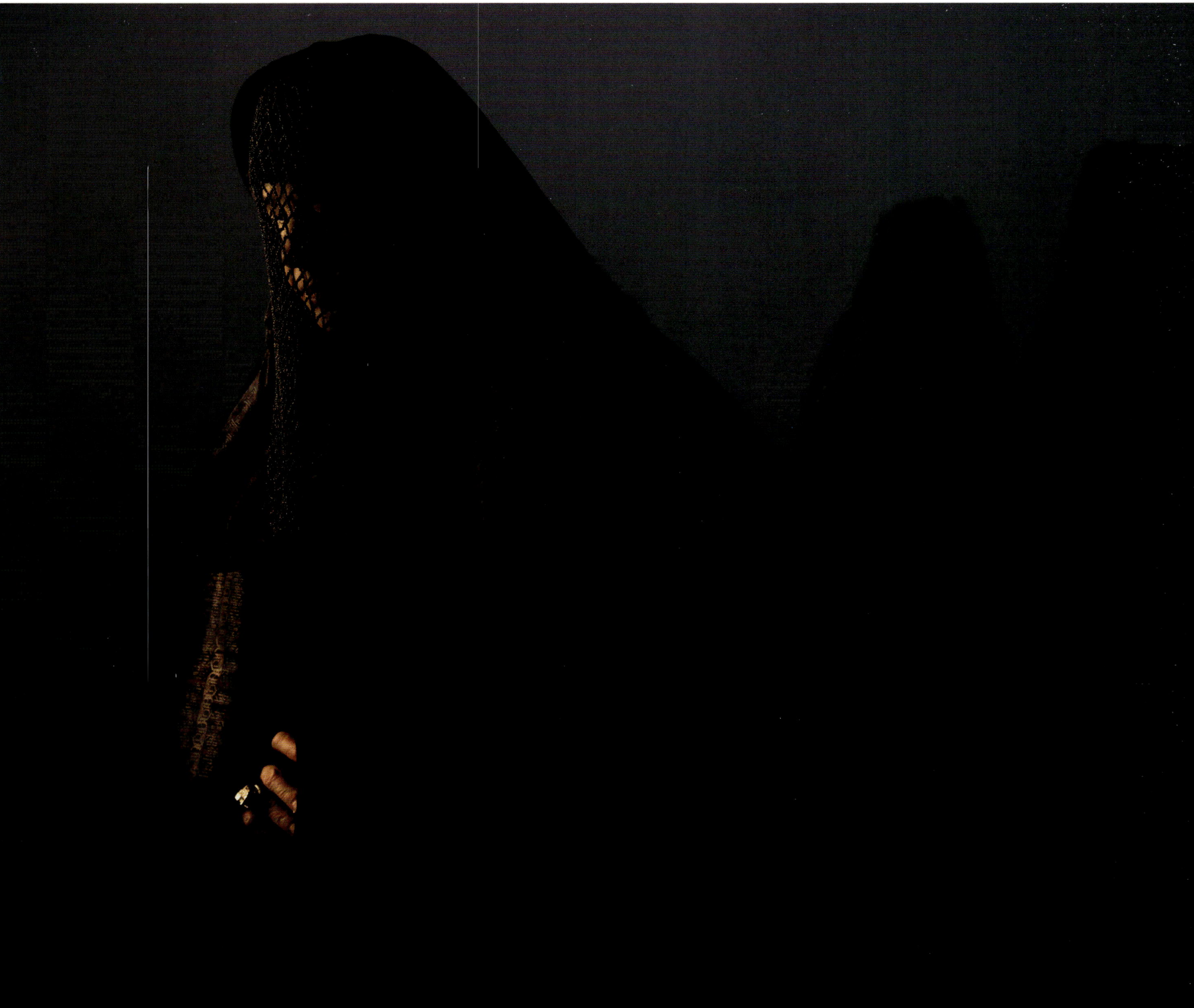

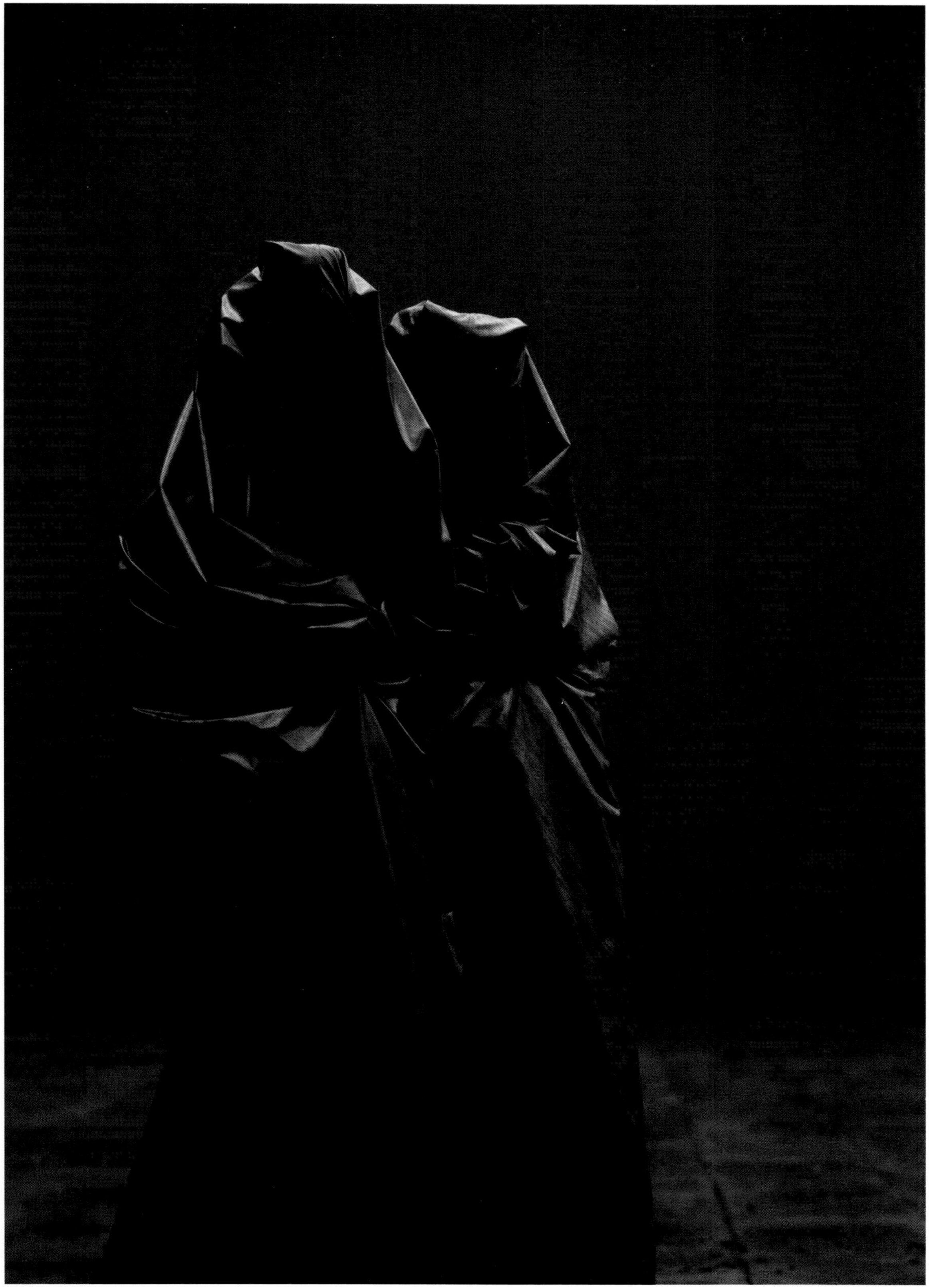

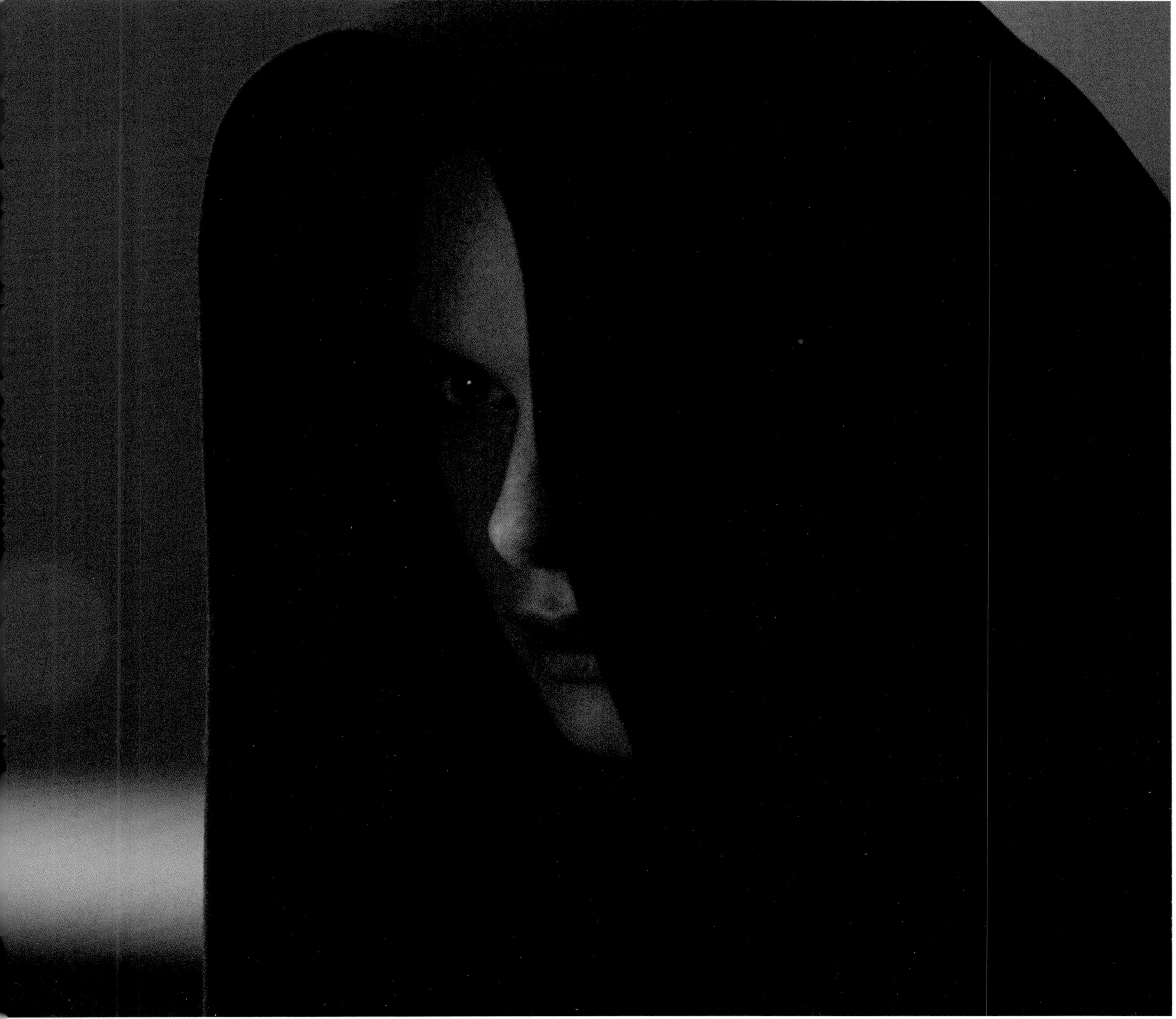

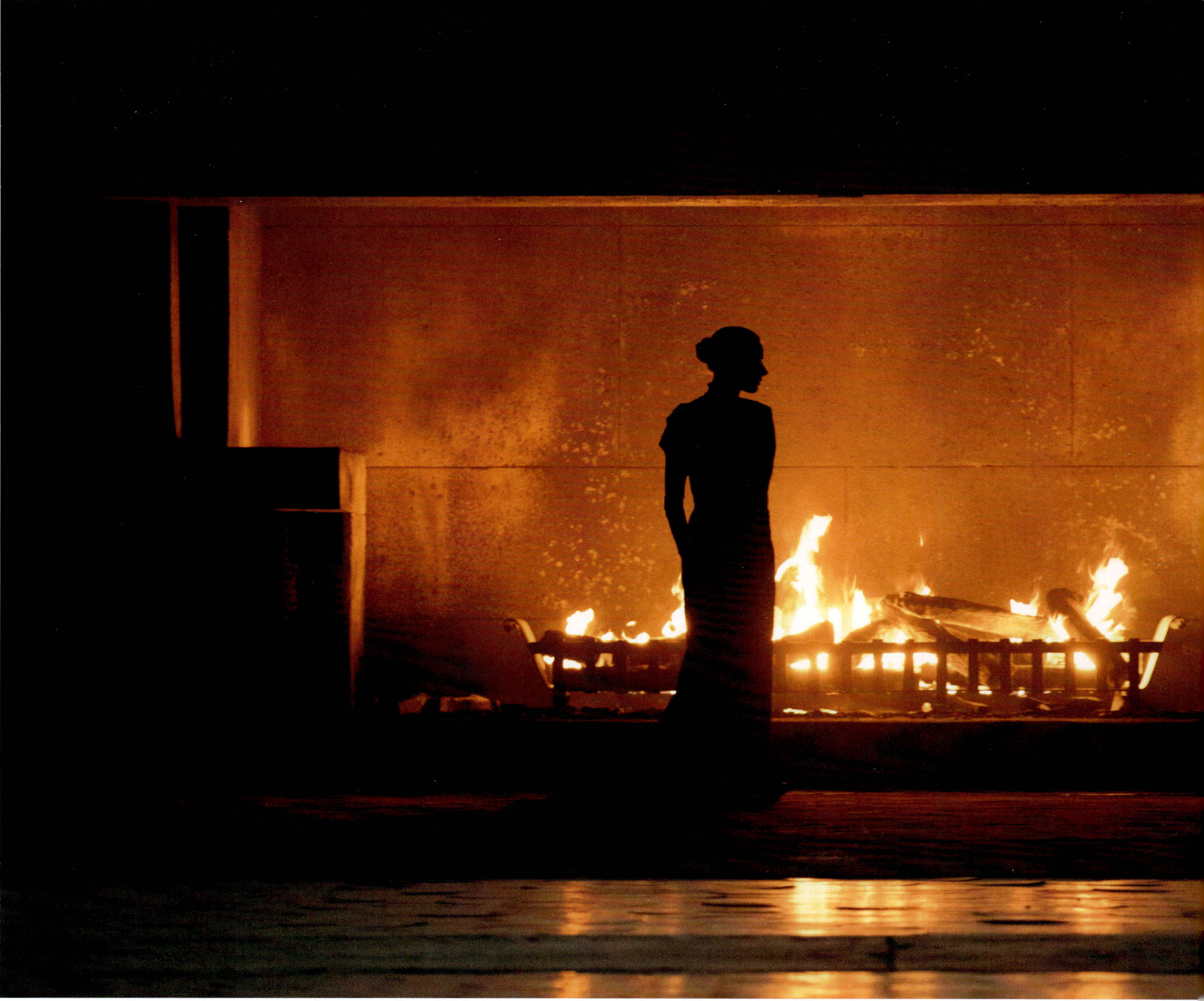

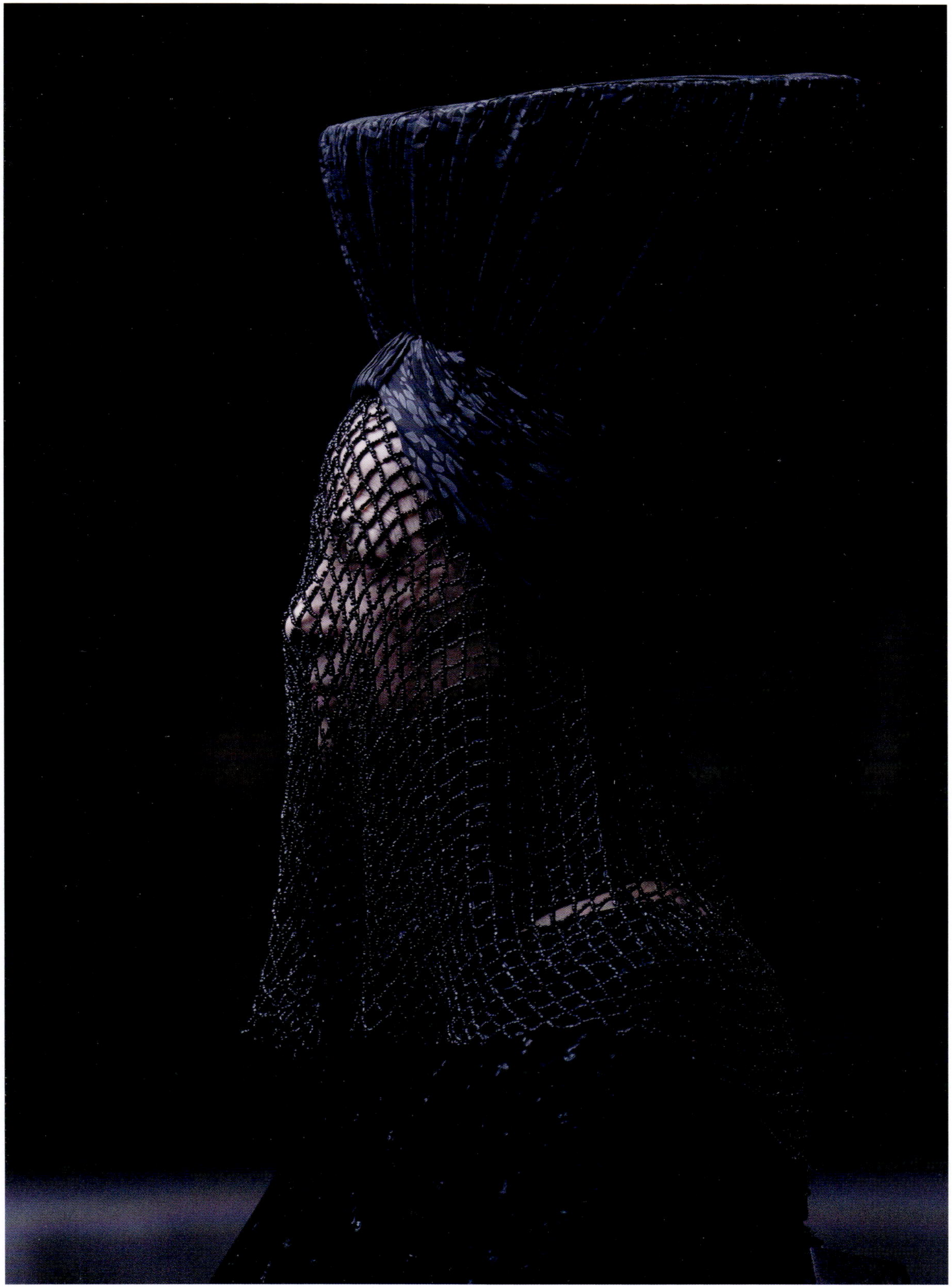

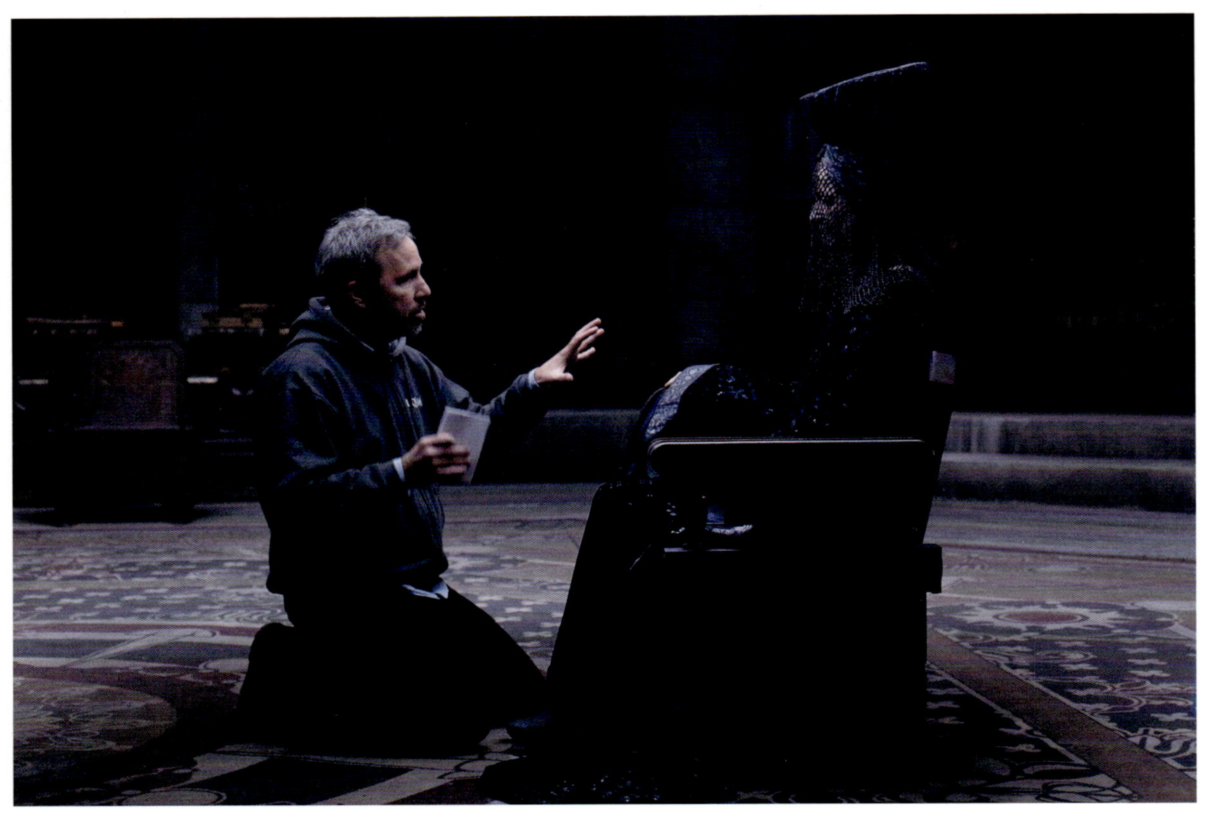

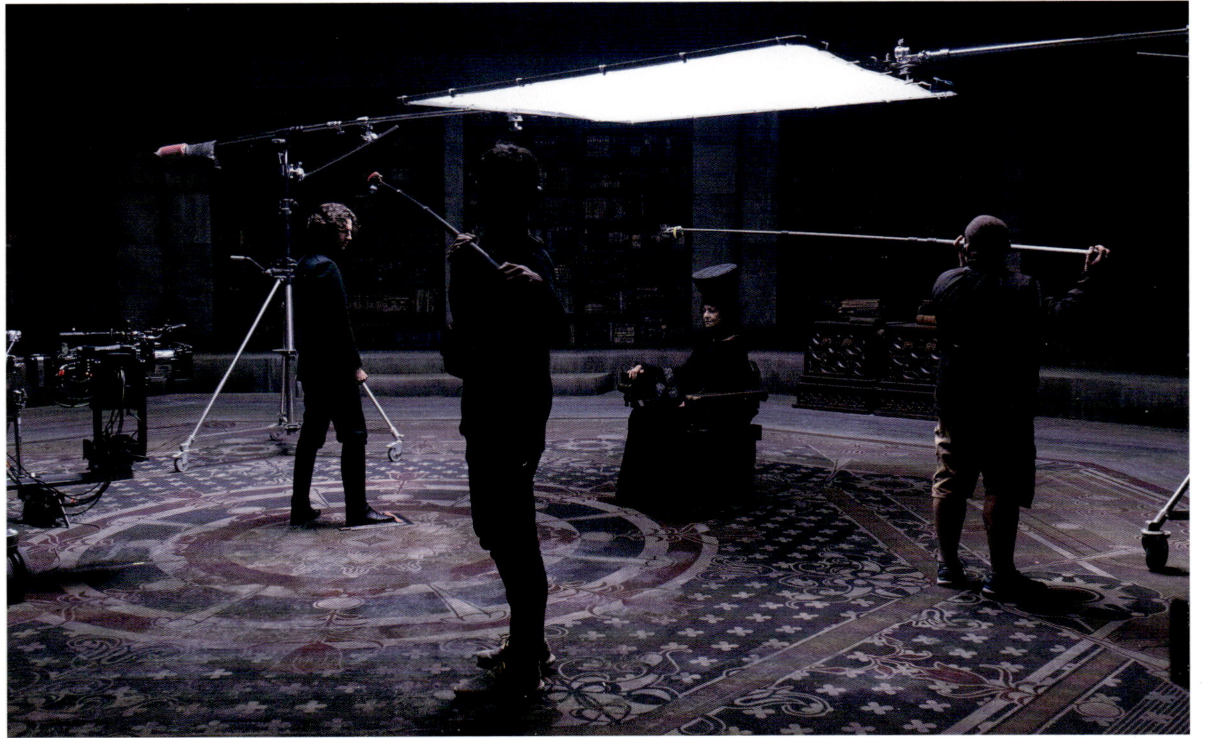

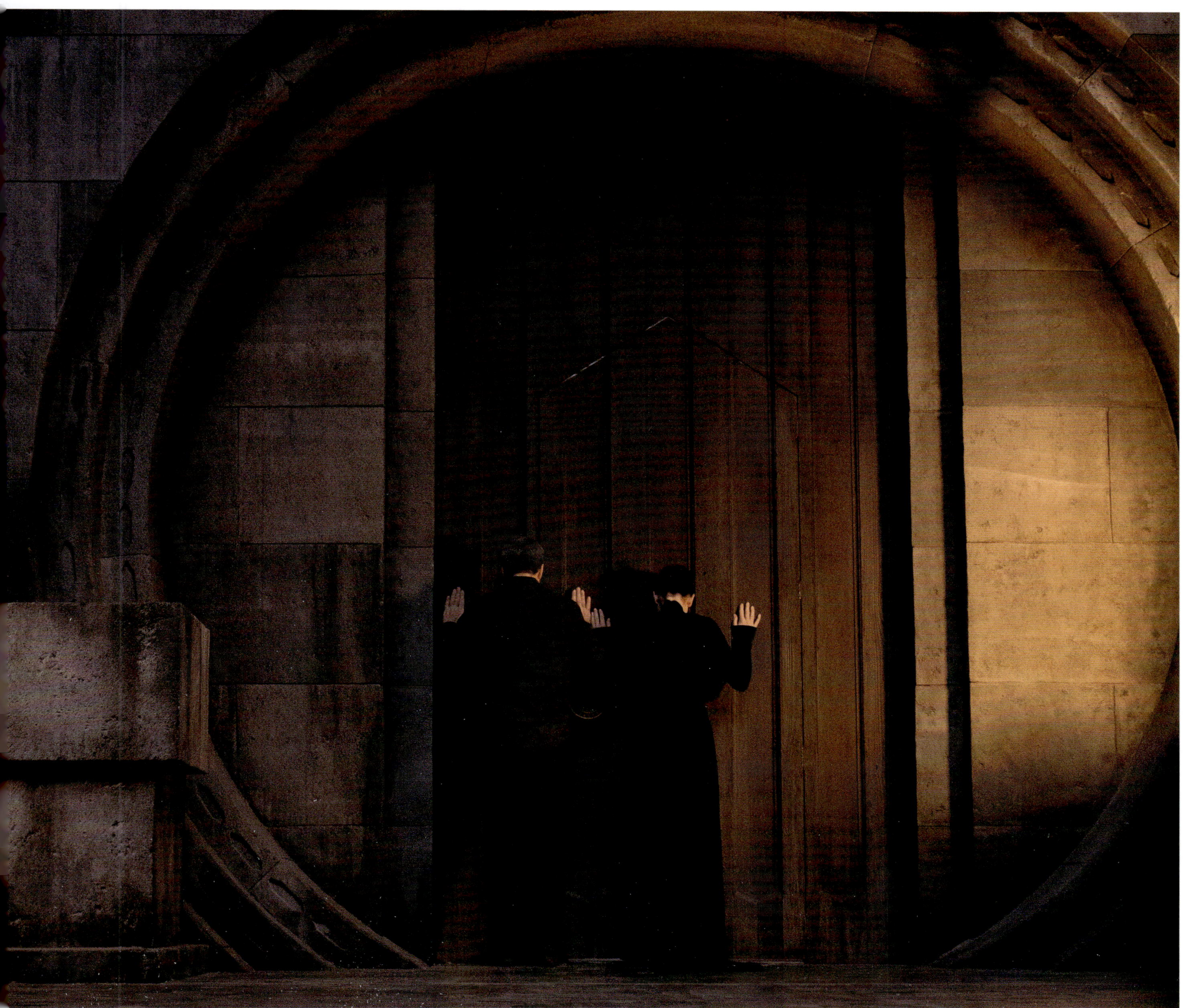

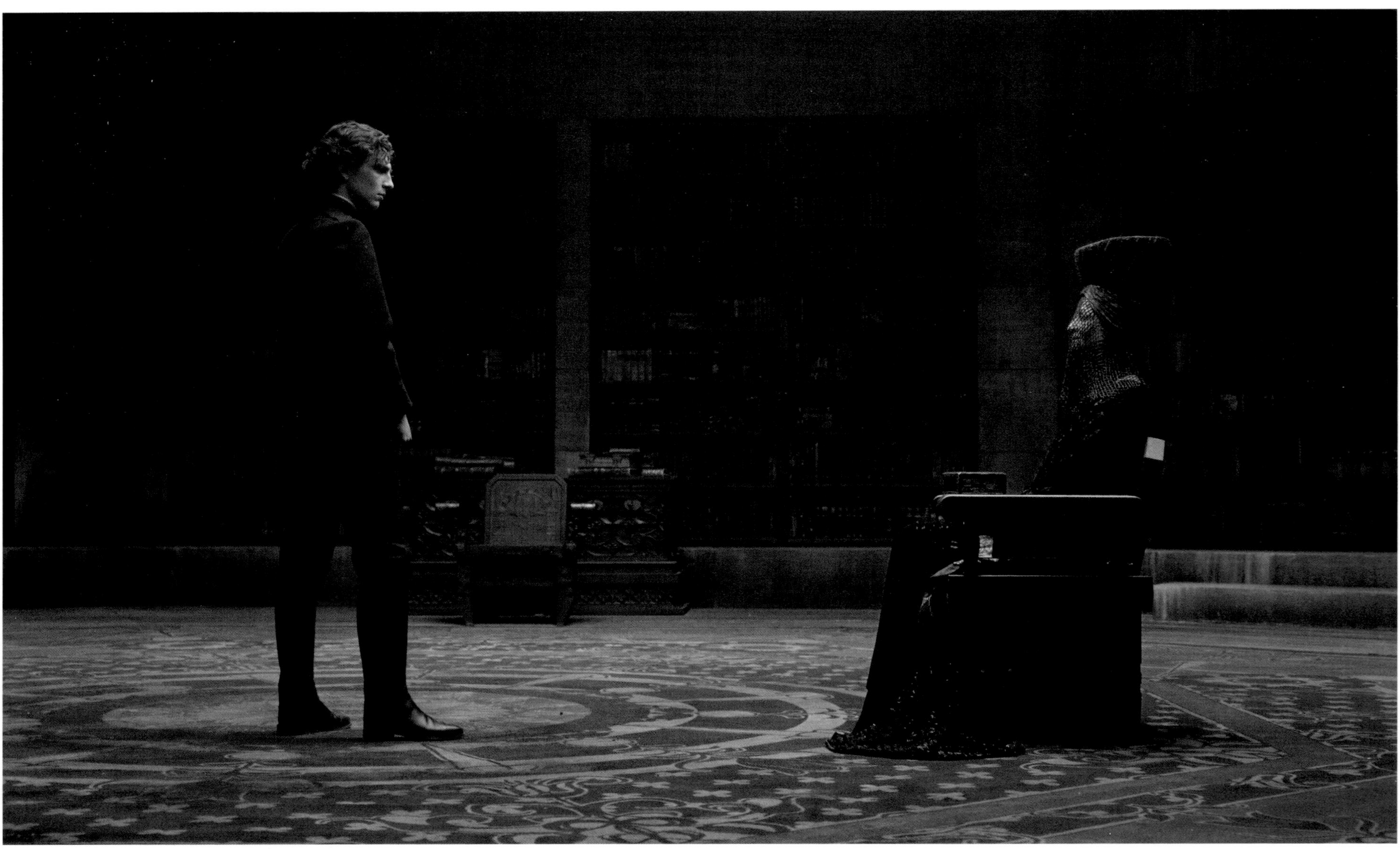

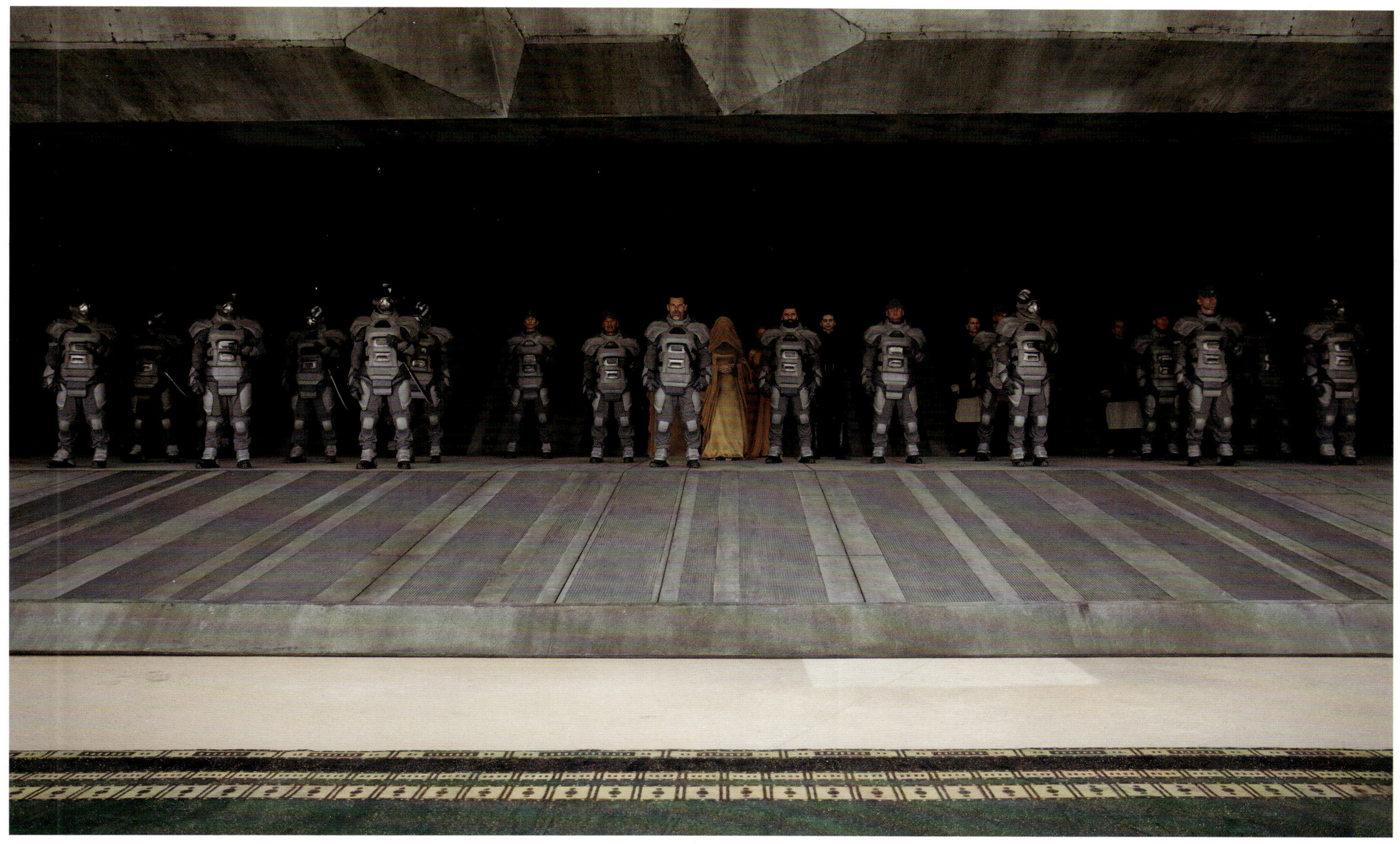

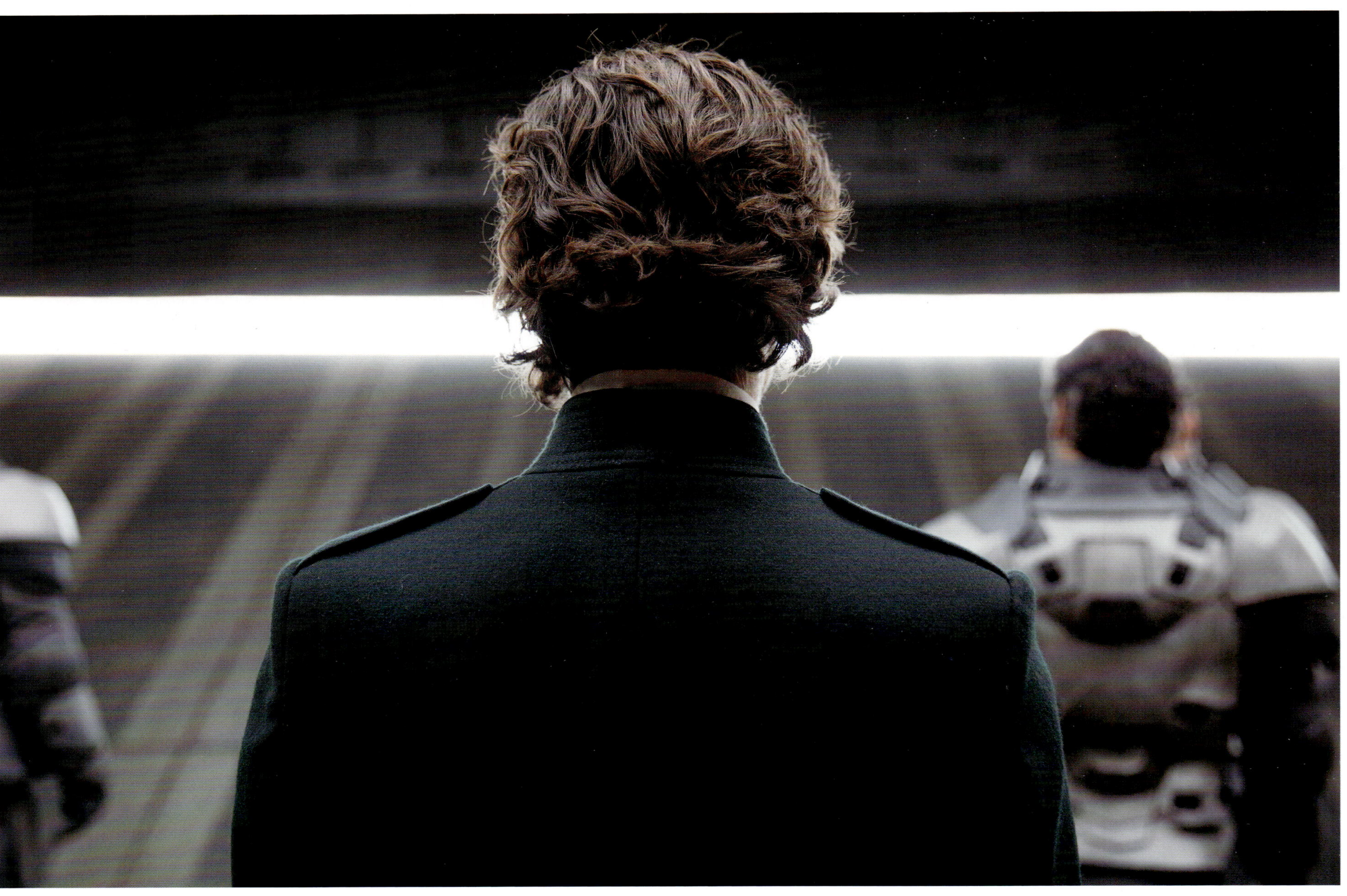

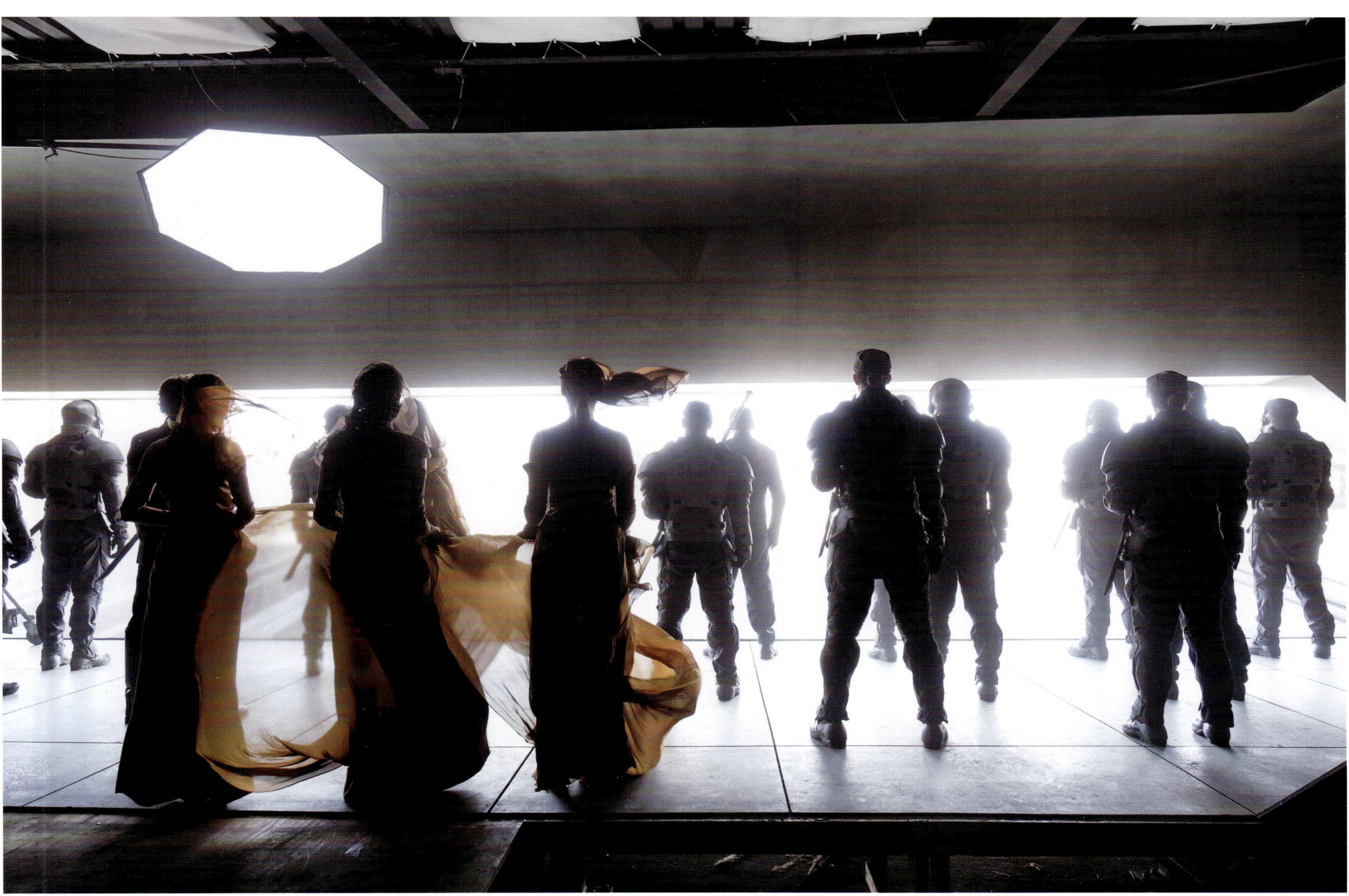

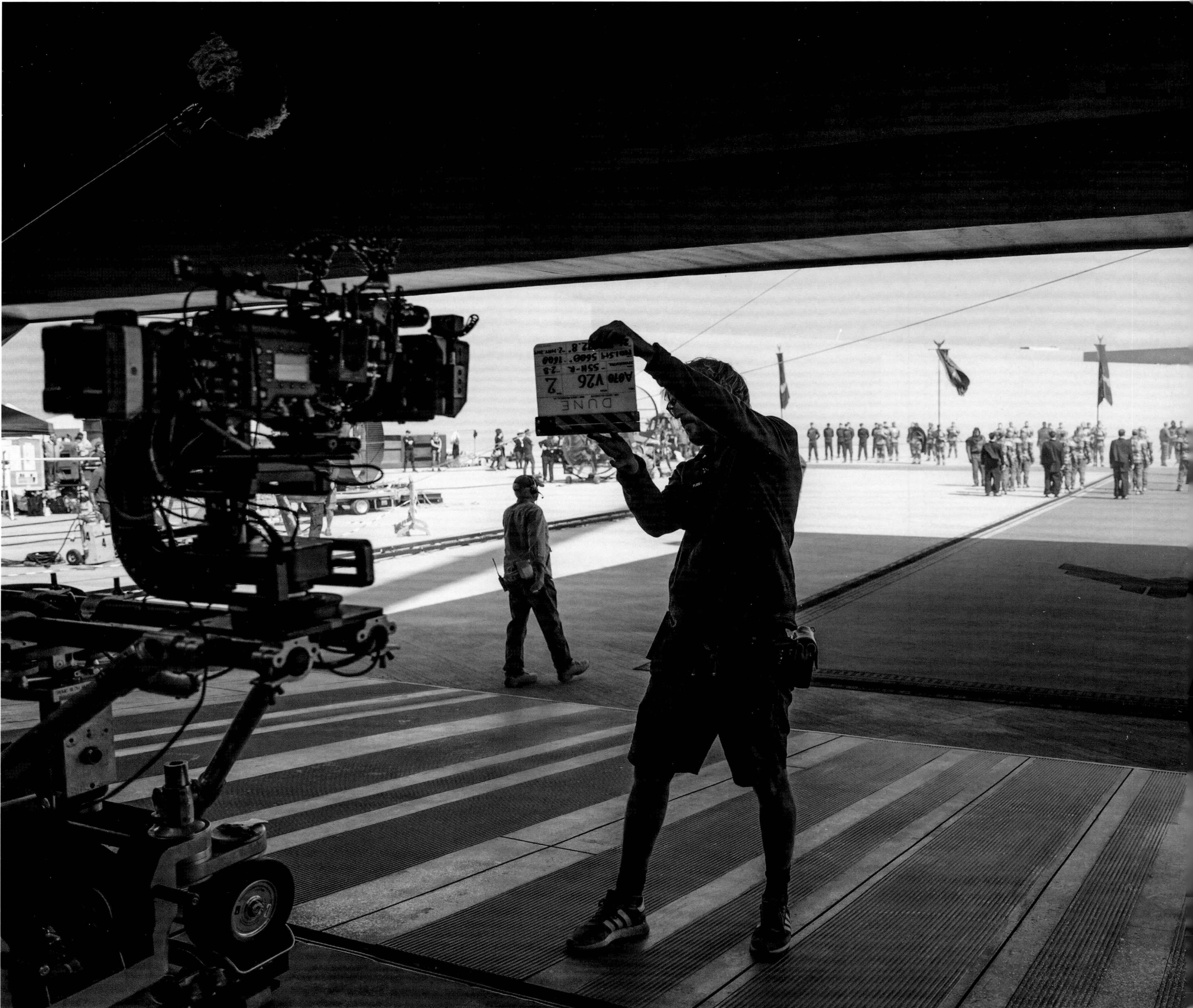
DUNE
A070 V26 2
SSN-R   -28
Rolsi9 5600' 1600
72.8"

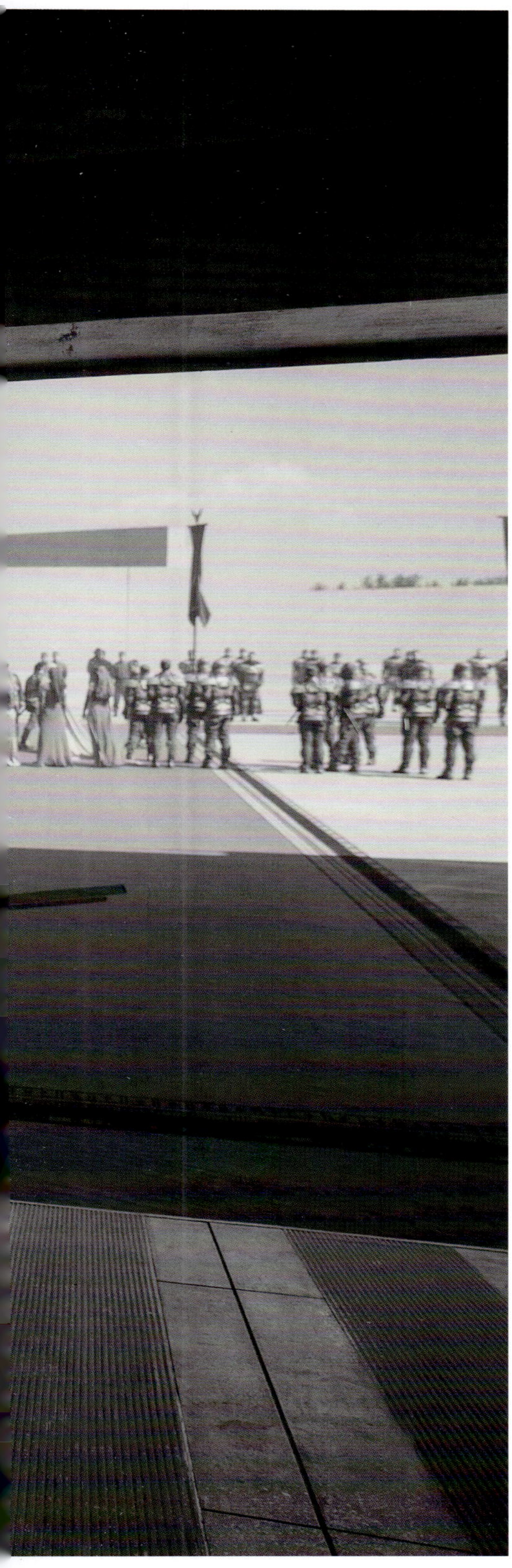

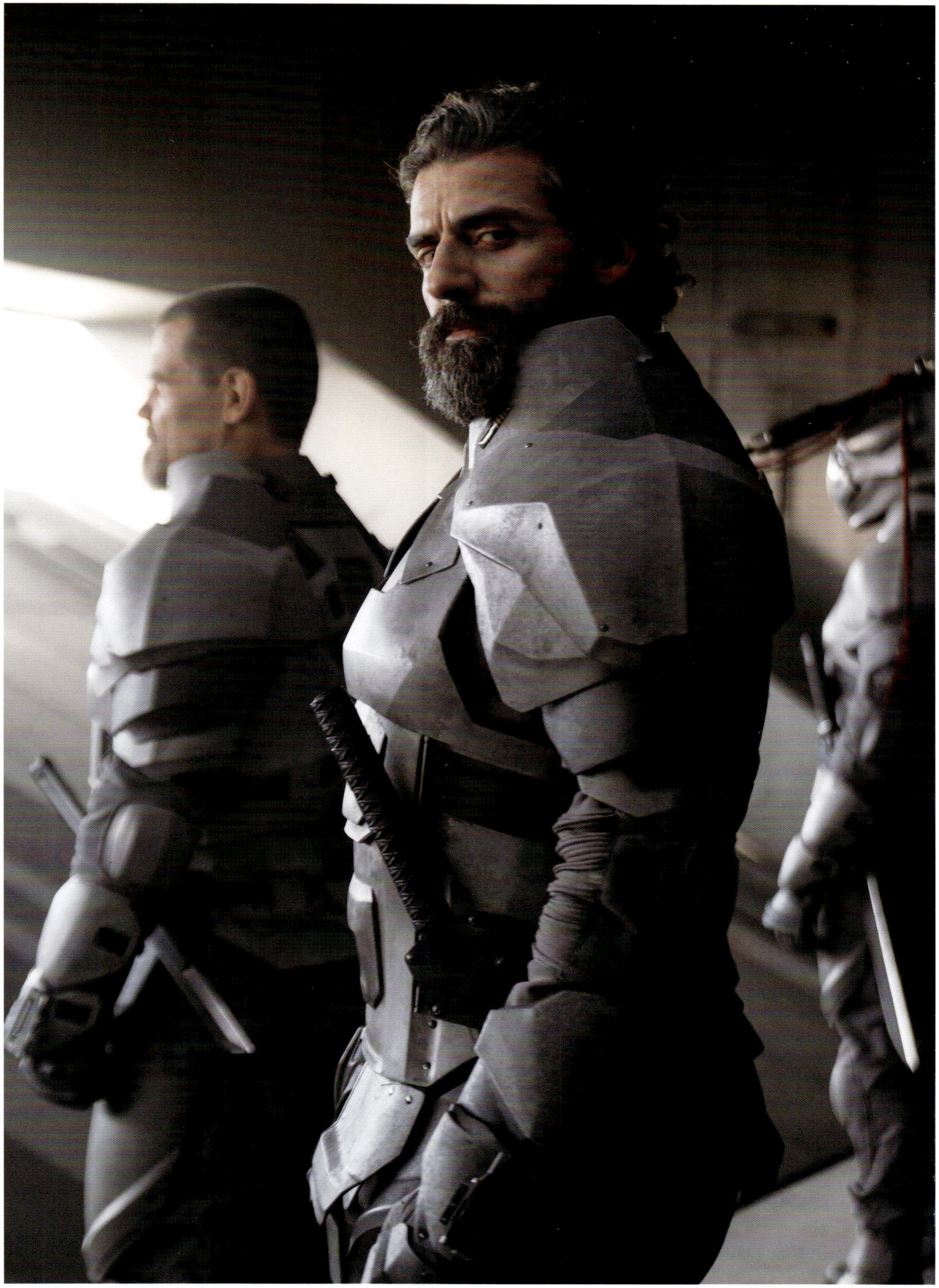

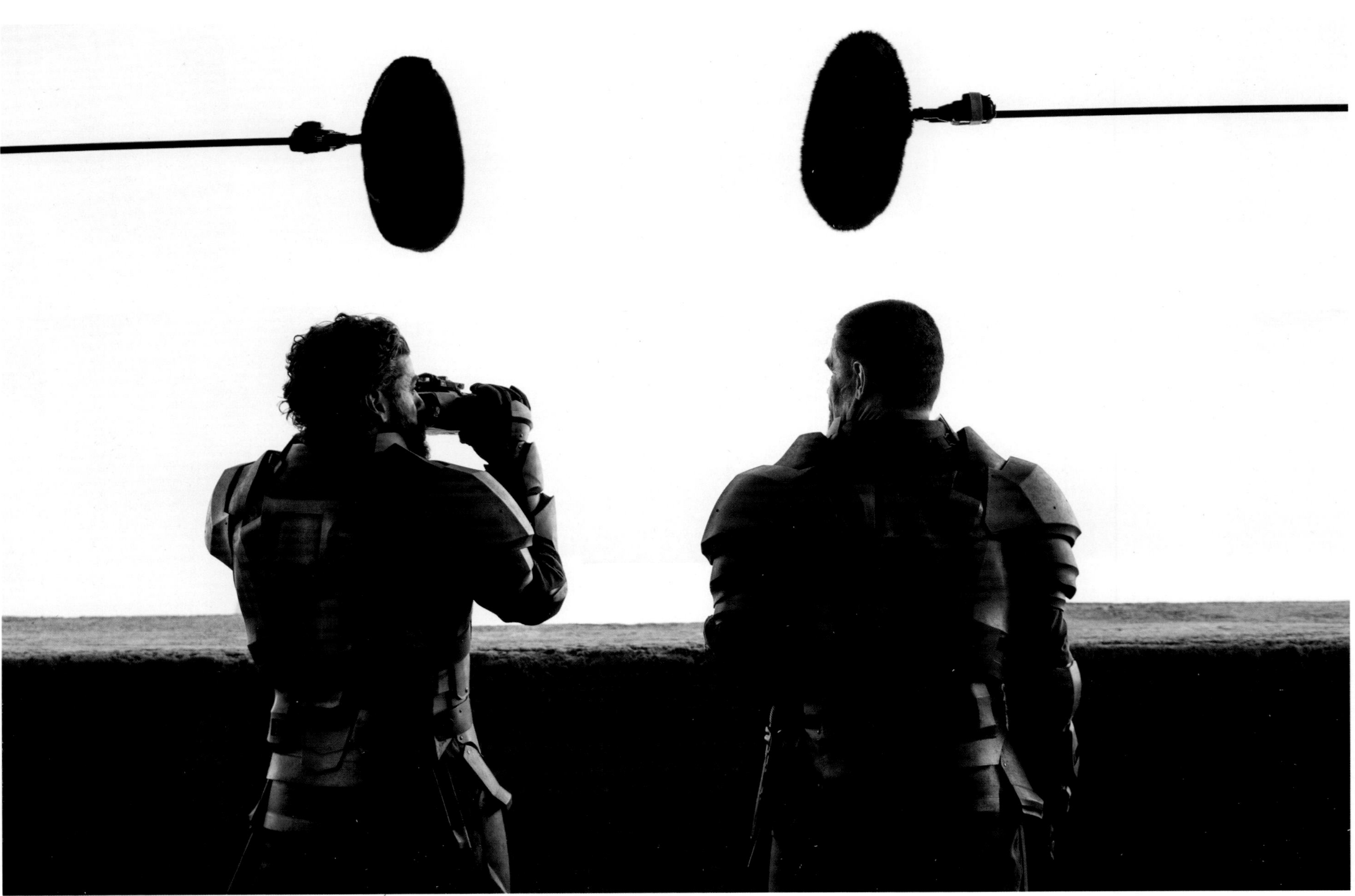

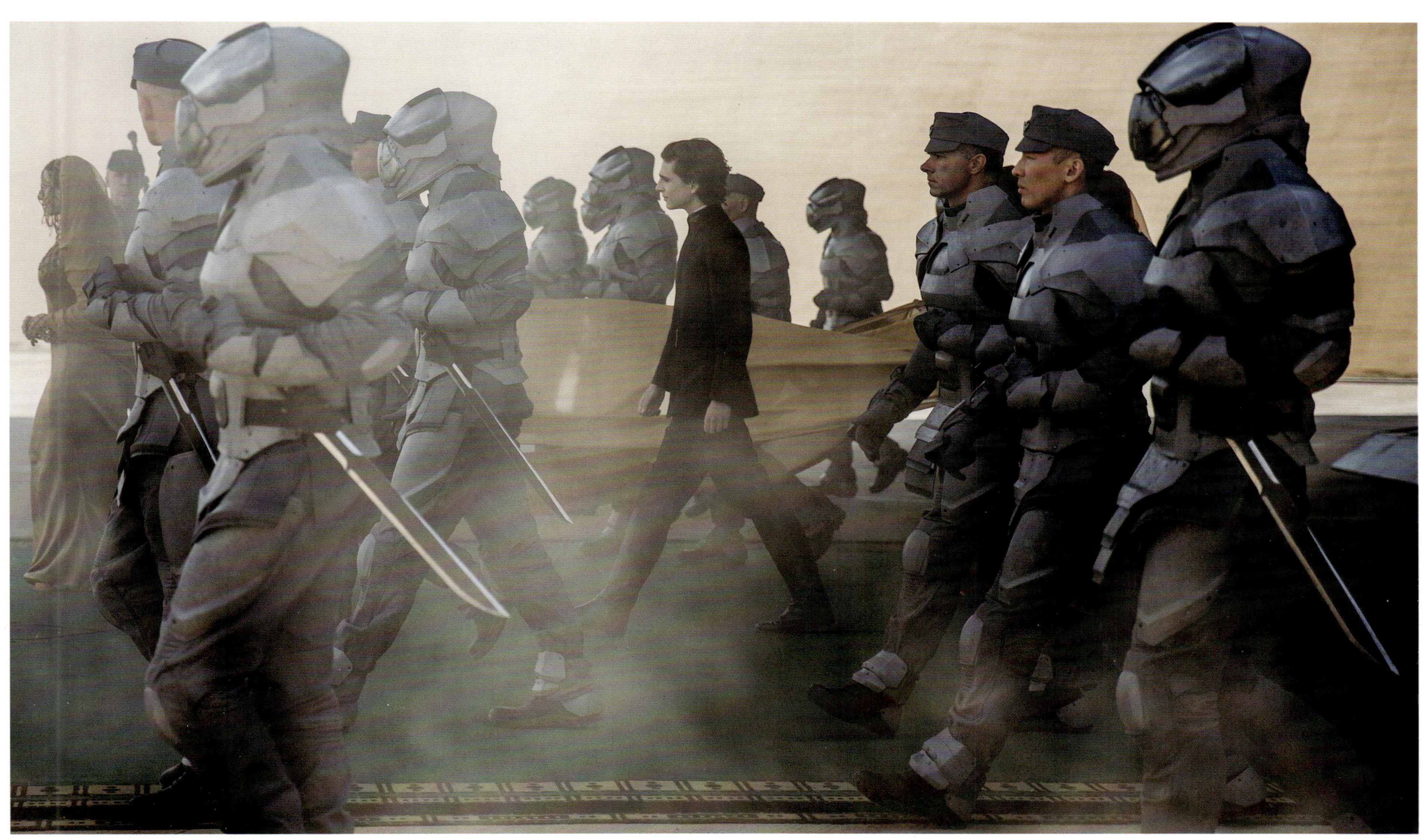

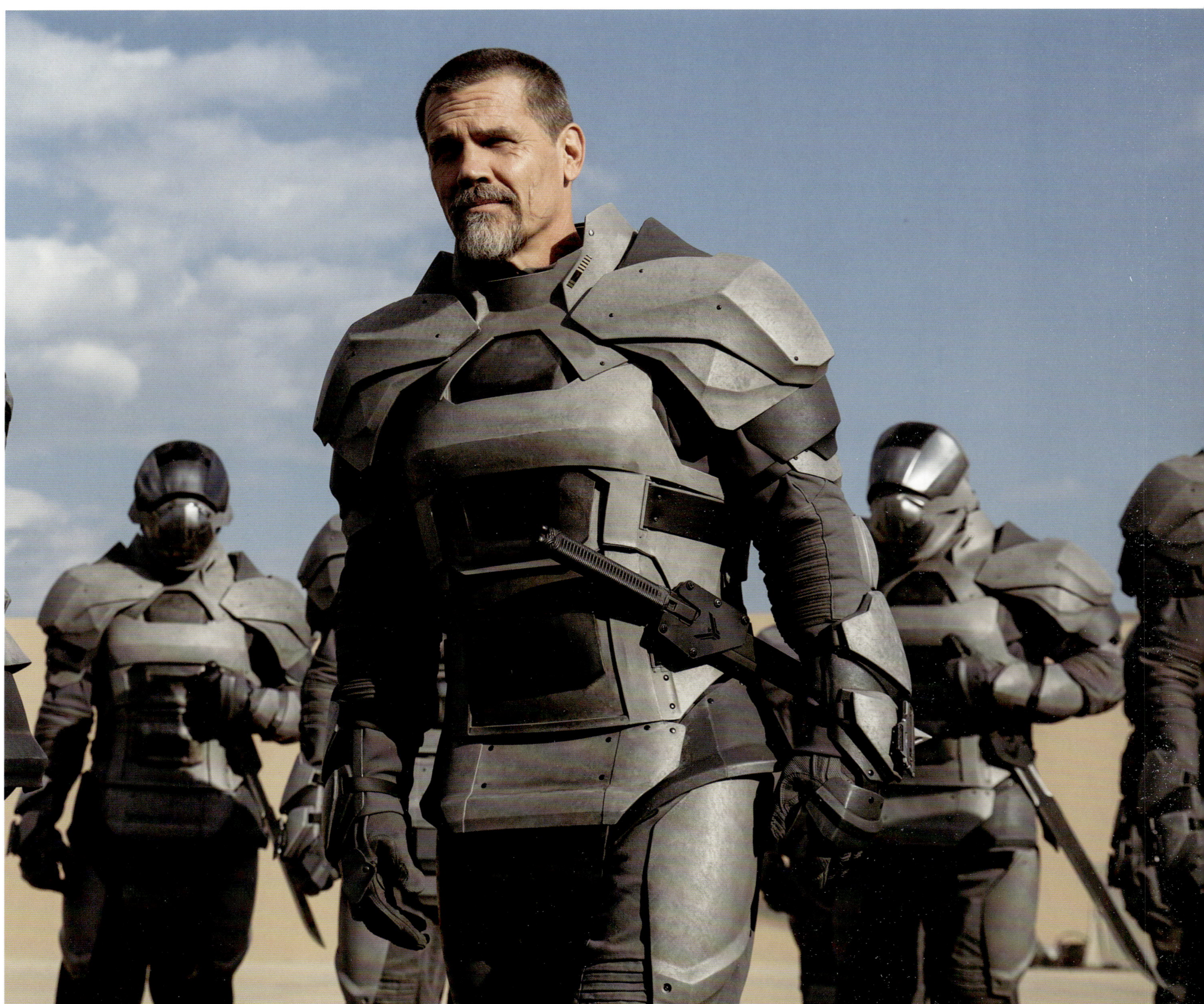

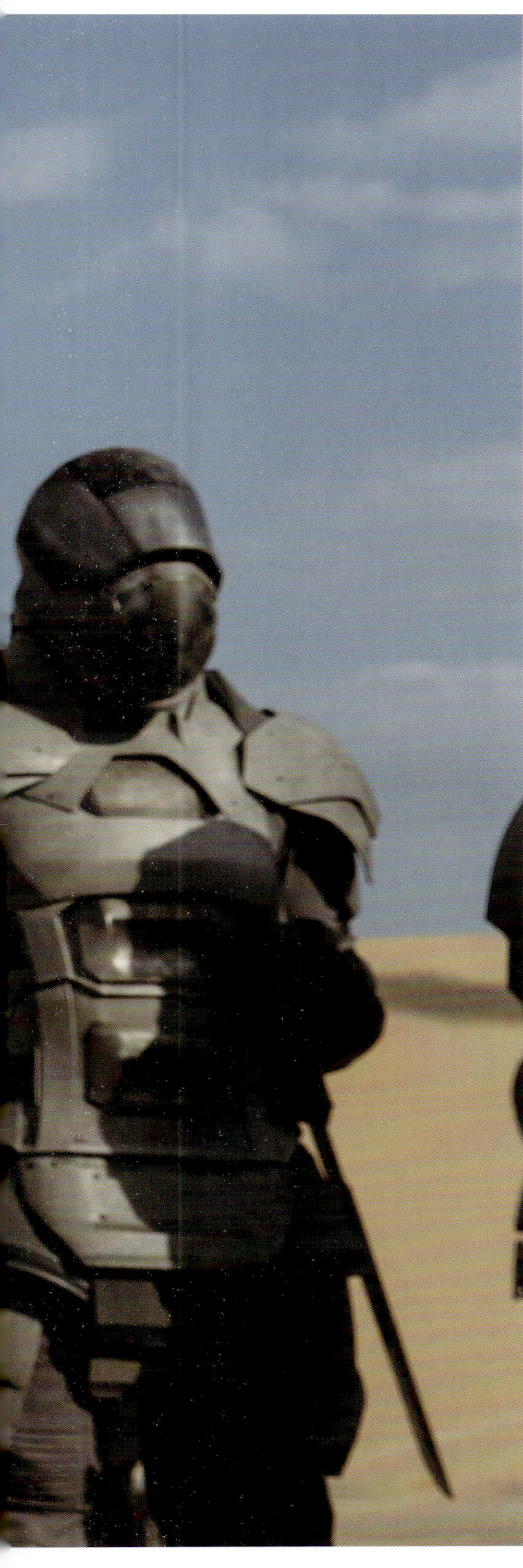

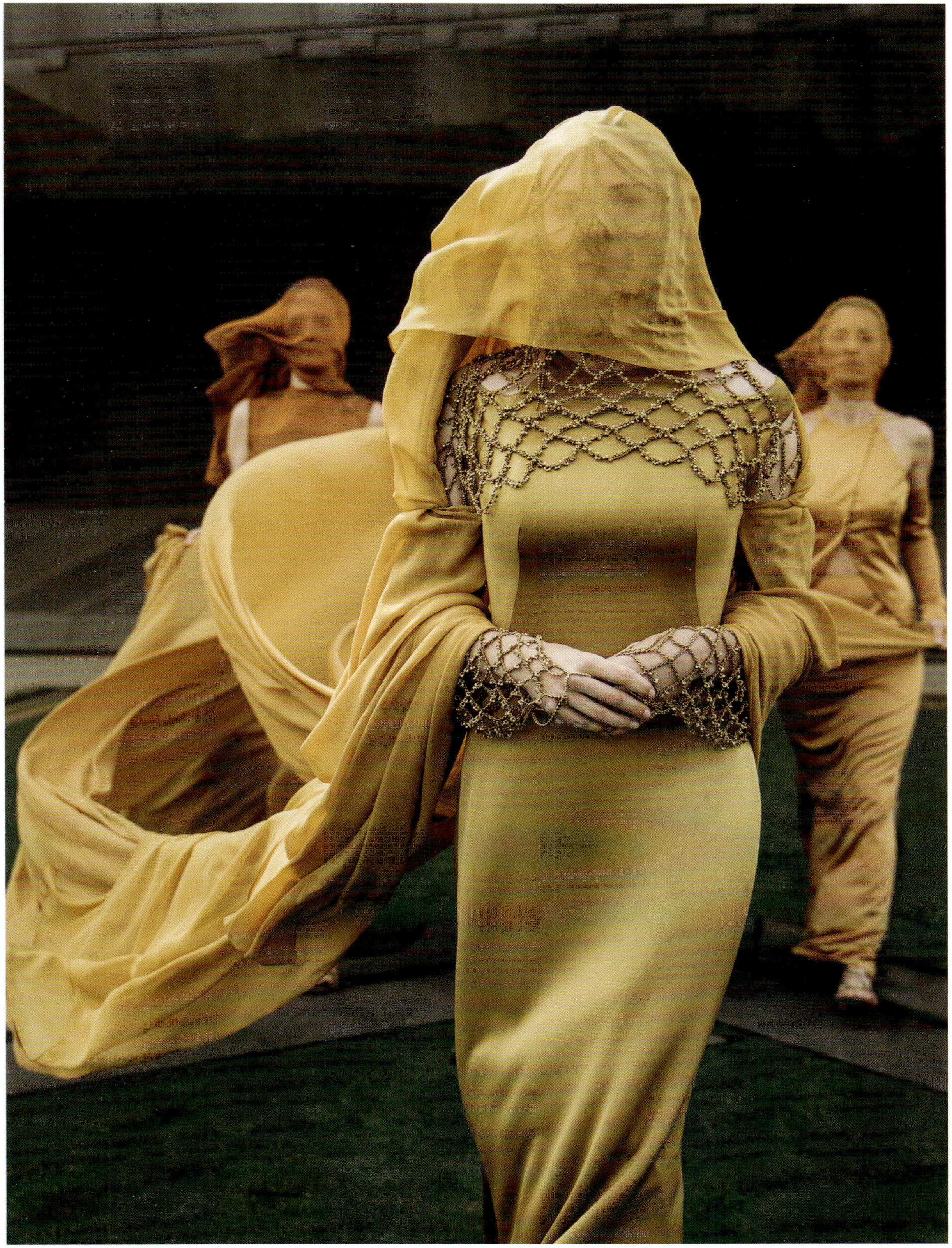

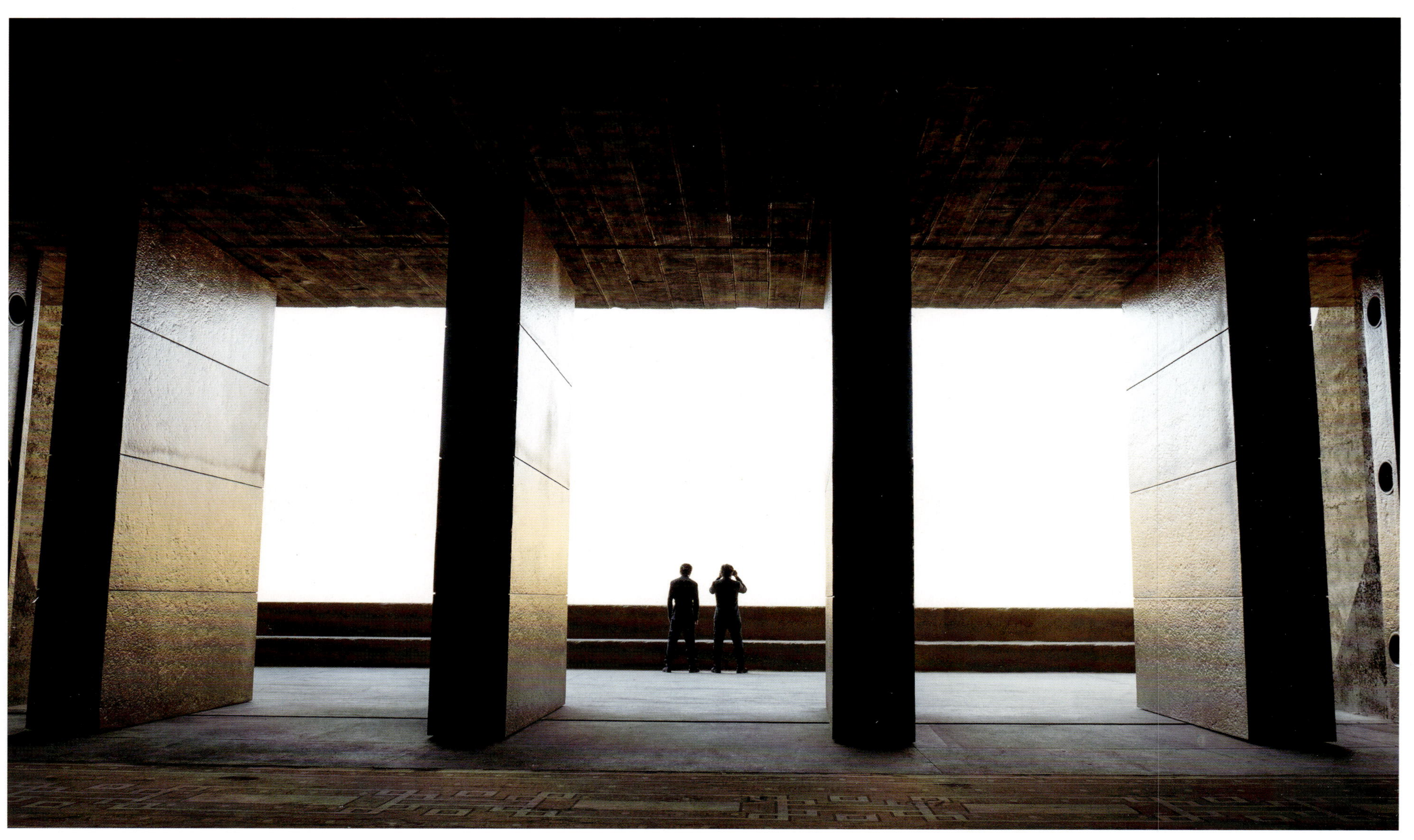

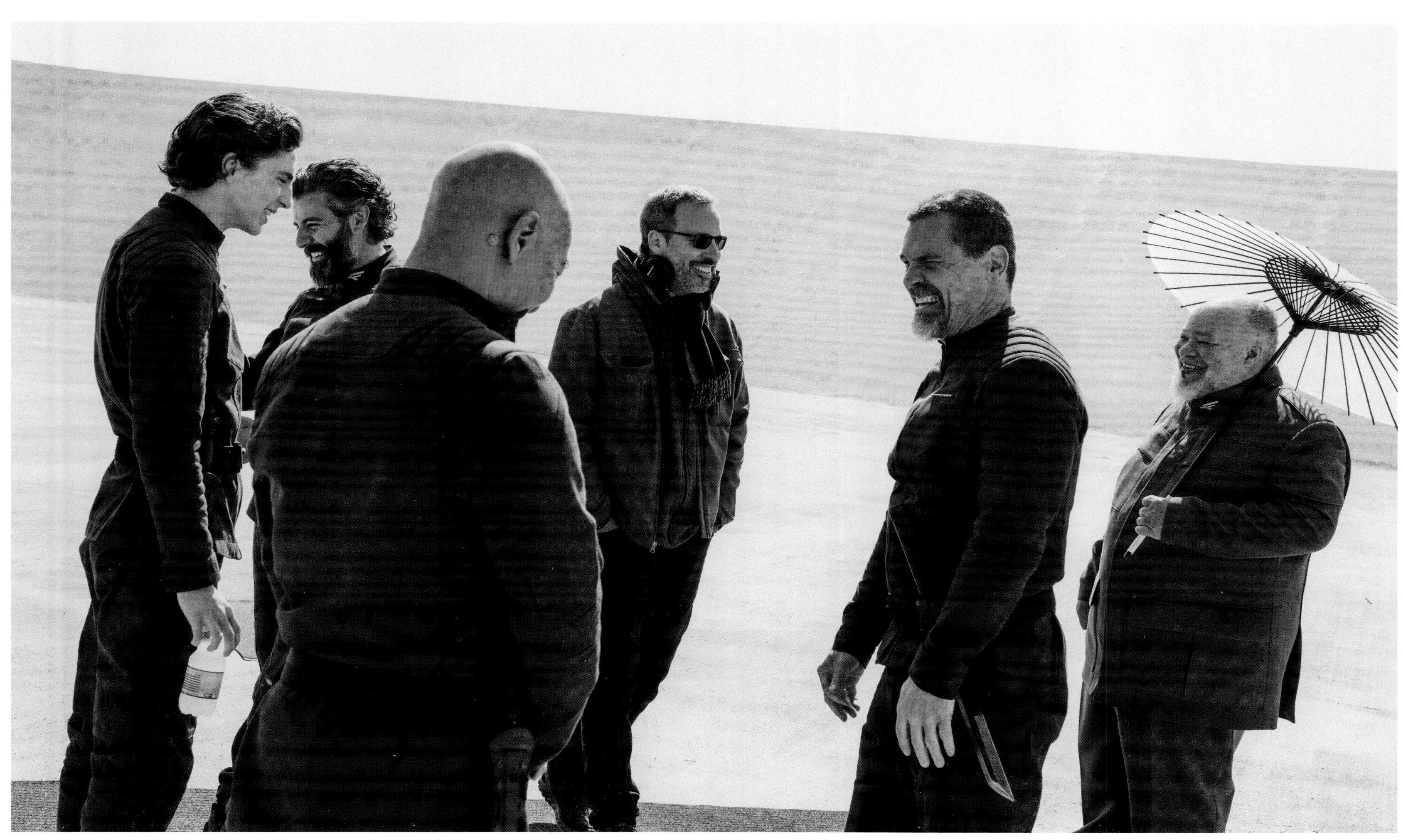

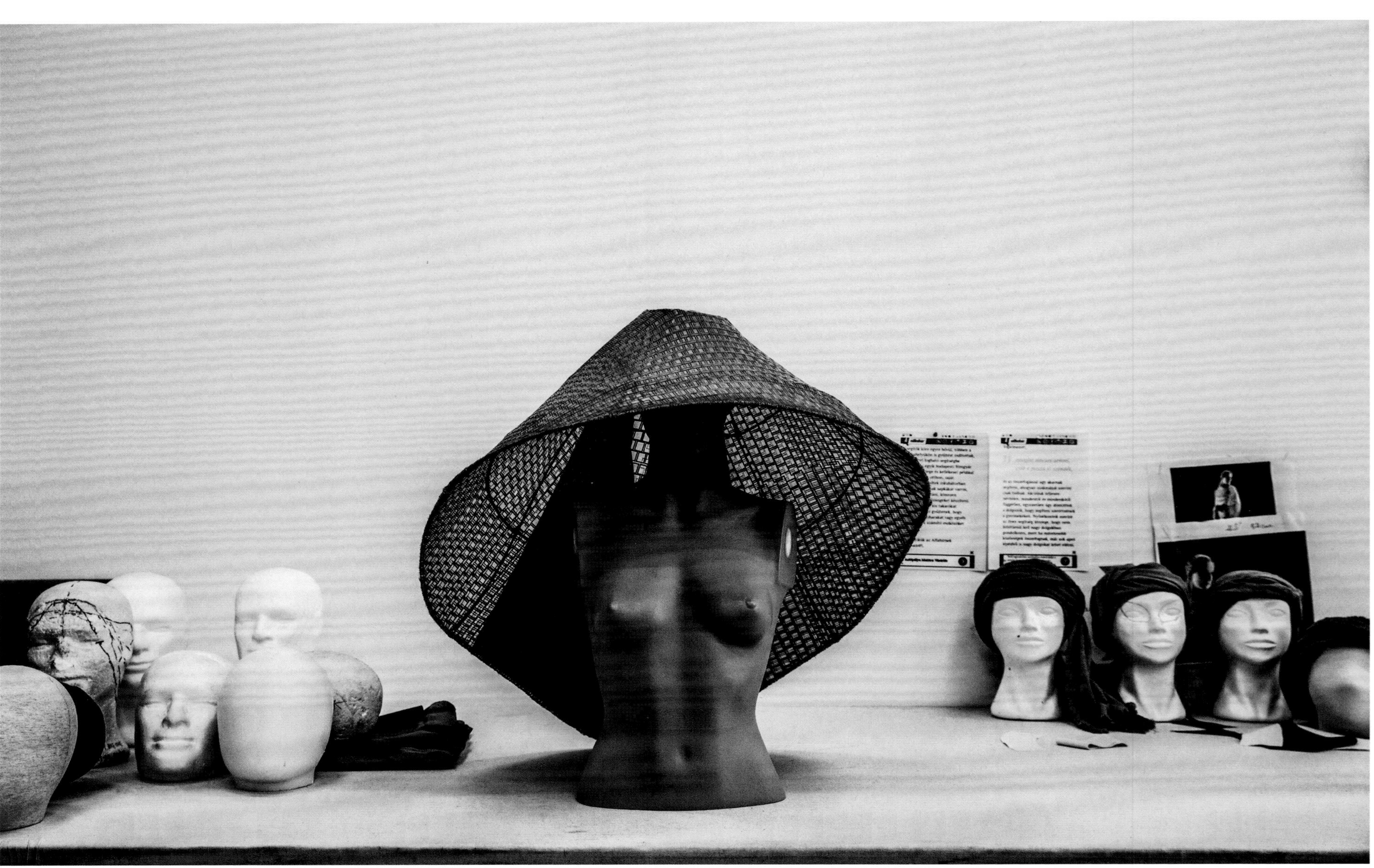

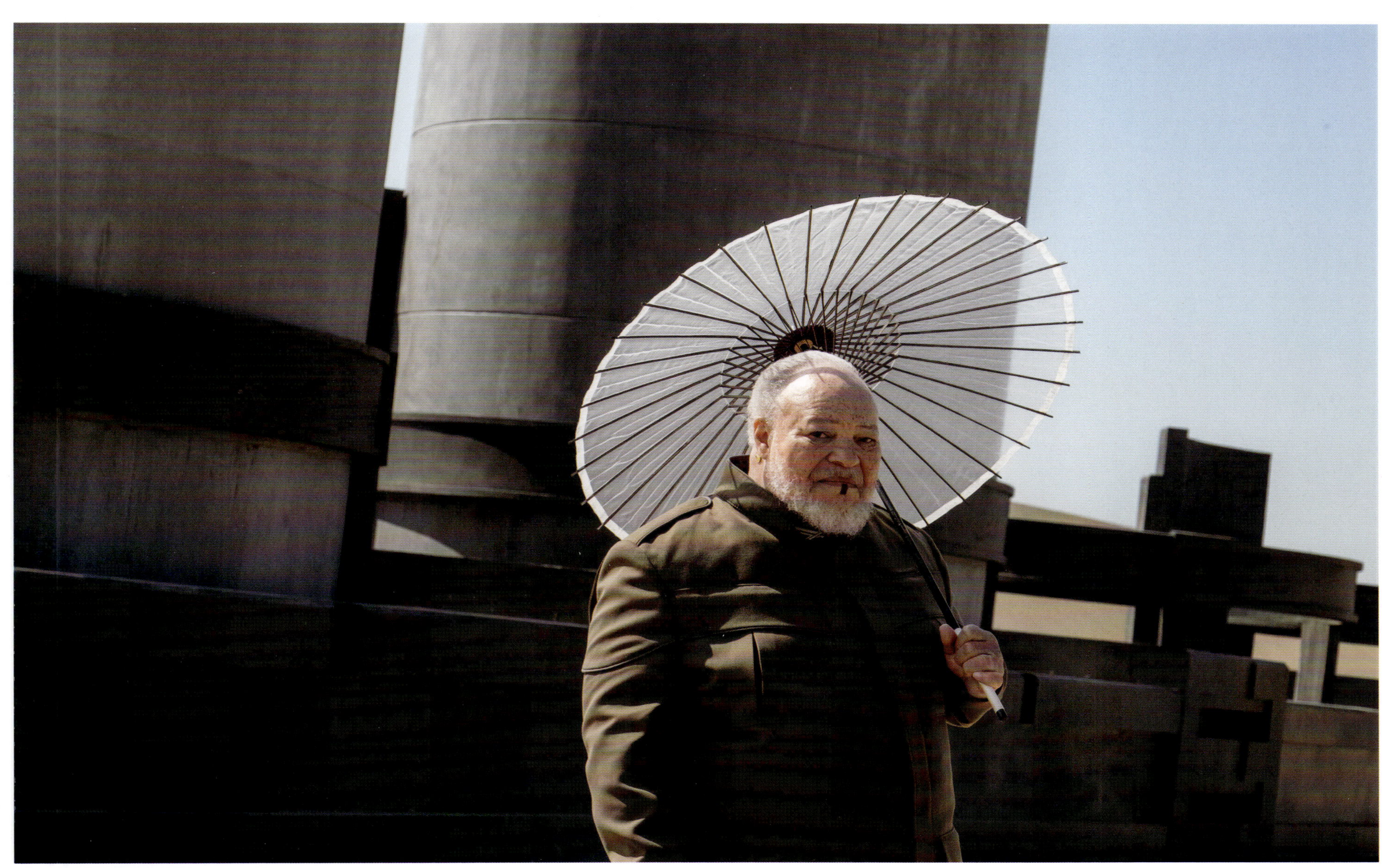

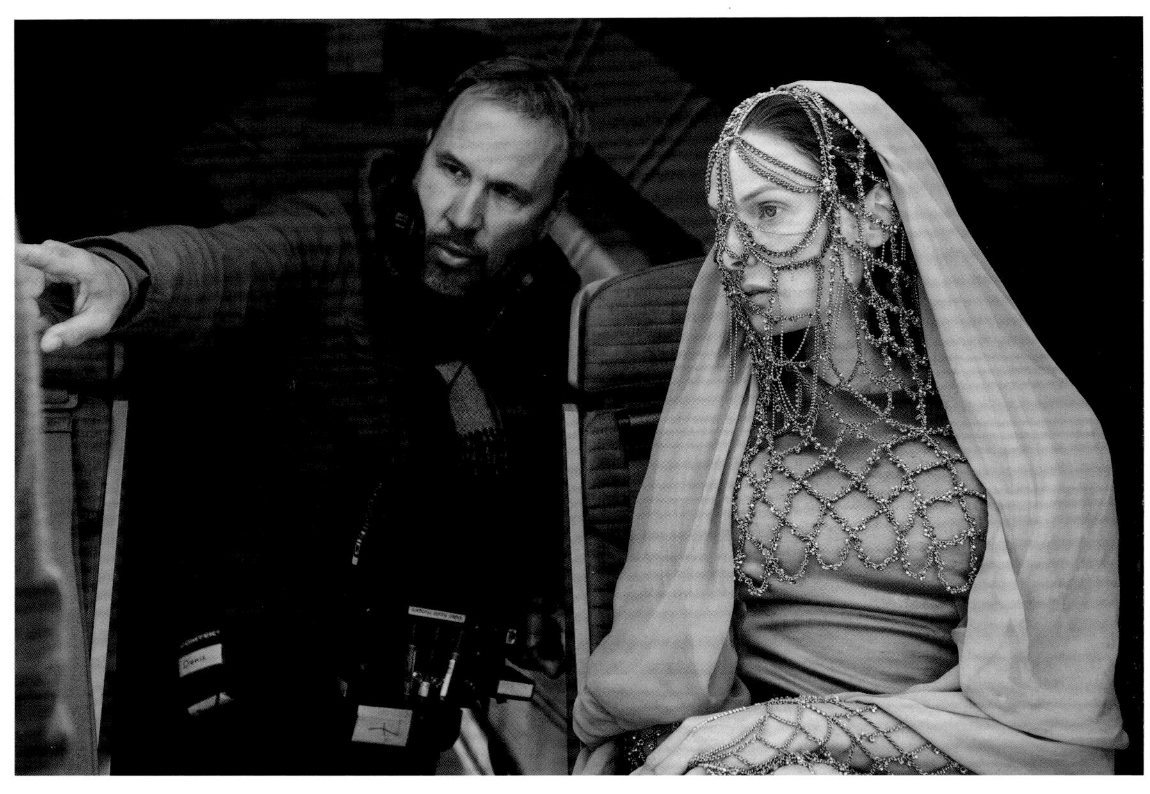

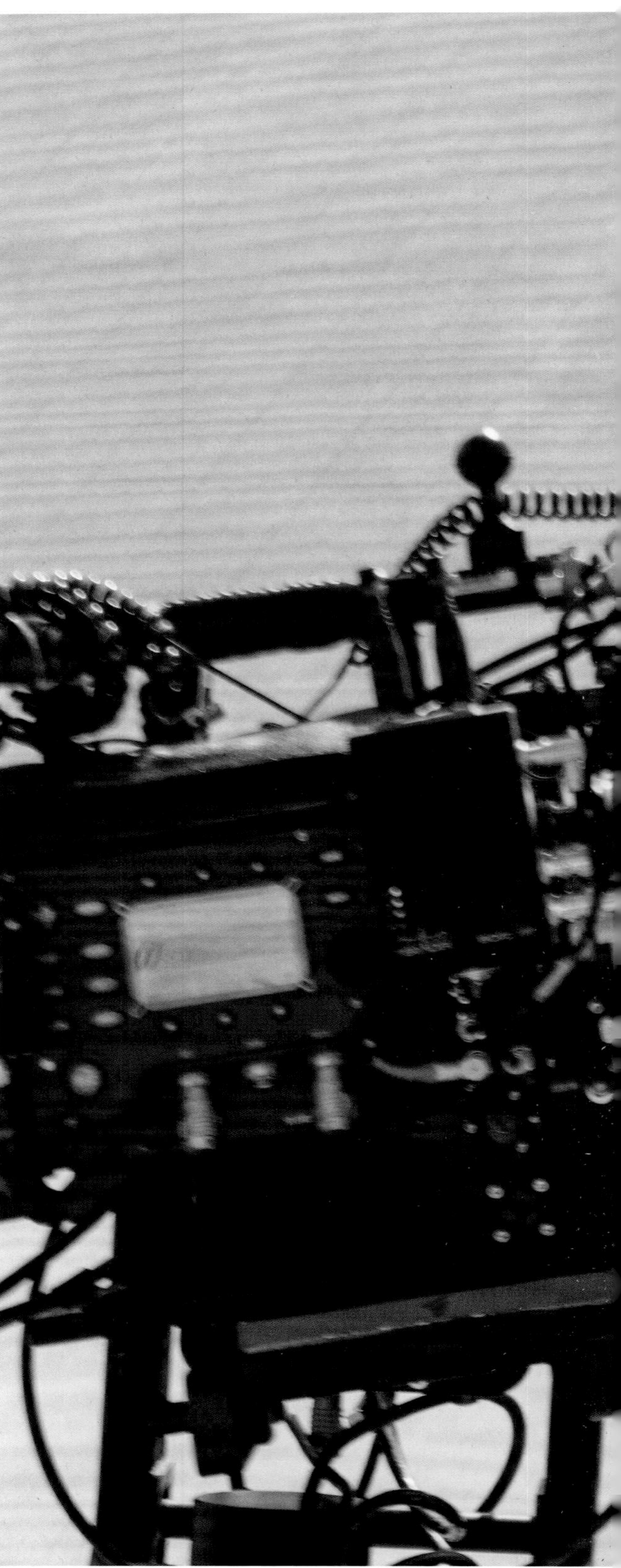

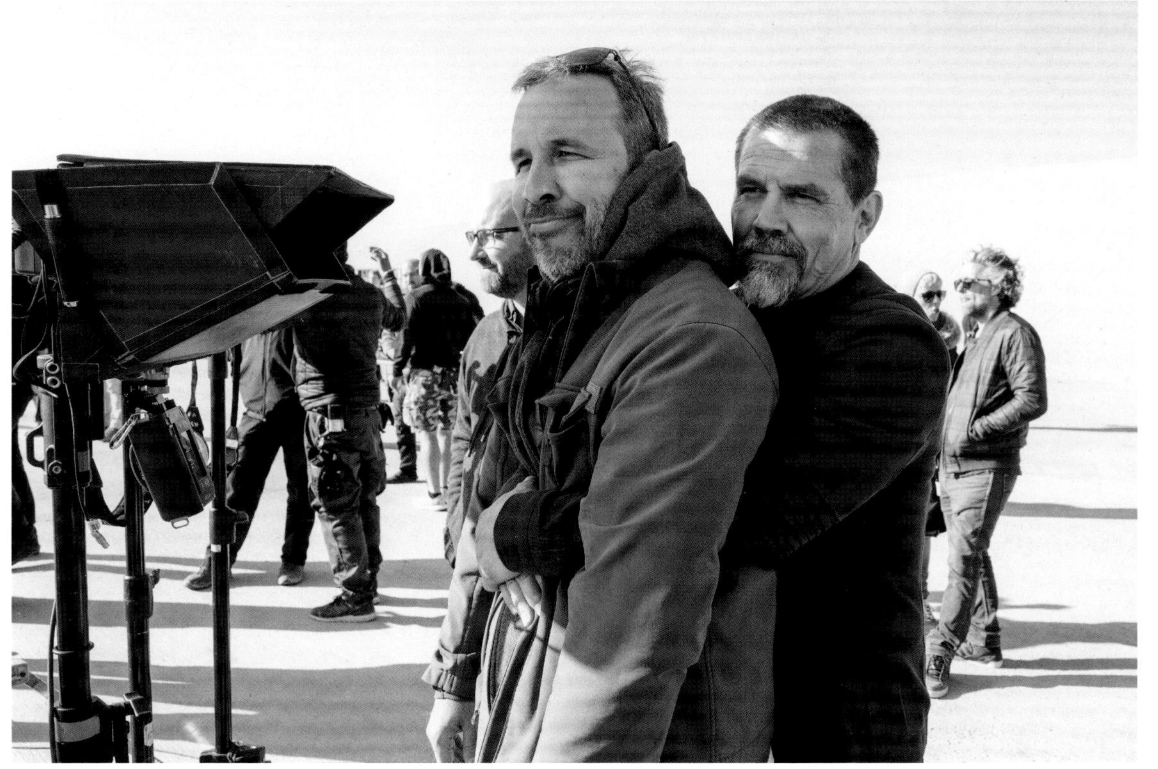

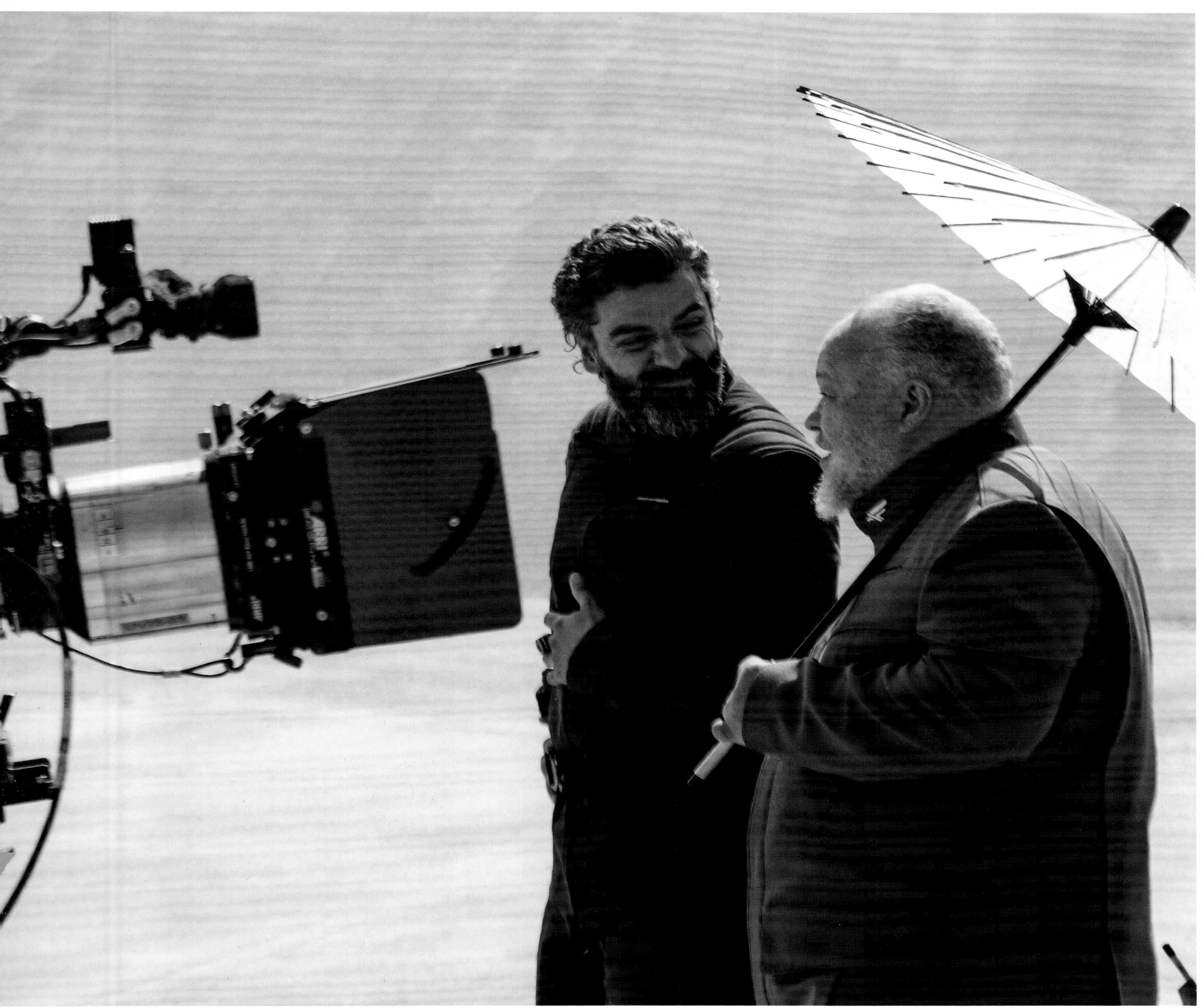

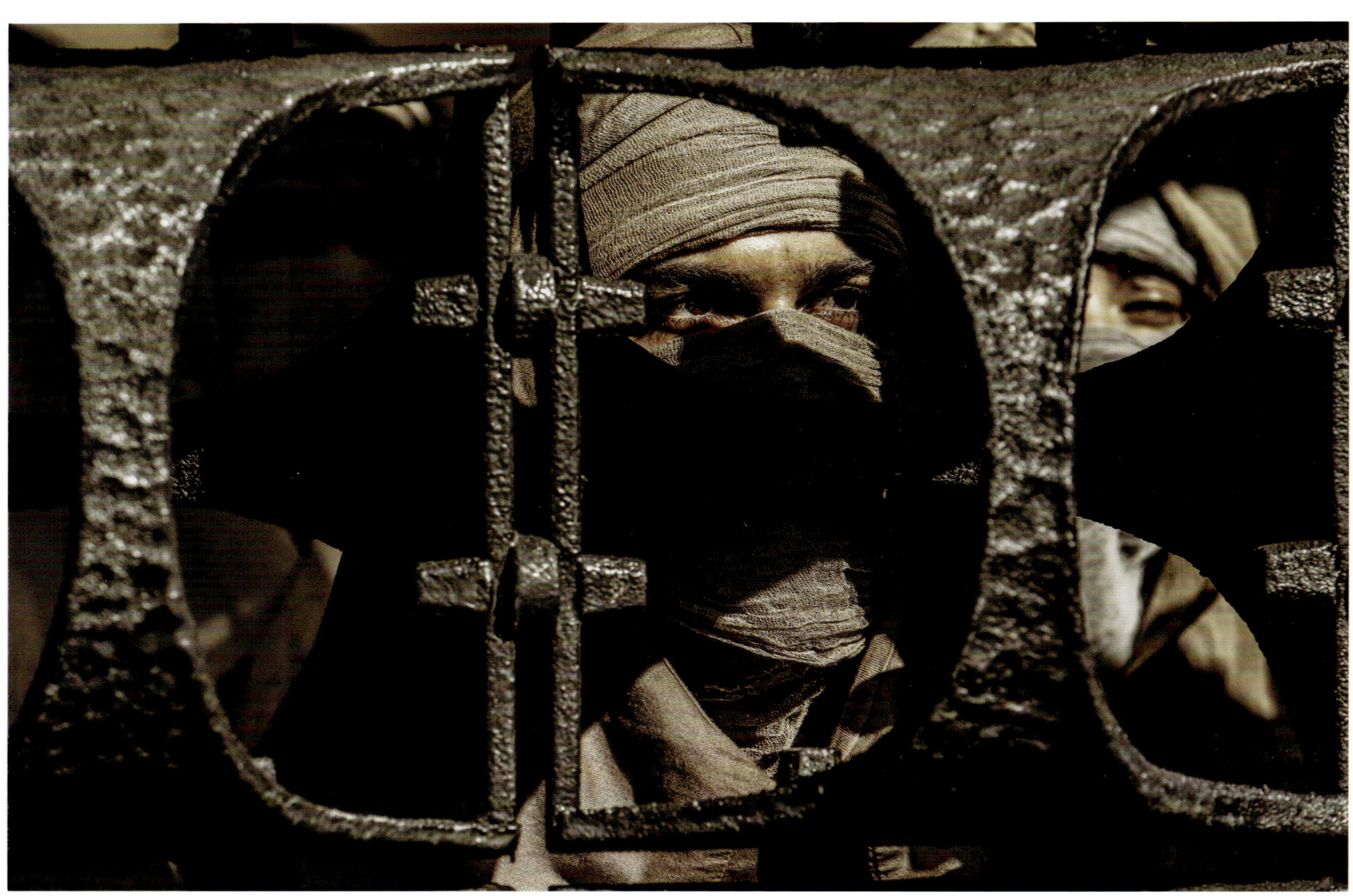

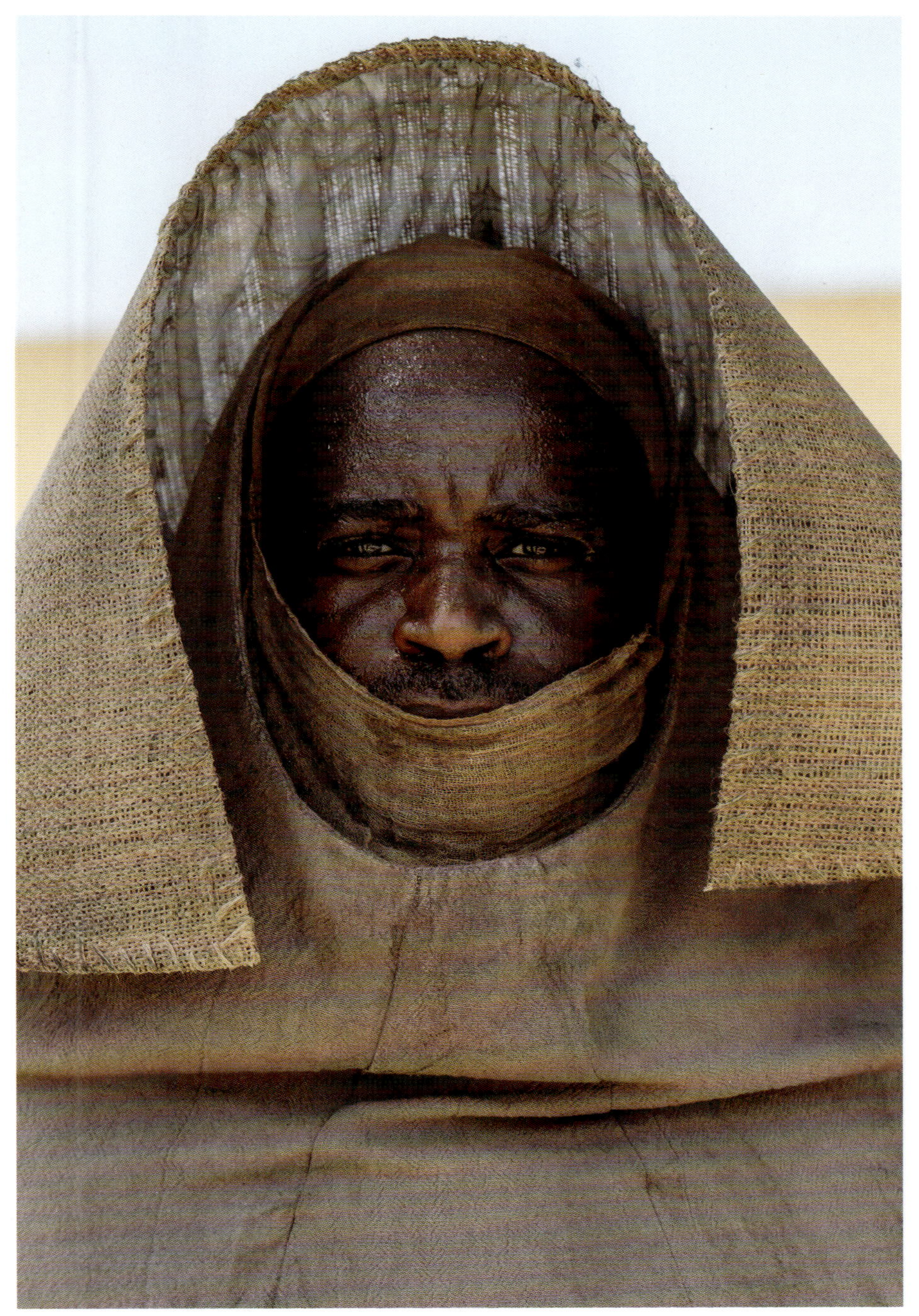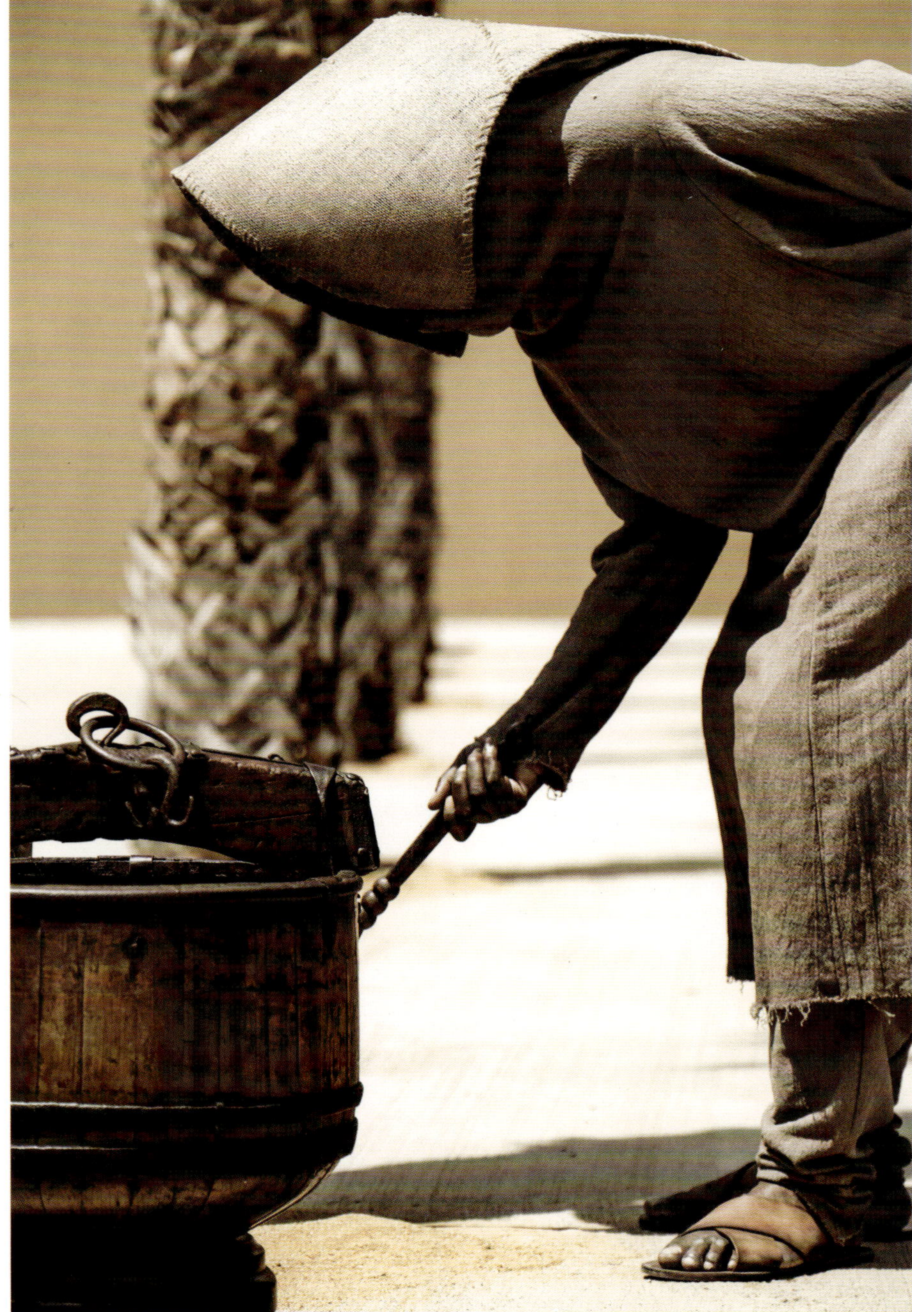

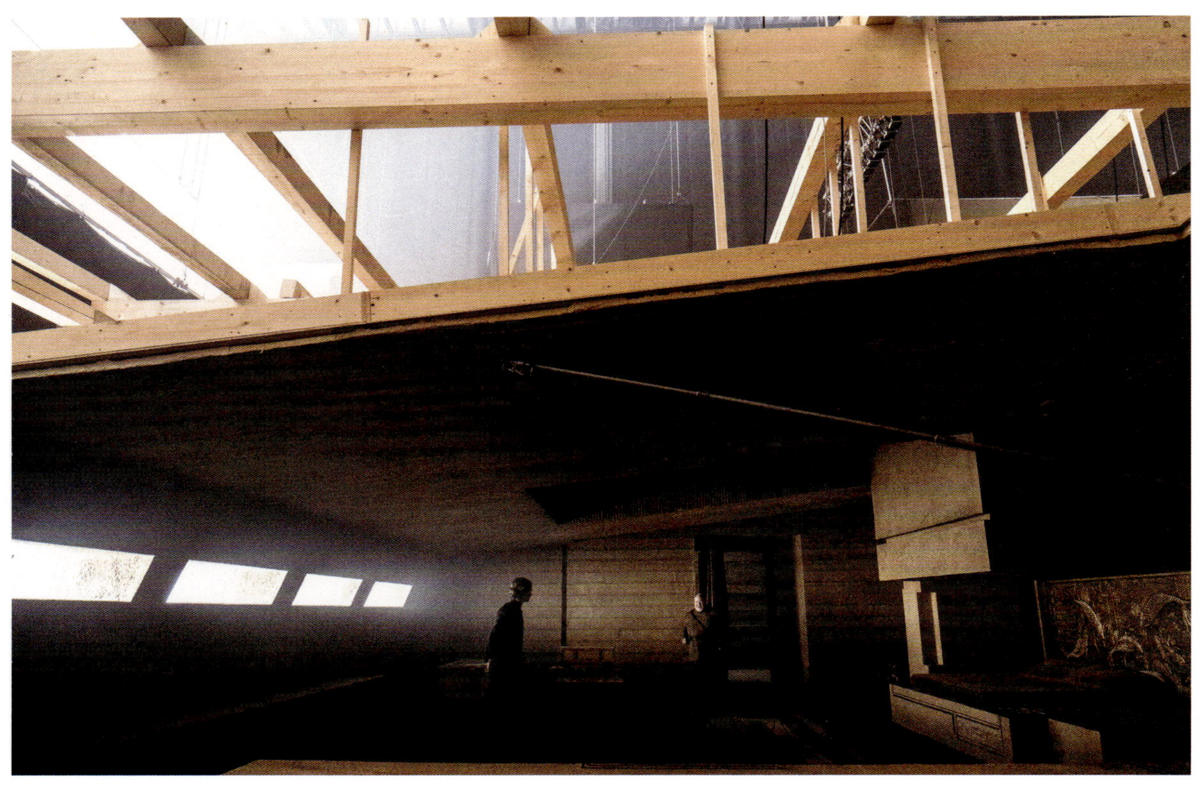

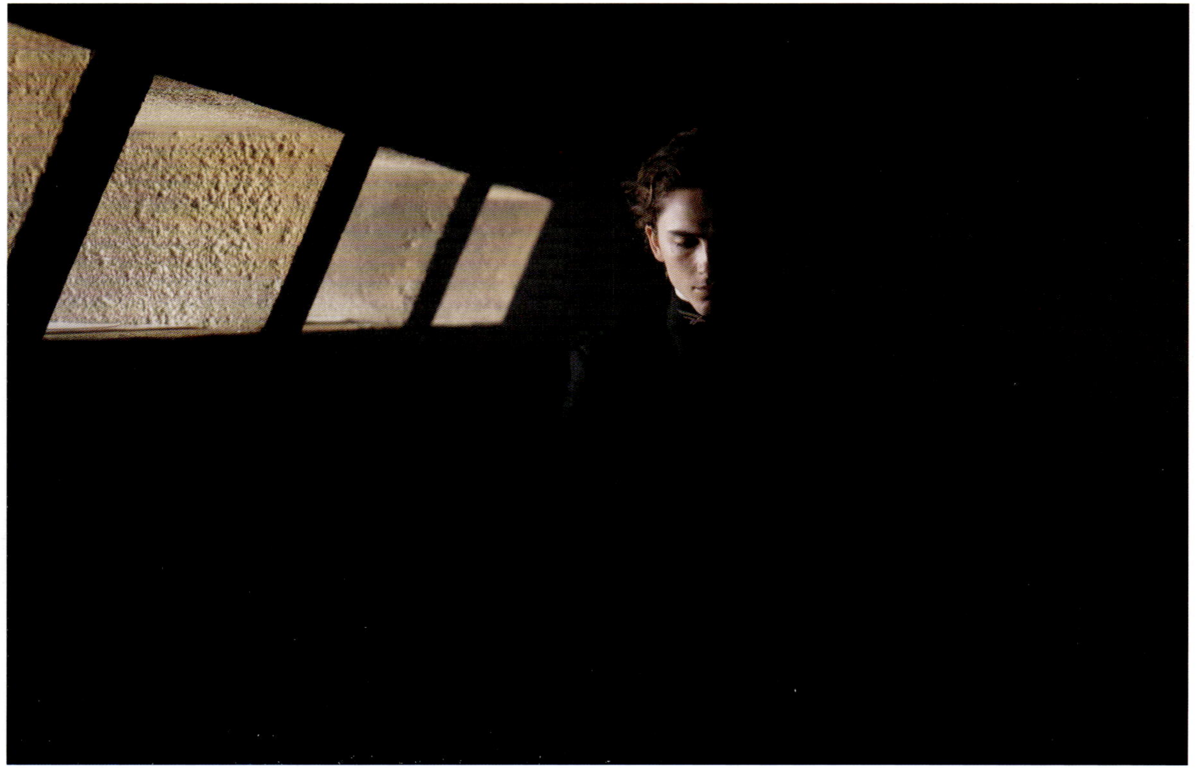

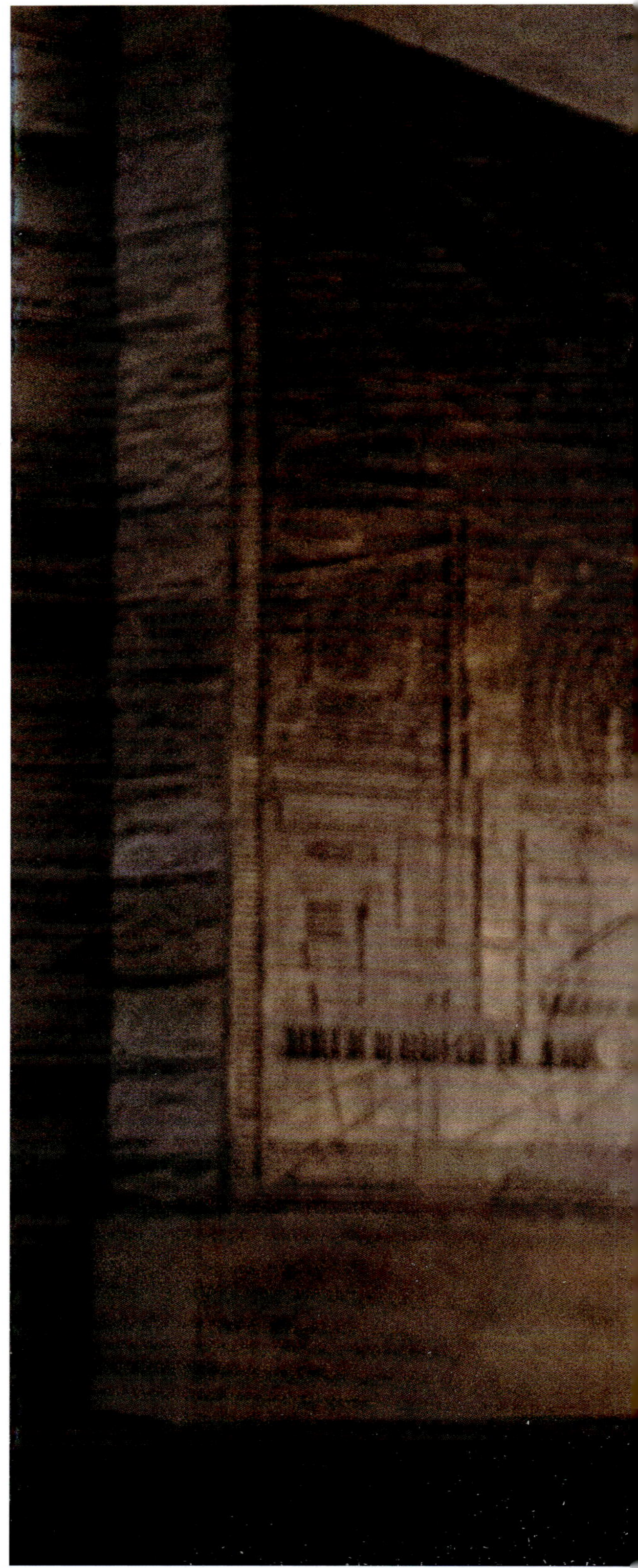

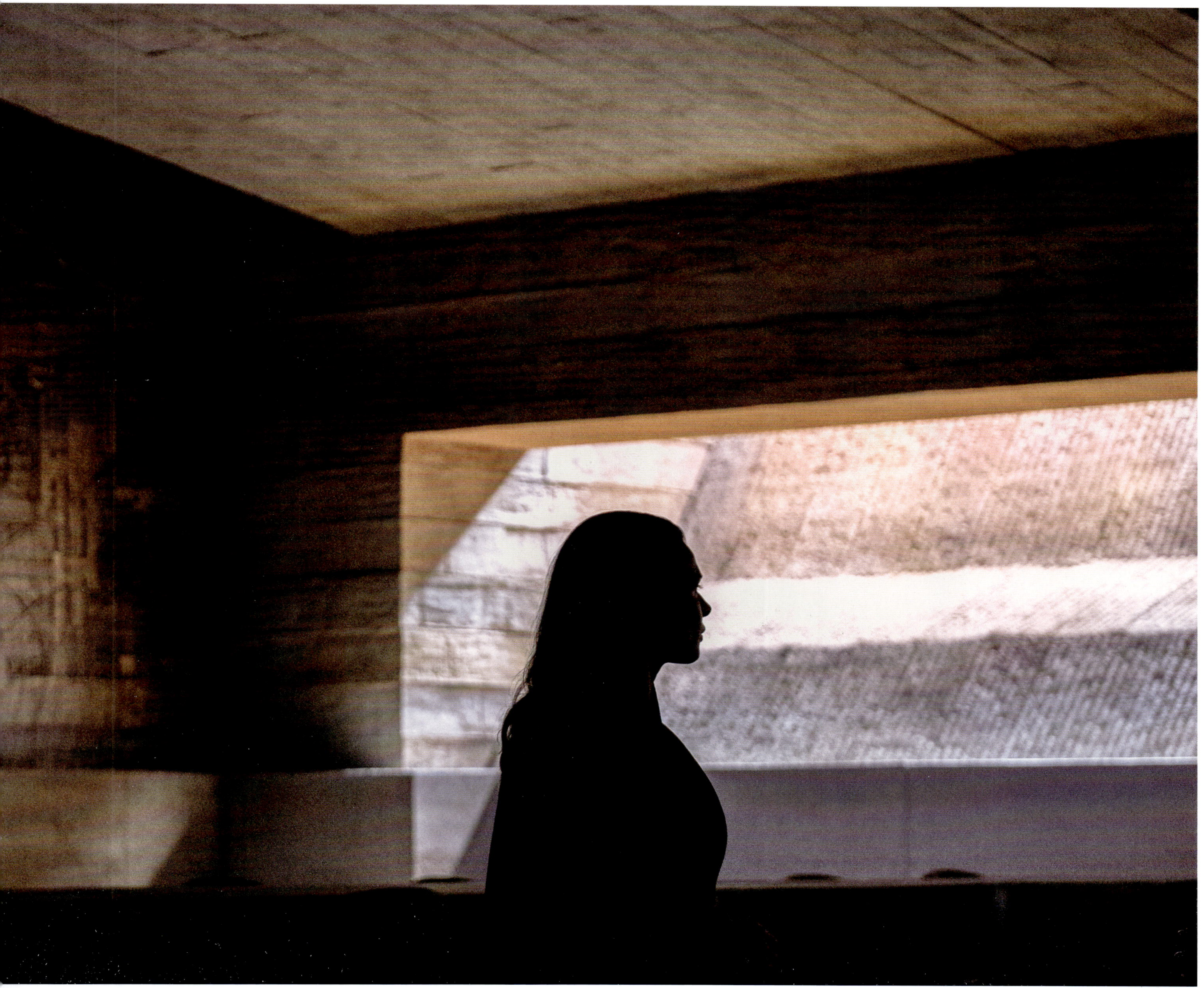

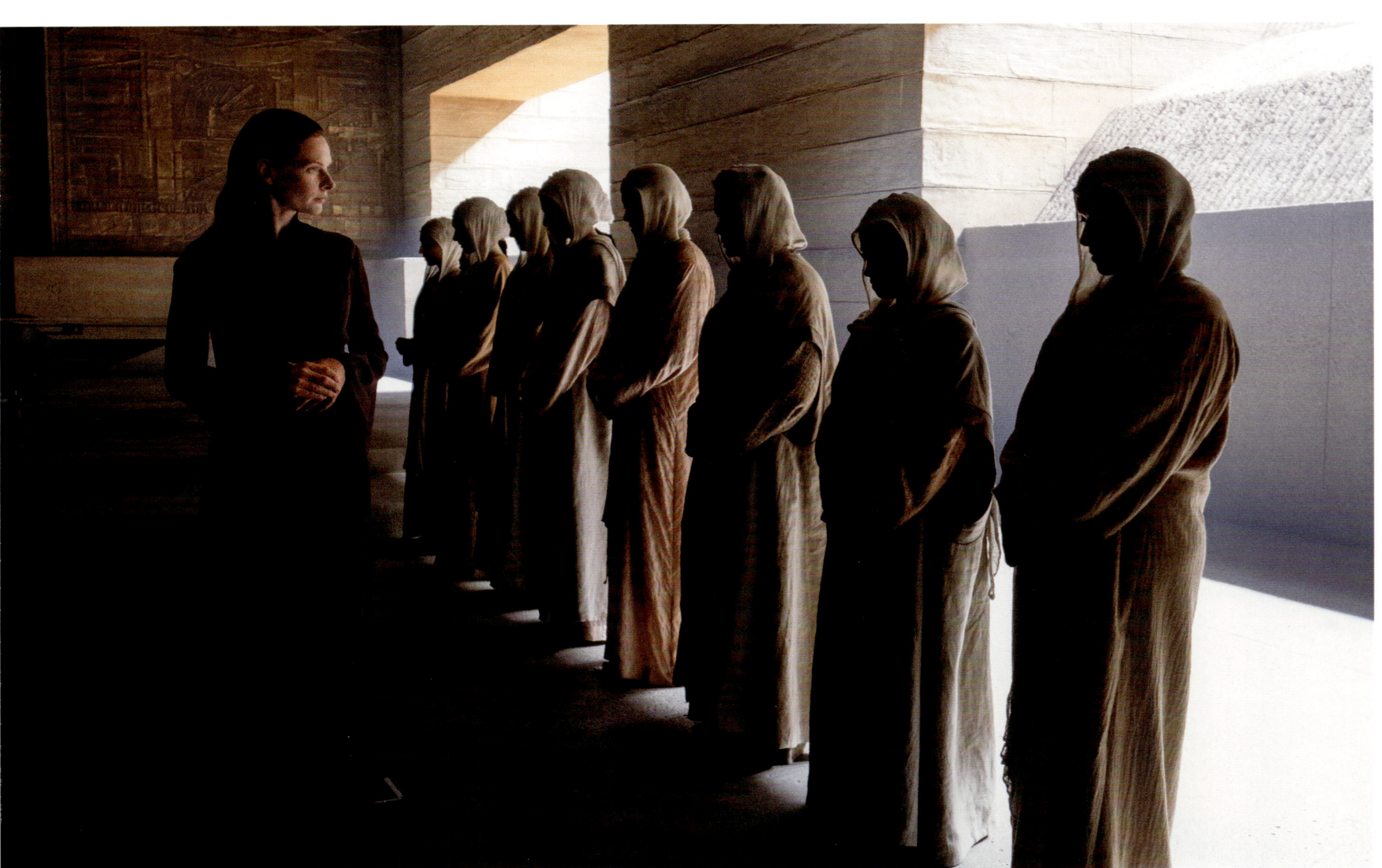

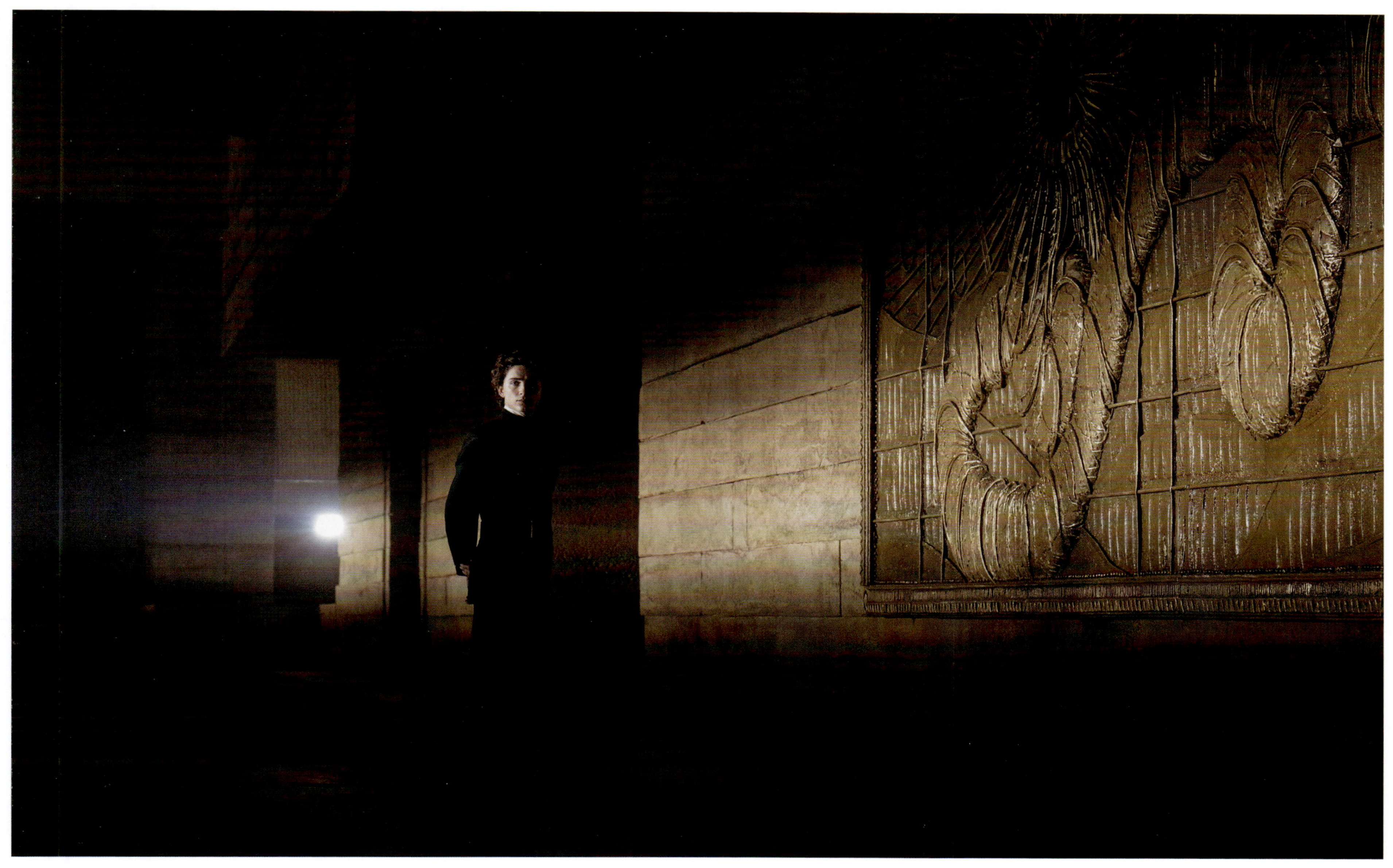

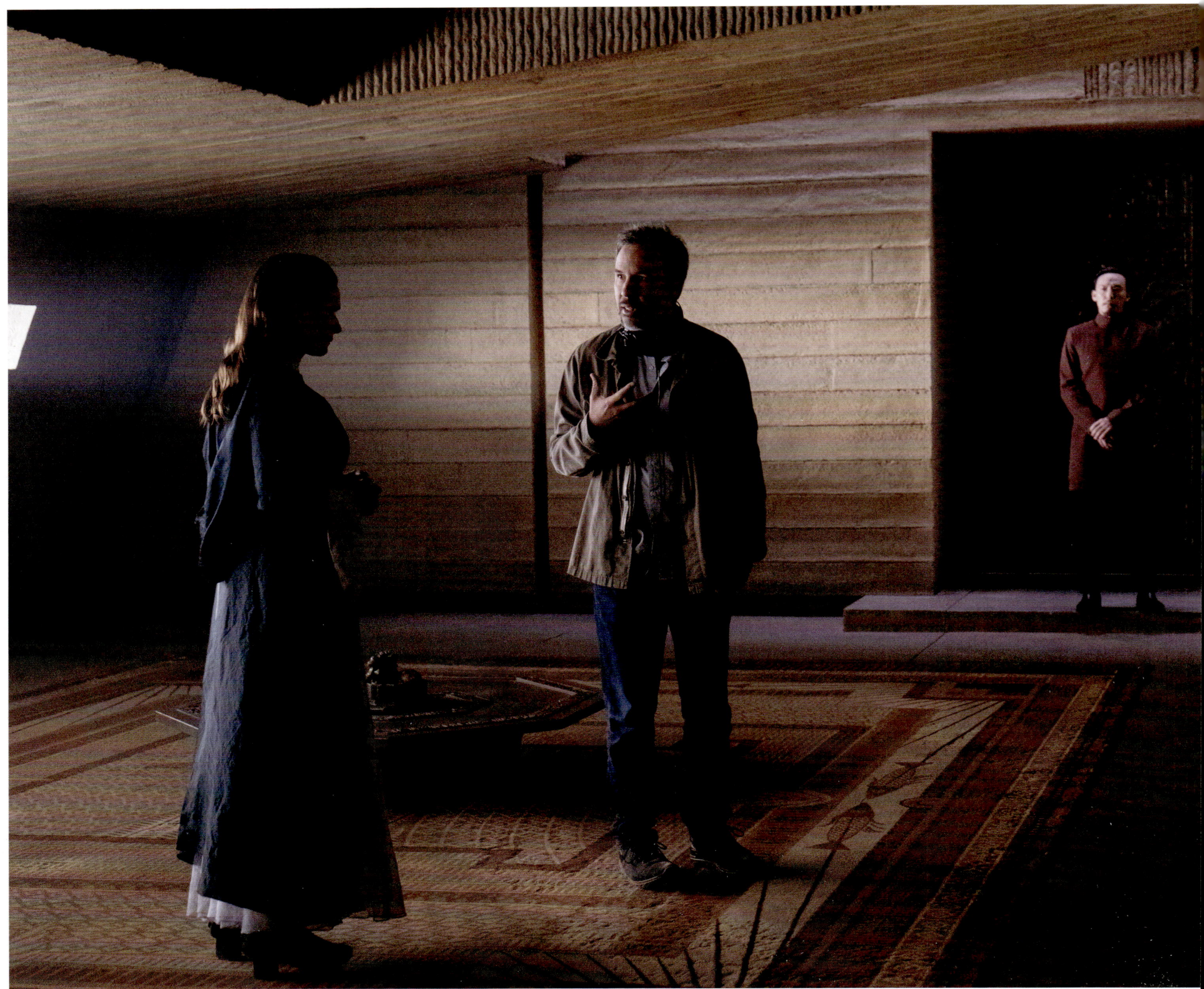

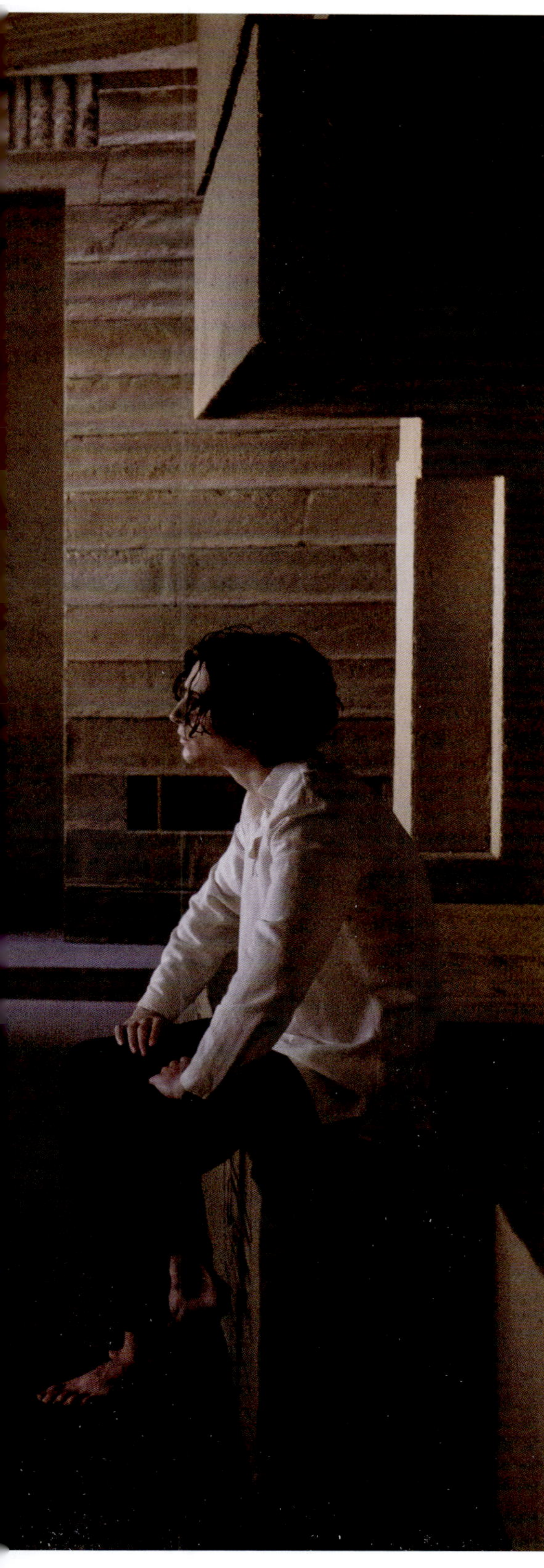

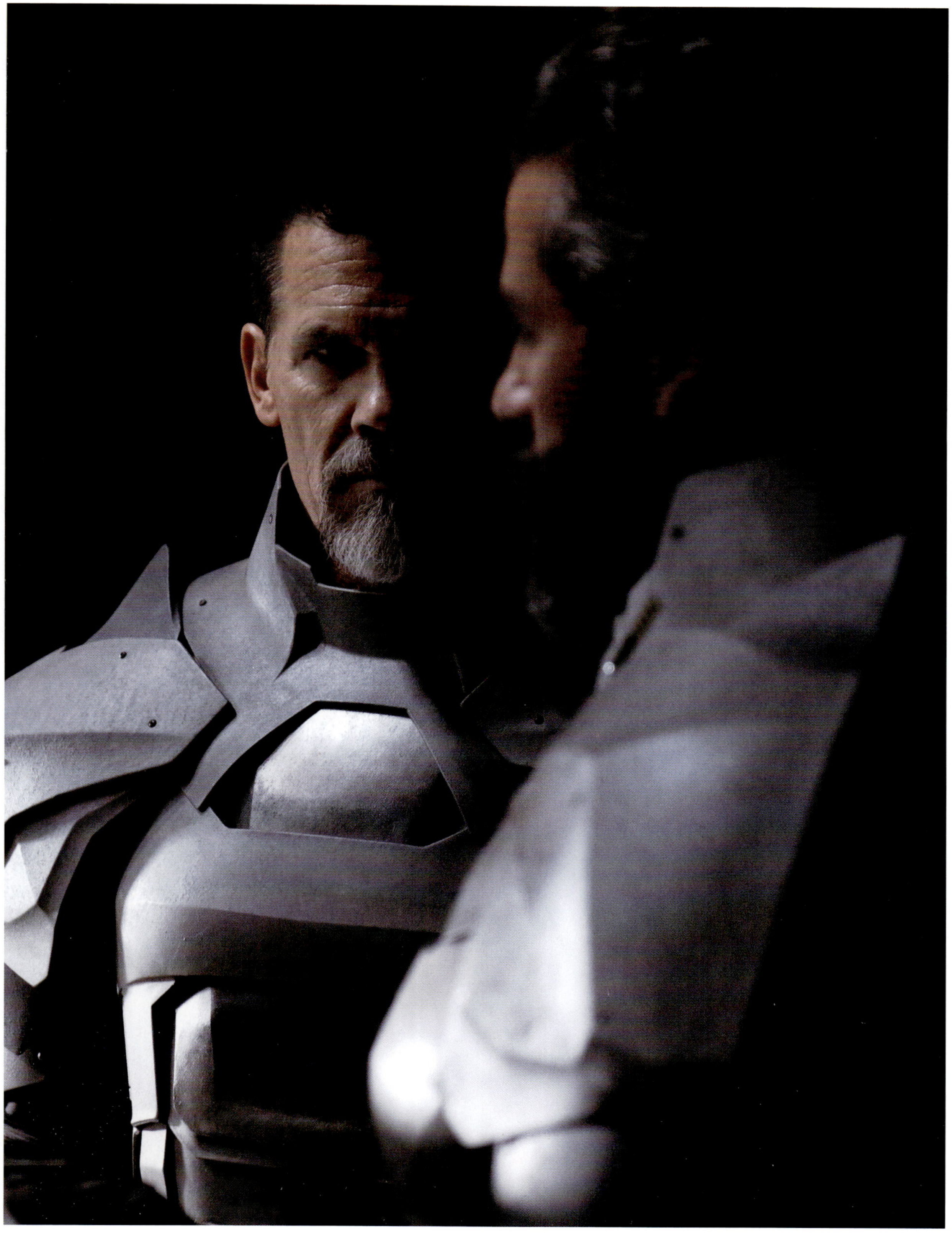

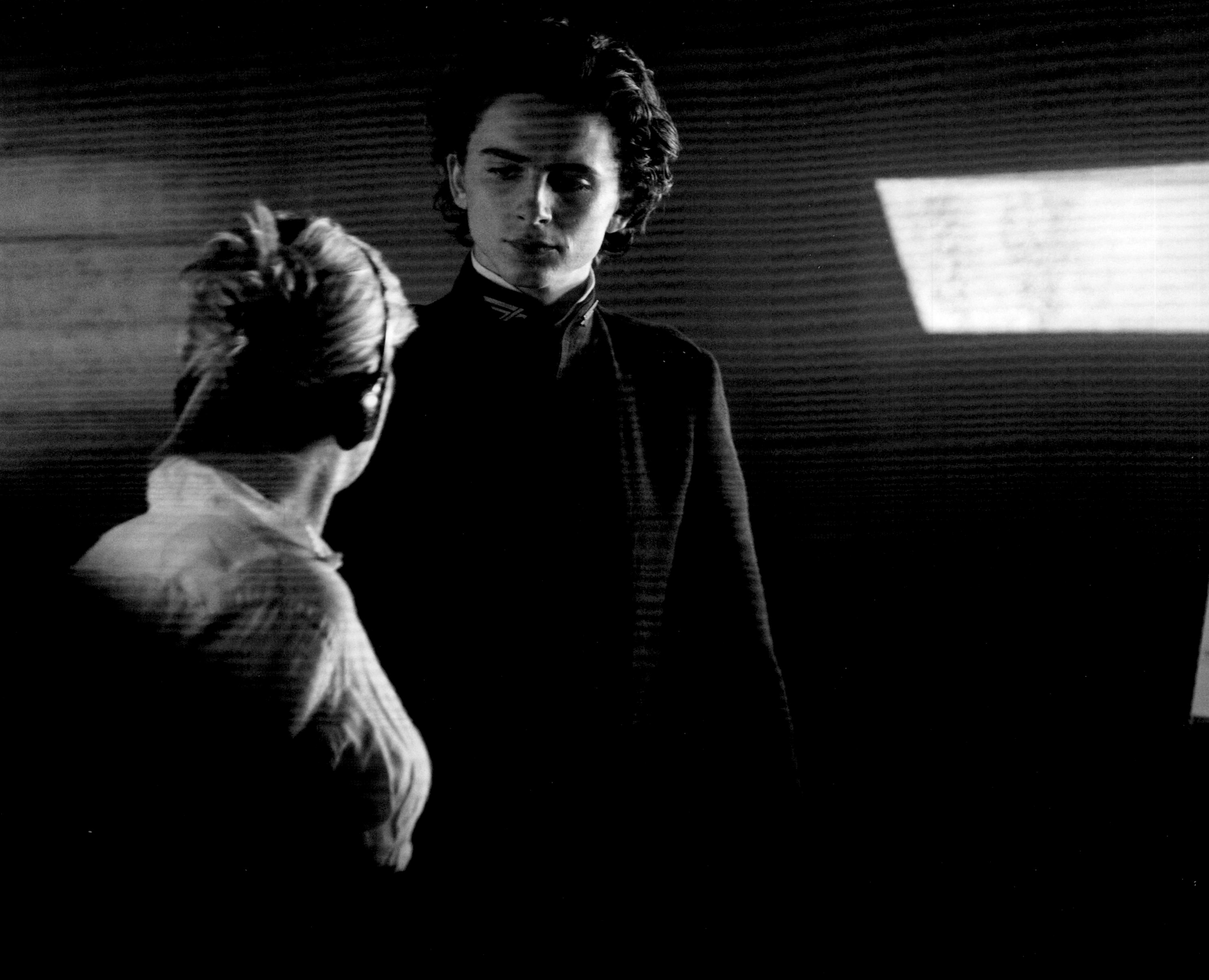

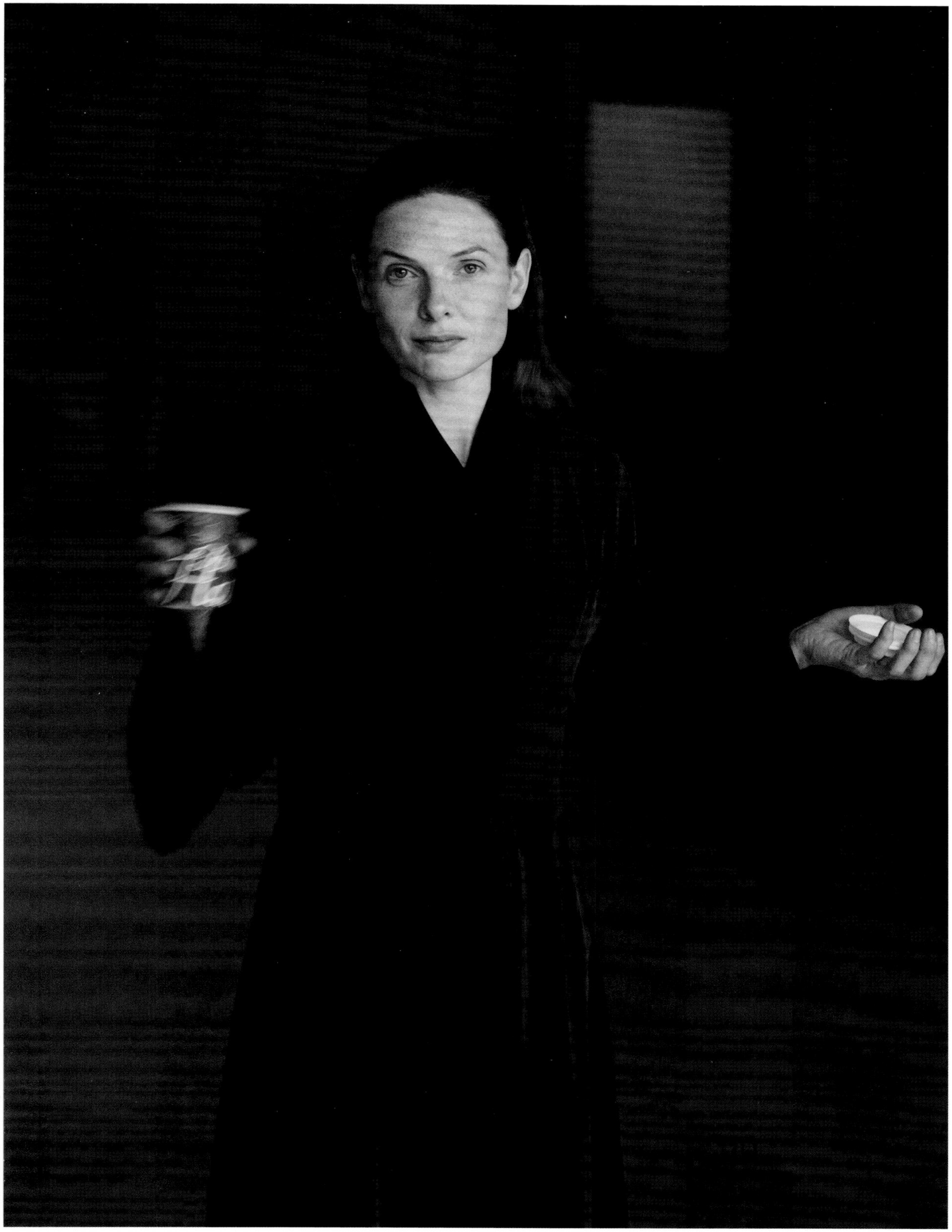

THE TRUE MAGIC OF this production was not just the various elements of the filmmaking process but the people at the heart of it. Denis introduced me to the worlds of Caladan, Arrakis, and Giedi Prime, but production designer Patrice Vermette invited me to step into them and experience the awe-inspiring sets he and his team built from the grains of Frank Herbert's imagination. Cinematographer Greig Fraser, who painted with light and showed us how to see the magic, shared his color palettes and tones with me so that I could ensure the photography reflected the look of the film. Paul Lambert, luminary of visual effects, who immersed our physical world into another universe, gave me insight into the details my eyes and camera could not yet see. The ensemble cast, who came together as a meteor shower of talent, lit up the set and screens alike, engaging with my lens and allowing me a deeper level of access to their characters and performances.

This collaboration between direction and design is the product of years of hard work behind the scenes. When a shooting crew step onto a set, they are immediately immersed in a physical world that is the result of thousands of hours of design, creation, and construction. Every detail has been carefully produced to form a vivid new world on camera.

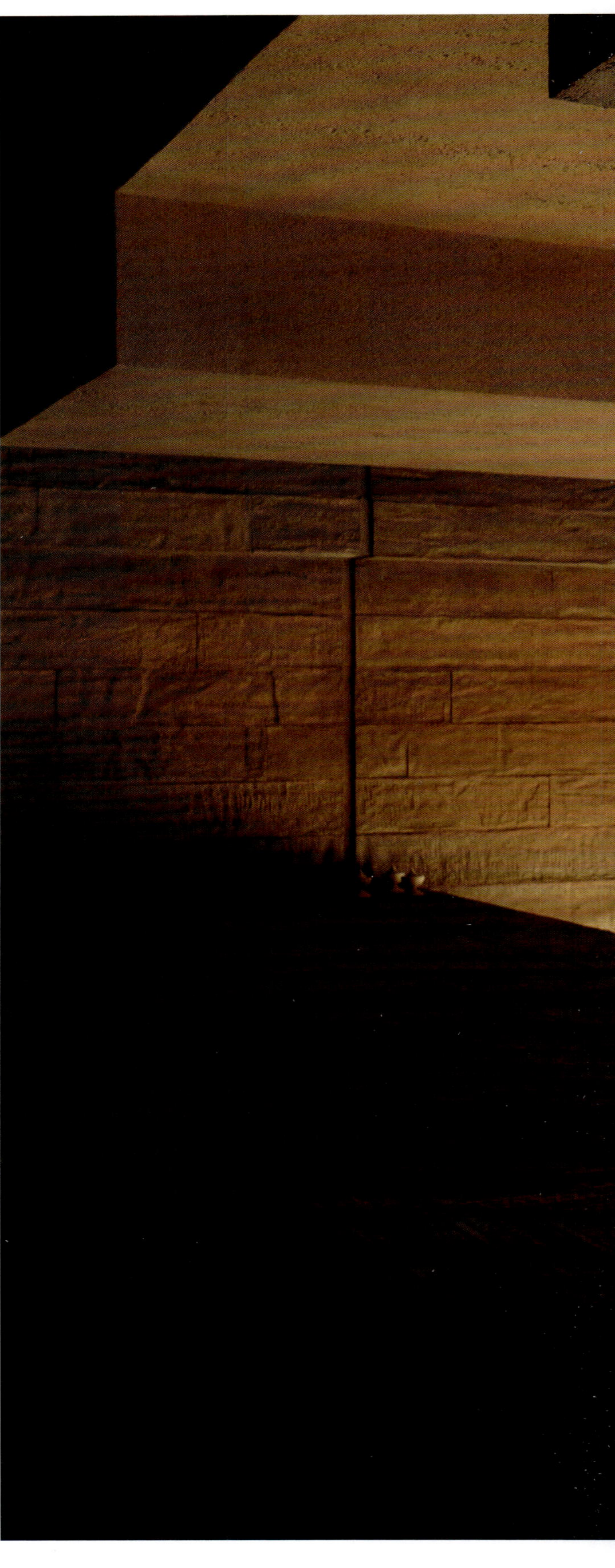

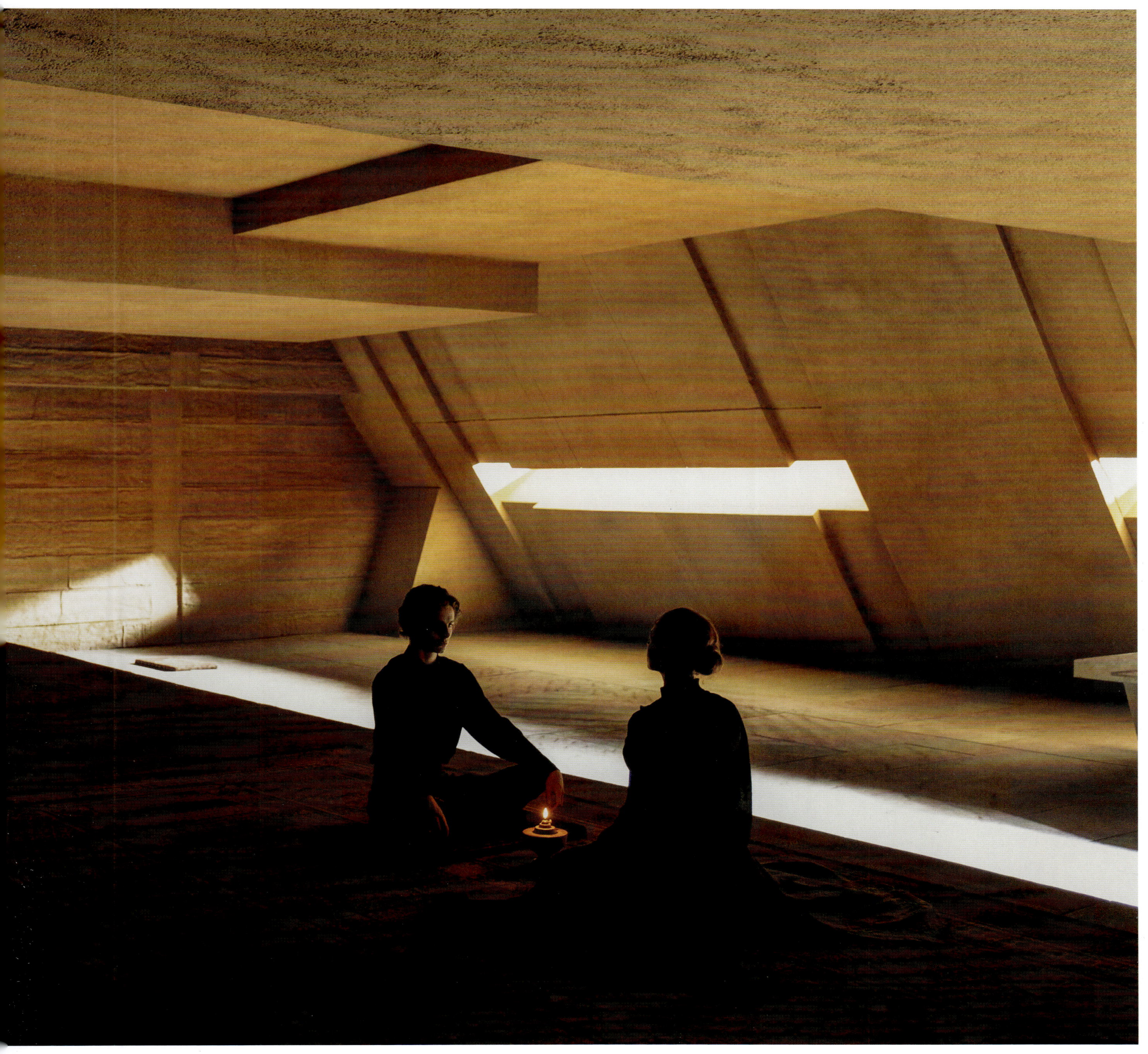

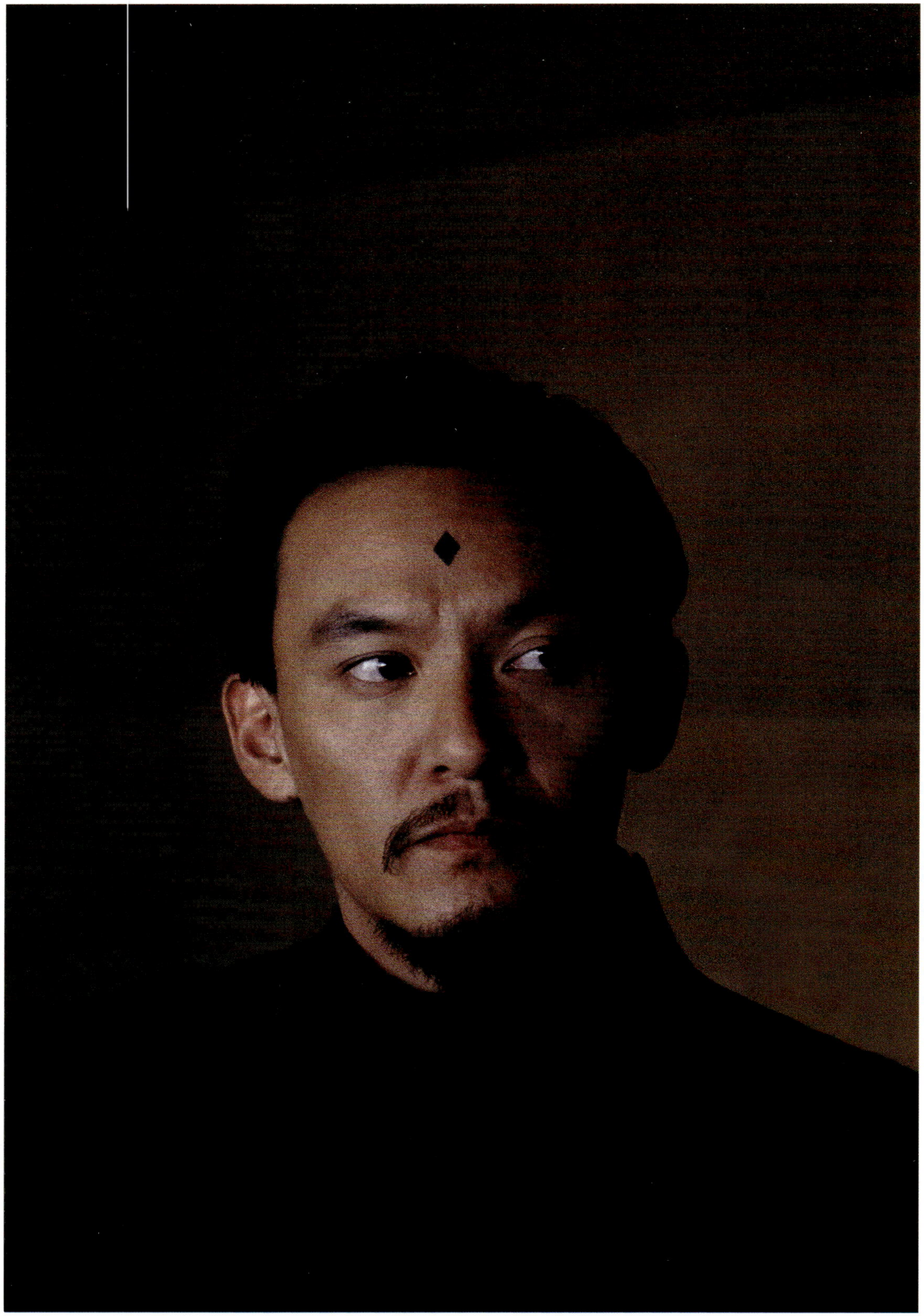

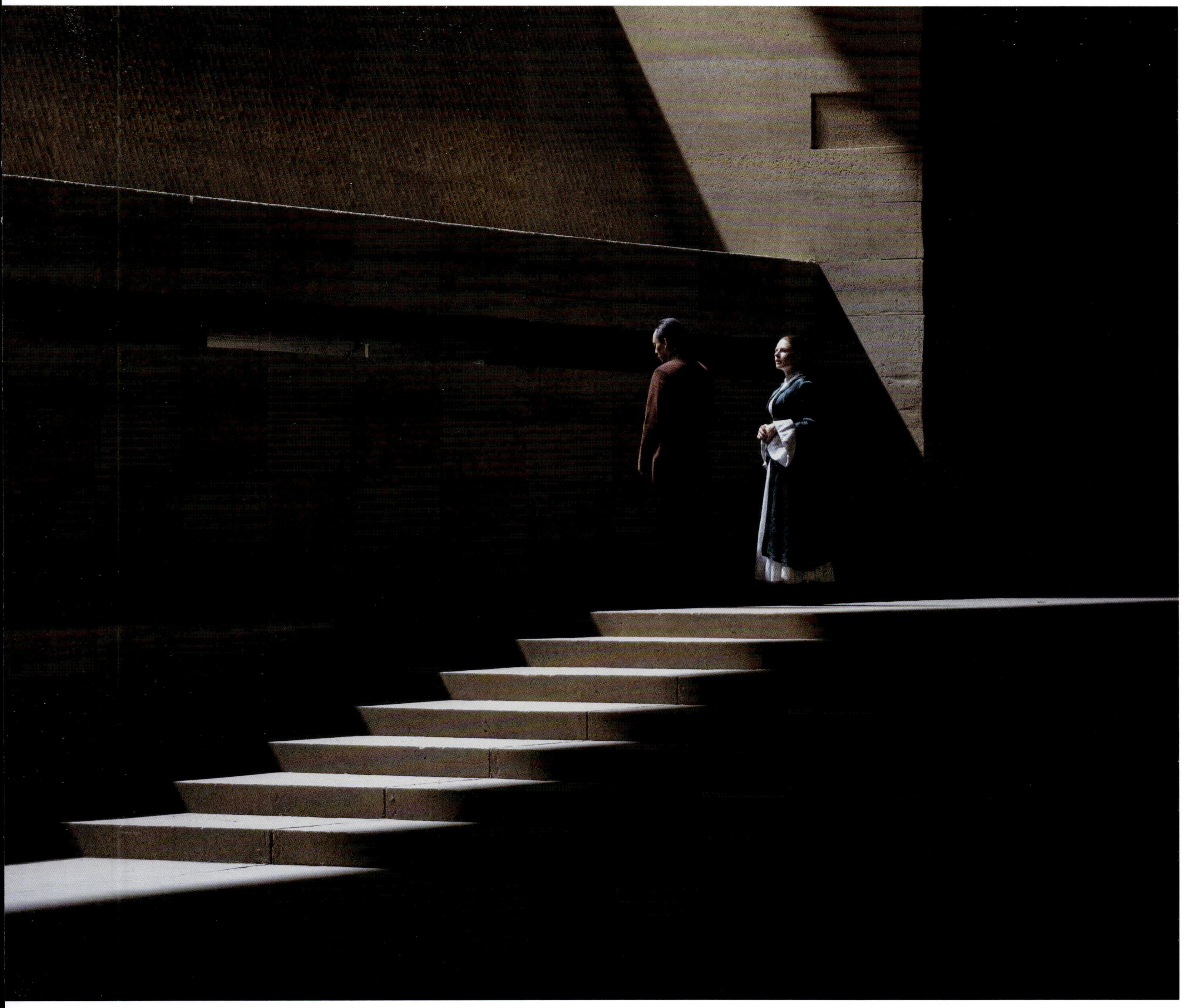

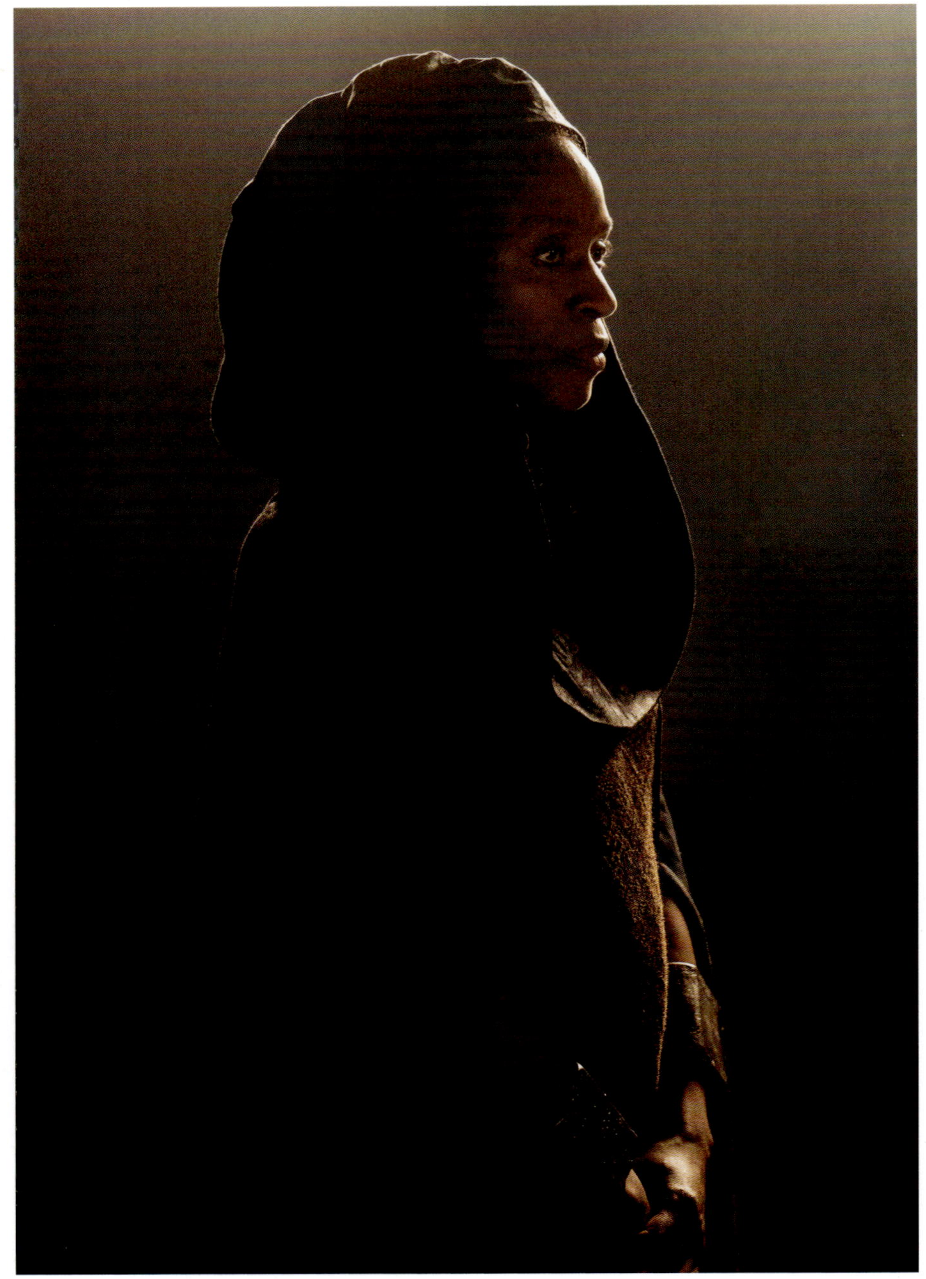 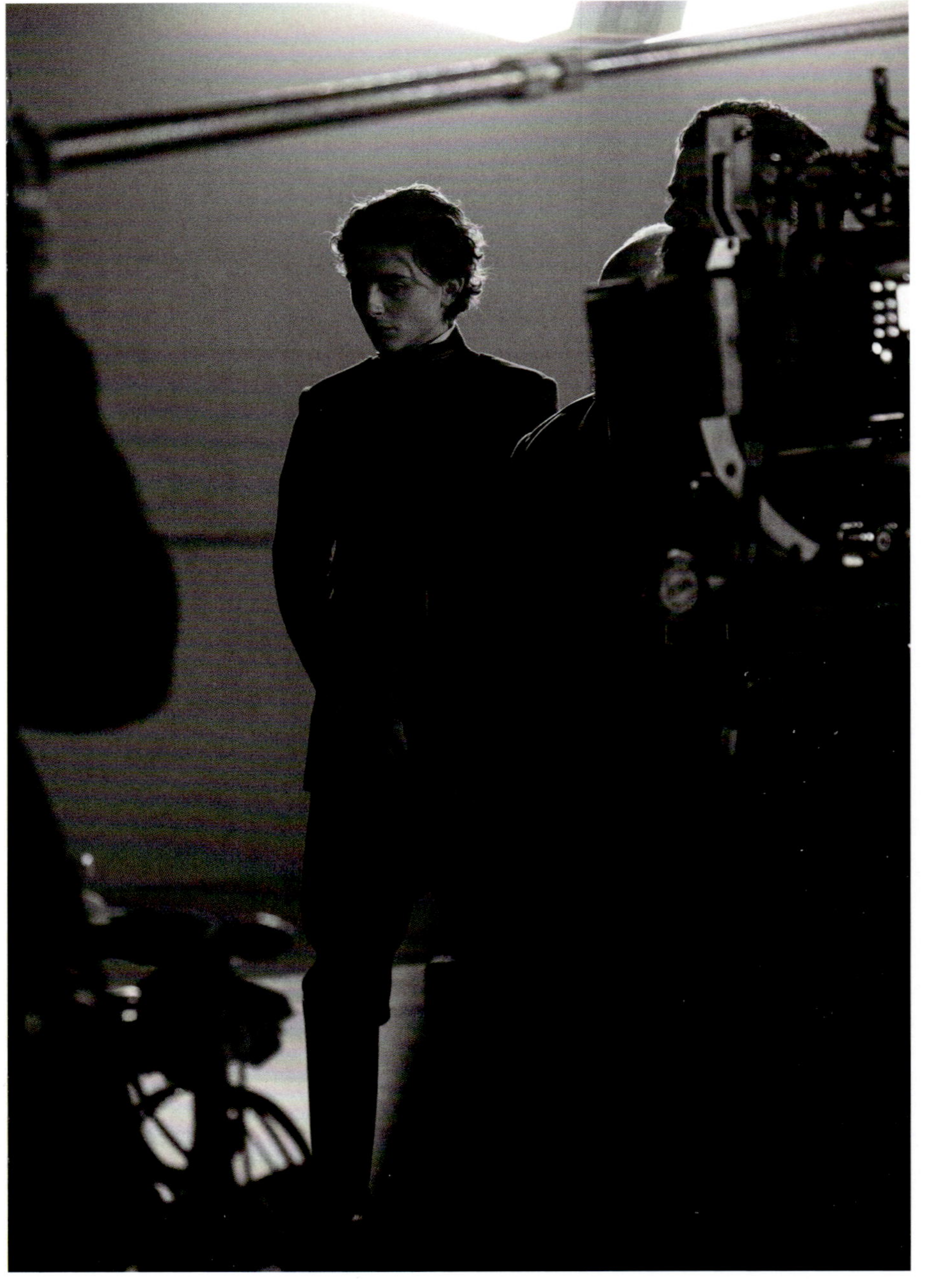

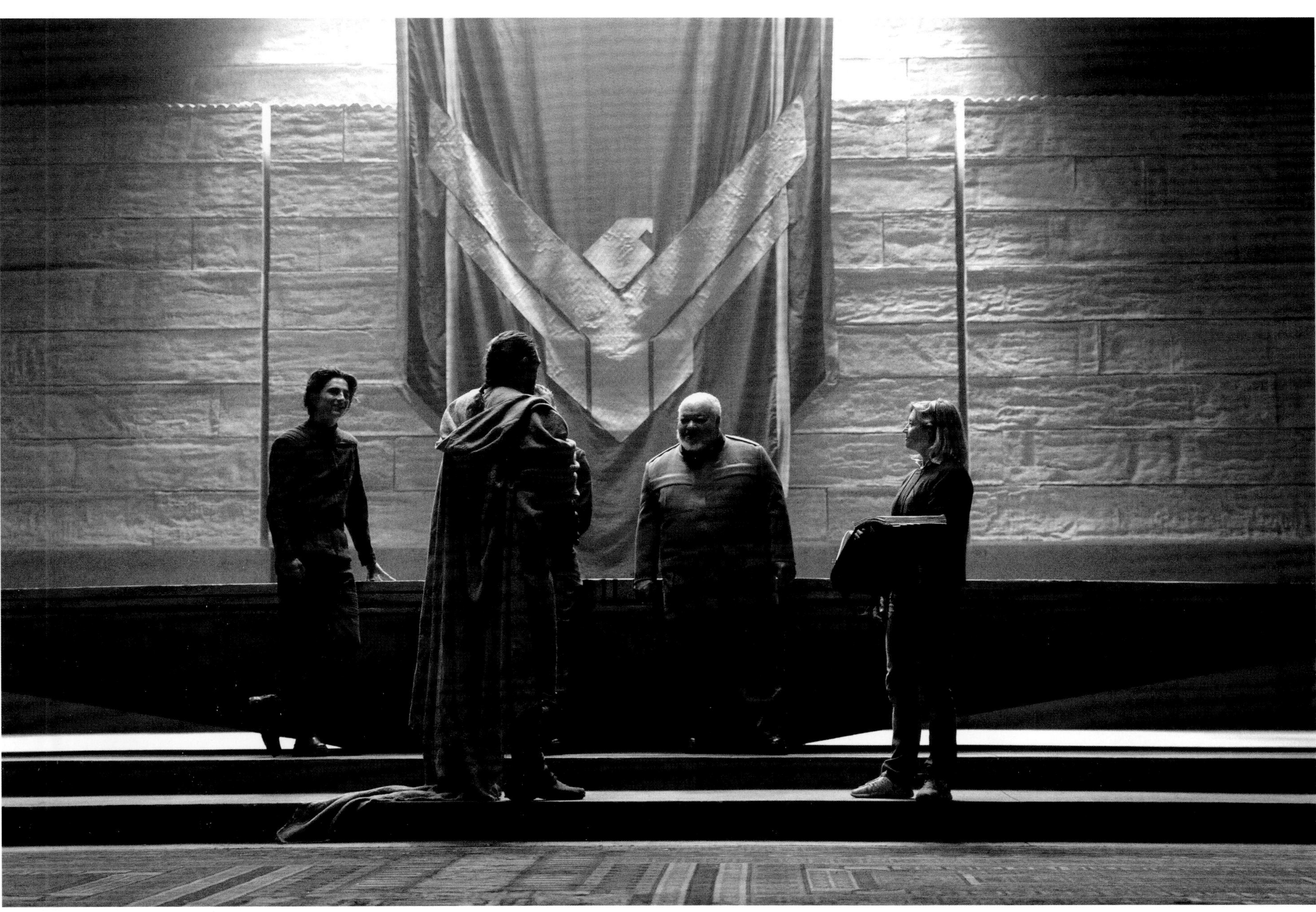

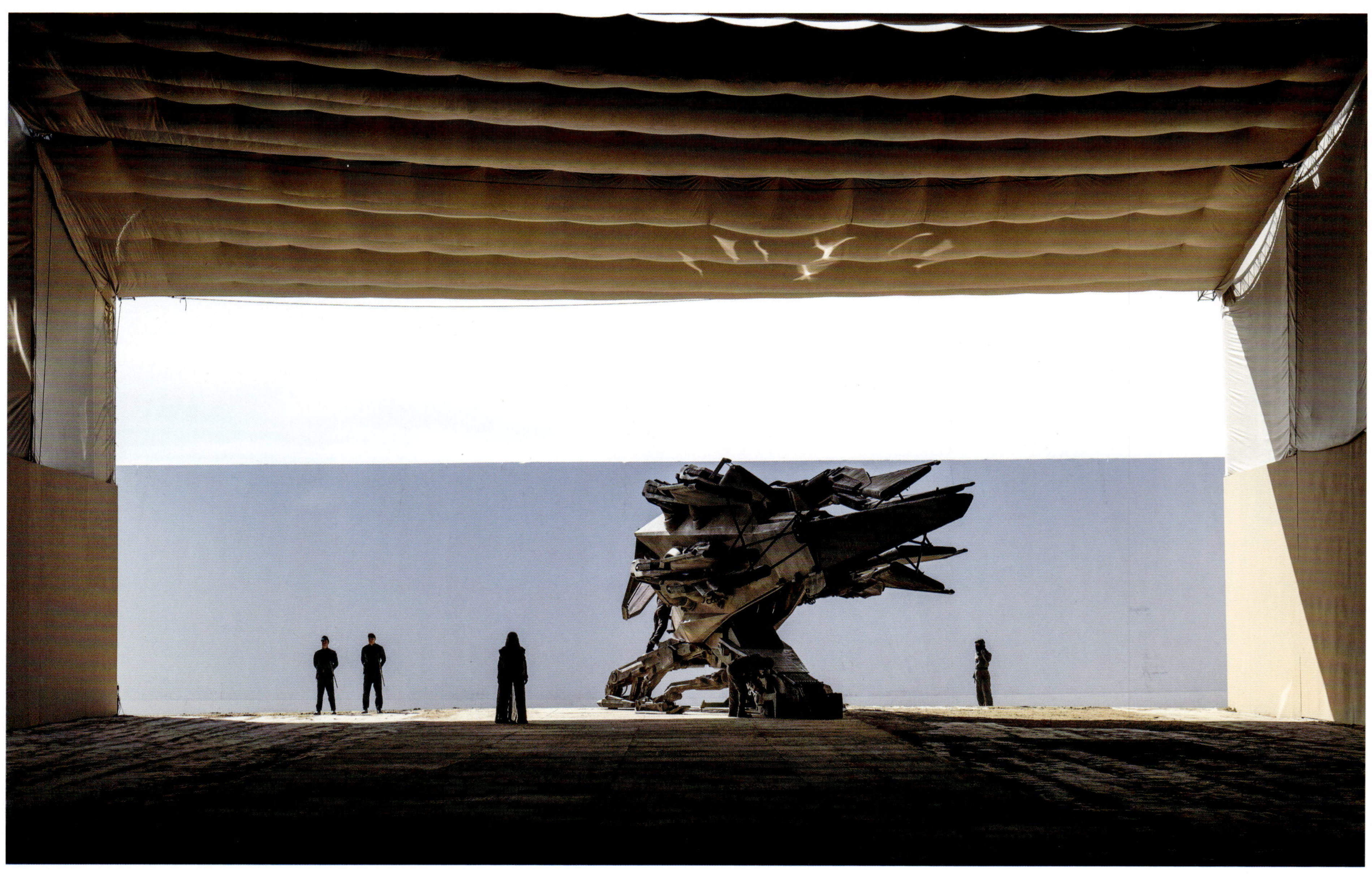

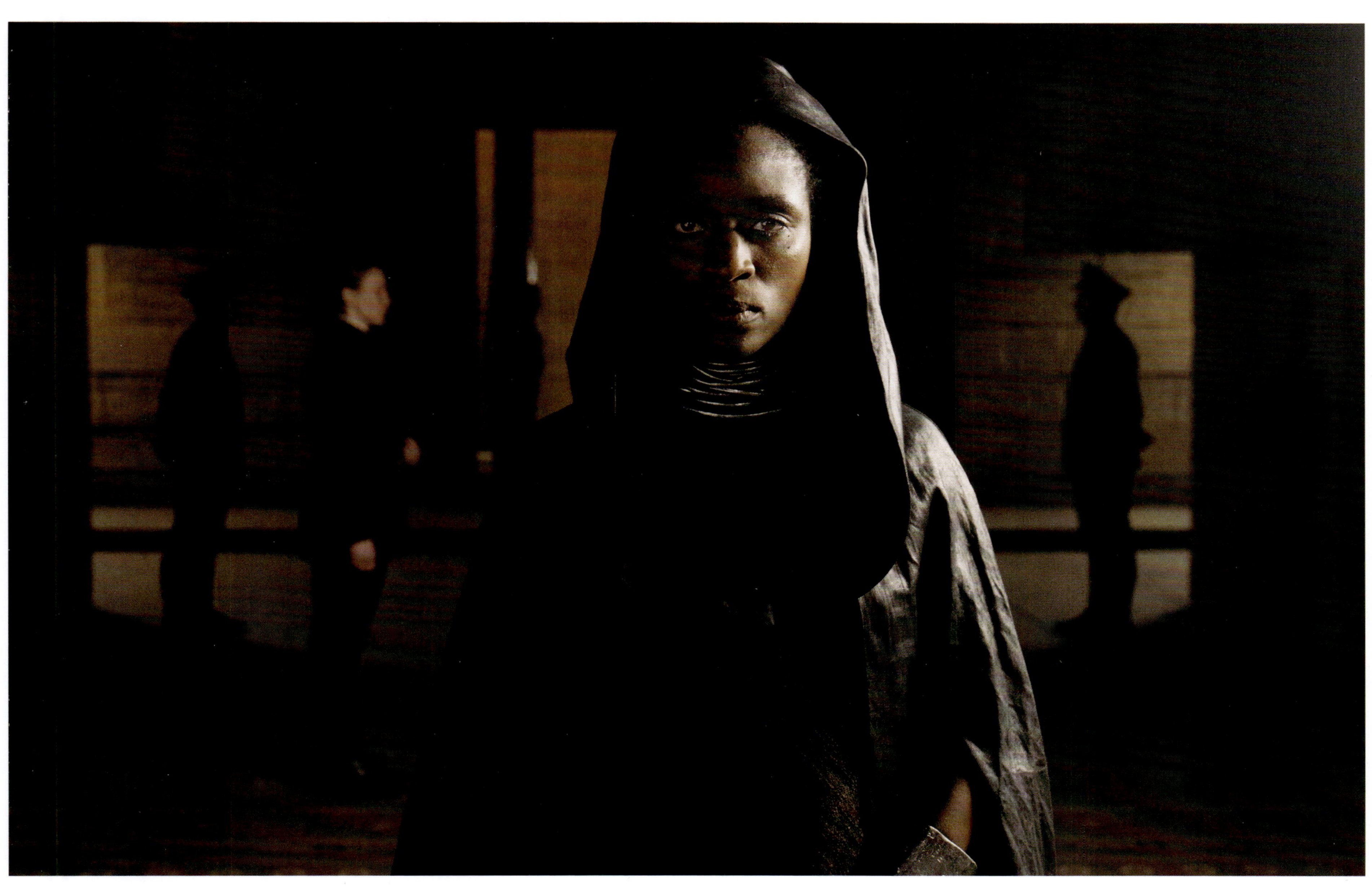

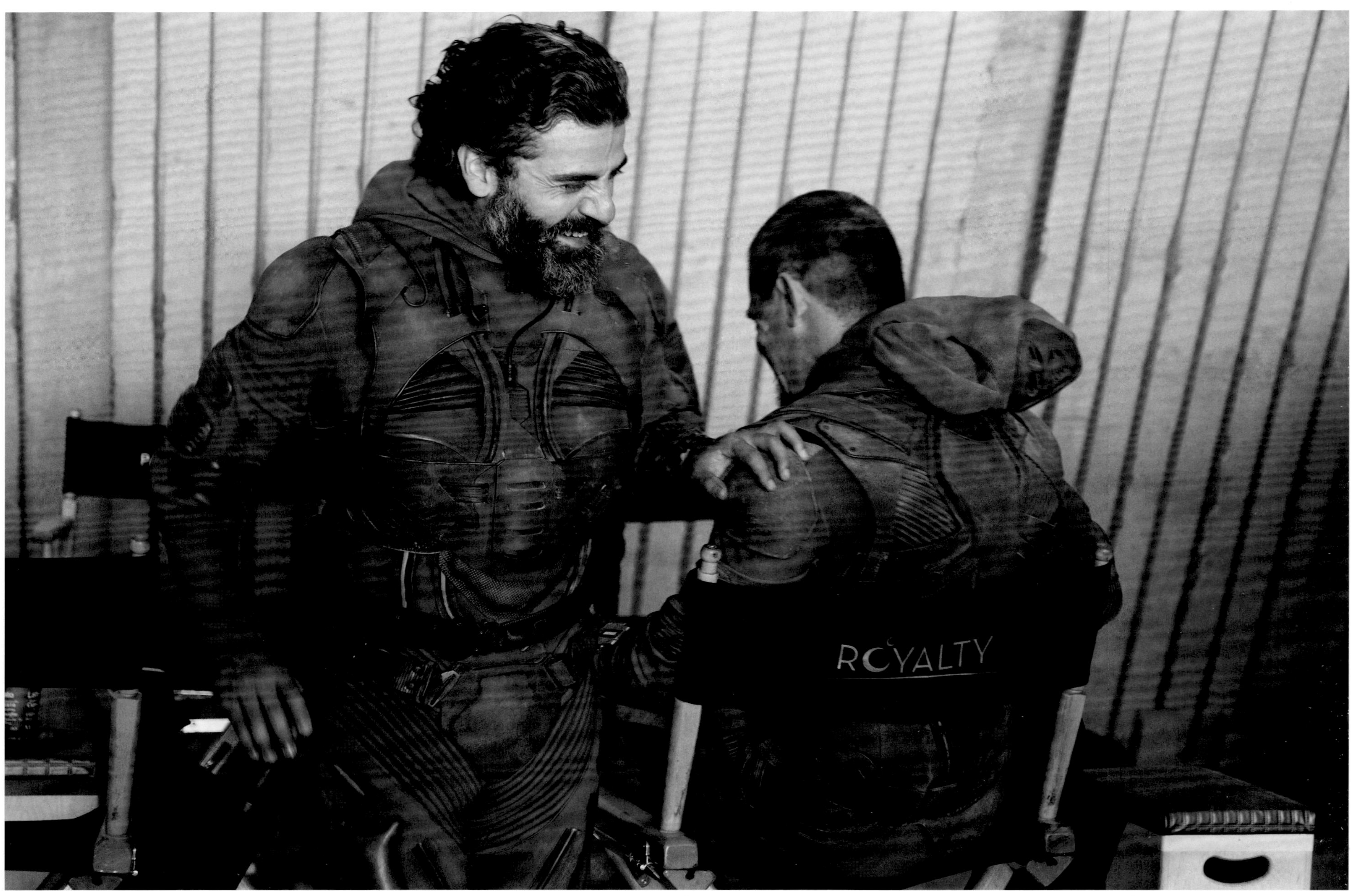
ROYALTY

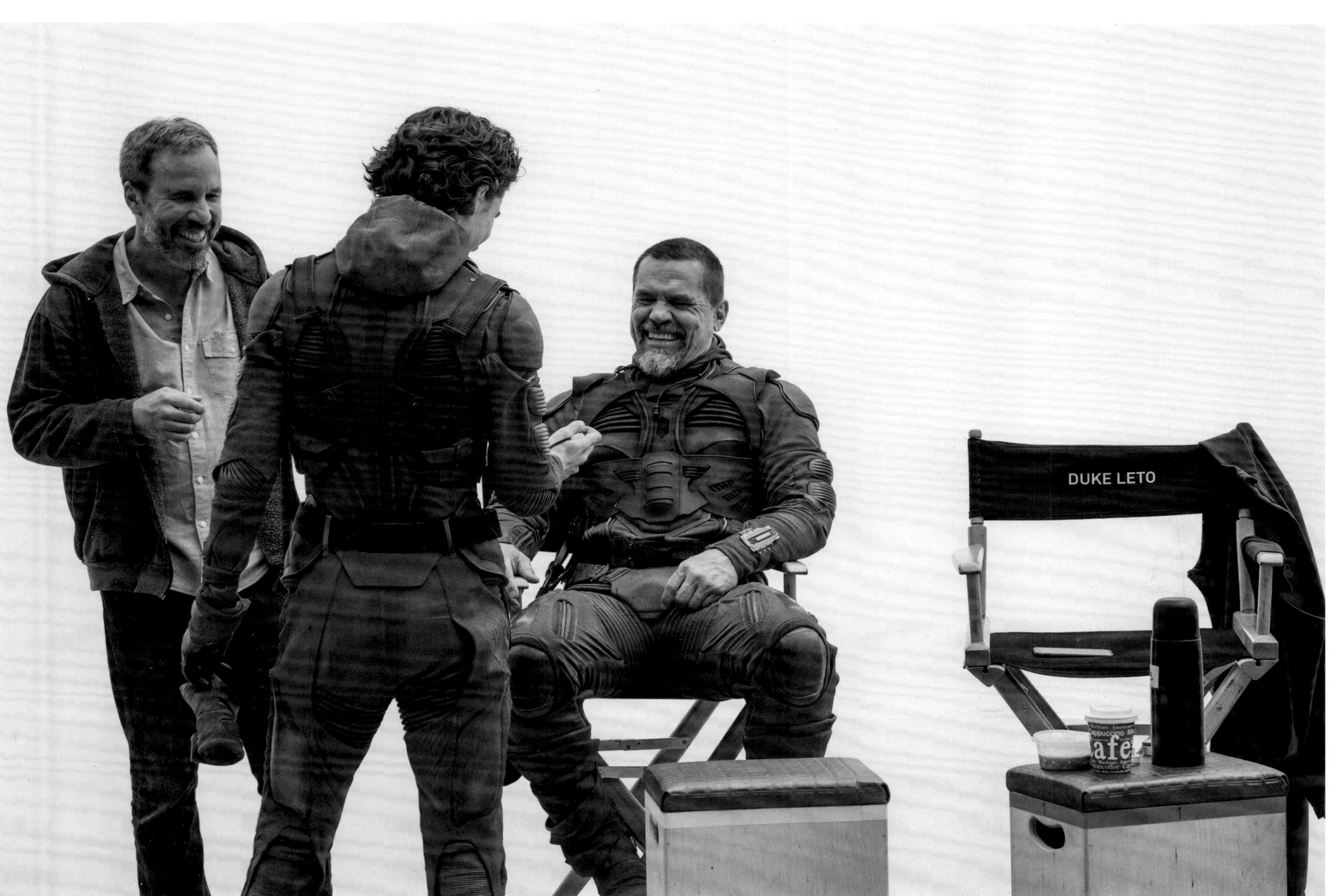
DUKE LETO

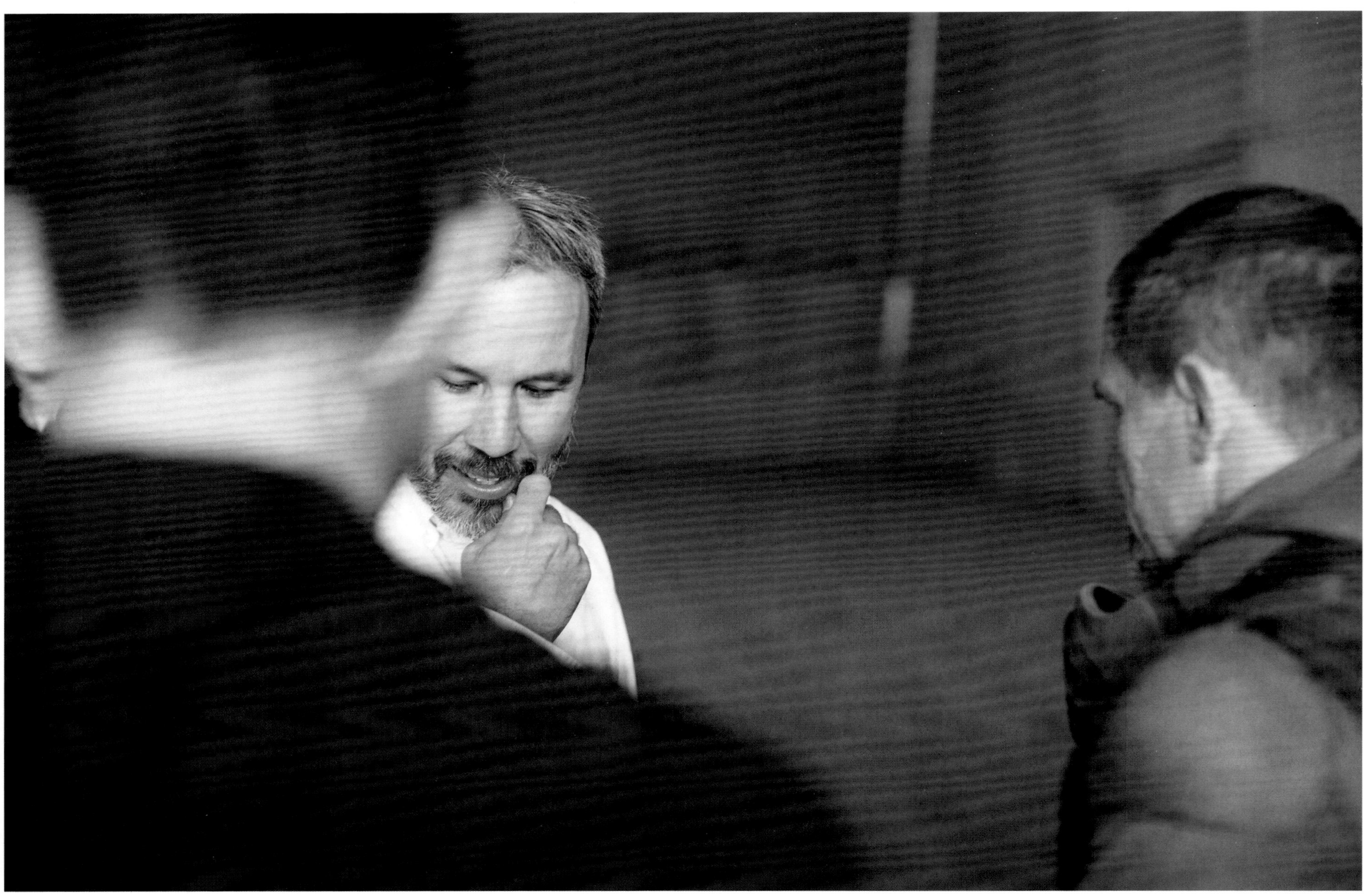

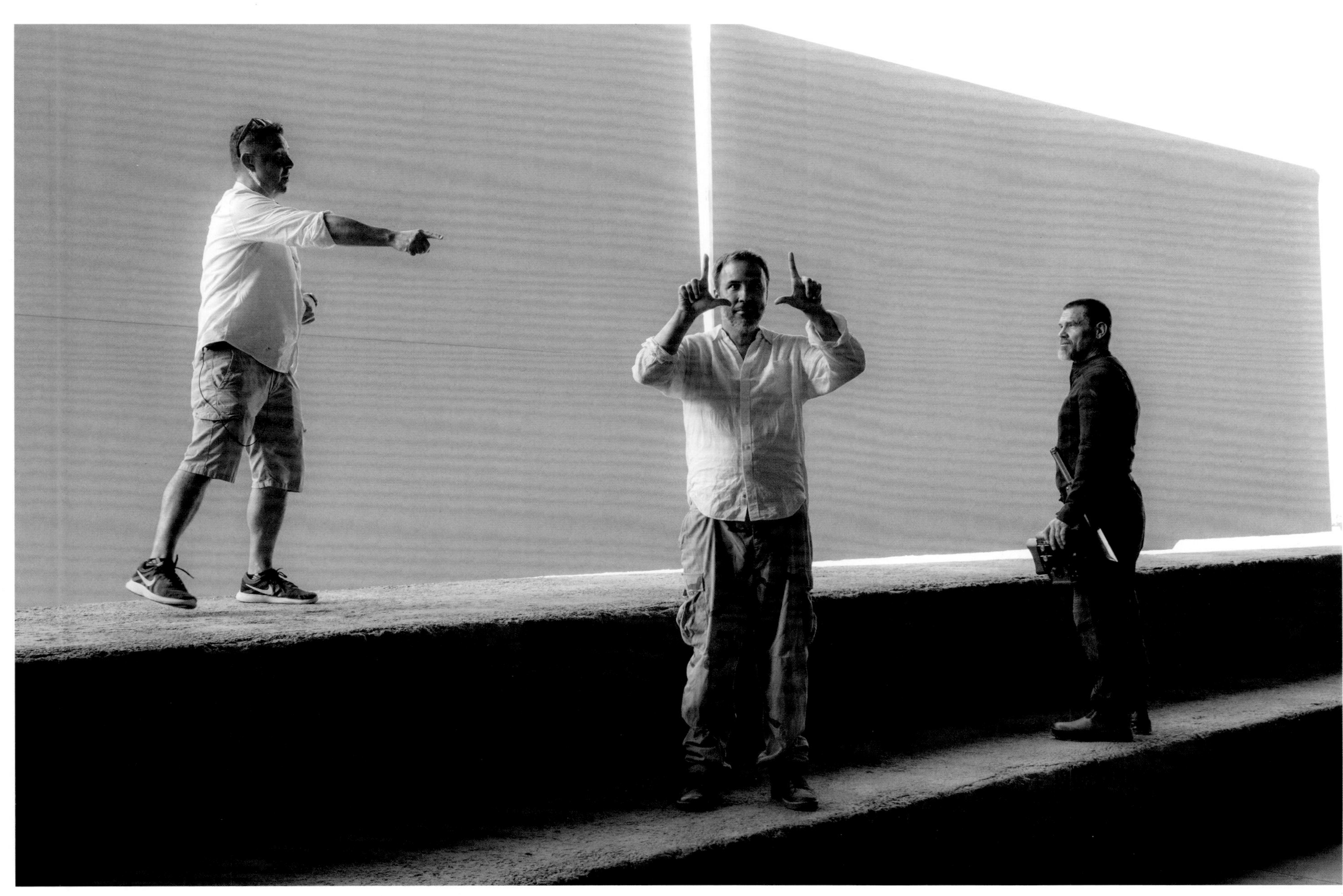

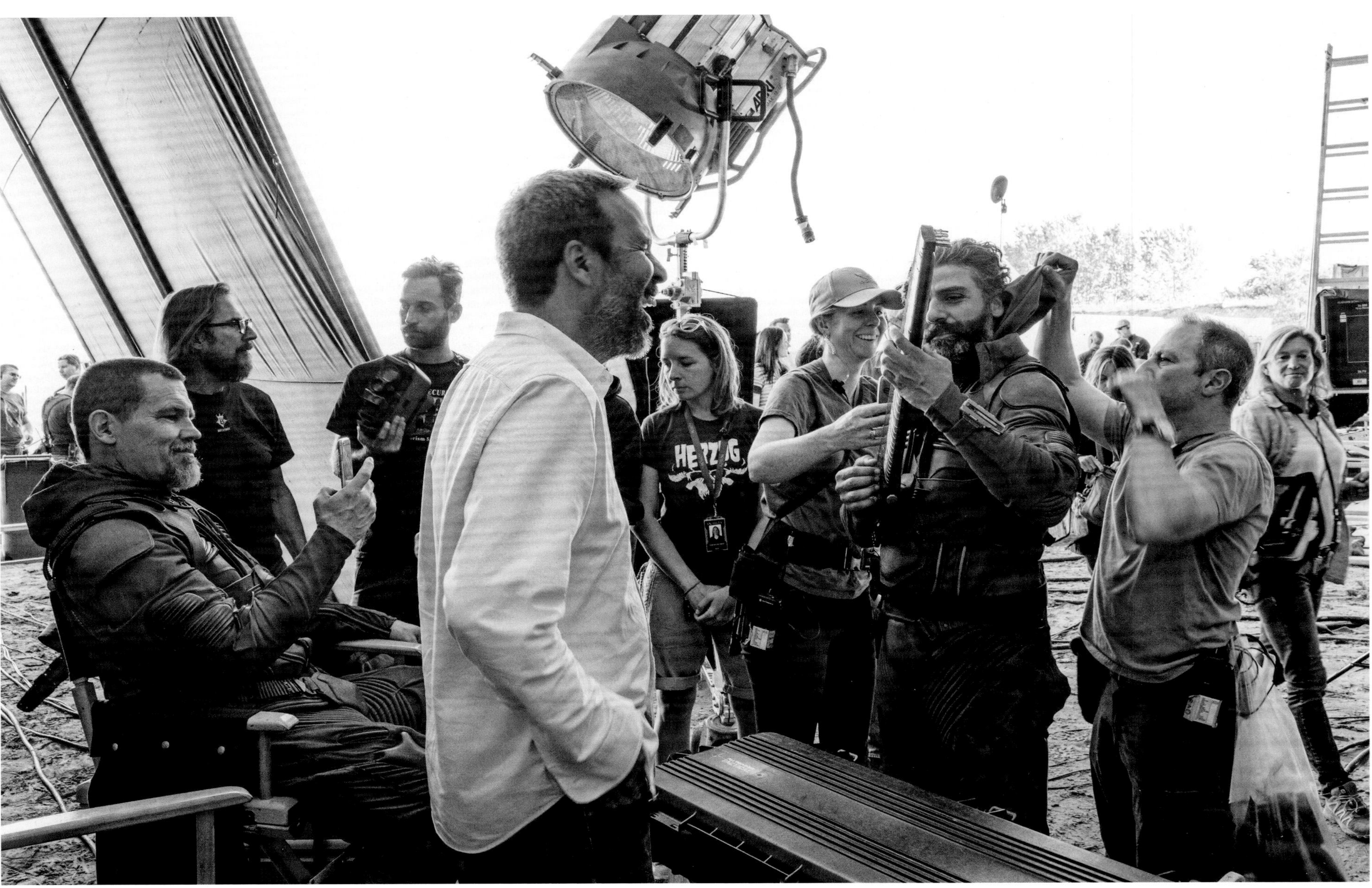

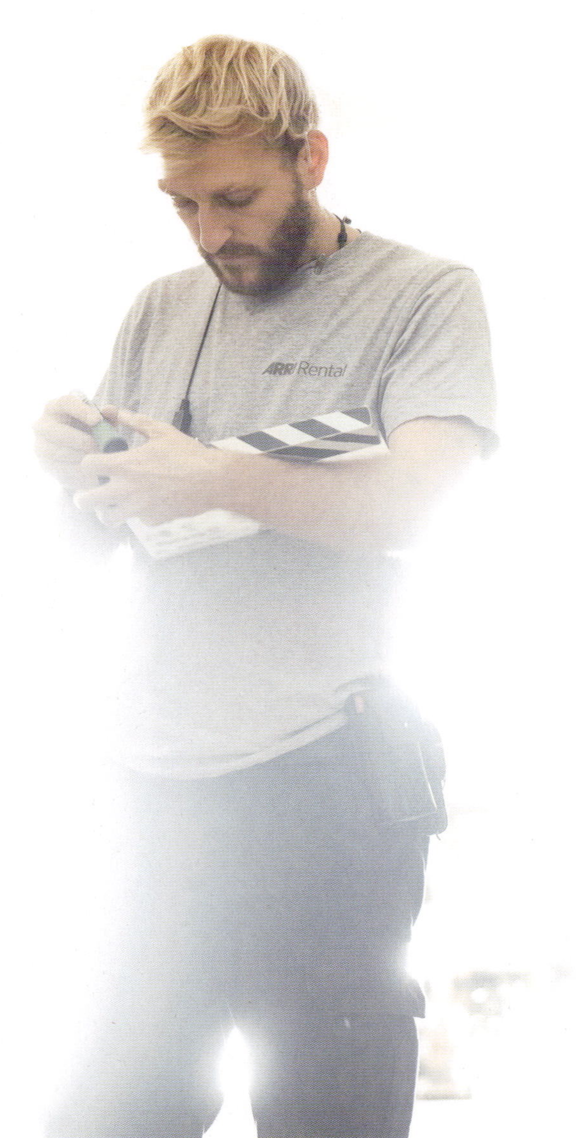
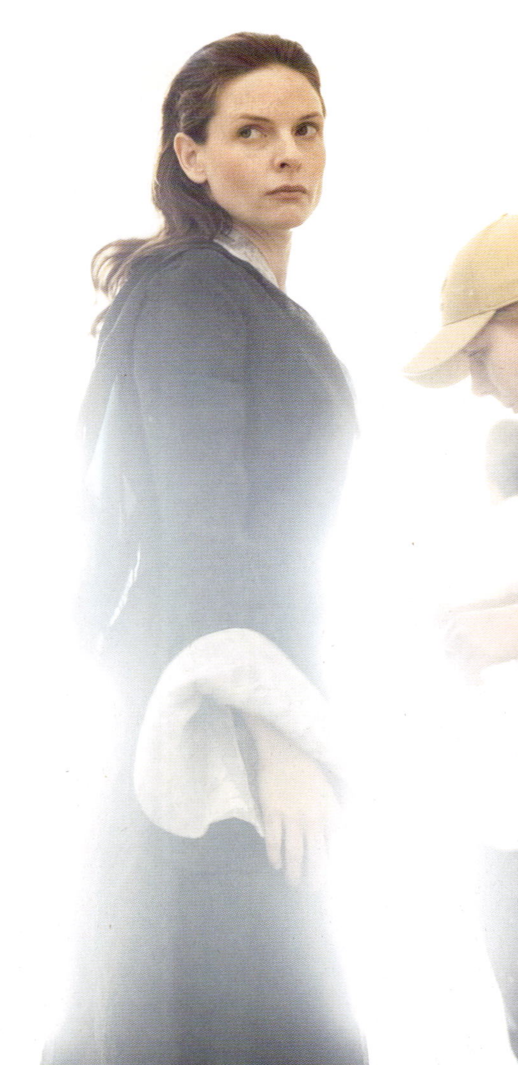
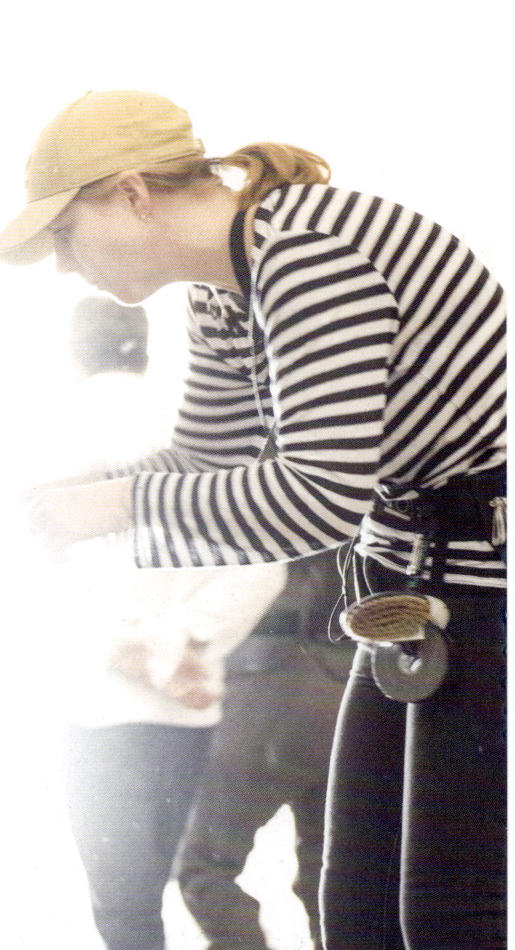

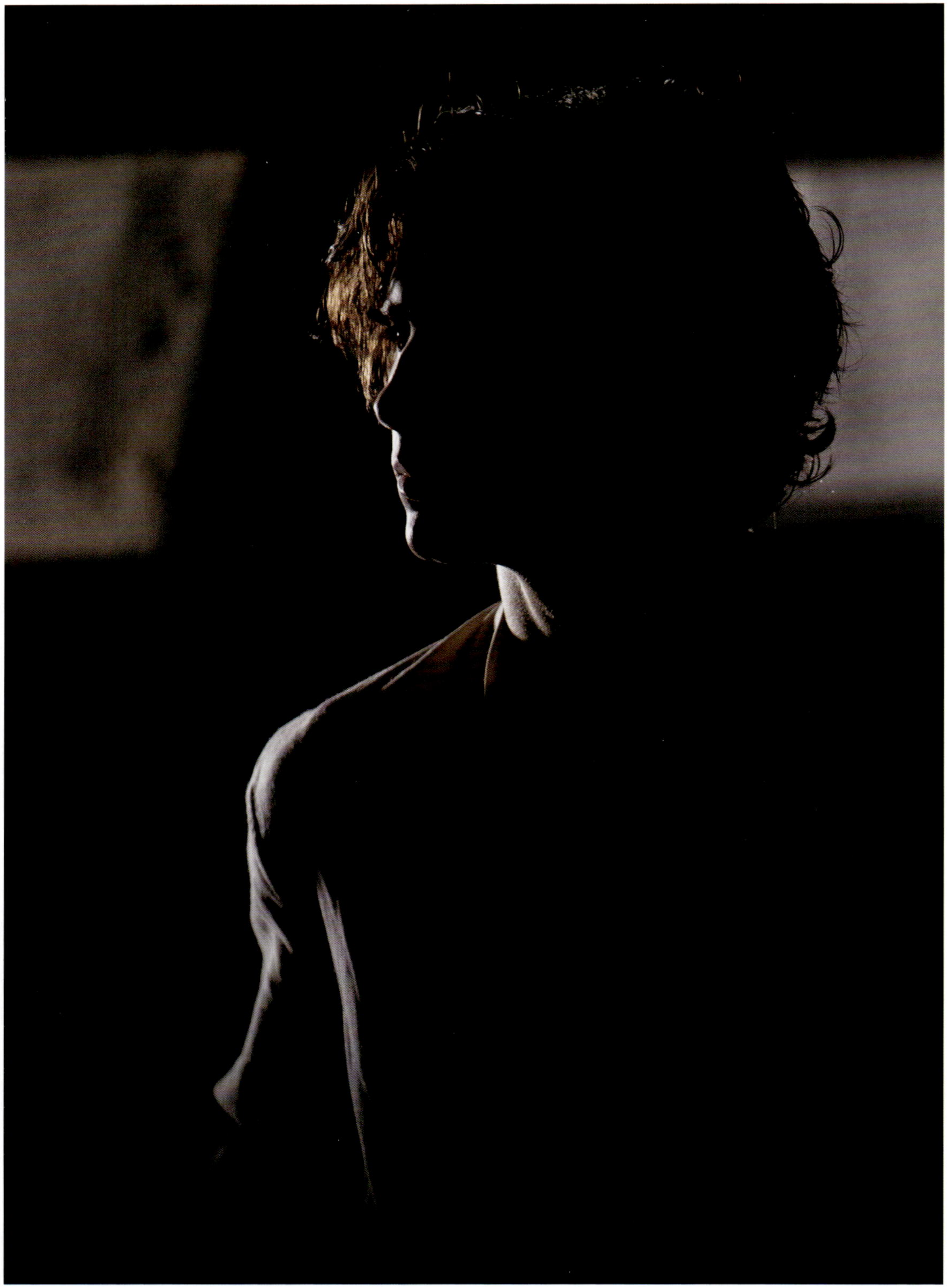

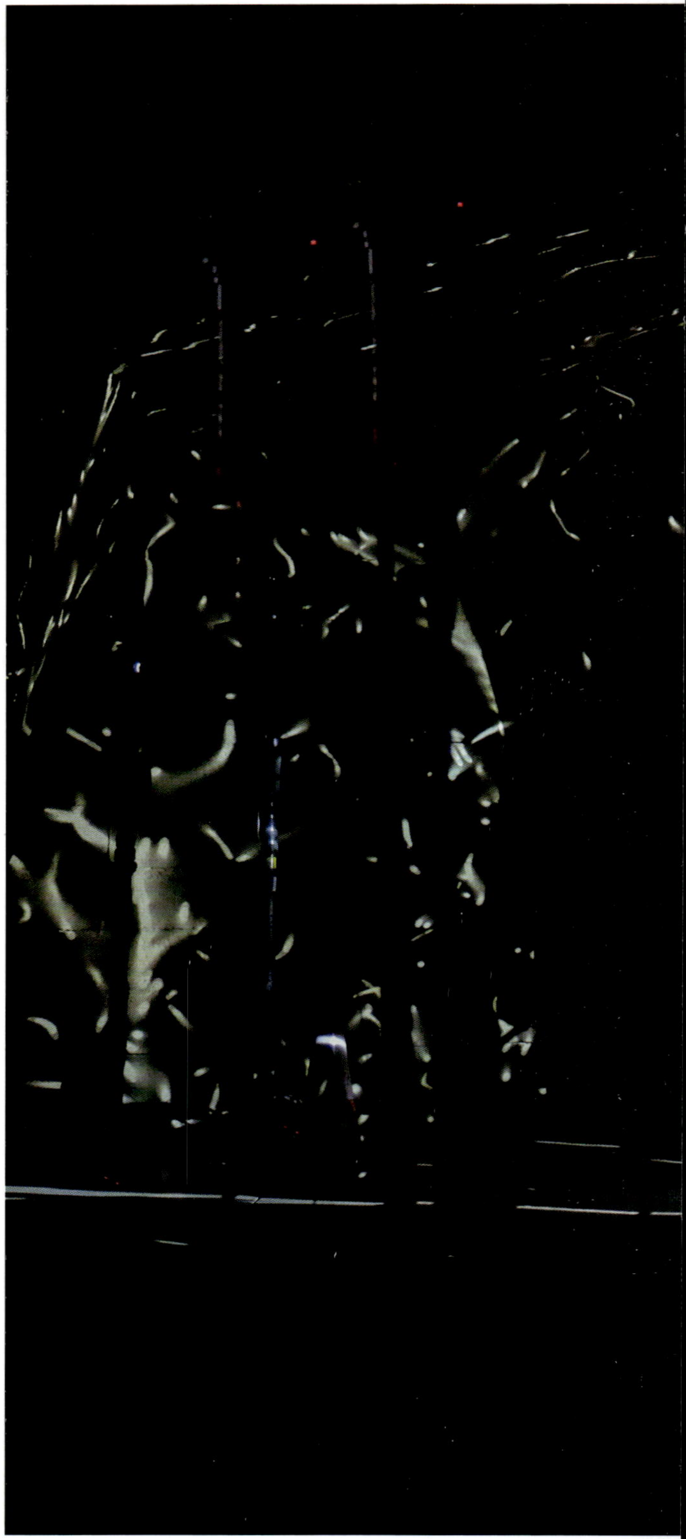

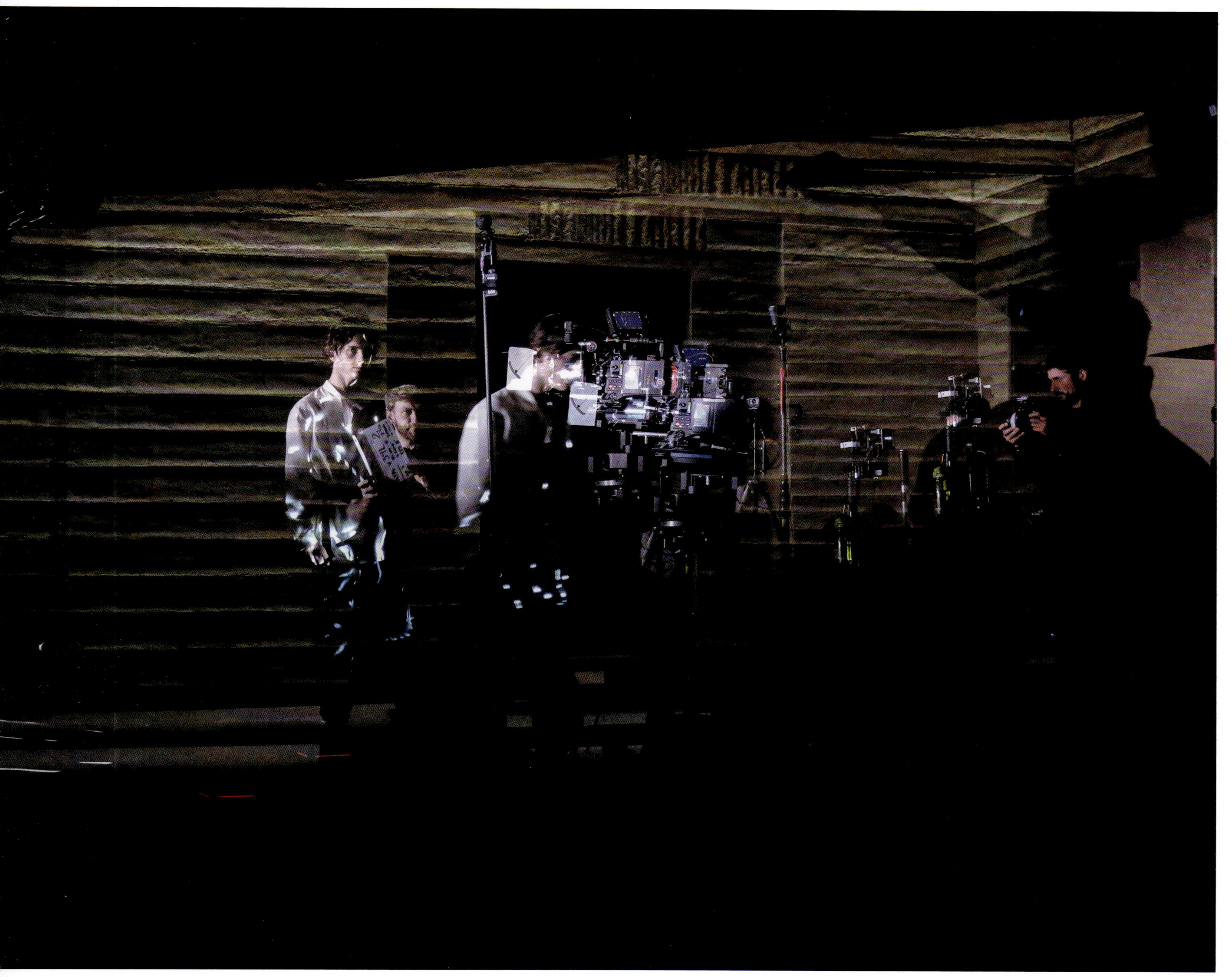

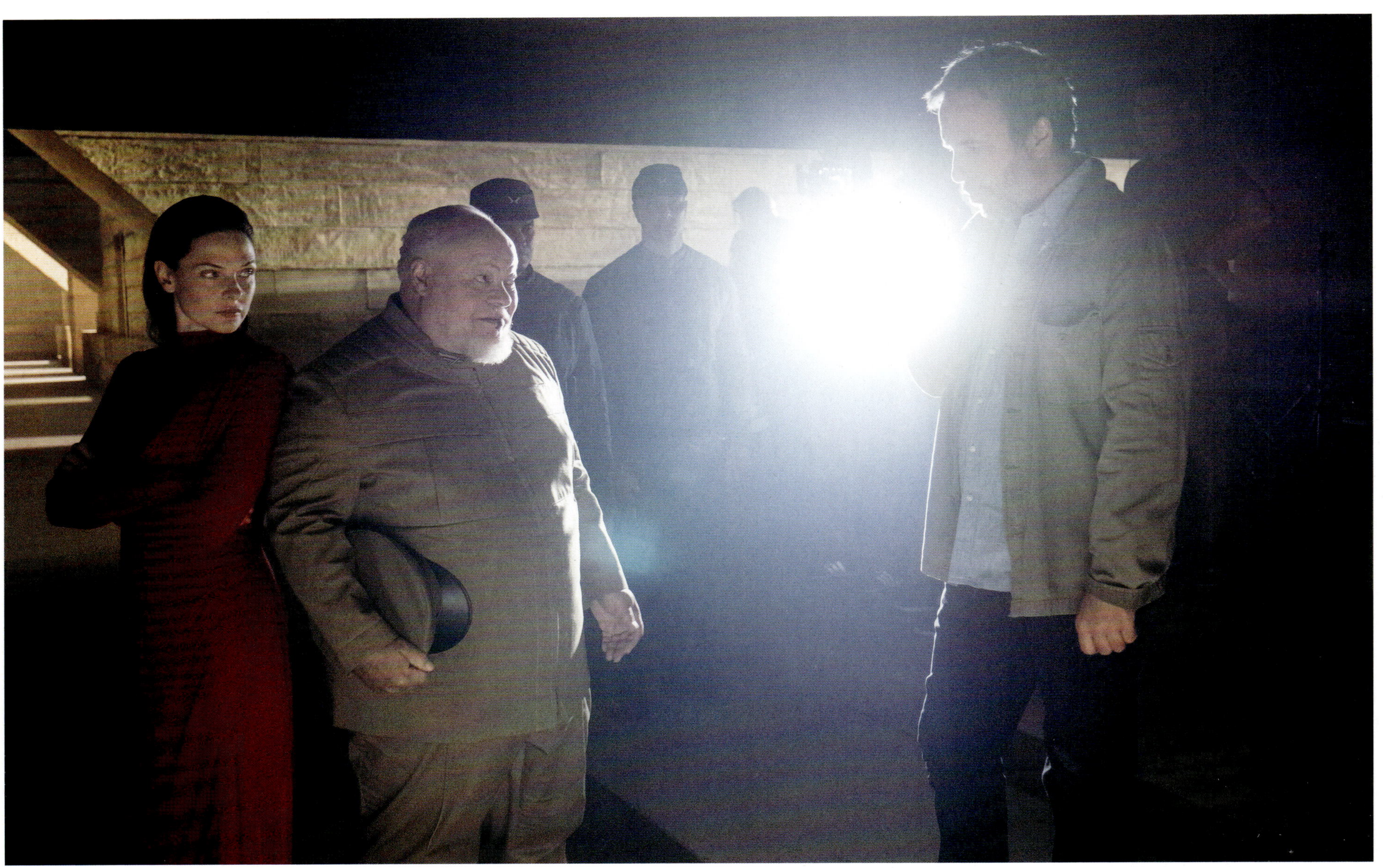

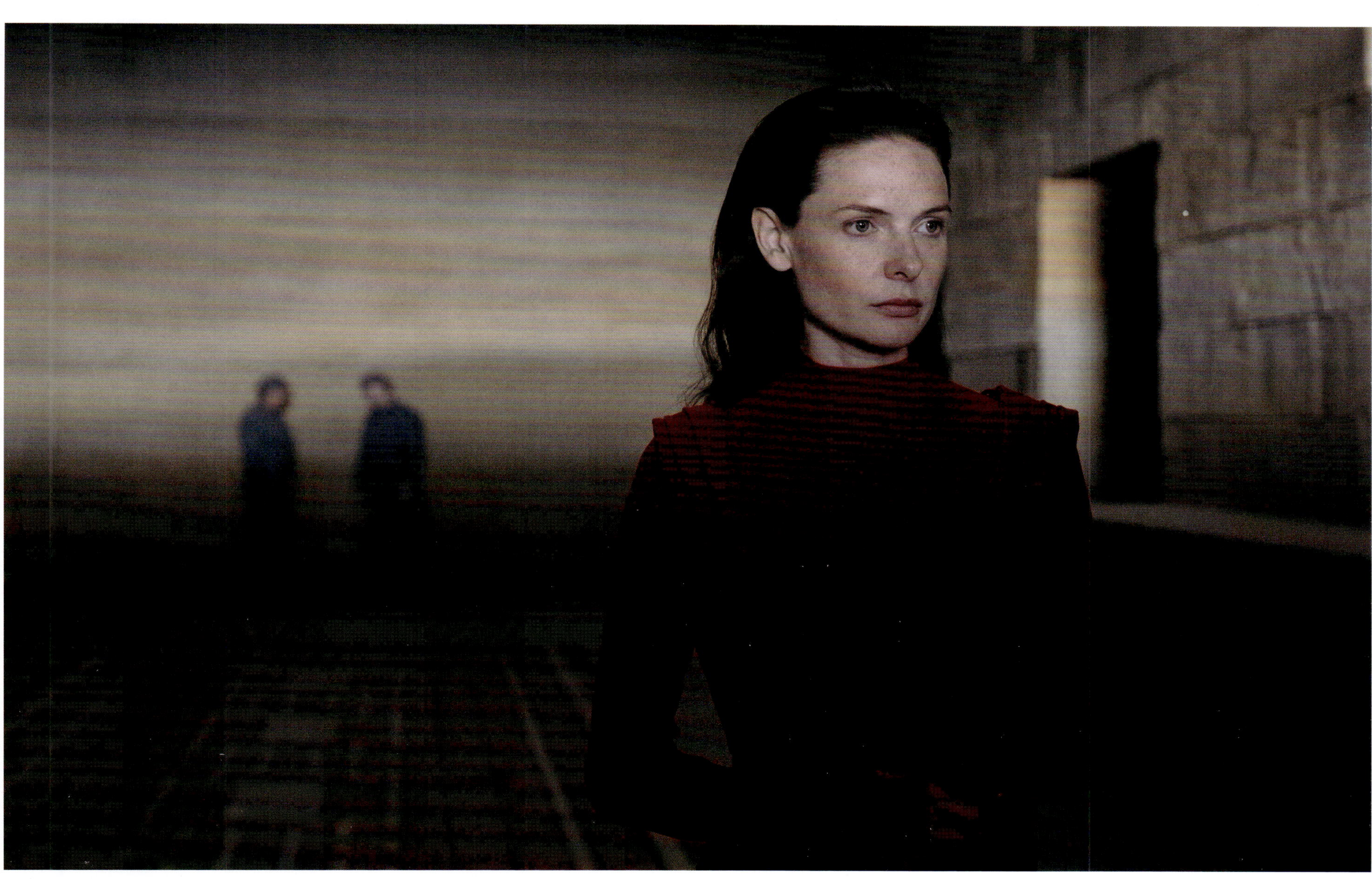

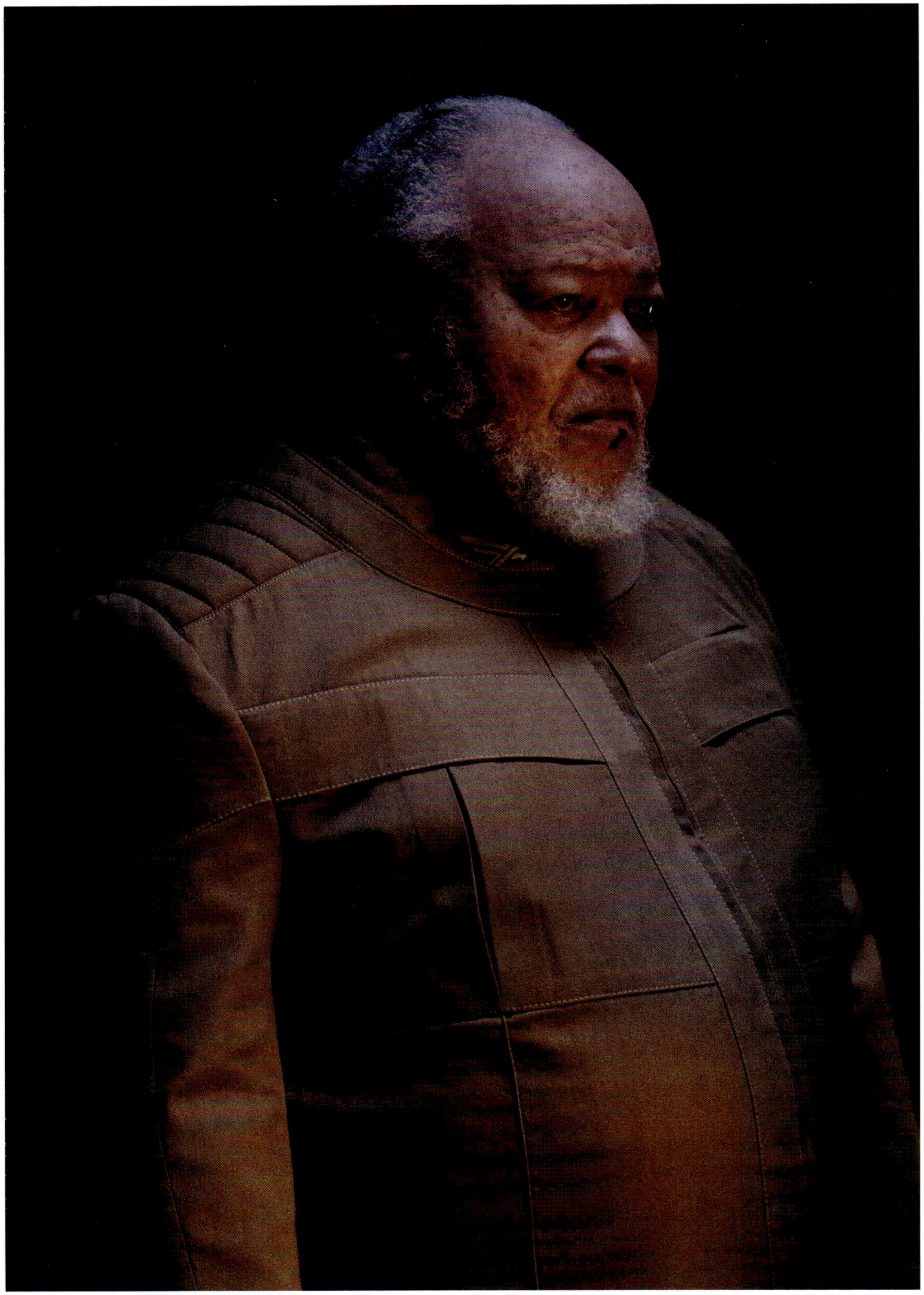

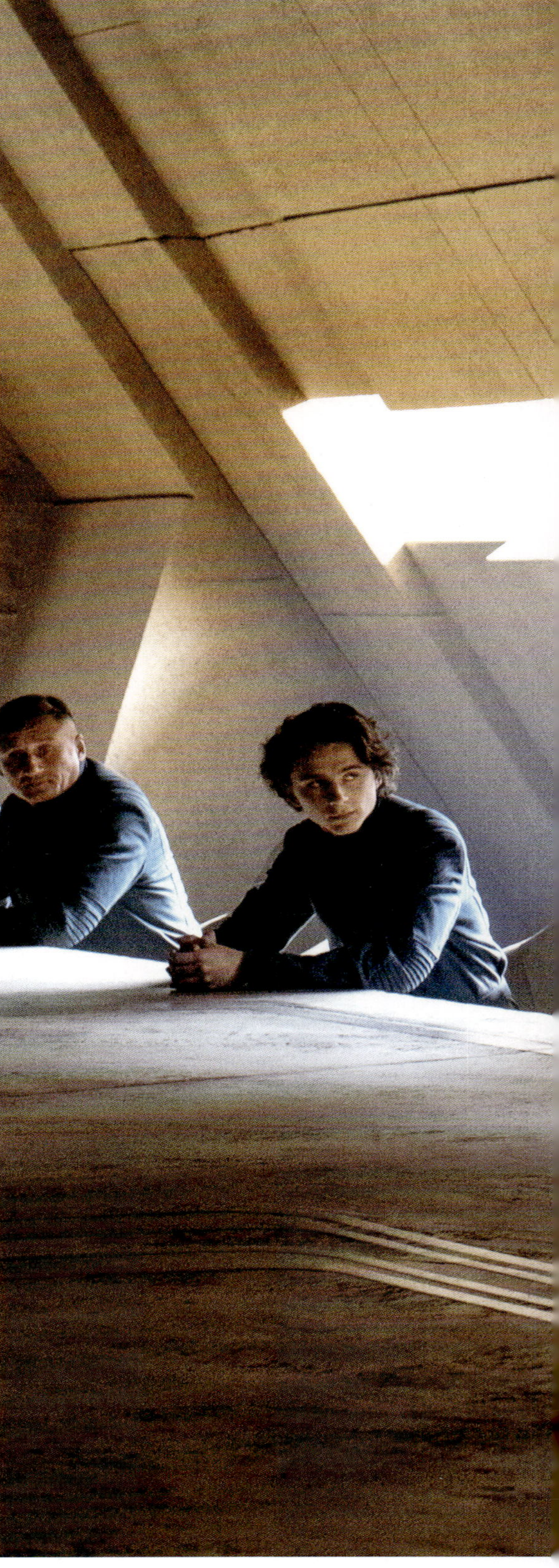

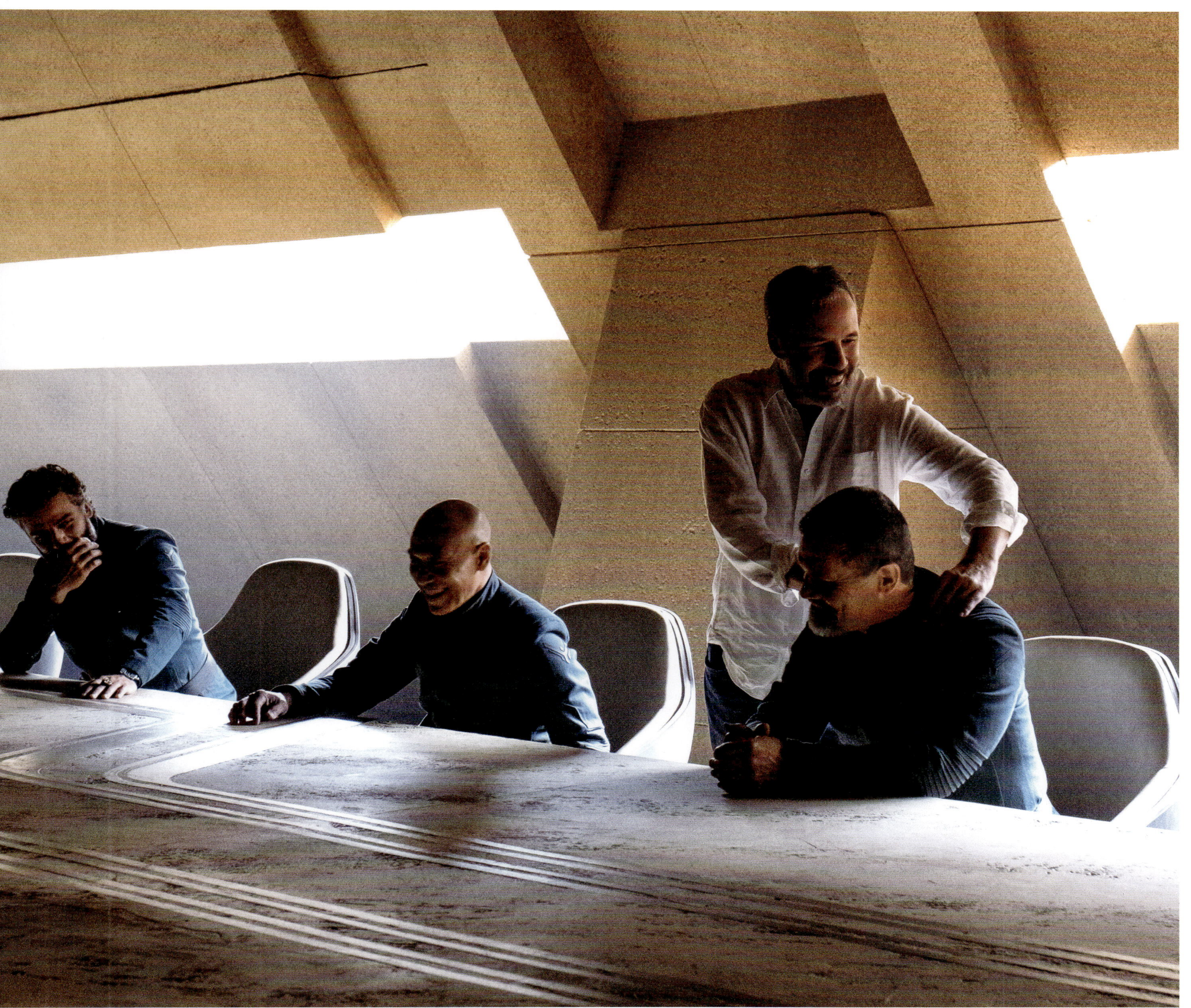

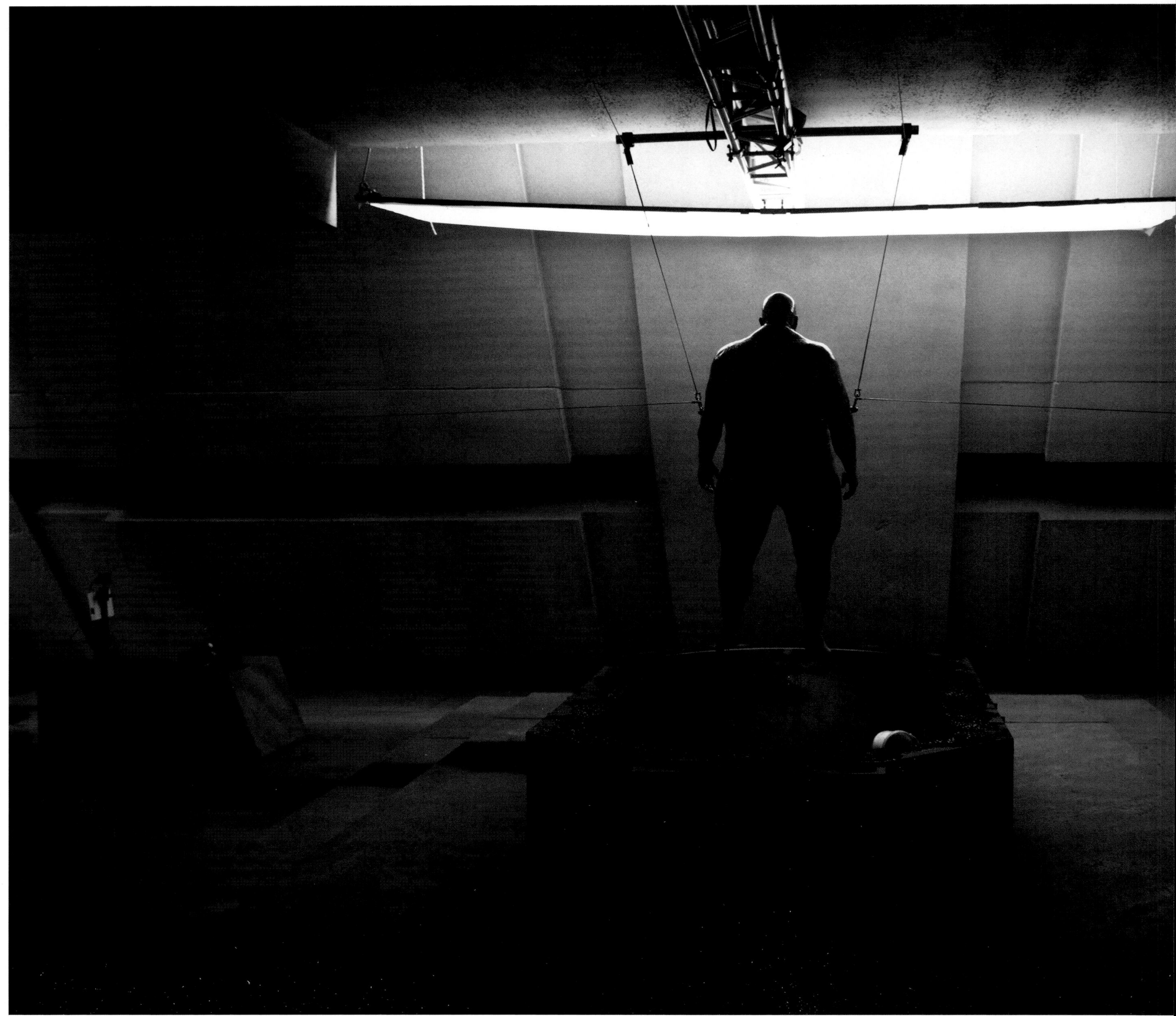

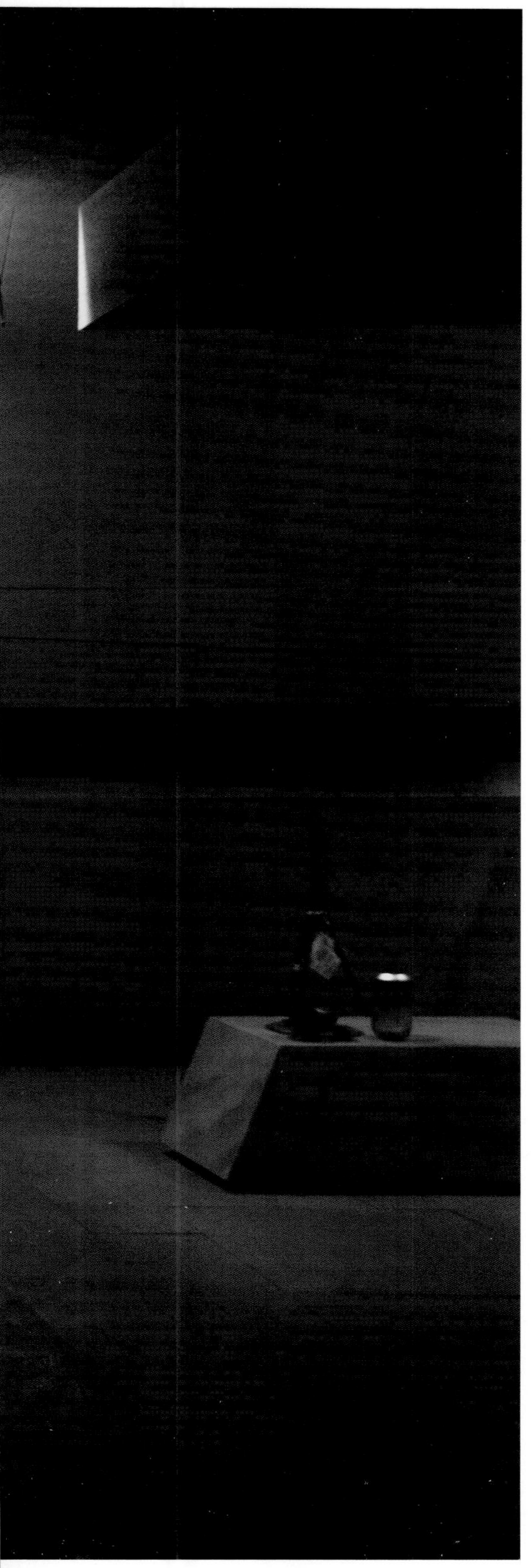

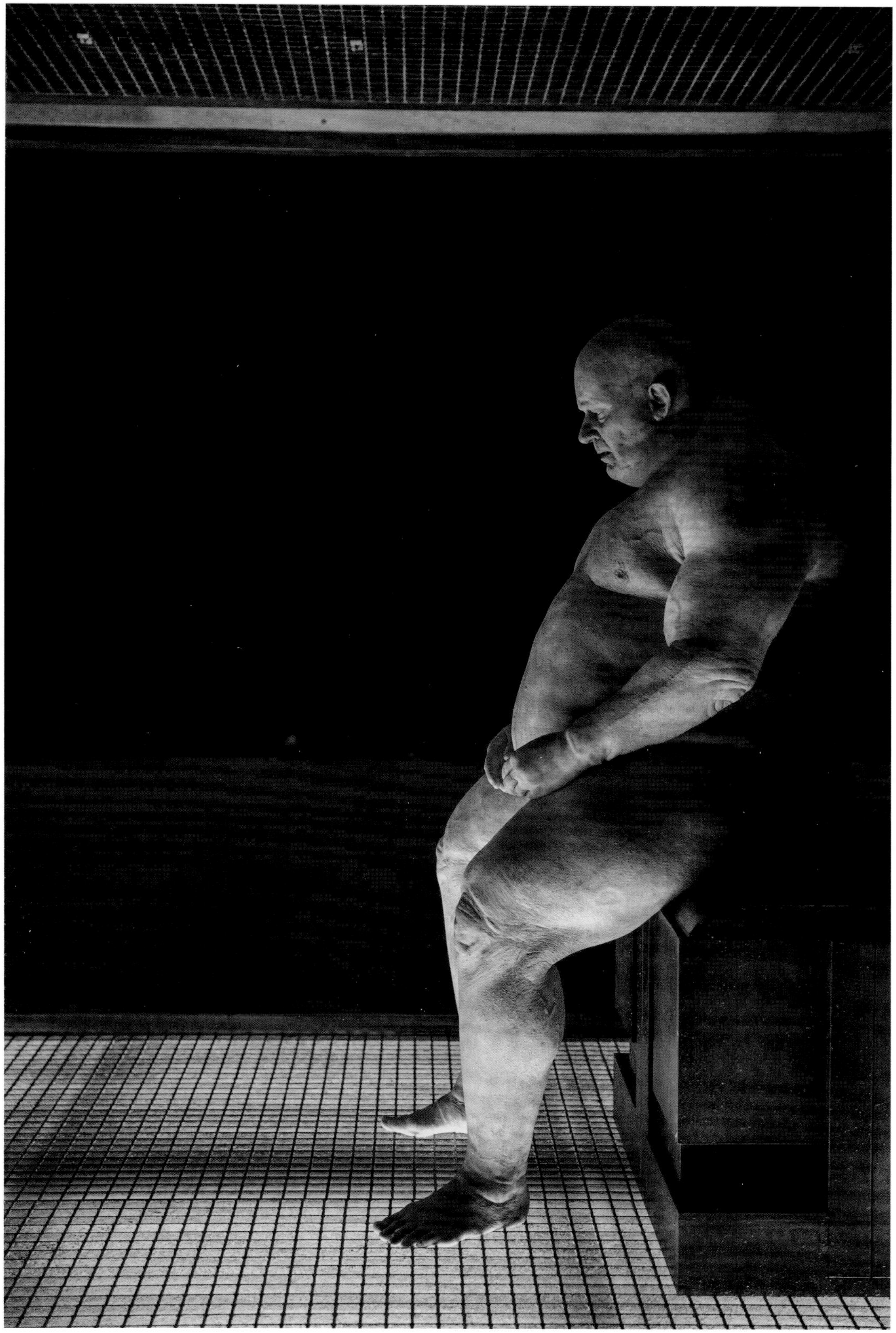

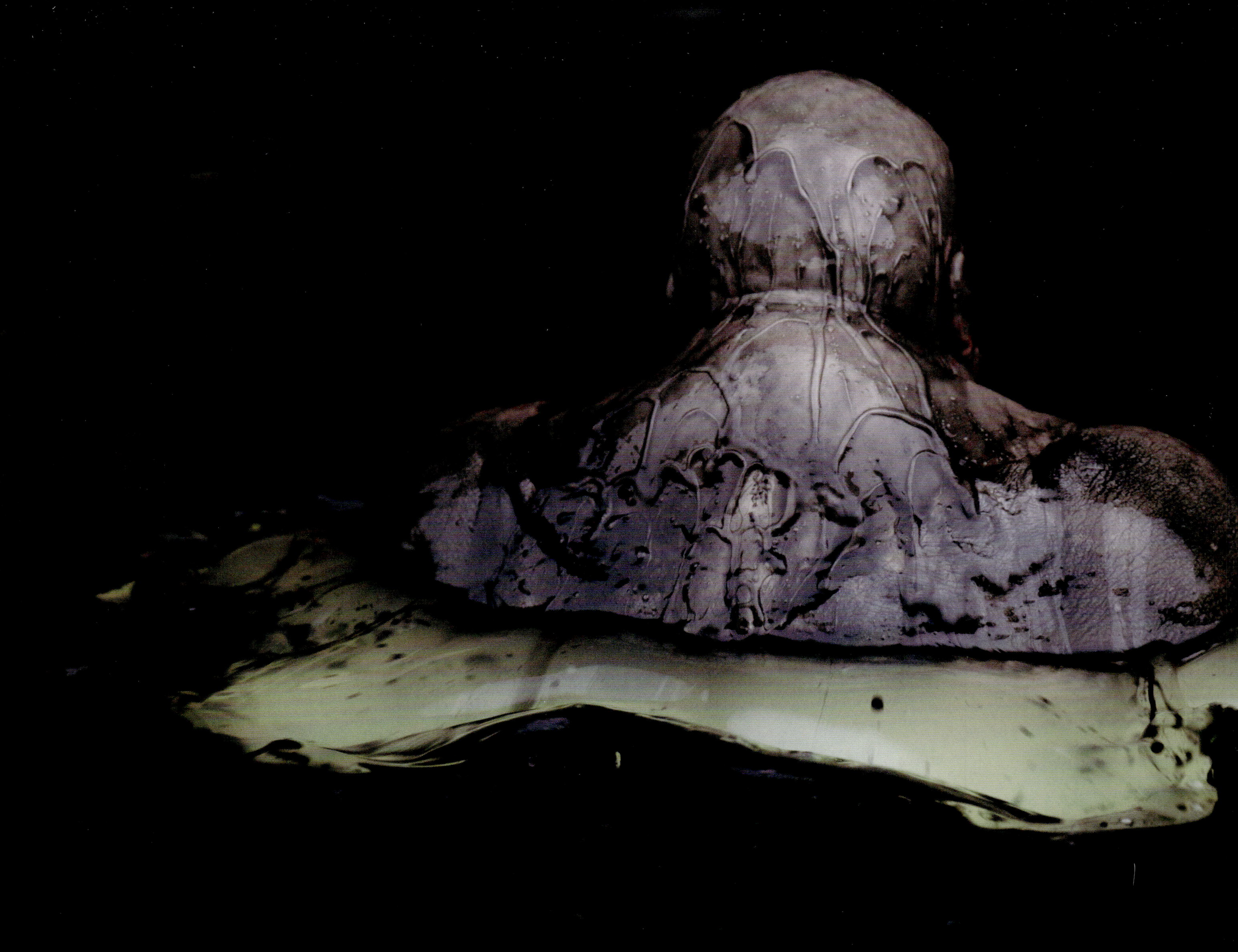

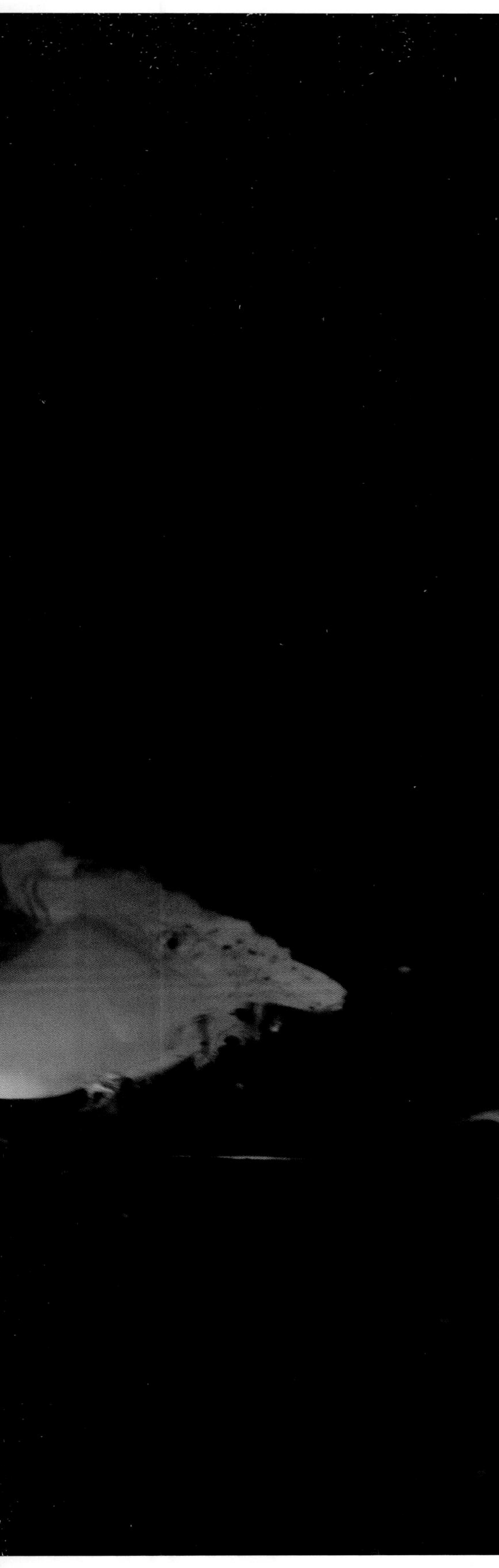

THE DAY-TO-DAY PROCESS OF making a film is effectively the same: Prep, light, set up, and shoot until the coverage is complete and meets the director's satisfaction. However, no day is ever really the same. Each set, character, and scene comes with a whole new array of discoveries and challenges. From one day to the next, the tone and environment can be at completely opposite ends of the spectrum, so the crew are usually ready for anything, but nothing could have prepared us for the Baron's arrival on set.

Stellan Skarsgård, hidden in a convincingly hideous disguise, shimmied onto the set with a leash-like tube between his legs attached to a cooling machine that kept him from overheating inside the intricate and incredibly realistic full-body prosthetics. With heartfelt laughter, dancing, and playful banter between takes, he kept us connected to the man behind the character. As he sank into the Baron's greasy bath, we watched the prosthetics team put their final touches on the suit and the special effects technicians pour more black oil (a concoction of beeswax and vegetable oil) into the tub around him. With a final nod of approval from Denis, the cameras rolled, and for the length of each take, we witnessed Stellan disappear as the Baron came to life.

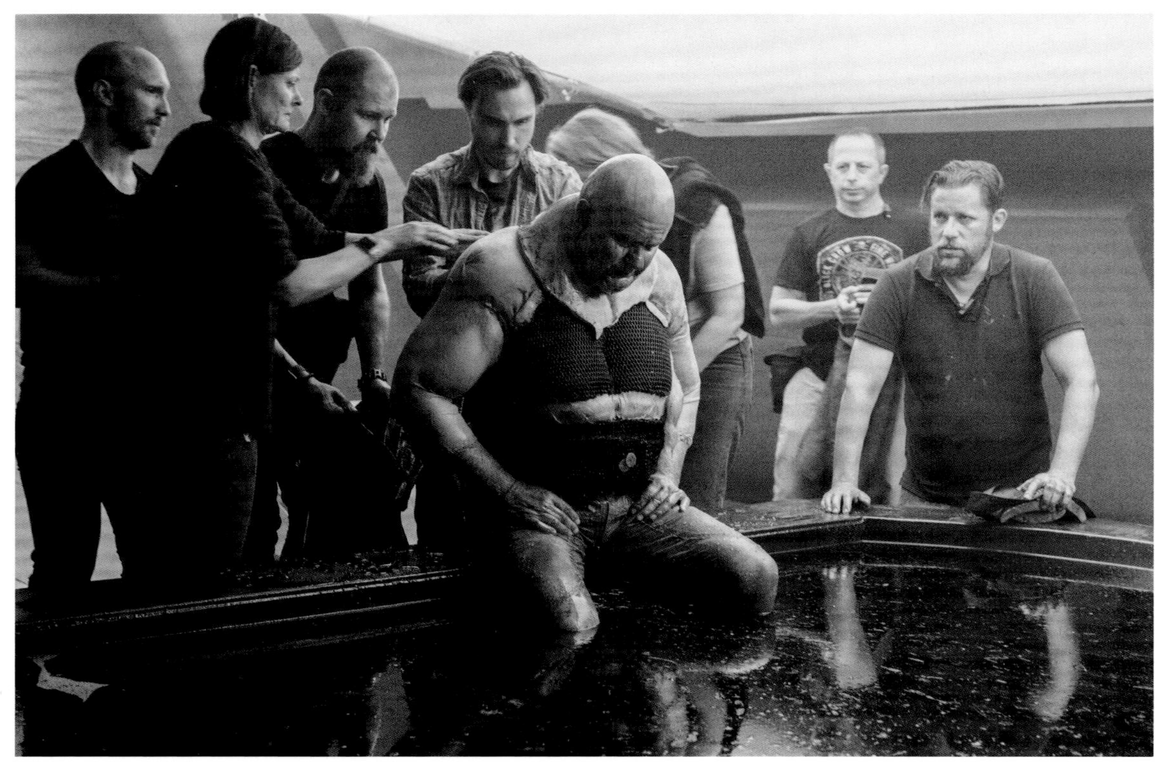

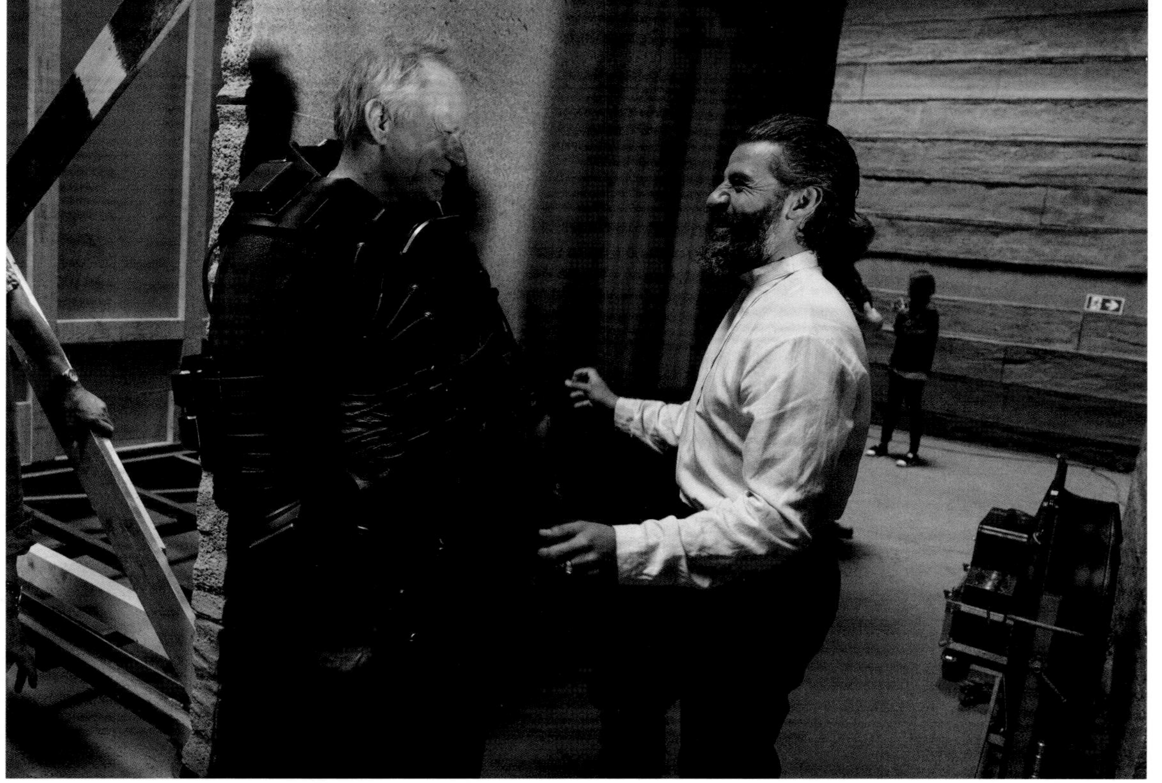

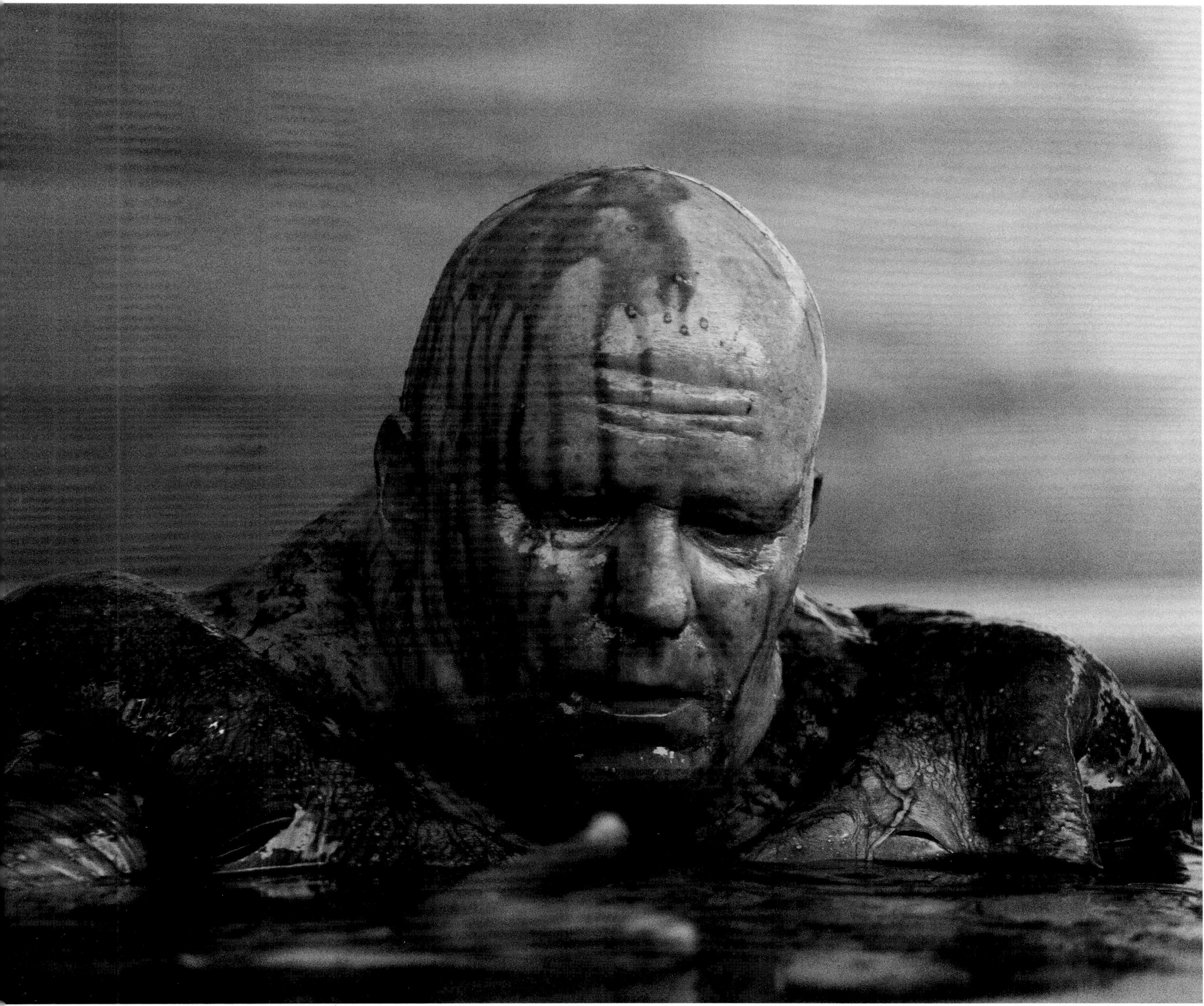

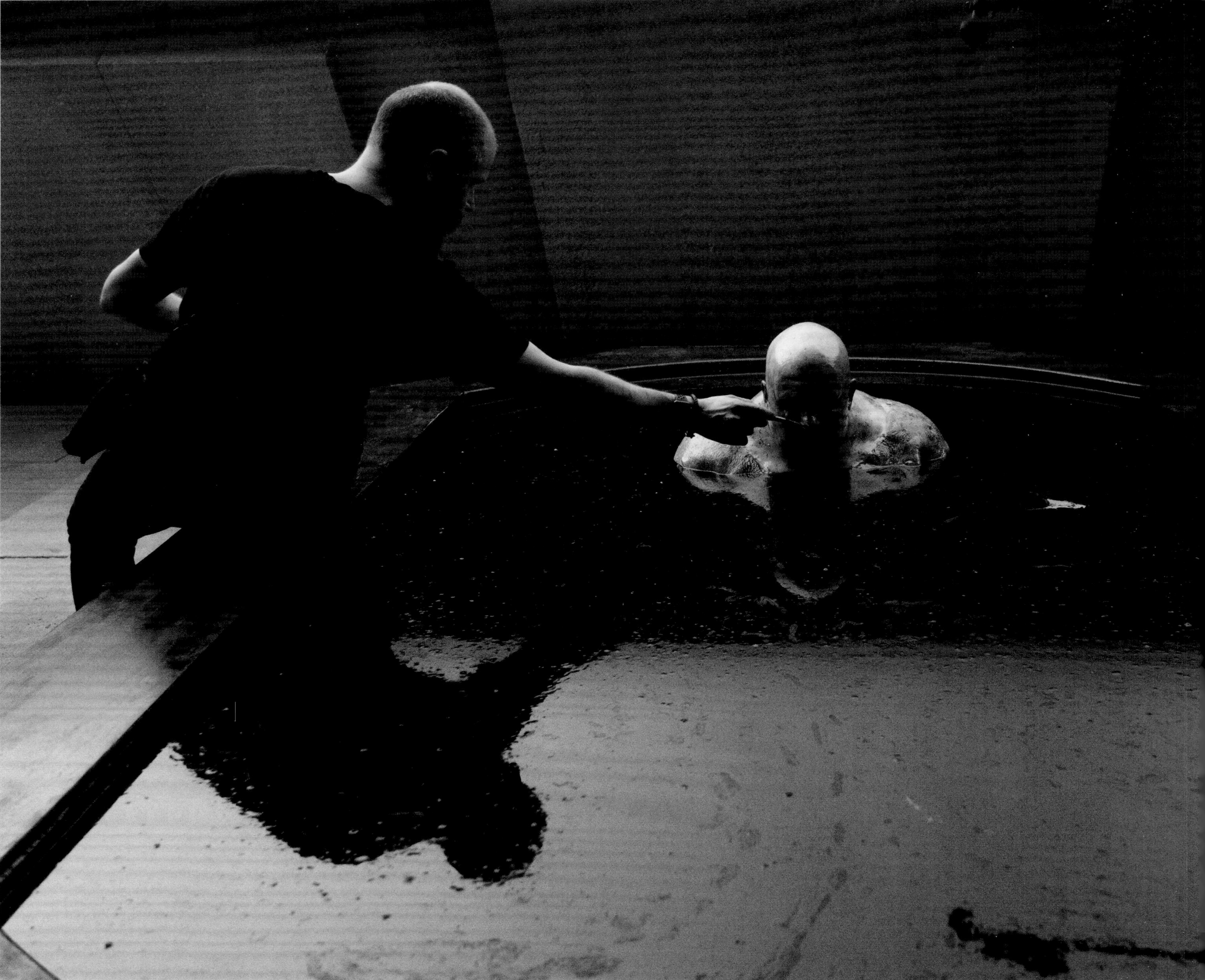

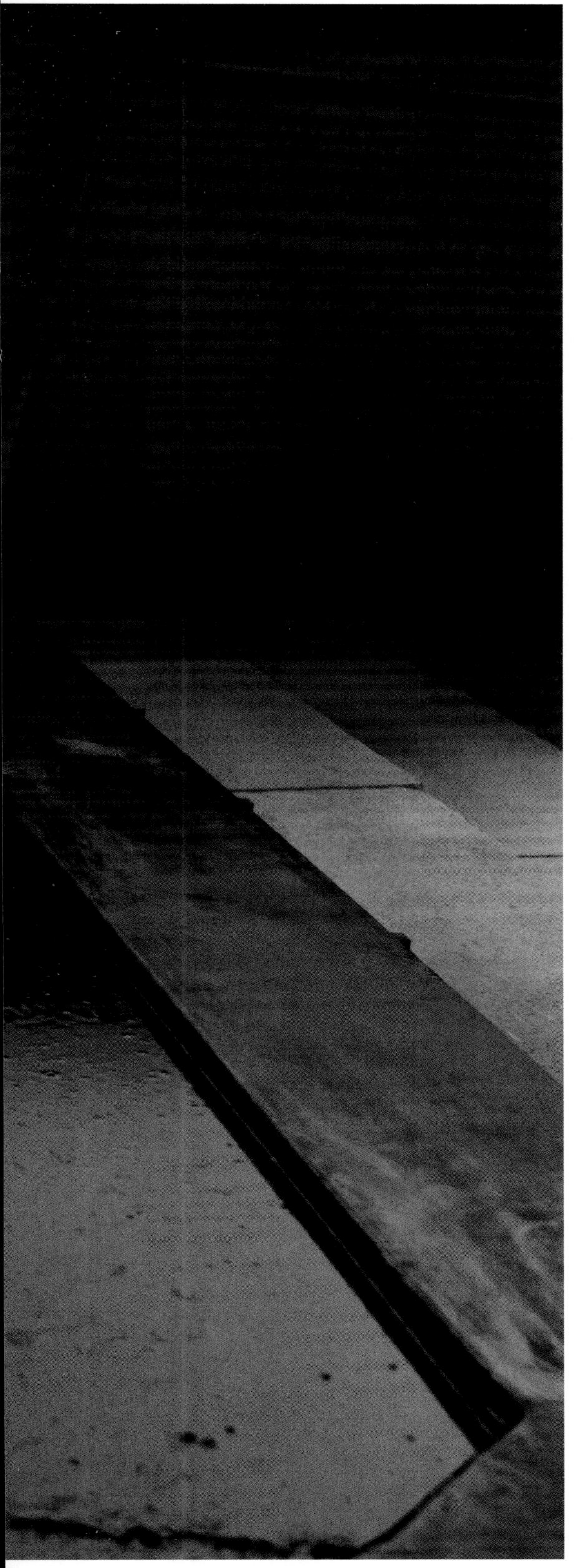

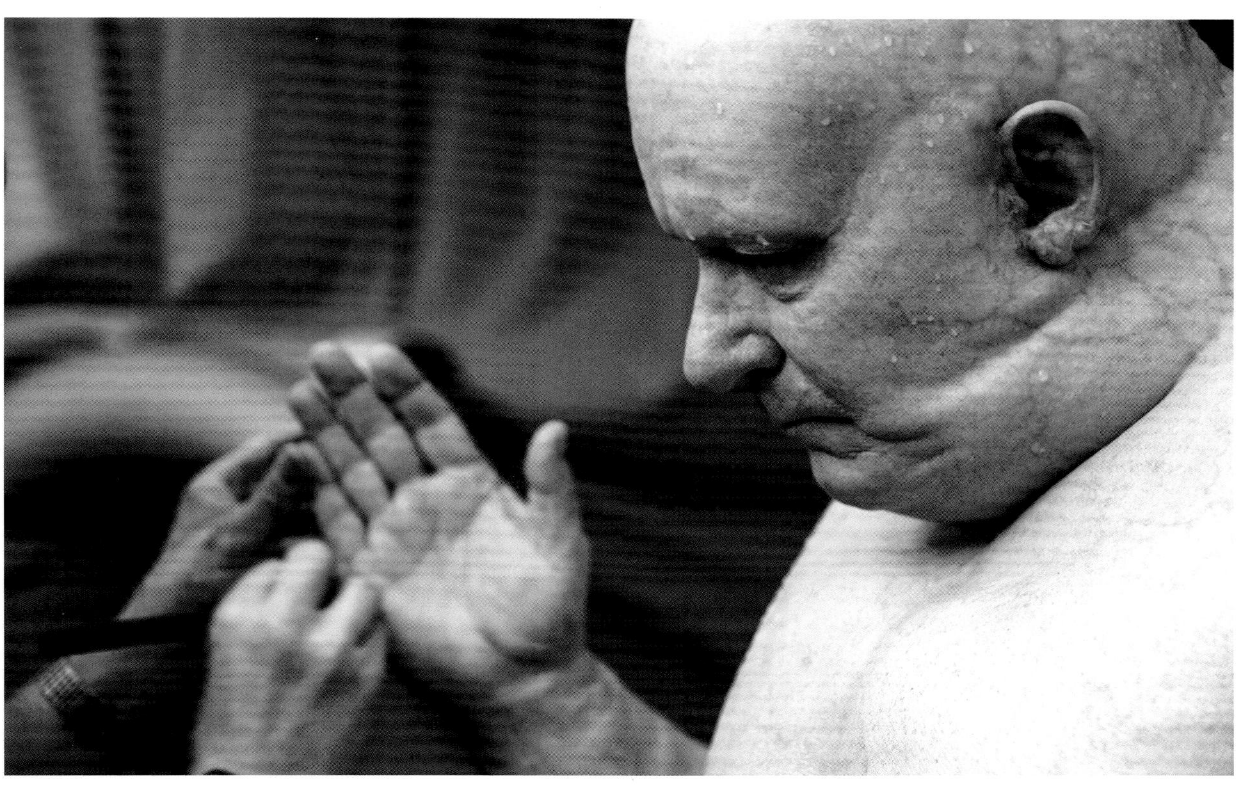

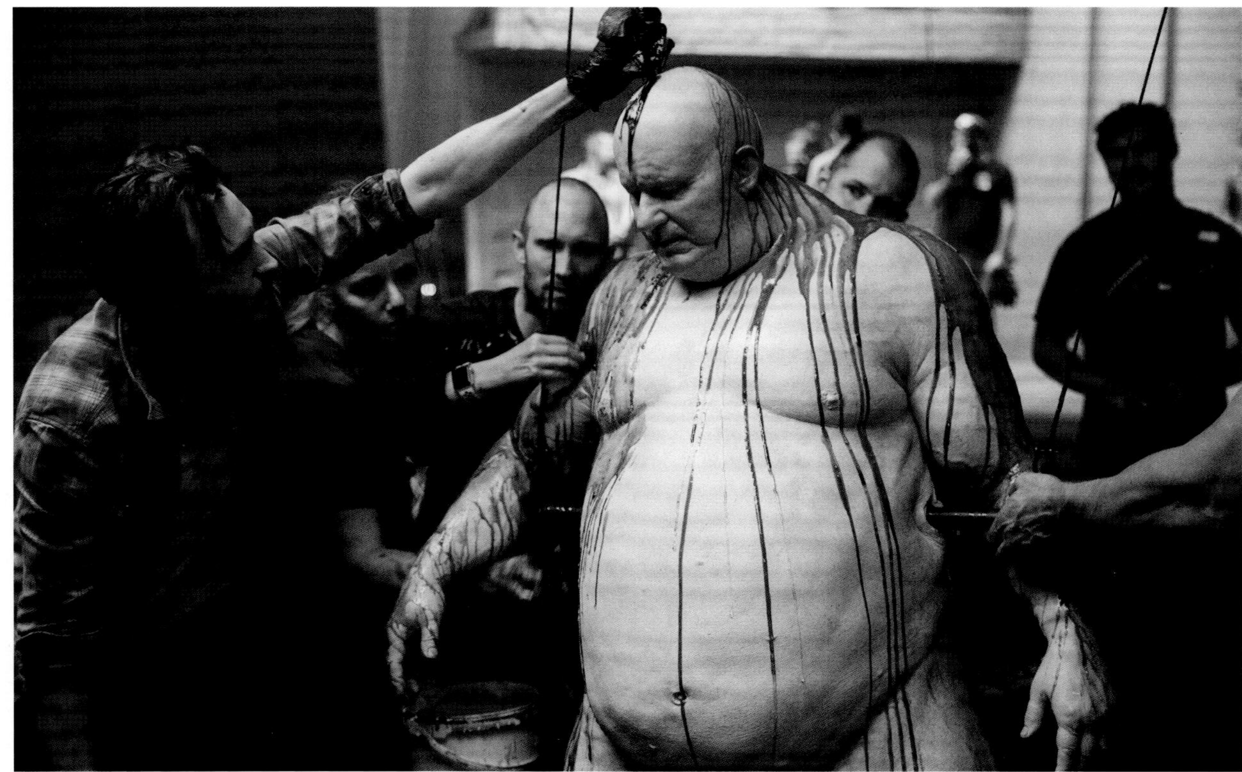

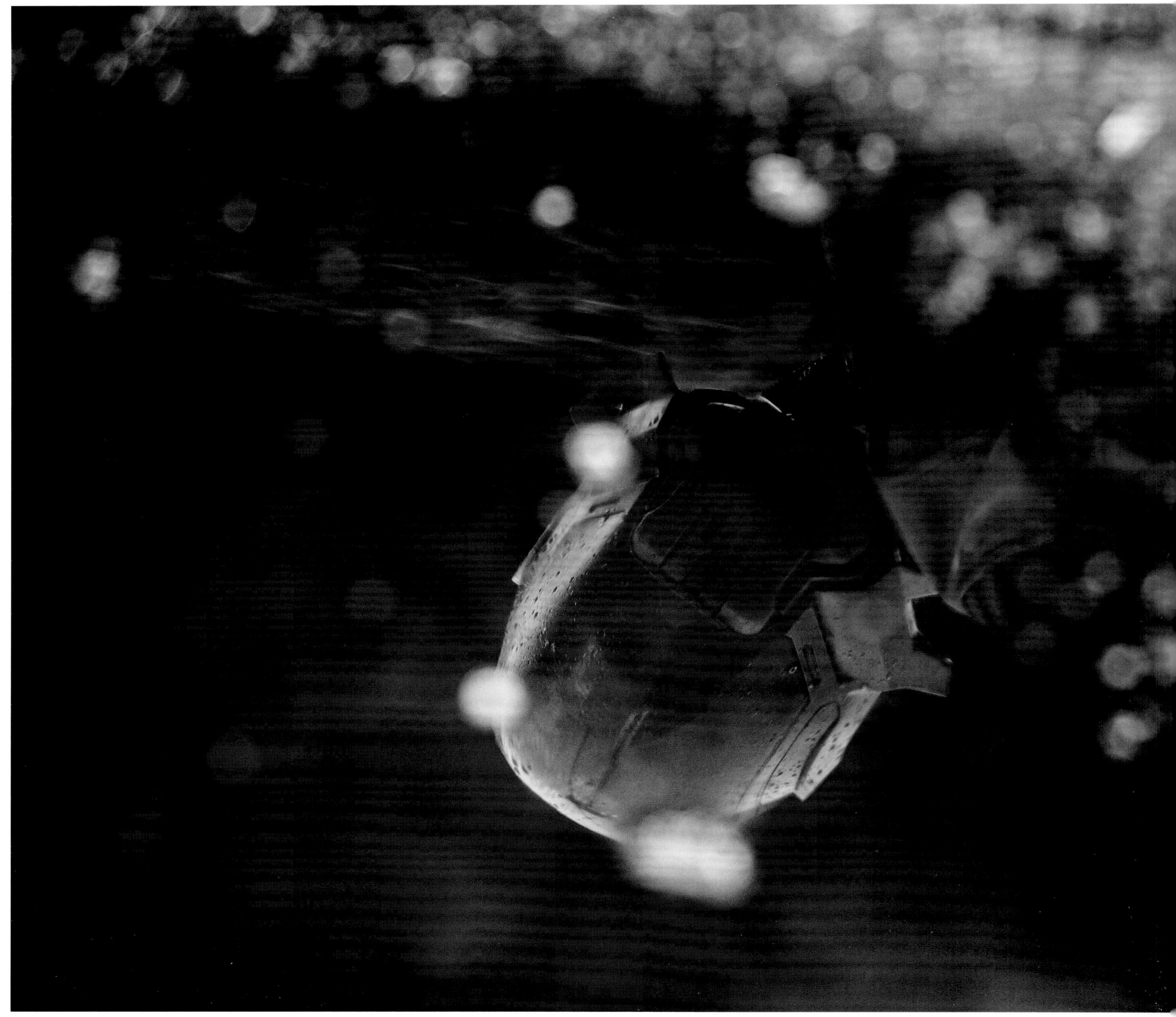

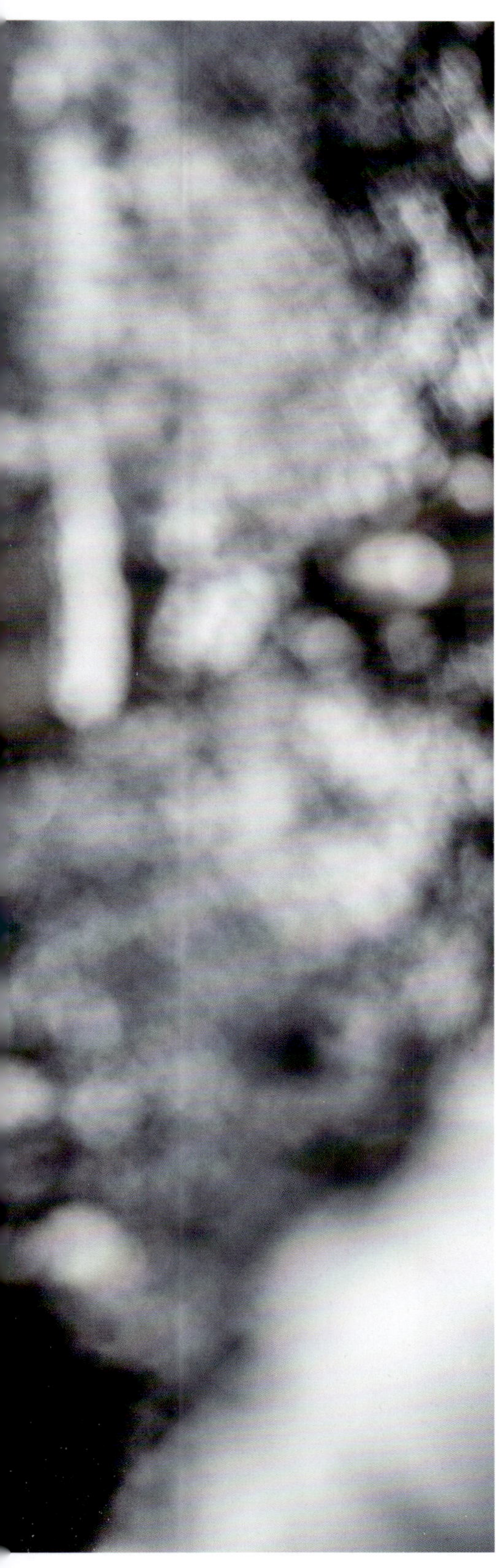

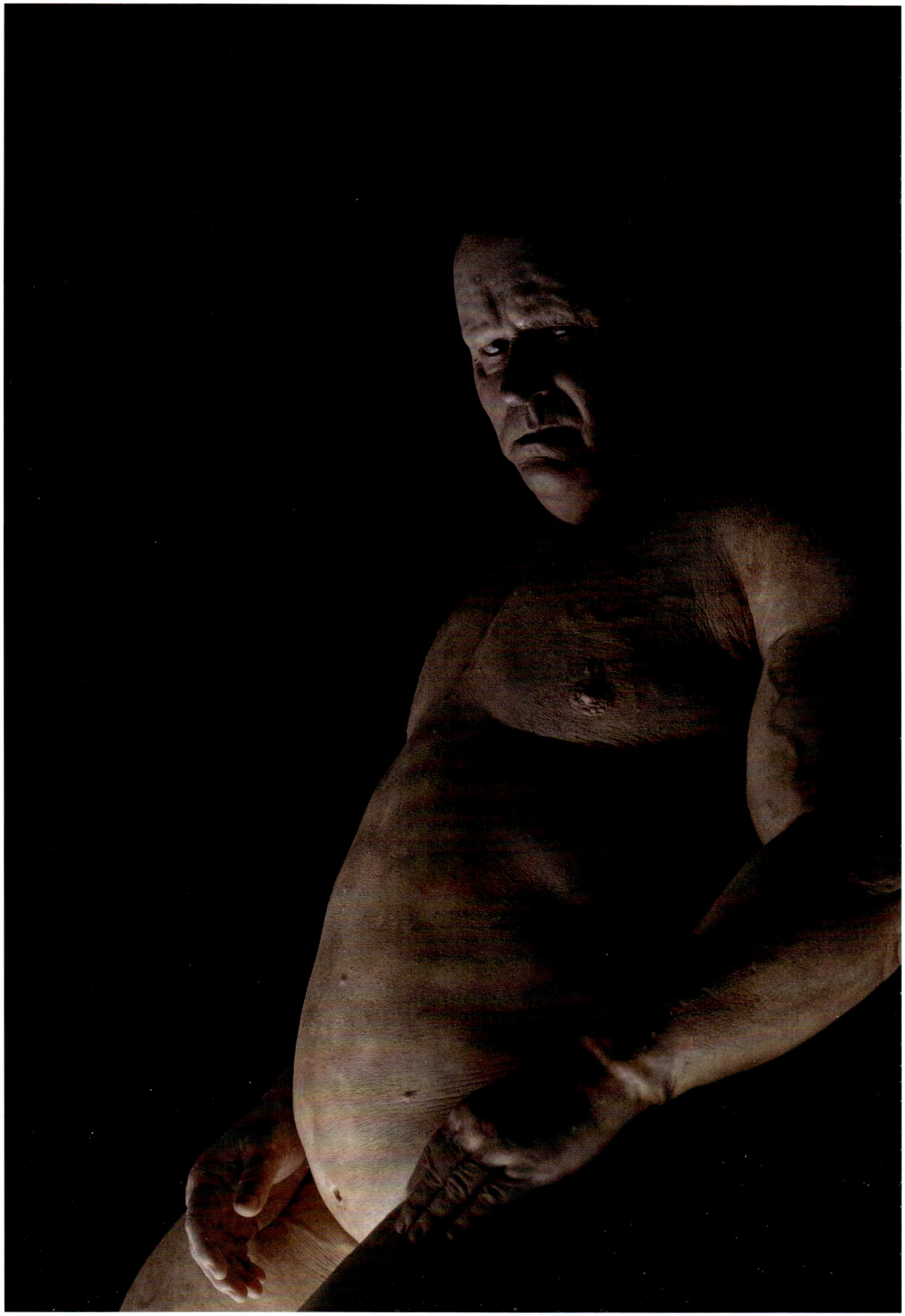

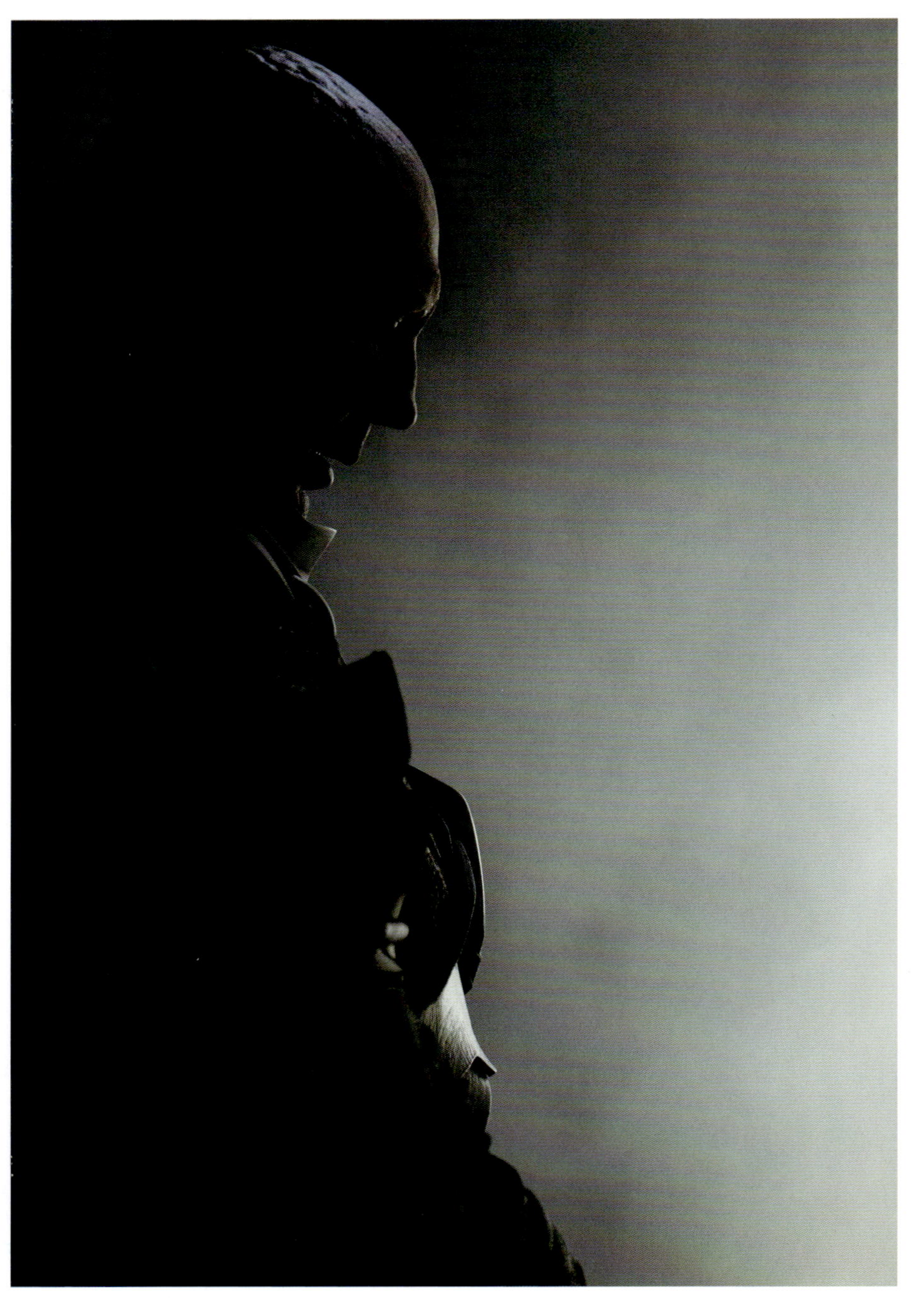
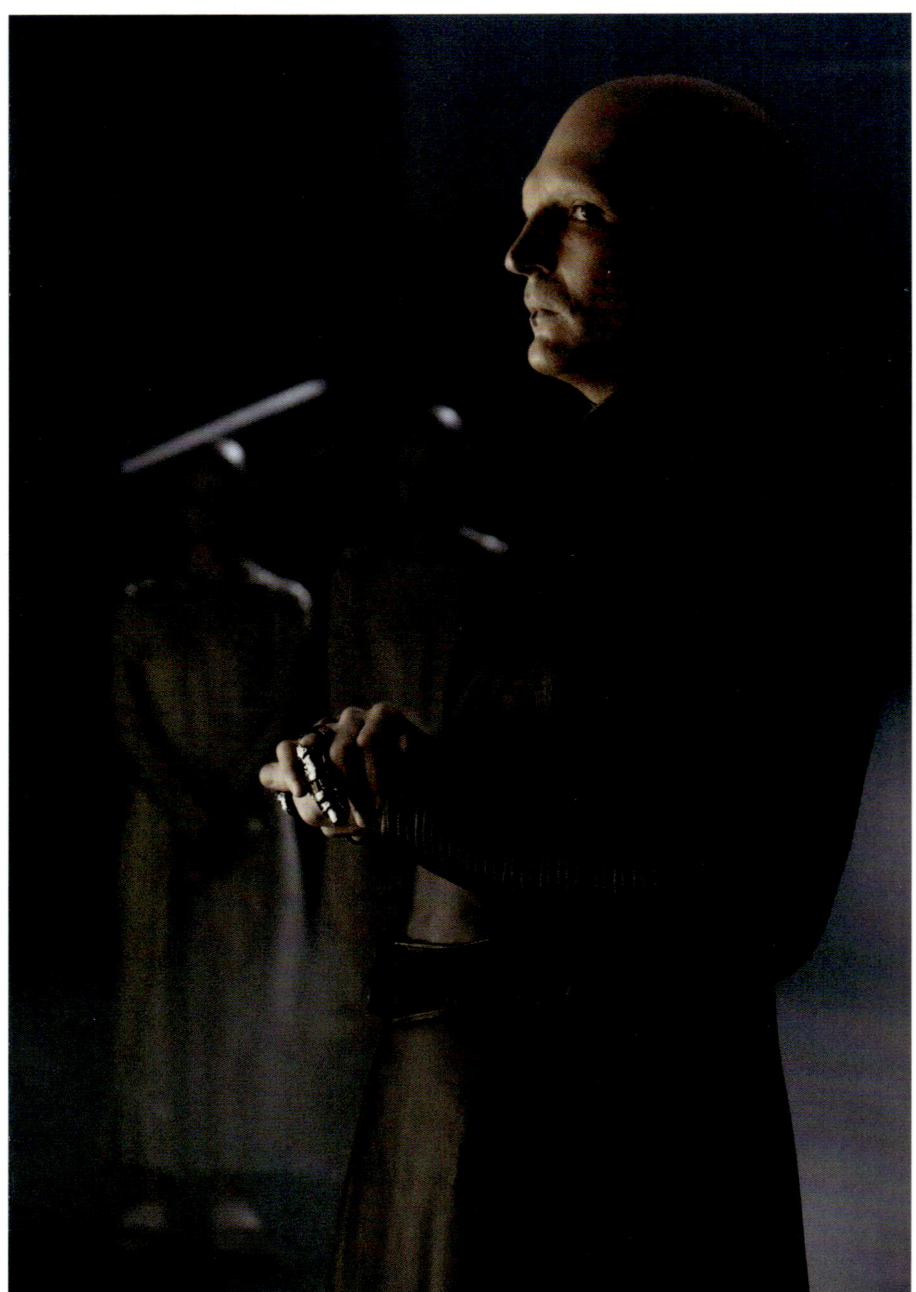

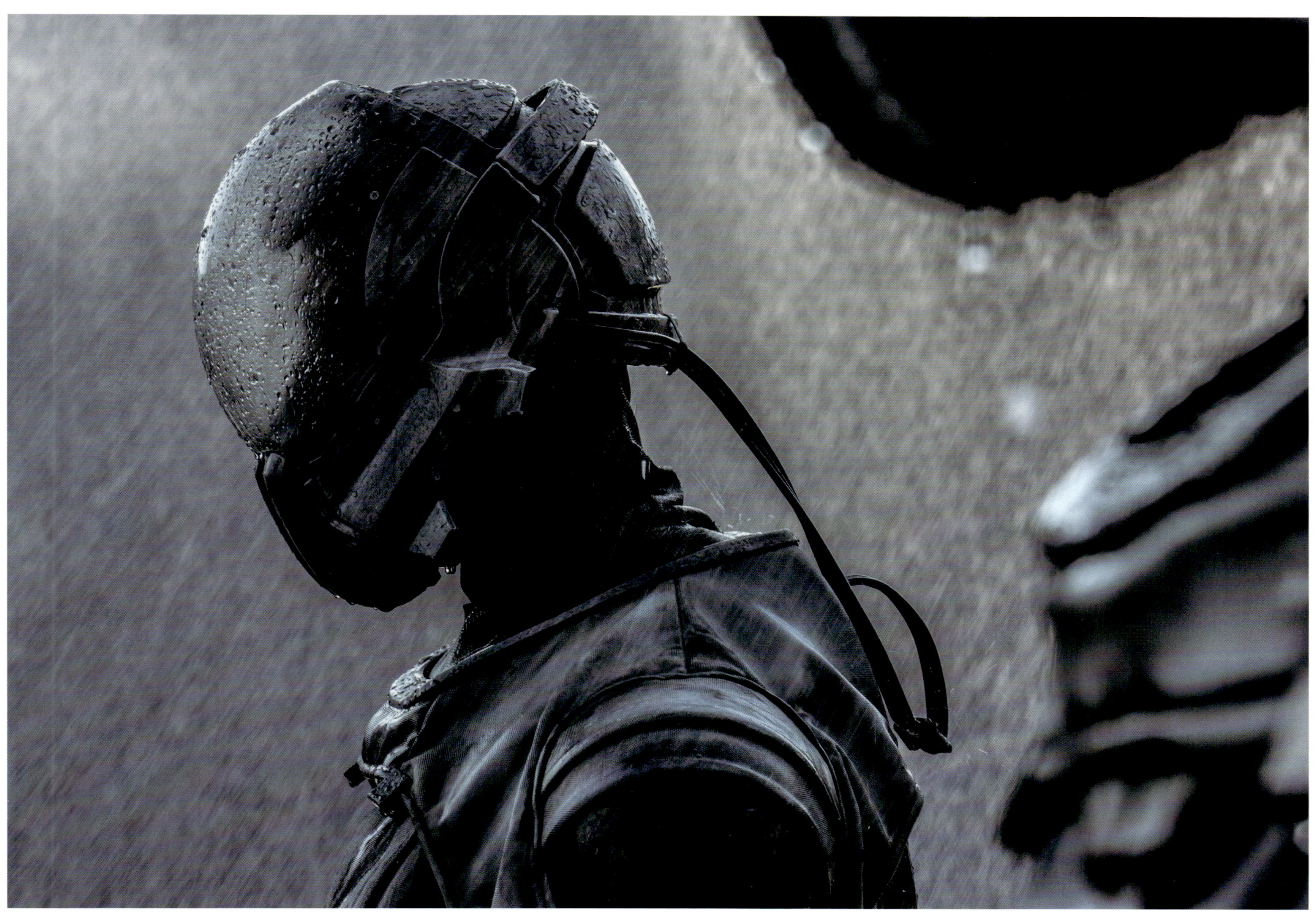

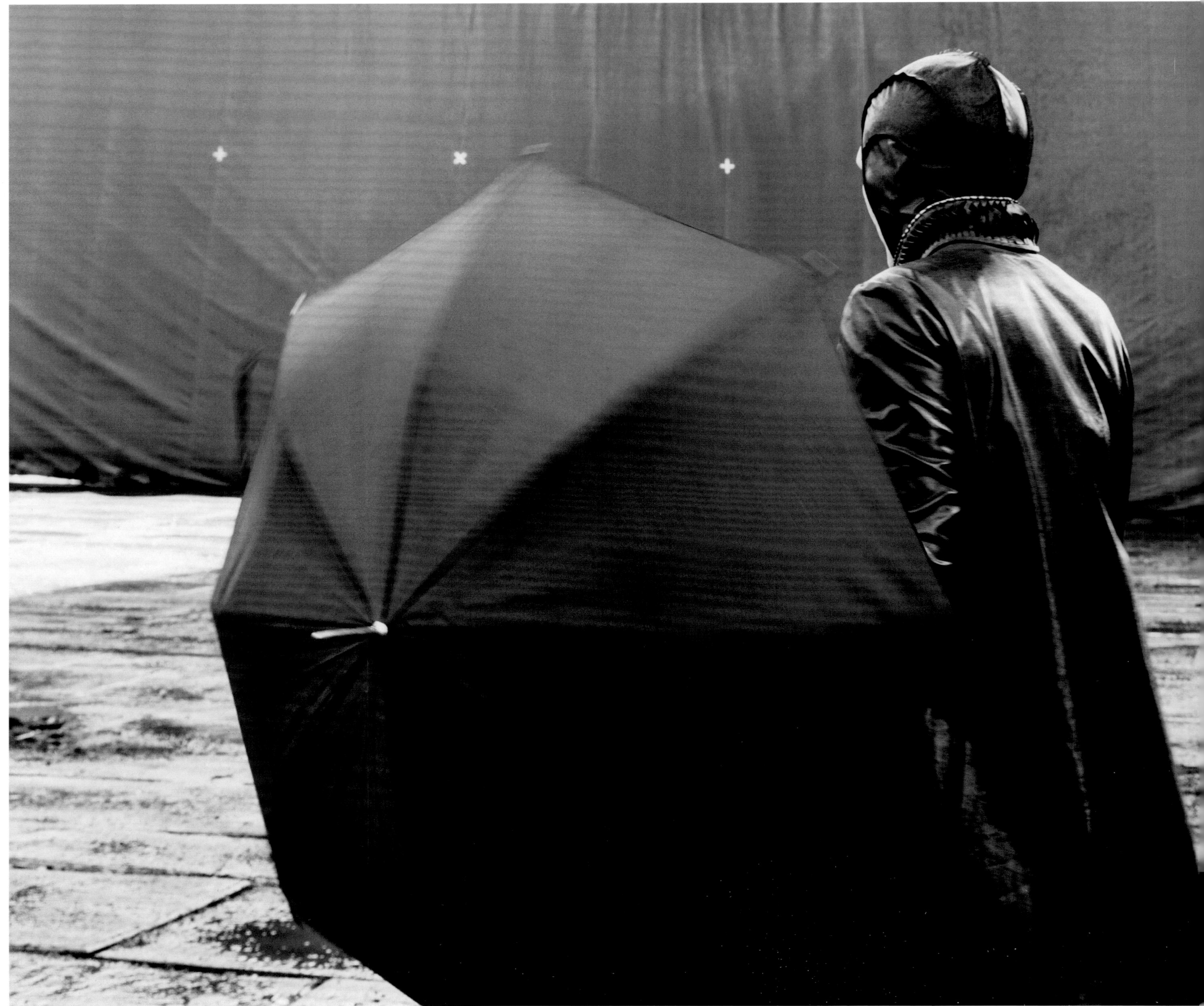

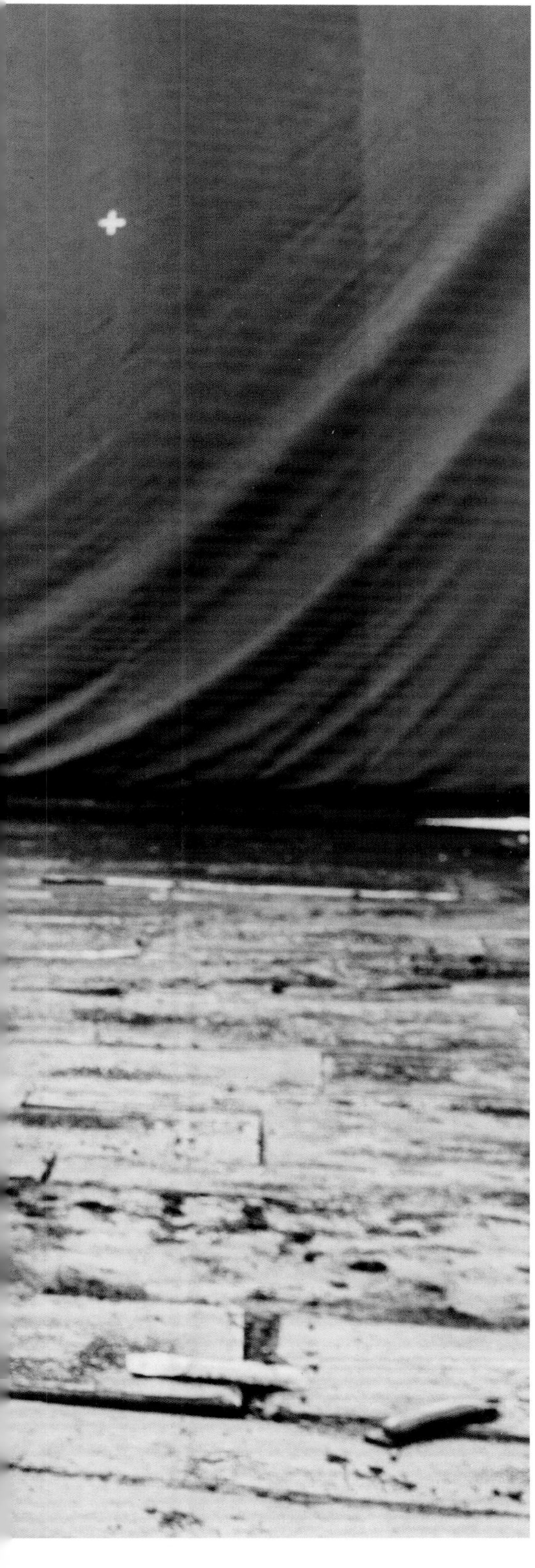

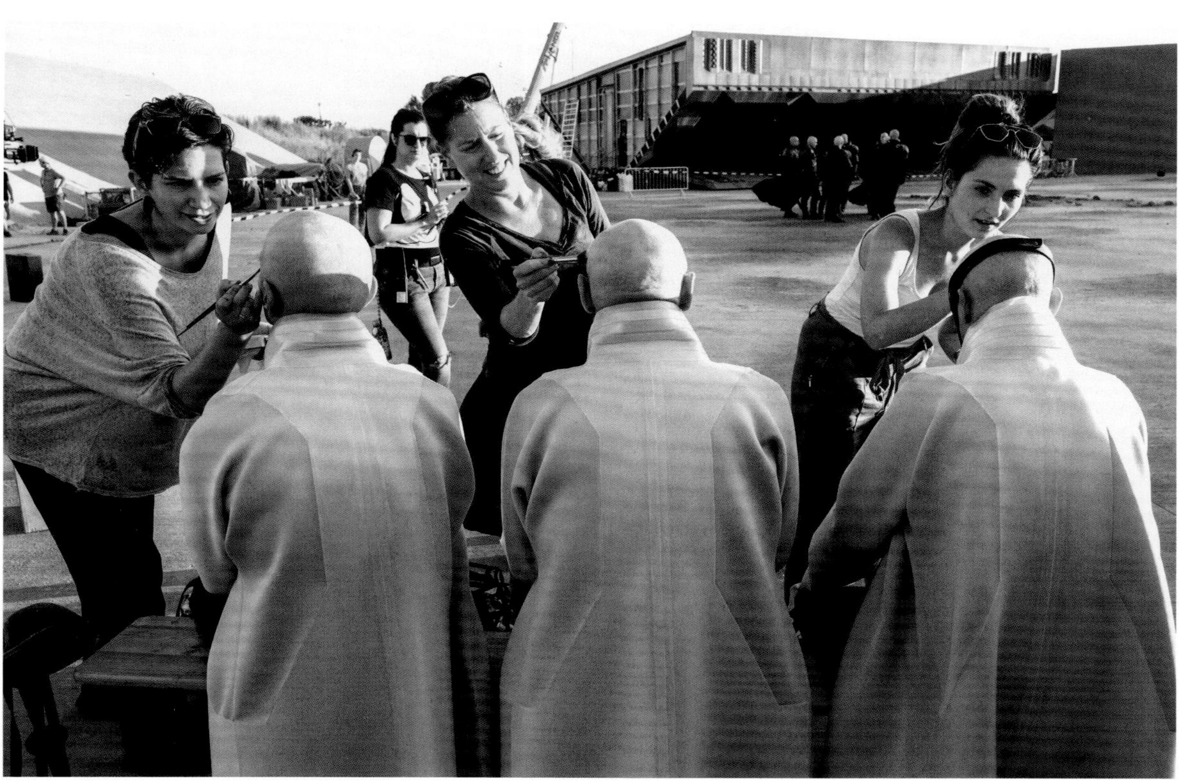

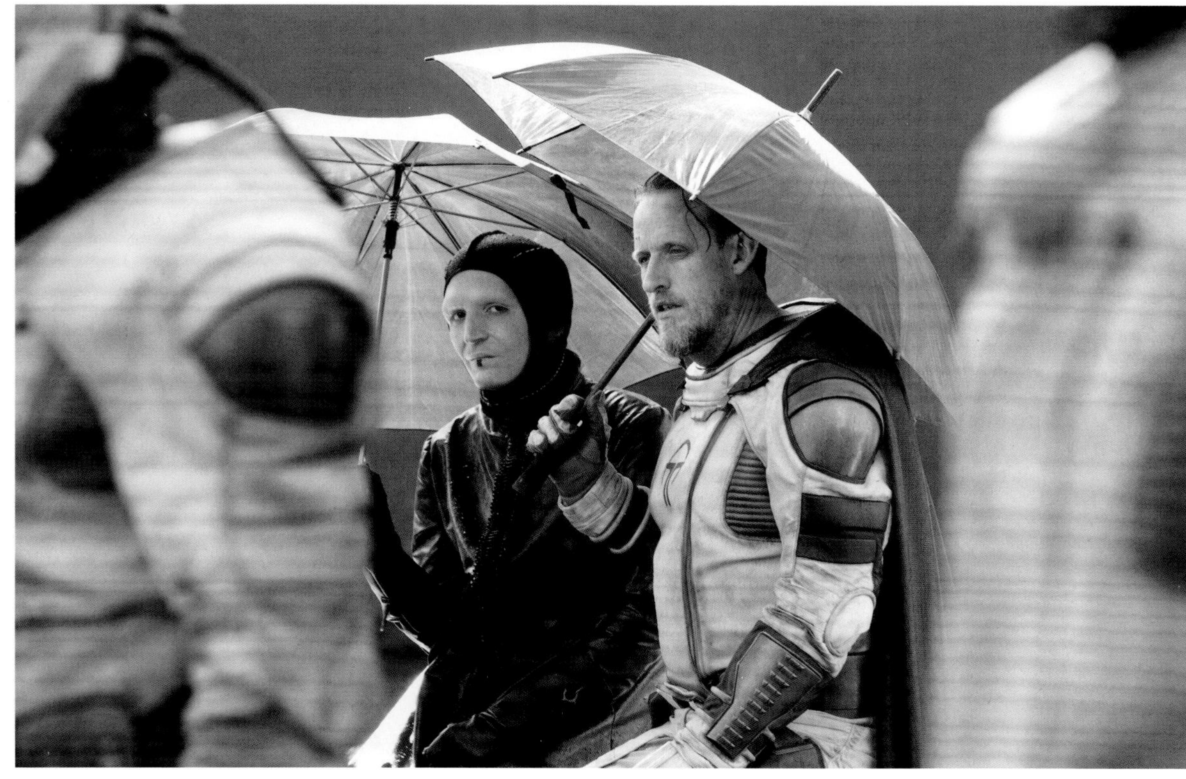

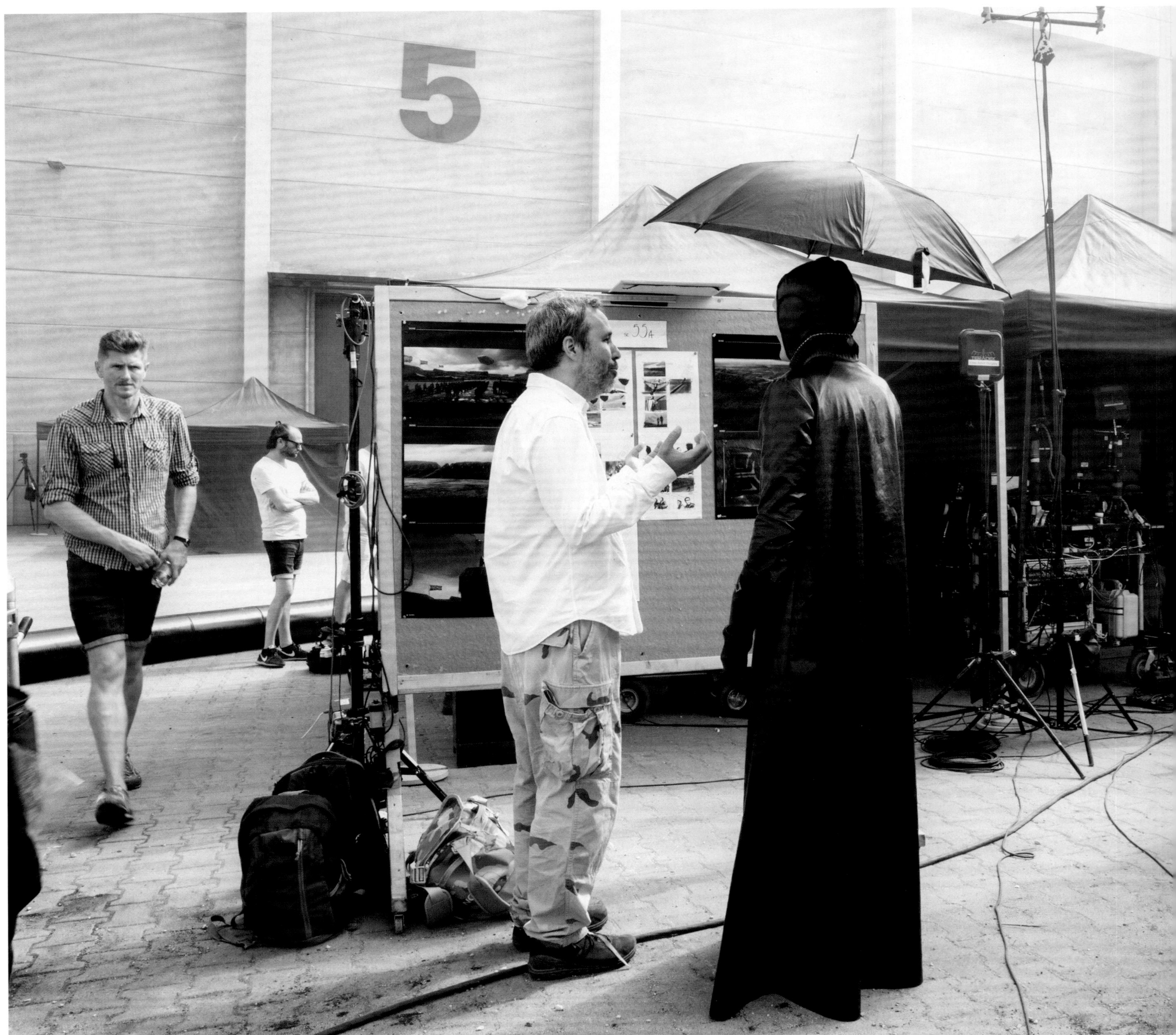

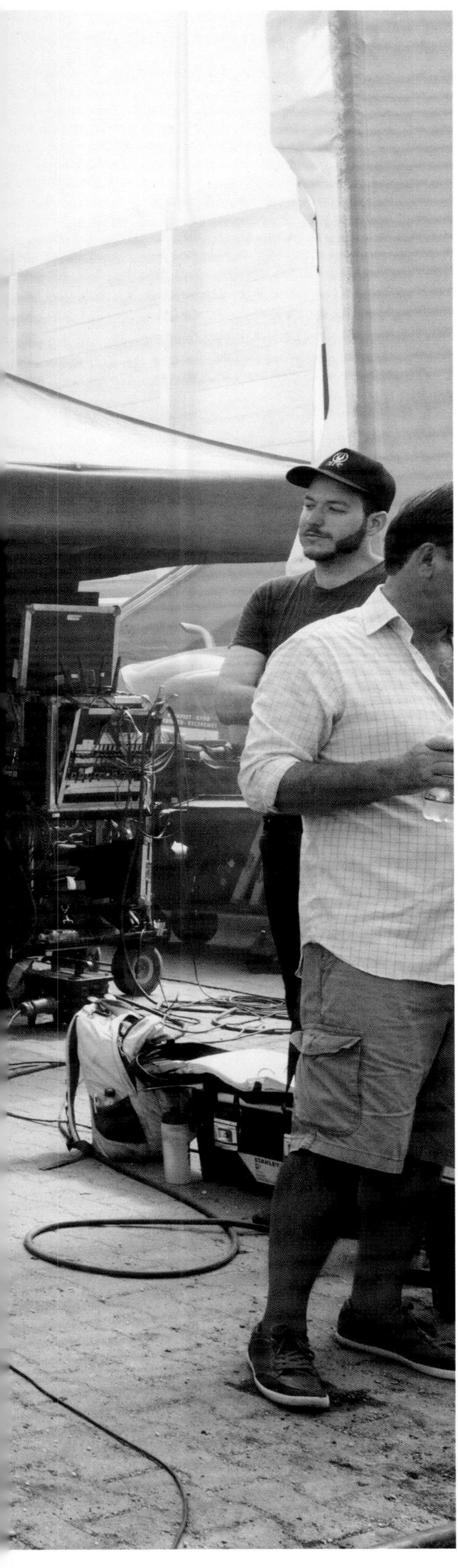

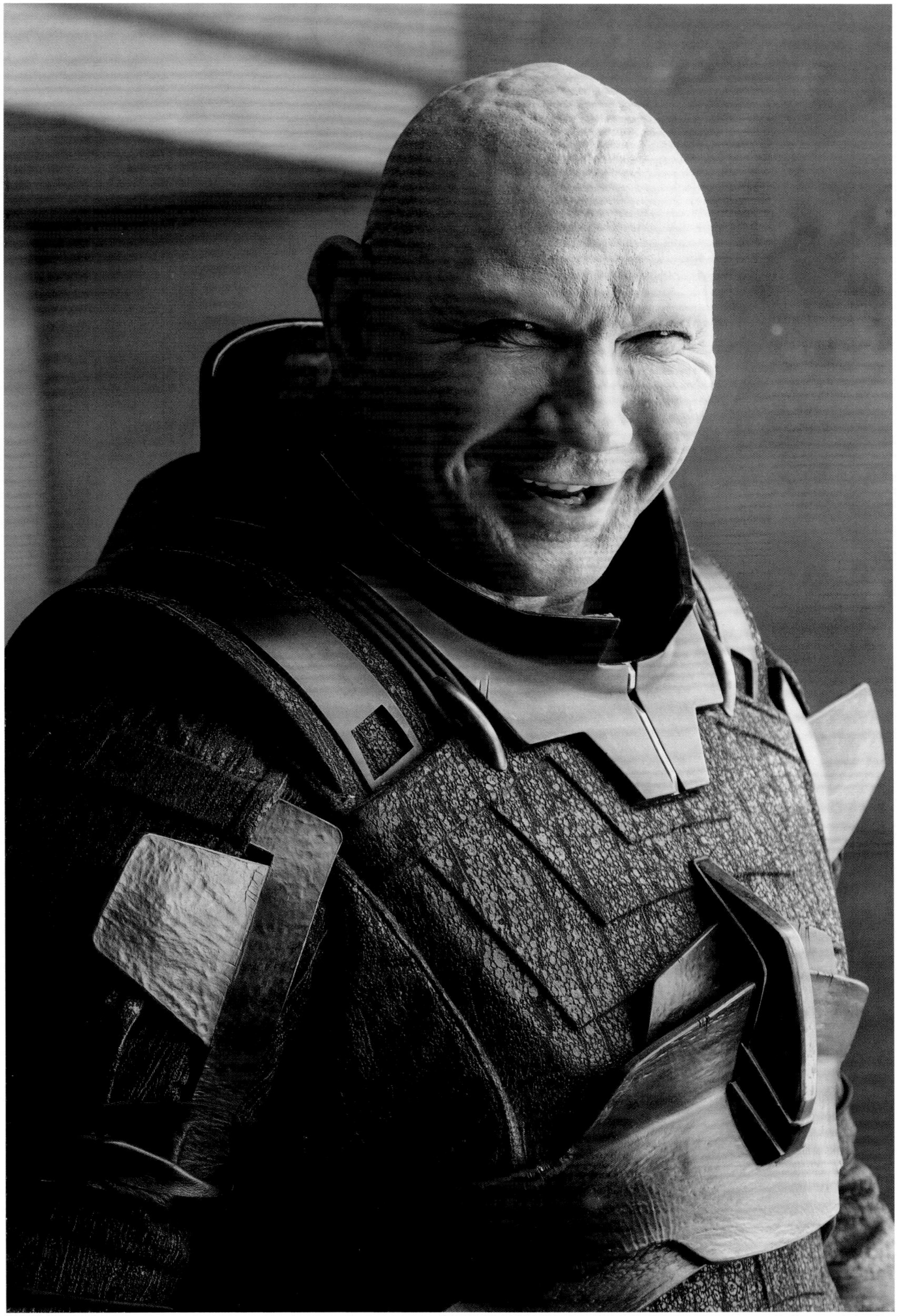

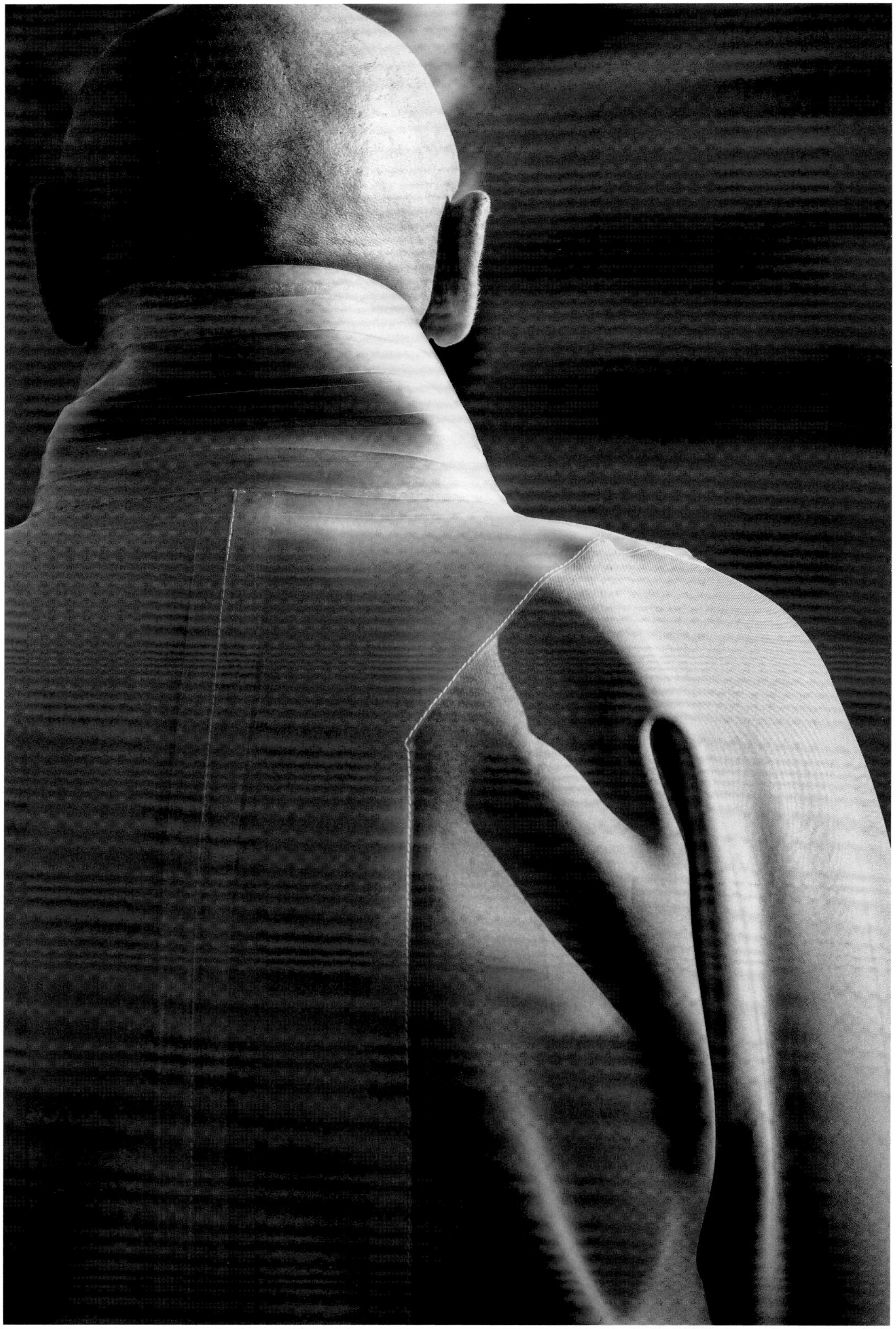

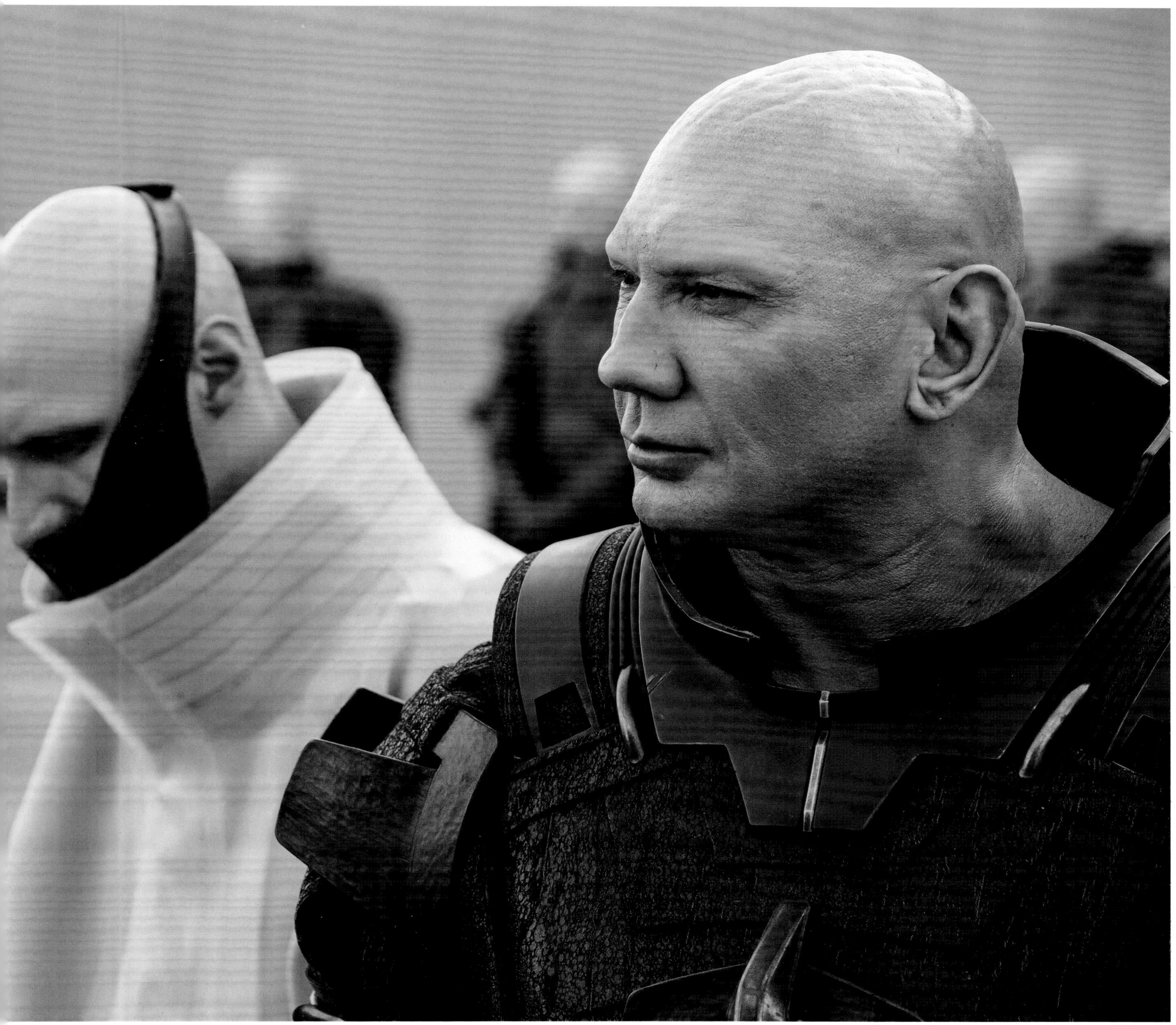

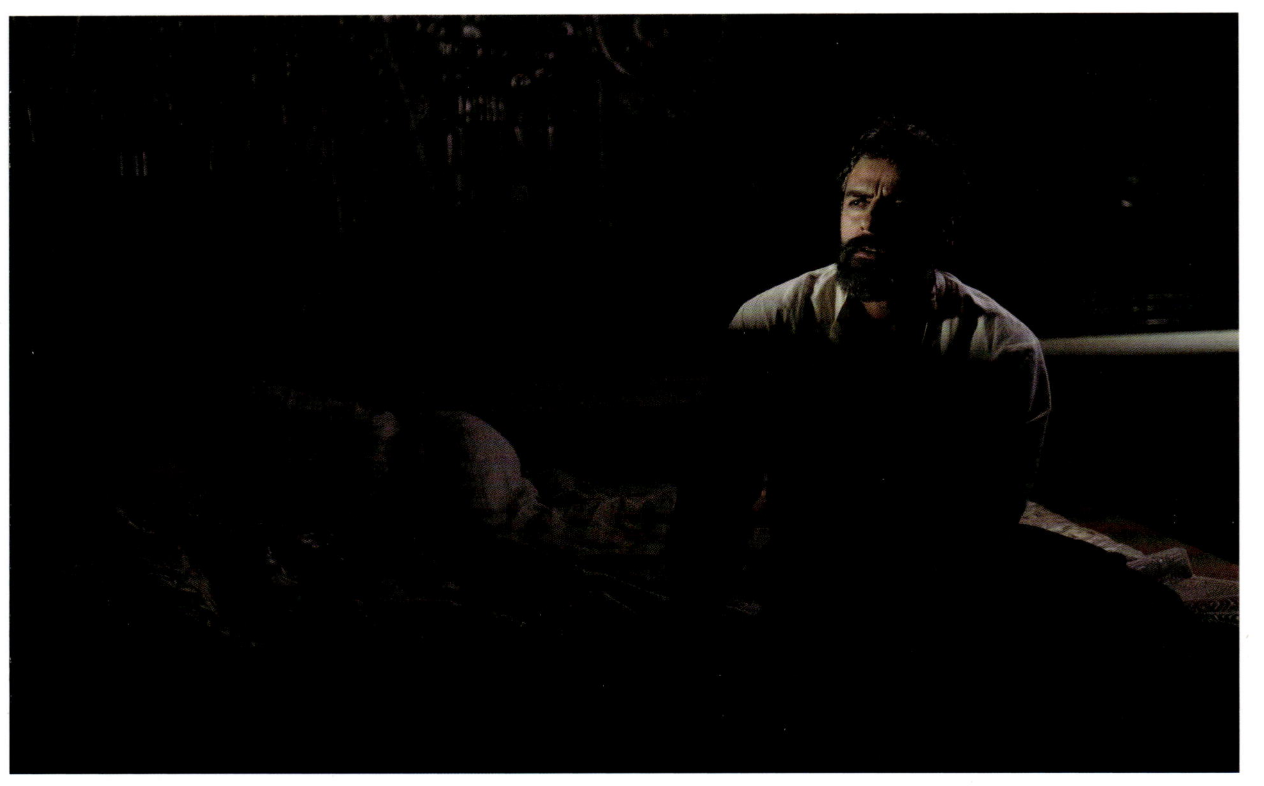

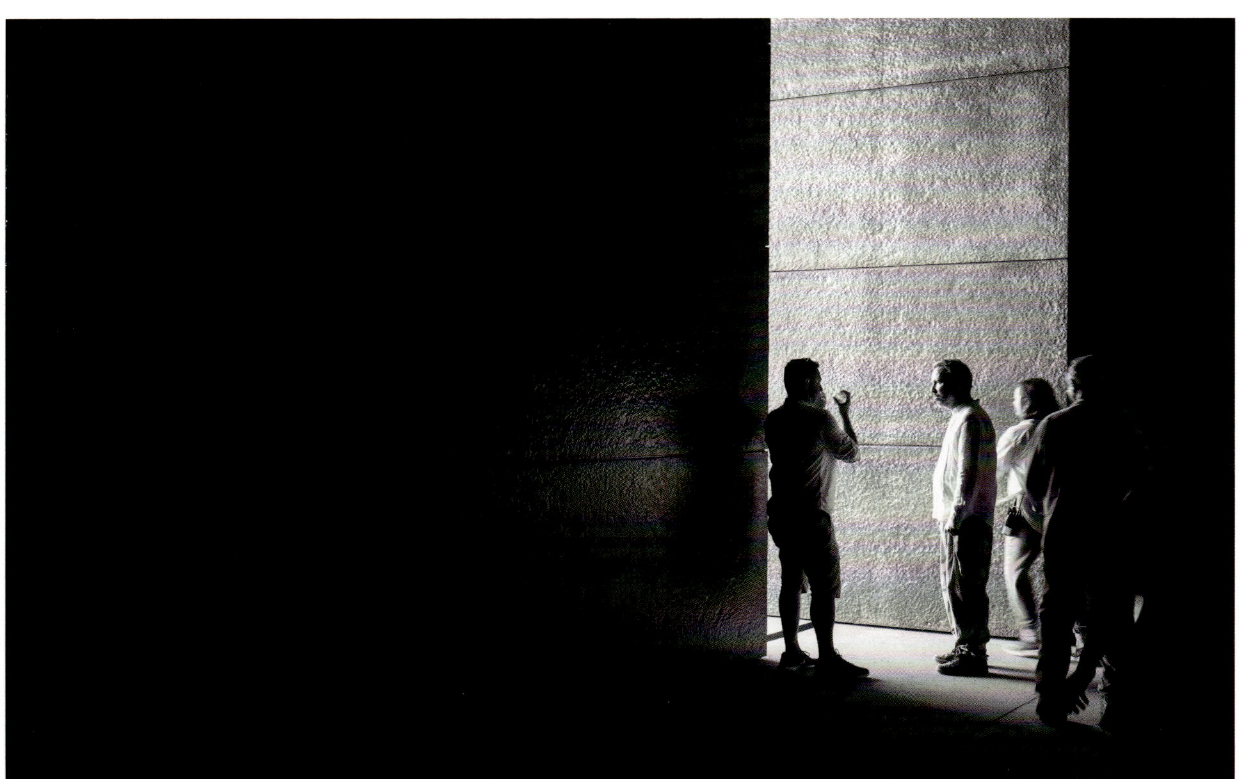

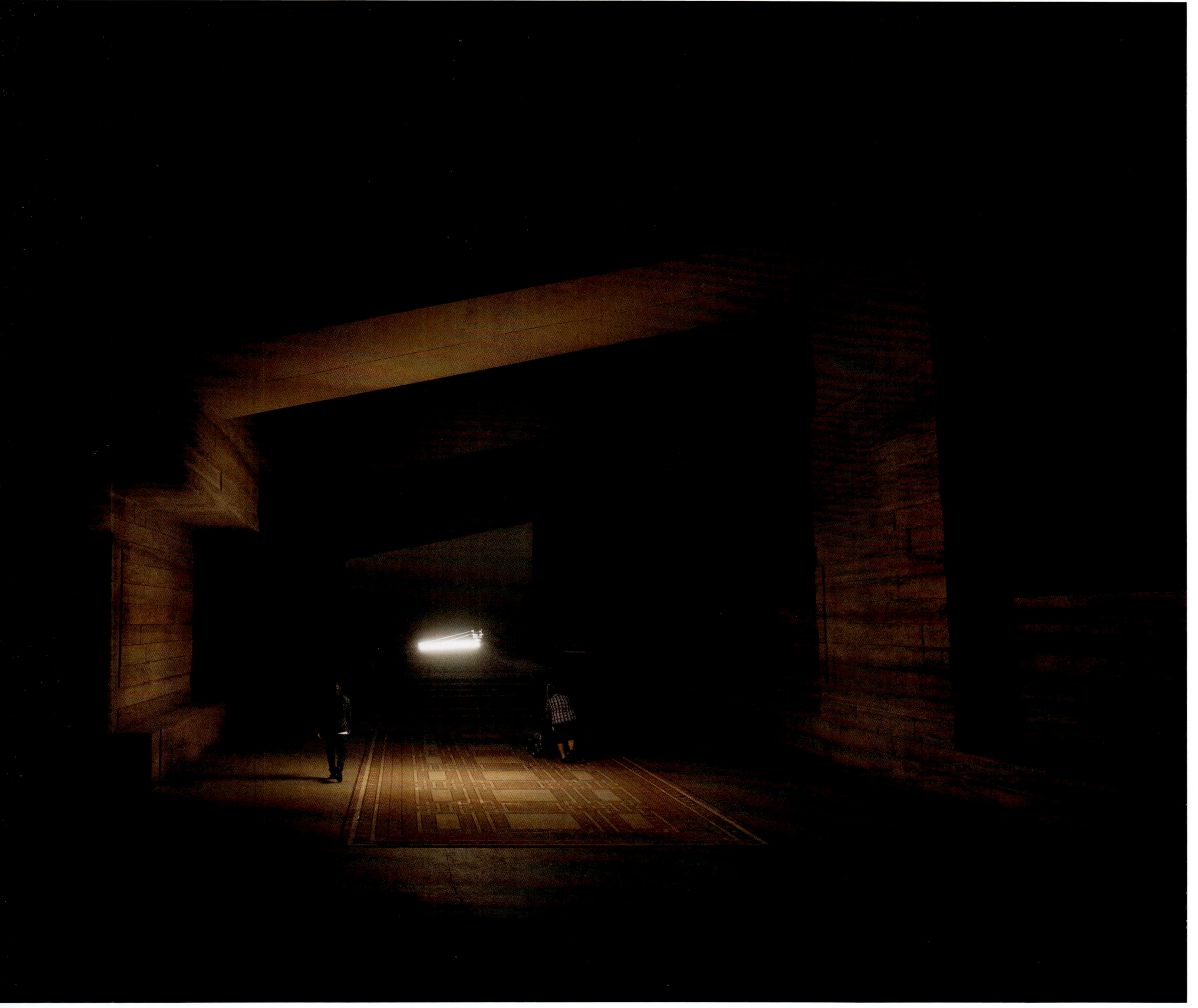

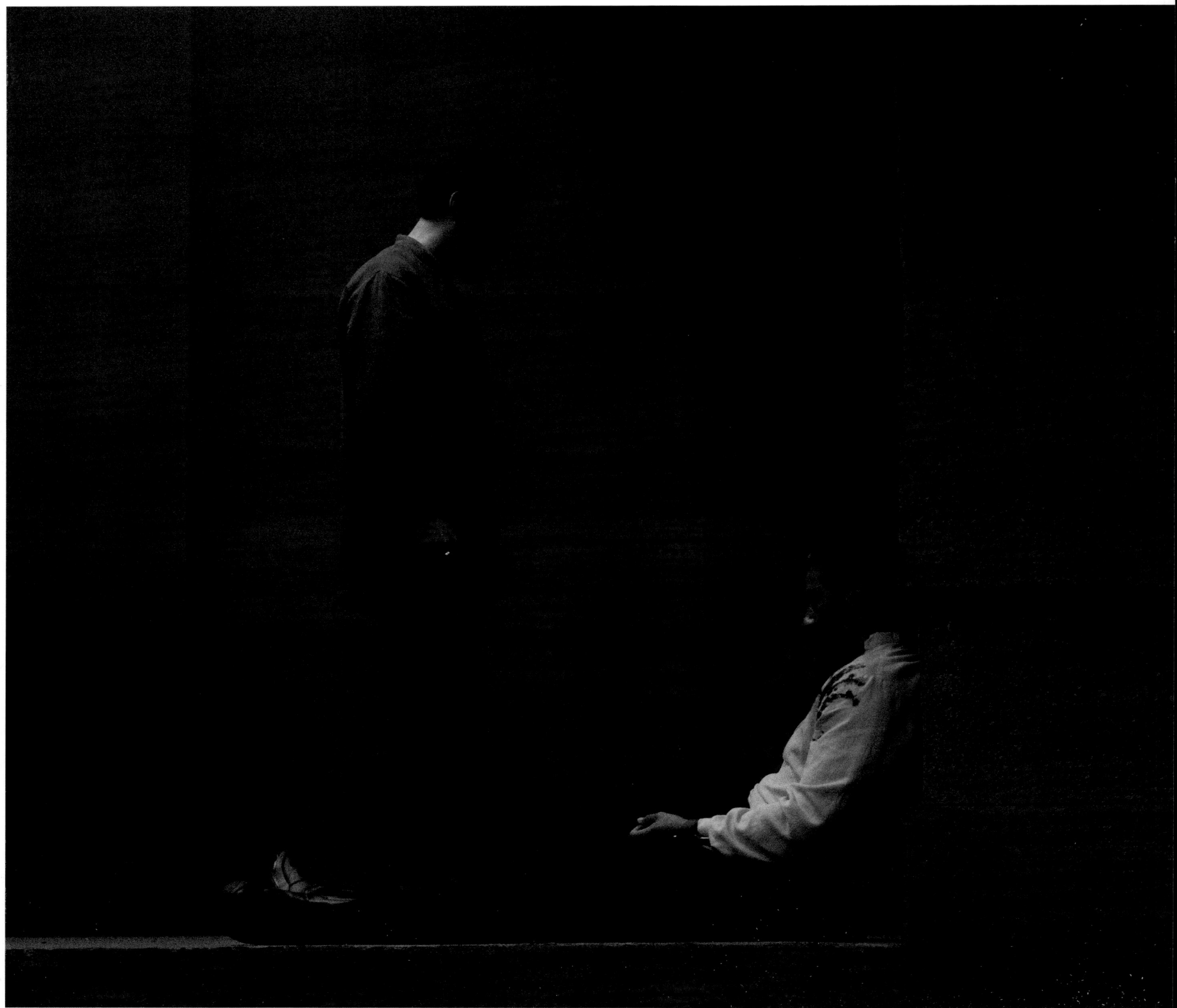

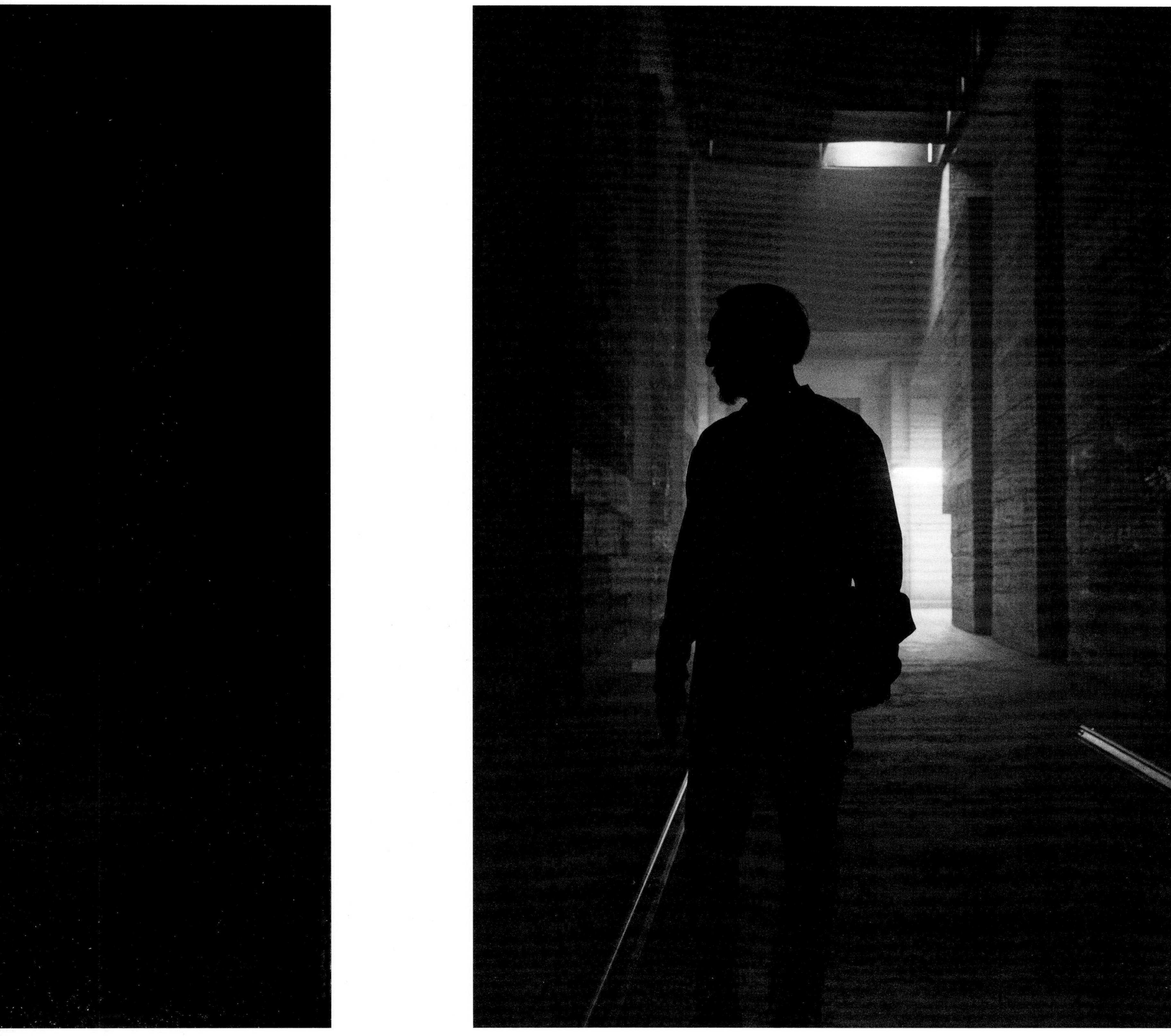

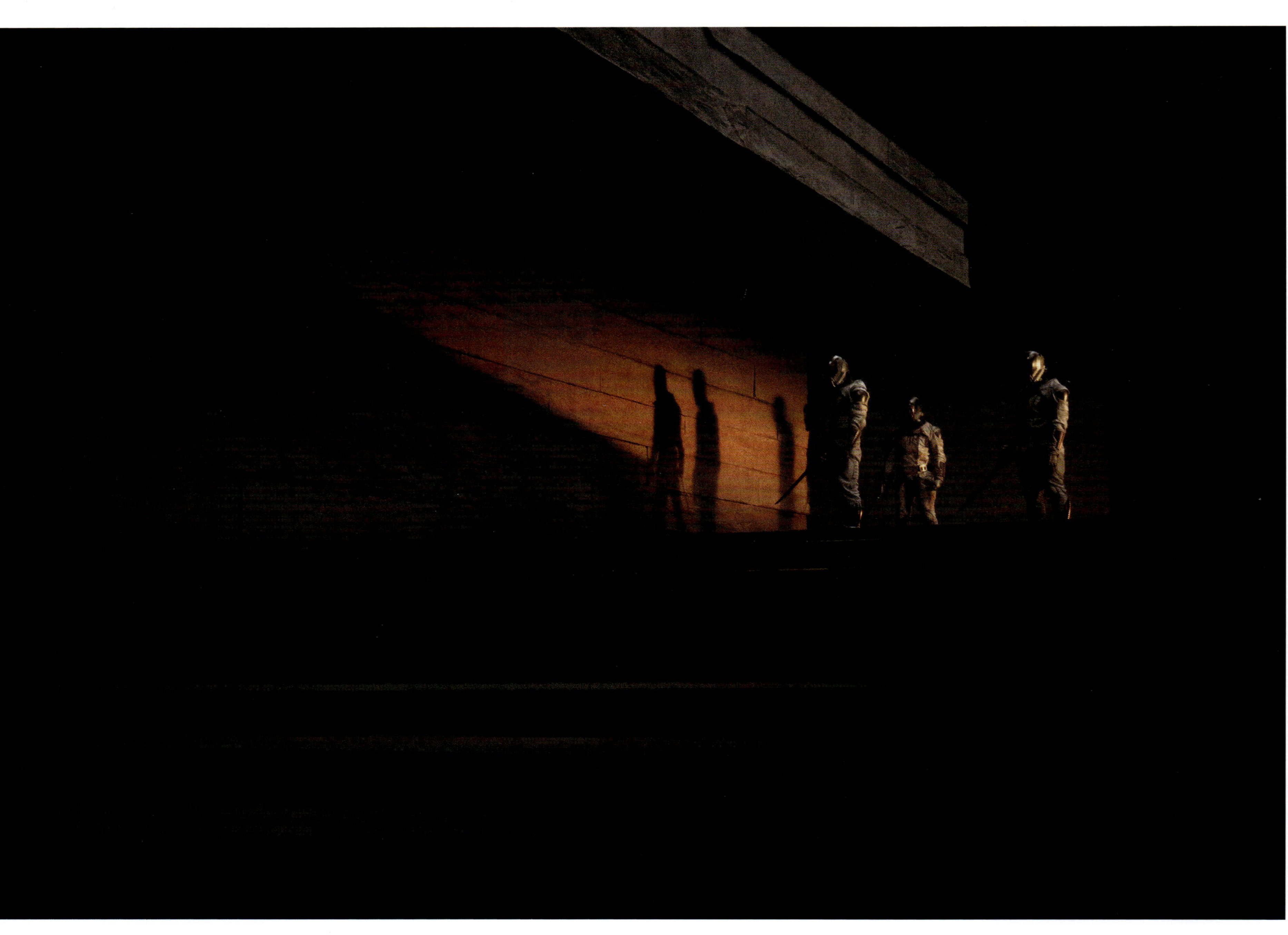

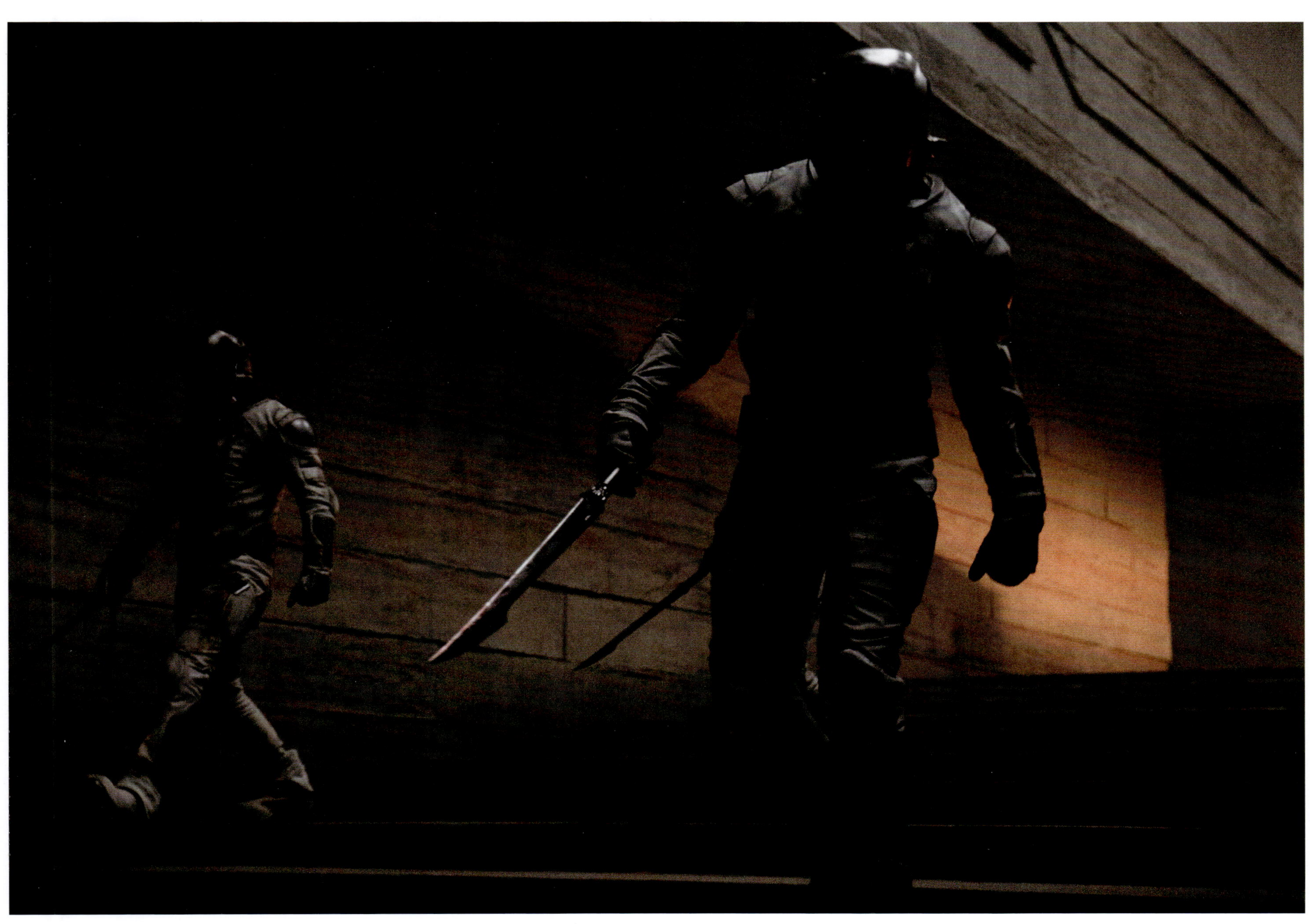

THERE ARE MANY MOMENTS during a production that become
personal memories for the cast and crew. Most are not caught
on camera, but every now and then, the moment is visual,
and I can capture it. We filmed the sequence in which the
invading Sardaukar, the elite Harkonnen warriors first created
by Frank Herbert, infiltrate the Arrakeen Residency on a stage in
Budapest. On set, I had squeezed into a small space beneath
the movie camera, which was positioned in a tight corner at
the bottom of a dark staircase.

The Sardaukar came one by one, swords in hand, down the
steps past us. Only a few feet beyond the camera was the set
wall, with a narrow path off to the right. This was the exit route the
performers were supposed to use after they left the camera's
frame. Unfortunately, the actors couldn't see much through their
dark helmets on the low-lit set, and as they reached the wall, they
stopped. Rather than making their exit, they remained, faces to
the wall, leaning into those who had stopped before them.

Off camera, we watched these men turn into life-size wind-
up toy soldiers, stopping one by one in an ever-growing huddle
at the set wall. It's important to keep quiet during a take so the
performers and sound department can do their work, but stifled
giggles crept through the whole crew. It was a moment that I
couldn't have described without the help of this photograph.

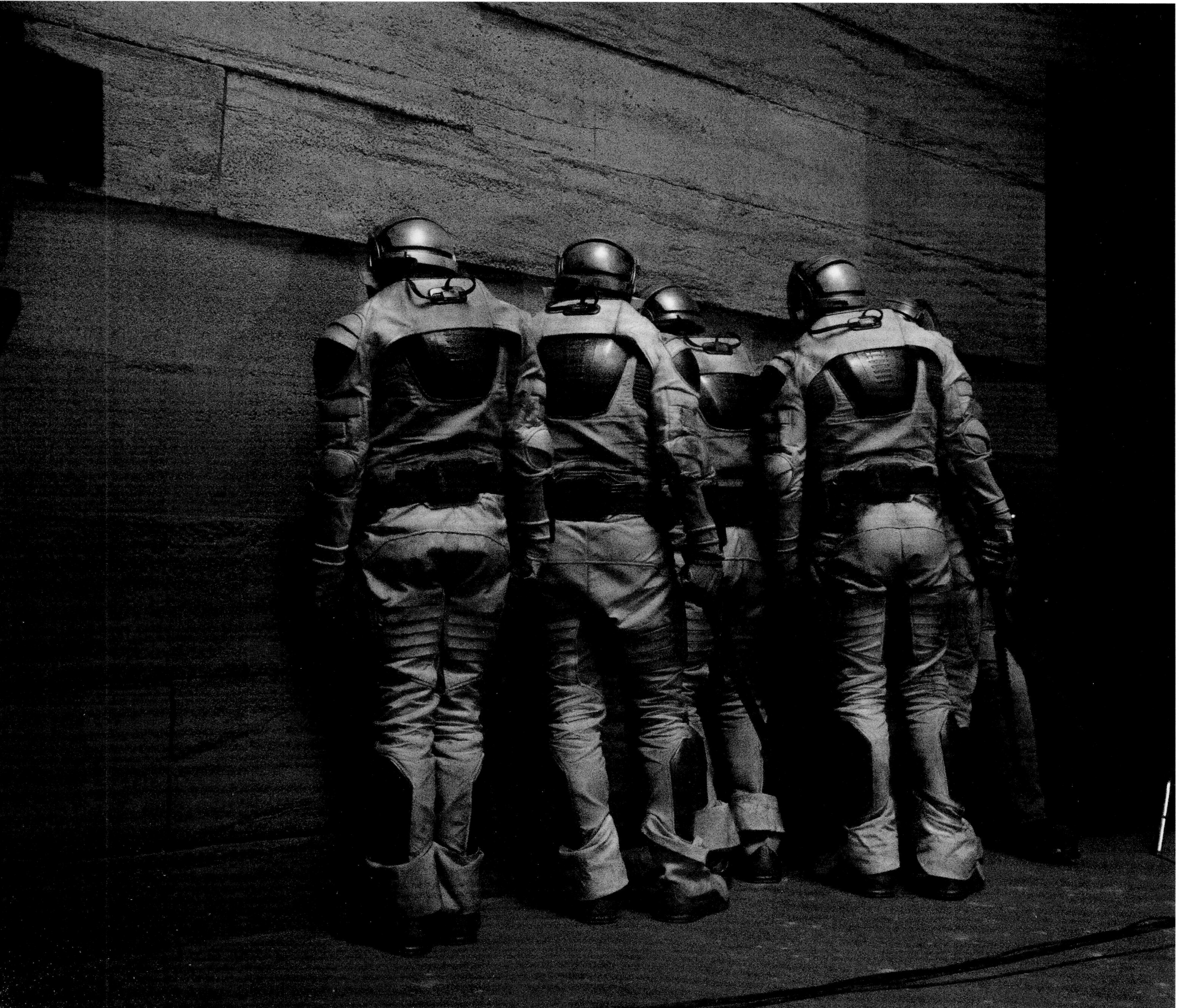

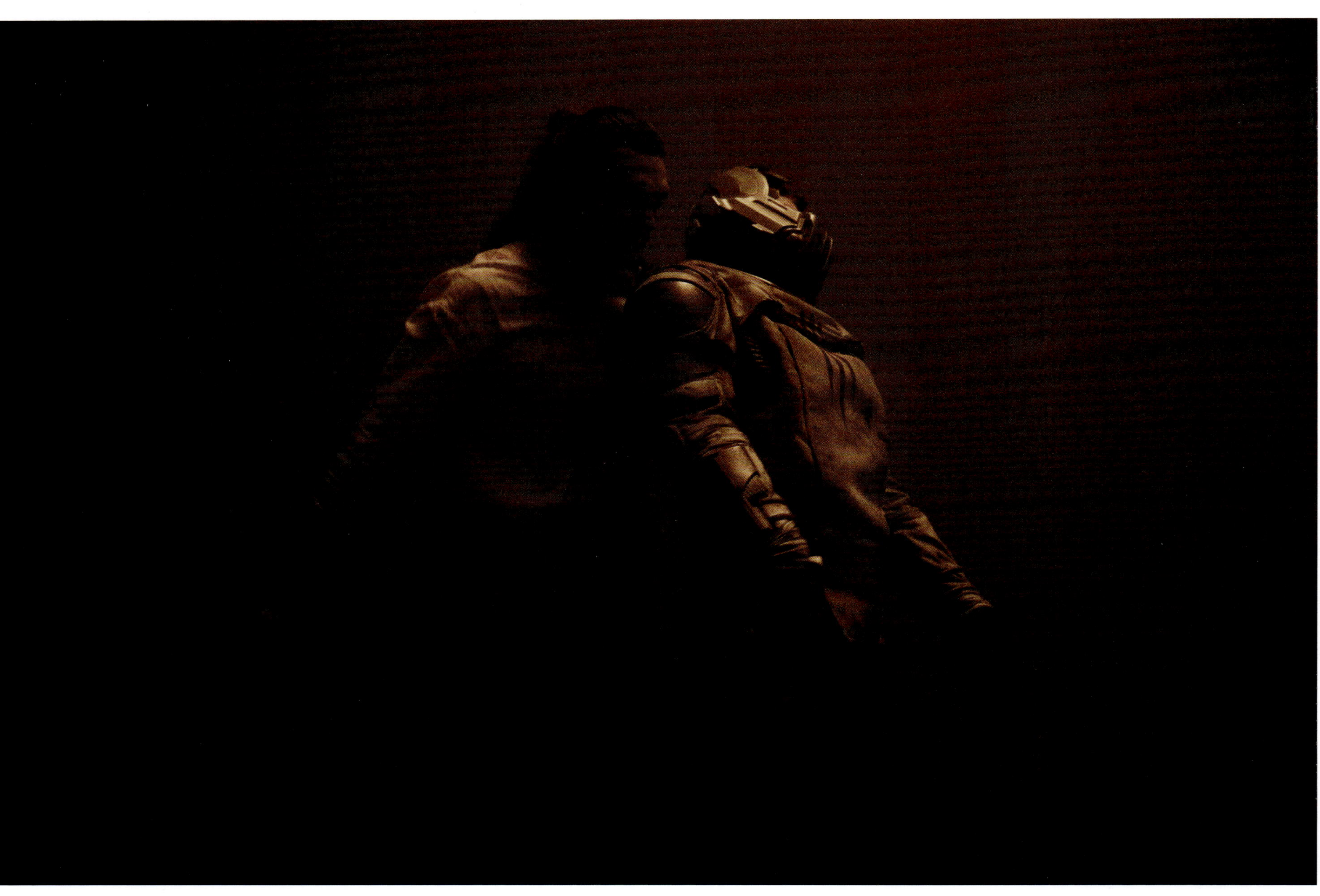

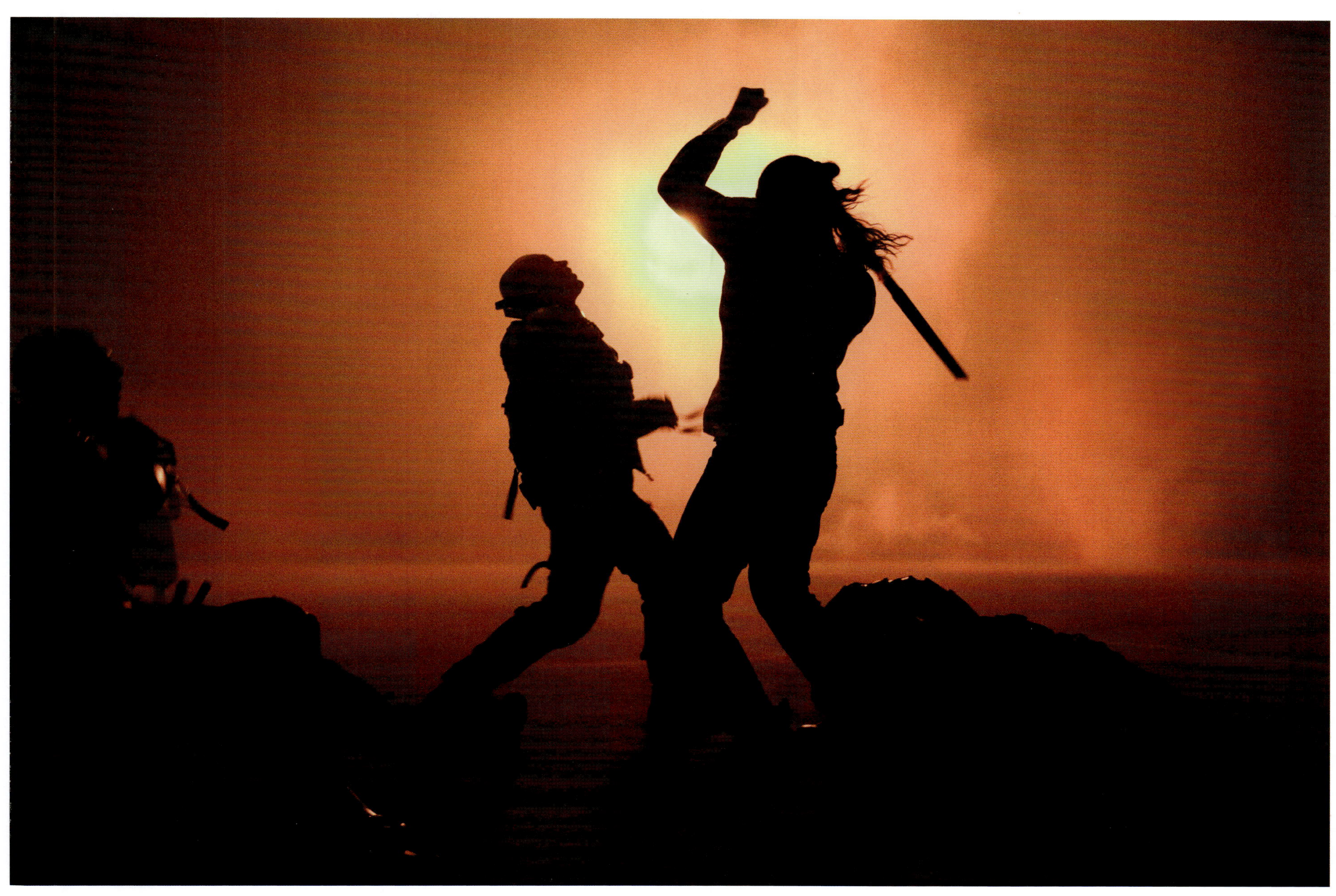

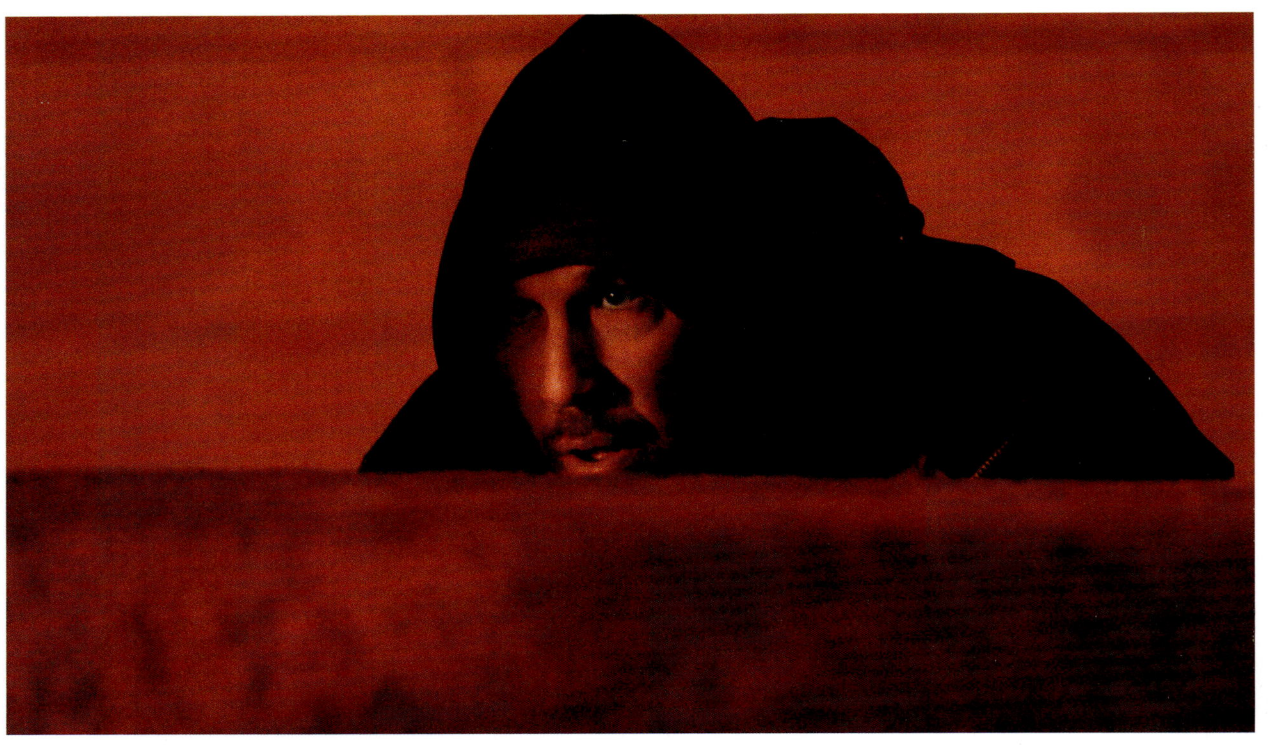

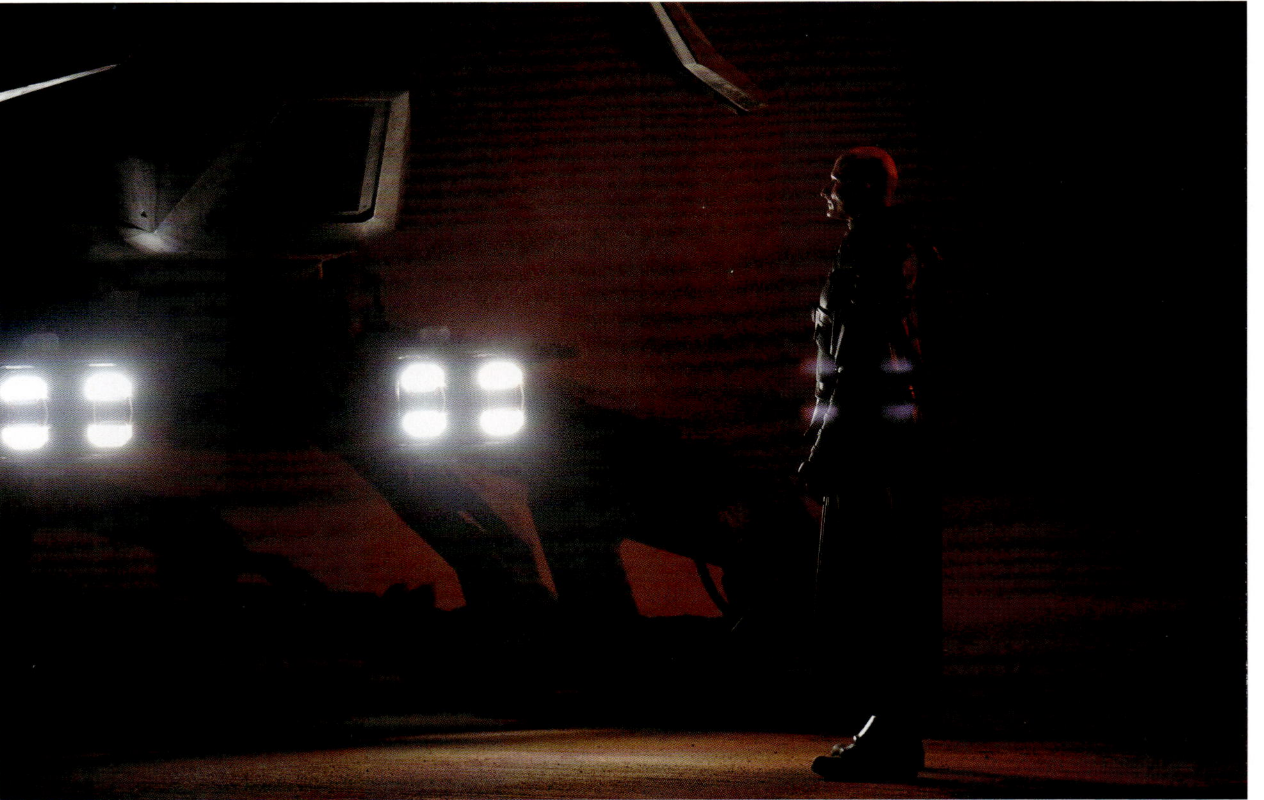

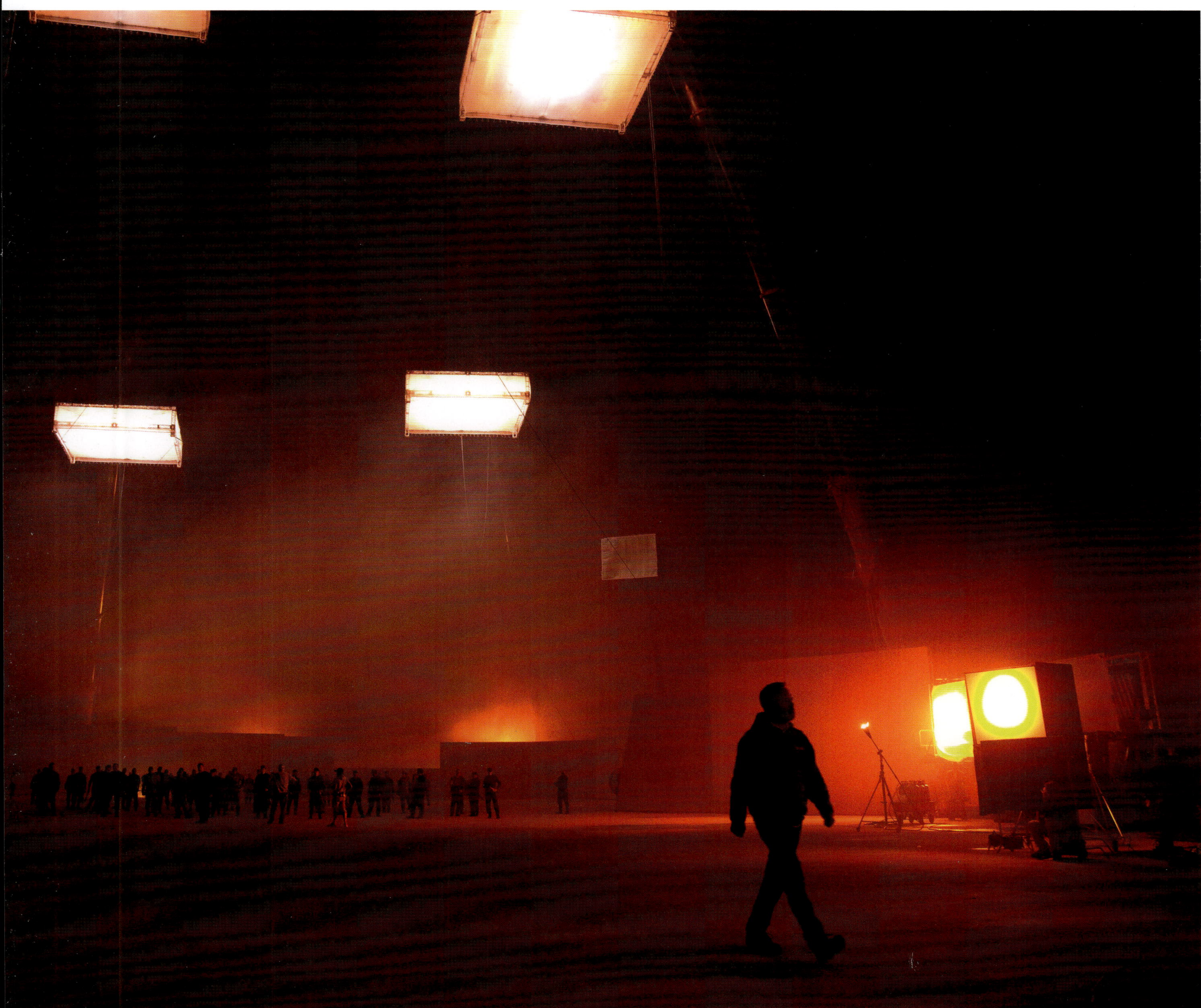

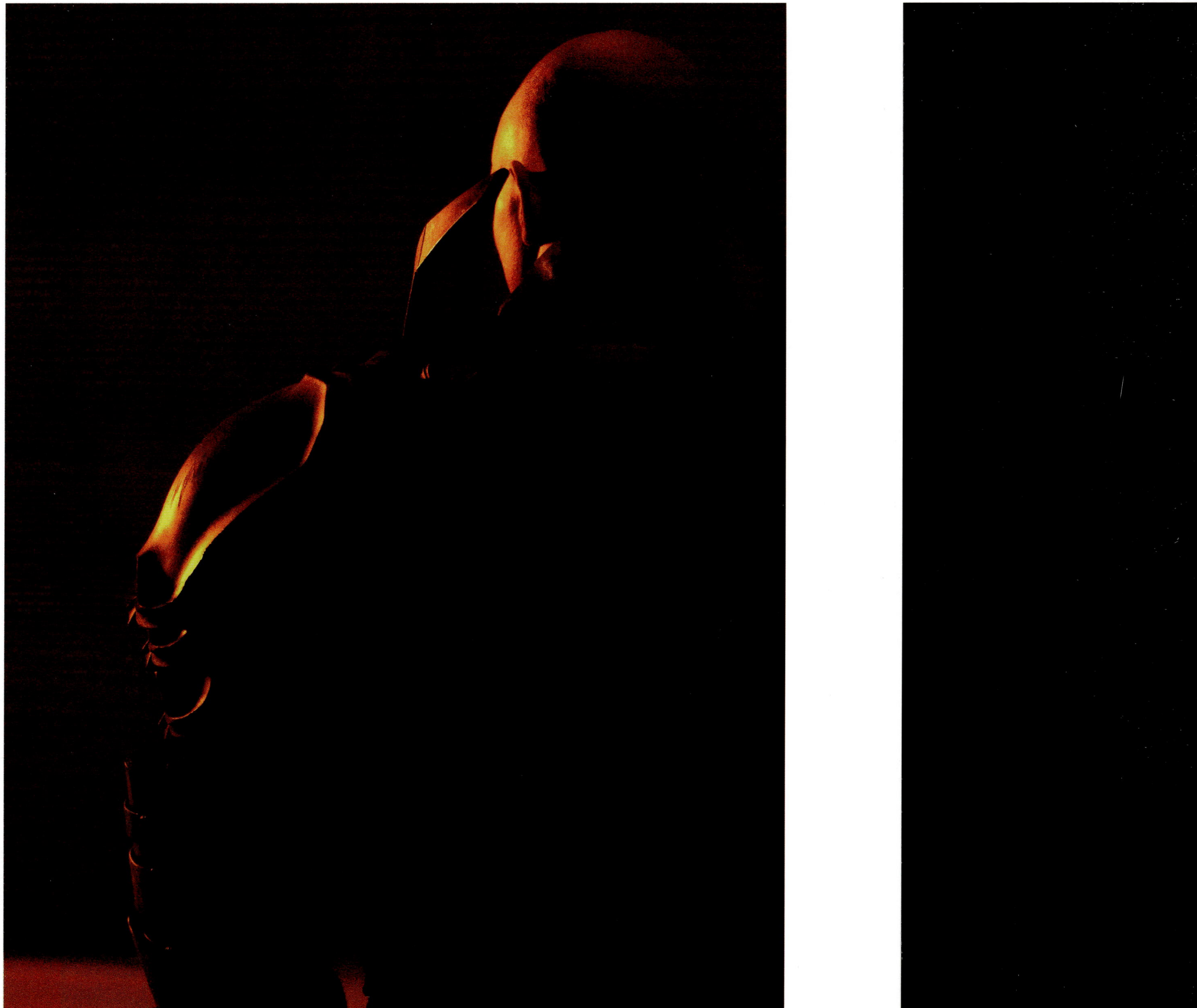

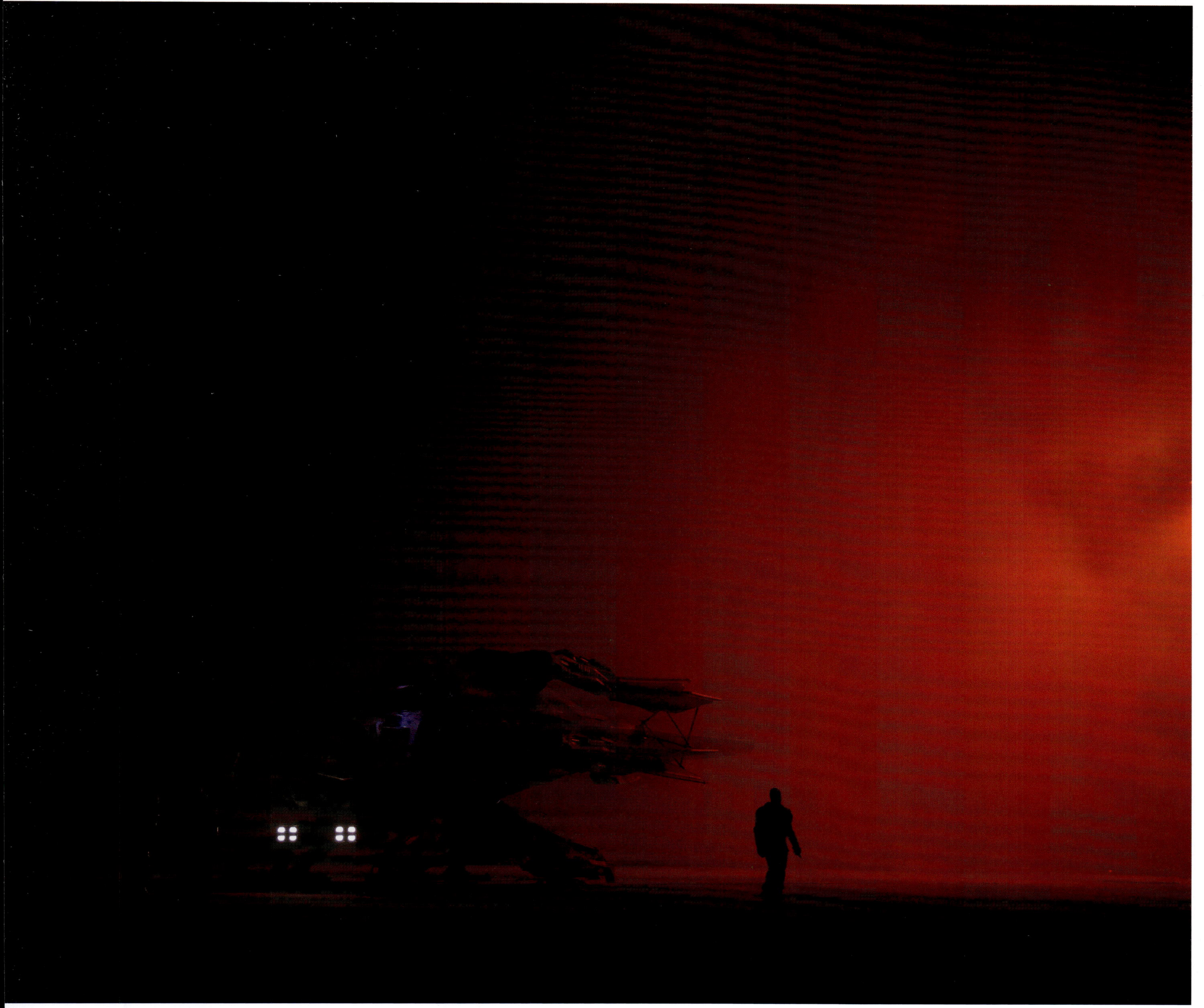

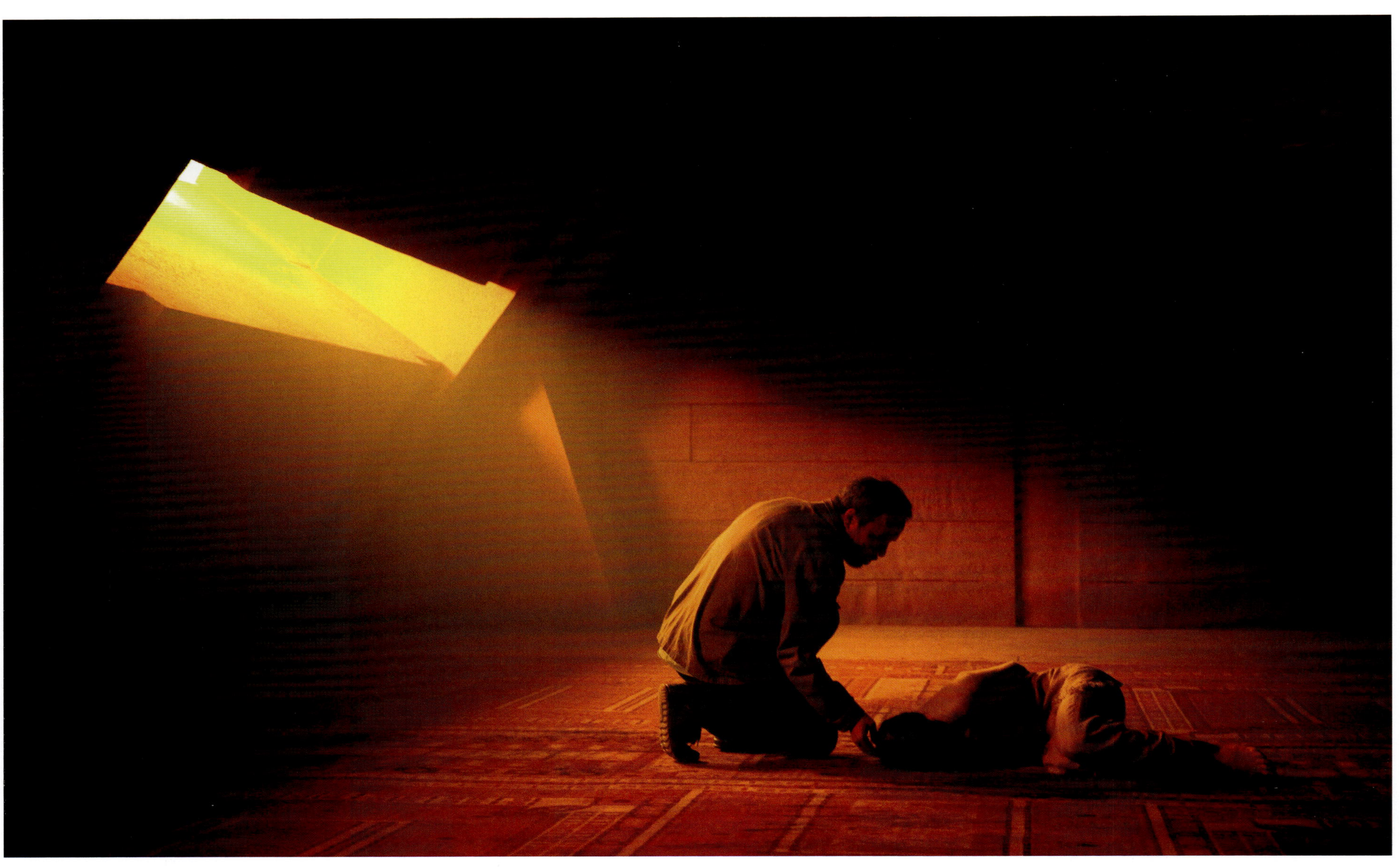

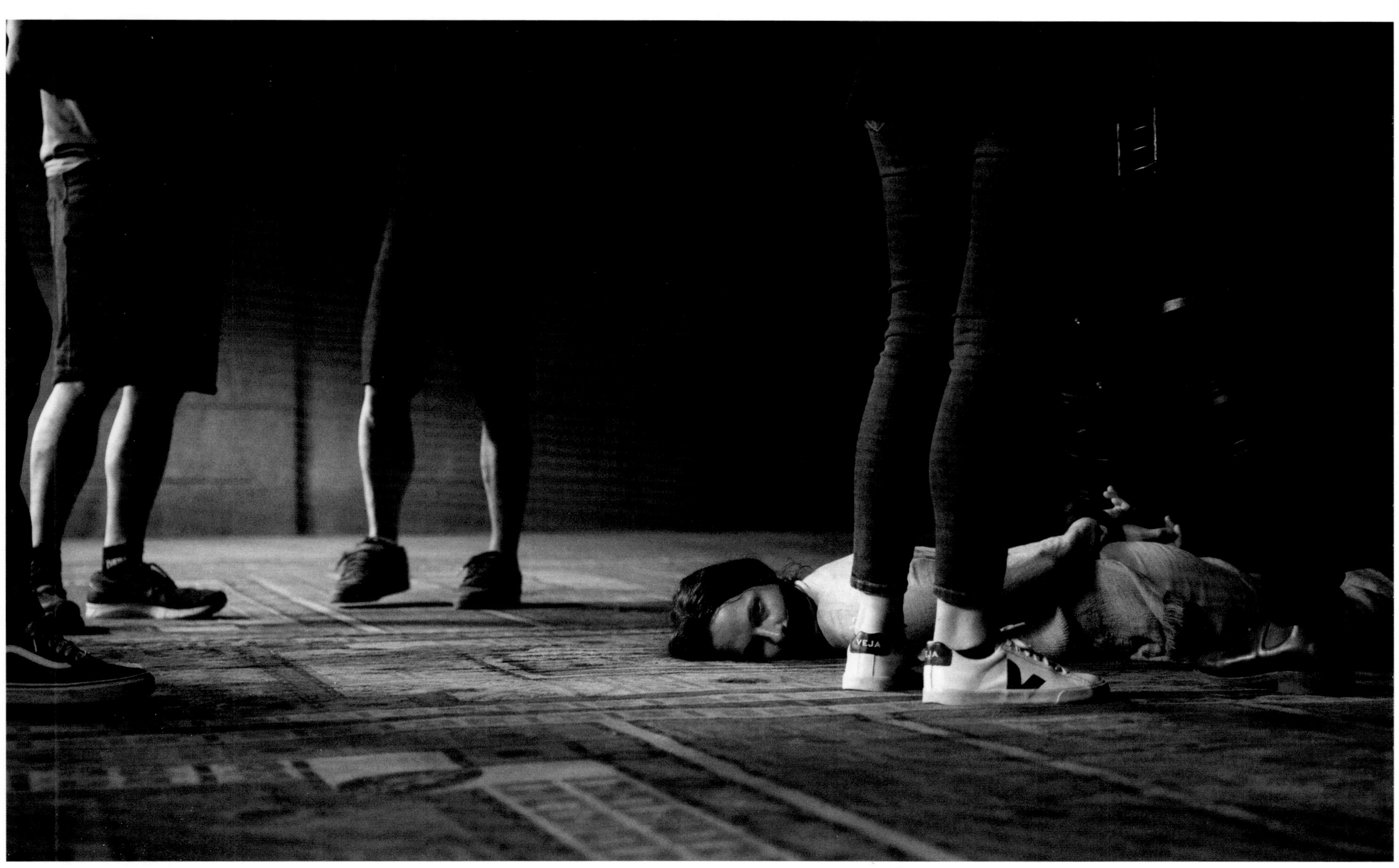

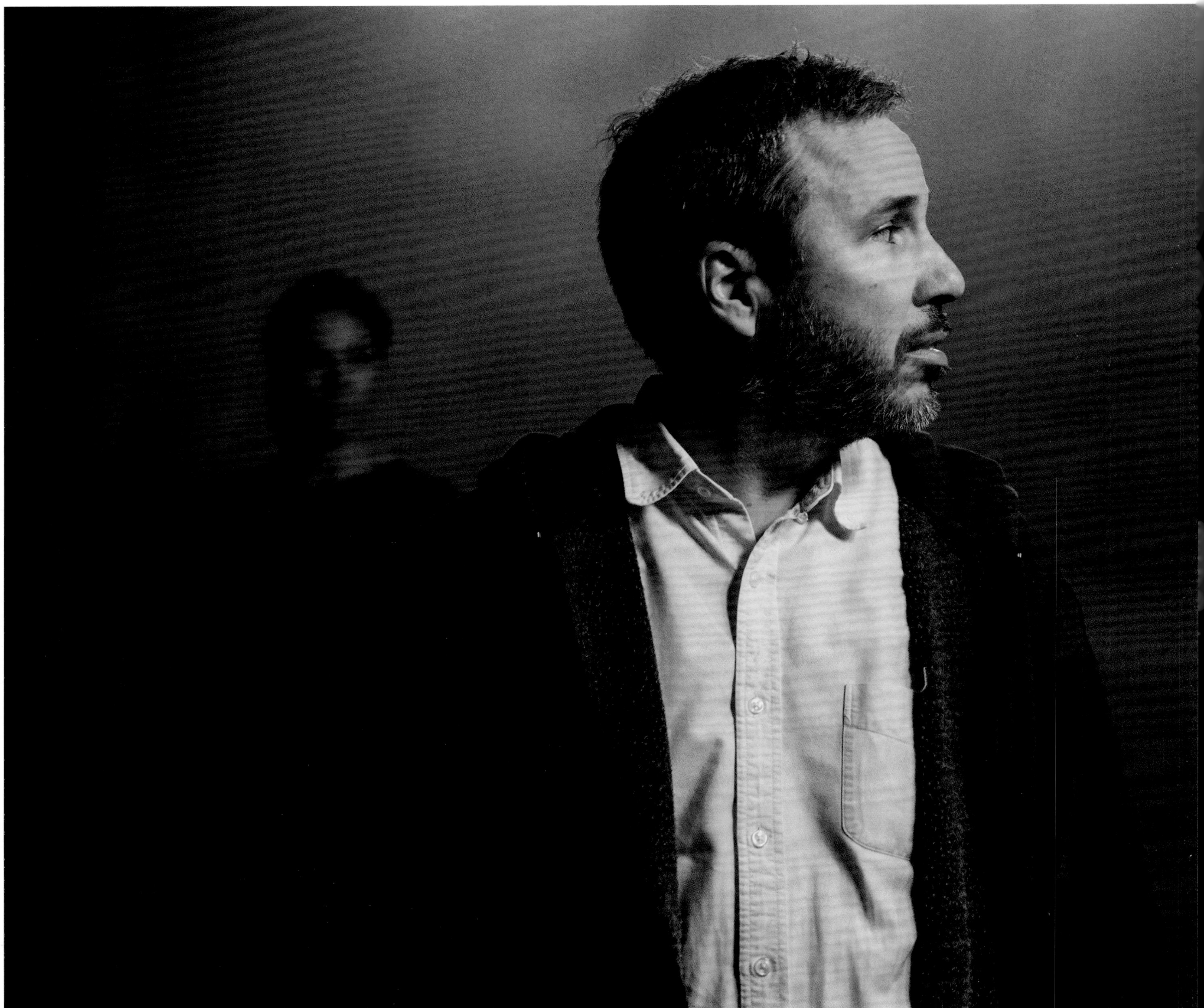

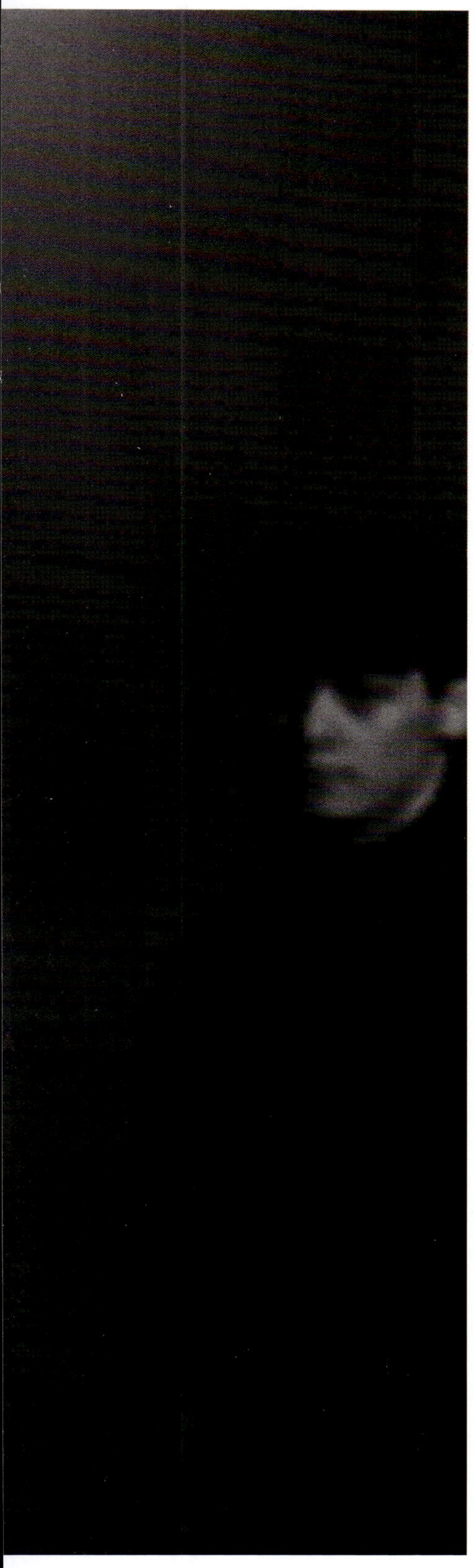

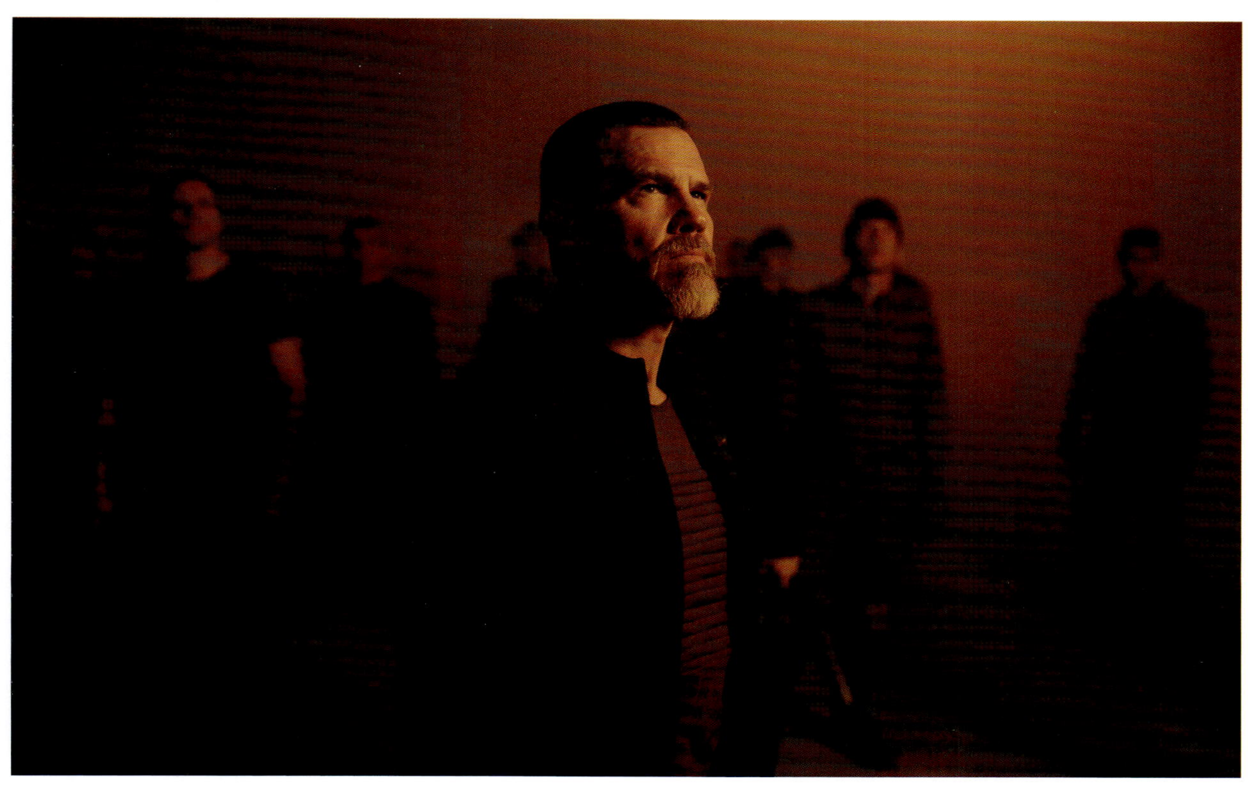

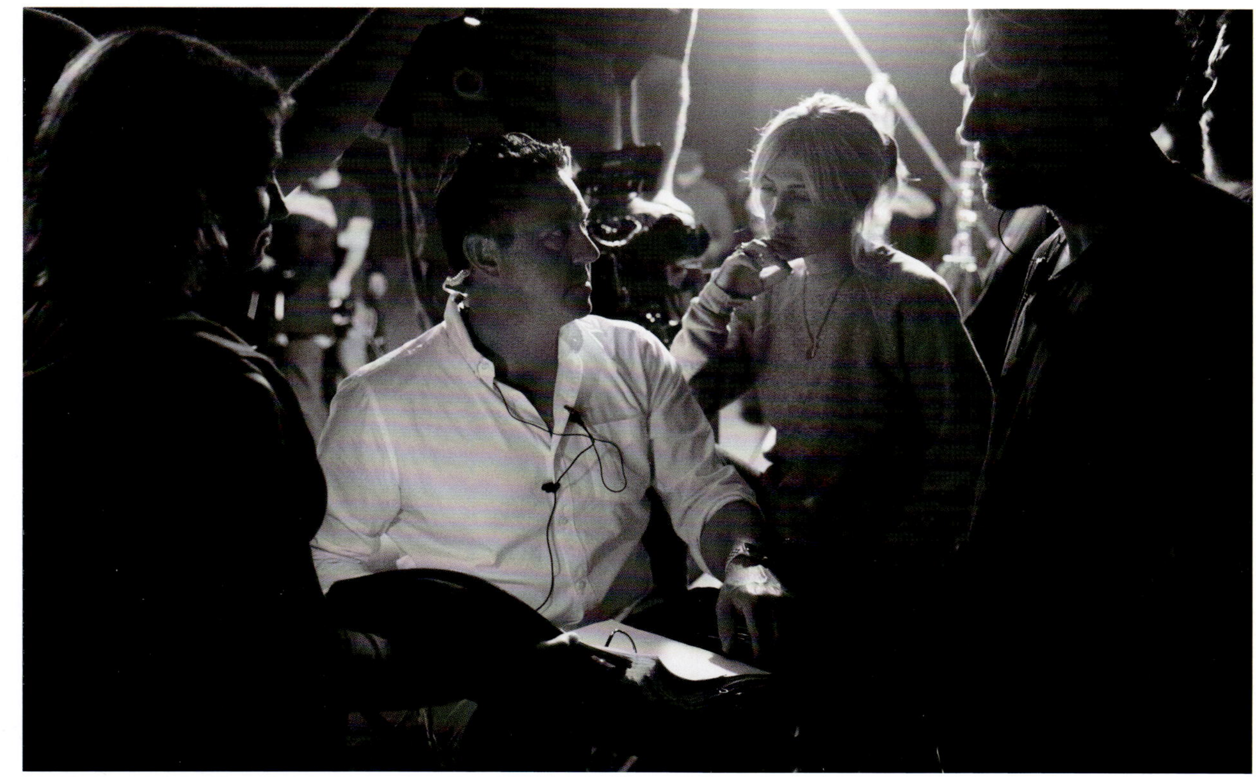

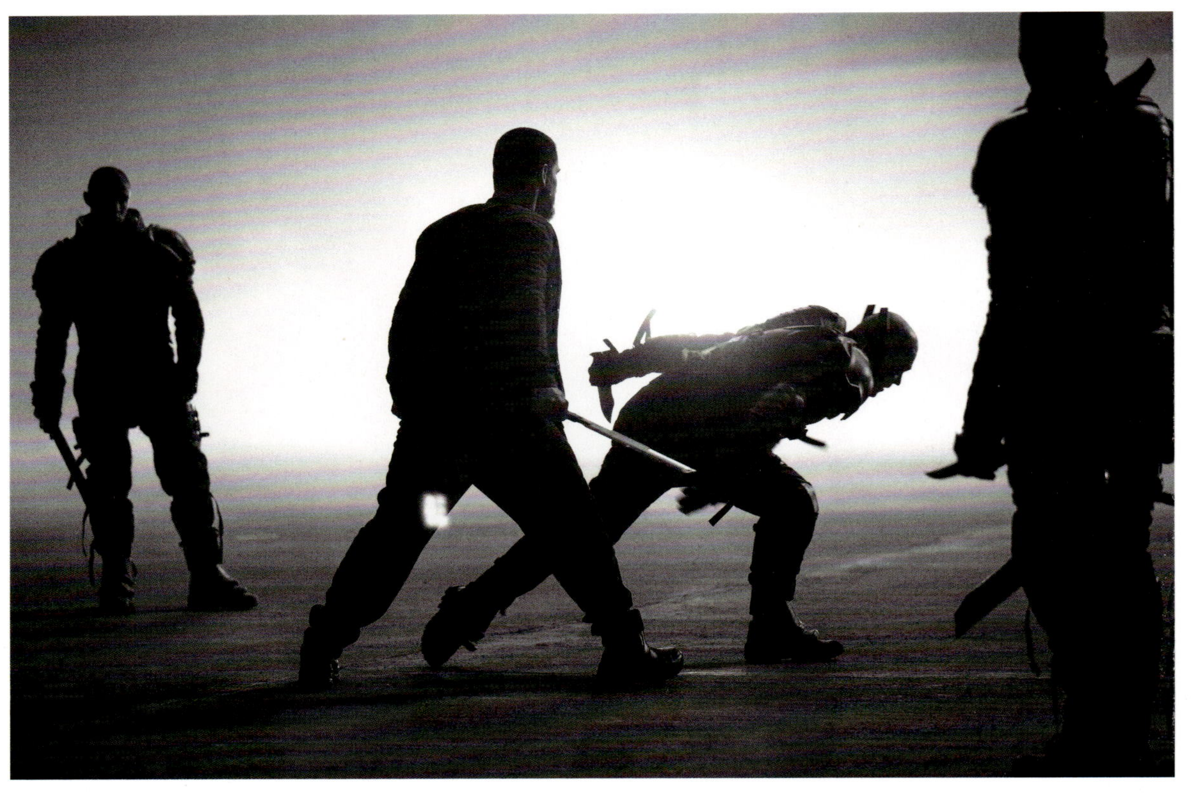

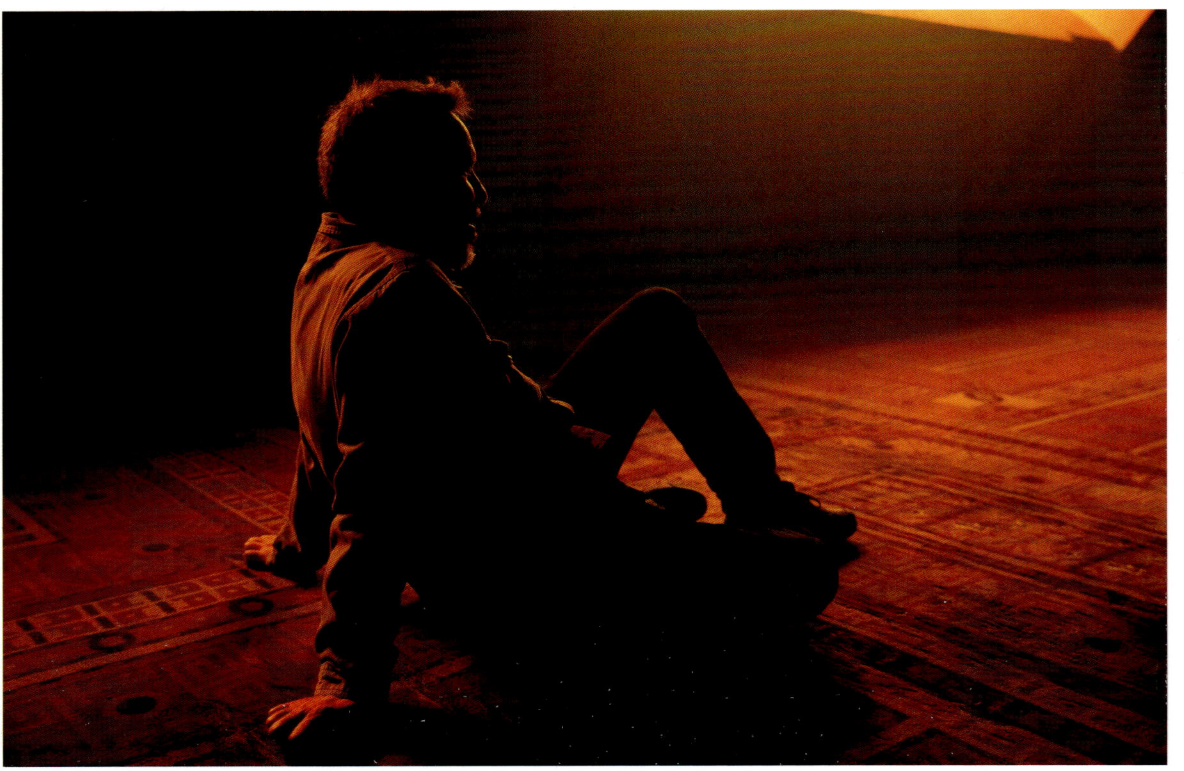

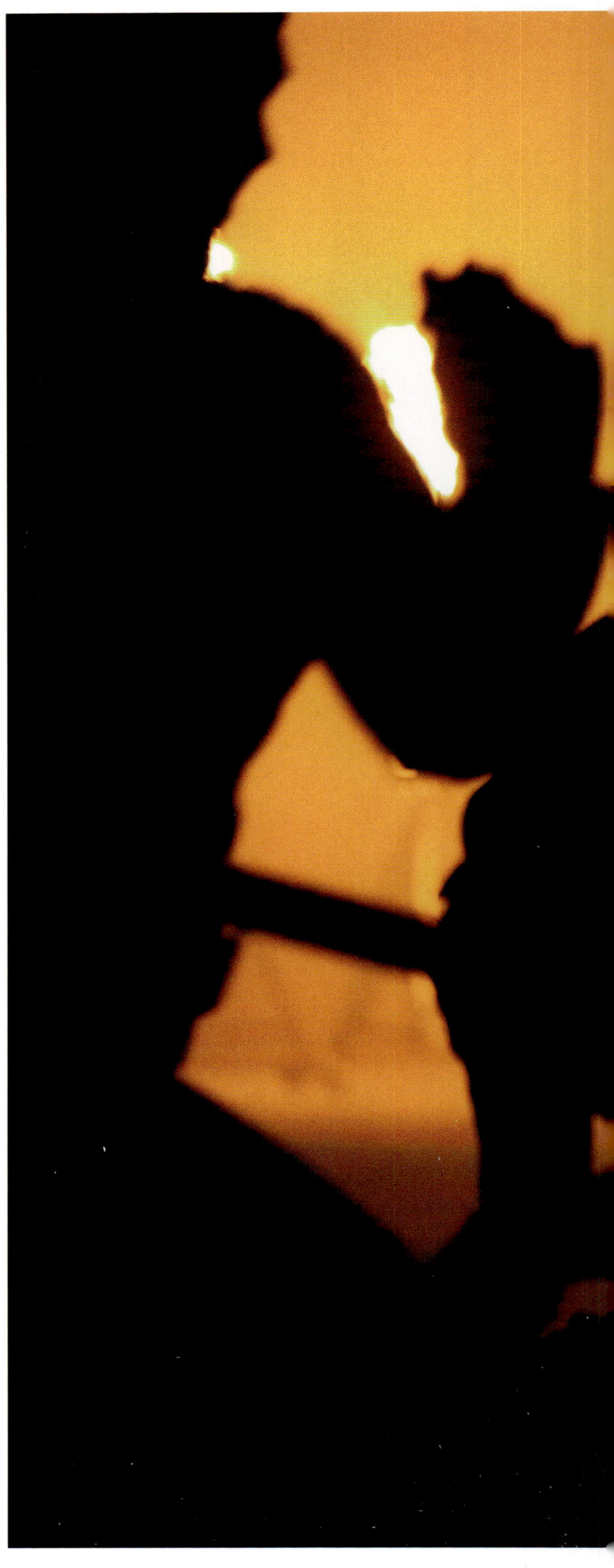

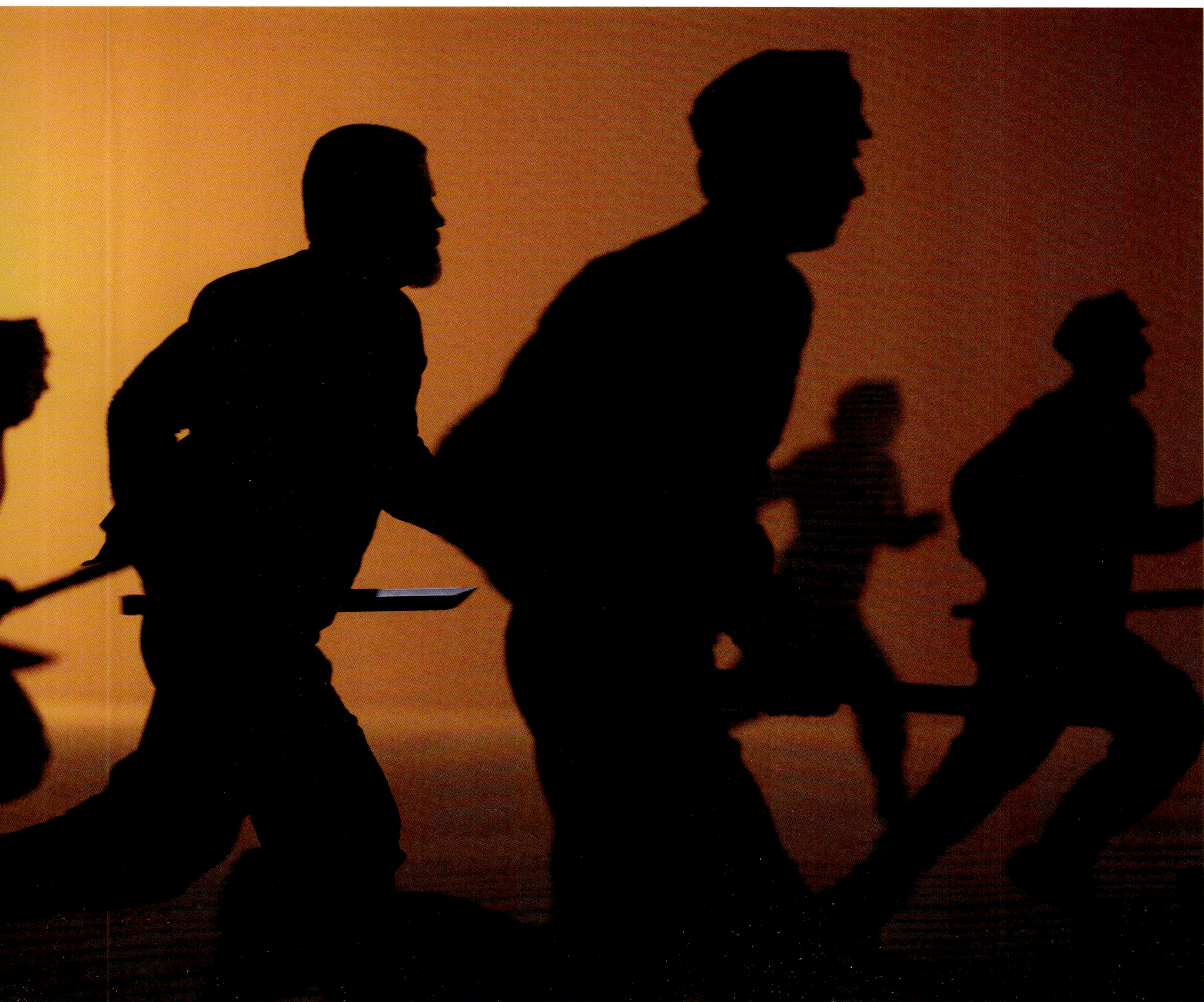

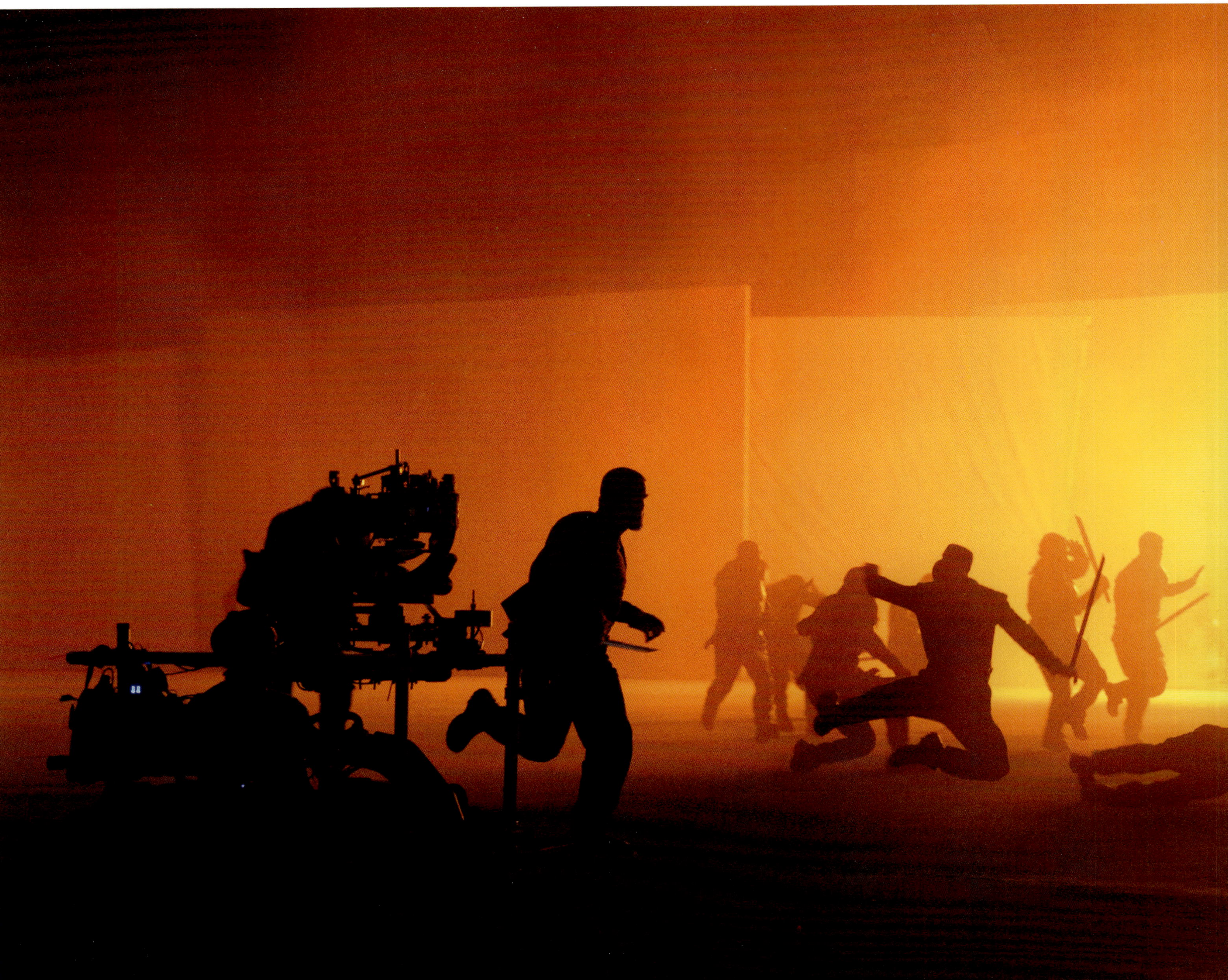

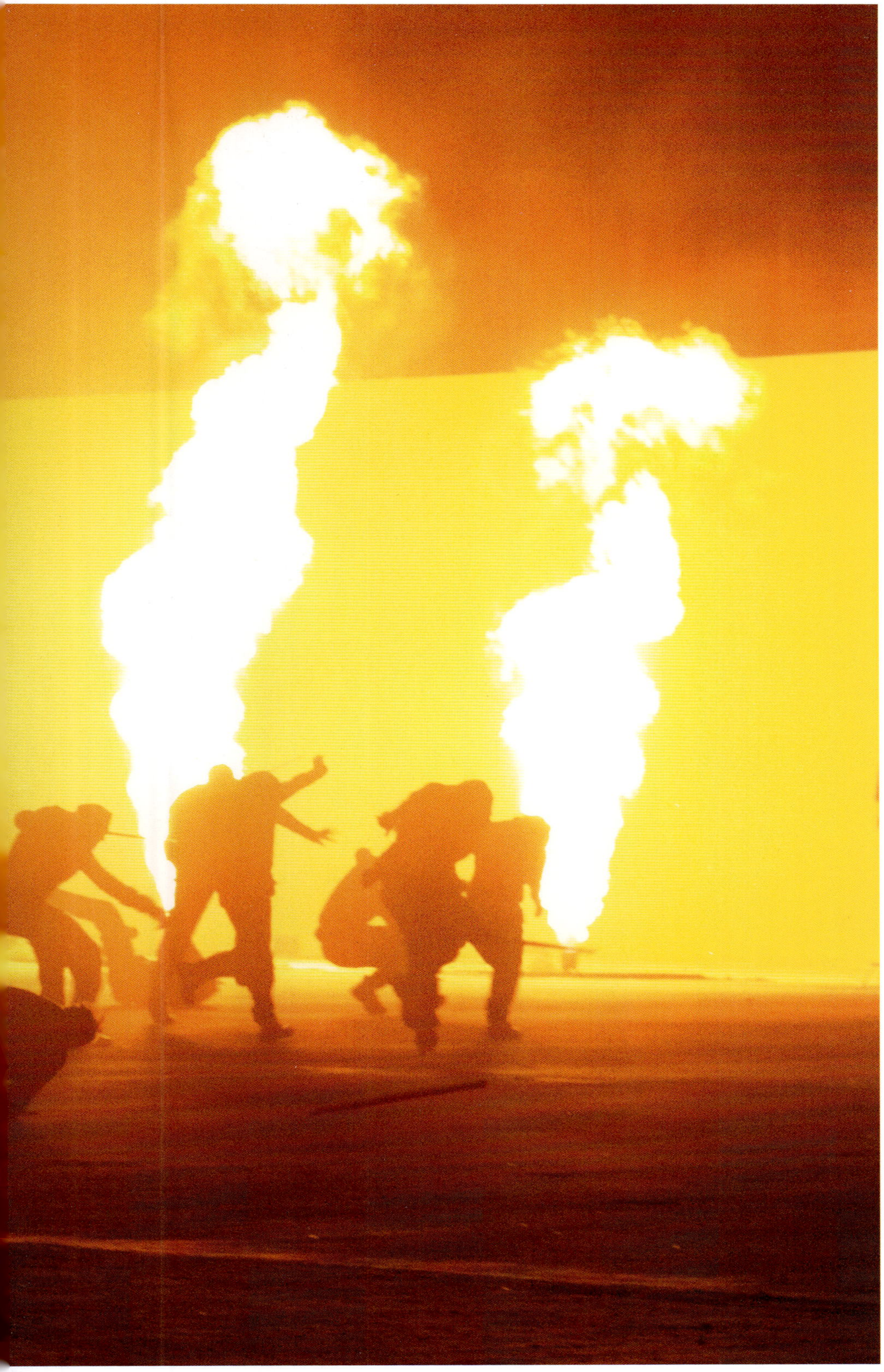

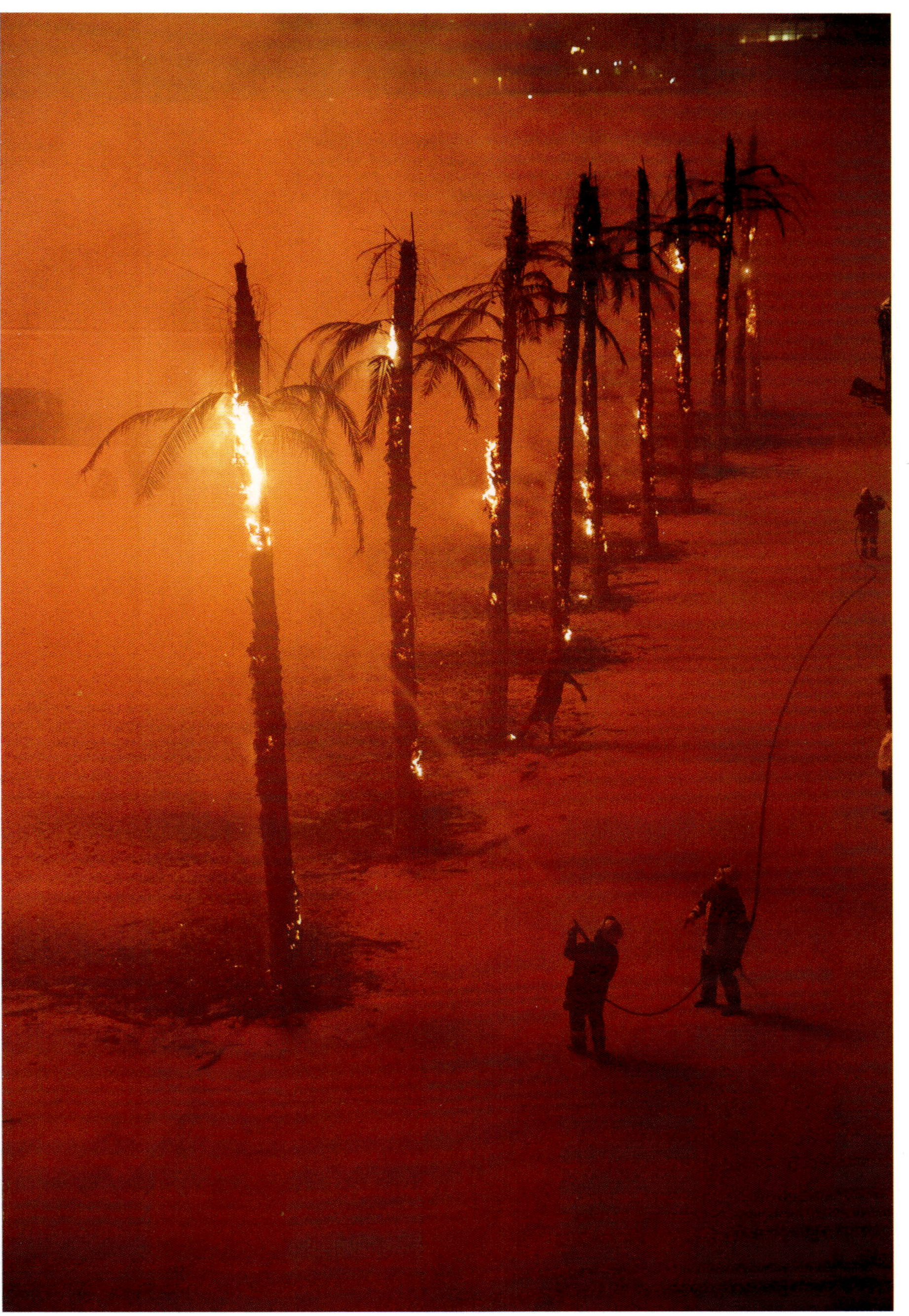

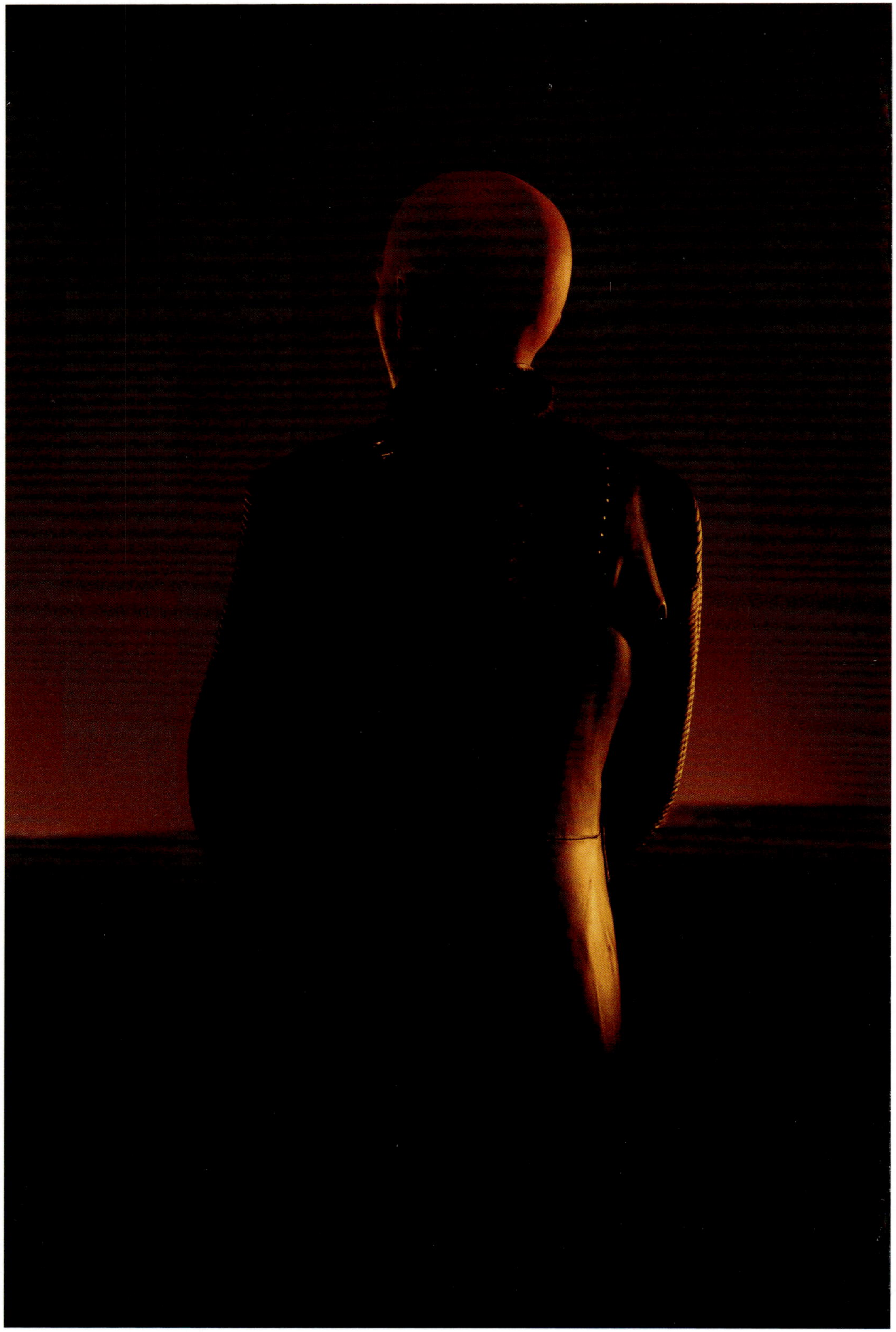

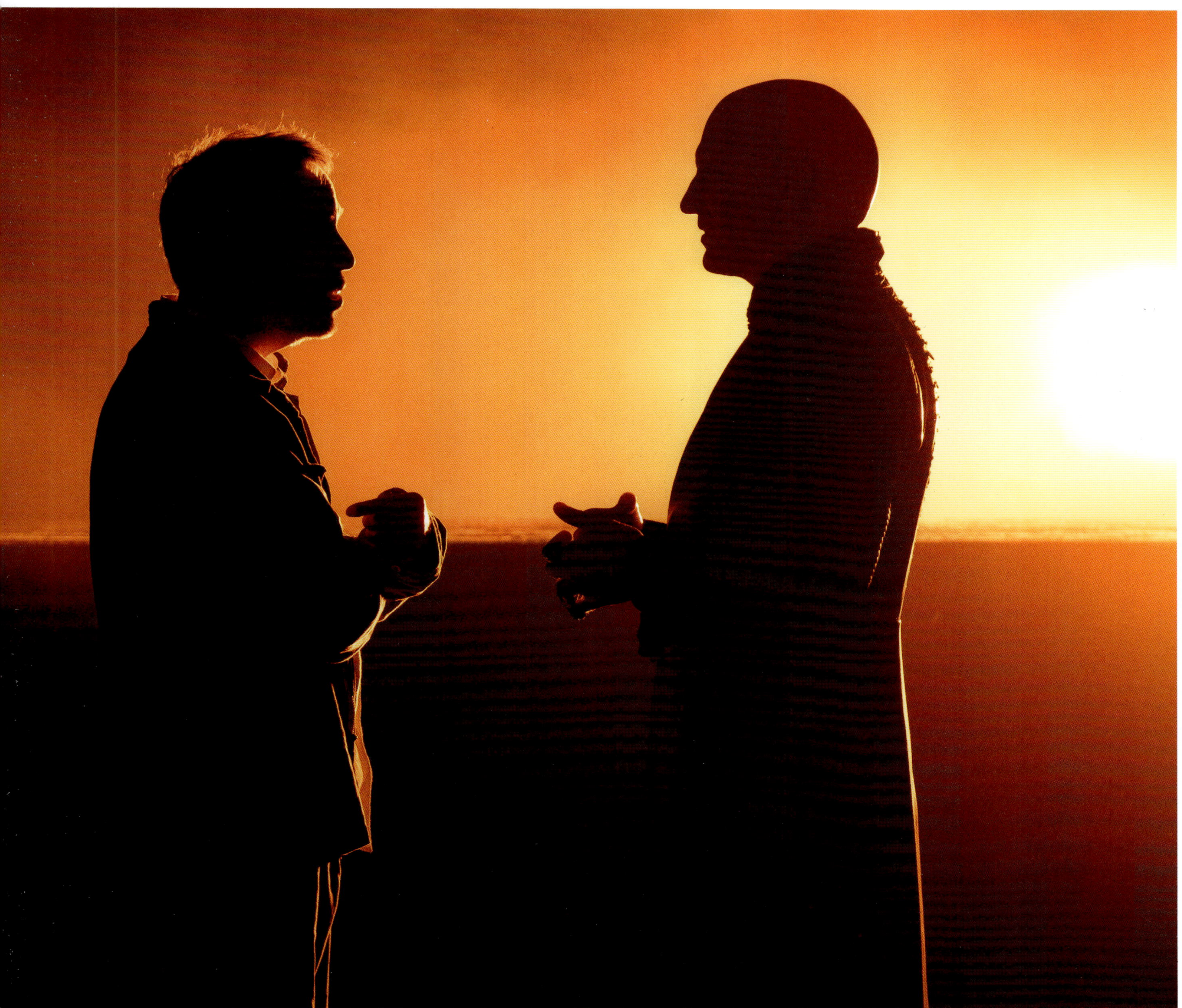

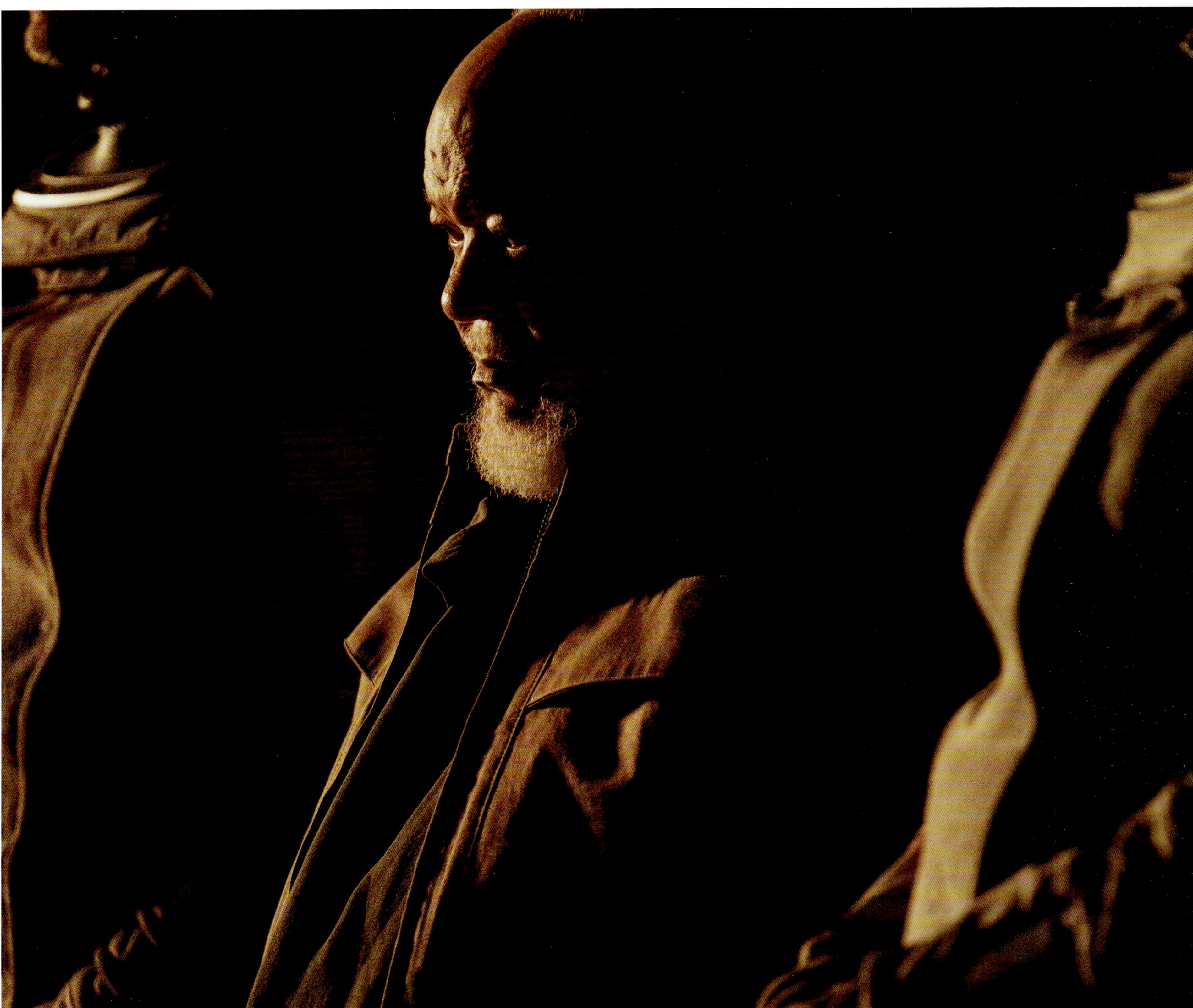

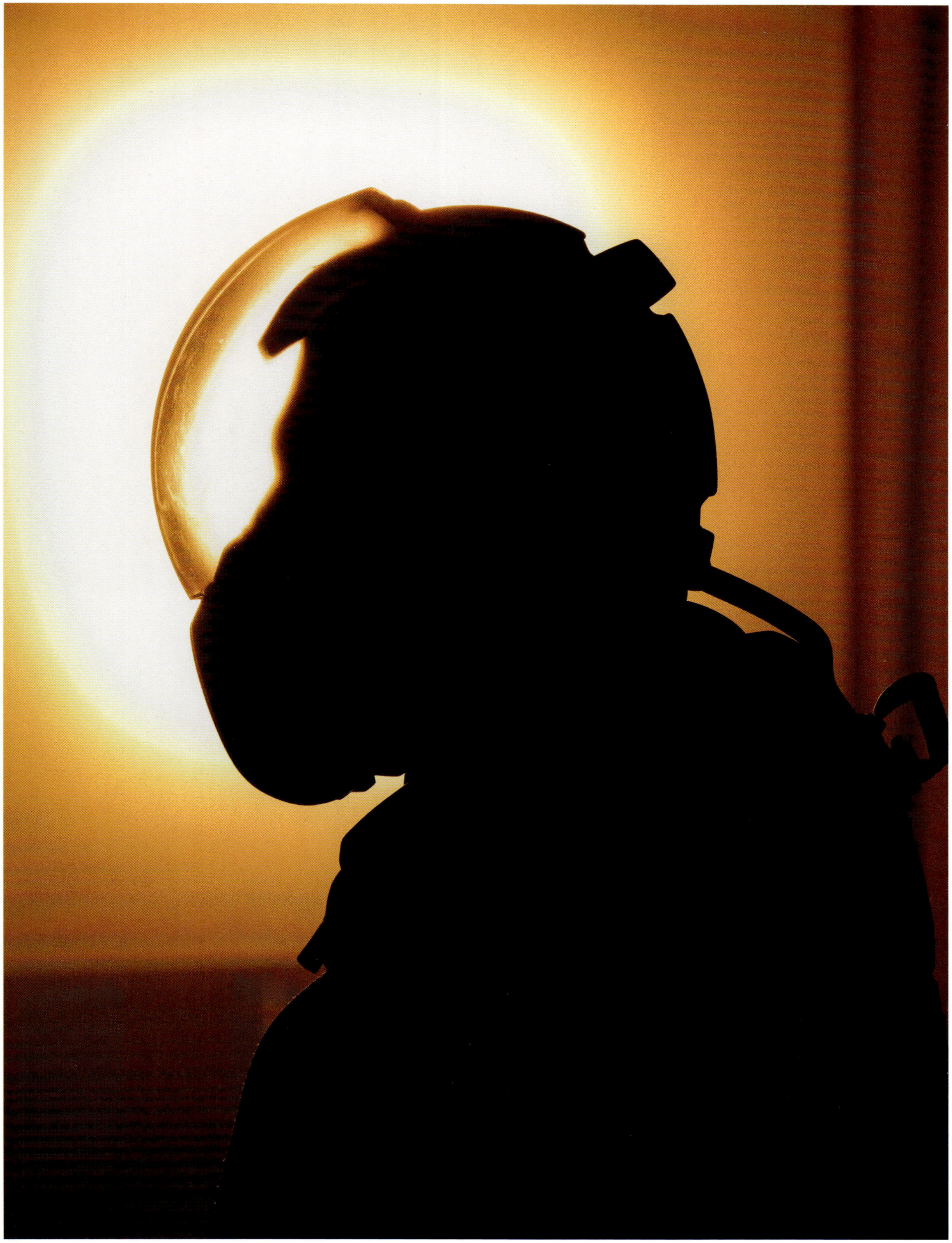

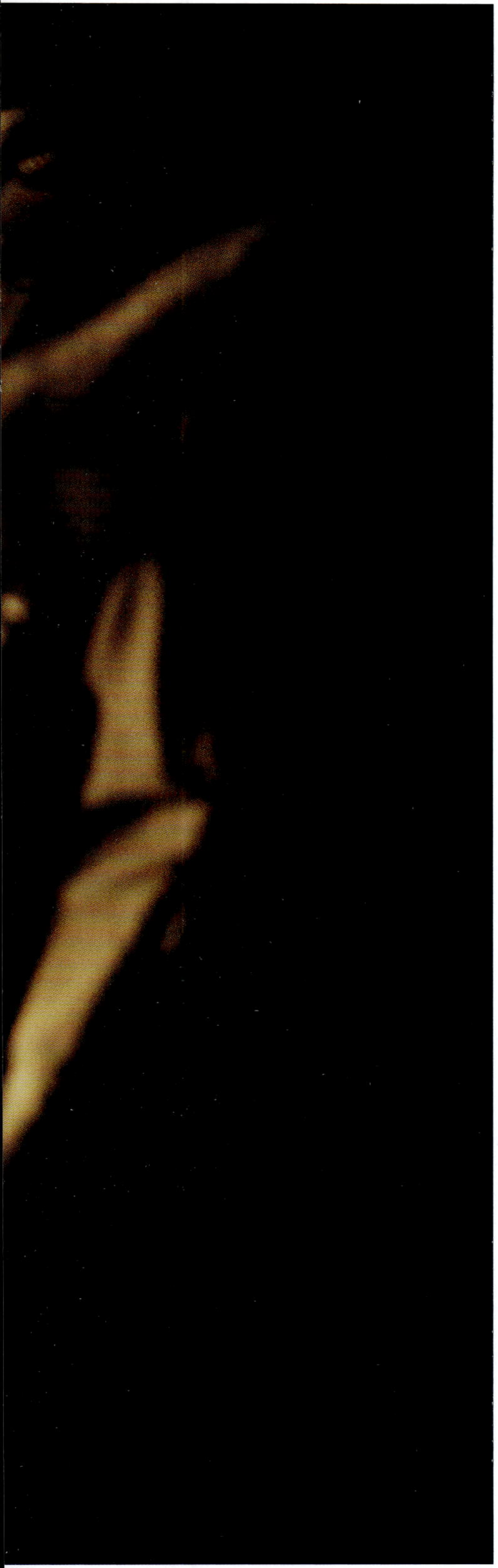

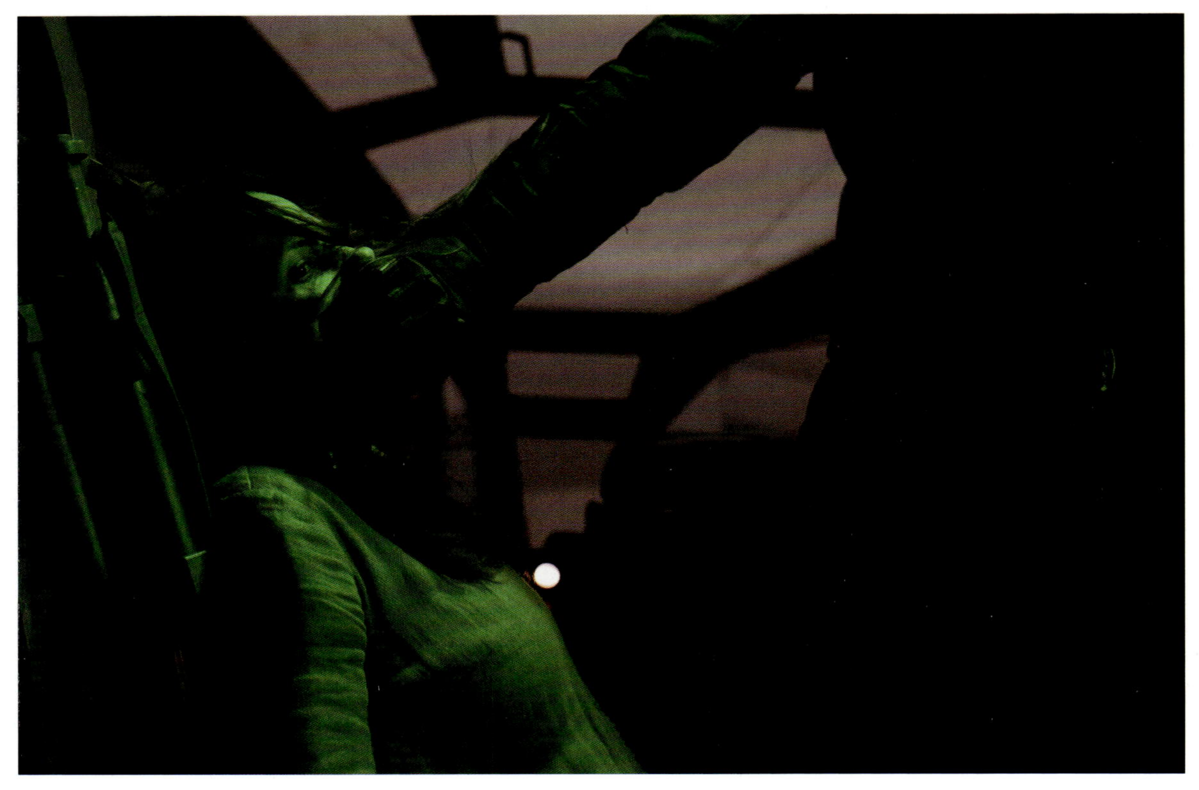

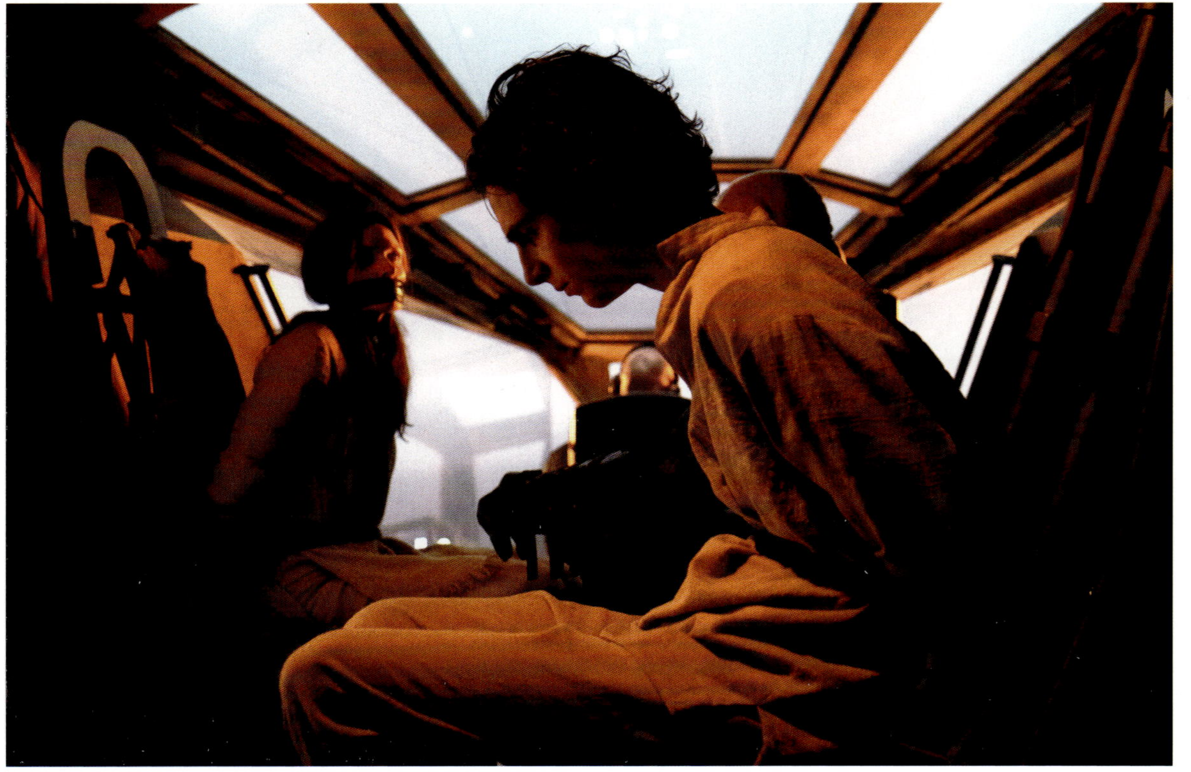

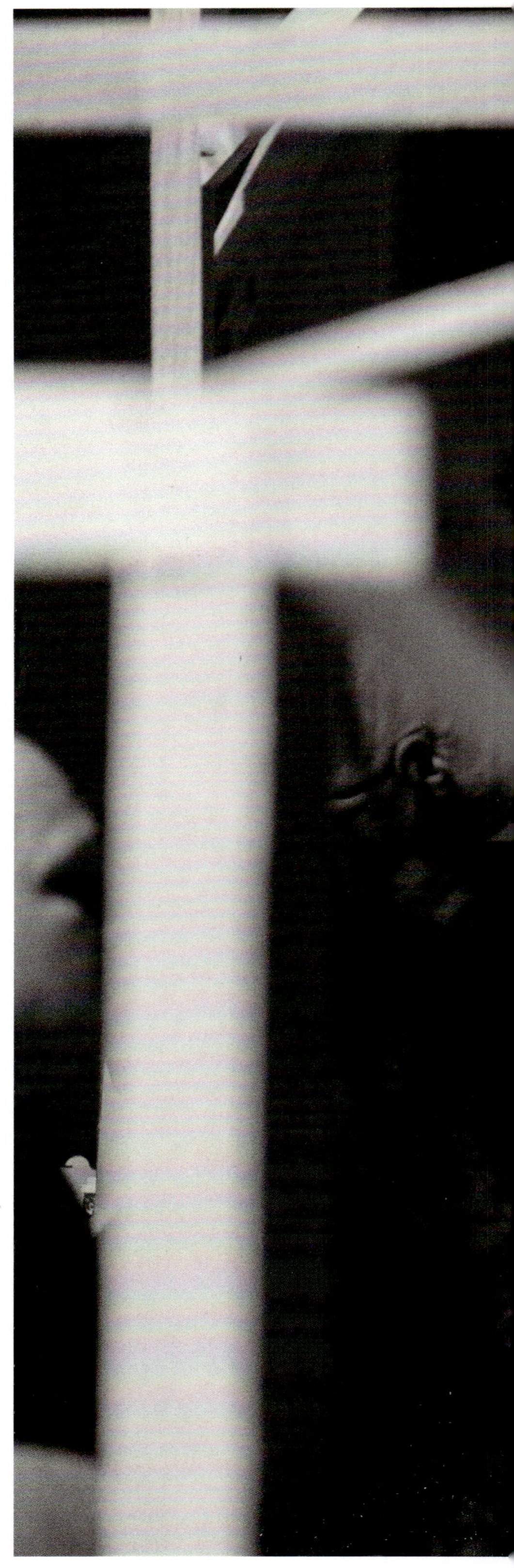

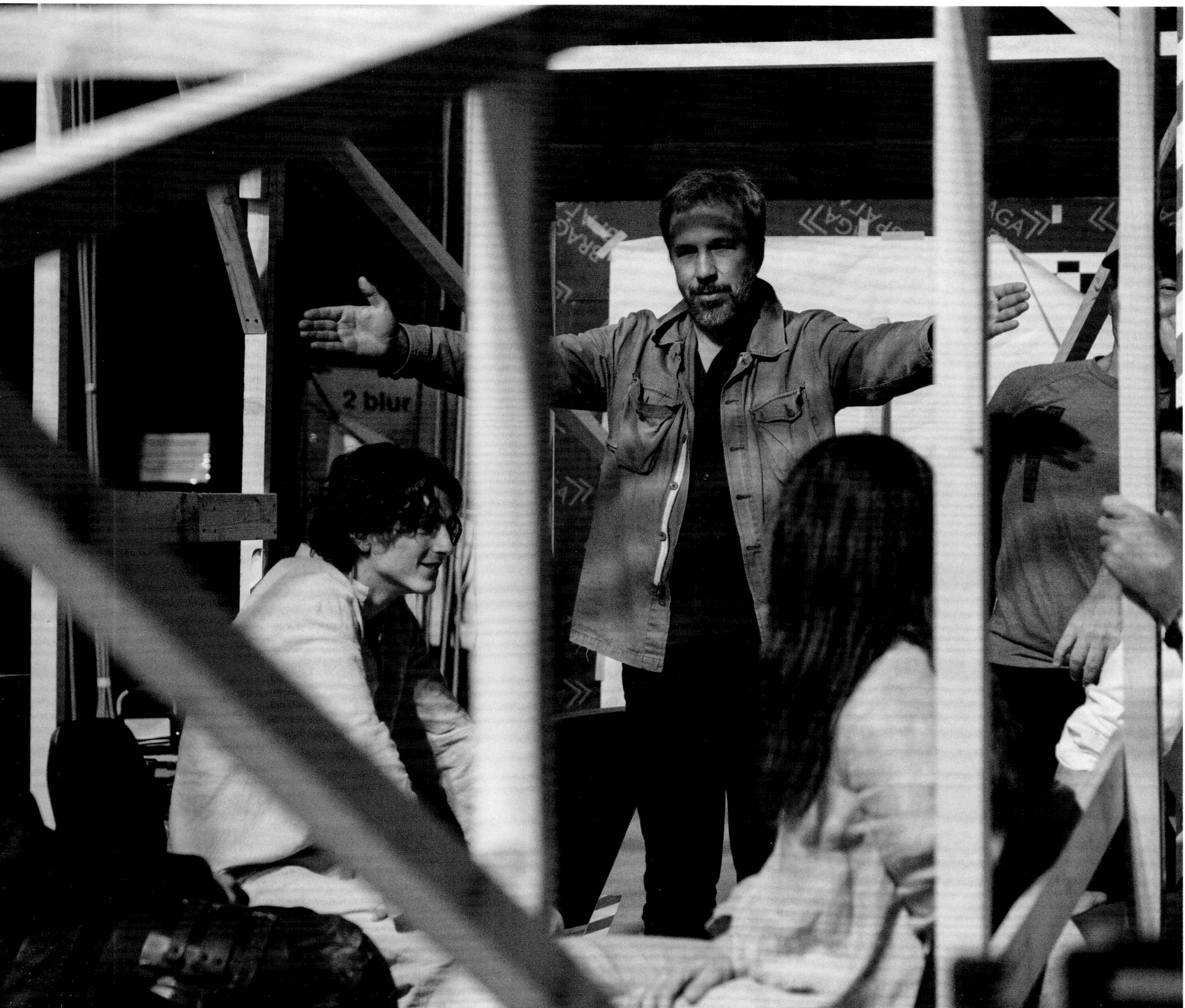
2 blur

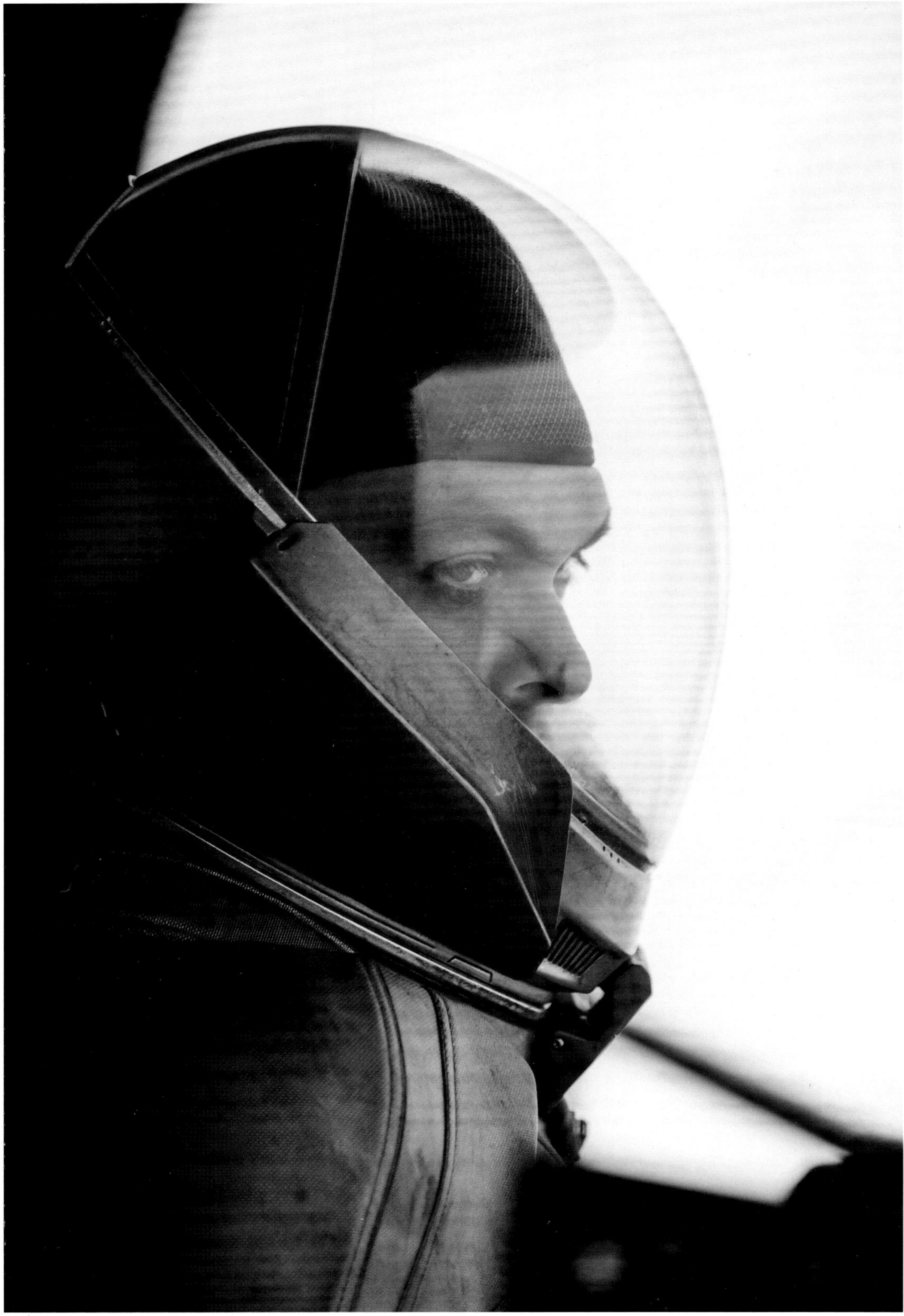

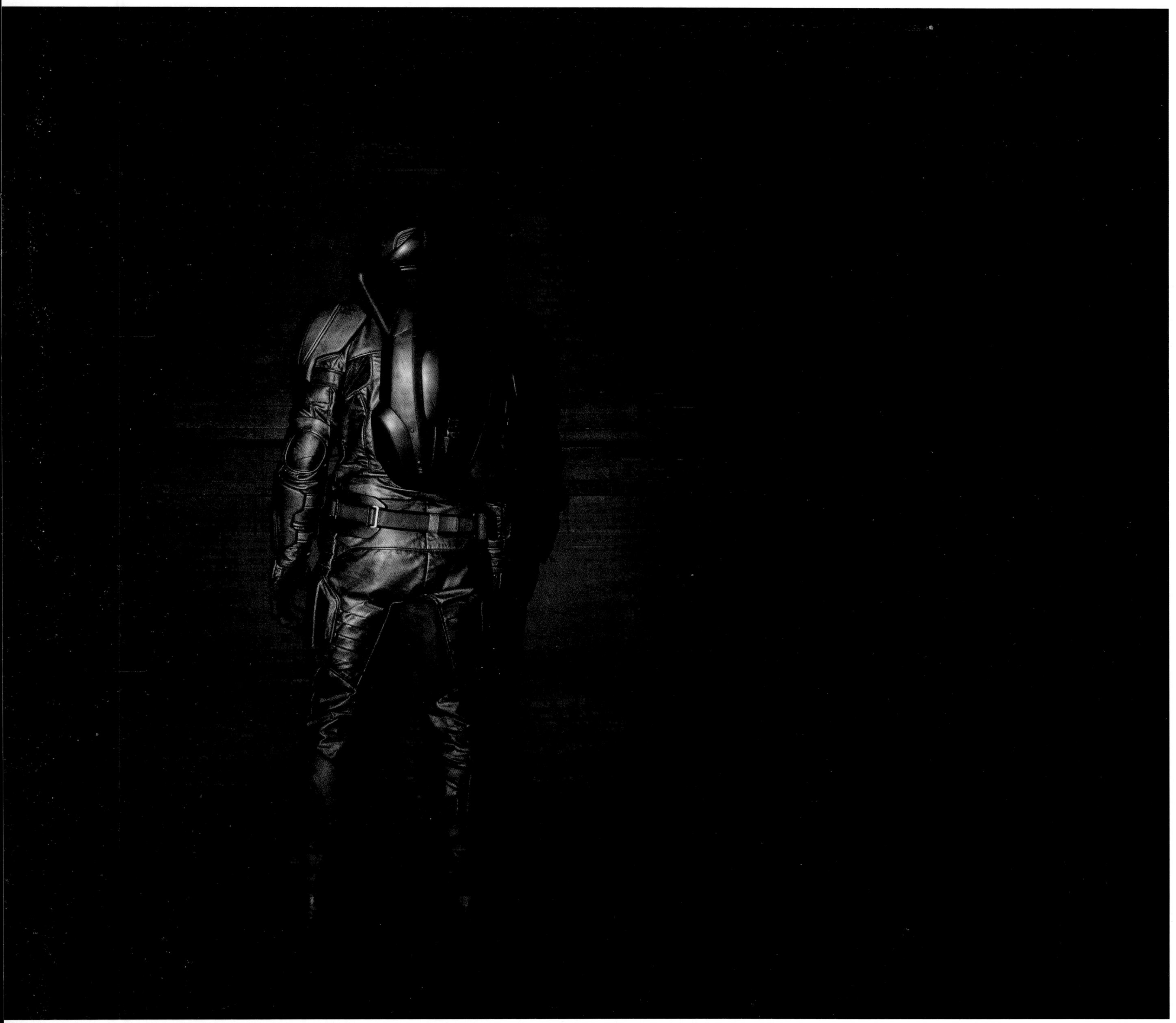

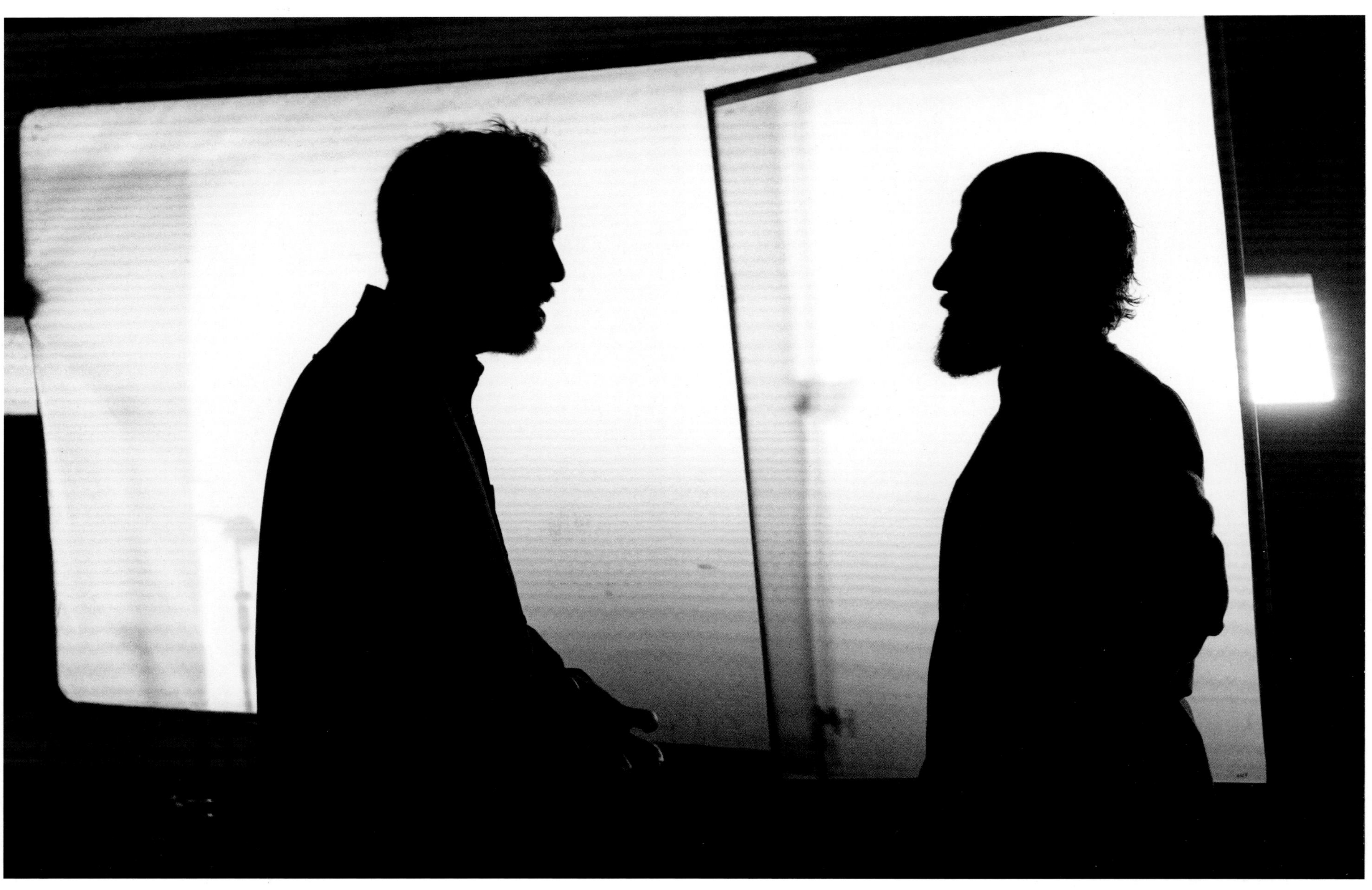

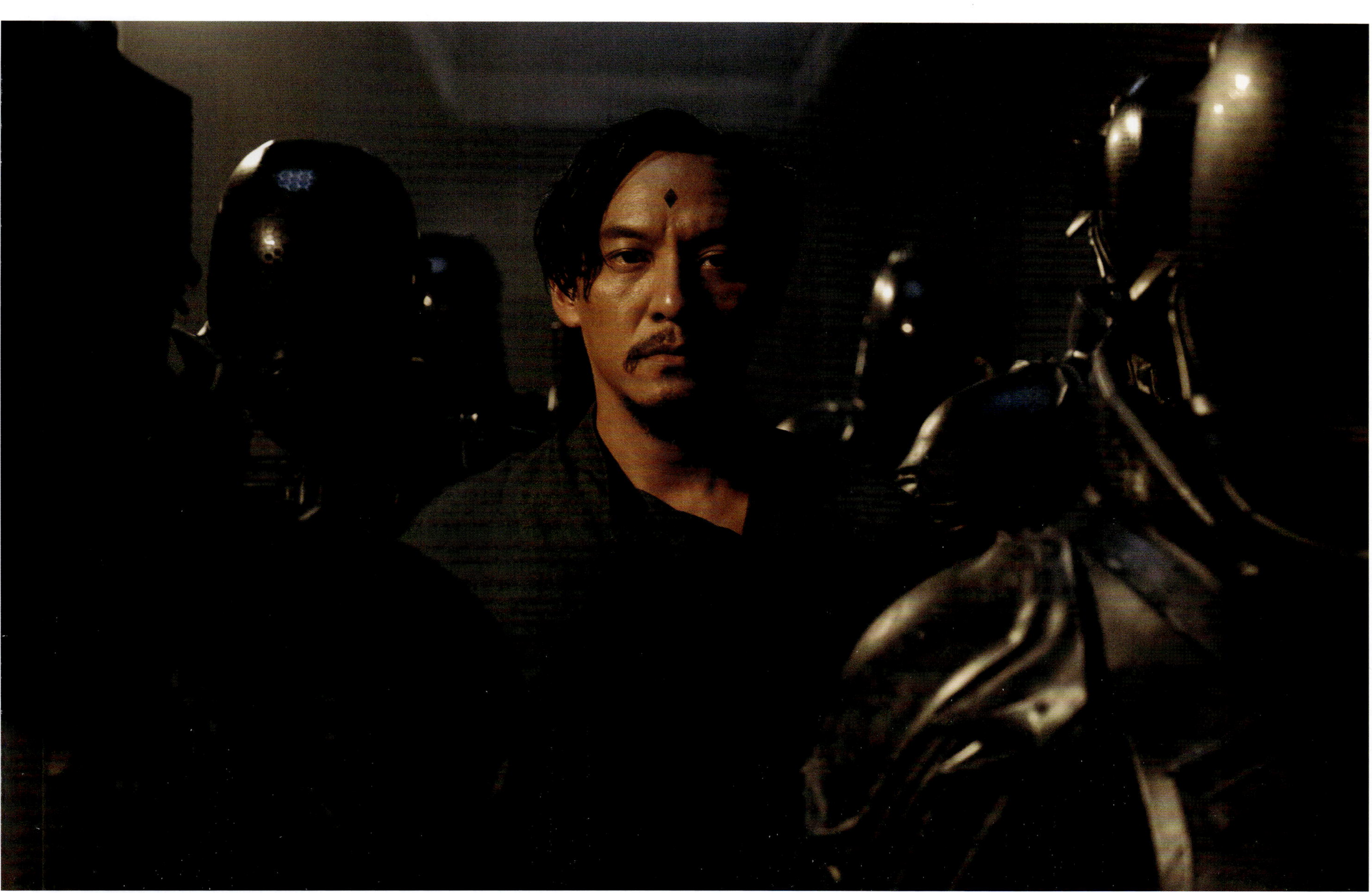

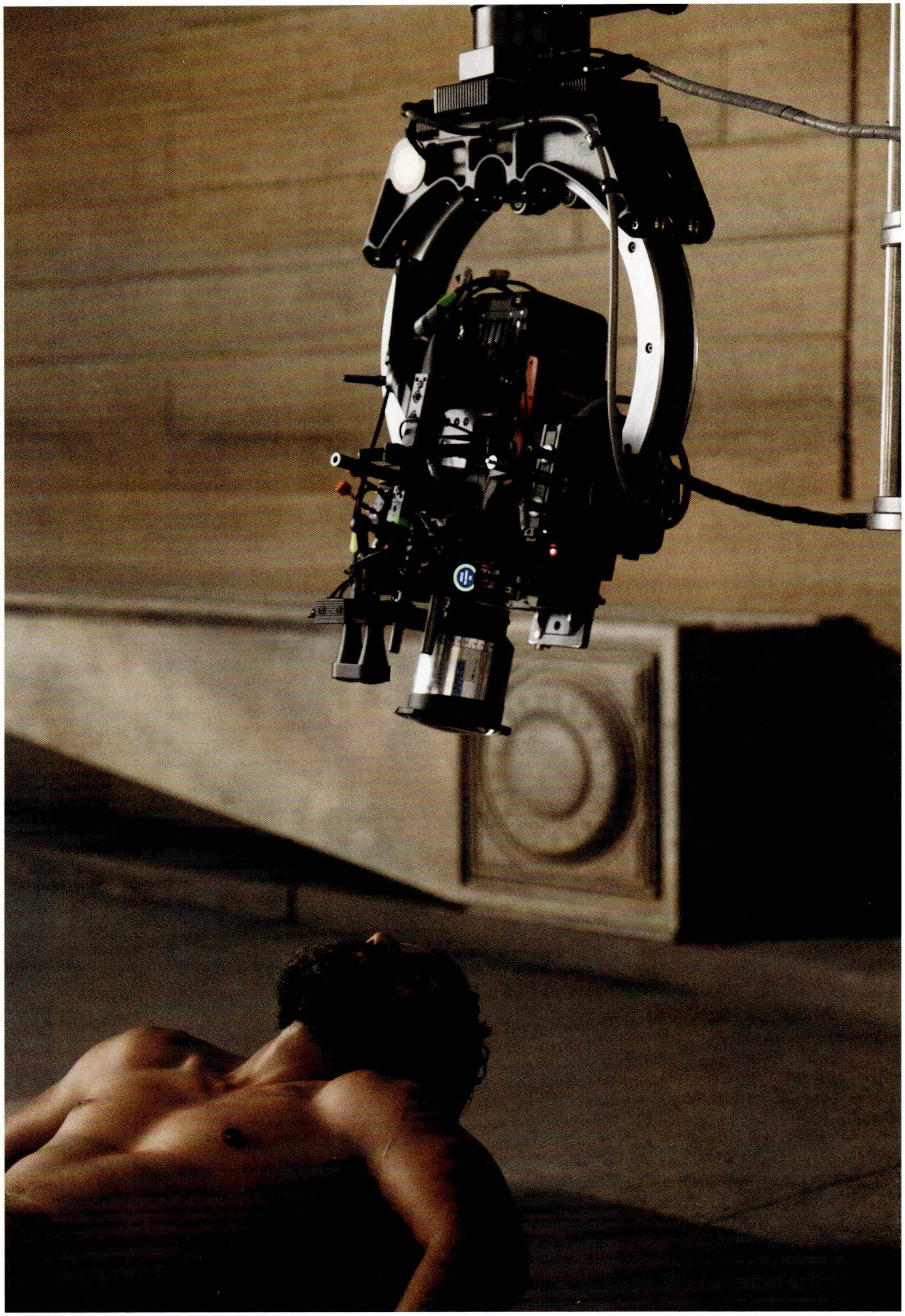

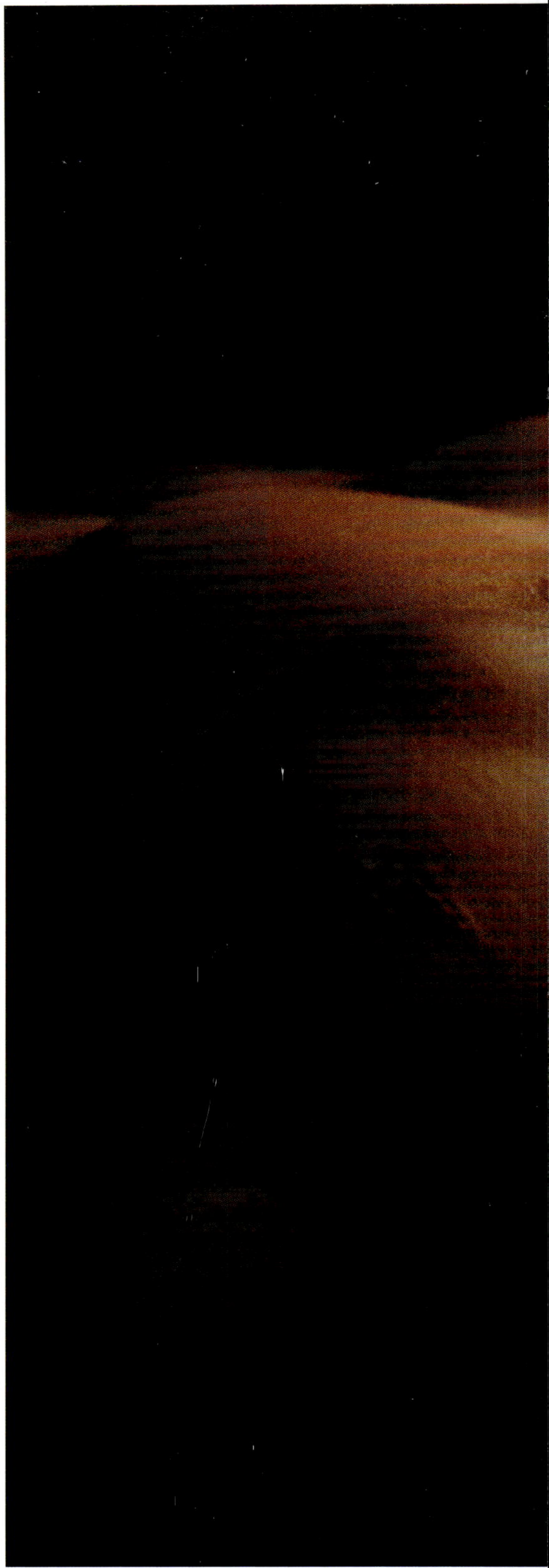

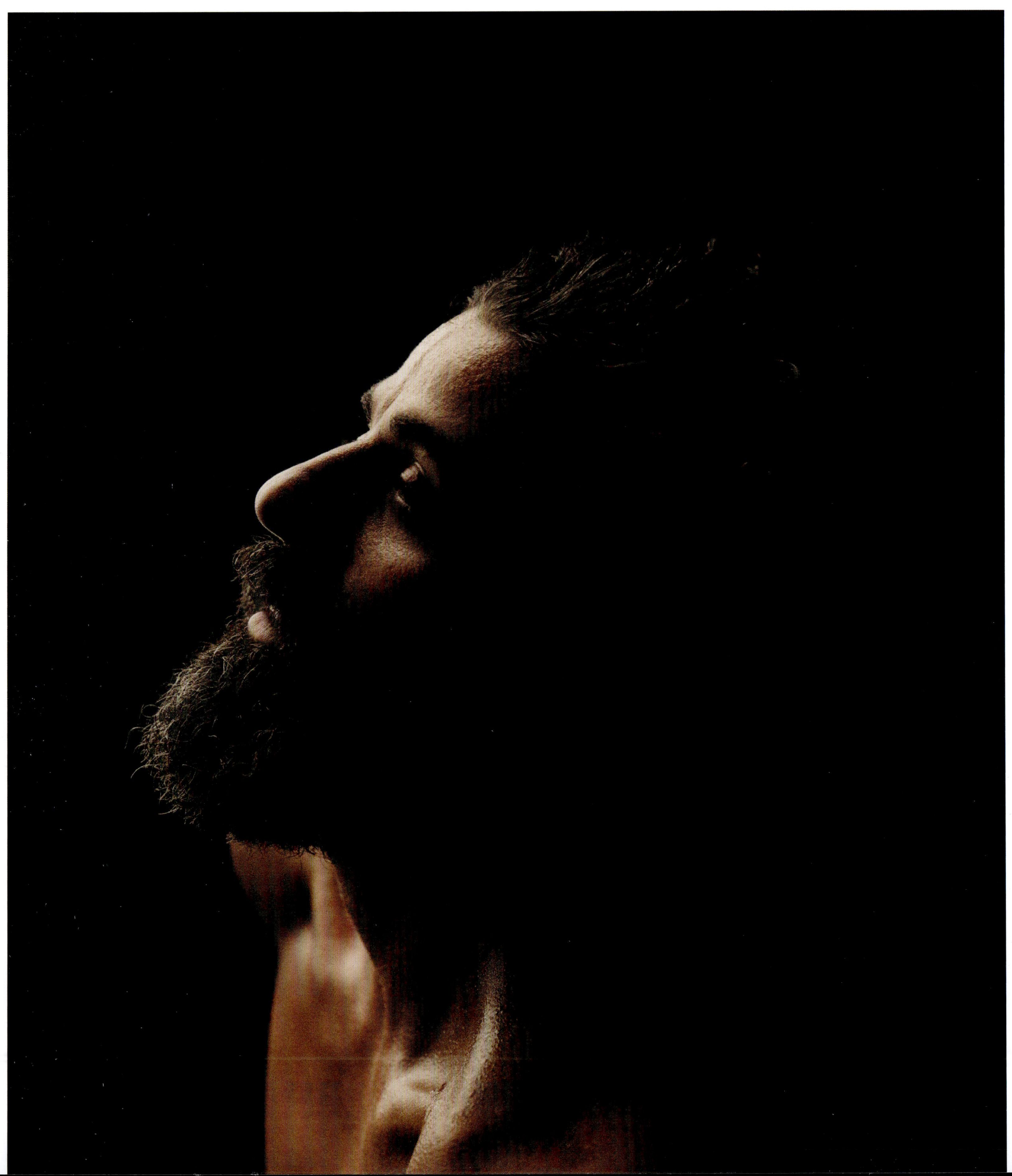

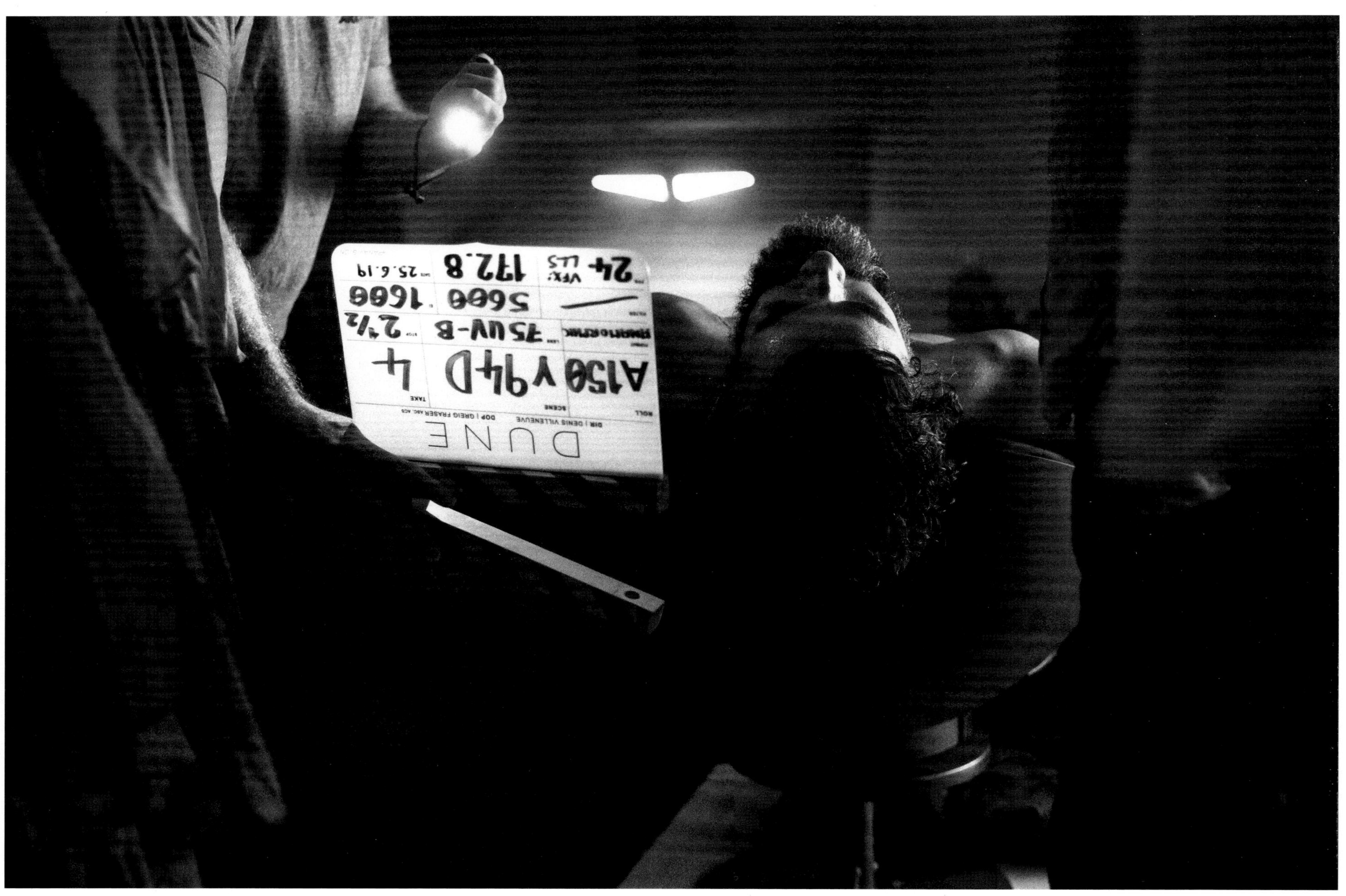

DUNE
ROLL
DIR DENIS VILLENEUVE DOP GREIG FRASER ASC ACS
SCENE A150 Y94D TAKE 4
75 UV-B 2½
5600 1666
VFX: ILS 24 172.8 25.6.19

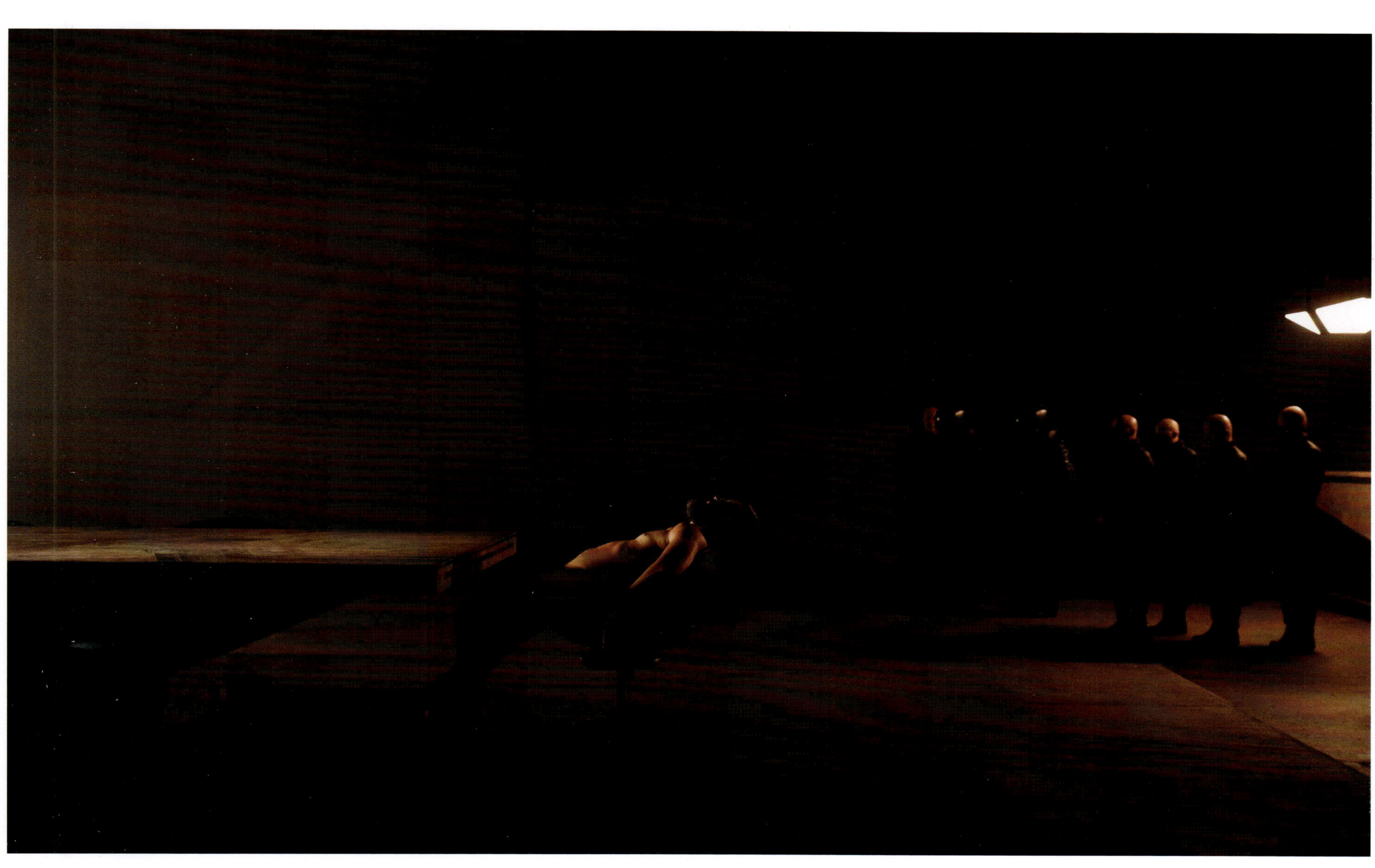

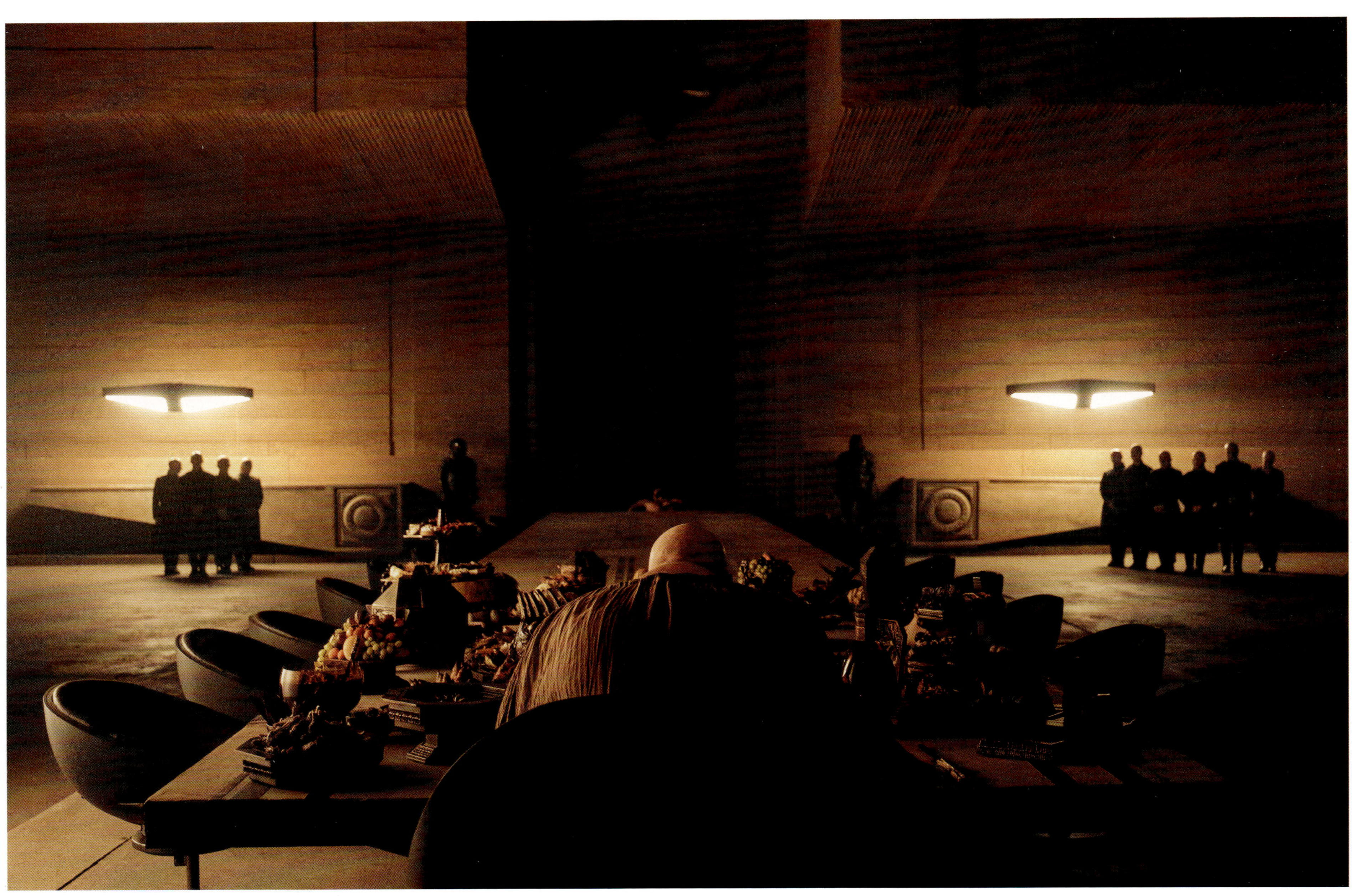

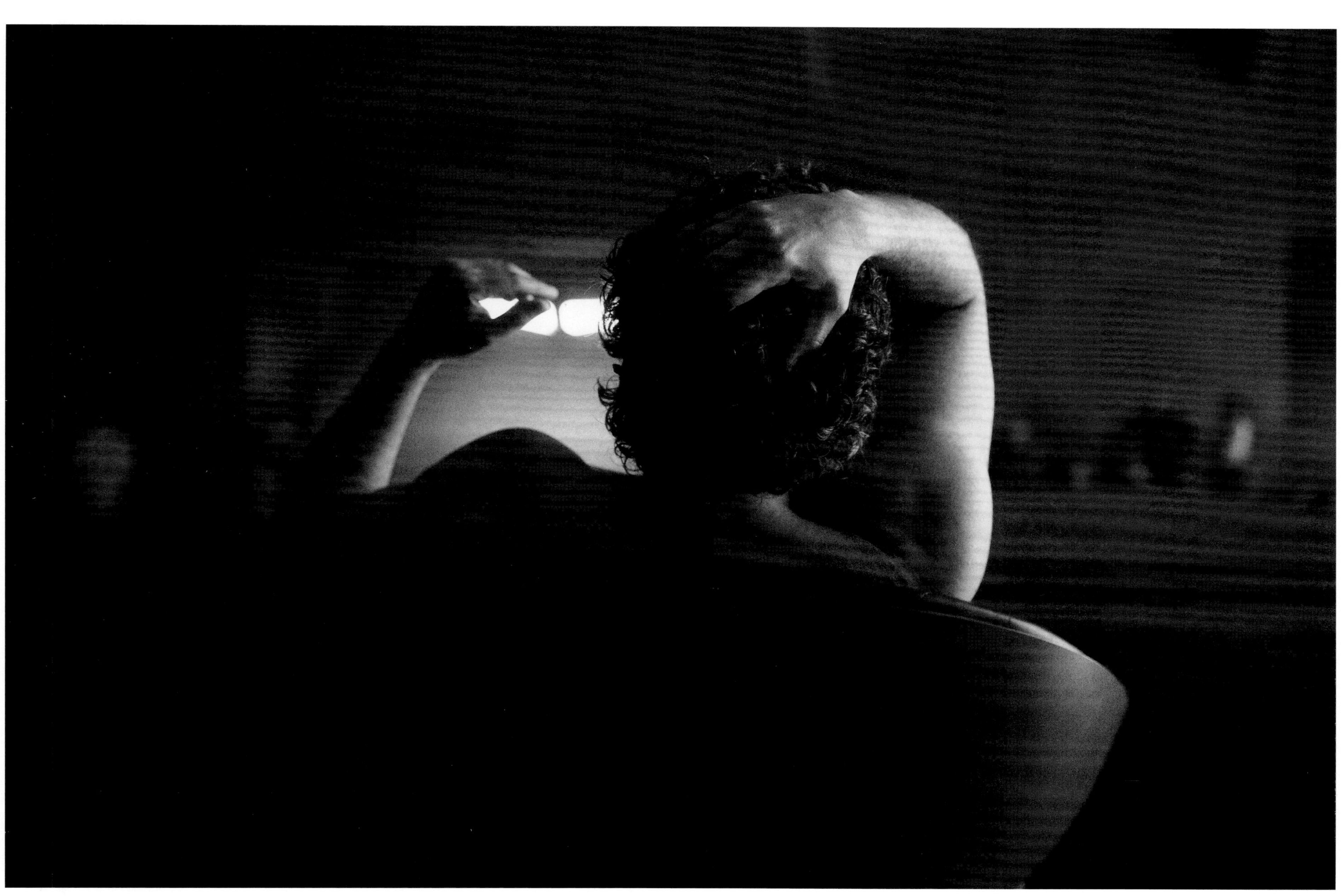

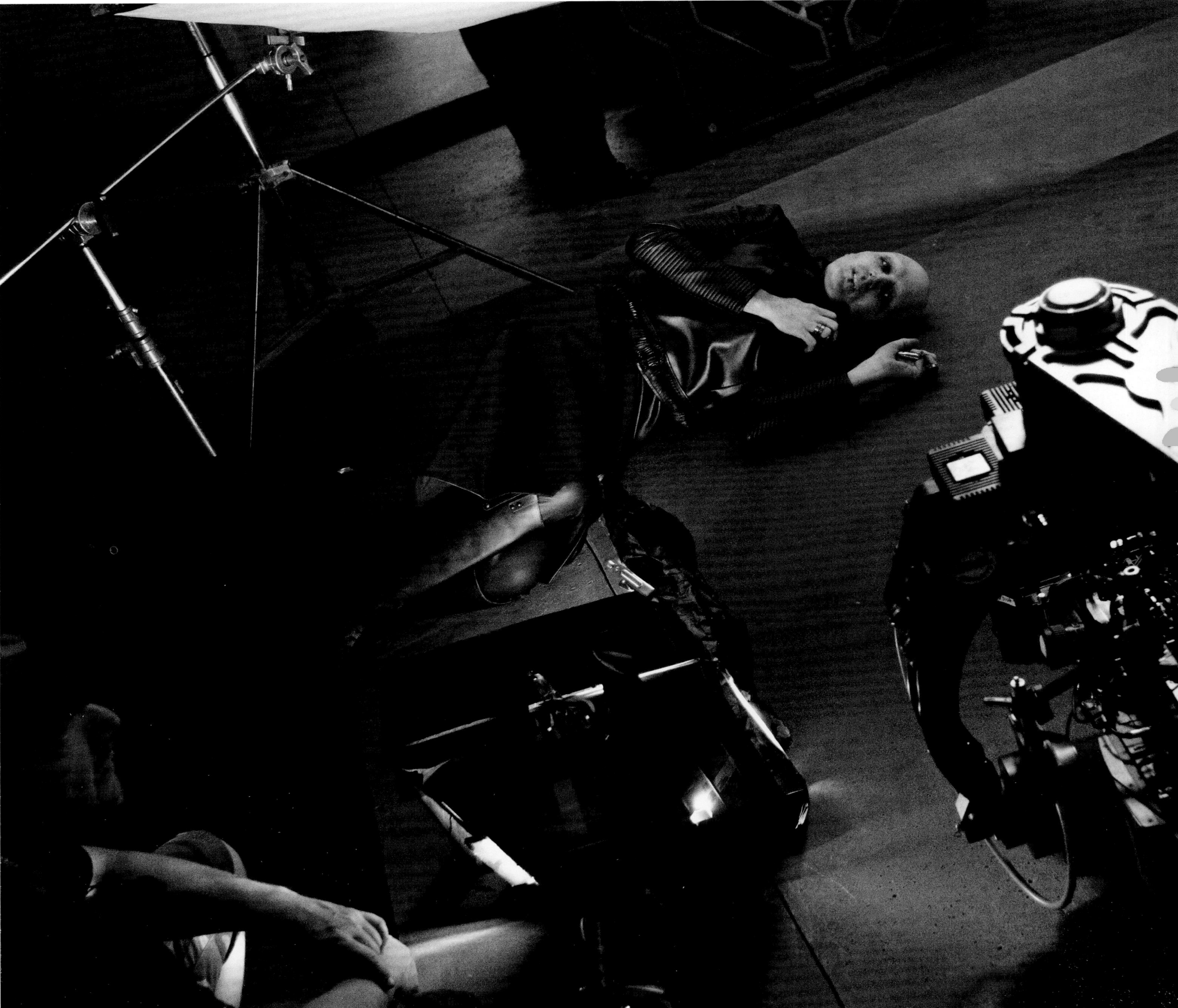

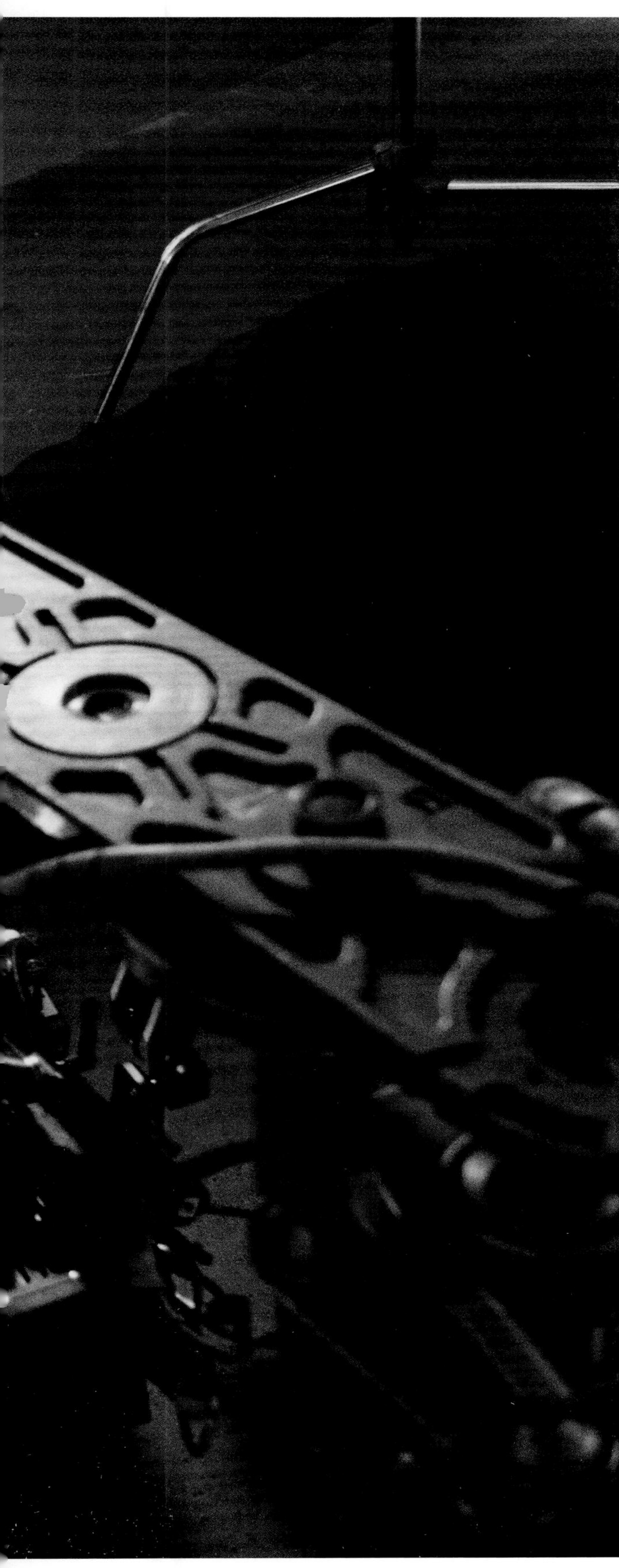

ONE OF THE STRANGEST things about working on a film production like *Dune* is the difference between the experience and the film itself. A haunting, gritty science fiction film on screen, the production was full of joy and operated with an atmosphere of zen-like productivity. An overlap of emotion between the two only seemed to show itself on the days we had to say goodbye, both on screen and off.

The deaths of Duke Leto and Piter de Vries in the same scene made for a dark but electrifying week. A death scene is never easy, but Oscar Isaac brought such a tragic quietude to the demise of the Duke, while David Dastmalchian's extraordinary talent for evoking terror was matched by his ability to endure the length of each take, frozen rigid by poison, for Piter's last moments. Off camera, both Oscar and David were congratulated with hugs and laughs and a sense of sadness. Parting ways with characters was difficult but usually meant we were moving on to another scene, another set. Saying goodbye to these incredible performers who had been a part of our family on the road was a much harder farewell, but such is the nature of making a movie.

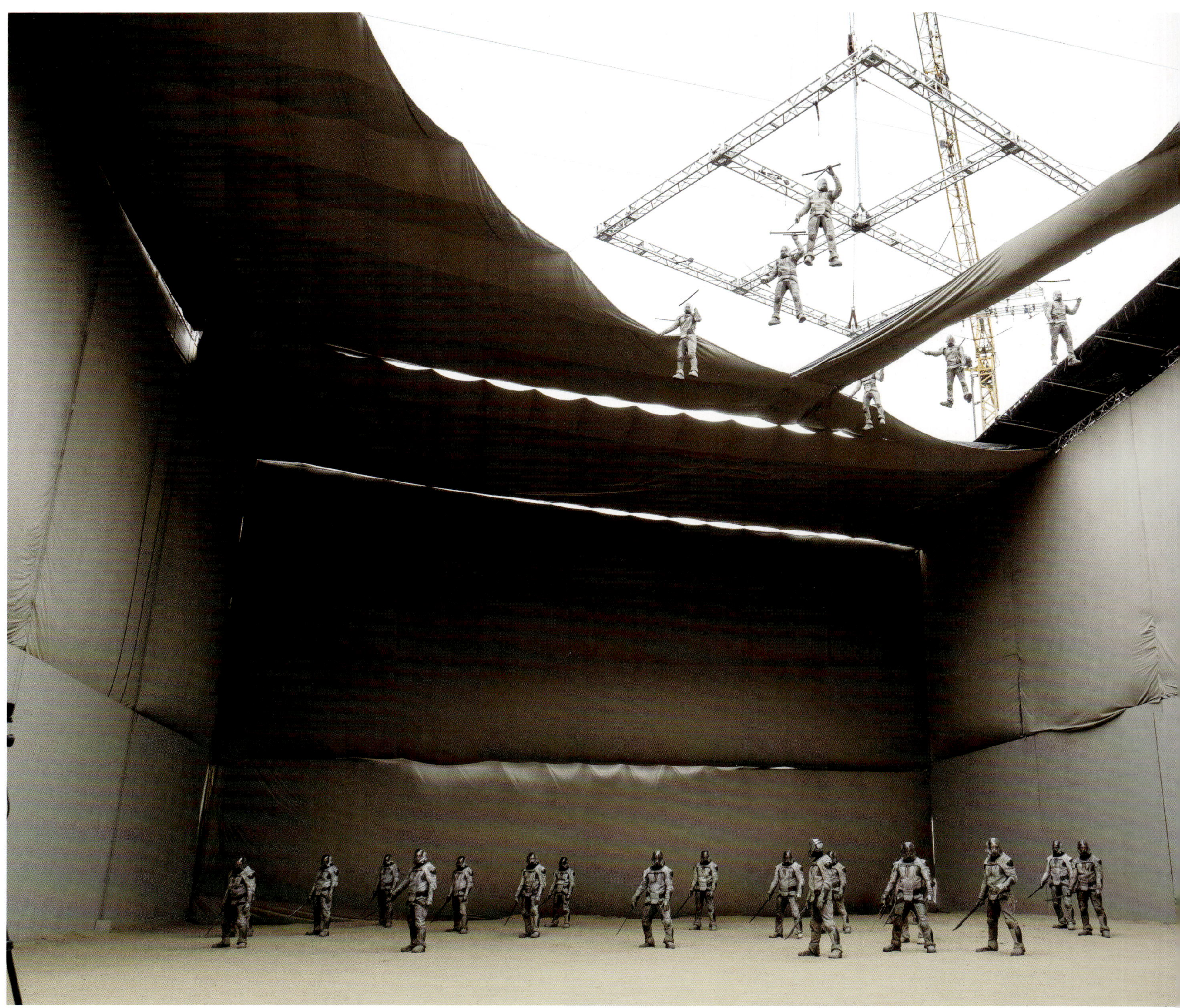

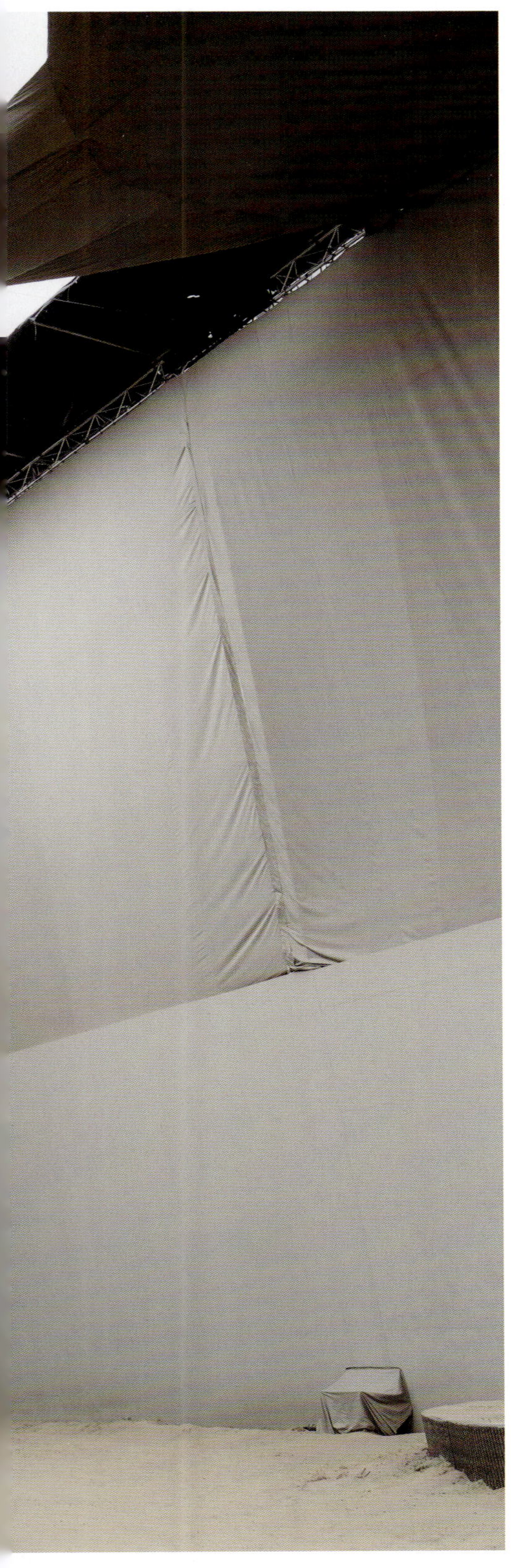

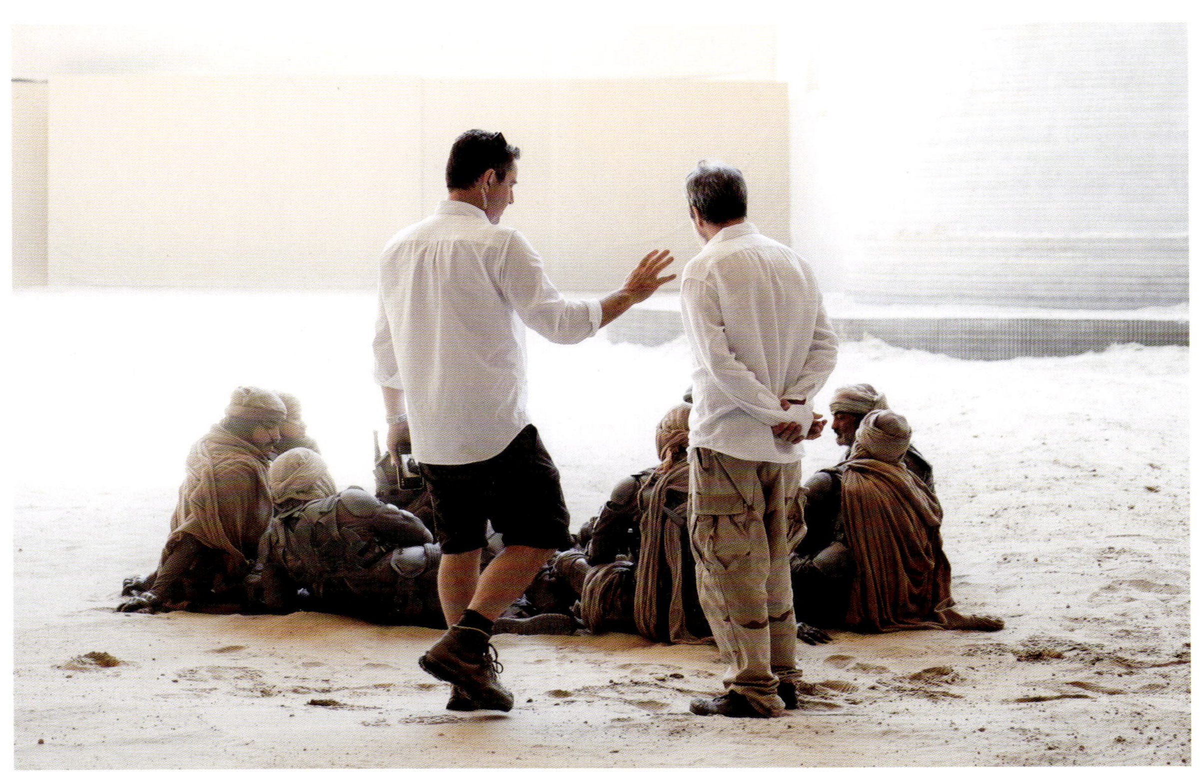

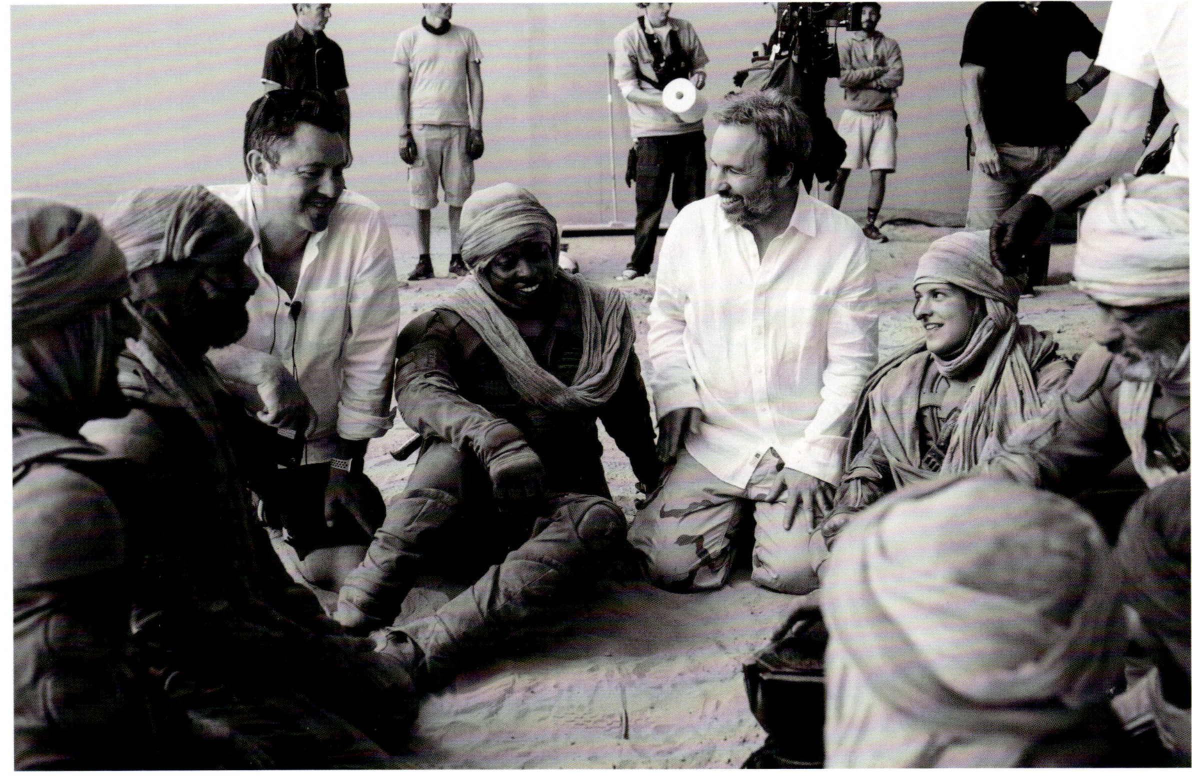

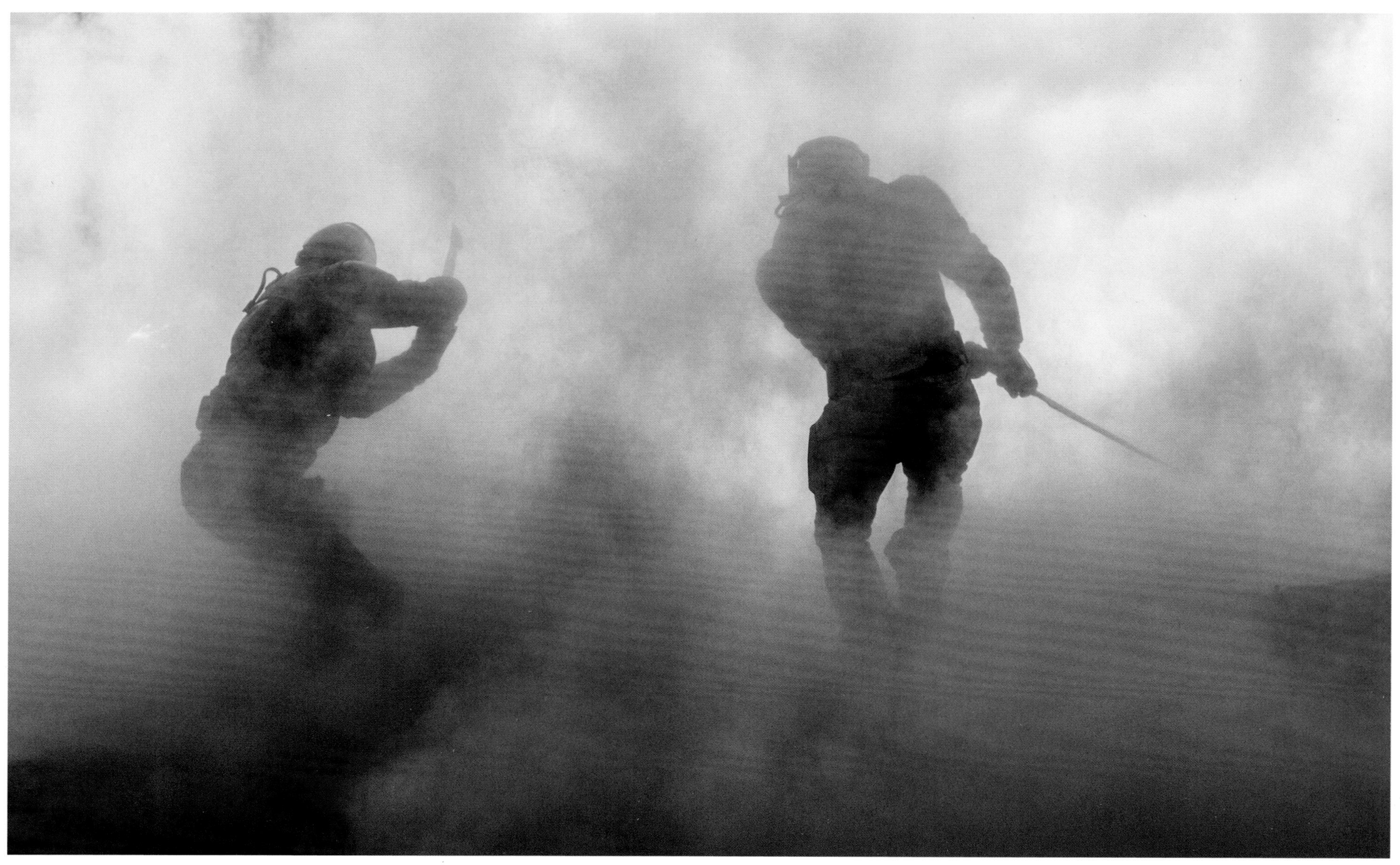

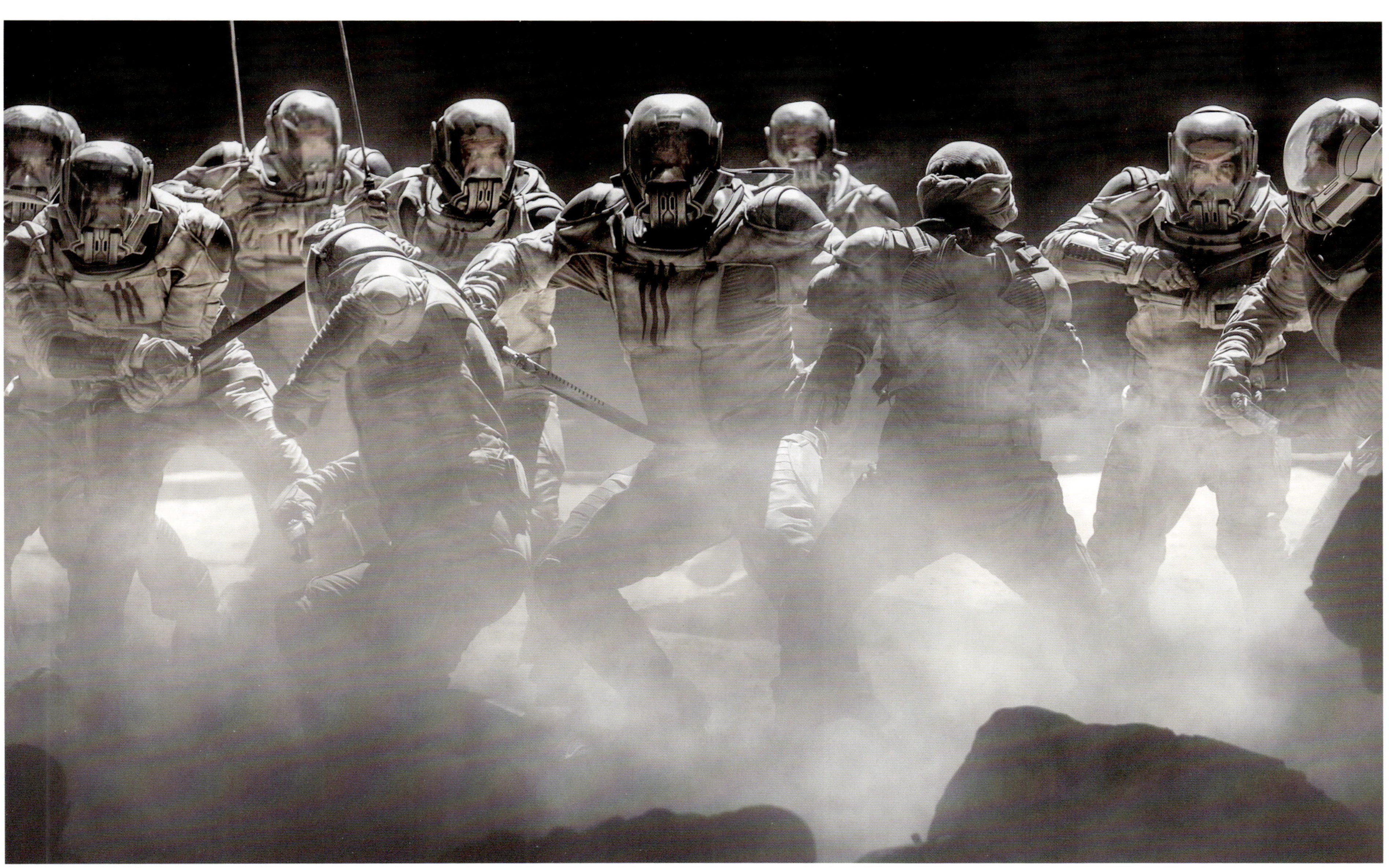

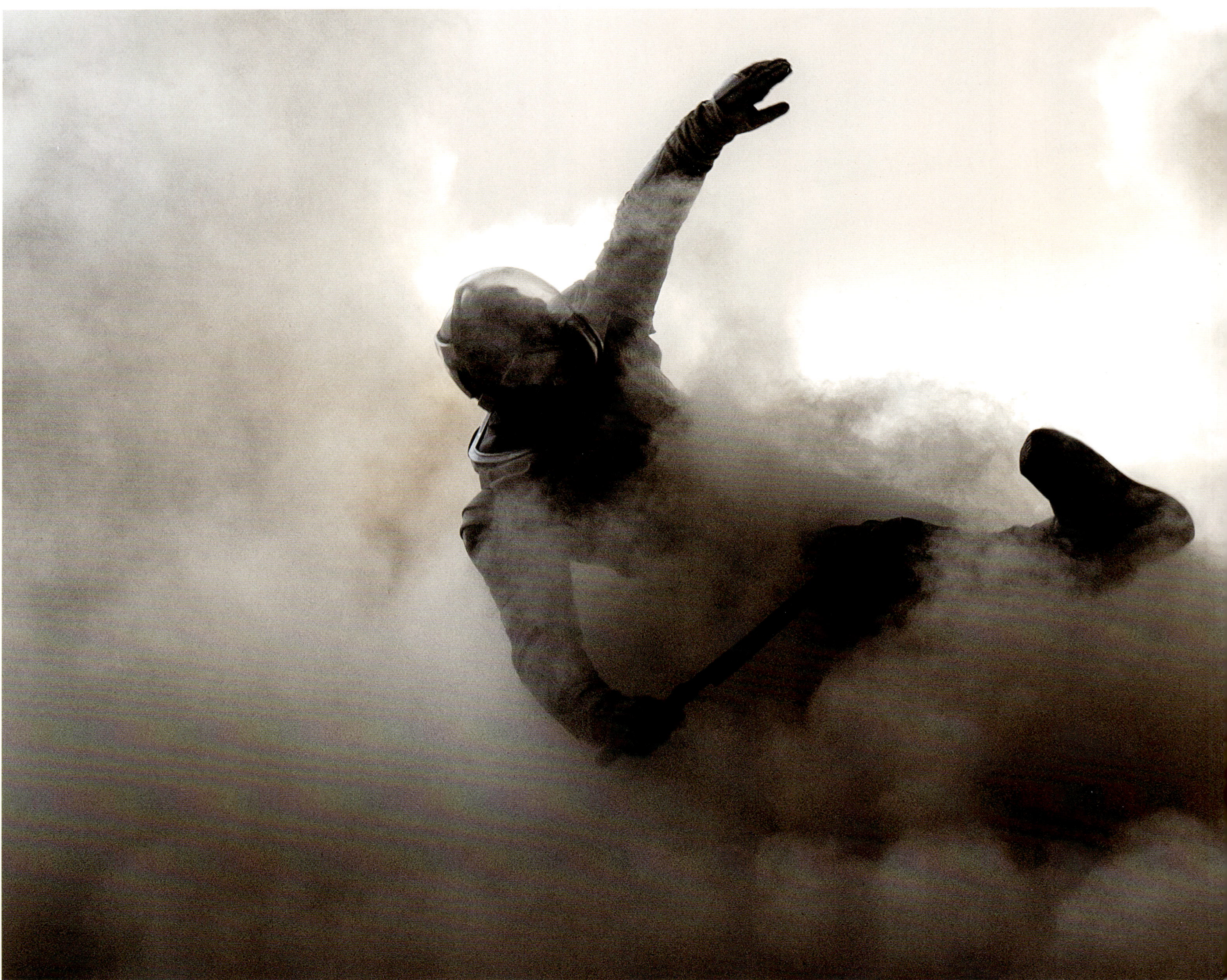

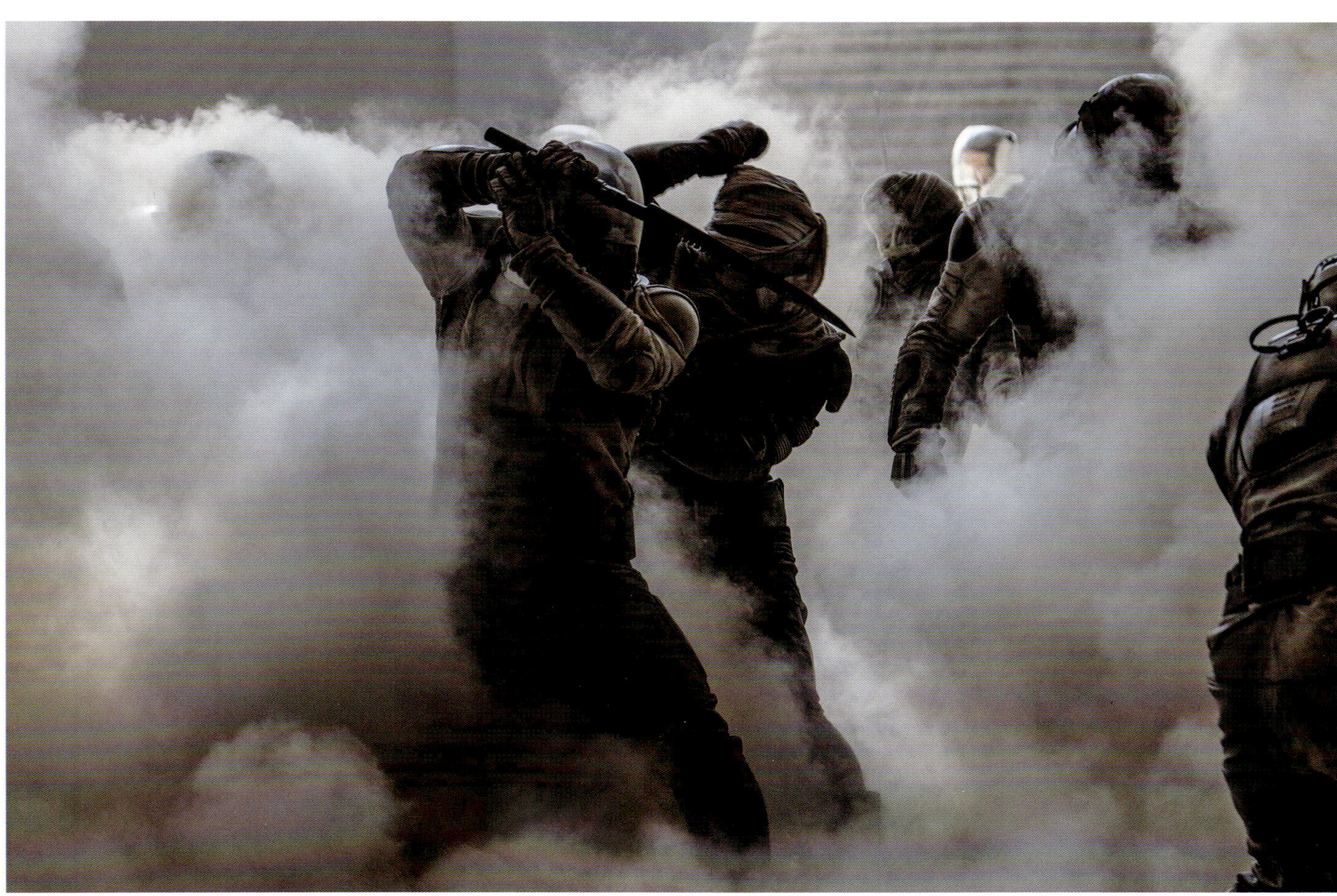

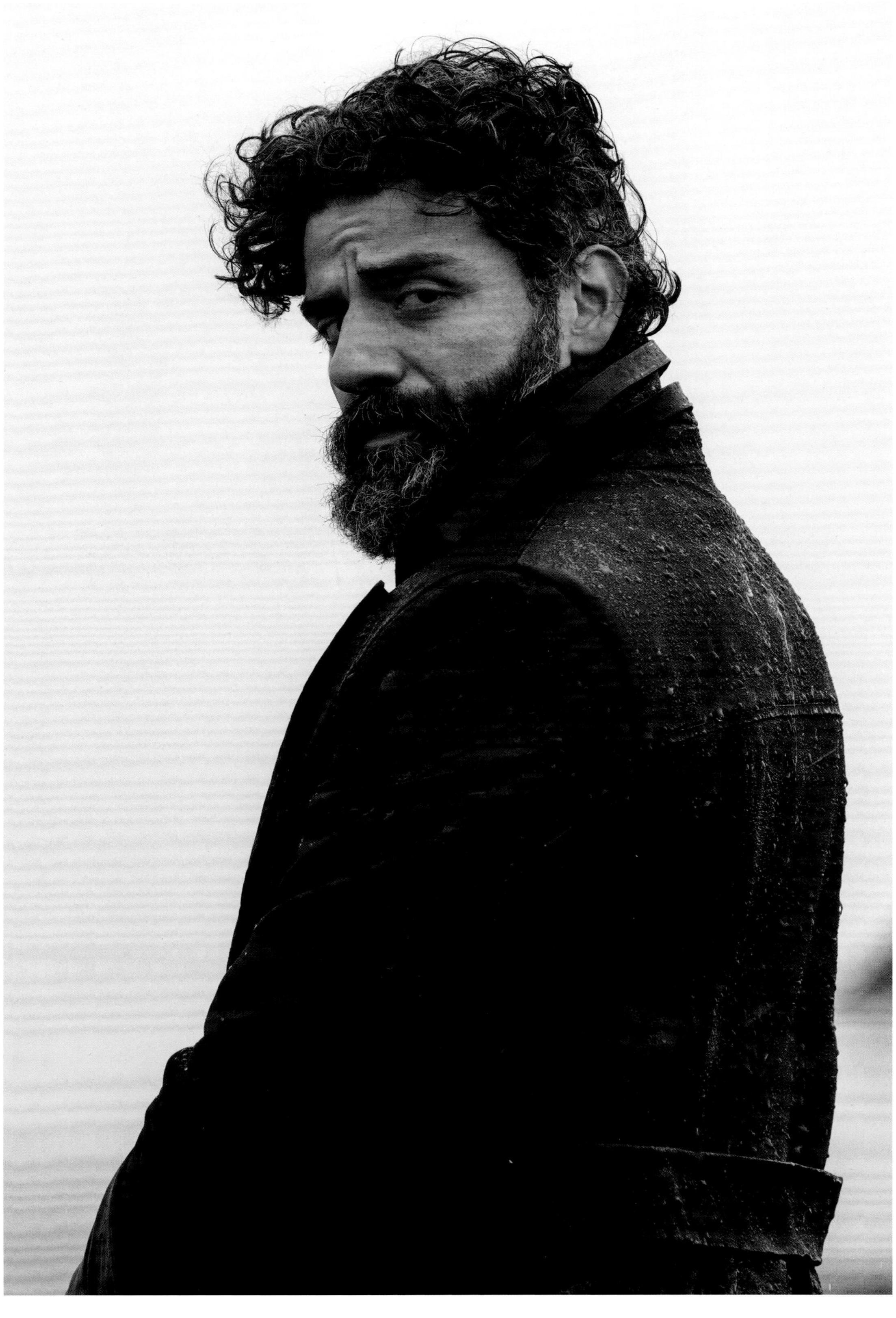

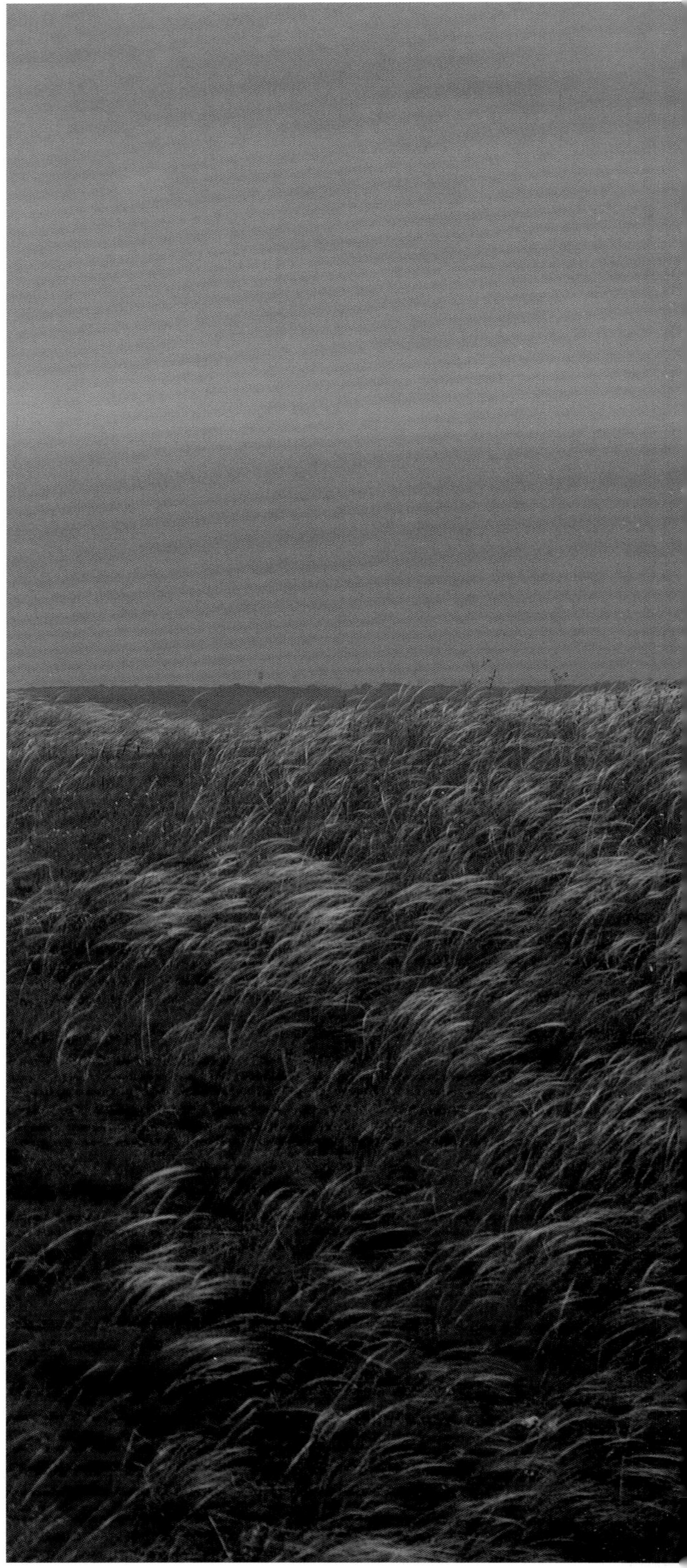

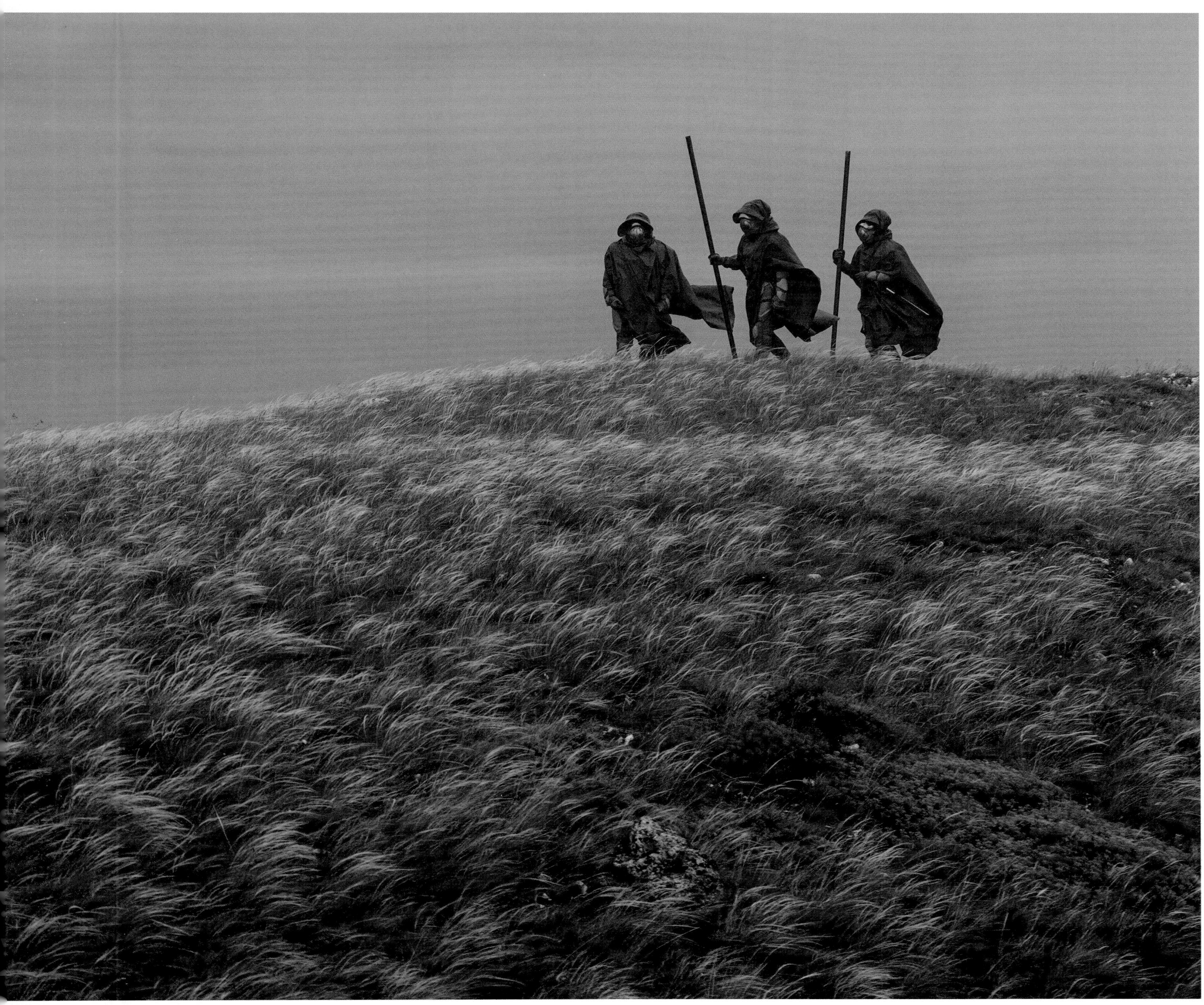

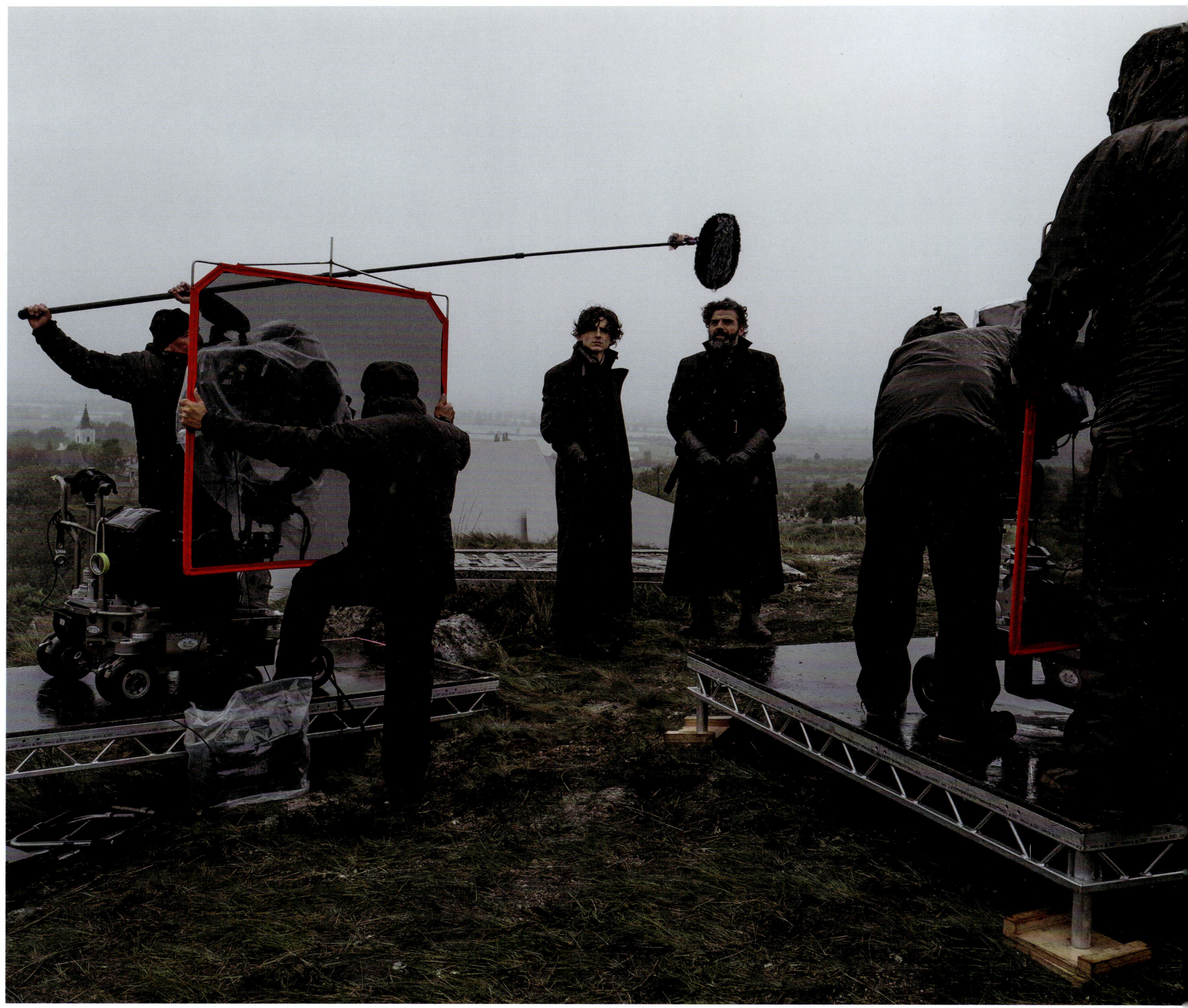

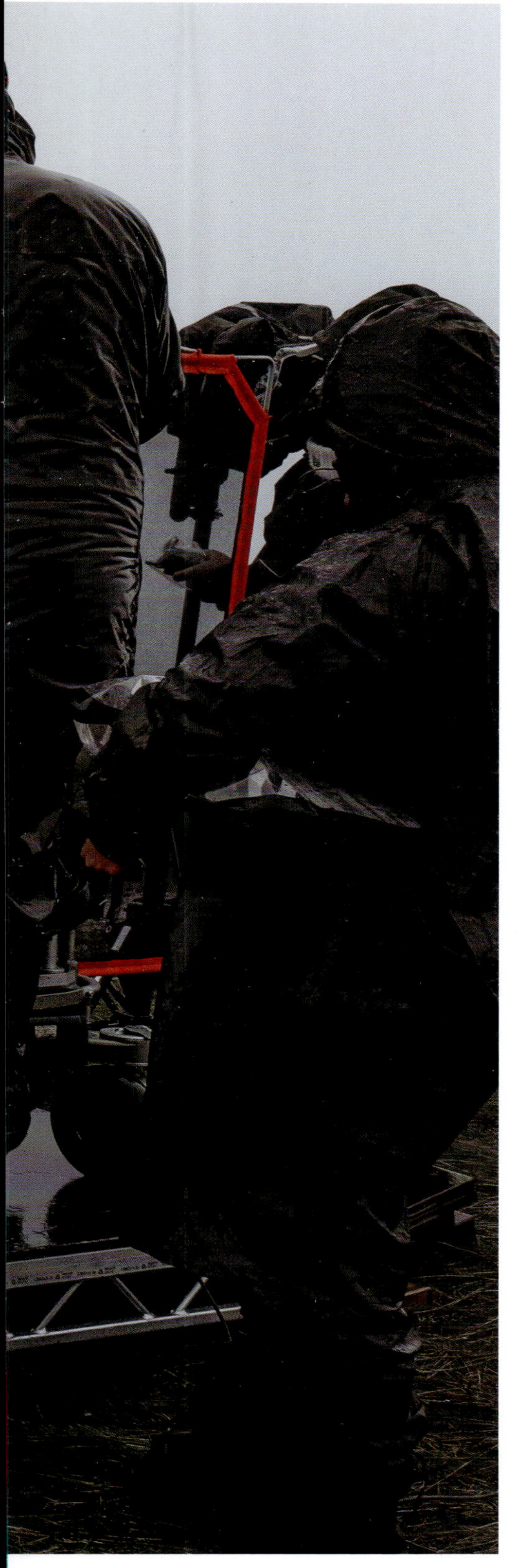

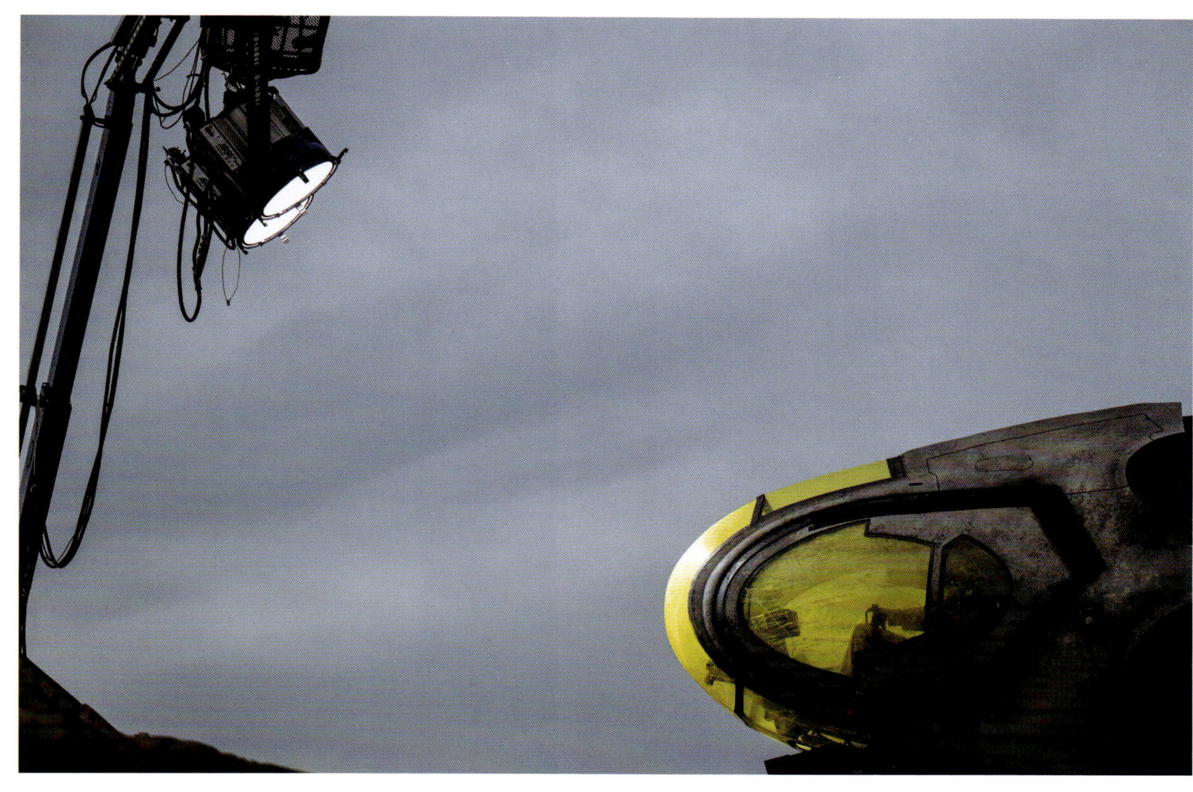

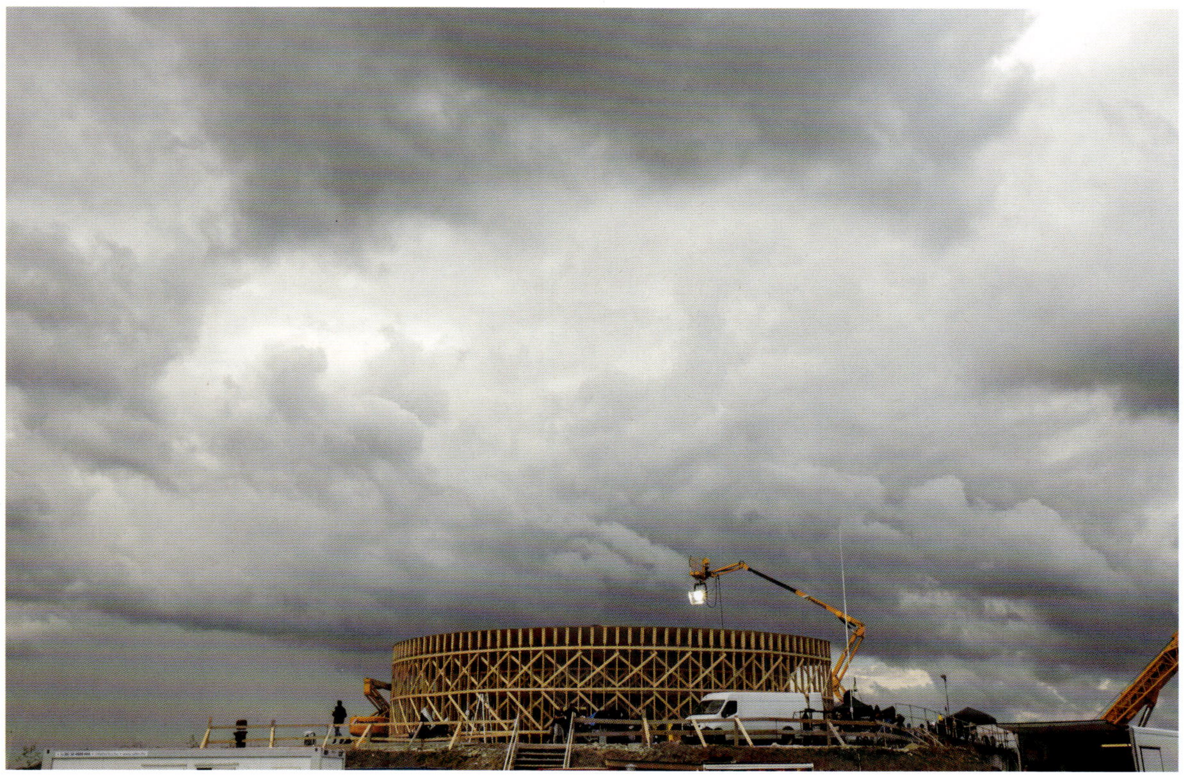

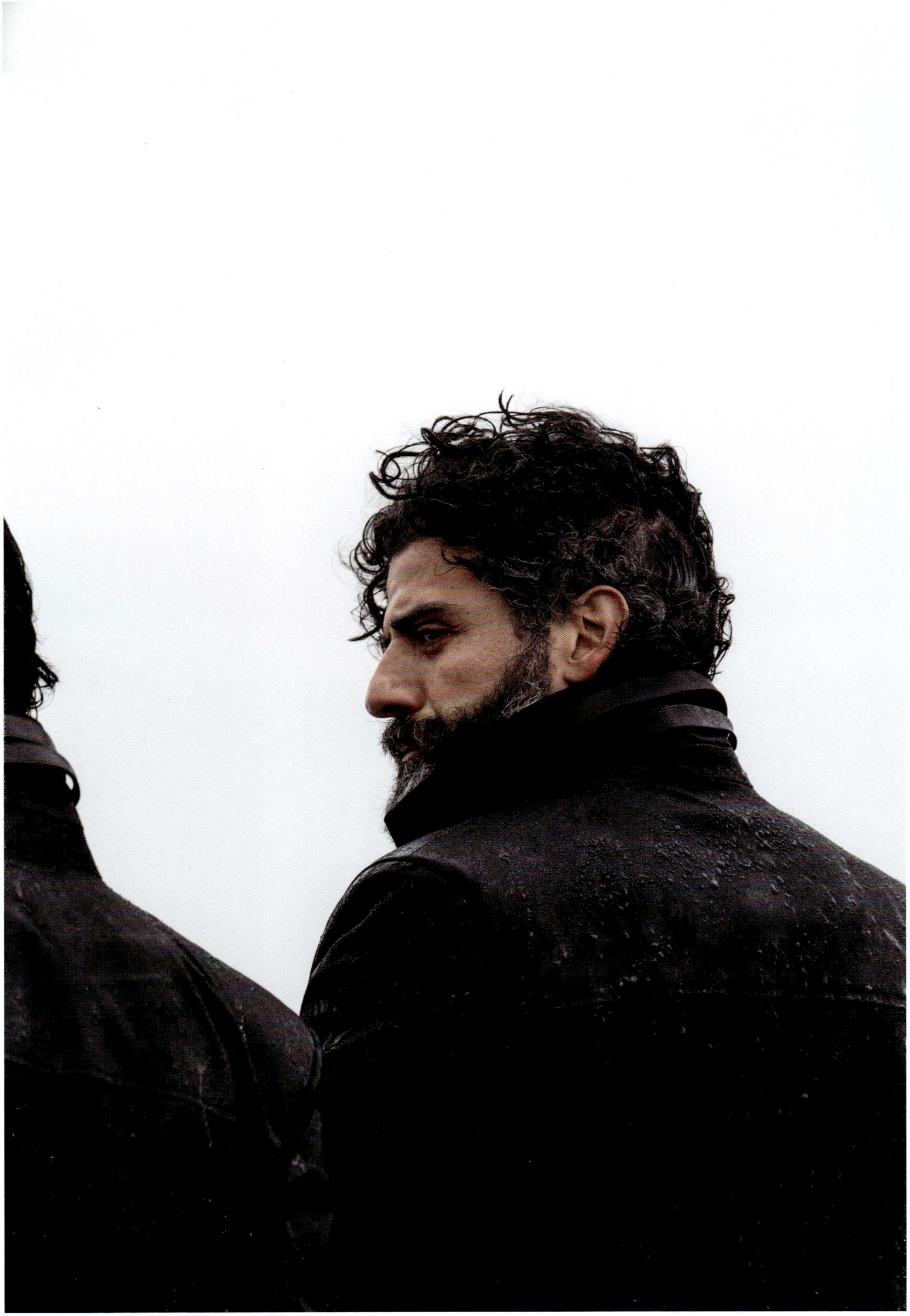

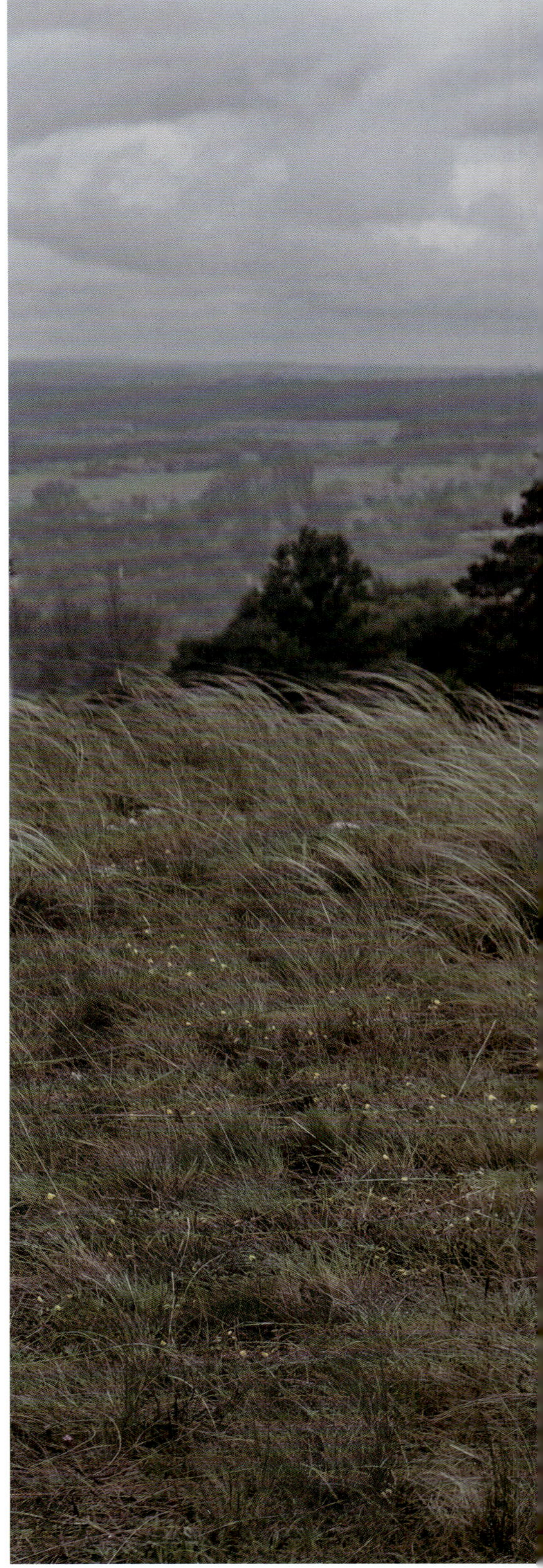

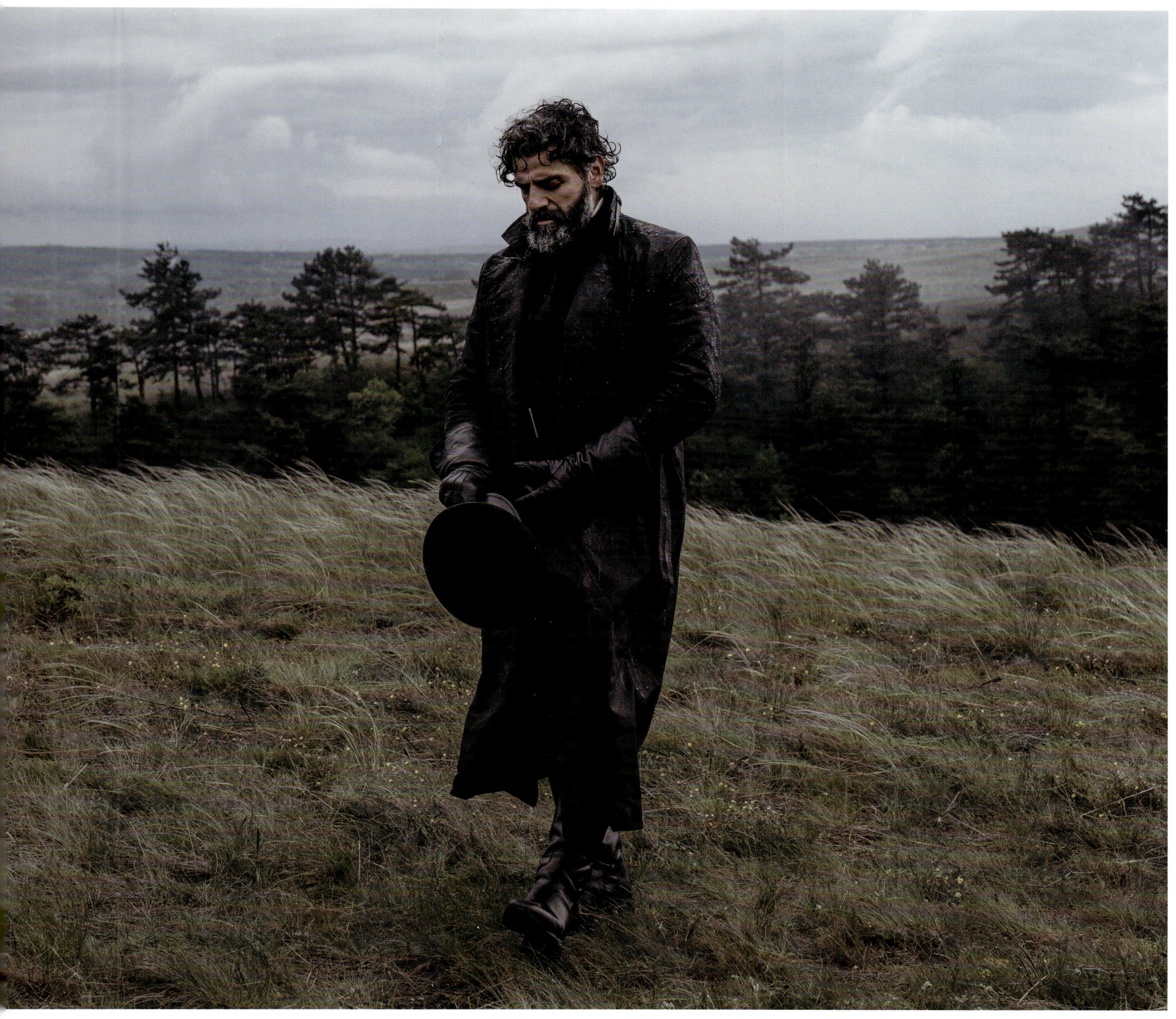

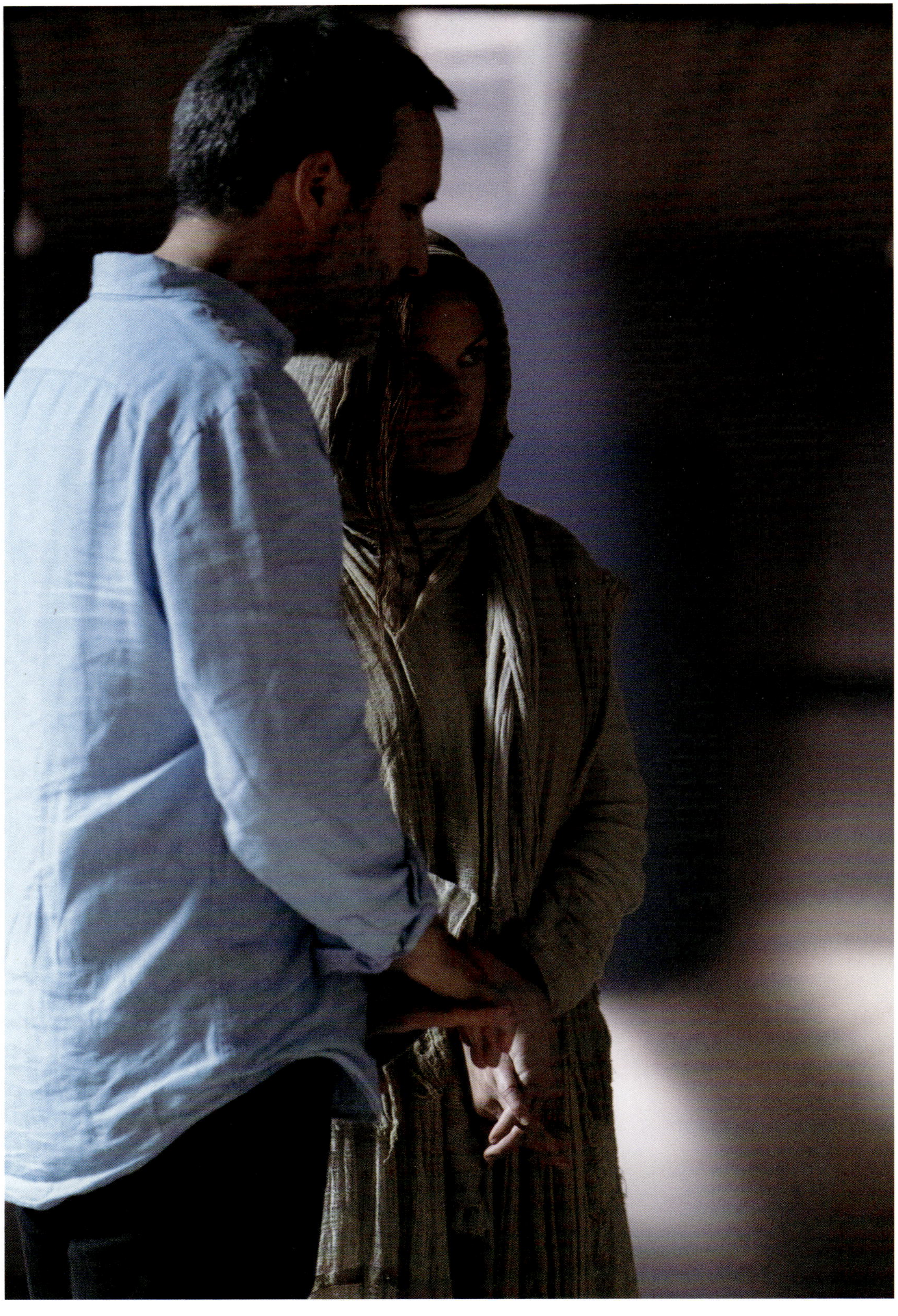

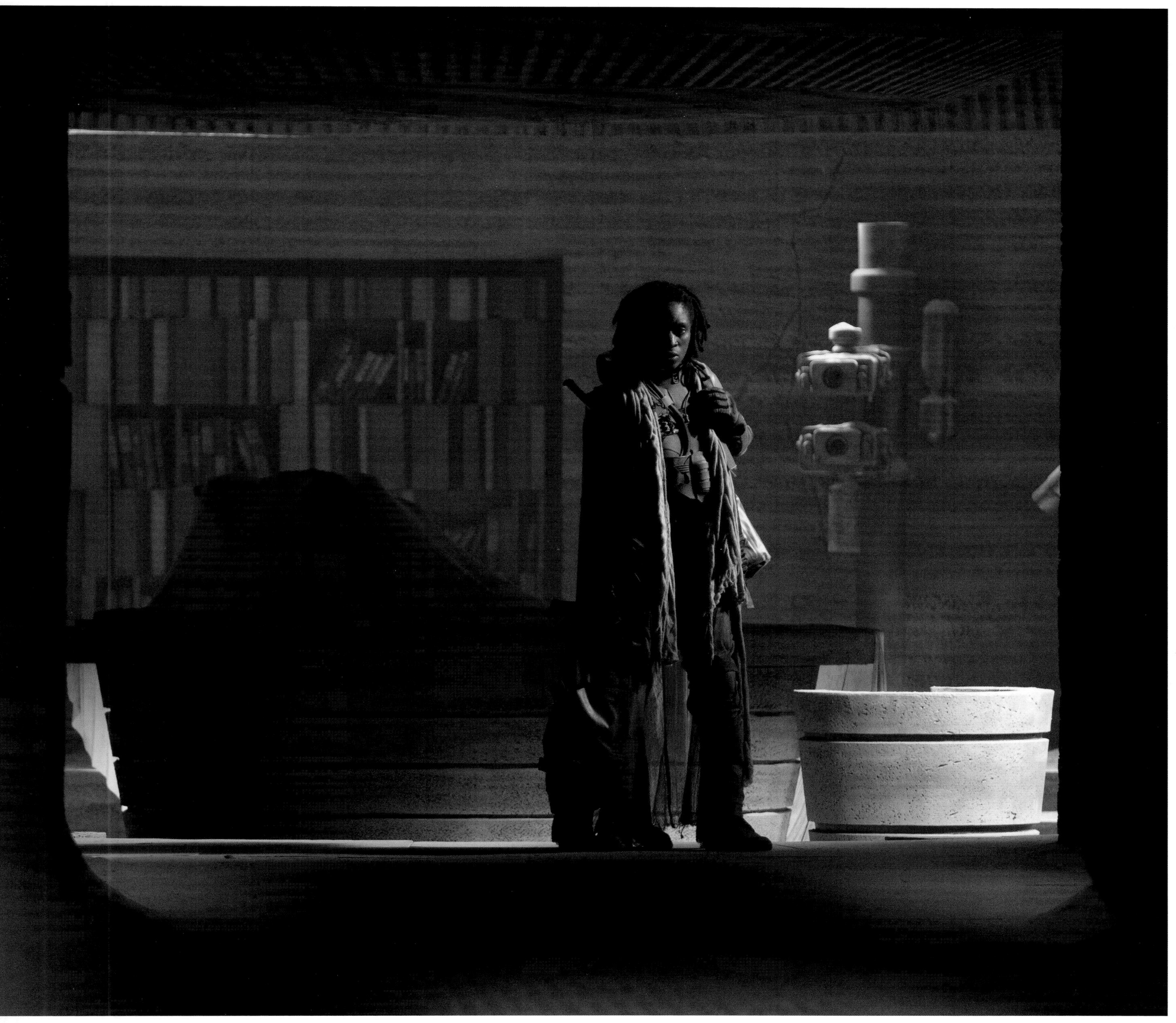

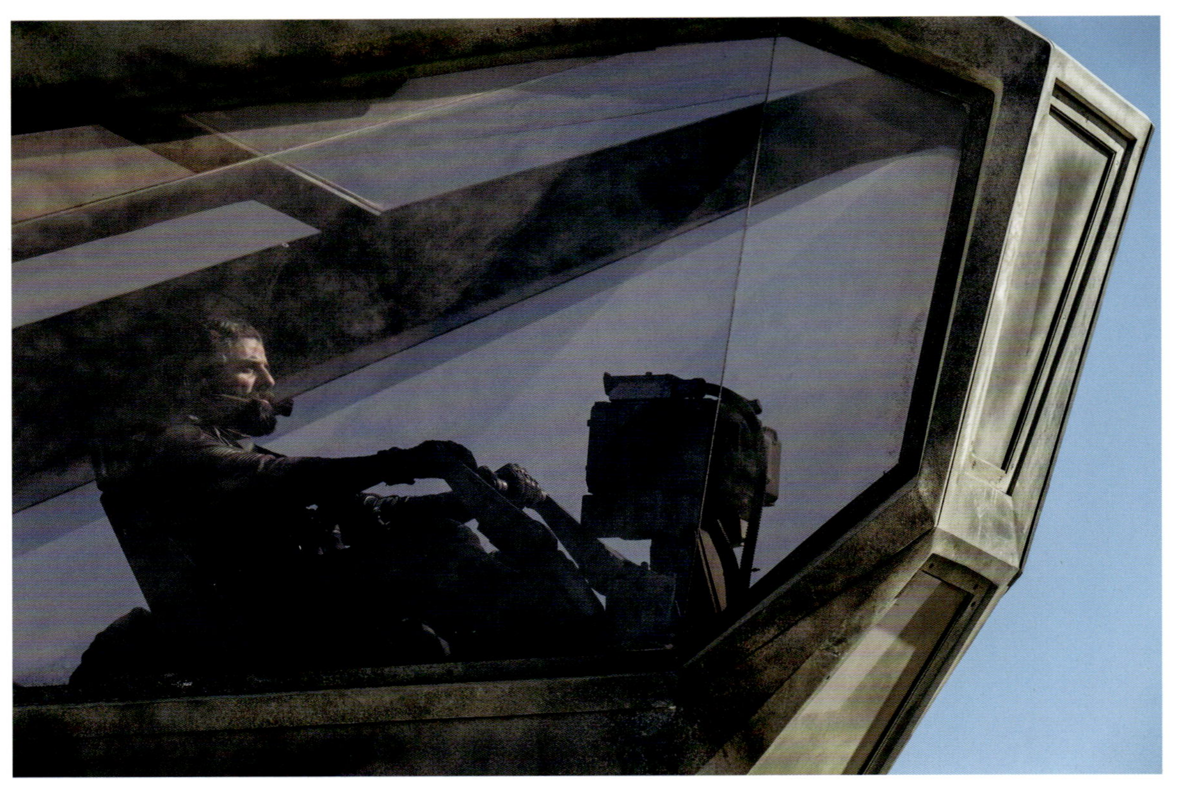

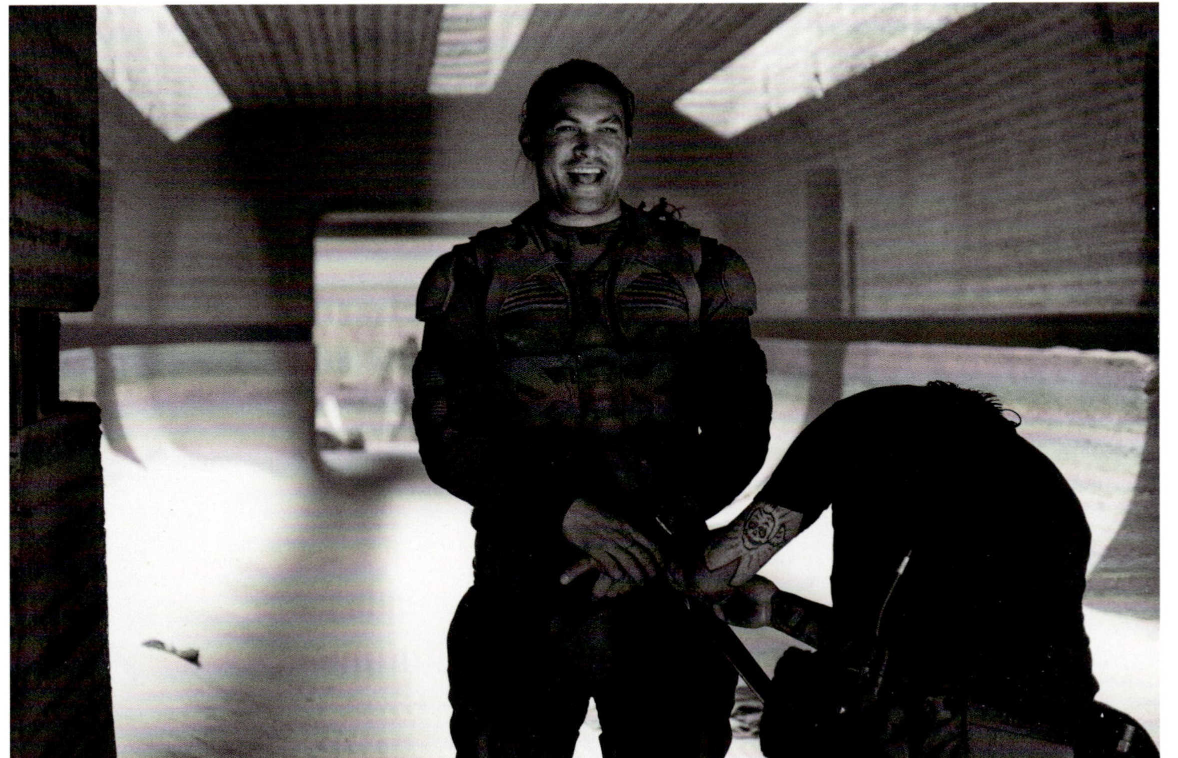

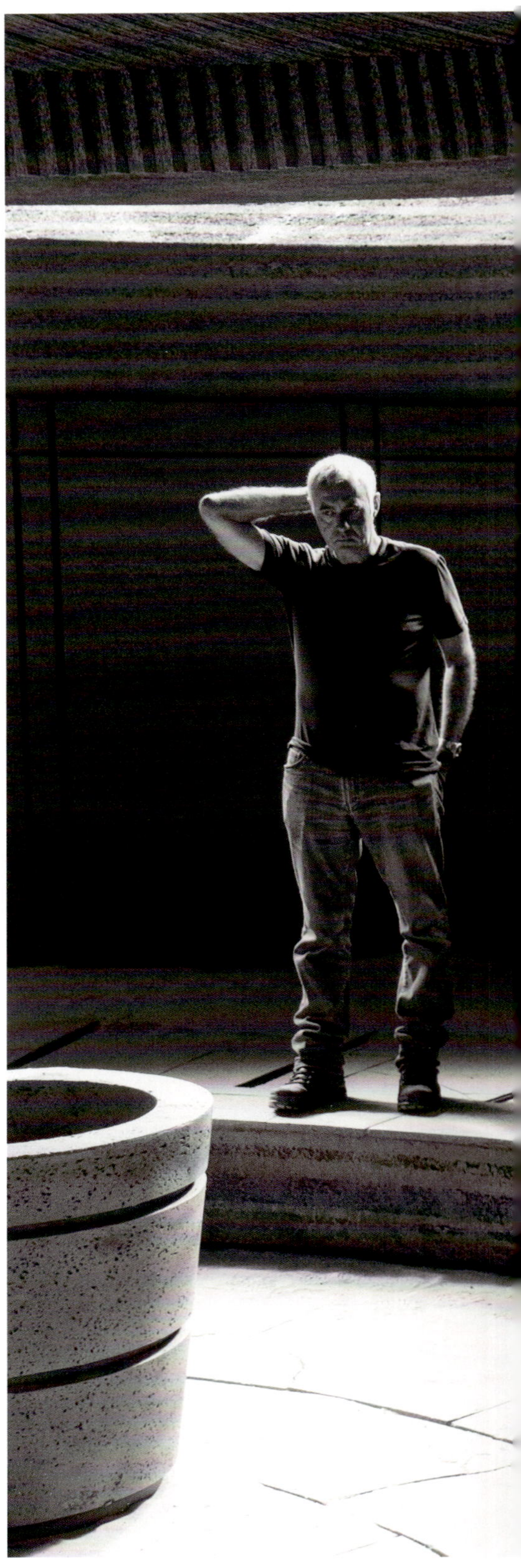

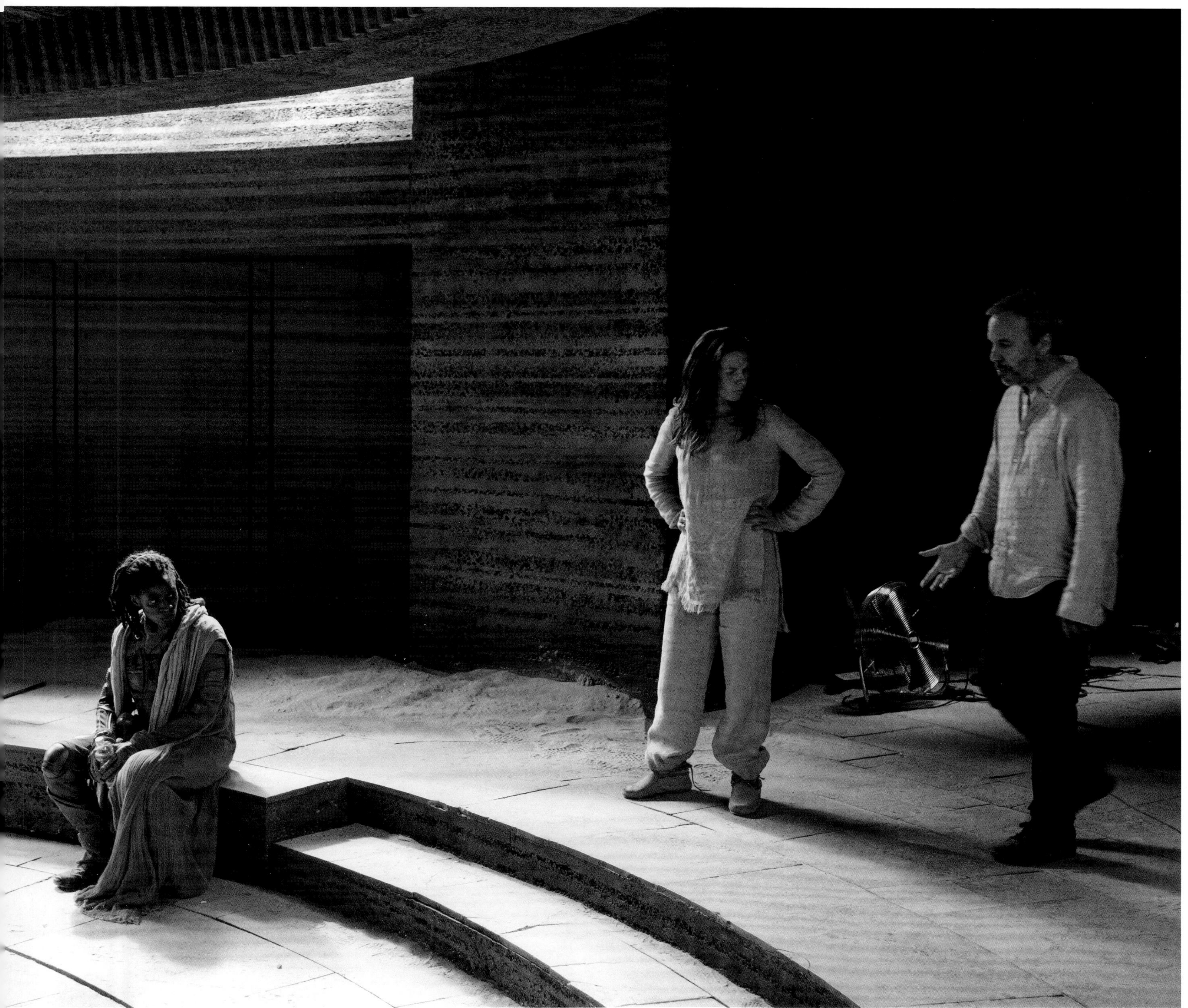

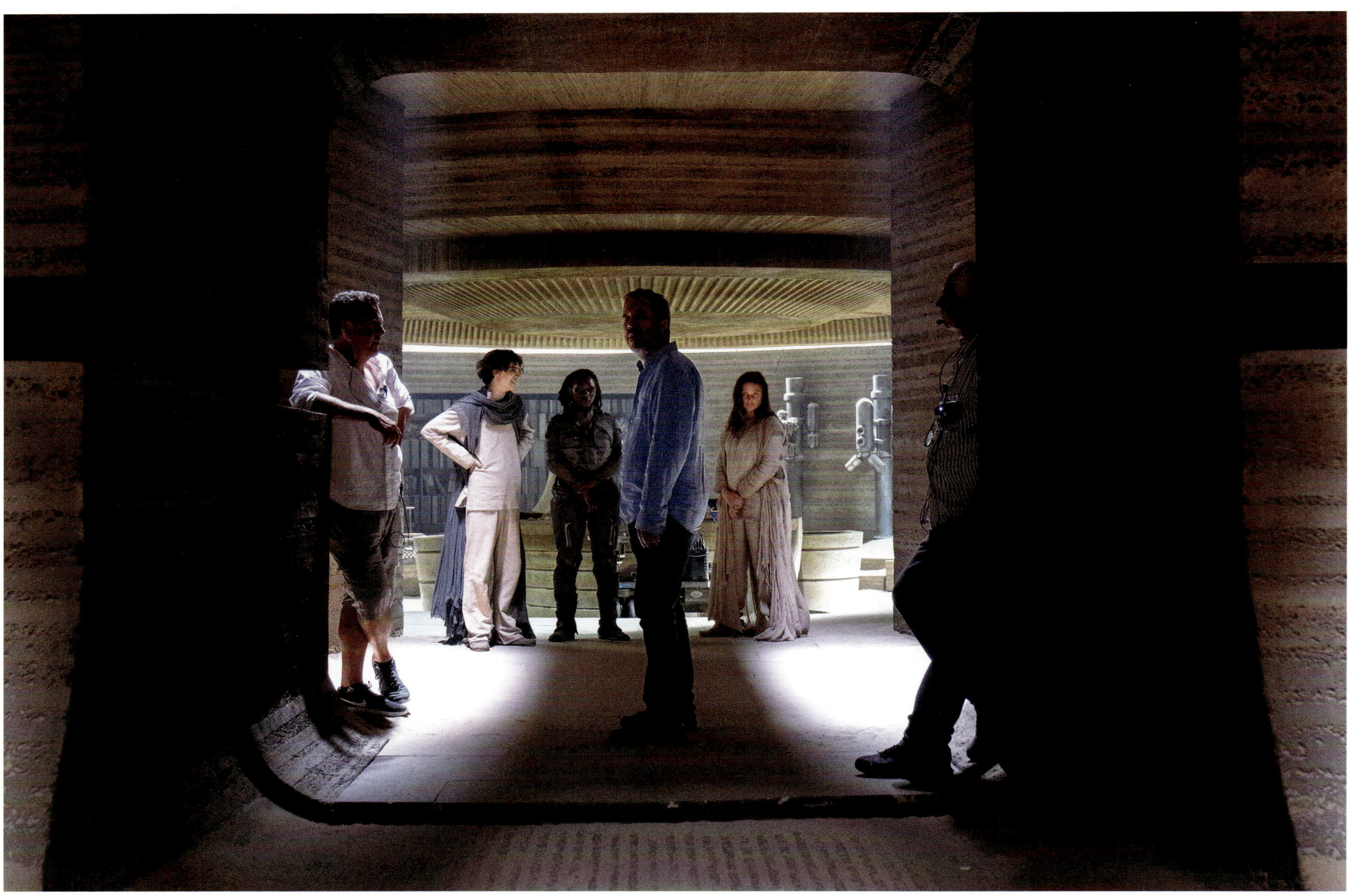

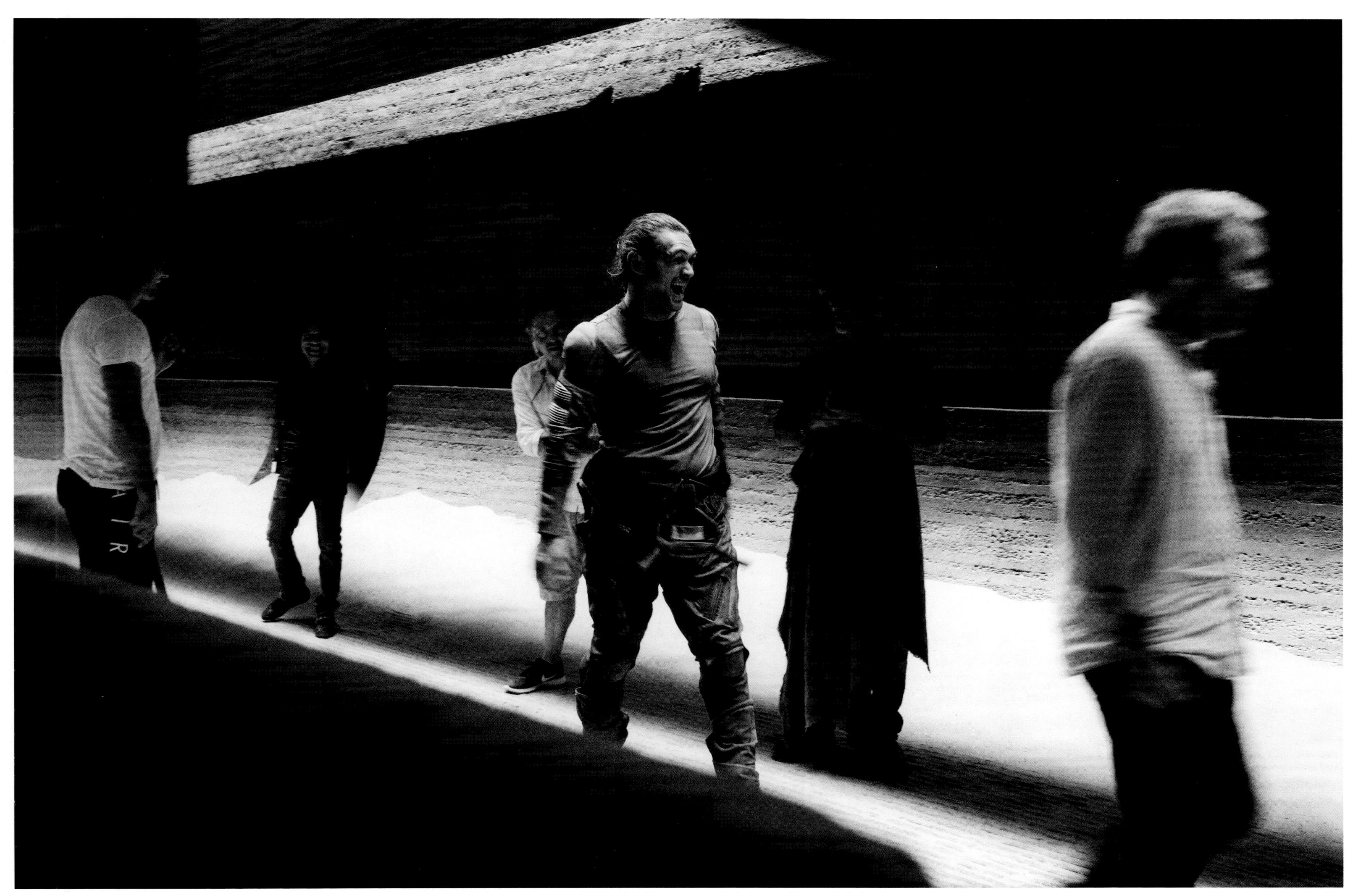

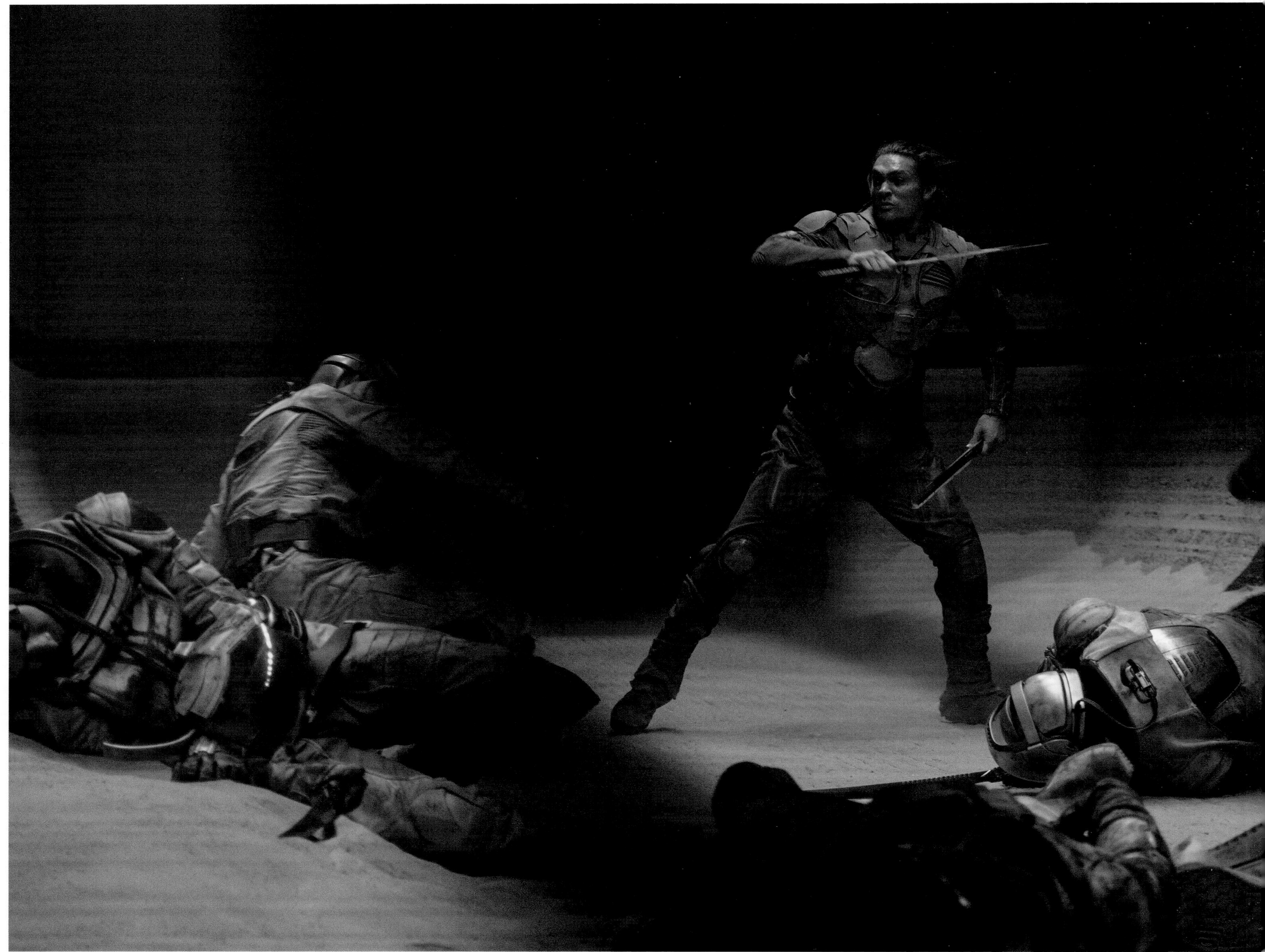

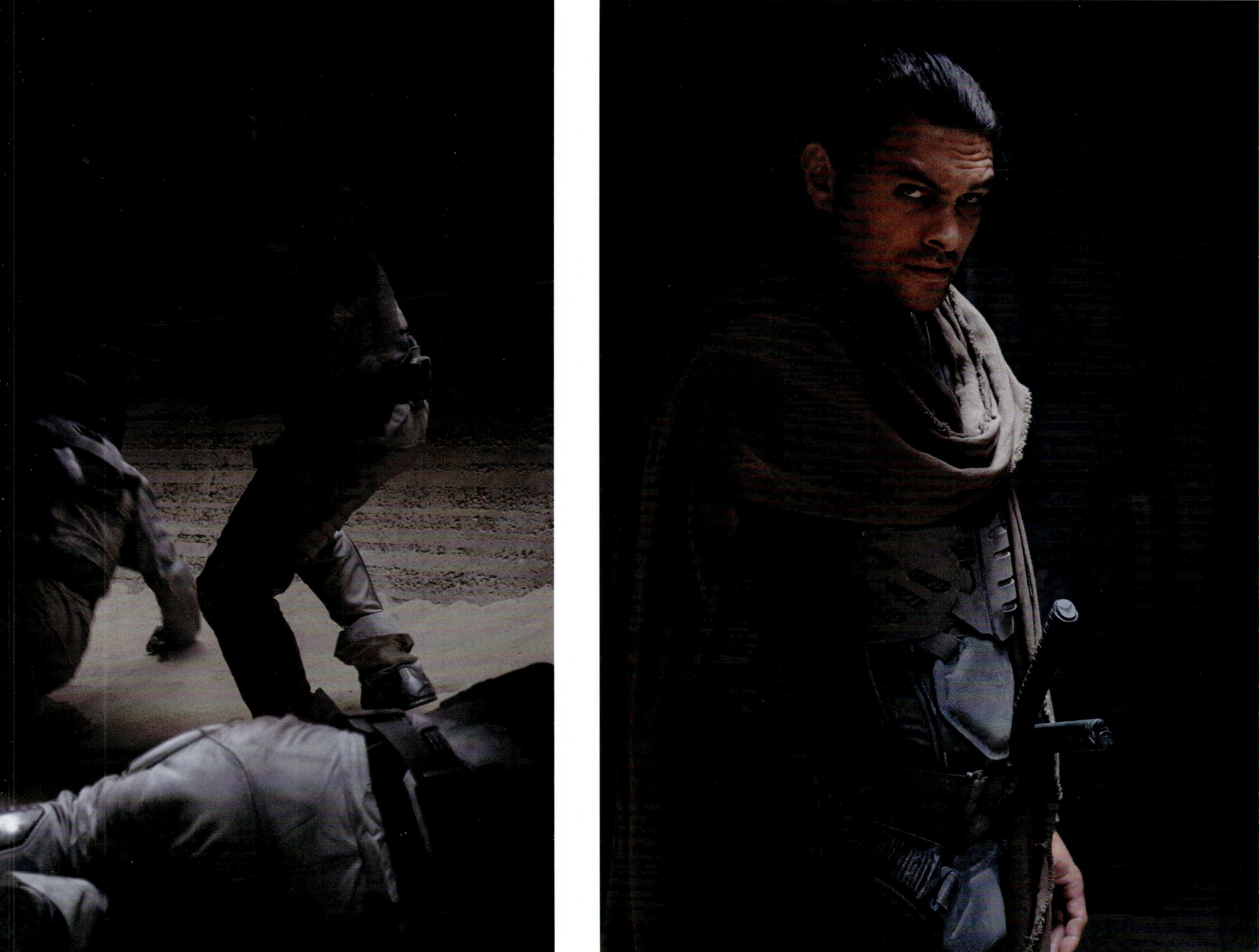

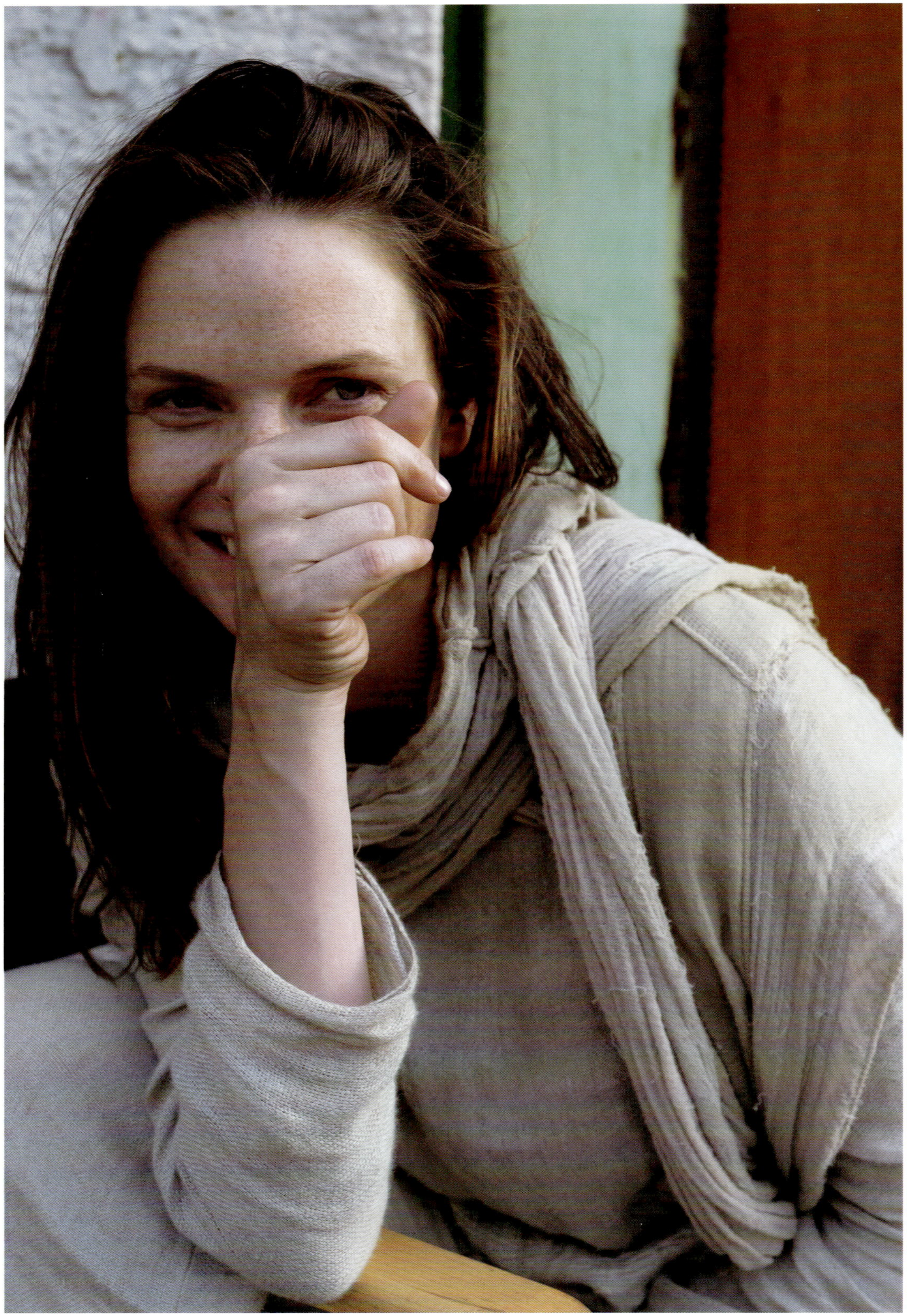

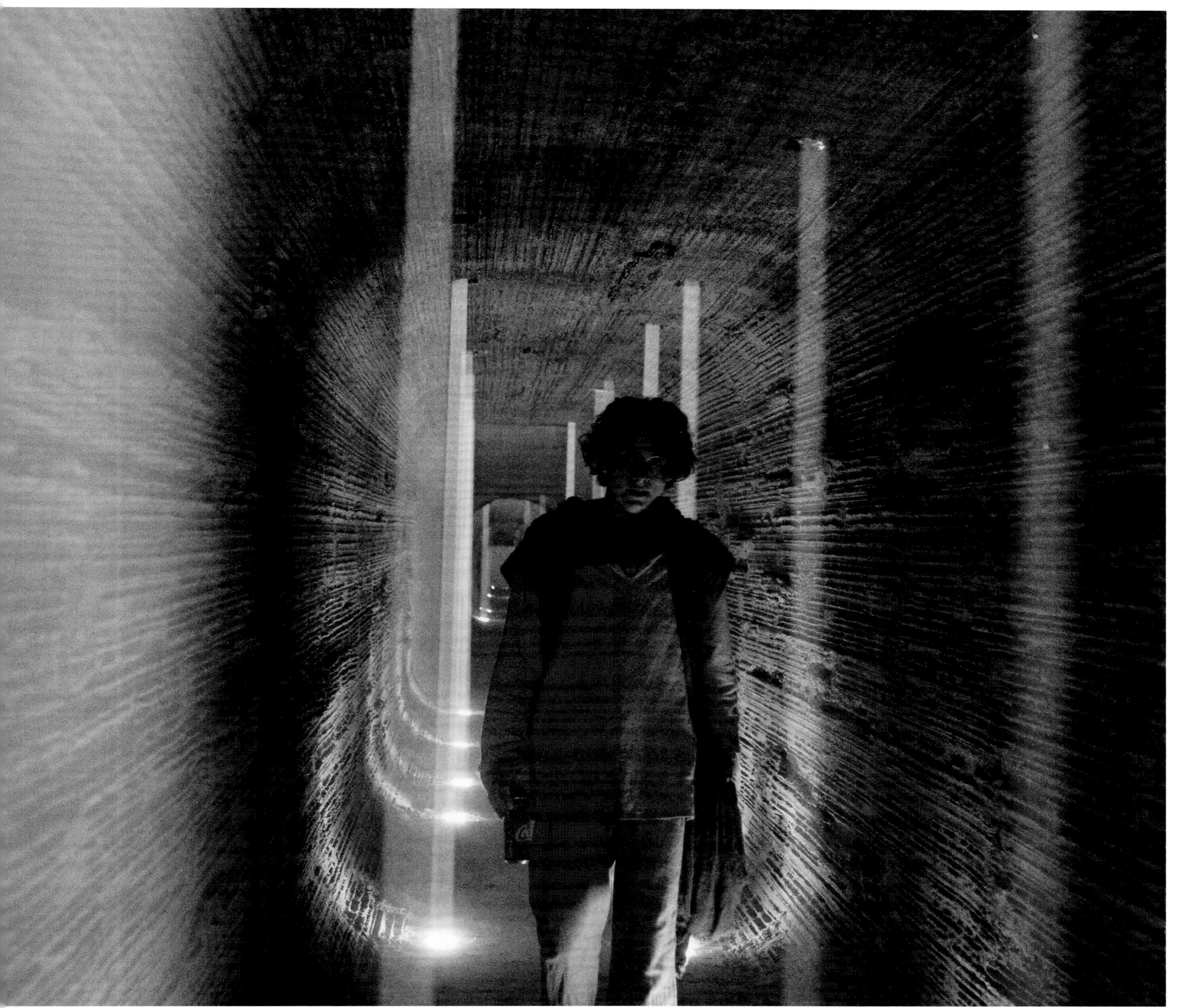

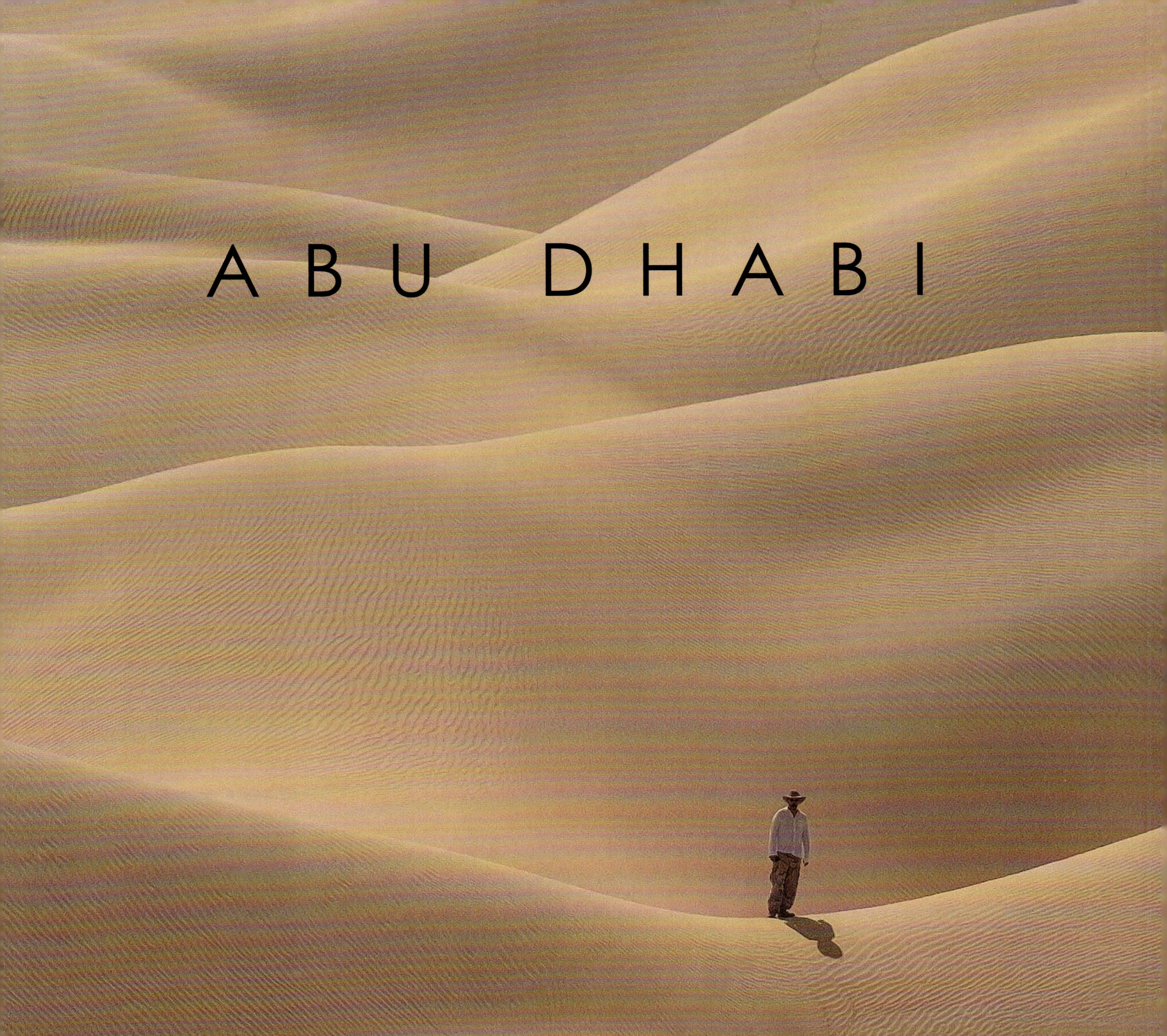
ABU DHABI

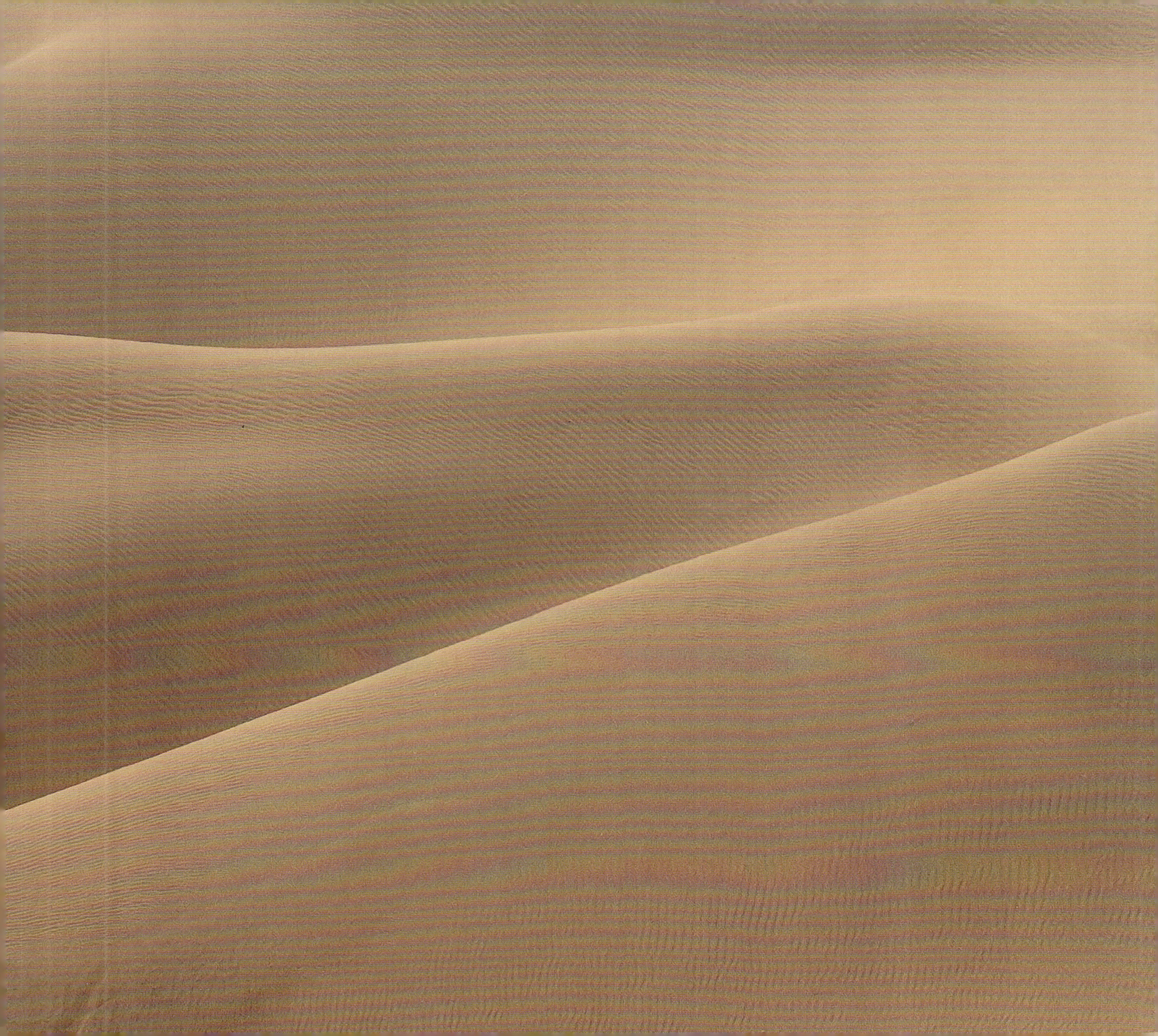

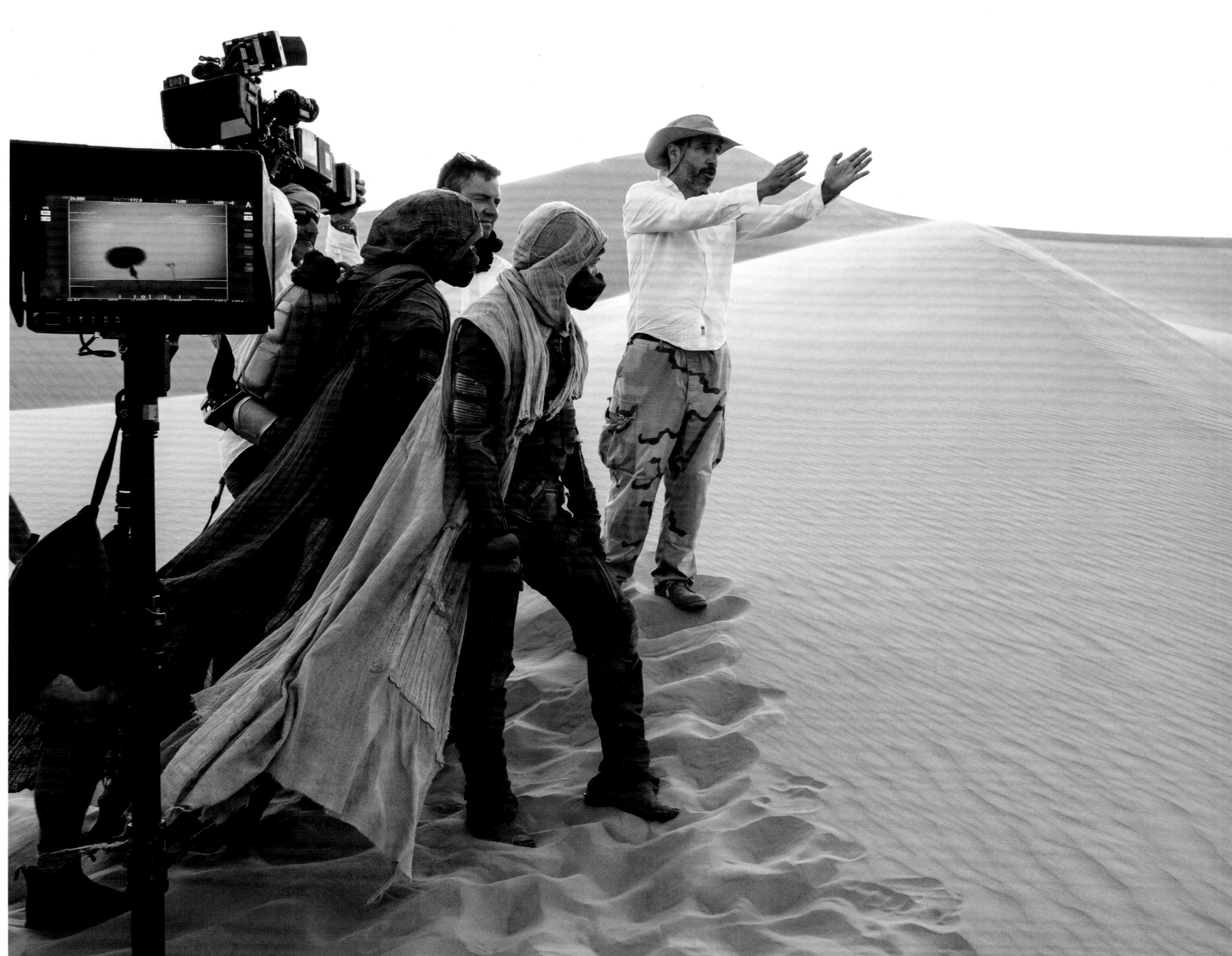

WORKING WITH DENIS AND watching him bring his vision to life was like witnessing a wizard conducting an orchestra of magicians. In the early days of production, I asked him if he was comfortable with me taking photographs of him while he interacted with the cast. These are important moments for me to capture, but they are often private and not intended for the camera. Denis's only stipulation was a challenge: Avoid the movie photo cliché of a director pointing or making a frame with his hands. It's something we have all seen too many times.

I loved this challenge the most. It not only gave me leave to push boundaries and think outside the box, it also invited me to share in Denis's energy as a director. I followed him wherever the process took him, be it on the floor of the set, looking up at a scene, or walking through a set, seeking out a character's point of view. I was able to connect with him through the lens, even when he caught a glimpse of my camera and jokingly made those very gestures he had instructed me to avoid!

There are a selection of these moments throughout this book, but this one in particular was important because it tells a story. Here is our leader and his crew, consciously keeping behind the off-camera line in the sand, guiding the organized chaos of the process while connecting us to the dunes. The desert was not just a location for this film, but a character in the story, so I tried to make sure it held its relevant space in the imagery.

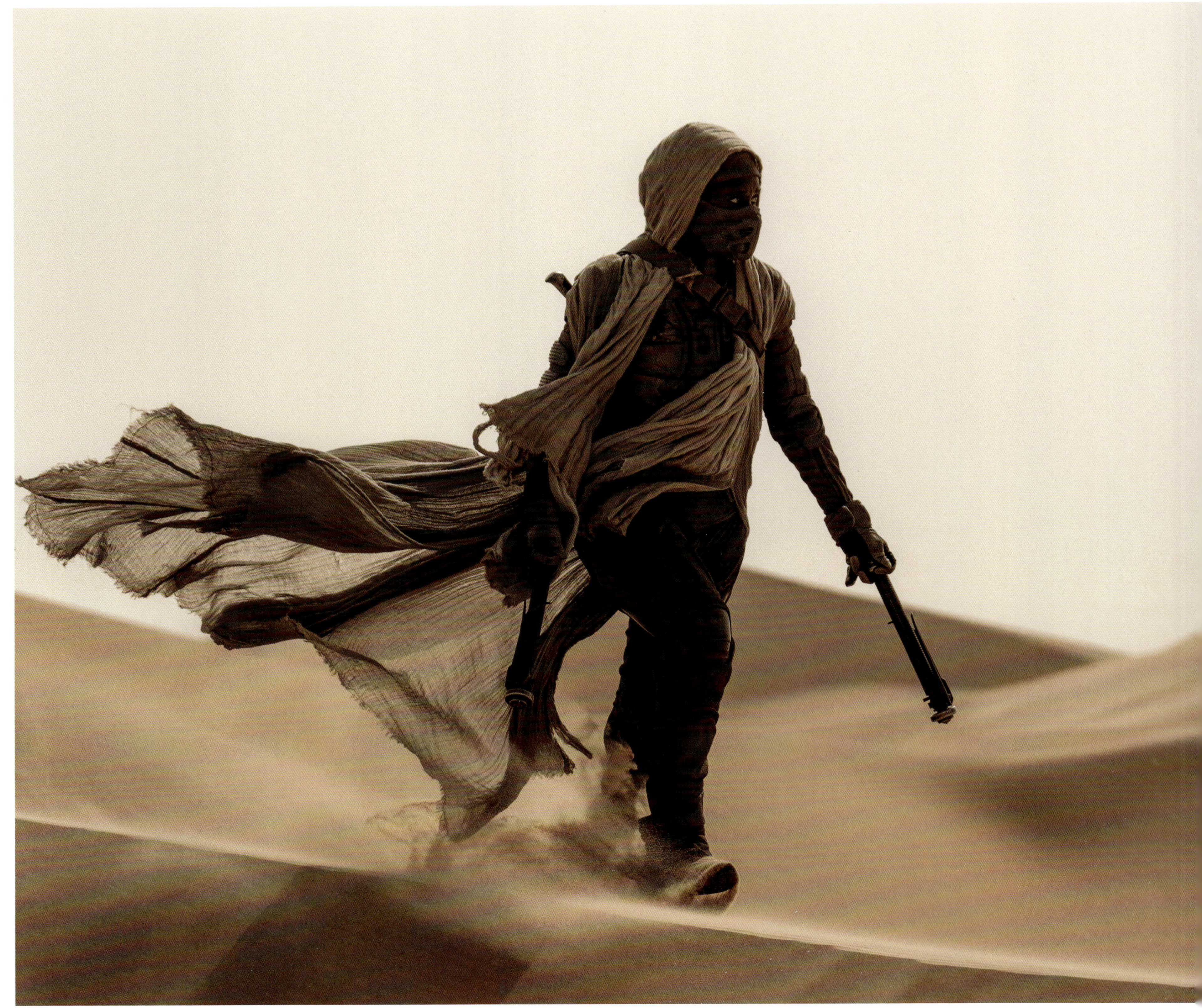

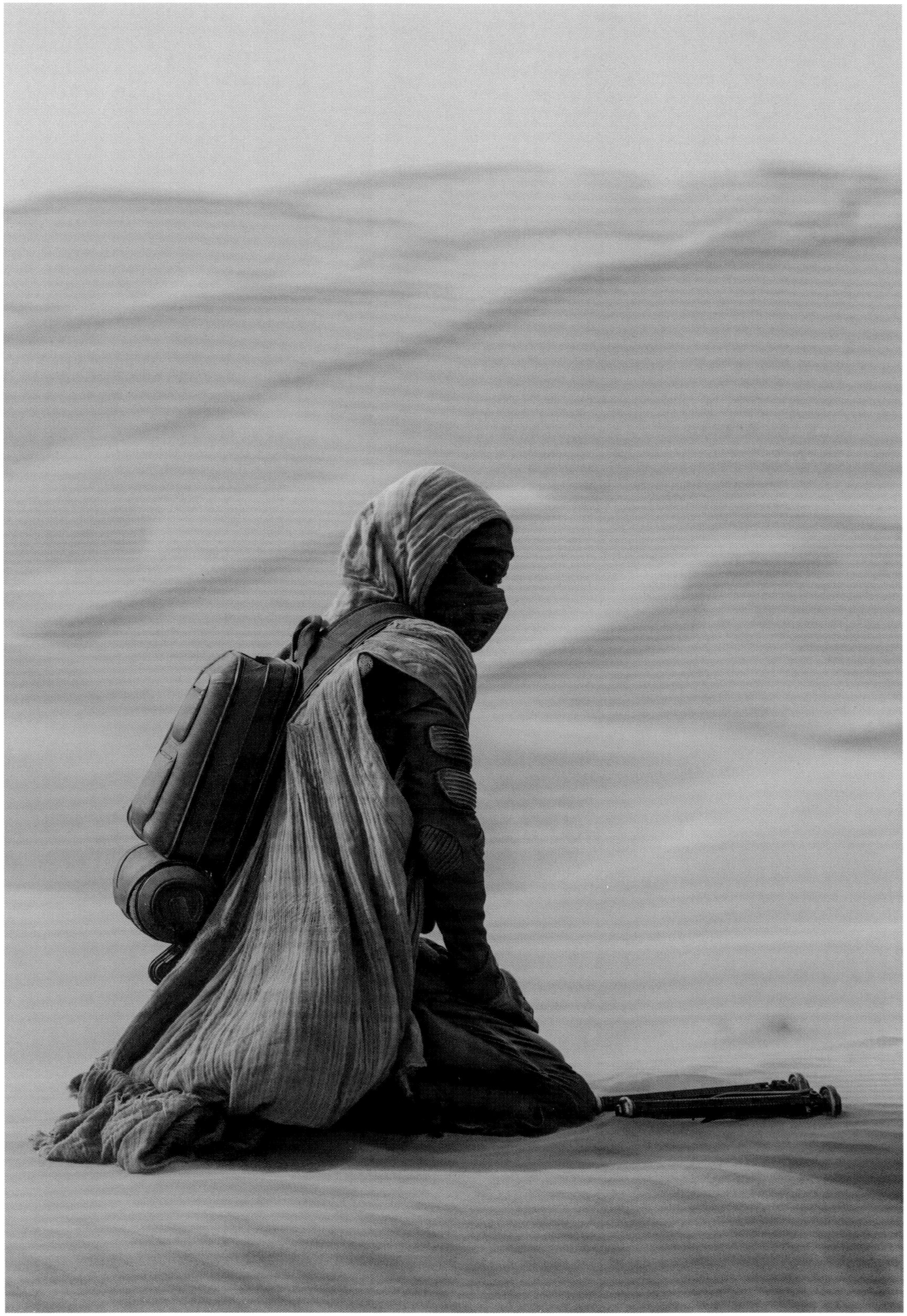

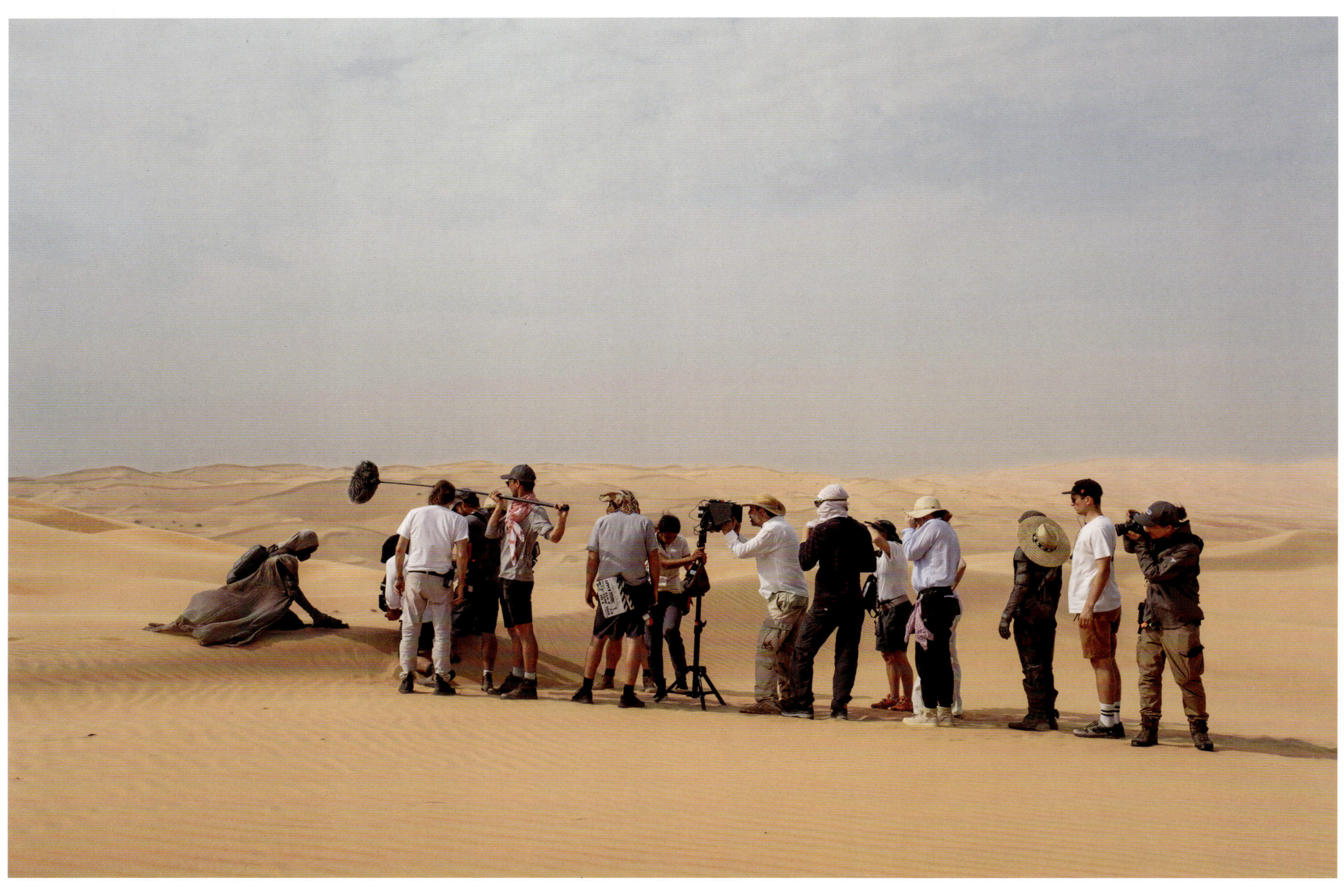

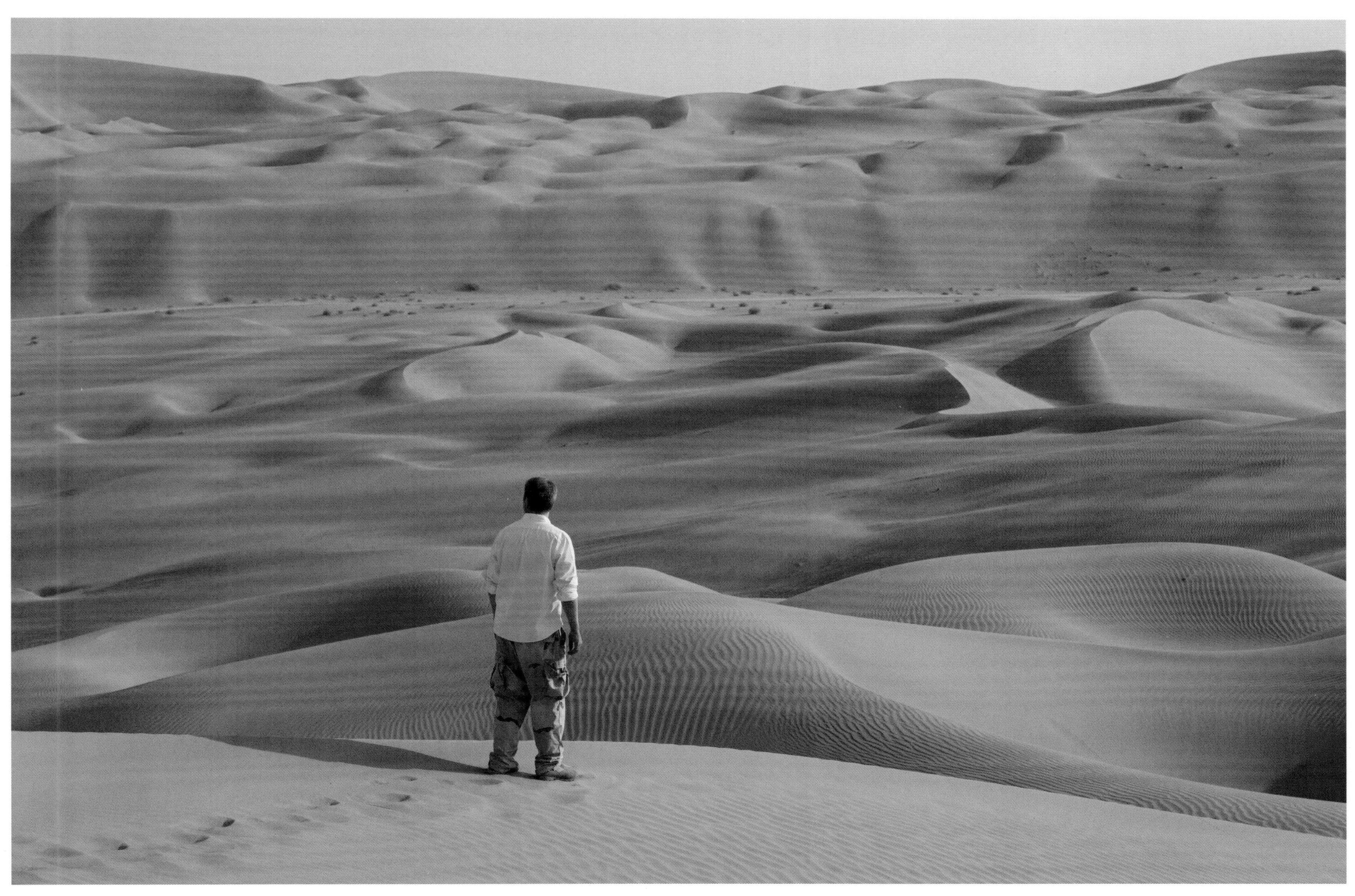

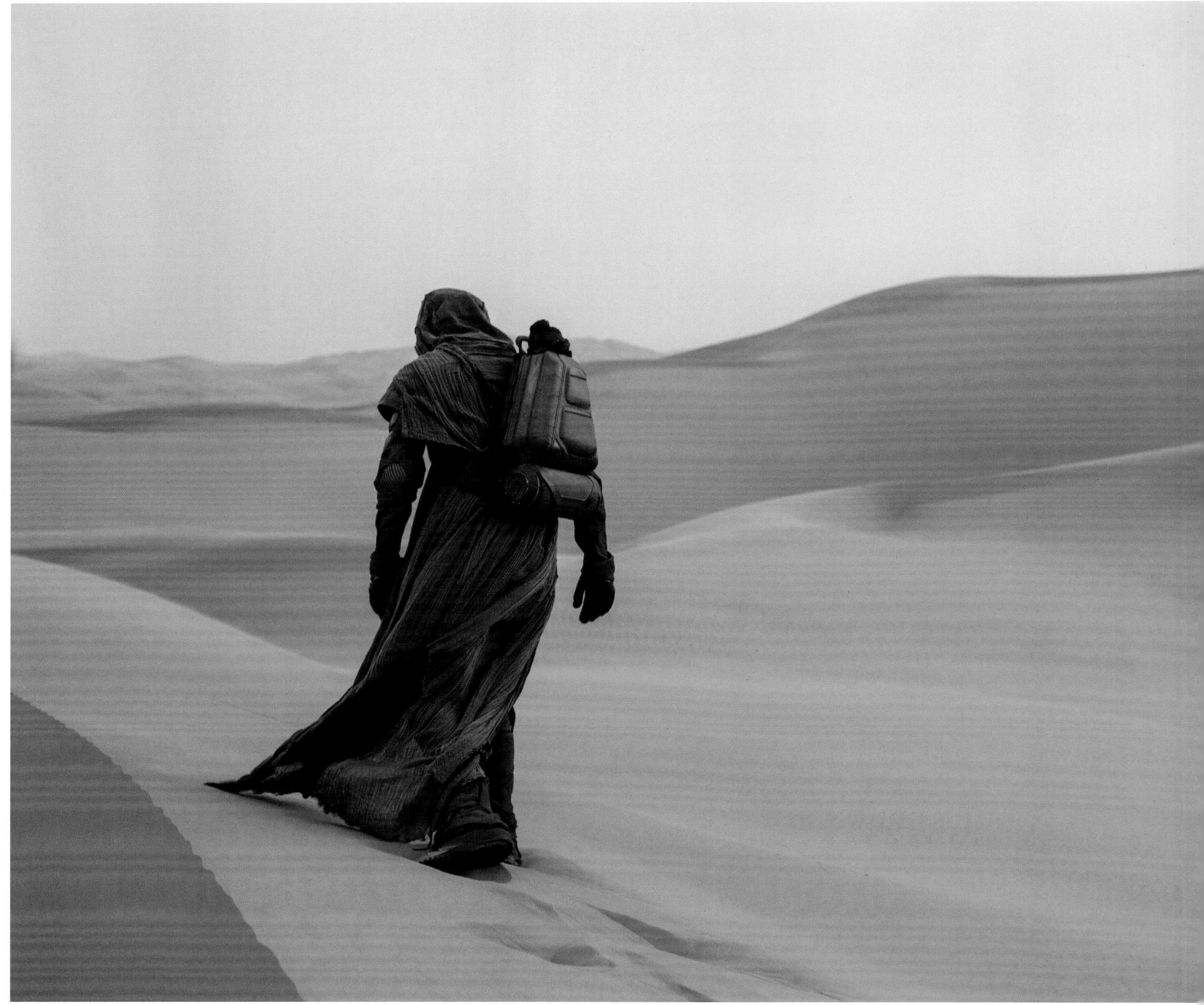

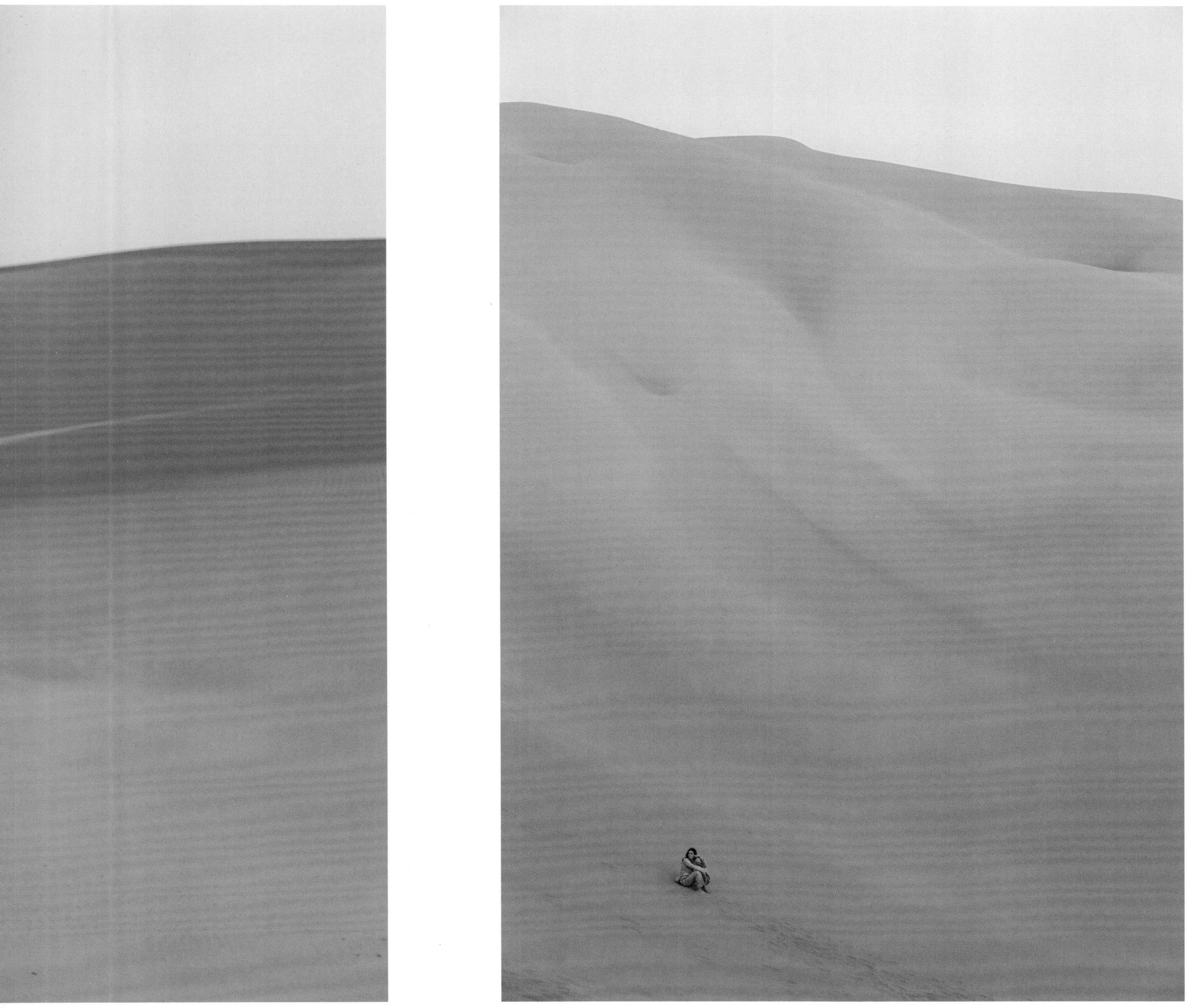

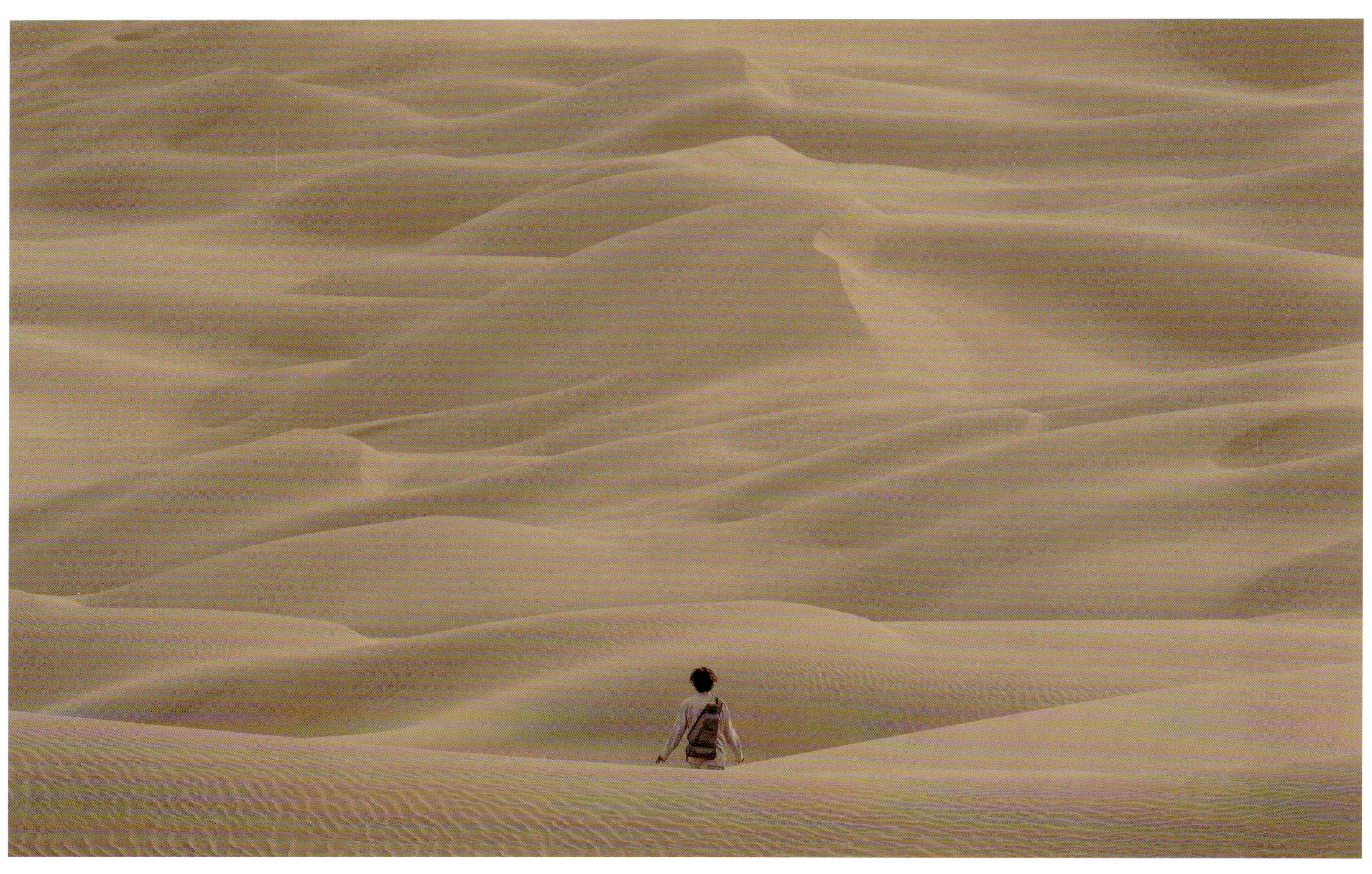

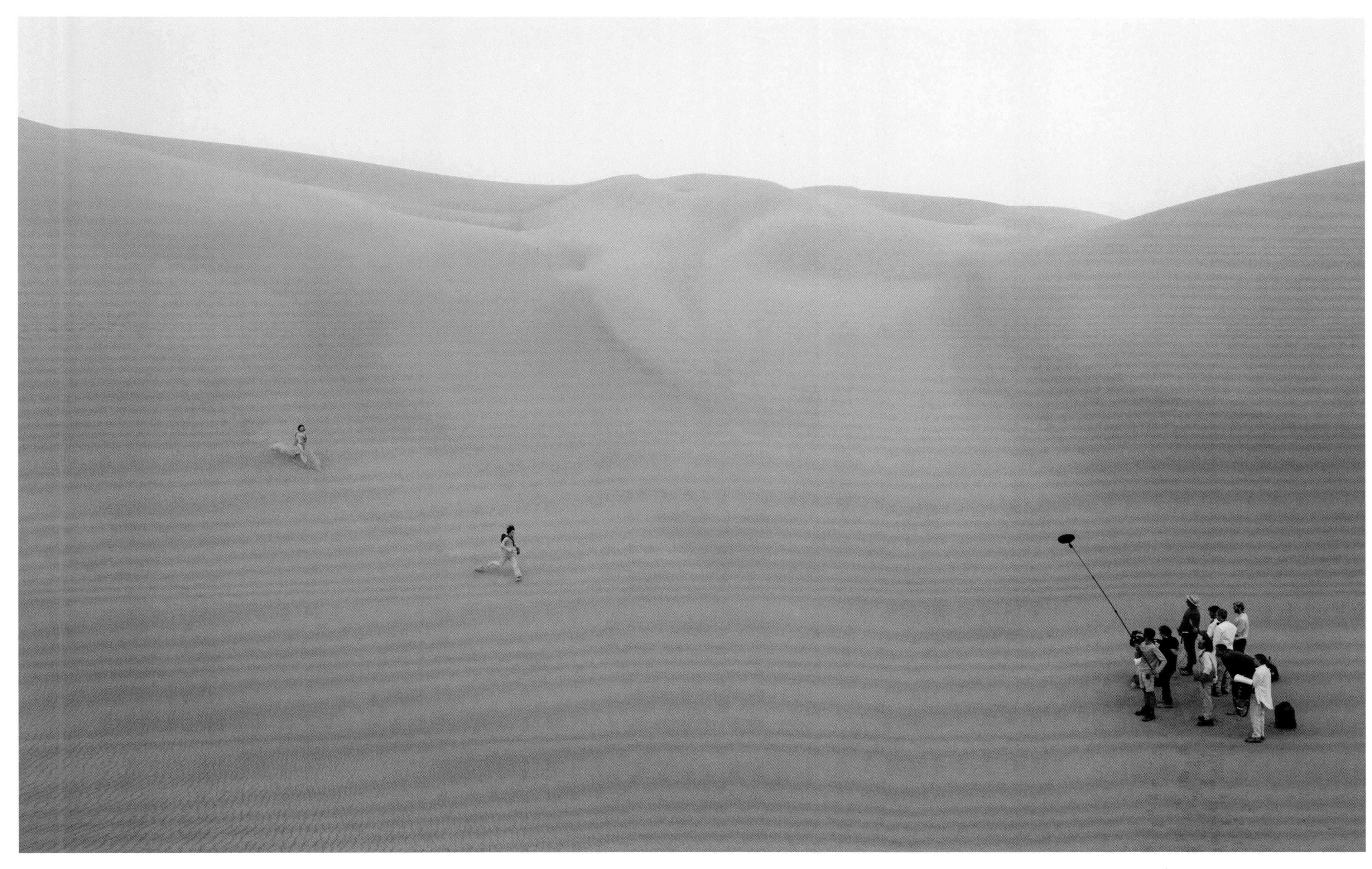

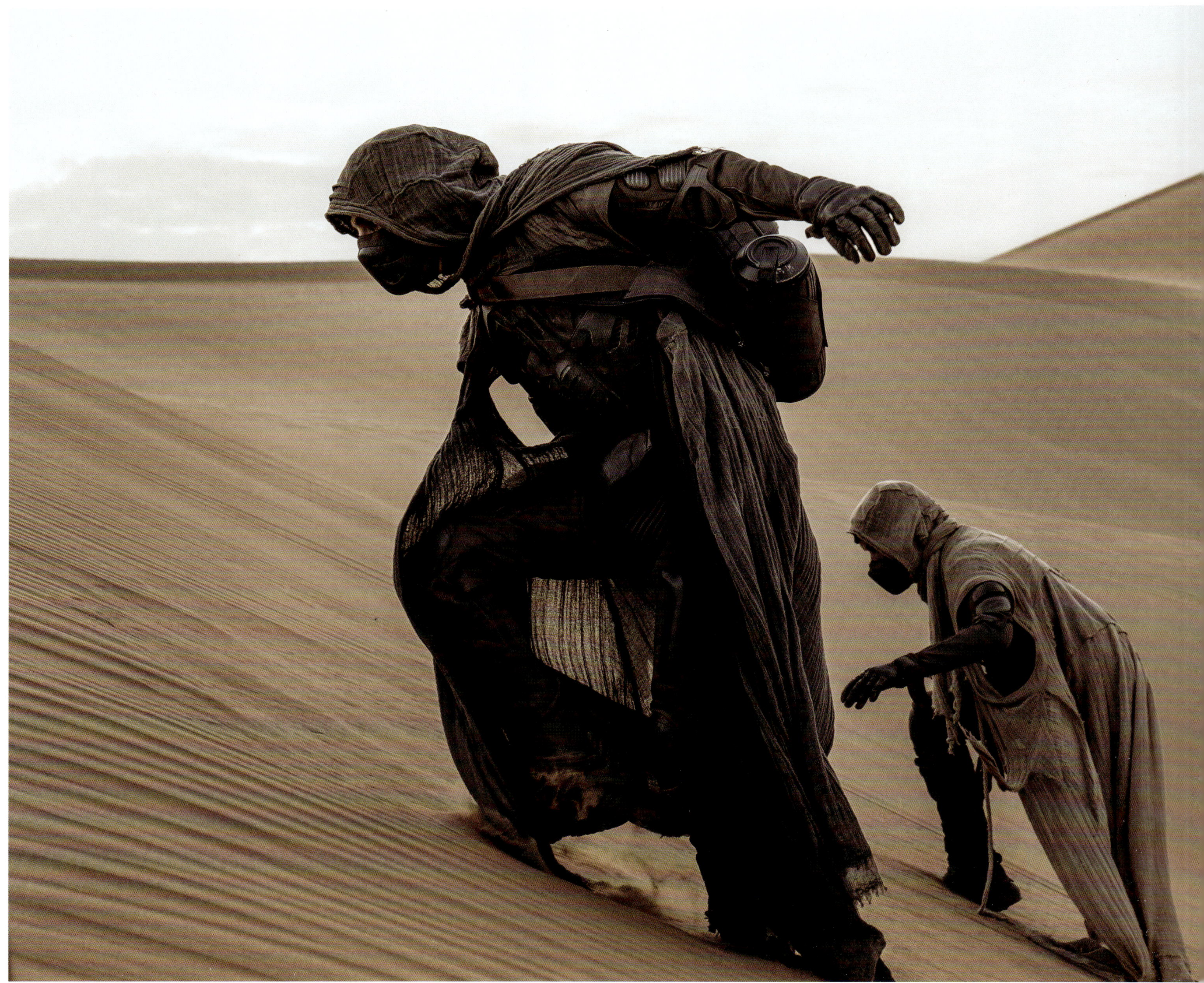

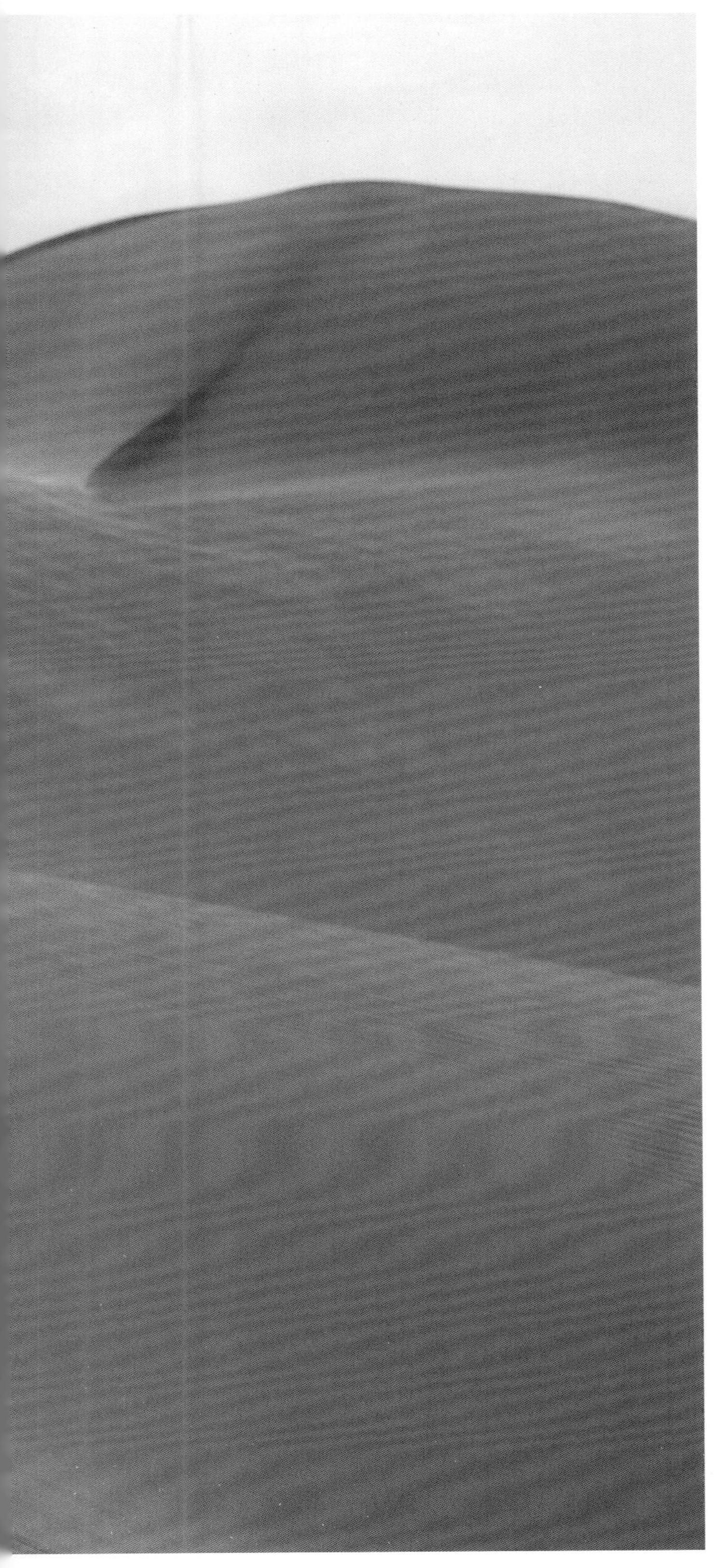

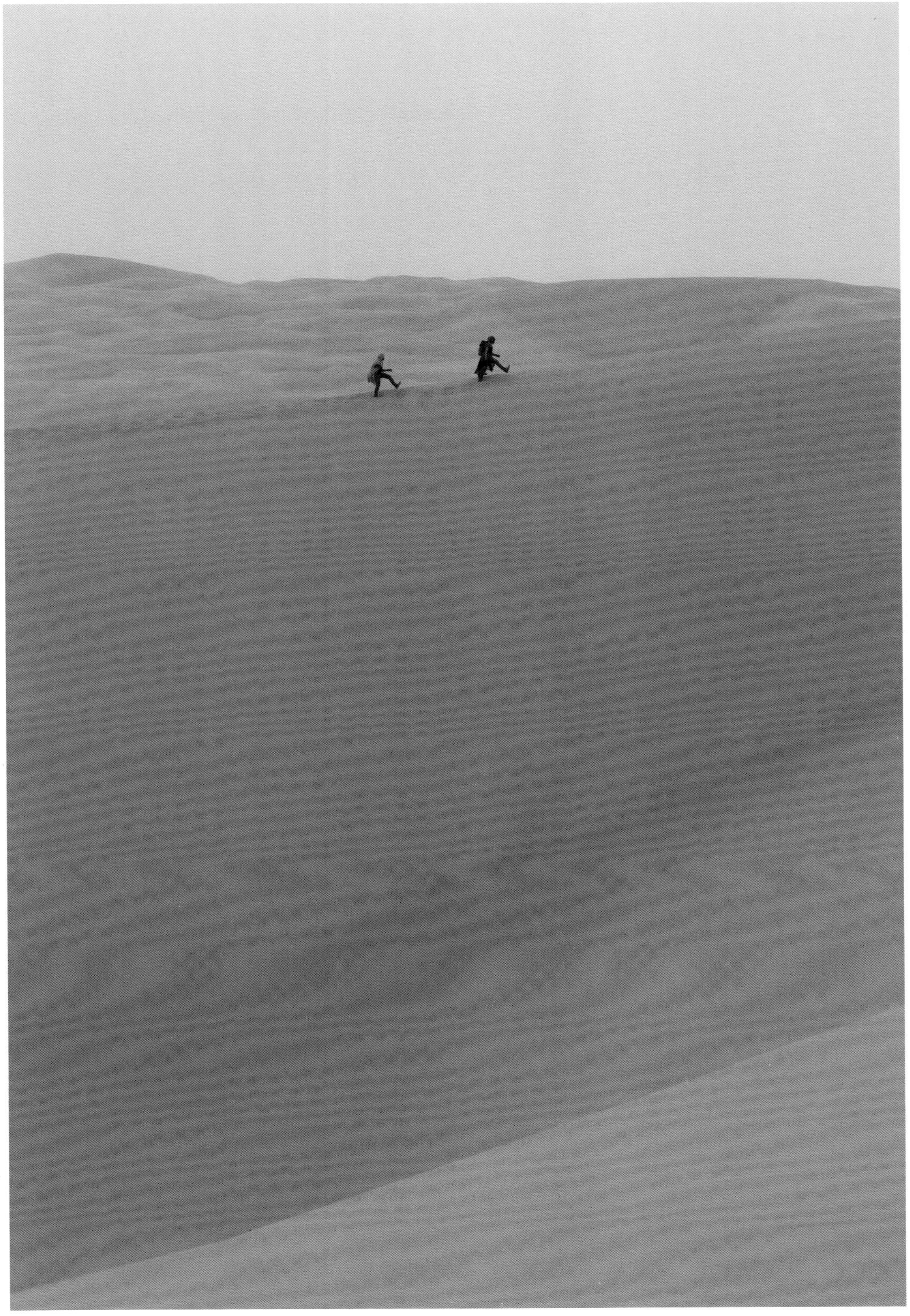

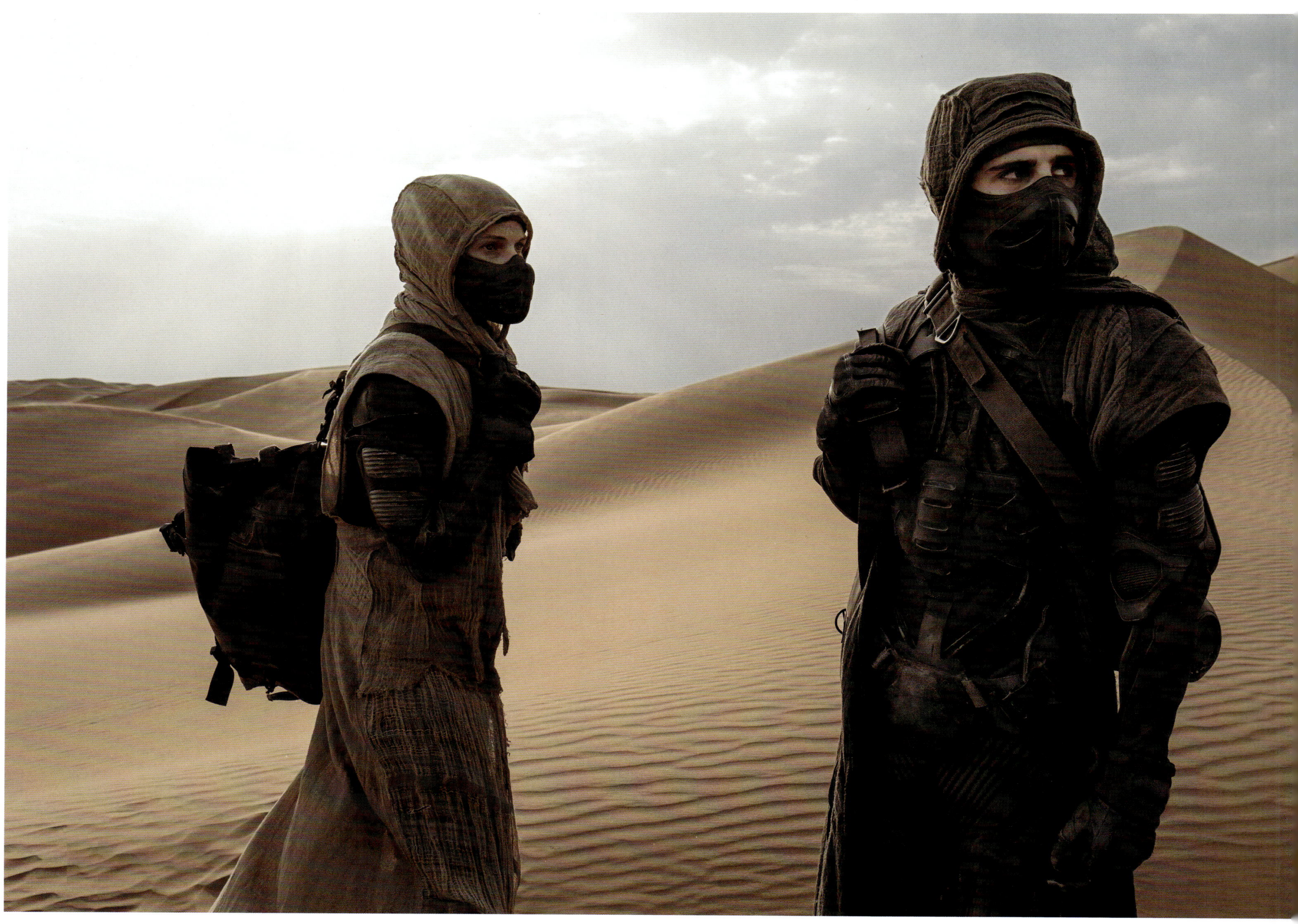

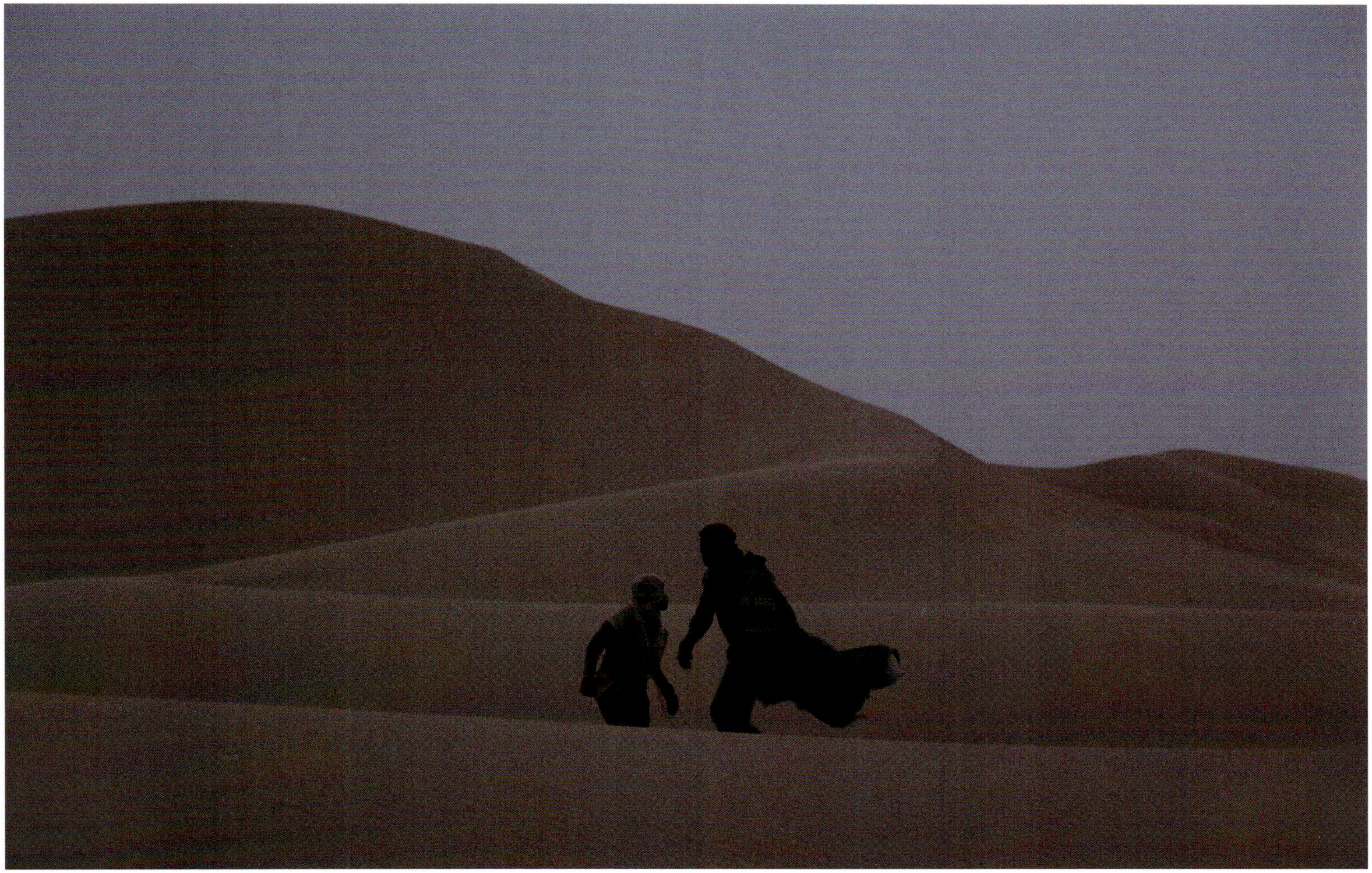

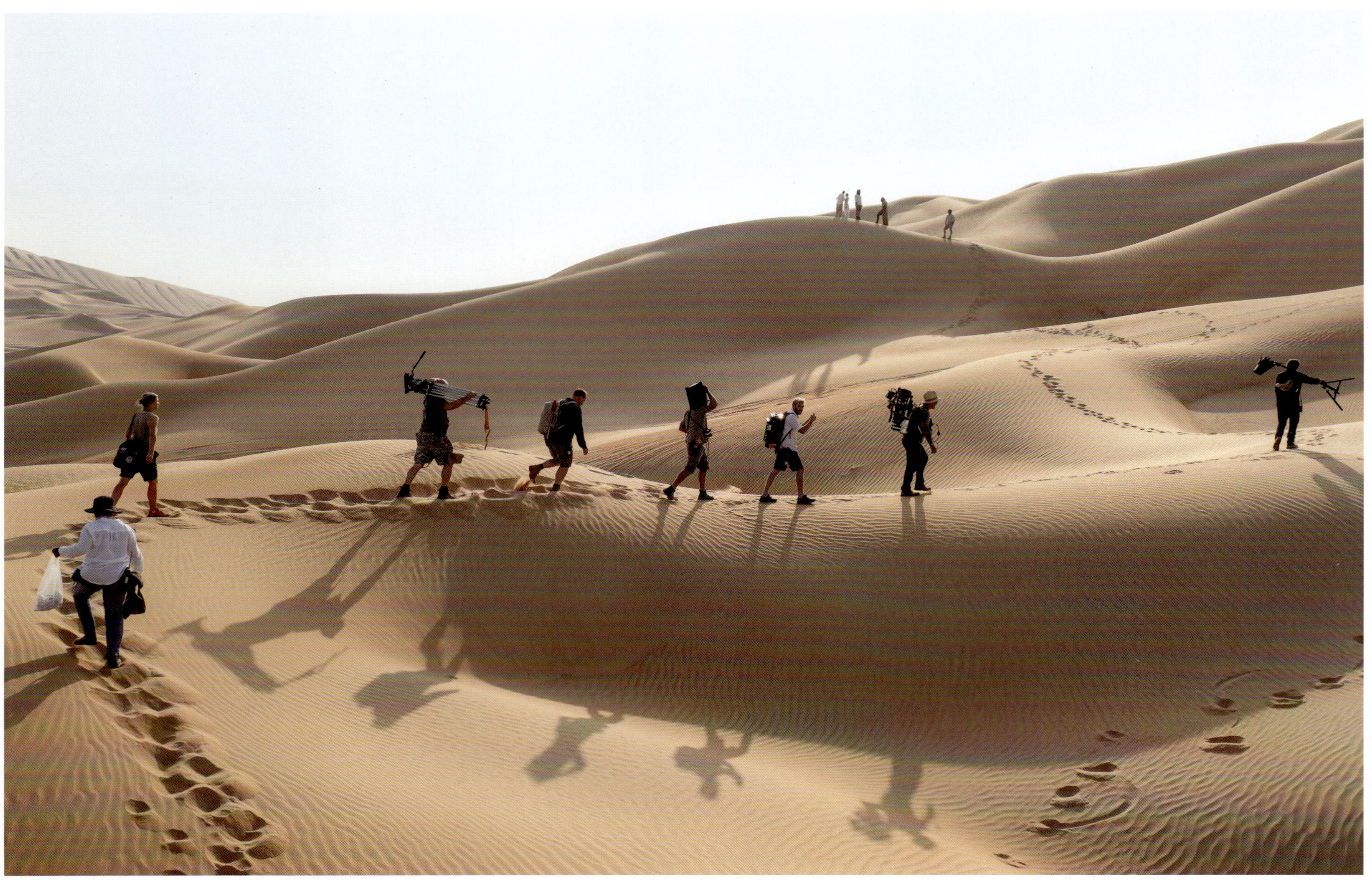

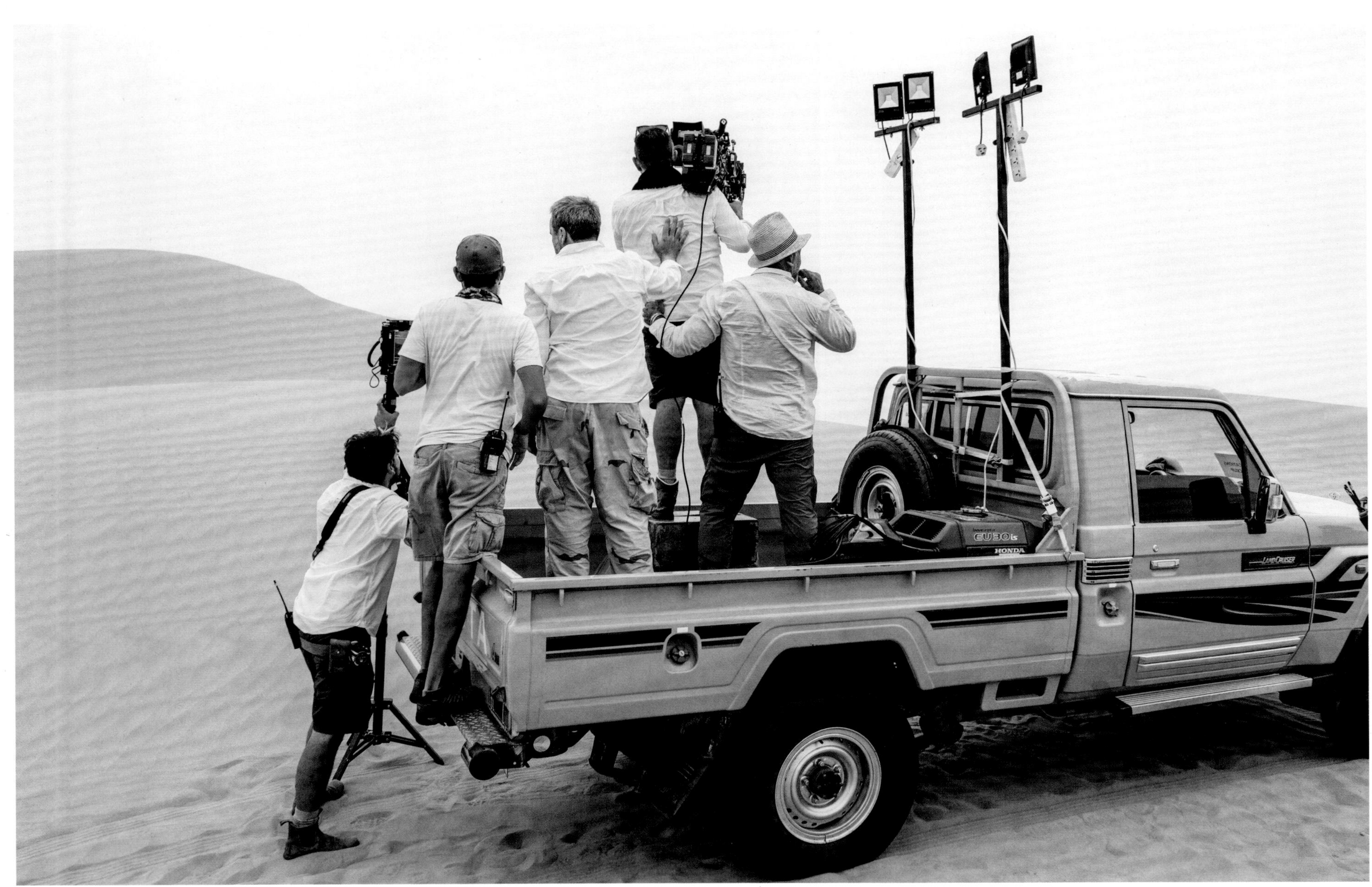

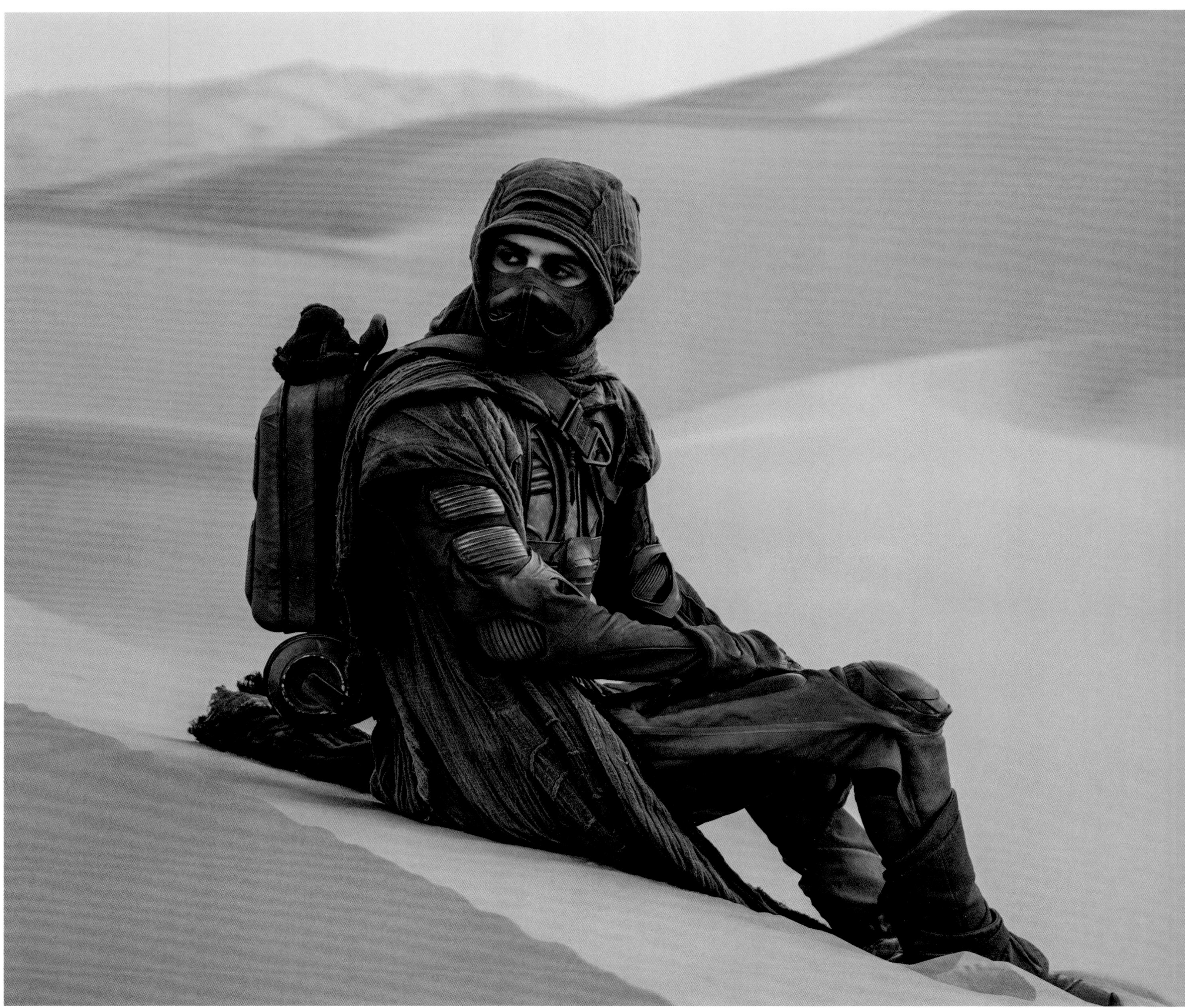

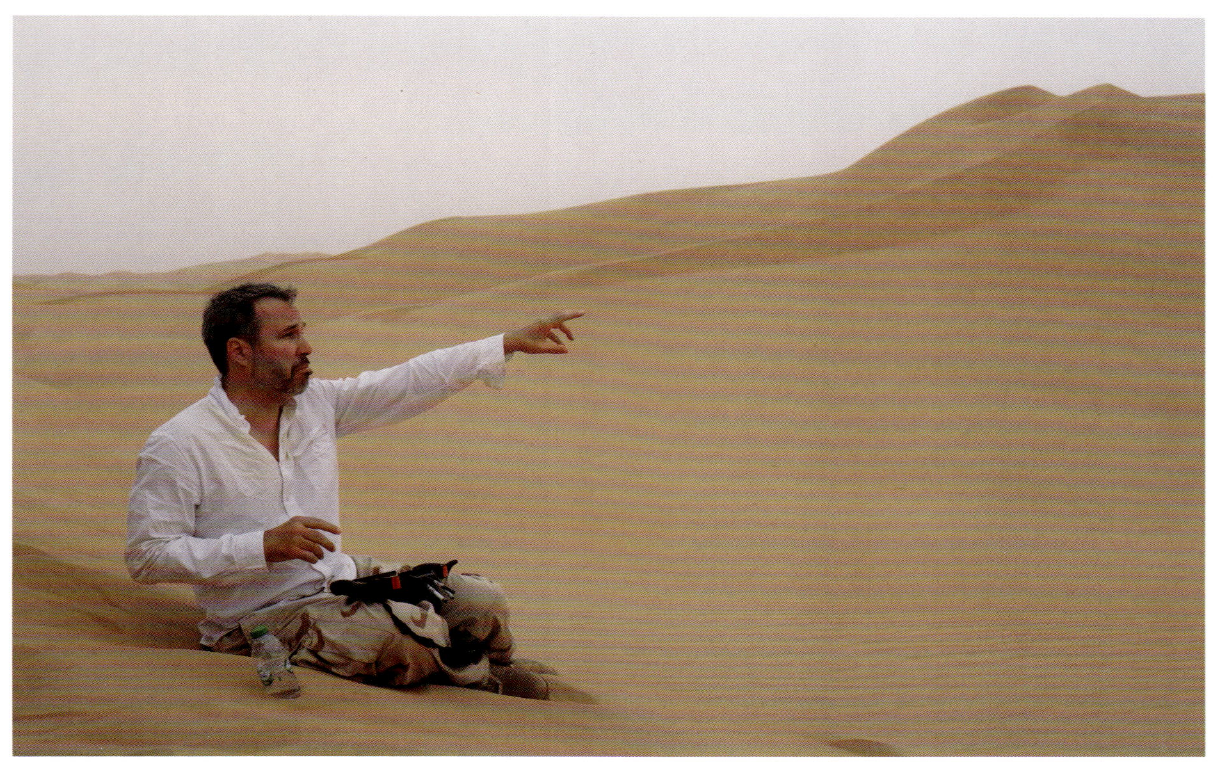

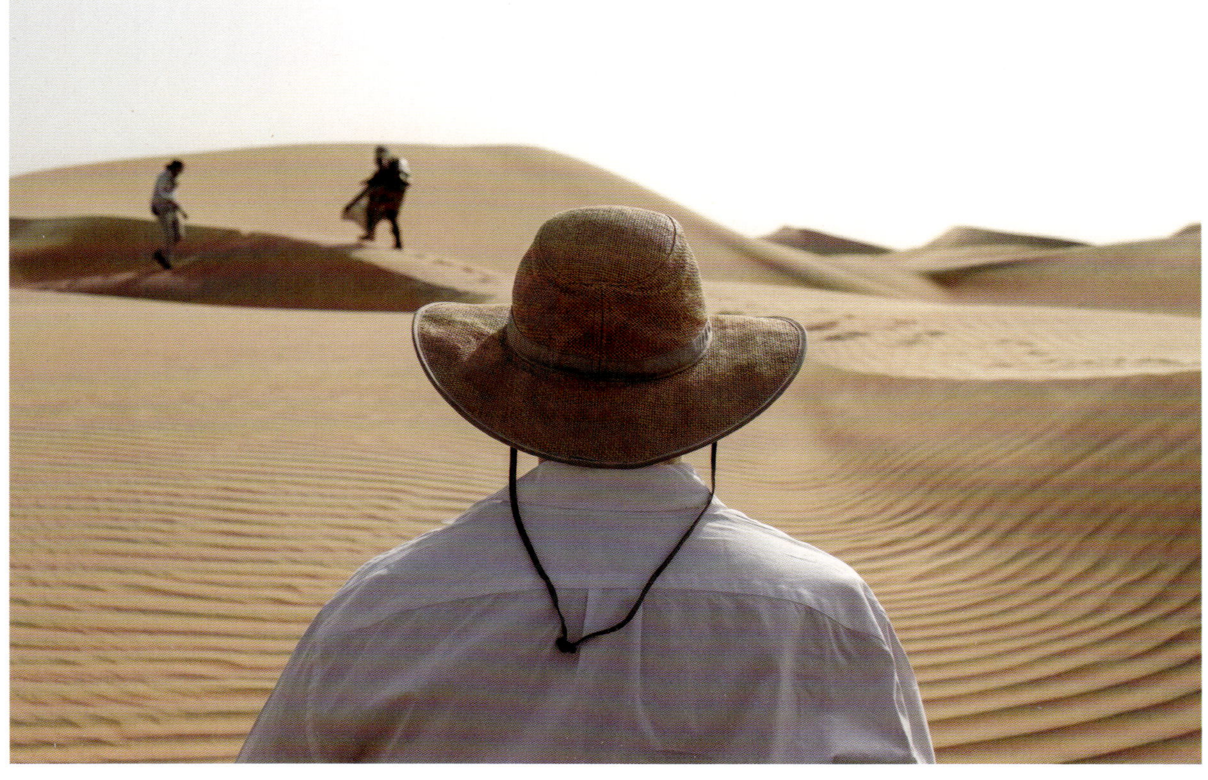

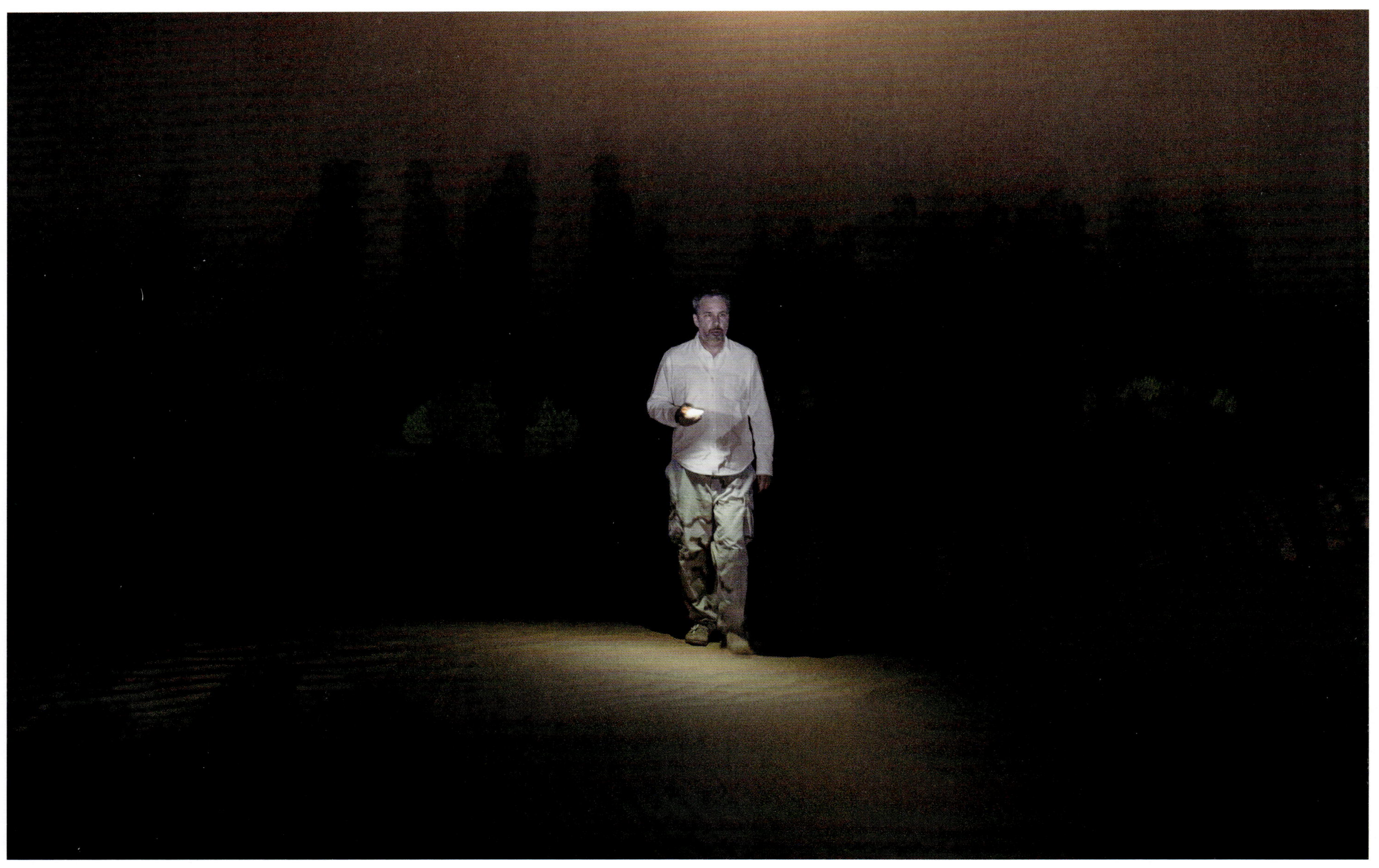

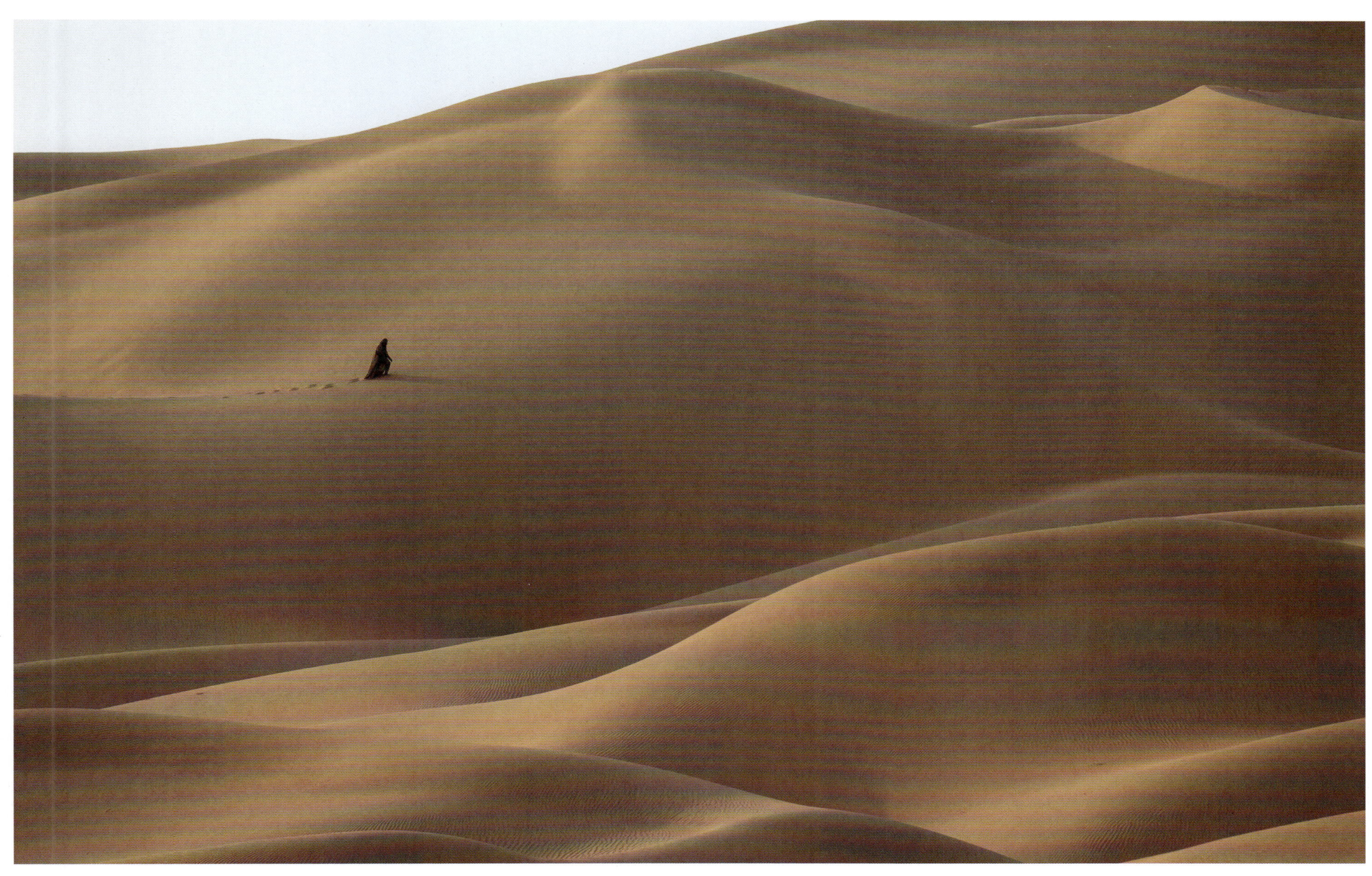

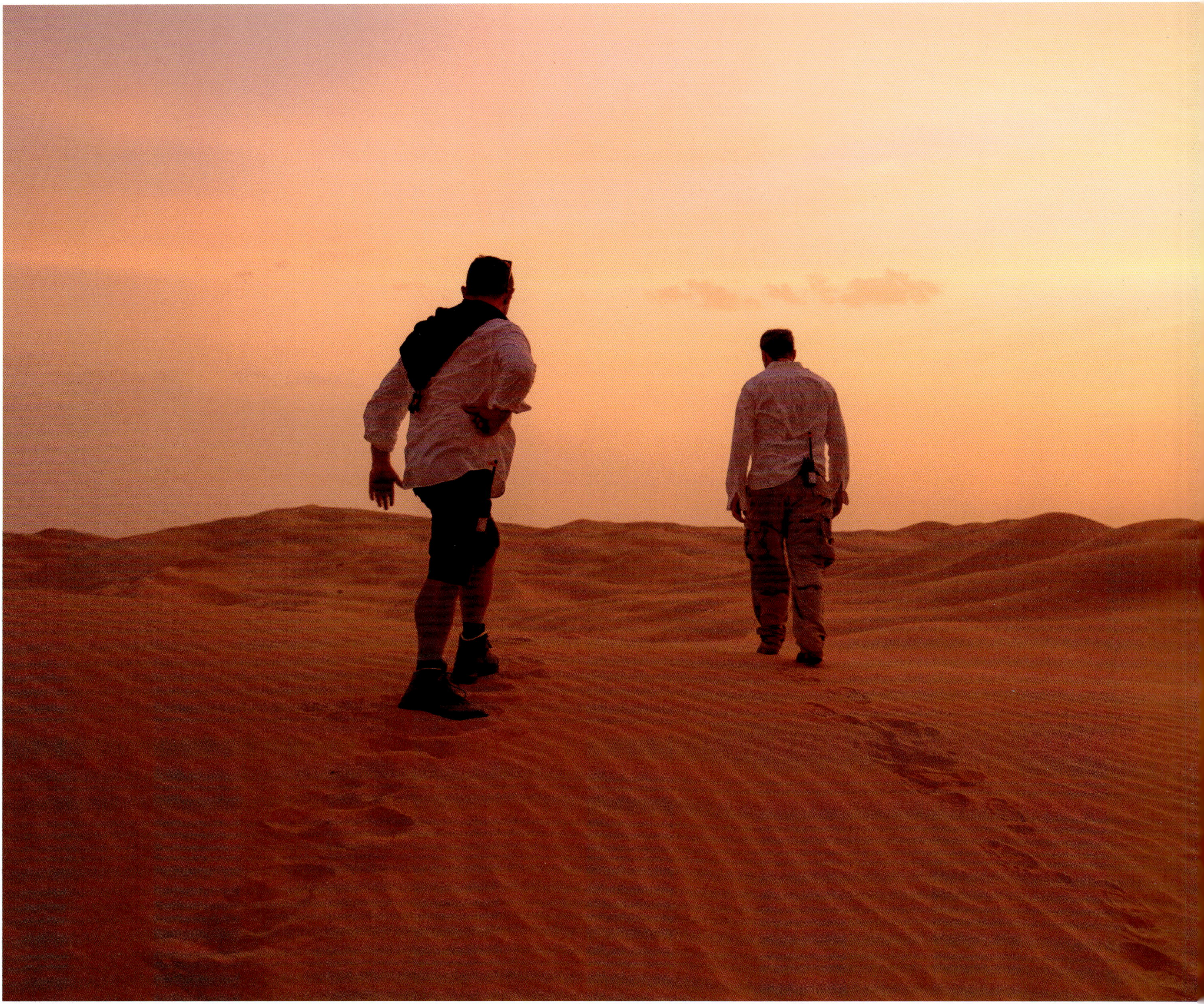

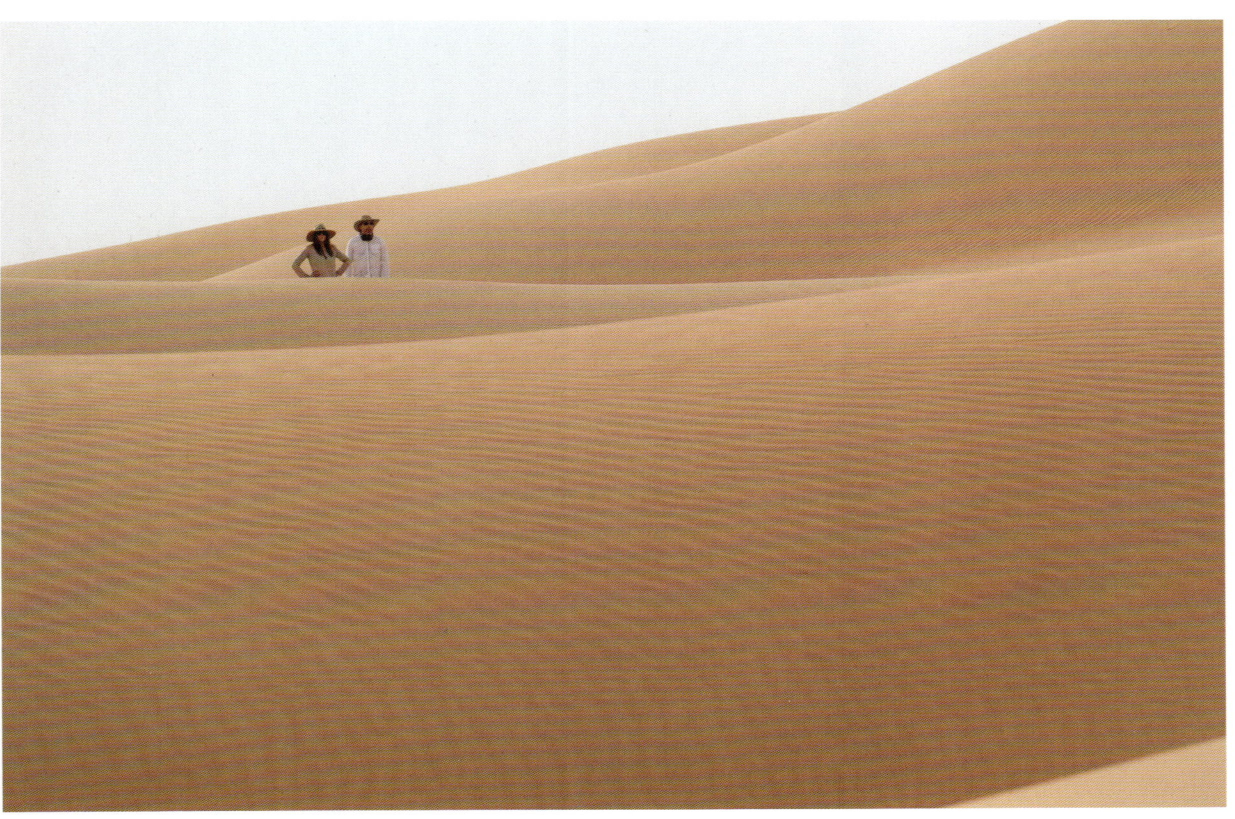

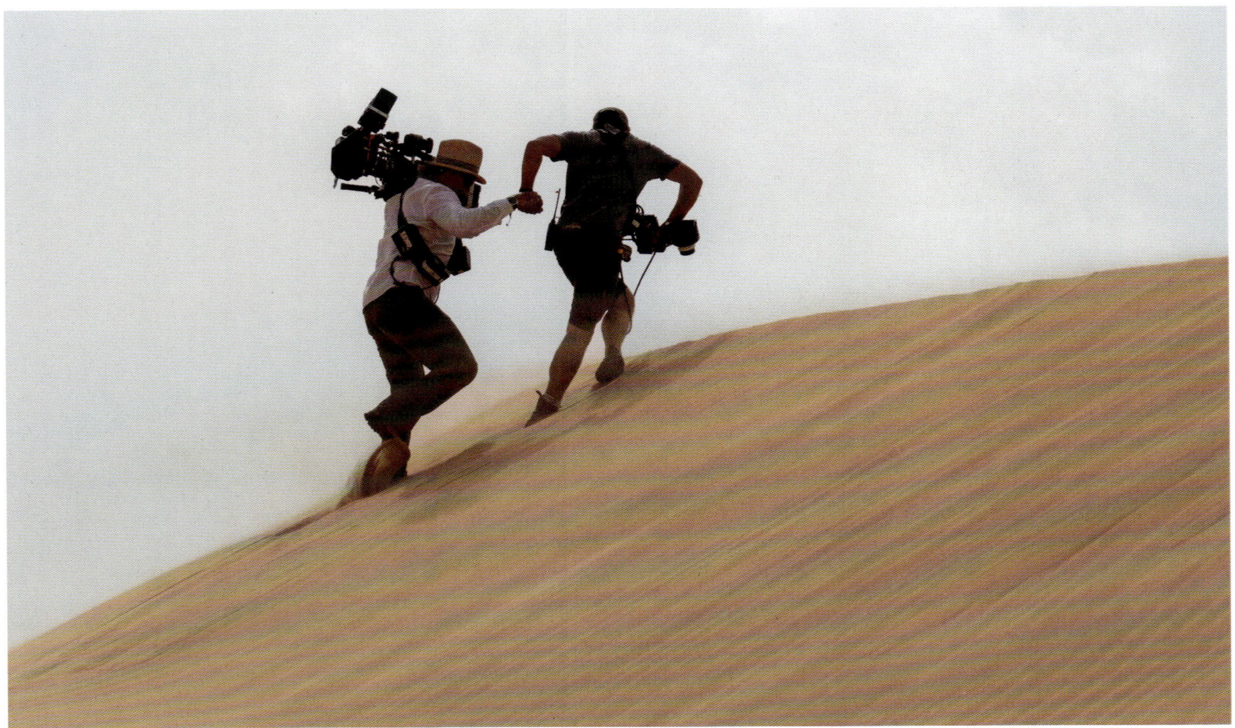

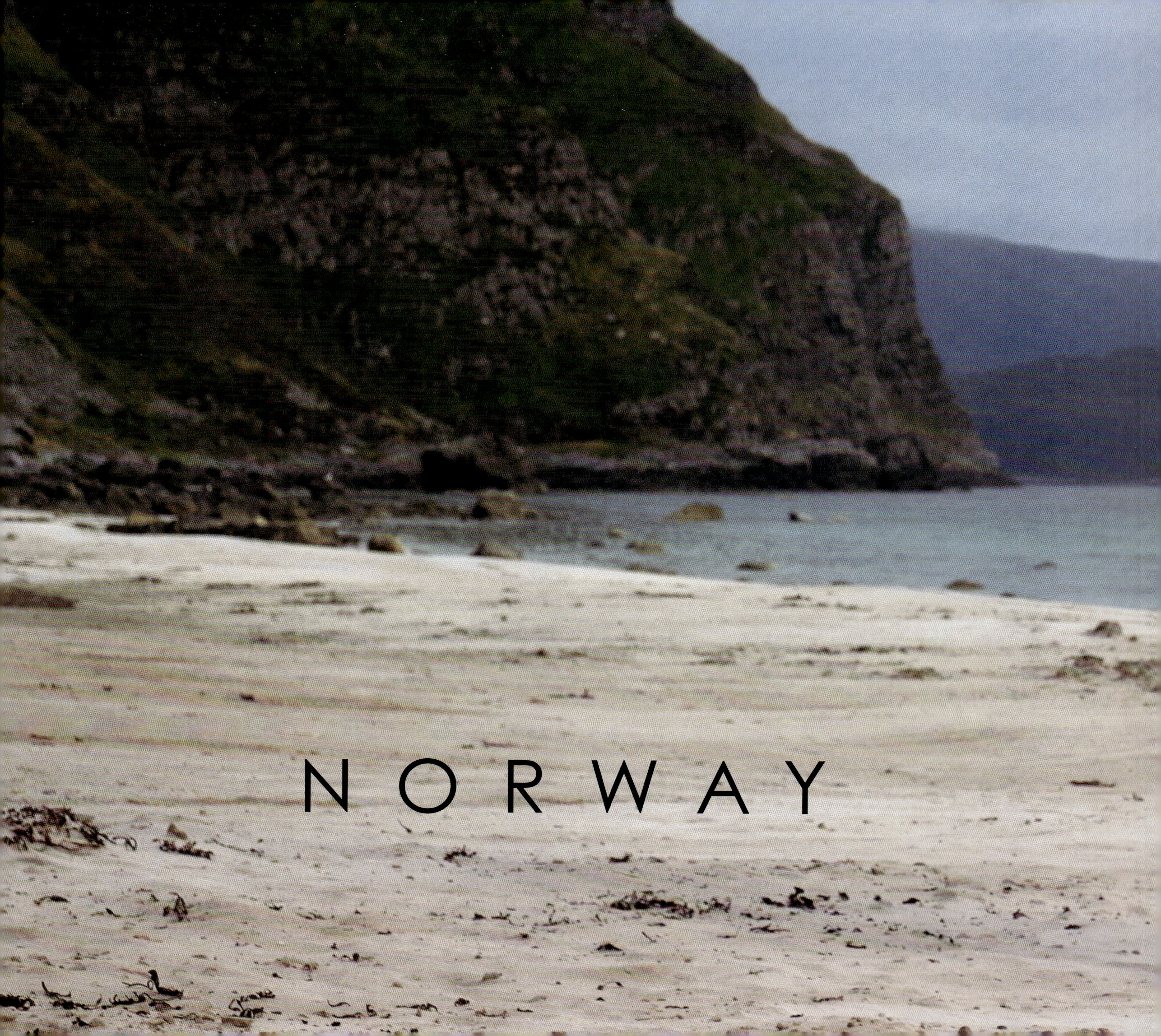
NORWAY

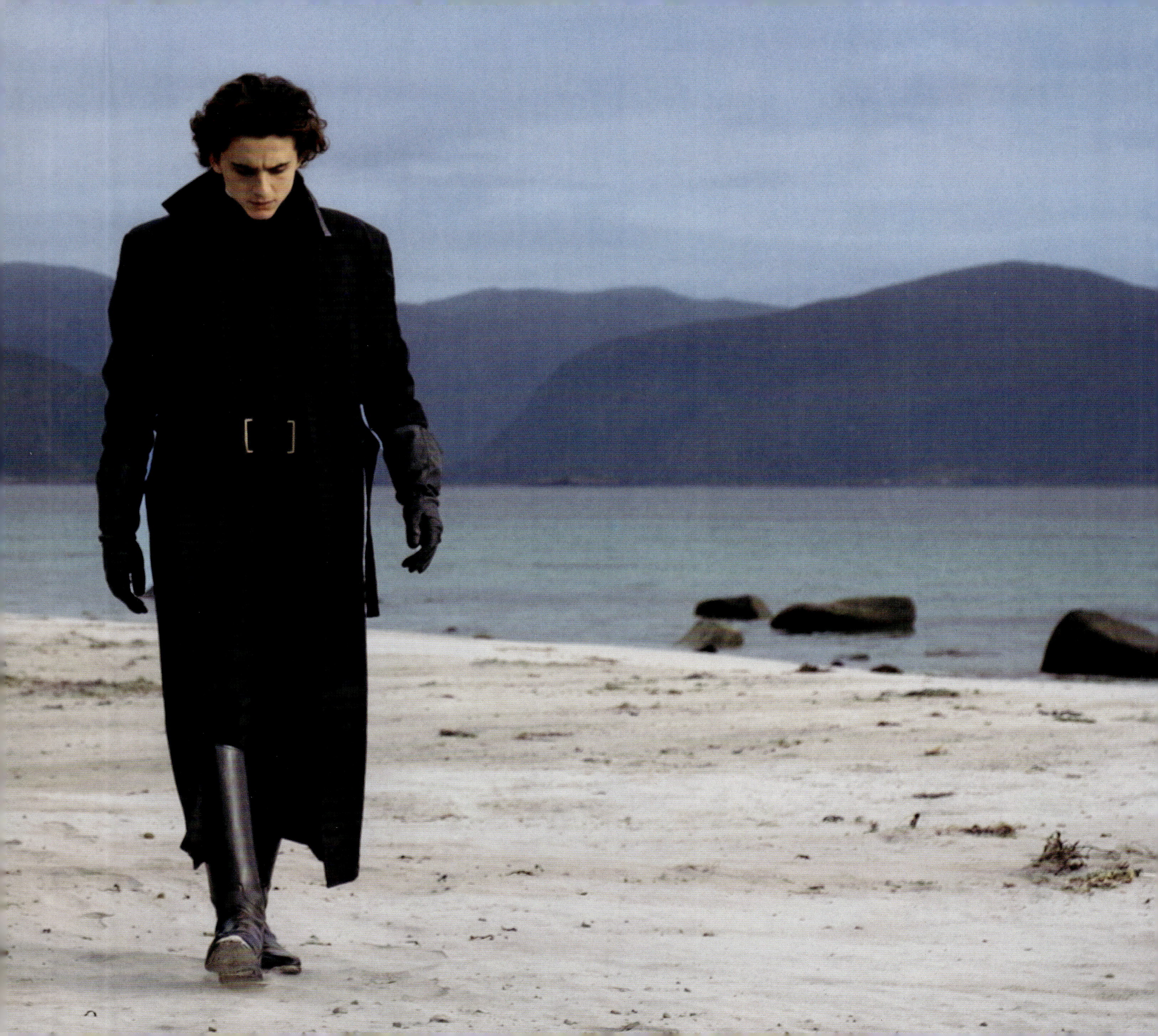

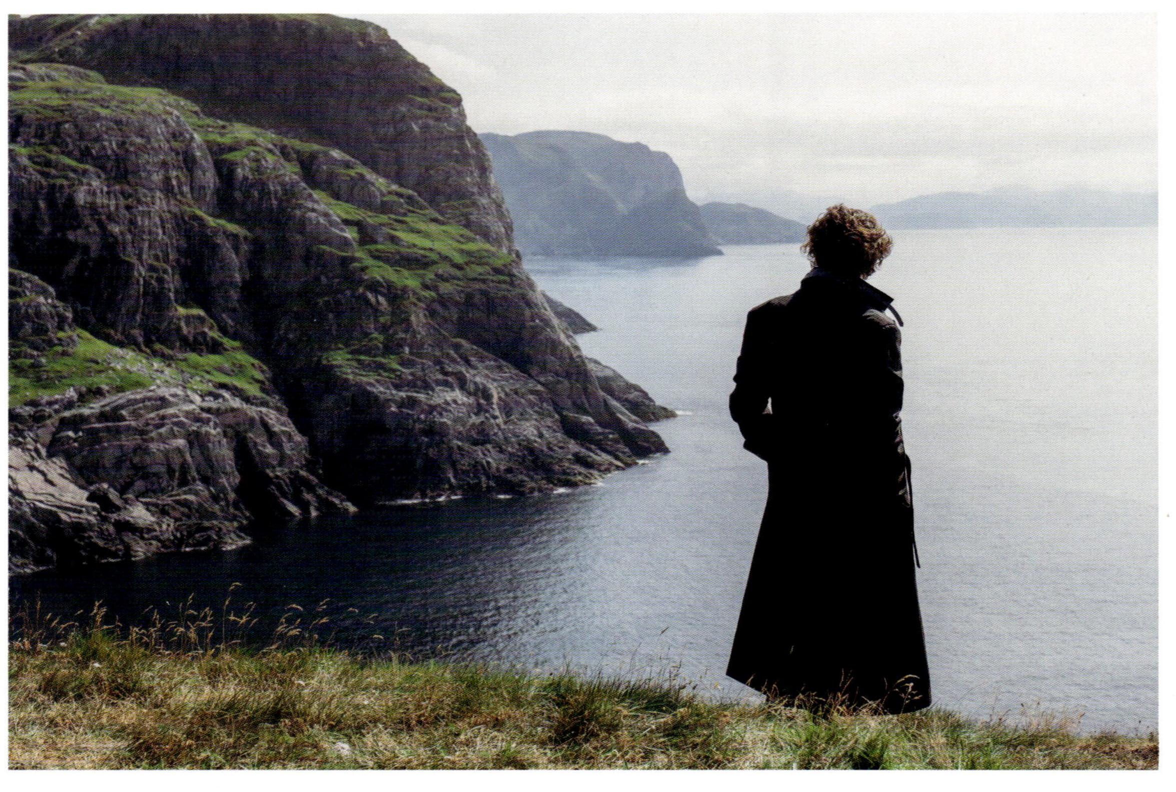

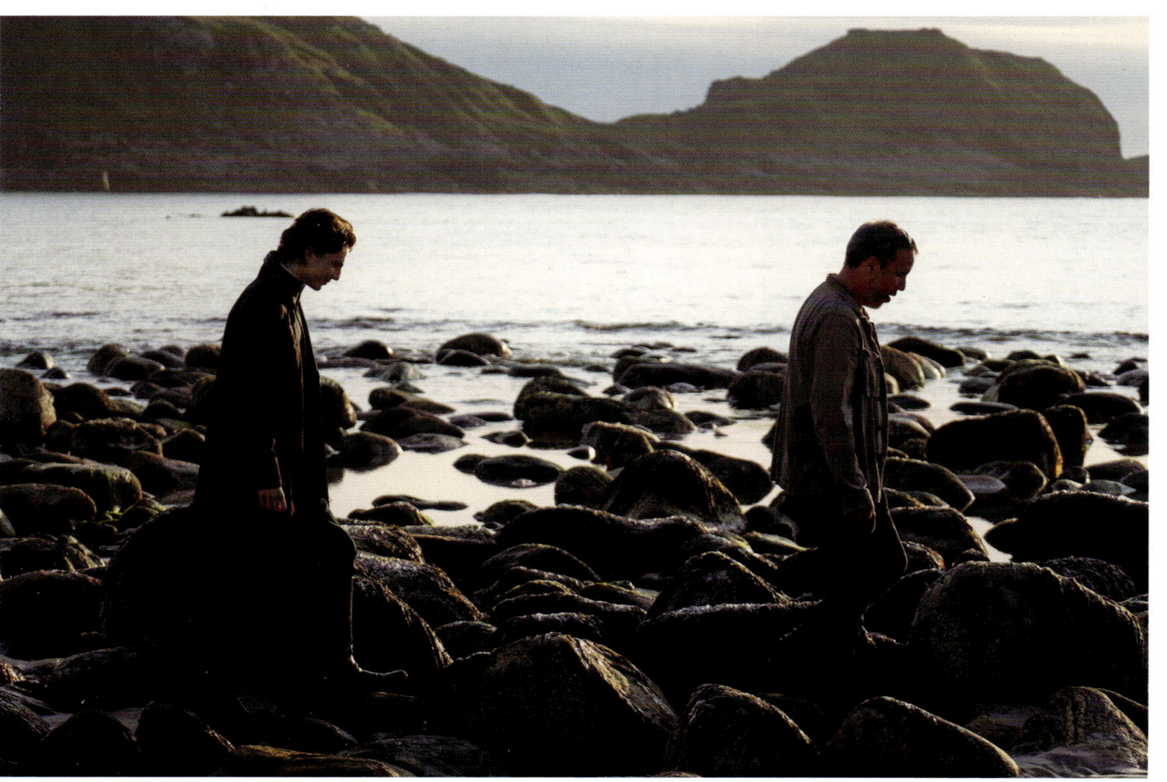

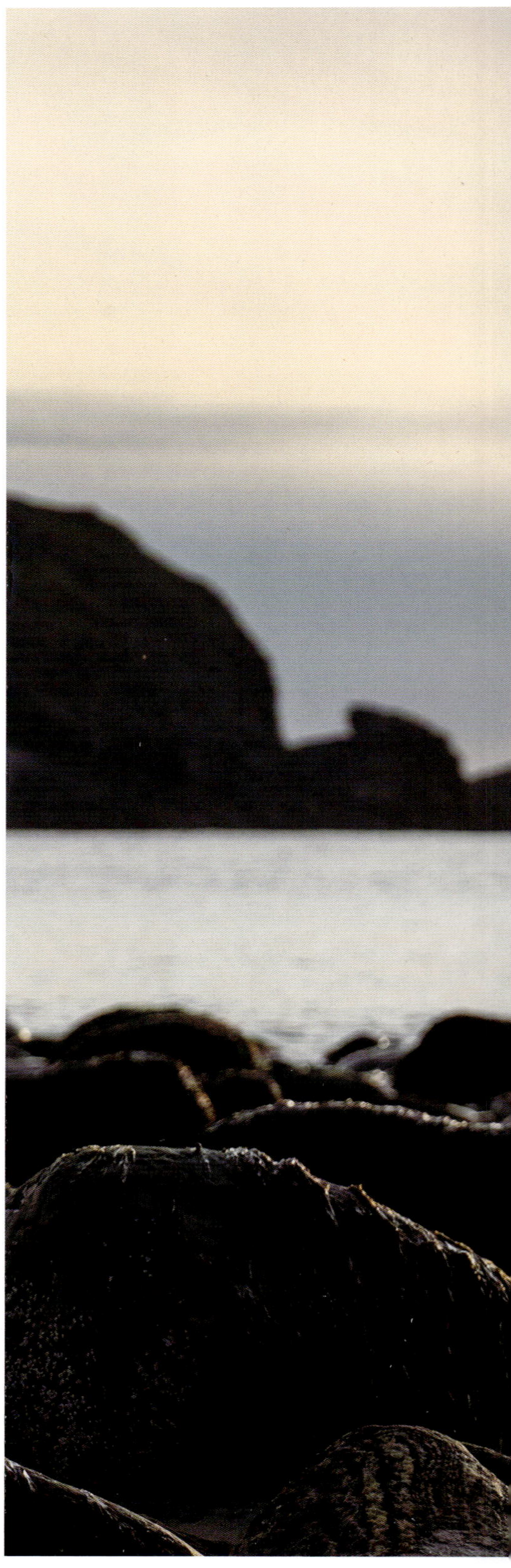

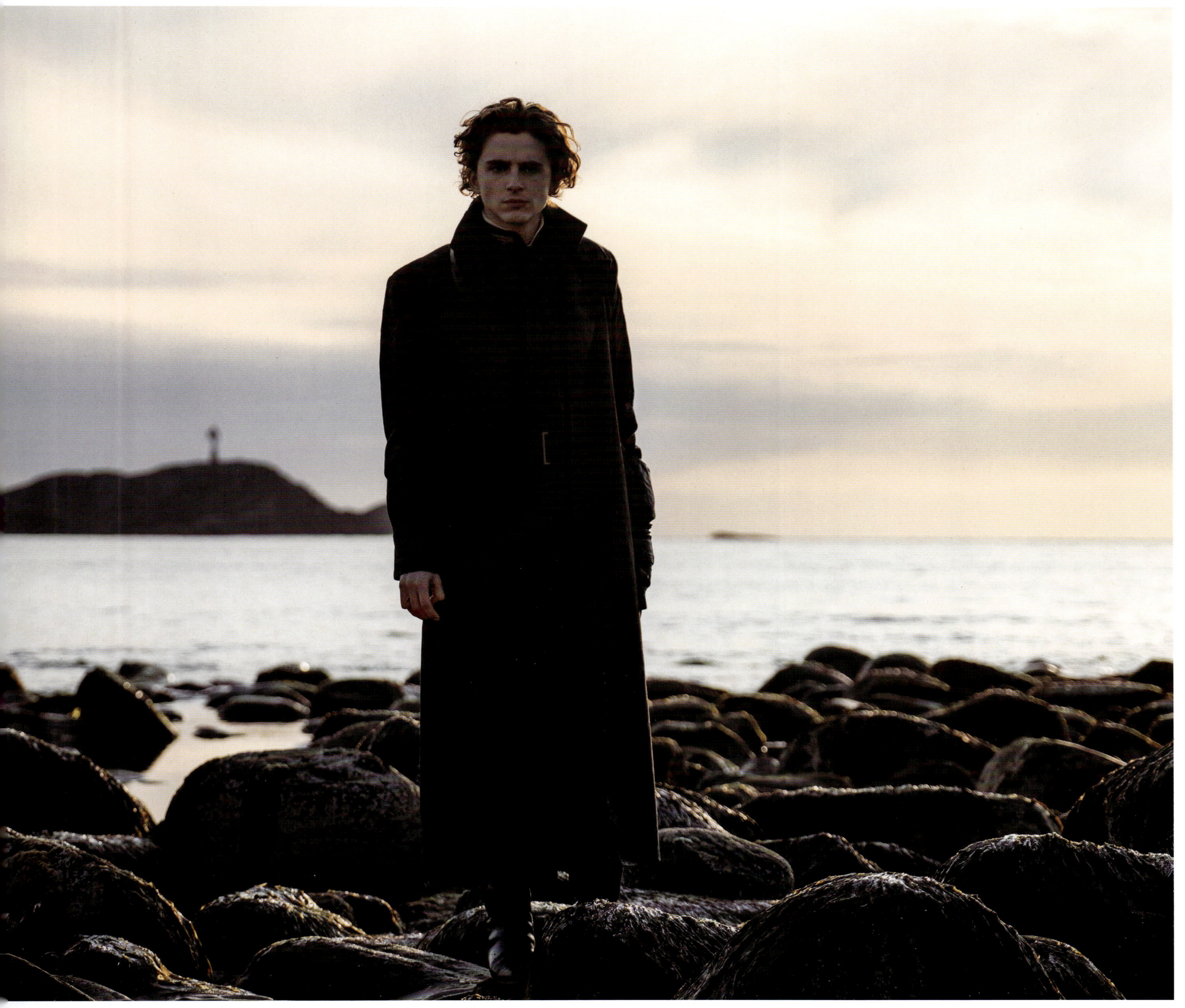

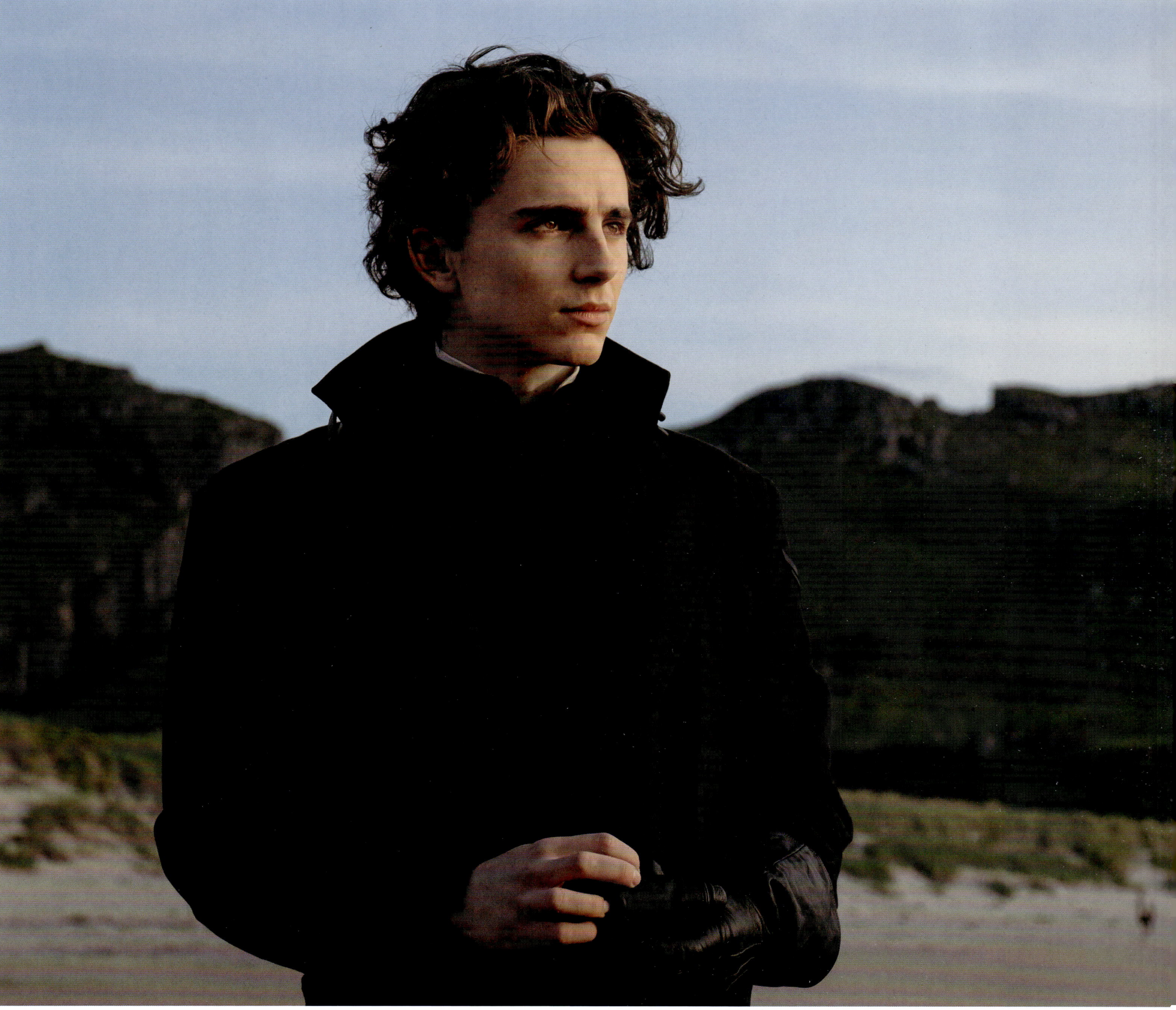

FOR MOST OF THE *Dune* crew, filming ended either in Budapest or Abu Dhabi; however, a skeleton crew went on to one final day of shooting on the coast of Norway. Stepping into the fresh chill of Norwegian air was a stark but welcome change from the muggy summer in Budapest and the excruciating heat of Abu Dhabi.

We spent the morning on a grassy cliff among the shaggy local goats before making our way down to the beach, where we filmed our last shot of the production. Like a diamond ring eclipse, our day in Norway was the final shining moment of this epic endeavor that had begun so many months ago. We had watched the twilights over a different planet in Wadi Rum, we had been to battle in Budapest, and we had watched the air turn red in the dunes of Abu Dhabi. It all culminated on this porcelain Norwegian beach, our crew of thousands dwindled down to about thirty. It was a beautiful and emotional ending to the journey, and as the sun set on the scene, so too did it set on our adventure. True to Frank Herbert's words, we had experienced greatness, and, as a crew, we had discovered a true "feeling for the myth" we were in.

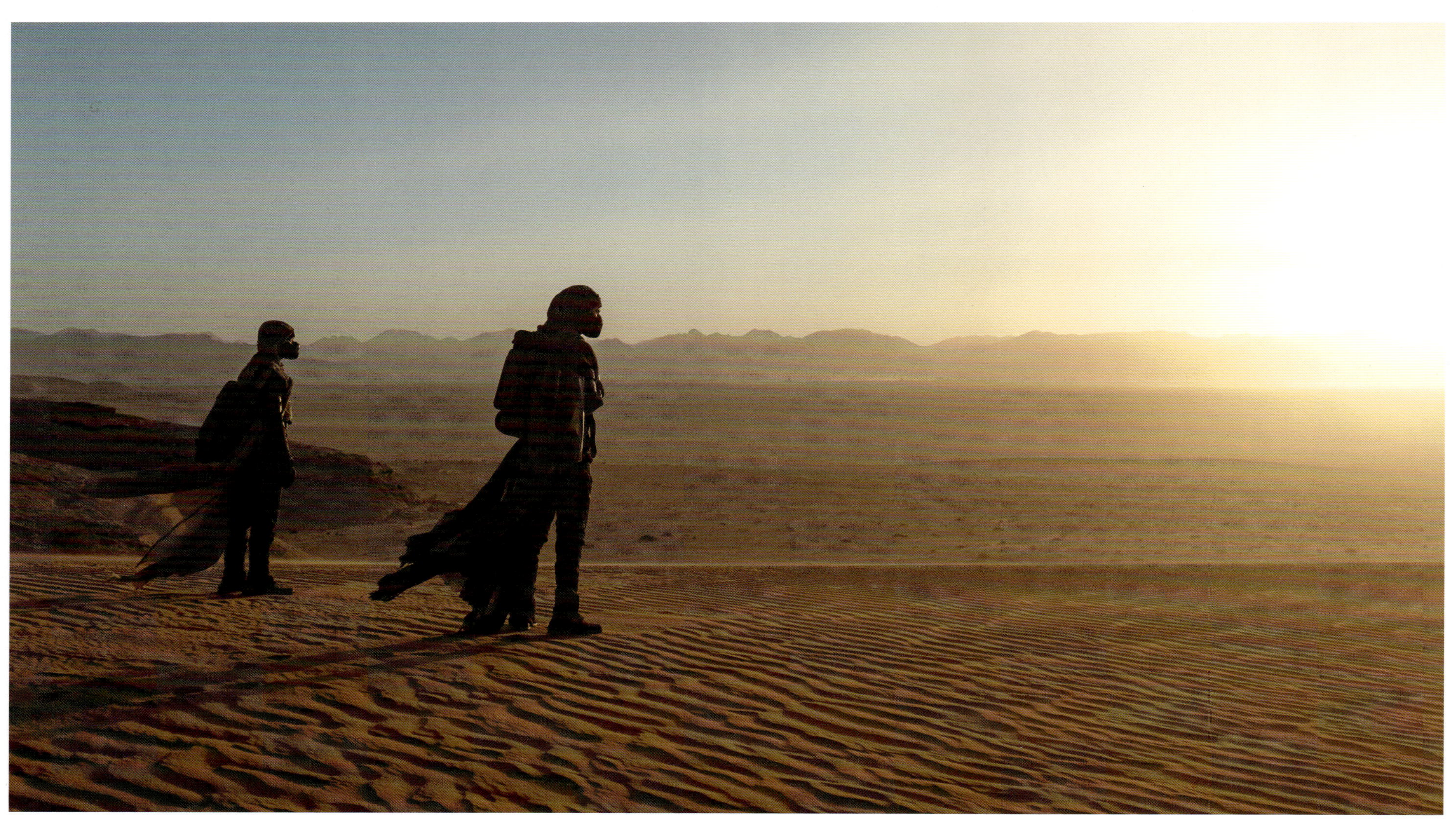

AFTERWORD:
THE VISIONARY OF *DUNE*
BY BRIAN HERBERT

FRANK HERBERT WAS HIMSELF a professional photographer, in addition to his better-known skills as the genius author of *Dune*, which has the mysterious desert world of Arrakis at its core. His classic novel has been read by millions of people around the world and translated into more than forty-five languages.

There certainly are a lot of people who have been playing in Frank Herbert's sandbox over the years, including authors such as myself, artists, filmmakers, game makers, merchandise manufacturers, literary agents, publishers, entertainment attorneys, and movie and television studio executives. My father's incredible *Dune* universe has expanded exponentially, and it has been my privilege to manage his estate, along with my fellow officers, Kim Herbert and Byron Merritt.

When Frank Herbert taught me the craft of writing, I listened with rapt attention as he told me he liked to write scenes as if he were viewing them through a camera lens. When he spoke of this, he showed me his first description of the Baron Harkonnen in *Dune*, whom he described over several pages as if seen through a camera lens that was opening very slowly, a little at a time. The chapter begins:

It was a relief globe of a world, partly in shadows, spinning under the impetus of a fat hand that glittered with rings. The globe sat on a freeform stand at one wall of a windowless room whose other walls presented a patchwork of multicolored scrolls, filmbooks, tapes and reels. Light glowed in the room from golden balls hanging in mobile suspensor fields.

An ellipsoid desk with a top of jade-pink petrified elacca wood stood at the center of the room. Veriform suspensor chairs ringed it, two of them occupied. In one sat a dark-haired youth of about sixteen years, round of face and with sullen eyes. The other held a slender, short man with effeminate face.

Both youth and man stared at the globe and the man half-hidden in shadows spinning it.

A chuckle sounded beside the globe. A basso voice rumbled out of the chuckle . . .

The Baron is not seen yet, but he speaks from the shadows. Then Frank Herbert writes, *"The fat hand descended onto the globe, stopped the spinning . . . ."* And: *"The fat hand moved, tracing details on the surface."* Dialogue ensues, and narrative, while the Baron moves *"within the shadows beside the globe . . . a shadow among shadows."*

Over several pages, the reader does not see any more of the evil, shadow-immersed antagonist than this, as the Baron, Feyd-Rautha, and Piter de Vries plot against Duke Leto. The reader sees no more of the Baron than his fat hand, and only hears his deep, basso voice. It is not until the very end of the chapter that Frank Herbert opens the camera lens all the way, to reveal his monstrous villain in startling detail:

The Baron moved out and away from the globe of Arrakis. As he emerged from the shadows, his figure took on dimension— grossly and immensely fat. And with subtle bulges beneath folds of his dark robes to reveal that all this fat was sustained partly by portable suspensors harnessed to his flesh. He might weigh two hundred Standard kilos in actuality, but his feet would carry no more than fifty of them.

"I am hungry," the Baron rumbled, and he rubbed his protruding lips with a beringed hand, stared down at Feyd-Rautha through fat-enfolded eyes. "Send for food, my darling. We will eat before we retire."

As a young man, director Denis Villeneuve read *Dune* and loved it. He also saw the Universal Pictures adaptation of the novel that was released in 1984, a lavish, big-budget movie with a great cast and many fine elements. But it was not what he envisioned, not what he thought the great novel deserved.

Denis had his own vision of what the epic story should look like on film, and from an early age he dreamed of directing a *Dune* movie one day. Now that dream has come true in duplicate, as Frank Herbert's great book is so immense that it requires two movies. With *Dune: Part One* complete and released in 2021, Denis and his crew are filming *Dune: Part Two* in Budapest and at other sites, including the spectacular desert of Wadi Rum in Jordan.

For decades, fans who read *Dune* have been forming their own images of the desert world and of the other fascinating planets in the *Dune* universe. Frank Herbert brought these worlds to life on paper, using his expert knowledge of science and world-building, and his remarkable talent for writing passages poetically and in such great detail that a fan once told me he became thirsty just reading the desert scenes.

In my twenties when I read *Dune*, and later when I saw the 1984 movie, to me there seemed to be a disconnect between the book and film versions. In the movie I was thrilled by many scenes and enjoyed the acting, but it did not always follow the plot. Of equal concern to me, director David Lynch and director of photography Freddie Francis—both highly talented filmmakers—portrayed the *Dune* universe as too dark for my liking. I was not alone in feeling that way. Even producer Dino De Laurentiis had worried about this when he saw the raw footage, but his vision did not prevail.

Back in 1972, before Lynch and Francis were involved, David Lean was hired to direct the movie by producer Arthur P. Jacobs, who had optioned the book. If that project had not fallen apart, I am confident that the brilliant director would have made the *Dune* I envisioned, with echoes of his own classic *Lawrence of Arabia*— bright and fantastically beautiful desert scenes, expressing the majesty of the vast sea of sand. It would have been a big, sprawling, brightly illuminated movie, not a dark and gloomy one.

In the early 1960s, David Lean had filmed *Lawrence of Arabia* in Wadi Rum, the stunningly beautiful desert region of Jordan where the famous British officer T. E. Lawrence once led Arab tribes to victory against the Turks. There is no doubt about it; Lean would have filmed *Dune* there as well.

Denis Villeneuve knew all this of course, and he had the wisdom to film much of his first *Dune* movie in that exact location, bringing history, desert scenes, and the science fiction imagination of Frank Herbert onto the screen. For that movie, the Academy Awards honored cinematographer Greig Fraser with an Oscar at the 2022 ceremony. Everything came together well in *Part One*, and the movie won six Academy Awards, more than any other film that year.

I'm sure my father would have enjoyed being at the Dolby Theatre in Hollywood for the ceremony, along with the cast and crew. I can actually envision him at the gala event and participating in it, with his big, wonderful beard and huge personality.

Frank Herbert captivated millions of readers around the globe with his magnificent novel. As one of his readers who envisioned what the *Dune* universe should look like, I have written many best-selling *Dune*-series novels, with my co-author, Kevin J. Anderson. We have been playing in Dad's huge sandbox for more than 25 years, while for more than 50 years, filmmakers have been working to put together a film version. After the 1984 movie (which received mixed reviews), there was a popular six-hour TV mini-series called *Frank Herbert's Dune* that aired on the Sci-Fi channel in 2000. It followed the plot more carefully than the 1984 version, but had a limited budget.

Now, with *Dune: Part One* and *Dune: Part Two*, I feel we are in the midst of creating the definitive film version of *Dune*. The third time's the charm, as the saying goes—and filmmakers are finally getting it right, with the vision and budget to accomplish what fans want to see. For decades it's been like cutting and polishing a priceless gem in the process of translation to film, seeking just the right luster, the true beauty of the novel. Finally, that beauty is emerging.

Photography was a lifelong love for Frank Herbert. As I wrote in my Hugo-nominated biography of him, *Dreamer of Dune*, my father saved enough money at the age of ten to buy a

Kodak box camera with a flash attachment. When color film was introduced in the 1930s, he purchased a miniature camera and began developing his own film. He set up a darkroom in the basement of his parents' home.

In 1940 when he was 19, he was turned down for a job at the *Oregon Statesman* newspaper in Salem, Oregon, where the personnel manager told him no positions were open. Not taking no for an answer, the determined young man sought out the managing editor and pitched him instead, saying he had his own photographic equipment, and that he could perform many duties on the paper, like a utility man on a baseball team, playing whatever position was needed. He got the job. One of the photographs he took while working at the *Oregon Statesman*, at a charity fund-raiser called the Salem Chest, was of US senator Douglas McKay, who would later become Secretary of the Interior. McKay took a liking to the young man, which later proved beneficial to Frank Herbert when he became a speech writer for Republican Party candidates in the 1950s.

Before that, in 1941, young Frank worked at the *Glendale Star* in California as a reporter and photographer. He went on many aerial assignments and personal flights, and he took at least 5,000 aerial photographs. Then, during World War II, he was assigned to the immense Norfolk Naval Shipyard in Portsmouth, Virginia, where he served as a Photographer Second Class V-6 in the US Naval Reserve. After the war, Frank Herbert talked with his best friend, Howie Hansen, about opening a camera supply store, a business project that never came to pass.

By 1947, Frank was employed as a feature writer for the *Tacoma Times* in Washington state. He had grown a beard, and when going out on assignments in the blustery northwest weather he wore a trench coat and fedora, with a huge Kodak Medalist camera slung over his shoulder. I have a wonderful photograph of him, taken with him holding that camera.

When I was a small child and Dad worked for the *Press Democrat* in Santa Rosa, northern California, he allowed me to go with him into a darkroom he had built in our home, where he taught me how to develop photographs. To my delight he told me to count off one second at a time at exactly the right cadence, while each photo was developing in the darkness of the room, keeping the photographic paper in the chemical solution for exactly the right amount of time before removing it with print tongs: "One chimpanzee, two chimpanzee, three chimpanzee . . ." Each chimpanzee represented one second of time. He also took pictures of me that were published in the paper. And in every home we lived in after that, he set up his own darkroom, where I helped him.

By 1957 Frank Herbert was working as a freelance writer and photographer. One day he learned that Georges H. Westbeau and his wife, Margaret, had a famous lioness outside of town, Little Tyke, internationally renowned because it was a vegetarian and had never eaten meat. It had been featured in a film documentary and in the best-selling book, *Little Tyke*. Dad went

out there with his notepad and camera to put together a story for
a national magazine, and he took me along with him.

By the early 1960s, Frank Herbert was the night picture editor for
the *San Francisco Examiner*, and later a wine critic and features
writer there, often taking photographs that were published. As his
creative writing career took hold in the 1970s and '80s, he took
many photographs, especially on a trip to Ireland researching his
novel *The White Plague*, which became a worldwide bestseller.

My father liked to keep a camera tripod and camera
equipment in his study next to his writing desk, and in 1985 he
would proudly show me a trove of new camera gear he had
purchased for a trip he planned to the Himalayas. On a trek
accompanied by a famous Sherpa guide, he intended to
become the oldest man to climb Mount Everest, a dream that
never came to pass.

But many of Frank Herbert's dreams did come true, including
the tremendous success of his novel after a rocky start in which
it was rejected by more than twenty publishers. Then in 1983
at Churubusco Studios in Mexico City, near the site of the 1968
Olympic Games, he clicked the clapboard to start the cameras
rolling on the initial *Dune* movie, and he got to keep the
clapboard from the first take of the first scene.

I know my father would have liked to have been here today
to set the new films in motion, at the side of Denis Villeneuve. But
Frank Herbert already set those films in motion, didn't he—in the
pages of his masterpiece, *Dune*.

BRIAN HERBERT
SEATTLE, WASHINGTON
MARCH 2, 2023

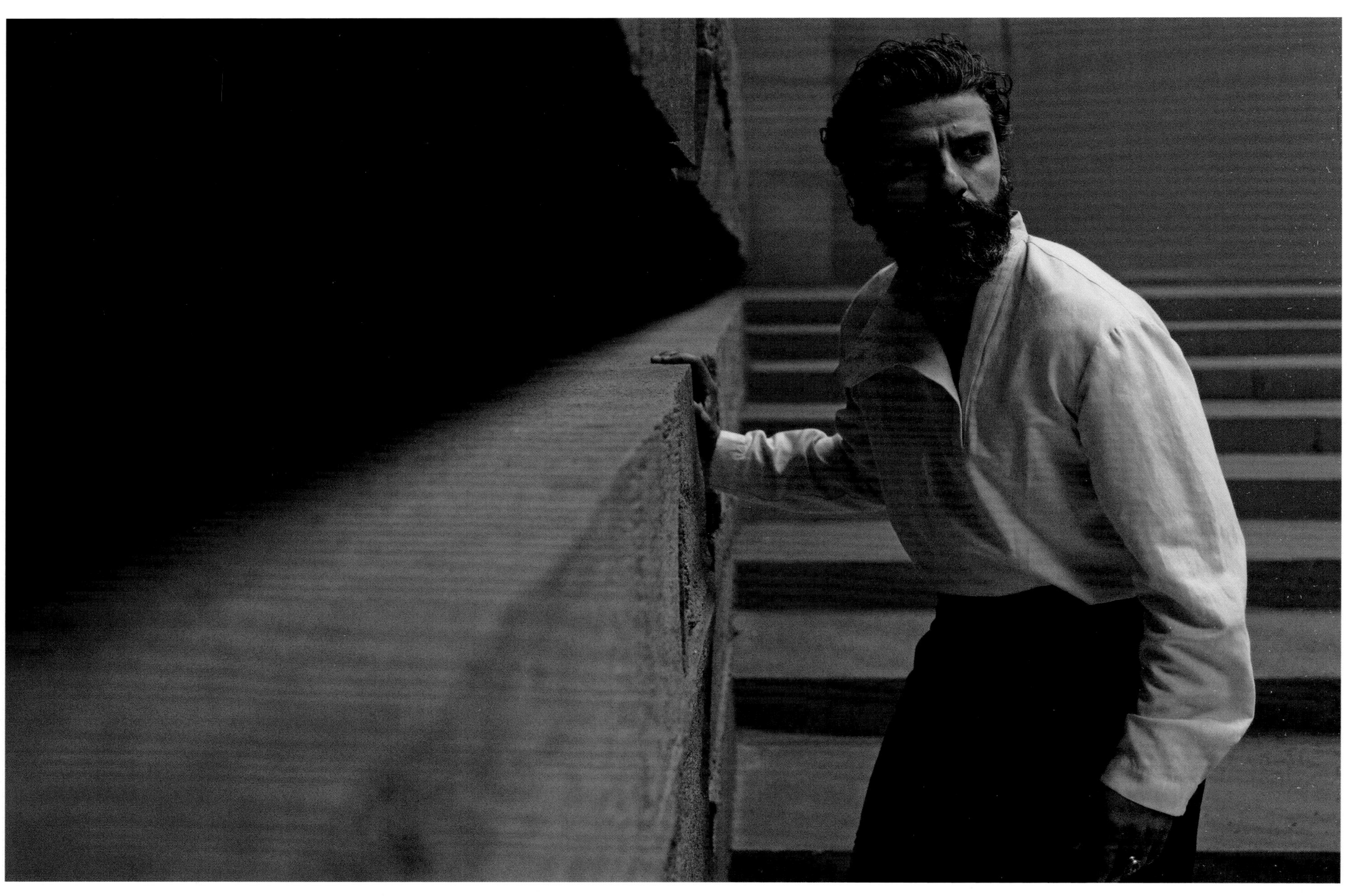

CAPTIONS

PAGE 1 Shooting a Duncan Idaho scene in the desert of Wadi Rum, Jordan. The scene would be omitted from the final film.

PAGE 2 Timothée Chalamet as Paul Atreides, disembarking from a life-size ornithopter prop in Jordan.

PAGE 4 Director Denis Villeneuve on the rocks of Wadi Rum.

PAGE 6 Executive producer Tanya Lapointe and director Denis Villeneuve in the dunes of Abu Dhabi.

PAGE 9 Josh Brolin as Gurney Halleck and Timothée Chalamet on the ramp of the ornithopter in Jordan.

PAGE 10 Sharon Duncan-Brewster as Dr. Liet Kynes in Wadi Rum.

PAGE 12 Rebecca Ferguson as Lady Jessica on the Arrakeen Residency set in Origo Studios, Budapest.

WADI RUM

PAGES 14–15 Rebecca Ferguson and Timothée Chalamet in Wadi Rum.

PAGE 17 Jason Momoa's stunt double, Kim Fardy, drops onto the rocks of Wadi Rum.

PAGES 18 AND 19 Timothée Chalamet in the Jordanian desert.

PAGE 20 The ornithopter, built by BGI Supplies, on location in Jordan.

PAGE 21 TOP Rebecca Ferguson and Timothée Chalamet with the ornithopter prop at night. **BOTTOM** Josh Brolin and Timothée Chalamet shoot a scene in which Halleck and Paul run to escape a sandworm.

PAGE 22 Timothée Chalamet films a scene in which Paul discovers spice in the desert of Arrakis.

PAGE 23 Josh Brolin on the ramp of the ornithopter.

PAGE 24 Boom operator György Mihályi alongside extras playing spice workers.

PAGE 25 Denis Villeneuve inside the cockpit of the ornithopter.

PAGE 26 In a sandstorm, Timothée Chalamet (far left) performs a scene with cinematographer Greig Fraser operating the camera, "A" camera first assistant Jake Marcuson pulling focus behind him, and other members of the grip and camera departments assisting.

PAGE 27 TOP (Left to right) Assistant director Tarik Afifi, Josh Brolin, Chalamet, set costumer Brad Holtzman, costume supervisor Lori Harris, and 3rd assistant director Teresa Orlando. **BOTTOM** Denis Villeneuve with the ornithopter.

PAGE 28 A Jordanian local cast as a spice worker.

PAGE 29 Sharon Duncan-Brewster and spice worker extras board the ornithopter prop during a simulated sandstorm.

PAGE 30 Wearing a stillsuit costume, Timothée Chalamet shoots a sandstorm scene.

PAGE 31 Sharon Duncan-Brewster as Dr. Liet Kynes.

PAGE 32 Denis Villeneuve with a group of spice worker extras.

PAGE 33 Timothée Chalamet films the sequence in which Paul Atreides rescues a group of spice workers from a sandworm.

PAGE 34 TOP A special effects technician kicks up sand with a blower in the desert. **BOTTOM** The cast and crew shoot with the ornithopter. The crew were required to stand behind the line of ropes to keep the sand at the location free of footprints.

PAGE 35 Sharon Duncan-Brewster and Josh Brolin with crew on the ornithopter.

PAGE 36 Jason Momoa as Duncan Idaho flanked by extras playing Fremen.

PAGE 37 TOP Momoa at sunset. **BOTTOM** Javier Bardem.

PAGE 38 Rebecca Ferguson, Jason Momoa, and Denis Villeneuve rehearse a scene.

PAGE 39 Sharon Duncan-Brewster and Ferguson share a laugh together between takes.

PAGE 40 Timothée Chalamet and Rebecca Ferguson film a scene at dusk in Jordan.

PAGE 41 The crew film in a small group to reduce footprints in the sand.

PAGE 42 A camera crane captures action performed by Timothée Chalamet and Rebecca Ferguson.

PAGE 43 TOP The crew film with a crashed ornithopter. **BOTTOM** Script supervisor Jessica Clothier and Denis Villeneuve discuss a scene in Wadi Rum.

PAGES 44–45 Timothée Chalamet and Rebecca Ferguson filming Paul and Lady Jessica's escape into the deserts of Arrakis.

PAGE 46 Duncan Idaho (Jason Momoa) after escaping the Harkonnens' invasion of Arrakeen.

PAGE 47 LEFT Sharon Duncan-Brewster as Dr. Liet Kynes in Wadi Rum.

PAGE 48 LEFT Assistant property master Brad Good, principal costumer Rewa Lewis, and Sharon Duncan-Brewster. **RIGHT** Fitting Duncan-Brewster's stillsuit costume: (Left to right) Lewis, Duncan-Brewster, lead senior special effects technician Till Hertrich, and Lori Harris.

PAGE 49 (Left to right) Camera assistant Tom Lane, Jessica Clothier (seated), digital imaging technician assistant Balázs Péter, camera trainee Ambrus Orosz, key grip Tommaso Mele, Greig Fraser, Jake Marcuson, first assistant director Chris Carreras, and Denis Villeneuve (seated).

PAGE 50 Rebecca Ferguson on the rocks of Wadi Rum.

PAGE 51 LEFT Jason Momoa as Duncan Idaho. **RIGHT** Sharon Duncan-Brewster as Dr. Liet Kynes.

PAGE 52 (Left to right) Chris Carreras, Timothée Chalamet, Greig Fraser, Jake Marcuson, Denis Villeneuve, boom operator György Mihályi, and Jessica Clothier in Wadi Rum.

PAGE 53 Villeneuve directs Chalamet and Rebecca Ferguson.

PAGE 54 Rebecca Ferguson and Timothée Chalamet perform the scene in which Paul and Lady Jessica change into their stillsuits.

PAGE 55 Ferguson and Chalamet climbing the rocks of Wadi Rum.

PAGE 56 Rebecca Ferguson as Lady Jessica.

PAGE 57 Timothée Chalamet as Paul Atreides.

PAGE 58 Rebecca Ferguson strikes a pose for the camera between takes in Wadi Rum.

PAGE 59 Paul Atreides (Timothée Chalamet) runs to escape a sandworm.

PAGES 60 AND 61 Rebecca Ferguson dances for Chiabella James's camera between takes.

PAGE 62 Dr. Liet Kynes (Sharon Duncan-Brewster) faces the Sardaukar.

PAGE 63 Winkler Tamás and Lucza Zsigmond alongside Ben Dilloway (center) as Sardaukar assassins.

PAGE 64 TOP Greig Fraser (far left) and Denis Villeneuve (center) with Javier Bardem (kneeling), Rebecca Ferguson, Timothée Chalamet, and Babs Olusanmokun as Jamis. **BOTTOM** (Left to right) Ferguson, Zendaya as Chani, Bardem, and Chalamet.

PAGE 65 Bardem with extras playing his Fremen companions.

PAGE 66 Timothée Chalamet and Zendaya in a moment between takes.

PAGE 67 Babs Olusanmokun prepares for a fight scene.

PAGE 68 Paul Atreides (Timothée Chalamet) arms himself against the Fremen.

PAGE 69 Lady Jessica (Rebecca Ferguson) disarms and captures Stilgar (Javier Bardem) with his crysknife.

Page 70 Babs Olusanmokun shades himself from the heat during a rehearsal in Wadi Rum.

PAGE 71 Timothée Chalamet and Olusanmokun film the scene in which Paul and Jamis fight.

PAGE 72 Javier Bardem rehearses his lines, which have been translated into Chakobsa, the Fremen language.

PAGE 73 Zendaya is filmed using a 16mm film camera in Wadi Rum.

PAGE 74 LEFT Timothée Chalamet. **RIGHT** Zendaya.

PAGE 75 LEFT Javier Bardem. **RIGHT** Rebecca Ferguson.

PAGE 76 LEFT Javier Bardem. **RIGHT** Zendaya.

PAGE 77 Babs Olusanmokun filming the final segment of the Paul/Jamis fight.

PAGE 78 Babs Olusanmokun in the heat of the fight scene.

PAGE 79 Olusanmokun and Timothée Chalamet filming the Paul/Jamis fight.

PAGE 80 Timothée Chalamet and Rebecca Ferguson in stillsuit costumes, complete with nose tubes.

PAGE 81 TOP Denis Villeneuve directs Zendaya. **BOTTOM** Ferguson, Javier Bardem, and Villeneuve share a laugh.

PAGE 82 Javier Bardem during rehearsals on location.

PAGE 83 The *Dune* crew film along a rocky ridge in Jordan.

PAGES 84–85 Performers dressed as Fremen cross a ridge in Wadi Rum.

BUDAPEST

PAGES 86–87 Extras portraying Sardaukar descend upon the Imperial Ecological Testing Station's Nexus set, built at Origo Studios in Budapest.

PAGE 89 Dressed in the Atreides uniform, Timothée Chalamet walks to the set on the Origo Studios backlot.

PAGE 90 Timothée Chalamet on the training room set.

PAGE 91 Josh Brolin with Gurney Halleck's arsenal of knives on the training room set.

PAGE 92 On the training room set, Josh Brolin performs stunt choreography with Timothée Chalamet.

PAGE 93 Brolin and Denis Villeneuve discuss a scene on the training room set.

PAGE 94 Denis Villeneuve directs Timothée Chalamet during filming of the training scenes.

PAGE 95 Gurney Halleck (Josh Brolin) and Paul Atreides (Chalamet) spar during the training sequence.

PAGE 96 Paul (Timothée Chalamet) with training mannequins on the training room set.

PAGE 97 Denis Villeneuve looks for a new angle while filming on the training room set.

PAGE 98 Lady Jessica (Rebecca Ferguson) trains Paul (Timothée Chalamet) in a scene deleted from the final film.

PAGE 99 Ferguson takes a moment to reflect during shooting on the Paul's bedroom set at Origo Studios.

PAGE 101 Filming the Bene Gesserit arrival scene on the exterior Castle Caladan set.

PAGE 102 Denis Villeneuve on the misty exterior Castle Caladan set.

PAGE 103 (Foreground) Reverend Mother Mohiam (Charlotte Rampling) with Lady Jessica (Rebecca Ferguson).

PAGE 104 Rebecca Ferguson in the mist during filming of the Bene Gesserit scenes.

PAGE 105 A hooded Ferguson and second unit cinematographer Katelin Arizmendi.

PAGE 106 Charlotte Rampling as Reverend Mother Mohiam with extras playing sisters of the Bene Gesserit.

PAGE 107 Two Bene Gesserit performers during the arrival scene.

PAGE 108 Charlotte Rampling films the Bene Gesserit departure scene.

PAGE 109 Rebecca Ferguson films the departure scene.

PAGE 110 Rebecca Ferguson on the interior Castle Caladan set, featuring a fully functioning fireplace.

PAGE 111 Charlotte Rampling as Reverend Mother Mohiam.

PAGE 112 TOP Denis Villeneuve directs Charlotte Rampling on the Castle Caladan library set at Origo Studios. **BOTTOM** (Left to right) Timothée Chalamet, first sound assistant Áron Havasi, Charlotte Rampling, and boom operator György Mihályi filming on the library set.

PAGE 113 Villeneuve and Rebecca Ferguson rehearse a scene that features the Castle Caladan library door.

PAGE 114 Timothée Chalamet and Charlotte Rampling film the gom jabbar scene, in which the Reverend Mother subjects Paul to a potentially deadly interrogation.

PAGE 115 Filming the Atreides's arrival on Arrakis on the backlot of Origo Studios: (Left to right from center) Roger Yuan (eighth from left) as Lieutenant Lanville, Josh Brolin, Rebecca Ferguson, Oscar Isaac, Chalamet, and performers playing Atreides soldiers.

PAGE 116 Filming the arrival on Arrakis from the point of view of Paul (Timothée Chalamet).

PAGE 117 Performers playing Atreides family members and soldiers during filming of the arrival scene.

PAGE 118 During shooting of the Arrakis arrival scene, camera assistant Tom Lane slates a shot of the disembarked Atreides coalition.

PAGE 119 Oscar Isaac and Josh Brolin in full Atreides armor for the arrival scene.

PAGE 120 Oscar Isaac and Josh Brolin film a scene on the Arrakeen Residency balcony set in which Duke Leto and Gurney Halleck look out over the city using binoculars.

PAGE 121 Lady Jessica (Rebecca Ferguson, far left) and Paul (Timothée Chalamet, center) flanked by Atreides soldiers in the arrival scene.

PAGE 122 An armored Josh Brolin with extras portraying Atreides soldiers on the Origo Studios backlot.

PAGE 123 Wearing Lady Jessica's arrival gown, and trailed by ladies in waiting, Rebecca Ferguson shoots the Arrakis arrival scene.

PAGE 124 Timothée Chalamet and Oscar Isaac on the Arrakeen Residency balcony set, constructed on the backlot at Origo Studios.

PAGE 125 Chalamet, Isaac, Roger Yuan, Denis Villeneuve, Josh Brolin, and Stephen McKinley Henderson, who portrays Thufir Hawat, share a laugh during a break in filming on the backlot.

PAGE 126 An Arrakeen hat design sits on a mannequin in the costume department at Origo Studios.

PAGE 127 Stephen McKinley Henderson holds Thufir Hawat's parasol during filming on the backlot.

PAGE 128 TOP Denis Villeneuve directs Rebecca Ferguson within an ornithopter cockpit. **BOTTOM** Josh Brolin hugs Villeneuve between takes on the backlot.

PAGE 129 Oscar Isaac and Stephen McKinley Henderson share a moment together between takes.

PAGE 130 A Pilgrim extra looks at the sacred palm trees through the Arrakeen Residency gates.

PAGE 131 The Arrakeen Residency gardener (Seun Shote) tends to the royal palm trees.

PAGE 132 TOP Timothée Chalamet and Stephen McKinley Henderson on the Paul's bedroom set. **BOTTOM** Chalamet on the Paul's bedroom set.

PAGE 133 Rebecca Ferguson on the Arrakeen Residency dining room set.

PAGE 134 Rebecca Ferguson and Golda Rosheuvel as the Shadout Mapes (third from right) with extras playing Arrakeen house staff on the Arrakeen Residency dining room set.

PAGE 135 Timothée Chalamet stands by the sandworm fresco on the Residency corridor set.

PAGE 136 Rebecca Ferguson, Denis Villeneuve, Chang Chen as Dr. Wellington Yueh, and Timothée Chalamet on the Paul's bedroom set.

PAGE 137 Josh Brolin with Oscar Isaac in full Atreides armor.

PAGE 138 Timothée Chalamet with Jessica Clothier on the Arrakeen Residency set.

PAGE 139 Rebecca Ferguson relaxes between takes on the Arrakeen Residency set.

PAGE 141 Timothée Chalamet and Rebecca Ferguson on the meditation room set.

PAGE 142 Chang Chen as Dr. Yueh.

PAGE 143 Chang Chen and Rebecca Ferguson on the Arrakeen Residency staircase set.

PAGE 144 LEFT Sharon Duncan-Brewster on the Duke Leto office set. **RIGHT** Timothée Chalamet during filming on the Duke Leto office set.

PAGE 145 Chalamet, Jason Momoa, Stephen McKinley Henderson, and Jessica Clothier rehearse lines on the Duke Leto's office set.

PAGE 146 Sharon Duncan-Brewster, in costume as Dr. Liet Kynes, stands next to an ornithopter on the Origo Studios backlot.

PAGE 147 Duncan-Brewster on the Duke Leto's office set.

PAGE 148 Oscar Isaac and Josh Brolin share a laugh on the set of *Royalty* (the code name for the *Dune* production).

PAGE 149 Denis Villeneuve, Timothée Chalamet, and Brolin crack each other up between takes.

PAGE 150 Denis Villeneuve directs Josh Brolin.

PAGE 151 Greig Fraser, Denis Villeneuve, and Josh Brolin rehearse on the Arrakeen Residency balcony set at Origo Studios.

PAGE 152 (Left to right) Josh Brolin, property master Doug Harlocker, property second assistant Krisztián Kis, Denis Villeneuve, assistant director Teresa Orlando, set costumer Rewa Lewis, Oscar Isaac, set costumer Brad Holtzman, and Jessica Clothier. Isaac is playing the baliset, a musical instrument prop created for Gurney Halleck's character, to entertain the crew between takes. The baliset scenes were deleted from the final film.

PAGE 153 Camera assistant Tom Lane, Rebecca Ferguson, and Rewa Lewis.

PAGE 154 Timothée Chalamet as Paul Atreides on the Paul's bedroom set.

PAGE 155 (Left to right) Chalamet, camera assistant Tom Lane, and Jake Marcuson filming the holographic desert bush projection on the Paul's bedroom set.

PAGE 156 Rebecca Ferguson, Stephen McKinley Henderson, and Denis Villeneuve rehearse a scene on the Arrakeen Residency set.

PAGE 157 Rebecca Ferguson on the Arrakeen Residency corridor set.

PAGE 158 Stephen McKinley Henderson as Thufir Hawat.

PAGE 159 An extra, Timothée Chalamet, Oscar Isaac, Roger Yuan, Denis Villeneuve, and Josh Brolin during a break in filming on the Duke Leto's office set.

PAGES 160 AND 161 Stellan Skarsgård as Baron Harkonnen on a Giedi Prime set at Origo Studios.

PAGE 162 Baron Harkonnen (Stellan Skarsgård), submerged in his healing bath.

PAGE 164 TOP The prosthetics team from Swedish company The Makeup Designers attend to Stellan Skarsgård's Baron Harkonnen prosthetics. **BOTTOM** Skarsgård and Oscar Isaac share a laugh on the Arrakeen Residency set.

PAGE 165 Baron Harkonnen (Skarsgård) soaks in his oily bath.

PAGE 166 Love Larson from The Makeup Designers touches up Stellan Skarsgård's Baron Harkonnen prosthetics on the Giedi Prime bathroom set.

PAGE 167 TOP Skarsgård's full-body makeup is finessed for the shoot. **BOTTOM** The special effects crew prepare Skarsgård before a take.

PAGE 168 On the backlot at Origo Studios, a Sardaukar soldier is reflected in a puddle on the rain-drenched Salusa Secundus set.

PAGE 169 Stellan Skarsgård on the Giedi Prime steam bath set at Origo Studios.

PAGE 170 LEFT Dave Bautista as Rabban Harkonnen. **RIGHT** David Dastmalchian as Piter de Vries with extras playing the Baron's servants.

PAGE 171 A Sardaukar soldier in the rain on the backlot at Origo Studios.

PAGE 172 David Dastmalchian twirls an umbrella on the backlot at Origo Studios.

PAGE 173 TOP Prosthetics makeup artists Niki de Jong, Márta Antal, and Athina Sapanidis provide final touch-ups to extras playing Harkonnen scientists. **BOTTOM** David Dastmalchian as Piter de Vries and Neil Bell as Sardaukar Bashar relax between takes on the backlot.

PAGE 174 Denis Villeneuve and David Dastmalchian discuss a scene on the backlot.

PAGE 175 Dave Bautista cracks a smile between takes.

PAGE 176 An extra portraying a Harkonnen technician, on the backlot.

PAGE 177 Daniel Scott Smith as a Harkonnen technician with Dave Bautista in a scene omitted from the final film.

PAGE 178 TOP Oscar Isaac and Rebecca Ferguson on the master bedroom set. **BOTTOM** Greig Fraser, Denis Villeneuve, and crew on the Arrakeen Residency balcony set.

PAGE 179 Jason Momoa shoots a scene, later deleted from the film, in which Duncan Idaho walks through a corridor on the Arrakeen Residency set. An electrician creates a moving glowglobe effect to the right of Momoa.

PAGE 180 Chang Chen and Oscar Isaac on the Arrakeen Residency set during the scene in which Dr. Yueh incapacitates Duke Leto.

PAGE 181 Chen as Dr. Yueh on the Residency corridor set.

PAGES 182 AND 183 Sardaukar soldiers invade the Arrakeen Residency.

PAGE 185 Extras portraying Sardaukar soldiers huddle against the set wall while filming the Arrakeen Residency invasion.

PAGES 186 AND 187 Duncan Idaho (Jason Momoa) attacks a Sardaukar soldier during the Harkonnen invasion sequence.

PAGE 188 TOP Denis Villeneuve looks for a camera position while filming the invasion sequence. **BOTTOM** On the backlot set, a Harkonnen soldier guards an ornithopter.

PAGE 189 Villeneuve crosses the backlot during shooting of the invasion scene.

PAGE 190 A Harkonnen soldier during filming of Duncan Idaho's escape from Arrakeen.

PAGE 191 Harkonnen soldiers with the ornithopter that Duncan Idaho steals during his escape.

PAGE 192 Denis Villeneuve directs Rebecca Ferguson in an abduction scene deleted from the final film.

PAGE 193 While filming the deleted abduction scene, Ferguson lies on the floor, ready for the next take.

PAGE 194 Denis Villeneuve directs extras playing Atreides soldiers on the backlot at Origo Studios.

PAGE 195 TOP On the backlot set, Josh Brolin and extras portraying Atreides troops shoot a scene in which they face the Harkonnen invasion. **BOTTOM** Jessica Clothier, Greig Fraser, second unit cinematographer Katelin Arizmendi, and visual effects supervisor Paul Lambert discuss the invasion sequence during filming.

PAGE 196 TOP Josh Brolin rehearses a fight scene with stuntmen playing Harkonnen soldiers. **BOTTOM** Denis Villeneuve reflecting on a scene between takes on the Arrakeen Residency set.

PAGE 197 On the backlot, Brolin and performers portraying Atreides soldiers film a shot in which their characters run into battle.

PAGE 198 Flame jets are ignited to simulate fires that erupt during the Harkonnen invasion as Josh Brolin and a group of stunt performers playing soldiers are filmed running into the fray.

PAGE 199 The Arrakeen Residency's burning palm trees are extinguished by the production's fire-safety professionals.

PAGE 200 David Dastmalchian on the backlot during filming of the Harkonnen invasion.

PAGE 201 Denis Villeneuve discusses a scene with Dastmalchian.

PAGE 202 Thufir Hawat (Stephen McKinley Henderson), under arrest by Harkonnen forces.

PAGE 203 A Sardaukar soldier silhouetted against the fiery backdrop created for the invasion sequence.

PAGE 204 TOP Lady Jessica (Rebecca Ferguson) during the scene in which Harkonnen forces abduct her and Paul and spirit them away in an ornithopher. **BOTTOM** Ferguson and Chalamet film the kidnapping scene in the ornithopter.

PAGE 205 Denis Villeneuve directs Chalamet and Ferguson during rehearsals in a makeshift version of the ornithopter cockpit set.

PAGE 206 Jason Momoa as Duncan Idaho on set at Origo Studios.

PAGE 207 Idaho in a scene omitted from the final film.

PAGE 208 Denis Villeneuve and Oscar Isaac on set at Origo Studios.

PAGE 209 Dr. Yueh (Chang Chen) is escorted by Harkonnen soldiers.

PAGES 210 AND 211 Filming Oscar Isaac as Duke Leto, whose character has been captured and stripped by the Harkonnens, on the Arrakeen Residency dining room set.

PAGES 212 AND 213 Oscar Isaac as the captured Duke Leto on the Arrakeen Residency dining room set.

PAGE 214 Baron Harkonnen (Stellan Skarsgård) feasts as Duke Leto (Oscar Isaac) awaits his destiny.

PAGE 215 Isaac takes a break while filming Duke Leto's death scene.

PAGE 216 David Dastmalchian performs Piter de Vries's death scene on the Arrakeen Residency dining room set.

PAGE 218 Stunt performers playing Sardaukar soldiers staging an attack on the Ecological Testing Station descend onto a set built between stages at Origo Studios.

PAGE 219 TOP Greig Fraser and Denis Villeneuve rehearse a scene with Fremen performers on the backlot. **BOTTOM** Fraser (kneeling left) and Villeneuve (kneeling right) share a laugh with the Fremen performers.

PAGES 220 AND 221 Performers playing Sardaukar soldiers during the Ecological Testing Station invasion sequence.

PAGE 222 A stuntman playing a falling Sardaukar soldier during the attack on the Ecological Testing Station.

PAGE 223 Fremen and Sardaukar performers battle on the Ecological Testing Station set.

PAGE 224 Oscar Isaac as Duke Leto at the Caladan cemetery location in Hungary.

PAGE 225 Extras at the Caladan cemetery set portray Atreides soldiers standing guard.

PAGE 226 Surrounded by crew, Timothée Chalamet and Oscar Isaac film a scene at the Caladan cemetery location.

PAGE 227 TOP An ornithopter built on a hilltop outside of Budapest and rigged for flight. **BOTTOM** The exterior of the ornithopter flight rig set.

PAGES 228 AND 229 Oscar Isaac during filming of the Caladan cemetery scene.

PAGE 230 Denis Villeneuve and Rebecca Ferguson rehearse a scene on the laboratory and office set, built at a steel mill in Budapest.

PAGE 231 Sharon Duncan-Brewster performs a scene on the office set.

PAGE 232 TOP Oscar Isaac films a scene on the flight rig in Budapest in which Duke Leto steers the ornithopter. **BOTTOM** Jason Momoa shares a laugh with assistant prop master Brad

Good between takes on the laboratory corridor set.

PAGE 233 Producer Joe Caracciolo, Sharon Duncan-Brewster, Rebecca Ferguson, and Denis Villeneuve rehearse a scene on the laboratory office set.

PAGE 234 Greig Fraser, Timothée Chalamet, Sharon Duncan-Brewster, Denis Villeneuve, Rebecca Ferguson, and first assistant director Chris Carreras during the shoot on the laboratory office set.

PAGE 235 Stunt double Kim Fardy, fight coordinator Roger Yuan, Greig Fraser, Jason Momoa, costumer Steven Constancio, and Denis Villeneuve between takes on the laboratory corridor set.

PAGE 236 On the laboratory corridor set, Jason Momoa performs the scene in which Duncan Idaho stages a heroic last stand against the invading Sardaukar soldiers.

PAGE 237 Momoa as Idaho on the laboratory corridor set.

PAGE 238 Rebecca Ferguson relaxes behind the scenes on the Testing Station laboratory and office set.

PAGE 239 Timothée Chalamet on the set of the testing station escape tunnel Paul uses to flee from the Sardaukar invaders.

ABU DHABI

PAGES 240–241 Denis Villeneuve in the dunes of Abu Dhabi's Liwa desert.

PAGE 242 In the Liwa desert, Denis Villeneuve directs Timothée Chalamet and Rebecca Ferguson in the sequence where Lady Jessica and Paul flee from enemy forces in Arrakis's deserts. Key grip Guy Micheletti and Greig Fraser can be seen behind Chalamet.

PAGES 244 AND 245 Sharon Duncan-Brewster in the deserts of Arrakis, where her character uses a device known as a thumper to summon sandworms.

PAGE 246 The crew, standing single file to protect the location from footprints, films Sharon Duncan-Brewster on a sand dune.

PAGE 247 Denis Villeneuve surveils a location in the Abu Dhabi desert.

PAGE 248 Paul Atreides (Timothée Chalamet) walks the dunes of Arrakis.

PAGE 249 Rebecca Ferguson takes a break from running up sand dunes.

PAGE 250 Timothée Chalamet in the dunes of Abu Dhabi.

PAGE 251 Timothée Chalamet and Rebecca Ferguson run across the dunes toward camera and crew during filming of Lady Jessica and Paul's escape from Harkonnen forces.

PAGES 252 AND 253 Paul (Timothée Chalamet) and Lady Jessica (Rebecca Ferguson) perform the sandwalk, a

Fremen technique designed to prevent detection by sandworms.

PAGES 254 AND 255 Wearing stillsuits, Lady Jessica (Rebecca Ferguson) and Paul Atreides (Timothée Chalamet) listen for sandworms on the dunes of Arrakis.

PAGE 256 The crew hike up the dunes, carrying cameras, costumes, and other filming equipment.

PAGE 257 Jake Marcuson, Jordanian assistant director Tarik Afifi, Denis Villeneuve, Greig Fraser, and key grip Guy Micheletti steady each other while filming from a truck bed.

PAGE 258 Timothée Chalamet wears Paul's stillsuit during the Abu Dhabi shoot.

PAGE 259 Denis Villeneuve directs the cast and crew in the dunes of the Liwa desert.

PAGE 260 Denis Villeneuve, illuminated by the lights of production vehicles, with his crew thrown into shadow before sunrise in the Liwa desert.

PAGE 261 A Fremen sandwalks across the dunes of Arrakis.

PAGE 262 Greig Fraser and Denis Villeneuve experience a red sunset, a phenomenon that occurs at the end of hot days in the desert.

PAGE 263 TOP Rebecca Ferguson and Villeneuve peer over the dunes before a scene. **BOTTOM** Jake Marcuson helps key grip Guy Micheletti up the steep dunes in the Empty Quarter.

NORWAY

PAGES 264–265 Timothée Chalamet on location in Norway for a scene in which Paul watches Atreides ships leave for Arrakis from a Caladan beach.

PAGE 266 TOP Timothée Chalamet on a cliff overlooking a Norwegian beach during filming of the exterior Caladan scenes. **BOTTOM** Chalamet and Denis Villeneuve block out a scene between takes in Norway.

PAGE 267 Timothée Chalamet on the rocky beach in Norway.

PAGE 268 Paul (Timothée Chalamet) watches his family's ships leave Caladan for Arrakis.

AFTERWORD

PAGE 270 Rebecca Ferguson and Timothée Chalamet on location in Wadi Rum.

CAPTIONS

PAGE 276 Oscar Isaac on the Arrakeen Residency set.

PAGE 281 Timothée Chalamet on the Castle Caladan library set.

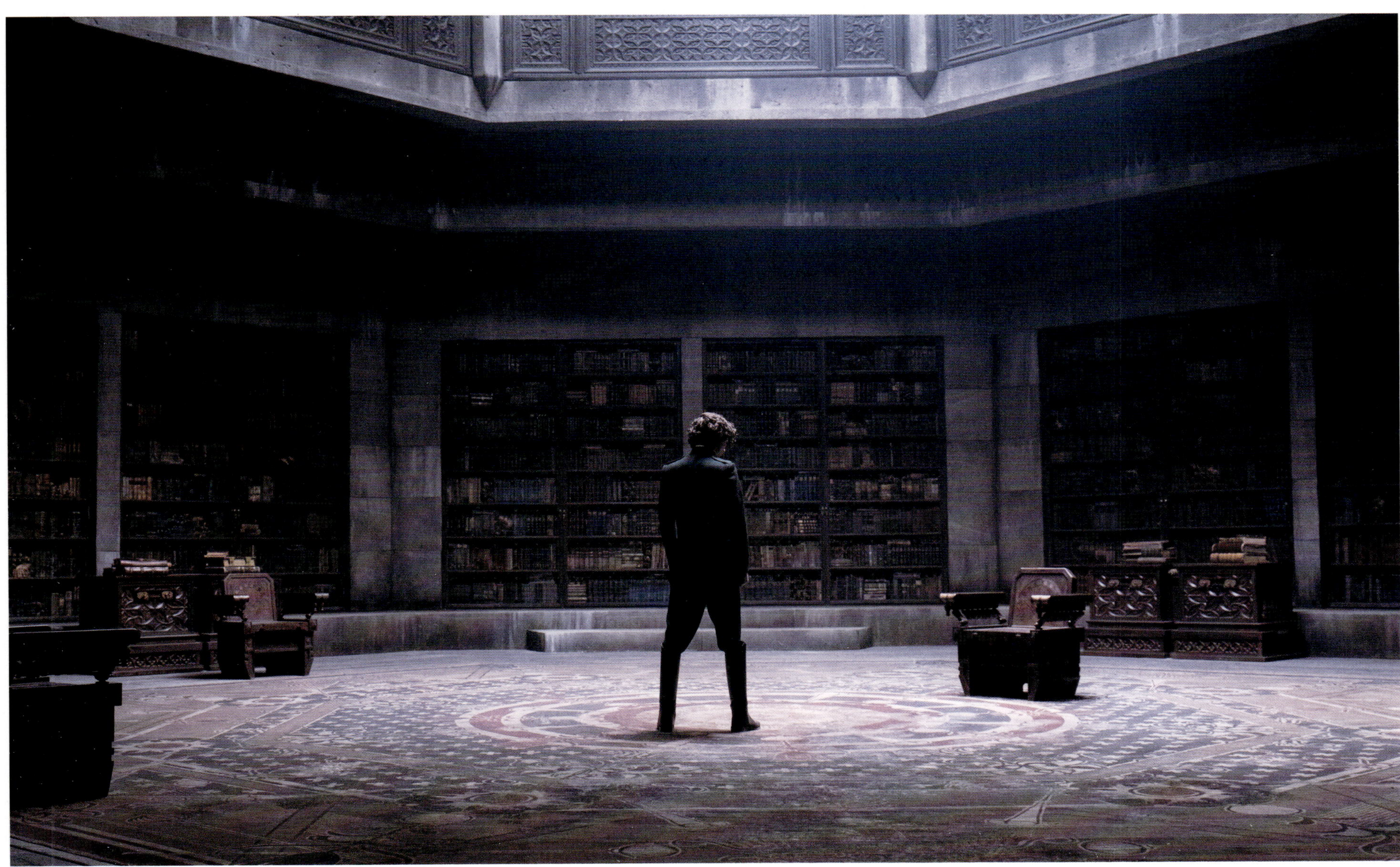

Publisher: Raoul Goff
VP of Licensing and Partnerships: Vanessa Lopez
VP of Creative: Chrissy Kwasnik
VP of Manufacturing: Alix Nicholaeff
VP, Editorial Director: Vicki Jaeger
Designer: Amazing15
Executive Editor: Chris Prince
Editorial Assistant: Savannah Jensen
Managing Editor: Maria Spano
Senior Production Editor: Katie Rokakis
Senior Production Manager: Joshua Smith
Senior Production Manager, Subsidiary Rights: Lina s Palma-Temena

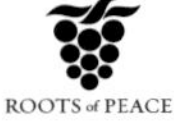
ROOTS of PEACE   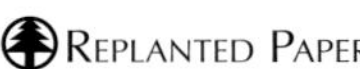REPLANTED PAPER

Insight Editions, in association with Roots of Peace, will plant two trees for each tree used in the manufacturing of this book. Roots of Peace is an internationally renowned humanitarian organization dedicated to eradicating land mines worldwide and converting war-torn lands into productive farms and wildlife habitats. Roots of Peace will plant two million fruit and nut trees in Afghanistan and provide farmers there with the skills and support necessary for sustainable land use.

Manufactured in China by Insight Editions
10 9 8 7 6 5 4 3 2 1

ACKNOWLEDGMENTS

This chapter of my life and career is one I am incredibly grateful to be able to hold on to, chronicled in these pages and shared with the world.

Thank you, Denis Villeneuve and Greig Fraser, for taking me on this adventure with you and giving me the freedom to have a perspective and create art in the process.

My sincerest gratitude to Tanya Lapointe not only for your generous contribution to this book but also for setting it in motion and guiding it to fruition.

Thank you to Chris Prince at Insight Editions and Robert Napton at Legendary for turning this project from just a suggested possibility into a hard-copy reality and to Tony Barbera at Warner Bros. for your generosity and support in the process.

Thank you to Rebecca Ferguson for being a muse and a champion to the story, the art, and the book.

Thank you to Frank Herbert whose brilliant imagination sent us on this remarkable journey.

And to the crew, thank you for giving your blood, sweat, and tears to this film and every image in this collection. I am humbled by your unparalleled support and collaboration, and I am proud to have been on this journey with you.

– Chiabella James

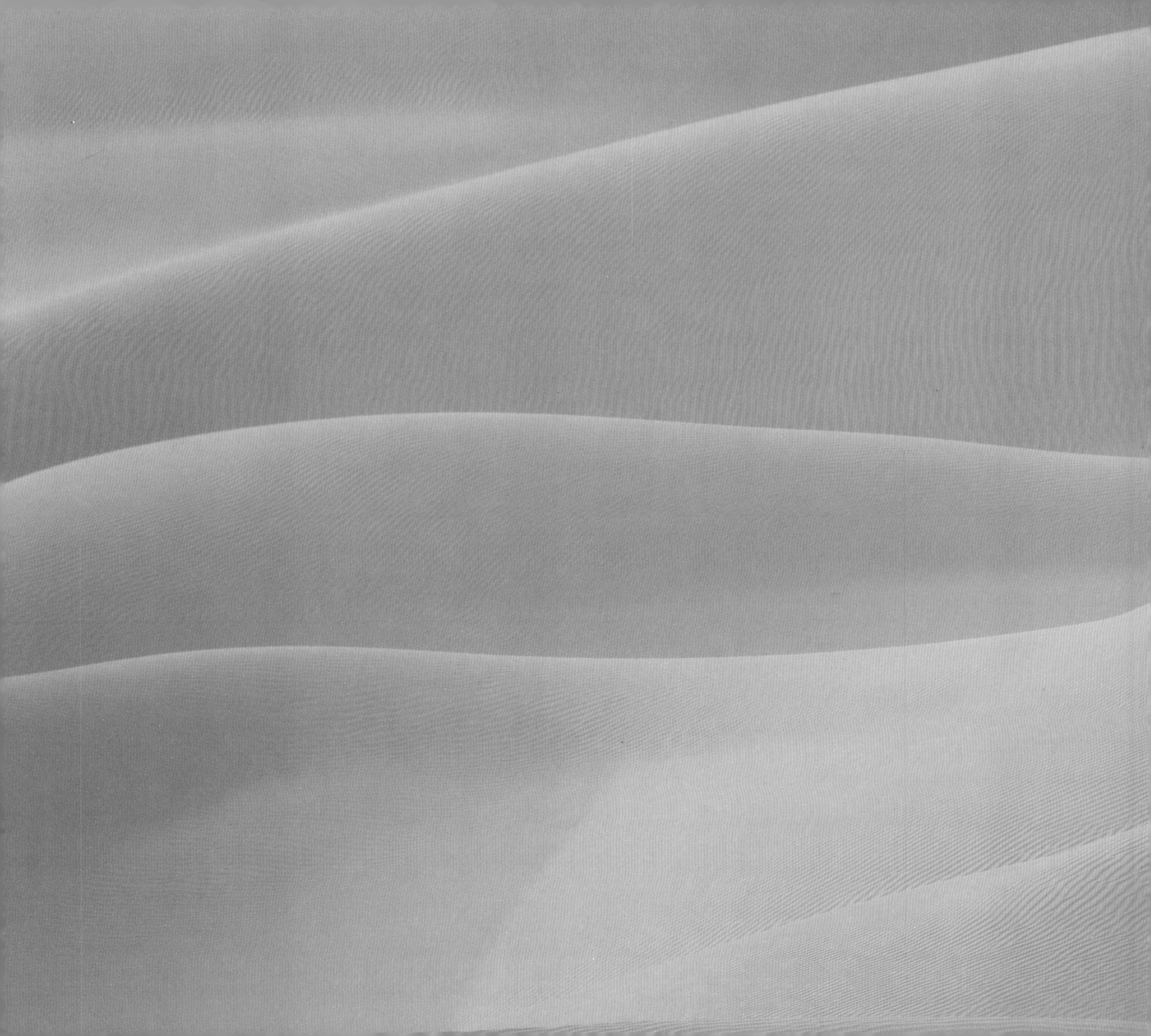